# THE ASHGATE RESEARCH COMPANION TO MORAL PANICS

*I know of no other book that comes close to providing such a comprehensive look at the history of approaches to understanding moral panics, along with contemporary applications and prospects for future development.*

Barry Glassner, Lewis and Clark College, USA, and author of
*The Culture of Fear: Why Americans Are Afraid of the Wrong Things*

ASHGATE
**RESEARCH**
COMPANION

The *Ashgate Research Companions* are designed to offer scholars and graduate students a comprehensive and authoritative state-of-the-art review of current research in a particular area. The companions' editors bring together a team of respected and experienced experts to write chapters on the key issues in their speciality, providing a comprehensive reference to the field.

# The Ashgate Research Companion to Moral Panics

*Edited by*

CHARLES KRINSKY

*University of California, Irvine, USA*

ASHGATE

Published by
Ashgate Publishing Limited
Wey Court East
Union Road
Farnham
Surrey GU9 7PT
England

Ashgate Publishing Company
110 Cherry Street
Suite 3-1
Burlington, VT 05401-3818
USA

www.ashgate.com

**British Library Cataloguing in Publication Data**
British Library Cataloguing in Publication Data
The Ashgate research companion to moral panics.
 1. Moral panics.
 I. Moral panics II. Krinsky, Charles.
 302.1′7-dc23

**Library of Congress Cataloging-in-Publication Data**
The Ashgate research companion to moral panics / [edited] by Charles Krinsky.
  p. cm.
 Includes bibliographical references and index.
 ISBN 978-1-4094-0811-6 (hbk. : alk. paper) – ISBN 978-1-4094-0812-3 (ebook) 1. Moral panics. 2. Moral conditions. I. Krinsky, Charles.
 HM811.A84 2012
 302′.17–dc23

2012030838

ISBN 9781409408116 (hbk)
ISBN 9781409408123 (ebk – PDF)
ISBN 9781409471738 (ebk – ePUB)

MIX
Paper from responsible sources
FSC
www.fsc.org   FSC® C018575

Printed and bound in Great Britain by
MPG Books Group, UK

Dedicated to the memory of my mother, Corinne Susman Krinsky

# Contents

# List of Illustrations

# List of Tables

# Notes on Contributors

**Joel Best** is Professor of Sociology and Criminal Justice at the University of Delaware. His most recent books include *The Stupidity Epidemic: Worrying about Students, Schools, and America's Future* (2010) and *Everyone's a Winner: Life in Our Congratulatory Culture* (2011).

**John J. Brent** is a doctoral student in the Department of Sociology and Criminal Justice at the University of Delaware. In 2007, he completed his MA in Criminal Justice at Eastern Kentucky University. He has published on building a theoretical foundation for criminal justice theory, the structural and cultural trends associated with illicit steroid use and trafficking, and methodological trends in criminology. He is currently working on an ethnographic study of the emotive frameworks and ontological rewards of those participating in illicit forms of fighting.

**Simon A. Cole** is Associate Professor and Chair of the Department of Criminology, Law and Society of the University of California, Irvine. He is the author of *Suspect Identities: A History of Fingerprinting and Criminal Identification* (2001) and *Truth Machine: The Contentious History of DNA Fingerprinting* (with Michael Lynch, Ruth McNally, and Kathleen Jordan 2008). He has written on identity theft (with Henry Pontell) and on the "CSI effect" (with Rachel Dioso-Villa). With Mary Bosworth, he is co-editor of the journal *Theoretical Criminology*.

**Chas Critcher** is *Emeritus* Professor of Communications at Sheffield Hallam University and Visiting Professor in Media and Communications at Swansea University. He studied at the Centre for Contemporary Cultural Studies of the University of Birmingham and co-authored *Policing the Crisis: Mugging, the State, and Law and Order* (with Stuart Hall, Tony Jefferson, John Clarke, and Brian Roberts (1978). His recent publications include *Moral Panics and the Media* (2003) and the edited volume, *Critical Readings in Moral Panics and the Media* (2006).

**Natália De' Carli** serves as Architect of the Federal University of Pernambuco. She received her Master's degree in Architecture from the University of Seville and is currently working toward her PhD at the same institution. She is a member of the research group, Out_Arquias.

**Bryan E. Denham** (PhD, Communications, University of Tennessee, 1996) holds the position of Campbell Professor of Sports Communication in the Department of Communication Studies of Clemson University, where he has worked since 1999. He is the author of approximately 50 journal articles and book chapters as well as 65 conference papers. "Folk Devils, News Icons and the Construction of Moral Panics," his 2008 *Journalism Studies* article addressing moral panics over "heroin chic," has become one of that publication's most downloaded articles. In 2010, he published "Amplifications of Deviance Surrounding Illicit Drug Use: Conceptualizing a Role for Film," which centers on deviance amplification in drug-related films, in *Communication, Culture and Critique*.

**Mary deYoung** serves as Professor of Sociology at Grand Valley State University. She is the author of *The Day Care Ritual Abuse Moral Panic* (2006) and more recently of *Madness: An American History of Mental Illness and its Treatment* (2010). She has written extensively on the satanic ritual abuse moral panic and has presented papers on the topic at national and international conferences.

**Erich Goode** is Sociology Professor *Emeritus* at Stony Brook University. He is the author or co-author of ten books, among them two editions of *Moral Panics: The Social Construction of Deviance* (with Nachman Ben-Yehuda 2009), nine editions of *Deviant Behavior* (2011), eight editions of *Drugs in American Society* (2012), and *Deviance in Everyday Life: Personal Accounts of Unconventional Lives* (2002). He has published over forty articles in academic journals and edited seven books of readings. He is semi-retired, lives in New York City, and is working on a study of deviance in memoir form.

**Alan Hunt** is Chancellor's Professor (cross-appointed in the Departments of Law and of Sociology and Anthropology) at Carleton University. He is the co-author, with Gary Wickham, of *Foucault and Law: Towards a New Sociology of Law as Governance* (1994) and the author of *Governance of the Consuming Passions: A History of Sumptuary Regulation* (1996) and *Governing Morals: A Social History of Moral Regulation* (1999). With Kevin Walby and Sale Spencer, he is the co-editor of *Emotions Matter* (2010).

**Brian V. Klocke** is Assistant Professor of Sociology and Criminal Justice at the State University of New York at Plattsburgh. He has published in *Men and Masculinities, Policing and Society, Sociology Compass*, and other journals. With Ellis Jones, Ross Haenfler, and Brett Johnson, he is the co-author of *The Better World Handbook: From Good Intentions to Everyday Actions* (2001).

**Charles Krinsky** holds a PhD in Comparative Culture from the University of California, Irvine, and an MA in Cinema Studies from New York University. He is the editor of *Moral Panics over Contemporary Children and Youth* (2008). He has taught at a number of colleges and universities, including Northeastern University, Arizona State University, Chapman University, the California State Polytechnic University, Pomona, as well as at Irvine. His research interests include the construction of gender and sexuality in American films and popular culture. Further information is available at http://beta-server.net/.

**Chrysanthi S. Leon**, JD, PhD, serves as Assistant Professor of Sociology and Criminal Justice at the University of Delaware. She is the author of *Sex Fiends, Perverts, and Pedophiles: Understanding Sex Crime Policy in America* (2011) and is currently a research fellow at the Legal Research Institute of the Boalt Hall School of Law.

**Jaime McCauley** is a PhD candidate in Sociology and Social Justice in the Department of Sociology and Anthropology of the University of Windsor. She also serves as Adjunct Professor of Sociology at Northern Kentucky University. Her research explores the gay marriage movement in the United States. She has also worked in the areas of moral regulation and moral panic, law and governance, and HIV/AIDS education.

**Máire Messenger Davies** is *Emerita* Professor of Media Studies at the University of Ulster and Visiting Professor in the School of Creative and Cultural Industries of the University of Glamorgan. A former journalist, holding a PhD in Psychology, she is the author of many publications on children and media, including her most recent book, *Children, Media and Culture* (2010).

**Toby Miller** is Distinguished Professor of Media and Cultural Studies at the University of California, Riverside, and Director of the University of California's study abroad program in Mexico. His many books include *The Avengers* (1997 and 1998) and *The Well-Tempered Self: Citizenship, Culture, and the Postmodern Subject* (1993). You can follow his lively adventures at http://www.tobymiller.org.

**Patricia Molloy** serves on the faculty of the Communication Studies Department of Wilfrid Laurier University. She holds a PhD in Education from the University of Toronto and has taught in the areas of war, cinema, popular culture, and women's studies at various universities in Toronto and southern Ontario. She has published extensively on narratives of war, violence, and sovereignty and on the construction of nationhood in films and other media.

**Glenn W. Muschert** is Associate Professor of Sociology at Miami University. His publications have appeared in *American Behavioral Scientist, Research in Social Problems and Public Policy, Sociological Inquiry*, and *Journalism and Mass Communication Quarterly*, among other journals.

**Julia Pearce** serves as Research Associate in the Department of War Studies of King's College, London. She is a social psychologist by training and her research interests include examining public information needs following terrorist events and exploring the concept of moral panic in relation to British responses to asylum seekers.

**Mariano Pérez Humanes** received his PhD in Architecture from the University of Seville, where he now serves as Professor in the Department of History, Theory, and Composition in Architecture. He is a member of the research group, Out_Arquias.

**Magdalena Rek-Woźniak** is a sociologist working as Researcher and Lecturer in the Department of Applied Sociology and Social Work of the University of Łódź. Her research interests include social inequalities and social policies (involving life-course policy analysis), the construction of social hierarchies in popular culture, and public discourses about social problems.

**Amanda Rohloff** is a PhD student in the School of Social Sciences of Brunel University. Her research interests include climate change, crime and deviance, media and popular culture, moral panics and moral regulation, punishment and social control, and social theory. She has authored or co-authored articles published in *New Zealand Sociology, Current Sociology, Sociology*, and *Crime, Media, Culture*.

**Willem Schinkel** serves as Associate Professor of Theoretical Sociology at Erasmus University Rotterdam. He is the author of *Aspects of Violence: A Critical Theory* (2010) and editor of *Globalization and the State: Sociological Perspectives on the State of the State* (2009).

**Pamela D. Schultz** is Professor of Communication Studies at Alfred University. Besides numerous journal and newspaper articles, she is the author of *Not Monsters: Analyzing the Stories of Child Molesters* (2005) and *A Critical Analysis of the Rhetoric of Child Sexual Abuse* (2000). Her current research focuses on law and public policy regarding child sexual abuse and sexual offenders, which she examines using construction theory and narrative analysis.

**Samantha A. Smith** received her PhD in Criminology, Law and Society from the University of California, Irvine in 2010. She is a behavioral research scientist for Northrop Grumman at the Defense Personnel Security Research Center, where she studies personnel security issues including investigative and adjudicative quality, cyber-behavior and cyber-security, and staff safety and security.

**Kenneth Thompson** is *Emeritus* Professor of Sociology at the Open University, having also taught at Yale University, Rutgers University, Smith College, Bergen University, and the University of California, Los Angeles. His publications include *Bureaucracy and Church Reform: The Organizational Response of the Church of England to Social Change, 1800–1965* (1970), *Sartre: Life and Works* (with Margaret Thompson, Facts on File 1984), *Beliefs and Ideology* (1986), *Media and Cultural Regulation* (1997), *Moral Panics* (1998), *Emile Durkheim* (2002), and two editions of *A Contemporary Introduction to Sociology* (with Jeffrey Alexander 2011).

**Tuukka Toivonen** is Junior Research Fellow at Green Templeton College, University of Oxford. His research centers on Japanese and comparative youth issues, social entrepreneurship, and the motivational processes of young workers. He is the co-author of *A Sociology of Japanese Youth: From Returnees to NEETs* (with Roger Goodman and Yuki Imoto 2011), the author of *Japan's Emerging Youth Policy: Making Young Adults Independent* (2012), and a leading member of his college's Future of Work program. For further information, visit http://www.tuukkatoivonen.com.

**Sheldon Ungar** serves as Professor of Sociology at the University of Toronto at Scarborough. His research centers on real-world events that produce social anxiety, including the nuclear arms race, emerging diseases, and global climate change. He has published articles in the *Sociological Quarterly*, *Social Problems*, the *British Journal of Sociology*, and other journals. Besides his continued interest in researching moral panics, his current work examines knowledge and ignorance, seeking to identify the effects of popular culture and new media on "cultural literacy." As part of his study of the cultural production of ignorance, he researches instances of the "silencing of science."

**Wojciech Woźniak** holds the position of Researcher and Lecturer in the Department of General Sociology of the University of Łódź. His research interests range from political and economic sociology, to social policy analysis, to the sociology of sports. His recent work examines public discourses in relation to social inequalities and social problems.

**Grazyna Zajdow** serves as Associate Head of School (Teaching and Learning) in Deakin University's School of History, Heritage and Society. Her research interests include women with drug and alcohol problems, self-help groups, state policies concerning the use of illicit drugs, and feminist sociology. She has published her scholarship in *Deviant Behavior*, *Health Sociology Review*, the *Journal of Australian Studies*, and other journals.

# Acknowledgments

I wish to thank Neil Jordan, Senior Commissioning Editor at Ashgate Publishing, whose patient guidance and considered advice were of immeasurable value in preparing this anthology.

Thanks are due, as well, to Phaedra Hernandez, whose able and uncomplaining assistance was essential to the completion of this project, Danka Valéria da Silveira Eiras, who generously volunteered her time and expertise to research and effect copyright clearances, and Mark Cermele, who expeditiously obtained the rights to reprint the trio of illustrations that enhance the contents of this volume.

At the Margaret Herrick Library of the Academy of Motion Picture Arts and Sciences, Lea Whittington, Reference Librarian, and Kristine Krueger, of the National Film Information Service, offered indispensable aid as I explored early motion picture history. Because of the service and support provided by Library Assistants David Moody and Nadya Iotova, conducting research at the Irvine-Katie Wheeler Library turned out to be a highly productive and decidedly congenial undertaking.

Working with the authors who contributed chapters (which, it should be noted, advance strikingly diverse critical perspectives) to *The Ashgate Research Companion to Moral Panics* turned out to be a sincere and consistent pleasure. Because of them, always ready to discuss and explain the finer points of their scholarship, assembling this collection became as great a learning experience for its editor as I believe utilizing it will be for its readers.

Finally, I am glad to have this chance to thank the professors and colleagues, some of only brief or geographically distant acquaintance, from whose aid and insights I have, at various times, gratefully benefited, including Rhona Berens, Shelly Stamp, Jeanine Basinger, Raul Fernandez, Jon Lewis, Alice Echols, Bernard Schissel, George E. Haggerty, and John Springhall.

# Introduction:
# The Moral Panic Concept

## Charles Krinsky

A moral panic may be defined as an episode, often triggered by alarming media stories and reinforced by reactive laws and public policy, of exaggerated or misdirected public concern, anxiety, fear, or anger over a perceived threat to social order. Details of the term's origin remain obscure, but its conceptualization began as an outgrowth of the politically engaged social perspective advanced by a group of leftist sociologists in the United Kingdom called the National Deviancy Conference (NDC). The NDC was formed in July 1968 in reaction to the Third National Conference of Teaching and Research on Criminology, held at the University of Cambridge, where, as the new organization's founders saw it, participants made the crucial mistake of treating deviance as an objectively discernible class of behaviors rather than an ascribed social category. In 1971, founding member Jock Young employed the term in "The Role of the Police as Amplifiers of Deviancy, Negotiators of Reality and Translators of Fantasy: Some Consequences of Our Present System of Drug Control as Seen in Notting Hill," his contribution to *Images of Deviance*, an anthology chiefly comprising papers originally presented at NDC meetings, edited by his friend Stanley Cohen (also an NDC founder). The next year, Cohen explored the idea in depth in *Moral Panics and Folk Devils: The Creation of the Mods and Rockers*, his analysis of media, public, and state responses to clashes between youth gangs that took place in Clacton and other resort towns along England's southeastern coast in 1964. Both Young and Cohen may have been influenced in their choice of words by the brief appearance of the term in Marshall McLuhan's (1964) *Understanding Media: The Extensions of Man* (xxxv).

In the decades that followed, the study of moral panics proceeded in two intersecting yet distinct waves. In the late 1970s and the 1980s, the relatively few moral panic researchers concentrated their efforts on expounding, corroborating, and elaborating the concept. By the early or mid-1990s, which Kenneth Thompson (1998: 1) has aptly called "the age of the moral panic," these scholars were joined by many others newly engaged with the topic. Investigations of moral panics began to cut a deep and broad swath across varied academic fields and disciplines that included cultural studies, media studies, education, sociology, communication studies, religious studies, cultural anthropology, cultural geography, political science, criminology, literary studies, legal studies, philosophy of science, and gender and sexuality studies. At the same time, the notion of moral panic spread beyond the confines of university and college campuses, wending its way into the popular imagination. Paradoxically perhaps, though hardly unexpectedly, greater acceptance of the moral panics model among scholars, the media, and the public occasioned a concurrent critical strategy of questioning and evaluating its advantages and limitations as a framework for explaining the causes, structures, and functions of social, cultural, and political crises.

# First Wave

## Jock Young

In his chapter for Cohen's *Images of Deviance* (1971), Jock Young focuses on the phenomenon of deviance amplification, when sensational media coverage of deviant behaviors unintentionally increases rather than restrains apparent deviance. Young also mentions the related phenomenon of moral panic:

> The media, then—in a sense—can create social problems, they can present them dramatically and overwhelmingly, and, most important, they can do it suddenly. The media can very quickly and effectively fan public indignation and engineer what one might call 'a moral panic' about a certain type of deviancy. (Young 1971b: 37)

To a great degree, moral panics take place in the media. During moral panics, media coverage, rousing public fears over a reputed social problem, also assists appreciably in constructing that problem.

While the term itself appears nowhere in the book, in *The Drugtakers: The Social Meaning of Drug Use*, published the same year as *Images of Deviance*, Young presents the sort of critical viewpoint that would become closely associated with moral panic research:

> What has to be explained is why certain groups or individuals select particular drugs, outlining the significance of drugtaking not only to them but in the context of work and leisure in modern industrial societies. This done, we must go further and explain why certain drugs are labelled legal and others are totally prohibited; we must concern ourselves as much with the reasons for the social reaction against particular forms of drugtaking as with the causes of drugtaking itself. For the reasons behind prohibition disclose as much about the meaning of drugtaking in society as does analysis of the motivations

of the drugtaker. Moreover, it is the social reaction against the use of illicit drugs which, to a considerable extent, shapes and buffets the way in which the drugtaker lives; circumscribing his activities, and even structuring the effects of the drugs that he normally takes. (1971a: 10)

Human behaviors acquire their meanings within specific social contexts. Disapproving social reactions to deviant behaviors dictate their significance even for those who engage in them. Therefore, to understand deviance as fully as possible, researchers must explain not only the motives behind particular uncondoned activities, but also, and just as importantly, the fundamental causes of society's responses.

Throughout his study, Young (1971a: 94, emphasis in original) delineates his preferred, "relativist" sociological standpoint, addressing its political implications as well, at one point stating,

The absolutist social scientist assumes social reactions against the deviant. He does not question, for example, why society reacts against the person who smokes marihuana but not those who smoke tobacco. In contrast, the relativist regards deviancy as not a property *inherent* in any activity but something which is *conferred* upon it by others. He turns the searchlight of inquiry, therefore, not only on the drugtaker but also on the people who condemn drugtaking. His interests are consequently wider than the absolutist for he must examine the power structure of society; explaining why certain groups have the ability to proscribe the behaviour of others and in what terms they legitimize their activities.

Going much further than simply proposing a novel research topic or method, Young stakes out a new relativist sociological position regarding both deviance and society. He admonishes scholars that societies and, more specifically, prevailing power relations define both deviant and condoned behaviors and groups. Shedding light on deviance, he contends, means casting a cold and critical eye on society and the structure of power.

## Stanley Cohen

It was Stanley Cohen's *Moral Panics and Folk Devils: The Creation of the Mods and Rockers* (2002), which, like Young's work, investigates divergent social reactions to deviance and their roles in constructing both deviant and condoned behaviors, that provided the definition of moral panic that subsequent researchers would most regularly cite. In this book, originally published in 1972, Cohen (2002: 1) describes at length the social response to deviance outlined by Young:

Societies appear to be subject, every now and then, to periods of moral panic. A condition, episode, a person or group of persons emerges to

3

become defined as a threat to societal values and interests; its nature is presented in a stylized and stereotypical fashion by the mass media; the moral barricades are manned by editors, bishops, politicians and other right-thinking people; socially accredited experts pronounce their diagnoses and solutions; ways of coping are evolved or (more often) resorted to; the condition then disappears, submerges or deteriorates and becomes more visible. Sometimes the object of the panic is quite novel and at other times it is something which has been in existence long enough, but suddenly appears in the limelight. Sometimes the panic passes over and is forgotten, except in folklore and collective memory; at other times it has more serious and long-lasting repercussions and might produce such changes as those in legal and social policy or even in the way the society conceives itself.

Cohen portrays moral panics as more or less discrete social processes. Though they may express ongoing public concerns about "something which has been in existence long enough," individual episodes emerge in response to dangers that appear to have surfaced suddenly. For Cohen, certain fairly well-defined steps occur in the development of moral panics. They commence when a person, group, or set of values, behaviors, or circumstances emerges as a perceived threat to social order. Frequently, they are sustained by moral crusaders, supported by media sensationalism, and enforced by state policies and practices. Then, they diminish or end, sometimes leaving behind sizable political and social changes.

In accord with Young's findings, Cohen emphasizes that, like the moral panics of which it is often a part, the process of deviance amplification is driven largely by the mass media. Early in his book, Cohen (2002: 8, emphasis in original) explains,

Much of this study will be devoted to understanding the role of the mass media in creating moral panics and folk devils. A potentially useful link between these two notions—and one that places central stress on the mass media—is the process of deviation amplification as described by [criminologist Leslie T.] Wilkins. The key variable in this attempt to understand how the societal reaction may in fact *increase* rather than decrease or keep in check the amount of deviance, is the nature of the information about deviance. As I pointed out earlier, this information characteristically is not received at first, it tends to be in such a form that the action or actors concerned are pictured in a highly stereotypical way. We react to an episode of, say, sexual deviance, drugtaking or violence in terms of our information about that particular class of phenomenon (how typical is it), our tolerance level for that type of behaviour and our direct experience—which in a segregated urban society is often nil. Wilkins describes—in highly mechanistic language derived from cybernetic theory—a typical reaction sequence which might take place at this point, one which has a spiraling or snowballing effect.

Stirring up moral panics, media direct their attention to "folk devils," that is, to deviant individuals or groups seen as embodying a new or extraordinary social threat. Sometimes, such coverage may have unexpected consequences, intensifying instead of suppressing the targeted deviance. In such cases, the scope of the deviance seems to spiral: provocative media reports on deviant or unconventional behaviors result in even more attention being paid to them, isolating those termed deviant from the rest of society, which often causes them to identify more strongly with each other, fostering greater deviance, and so on.

## Stuart Hall, Chas Critcher, Tony Jefferson, John Clarke, and Brian Roberts

In 1978, five scholars affiliated with Birmingham University's Centre for Contemporary Cultural Studies—Stuart Hall, Chas Critcher, Tony Jefferson, John Clarke, and Brian Roberts—published *Policing the Crisis: Mugging, the State, and Law and Order*, a critical examination of a nationwide moral panic over mugging that befell Britain in 1972–3. In this comprehensive work, Hall et al. (1978: 16, emphasis in original) offer a definition of moral panic arguably second only to Cohen's in its influence among scholars:

> When the official reaction to a person, groups of persons or series of events is *out of all proportion* to the actual threat offered, when 'experts', in the form of police chiefs, the judiciary, politicians, and editors *perceive* the threat in all but identical terms, and appear to talk 'with one voice' of rates, diagnoses, prognoses and solutions, when the media representations universally stress 'sudden and dramatic' increases (in numbers involved or events) and 'novelty', above and beyond that which a sober, realistic appraisal could sustain, then we believe it is appropriate to speak of the beginnings of a *moral panic*.

Like Cohen, Hall et al. examine the typical or exemplary progression of moral panics. Likely to be recognized only *in media res*, moral panics gain momentum as politicians and other moral crusaders join forces to define and combat a perceived social threat through public discourse, the law, and public policy.

The affinity with Cohen's work runs deep: part of the authors' program in *Policing the Crisis: Mugging, the State, and Law and Order* was to revise and expand Cohen's moral panics model in light of recent political developments in the United Kingdom and the United States:

> And part of our intention is certainly to situate the 'moral panic' as one of the forms of appearance of a more deep-seated historical crisis, and thereby to give it greater historical and theoretical specificity. This relocation of the concept on a different and deeper level of analysis does not, however, lead us to abandon it altogether as useless. Rather, it helps us to identify the 'moral panic' as one of the principal surface

> manifestations of the crisis, and in part to explain how and why the crisis came to be *experienced* in that form of consciousness, and what the displacement of a conjunctural crisis into the popular form of a 'moral panic' accomplishes, in terms of the way the crisis is managed and contained. We have therefore retained the notion of the 'moral panic' as a necessary part of our analysis: attempting to redefine it as one of the key ideological forms in which a historical crisis is 'experienced and fought out'. (Hall et al. 1978: 221, emphasis in original)

Hall et al. align Cohen's processual model of moral panics with a Marxist critique of false consciousness. In response to "a conjunctural crisis," that is, to the growing difficulty of forming consensus because of the inherent conflict between capitalism and social progress, moral panics divert potential dissenters' attention toward imagined or misrecognized social threats. Moral panics, they conclude, must be understood not merely as occasional incidences of public concern and fear, but as diversionary manifestations, intended to maintain the *status quo*, of a continuing historical crisis.

Whereas Young (1971) and Cohen (1972) spoke of deviance amplification, Hall et al. (1978: 225) describe the "signification spirals" that commonly accompany moral panics:

> In the public signification of troubling events, there seem to be certain thresholds which mark out symbolically the limits of societal tolerance. The higher an event can be placed in the hierarchy of thresholds, the greater is its threat to the social order, and the tougher and more automatic is the coercive response. ... The use of convergences and thresholds together in the ideological signification of societal conflict has the intrinsic function of escalation. One kind of threat or challenge to society seems larger, more menacing, if it can be mapped together with other, apparently similar, phenomena — especially if, by connecting one relatively harmless activity with a more threatening one, the scale of the danger implicit is made to appear more widespread and diffused. (1978: 225–6)

Building on the notion presented by Young and Cohen, Hall et al. discuss not just amplification (that is, an intensification or extension) of deviance, but rather escalation or accretion in its meaning. In the authors' view, the limits of social tolerance are relative: sanctions against harmful or socially threatening activities tend to be stronger than those against deprecated but largely innocuous behaviors. However, in the signification spiral propelled by moral panics, less dangerous activities become identified as symptoms or precursors of superficially similar but more destructive behaviors. Because both types of behavior are now taken to express a single pervasive menace, activities that were once discouraged but socially tolerated become almost as blameworthy as far more perilous or troublesome ones.

# Second Wave

## Erich Goode and Nachman Ben-Yehuda

Erich Goode and Nachman Ben-Yehuda's *Moral Panics: The Social Construction of Deviance* (2009), first published in 1994, includes a comprehensive analysis of the typical characteristics of many moral panics. Increasingly used as a frame for studying the phenomenon, this conceptualization became known by some scholars as the attributional model, so called in contrast to Cohen's concentration on the social and cultural development of episodes, which in this context came to be referenced as the processual model (see Critcher: 2010, Klocke and Muschert: 2010). Goode and Ben-Yehuda's (2009: 37–43) itemization of five key attributes of moral panics can be summarized as follows:

1. Concern. There must be a measurable increase in the level of anxiety arising from the conviction that a group's behaviors pose a substantial threat to society, a response seen by those who experience it as a reasonable reaction to a definite social menace.
2. Hostility. The source of the alleged social menace must be viewed with enmity or resentment as a readily identifiable group independently responsible for the danger its behaviors pose to society.
3. Consensus. Substantial agreement that a threat to society exists need not be achieved throughout society, but must be achieved within a segment of the public large or powerful enough to defuse opposition to its preferred definitions or policies.
4. Disproportionality. The intensity of public concern over a perceived social threat must be out of proportion to the measurable or demonstrable level of danger posed.
5. Volatility. Moral panics tend to arise suddenly and dissipate quickly, sometimes leaving behind enduring social changes.

While their consideration of the structural characteristics of moral panics represents a distinct shift in perspective from Cohen's attention to their progression over time, that Goode and Ben-Yehuda contextualize their own work by cogently analyzing Cohen's ideas throughout their book suggests that their intention was to supplement rather than displace his processual model.

Nearly as influential as their presentation of the typical properties of moral panics has been Goode and Ben-Yehuda's (2009: 51–72) concise taxonomy of commonly held scholarly models of, or theoretical perspectives on, the evolution of such episodes. Goode and Ben-Yehuda detail three main models or theories tacitly employed by moral panic scholars:

1. The grassroots model suggests that the public itself creates and maintains most or the most important moral panics. While the media or moral crusaders take

the lead in spreading and reinforcing moral panics, they do so in response to widespread concerns among the public.

2. According to the elite-engineered model, during moral panics, "The richest and most powerful members of the society consciously undertake campaigns to generate and sustain concern, fear, and panic on the part of the public over an issue that is not generally regarded as terribly harmful to the society as a whole" (Goode and Ben-Yehuda 2009: 62).

3. Concerning the interest-group perspective, which they call, "By far, the most common approach to moral panics (2009: 67)," Goode and Ben-Yehuda (citing sociologist Howard S. Becker) note, "Rule creators and moral entrepreneurs launch crusades, which occasionally turn into panics, to make sure that certain rules take hold and are enforced" (2009: 67).

As their text nears its conclusion, Goode and Ben-Yehuda (2009: 226) make plain their own conviction that all moral panics models must remain incomplete and tentative because episodes are, above all, variable and inconstant:

> As we have seen throughout this book, moral panics make up an extremely diverse collection of events. We do not find that they go through specific, predetermined stages, with a beginning, a middle, and a predictable end. … Their locus may be society-wide, or local and regional; more specifically, and broad, society-wide panic may be evident in all or nearly all communities nationally, or may or may not explode in certain specific locales, or alternatively, a panic may be extremely brief, lasting as little as a month or two …. Or they may be more long term and run their course only after several years. Some of the longer panics may represent the temporally limited portion of a much longer-range concern.

In discussing the attributes of moral panics as well as scholars' perspectives on the phenomenon, Goode and Ben-Yehuda offer tools for examining the causes, structures, and effects of moral panics rather than a classification system into which any given episode might readily be placed.

## Angela McRobbie and Sarah L. Thornton

In "Rethinking 'Moral Panic' for Multi-Mediated Social Worlds" (1995), cultural studies scholars Angela McRobbie and Sarah L. Thornton contend that, to remain useful to researchers, the moral panic concept must be revised to account for the social and cultural transformations wrought by a rapidly changing media landscape. They contend that as mass media have become both more culturally central and more fragmented, the viewpoints they entertain have grown in number and diversity, and the folk devils targeted during moral panics have a far greater capacity to air their own opinions than was often the case when the concept was first advanced:

One of the main aims of pressure groups is timely intervention in relevant moral panics—to be able to respond instantly to the media demonization of the group they represent, and to provide information and analysis designed to counter this representation. The effectiveness of these groups and in particular their skills at working with the media and providing highly professional 'soundbites' more or less on cue make them an invaluable resource to media machinery working to tight schedules and with increasingly small budgets. They allow the media to be seen to be doing their duty by providing 'balance' in their reporting. At the same time, they show how 'folk devils' can and do 'fight back'. (McRobbie and Thornton 1995: 566)

According to McRobbie and Thornton, as niche media with limited budgets seek audiences by broadcasting reproving and nonconforming perspectives alike, the boundaries between moral crusaders and folk devils have become less distinct. Those whose behaviors crusaders deem deviant can access the means of offering their opposing perspectives.

McRobbie and Thornton's (1995: 567) criticism of the moral panic concept extends to questioning whether it might not be inherently inaccurate and unuseful:

The delicate balance of relations which the moral panic sociologists saw existing between media, agents of social control, folk devils and moral guardians, has given way to a much more complicated and fragmented set of connections. Each of the categories described by moral panics theorists has undergone a process of fissure in the intervening years. New liaisons have been developed and new initiatives pursued. In particular, two groups seem to be making ever more vocal and 'effective' intervention: pressure groups have, among other things, strongly contested the vocality of the traditional moral guardians; and commercial interests have planted the seeds, and courted discourses, of moral panic in seeking to gain the favourable attention of youthful consumers.

This leads us to query the usefulness of the term 'moral panic'—a metaphor which depicts a complex society as a single person who experiences sudden fear about its virtue. The term's anthropomorphism and totalization arguably mystify more than they reveal. Its conception of morals overlooks the youthful ethics of abandon and the moral imperatives of pressure groups and vocal experts. In the 1990s, we need to acknowledge the perspectives and articulations of different sectors of society. New sociologies of social regulation need to shift attention away from the conventional points in the circuit of implication and control and look instead to these other spaces.

Earlier scholars asserted that social control was imposed on folk devils by media and moral crusaders through moral panic. As the social relations between media, moral crusaders, and folk devils have broken apart and become more changeable, an analytic model of society as a single organism subject to intermittent moral panics no longer has any validity. Youth, frequent choices as folk devils, nevertheless have exceptional power as consumers, and clear distinctions between moral guardians and folk devils can no longer be assumed.

## Kenneth Thompson

In *Moral Panics* (1998), Kenneth Thompson presents a systematic review of the concept's development that highlights the substantial reconsideration of the model that took place in the 1990s. Looking back on the 1980s, he ventures a reason for the relative dearth of moral panics analyses after Hall et al.'s *Policing the Crisis: Mugging, the State, and Law and Order* (1978):

> In the 1980s, however, the focus of sociologists turned to the rise of the New Right economic policies and ideology, involving economic deregulation coupled with cultural and moral re-regulation. The concept of moral panic seemed less relevant because it appeared to focus on episodic and discrete events, giving too much attention to symptoms rather than focusing directly on political-economic developments and their relationship to ideological trends. Other sociologists dispensed with the concept because it seemed to involve subjecting 'representations' to the judgement of the 'real', rather than concentrating on the operations of representational systems in their own right. (Thompson 1994: 140)

Thompson identifies two coinciding causes for many researchers' lack of interest in the moral panics model at the time, one related mostly to the politics of the 1980s, the other to the limitations of the concept itself. First, the New Right's association of "free market" policies with moral regulation highlighted the enduring causal relationship between economics and social relations, which the notion of moral panics as discrete episodes seemed not to address. Second, the assumption of clear and substantial distinctions between "representations" and the "real" involved in the moral panics model failed to engage scholars who saw laws, economics, public policy, and social identities as jointly forming comprehensive "representational systems" (a viewpoint, it might be added, that the rising neoliberalism of the 1980s appears to confirm).

Turning his attention to the revival of moral panic research in the 1990s, Thompson (1998: 140–41) finds both conceptual and historical reasons for the model's resurgence (as he did for its earlier neglect):

It is only recently, in the 1990s, that the continuing rapid succession of phenomena commonly described as 'moral panics' began to force a reappraisal, and we have reintroduced the possibility of regarding moral panics as symptomatic of developments that are of wider significance, rather than viewing them simply as unrelated episodes of collective behaviour.

The reappraisal takes account of a number of changes. The first set of changes are structural: such as economic restructuring and deregulation, immigration and international population flows, changes in the division of labour (including the domestic division of labour and gender roles). These changes have profoundly unsettling effects that leave people anxious and at risk. The second set are technological—changes in communication technologies, such as computerized newspaper production, satellite broadcasting, cable, video and the Internet. These have increased competition between sources of information and entertainment, and make regulation more problematical. … Third, and relatedly, there have been cultural changes—increased 'multiculturalism' in the broadest sense, fragmentation of cultures, and conflicts over identity, lifestyles and morals. Furthermore, the culture industries have become more central to economic and social life, and so there is a constant drive to promote cultural changes, which can provoke resistance and conflict. They also entail increased efforts at cultural and moral re-regulation, with the development of expert regulatory authorities, and the exercise of power through fixing discursive formations, and surveillance.

Thompson's description of recent reconsiderations of the concept recalls Hall et al.'s view that moral panics may be seen as misleading expressions of enduring social and economic conflicts. He asserts that the proliferation of moral panics in the 1990s led to a re-evaluation of the model as researchers began to realize that rather than representing a series of unrelated upsurges in levels of public concern, successive episodes were collectively indicative of ongoing, large-scale, and unsettling social, economic, and cultural changes. Thompson concludes that scholars have revised the concept of moral panic in light of economic change, the growing importance as well as the greater fragmentation of mass media (an evident allusion to McRobbie and Thornton's work), and increasing cultural diversity.

## Sheldon Ungar

Like McRobbie and Thornton, Sheldon Ungar proposes re-evaluating and revising the concept of moral panic in keeping with recent changes in the cultural and political functions performed by media in various societies. In "Moral Panic versus the Risk Society: The Implications of the Changing Sites of Social Anxiety" (2001: 277),

Ungar calls on scholars to revisit the moral panics model in relation to the somewhat similar but distinct phenomenon of risk society crisis:

> Risk society issues do not generally fit a top-down model. If responses to nuclear reactors are prototypical, panics appear to require some catalytic real-world event that is given direction by interest groups and carried forward by elements of the informed public, often as part of social movement organizations .... Significantly ... political authorities and large actors often find themselves the target of such activities and have encountered strong resistance in their efforts to influence long-term public opinion ....
>
> From a social constructionist perspective, claims making pertaining to moral panics can derive more from a shift in moral boundaries than either the objective standing of a condition or new evidence. ... Moreover, claims may be about valence issues (these are one-sided issues, as in hard drug use) or involve relatively disproportionate power on the contending sides, as folk devils are pitted against better-organized and more powerful groups. With the risk society, issues tend to be warranted more by scientific findings or claims, with scientists, for all their public liabilities, playing a central role in the cast of claims makers. Given scientific uncertainties, the likelihood that the media's attempt to strike an equilibrium will be greater for 'factual' than for moral claims ..., and the chance that the powerful will find themselves targeted, a more equal balance of power between rival claims makers is anticipated with risk issues.
>
> In short, moral panic has conventionally focused on social control processes aimed at the moral failing of dispossessed groups. Risk society issues tend to involve diverse interest groups contending over relatively intractable scientific claims. However, the former have come closer to the latter as diverse media and attention to a broader range of voices allow folk devils to contest the setting of moral boundaries. Social regulation processes, in other words, have become less predictable and more fractious.

Adopting the notion of risk society (societies where media play a crucial role in reporting on, and managing public reaction to, the dangers, such as global warming or nuclear accidents, associated with late modernity) from German sociologist Ulrich Beck (1992), Ungar notes several crucial differences between risk society crises and moral panics. Moral panics typically involve "valence issues," that is, contests over contrasting behavioral goals (ending illicit drug use vs putting a stop to both illicit and recreational drug-taking, for instance) in which one alternative is presented as morally superior to the other. Risk society crises, on the other hand, may have no clear moral component, and the most effective response to a perceived problem, and even the nature of the problem itself, may be difficult to determine. Though fueled by misrecognition of, for example, folk devils or the actual goals of public policy, moral panics nevertheless focus on apparently understandable dangers posed by supposedly readily identifiable individuals, groups, or behaviors. Corporations and governments are likely to become the focus of risk society crises, while moral panics usually center on marginalized individuals or groups. Yet, as folk devils have acquired the means to fight back (like Thompson, Ungar here alludes to McRobbie and Thornton's work), moral panics and risk society crises have become more alike at least in respect to their targets' capacity to mount successful counter-offensives.

## The Ashgate Research Companion to Moral Panics

In necessarily broad outline, the preceding consideration of researchers' particularizing, questioning, and emending of the moral panics model describes the scholarly debate into which the present anthology enters. *The Ashgate Research Companion to Moral Panics* is organized thematically into six main parts: "The Evolution of the Moral Panic Concept," "Sex Panics," "Media Panics," "Moral Panics over Children and Youth," "Moral Panics and Governance," and "The Future of the Moral Panic Concept." Each section treats a major topic or proposition often deliberated in current research, each begins with a brief overview intended to draw connections between the chapters contained within it, and other recent scholarship, including pertinent texts not remarked upon above.

Moral panics are characteristically media driven and, reflecting the variety of forms that public discourses may take, the definition of media texts recognized by the contributors to this volume is extremely (though not limitlessly) wide in scope. It encompasses, for example, films, television programs, newspaper reports, videogames, online posts, laws, photographs, podcasts, political speeches and statements, government documents, protest signs and car window stickers, mass actions, and scholarly articles.

The critical perspectives presented in *The Ashgate Research Companion to Moral Panics* cross both national borders and disciplinary boundaries. This anthology collects research examining social problems pertinent to, among other countries, Canada, the United States, Brazil, the United Kingdom, the Netherlands, Poland, Australia, and Japan. Mostly but not exclusively employing qualitative research methods, its contributors draw on ideas and utilize techniques developed in disciplines and fields of study such as philosophy, sociology, cultural anthropology, literary studies, international studies, economics, immigration studies, education, policy studies, cultural geography, communication studies, social history, the philosophy of science, film studies, social psychology, media studies, architecture, city planning, legal studies, criminology, performance studies, visual studies, political science, and cultural studies

Rather than literature reviews or review essays, the succeeding chapters comprise new research efforts centering on historical and especially contemporary issues concerning moral panics, which should be useful to researchers because they engage insightfully and persuasively with scholarly conceptualizations of the phenomenon. Importantly, this collection includes both significant elaborations on and informed critiques of the moral panics model.

Besides researchers, this volume's thorough treatment of its subject, inclusion of a range of perspectives, and clear thematic organization should appeal to undergraduate and graduate students, college and university professors, and many others interested in studying social problems and cultural issues. Of the two appendices that follow the contributors' chapters, one, meant to facilitate the book's use in classrooms and on course reading lists, offers alternative ways to organize the chapters according to various themes, while the other, designed to assist researchers, constitutes an extensive bibliography of scholarly texts on moral panics and related topics.

It is hoped that a diverse readership will judge *The Ashgate Research Companion to Moral Panics* clearly written, amply informative, easily utilized, and readily applicable to research practice. Perhaps not a few may find it enjoyable as well.

# References

Cohen, S. (ed.) 1971. *Images of Deviance*. Harmondsworth: Penguin Books.

Cohen, S. 2002 (1972, 1980). *Folk Devils and Moral Panics: The Creation of the Mods and Rockers*. 3rd Edition. London: Routledge.

Goode, E. and Ben-Yehuda, N. 2009 (1994). *Moral Panics: The Social Construction of Deviance*. 2nd Edition. Malden: Wiley-Blackwell.

Hall, S., Critcher, C., Jefferson, T., Clarke, J., and Roberts, B. 1978. *Policing the Crisis: Mugging, the State, and Law and Order*. Critical Social Studies. Houndmills: Palgrave Macmillan.

Klocke, B.V. and Muschert, G.W. 2010. A hybrid model of moral panics: synthesizing the theory and practice of moral panic research. *Sociology Compass*, 4(5), 295–309.

McLuhan, M. 1964. *Understanding Media: The Extensions of Man*. New York: McGraw-Hill.

McRobbie, A. and Thornton, S.L. 1995. Rethinking 'moral panic' for multi-mediated social worlds. *British Journal of Sociology*, 46(4), 559–74.

Thompson, K. 1998. *Moral Panics*. Key Ideas. Milton Park: Routledge.

Ungar, S. 2001. Moral panic versus the risk society: the implications of the changing sites of social anxiety. *British Journal of Sociology*, 52(2), 271–91.

Young, J. 1971a. *The Drugtakers: The Social Meaning of Drug Use*. London: MacGibbon and Kee.

Young, J. 1971b. The role of the police as amplifiers of deviancy, negotiators of reality and translators of fantasy: some consequences of our present system of drug control as seen in Notting Hill, in *Images of Deviance*, edited by S. Cohen. Harmondsworth: Penguin Books, 27–61.

# PART I
# THE EVOLUTION OF THE MORAL
# PANIC CONCEPT

# Overview of Part I

As interest in the topic has continued to grow, some of the path-breaking sociologists who first devised the moral panics model have re-entered the scholarly debates over the concept in order to clarify their original intentions. For example, Jock Young, whose essay, "The Role of the Police as Amplifiers of Deviancy, Negotiators of Reality and Translators of Fantasy: Some Consequences of Our Present System of Drug Control as Seen in Notting Hill" (1971), includes the earliest use of the term "moral panic" by a sociologist in print, recently recalled that he and other young British academics involved with the "new deviancy theory" of the 1960s and 1970s saw themselves as advocates of a radically innovative sociological perspective:

> The first level of advocacy was, thus, the appreciation and defemce of subculture; the second was to question the nature of social reaction. This corresponded to the rule of symmetry: that, in order to explain deviant behaviour, it was necessary to explain action and reaction and then, of course, subsequently, the impact of reaction upon action. As such, it invoked a notion of *subcultures in collision* and the necessity of a 'fully social theory' of deviance to explain both, say, the subcultures of youth and those of control, whether the police, journalists, lawyers, etc. But there was, as we have seen, a third level of advocacy, and that concerned the impact of social reaction, namely that secondary deviance was often more severe than primary deviance, secondary harm more of a problem than primary harm. This was the basis of the critique of the whole process of criminalization, of prison as producing the criminal just as the mental hospital constructed madness and treatment clinics produced addicts and alcoholics, etc. Irrationality was, therefore, shifted from the supposedly wanton youth or mindless drugtaker to the agents of control themselves, for the actions of authority through the process of deviancy amplification only made things worse.

In reaction against sociologists of deviance who, it seemed to them, treated criminality and deviance as readily classifiable behaviors or tendencies, Young and other new deviancy theorists advocated a wholesale critique of the social processes of criminalization and of the ascription of deviance. According to Young, the advocacy pursued by new deviancy theorists found expression in three crucial, interrelated concepts about society and deviance or, as Young puts it, expressed itself on three levels. First, rather than seeing mainstream society as a largely non-ideological configuration from which deviant groups diverge, new deviancy theorists saw both mainstream society and deviants as two distinct groups or subcultures, each with its own norms and deviations, that, in conflict with one another, mutually produce categorizations of normativity and deviance. Second, and tied to this viewpoint, instead of accepting deviance as a deviation from social norms to which mainstream society then reacts, new deviancy theorists asserted that both mainstream society and deviant groups act and react in relation to each other. Third, new deviancy theorists recognized no defining distinctions between primary deviance, that is, deviance from social norms, and secondary deviance, that is, further deviance produced as a result of being treated as deviant. They asserted, instead, that all deviance involves reacting to ascriptions of deviance (though acknowledging that being treated as deviant often amplifies deviance).

Young remembers that the various levels of advocacy pursued by new deviancy theorists coalesced in producing the moral panic concept. He relates that the new deviancy theorists' formulation of the moral panics model was inspired by the notion of moral indignation as advanced by Danish sociologist Svend Ranulf in the 1930s and elaborated upon by American criminologist Albert K. Cohen in the 1960s. Young (2009: 10) recounts,

> Albert Cohen conceived of moral indignation as what would now be described as a form of 'othering'—a process both of threat to identity and of confirmation. Further, that such a moral disturbance had an intensity of emotion, that it was a function both of attraction and repulsion. It was out of such an analysis of moral indignation (supplemented of course with notions of the moral entrepreneur ...), and moral passage ... that the concept of moral panic arose. Indeed, if moral indignation depicts the chronic condition of moral disturbance, moral panic is its acute form.

A variation on Friedrich Nietzsche's (1996: 22, emphasis in original) conceptualization of *"ressentiment"* (put simply, profound hostility displaced onto a scapegoat), moral indignation constitutes a discomfort or disquiet experienced by those who adhere to social norms concerning others' deviance from those standards. To Albert K. Cohen's (and before Cohen, Svend Ranulf's) notion of moral indignation, Young adds the insight that it constitutes an ongoing condition that may find episodic expression in moral panics Or, to use Young's (2009: 7) own words, "The folk devils conjured up out of moral indignation and prejudice are actually constructed by the forces of social control."

In "Whose Side Were We On? The Undeclared Politics of Moral Panic Theory" (2011), Stanley Cohen, whose *Folk Devils and Moral Panics: The Creation of the Mods and Rockers* (the first edition of which was published in 1972) remains the most widely influential work on the topic, responds to those critics (religious studies scholar Philip Jenkins among them) who aver that, assumedly because of their leftist social perspectives, he and indeed most researchers chose to analyze repressive moral panics (such as those over drugtaking, mods and rockers, or mugging) that obscured the actual causes of social problems and extended social control over outsiders, strategically ignoring any moral panics that might, in contrast, benefit society. Cohen (2011: 238) writes,

> But can anyone on 'our side' find a good, positive or approved moral panic? Jenkins, one of the few students of moral panic who explicitly poses the question, is also one of the few who stubbornly stands outside the liberal consensus. He repeats the familiar charge that moral panic theory ensures (by circular logic) that its claims to objectivity will always sound bogus or exaggerated: 'Whoever heard of a legitimate panic or of well-founded hysteria?' ... Cases are still chosen, he claims, because of their suitability for debunking by liberals. Moral panic is another term of political correctness (a poor argument as there have in fact been numerous moral panics around child abuse).

Cohen retorts that he and other new deviancy theorists wrote of moral panics that denied the causes of social problems and maintained the *status quo* because that was how such episodes occurred in the 1970s. He adds that by the 2000s, many potentially beneficial moral panics over corporate crime, crimes of the state, and environmental crimes were taking place, furnishing a detailed and enumerated summary of the many differences between moral panics of the 1970s and those of the twenty-first century:

> New forms and features of moral panics are already emerging—trying to adapt in evolutionary-like style to the new conditions of postmodernity. Here are a few; their final shape is not yet clear.
>
> 1. It is easier for us (sociological critics of moral panics) to identify with the kind of moral entrepreneurs behind new panics than with traditional entrepreneurs. We are closer to them in social class, education and ideology. Moreover we are more likely to agree with them about the distinction between moral panic (the problem is taken too seriously) and denial (the problem is not taken seriously enough).
> 2. The alliances between political forces are now more plastic and flexible. Panics about 'genuine' victims (of natural disasters, for example) generate more consensus than uncertain, or even 'unworthy', victims such as the homeless.
> 3. Traditional moral panics are elite engineered. The new panics may not be entirely populist, but do give more space to social movements, identity politics and victims.

4. Theoretically there can be 'negative' moral panics (the traditional ones that criminologists so readily detect, expose and criticize) but also 'positive' ones where we approve the values beyond the 'panic' but not the label itself. It sounds considerably more sensible to talk of an 'approved crusade' than an 'approved panic'. But this would lose precisely the particular connotation of 'panic' that one wants to retain!

5. The dominant tone of new panics is no longer non-interventionist. Indeed, more intervention is the (literally) observable index of success, in particular the construction of more laws, rules, contracts and regulations. The social bases of the new criminalizers ... is surely of interest—either (1) they are post-liberals who come from a decriminalizing generation—private morality is not the business of the state, net-widening leads to the hidden extension of state power, and so on, or (2) they are part of the new right—they are against state power that takes the form of regulation over health, welfare, disease risk, protection, 'hate' and the environment, but private morality (sexuality, abortion, lifestyles) should become even more the business of the state. They also have few problems with the extension of the correctional system.

6. Certain new moral panics can be understood as 'anti-denial' movements. The message is that the denial—cover-up, evasion, normalization, turning a blind eye, tolerance, and so on—of certain social conditions, events and behaviours is morally wrong and politically irrational. Acknowledgement becomes the slogan. The previously denied realities must now be brought to public attention, their dangers exposed, their immorality denounced. (Cohen 2011: 240–41)

Cohen details the many differences between current and past moral panics, contending, for example, that those who act as moral entrepreneurs are now more easily identified with by sociologists, episodes are less often elite engineered than in the past, the political alliances that support moral panics are more flexible and changing than those of the 1970s, and in some cases the victims identified in moral panics, such as survivors of natural disasters, more readily generate consensus (or, in other words, are less often chosen for political purposes). Pointedly, at the same time that he isolates apparently objective distinctions between new and older moral panics, he both questions the assertion that he and other new deviancy theorists were overly subjective in their analyses of moral panics and casts doubt on the notion that later researchers such as Jenkins can claim substantially greater objectivity. For instance, in comparing victims of natural disasters with the homeless, he implies that while some victims at the center of current moral panics may be seen as ideologically neutral, others are certainly not. Additionally, in employing such terms as "post-liberals" and "new right," Cohen emphasizes that later moral panic researchers are no more apolitical than the new deviancy theorists whom they oppose.

## The Evolution of the Moral Panic Concept

Like Jock Young and Stanley Cohen in the works discussed above, the authors collected in part one of *The Ashgate Research Companion to Moral Panics* take backward glances at the moral panics model in order to increase its usefulness for current researchers. In chapter one, "The Genealogy and Trajectory of the Moral Panic Concept," Erich Goode and Nachman Ben-Yehuda look at the political inspiration for the moral panics model. They contend that as the structure of society has changed, so has the concept. They trace its genealogy back to the young British sociologists of the National Deviancy Conference and the cultural ferment of the 1960s.

Chapter two, Toby Miller's "Tracking Moral Panic as a Concept," traces the development of the moral panic concept once it left college and university campuses. In Miller's view, as academics' power to determine its meaning diminished, the notion of moral panic took on a life of its own. Miller concludes that paying attention to the meanings that moral panic has accrued in popular culture may enable us to make it a useful tool in effecting progress in the United States.

Chapter three, "Assemblages of Moral Politics: Yesterday and Today," by Alan Hunt, identifies moral panics as intense, usually short-lived elements of ongoing moral regulation projects. Noting that such episodes do not always have a clear moral aspect, Hunt suggests that moral regulation comprises assemblages of diverse elements whose composition varies over time and where no single component determines the overall trajectory.

In chapter four, "The Problems with Moral Panic: The Concept's Limitations," Joel Best recommends that while some of its originators continue to defend the concept, contemporary researchers might be better advised to assess its problems clearly. As his endeavor in this direction, Best (like Goode and Ben-Yehuda) tracks the evolution of the moral panics model as far back as the National Deviancy Conference.

## References

Cohen, S. 2011. Whose side were we on? The undeclared politics of moral panic theory. *Crime, Media, Culture,* 7(3), 237–43.

Cohen, S. 2002 (1972, 1980). *Folk Devils and Moral Panics: The Creation of the Mods and Rockers.* 3rd Edition. London: Routledge.

Hall, S., Critcher, C., Jefferson, T., Clarke, J., and Roberts, B. 1978. *Policing the Crisis:*

*Mugging, the State, and Law and Order*. Critical Social Studies. Houndmills: Palgrave Macmillan.

Jenkins, P. 2009. Failure to launch: why do some social issues fail to detonate moral panics? *British Journal of Criminology*, 49(1), 35–47.

Nietzsche, F. 1996 (1887), *On the Genealogy of Morals*, translated by D. Smith. Oxford World's Classics. New York: Oxford University Press. Originally published as *Zur Genealogie der Moral: Eine Streitschrift*. Leipzig: C.G. Naumann.

Young, J. 2009. Moral panic: its origins in resistance, ressentiment and the translation of fantasy. *British Journal of Criminology*, 49(1), 4–16.

# The Genealogy and Trajectory of the Moral Panic Concept

## Erich Goode and Nachman Ben-Yehuda*

The Ten Commandments notwithstanding, no ideas drop fully formed from the heavens; all concepts, theories, and principles grow from the ground up, out of the rich soil of context, culture, communication, and human contact. The moral panic is no exception. Exaggerated or misplaced accusations of believed moral wrongdoing, the persecution of innocent parties, and the fear, suspicion, or concern that certain individuals, groups, or categories threaten a community's or a society's well-being, way of life, and moral order stretch back to the dawn of humanity. But it was not until the early 1970s that academics identified, conceptualized, and named the phenomenon of widespread concern over a nonexistent or minor moral threat in the form of a sociological concept.

In 1964, a series of scuffles broke out in Clacton, a small resort town on England's east coast, between two youth factions, the mods (or modernists) and the rockers (delinquent rock and rollers). The damage totaled only a bit more than £500 (perhaps four times that in today's currency). But the police, unaccustomed to such rowdy vandalistic behavior, arrested nearly a hundred youths and the media reported these disturbances, and similar conflicts in other seaside resort towns, in sensationalistic, outraged stories bearing headlines such as "'Wild Ones' Invade Seaside—97 Arrests," and "Wild Ones 'Beat Up' Margate" (see illustrations 1.1, 1.2). These and comparable headlines and reports designated members of youth gangs as deviants, the "other," the enemy—in Stanley Cohen's term, a collective *folk devil*. To put an end to delinquent behaviors such as occurred at Clacton and elsewhere, members of Parliament called for stiffer penalties for "hooliganism" and other youth offenses and the House of Commons introduced and debated bills designed to address the problem of rowdy young people. In 1965, Cohen, then a graduate student at the London School of Economics (LSE), was struck by the "fundamentally inappropriate" reaction of the police, the media, and legislators to these minor incidents and decided to study this intriguing discrepancy (2002: 172).

* The authors would like to thank Jock Young and David Downes for sharing their recollections of the formation of the National Deviancy Conference.

Illustration 1.1    *Daily Mirror*, "'Wild Ones' Invade Seaside—97 Arrests,"
March 30, 1964

Illustration 1.2    *Daily Mirror*, "Wild Ones 'Beat Up' Margate," May 18, 1964

Between 1967 and 1969, Jock Young, another LSE graduate student and a friend of Cohen, while engaging in a participant observation study of marijuana use among bohemian residents of Notting Hill, a community in London, was struck by the stereotypes the police held of drug users, the moral indignation officers felt and expressed toward these young miscreants, and the degree to which police actions often escalated the unconventional behavior they presumably intended to stamp out. Young observed the same overreactions by law enforcement as Cohen, the same creation of deviant categories and characters practically out of whole cloth, and the same media exaggerations. In print, at just about the same time, both researchers referred to episodes of exaggerated concern that conventional, mainstream sectors of the society express toward marginal, unconventional persons and behavior as a *moral panic* (Young 1971a, 1971b, Cohen 2002).

A moral panic is the outbreak of moral concern over a supposed threat from an agent of corruption that is out of proportion to its actual danger or potential harm. The indictments that aggrieved parties lodge during the course of a moral panic episode are not always spurious—the threats named may be genuine—but such claims are by definition exaggerated concerning the seriousness, extent, typicality, direction, or inevitability of alleged harm or danger. Empirically assessed, the fear, concern, and outrage generated by certain conditions or behaviors are disproportionate to their objective threat. For each episode, the society, or a sector of the society, overreacts to a seeming danger in its midst. Over the years and in numerous locales, these perceived, supposed, or exaggerated threats have come from an array of sources, such as recreational drug use, accused child molesters, putative satanic ritual abuse, Jews, Chinese immigrants, pornography, comic books, alleged alien abductions, crime, and communism.

*Who* expresses this concern? The principal "actors" in the moral panic are the media, which publish or broadcast stories about a supposed threat; the public at large, the members of which feel, verbalize, or act on their concern; representatives of the legal system, including politicians and lawmakers, who propose and enact legislation and the police who enforce it; and social movement activists, who organize, recruit, proselytize, assemble, demonstrate, and lobby on behalf of their cause against the putative threat. These agents or actors in each sphere or realm of the moral panic manifest that a given threat *warrants* the expression of a given level of concern, by feeling, talking about, or acting out that sentiment. Actors express concern, whether in sentiment or actions, in these *separate but mutually interpenetrating* spheres; the concern of actors in one realm is not a valid measure or indicator of concern of actors in another. Concern among one set of actors is not necessarily always expressed by another set of actors. A media panic is a media panic even without public sentiment behind it. In a "classic" or full-blown moral panic, however, the concern of actors in all five realms is expressed.

The moral panic is defined by the following components. First, as we have seen, *concern*: members of the society feel anxious, worried, or fearful that something is wrong that must be corrected. Second, *hostility*: the public, or a segment of the public, believes that certain parties are engaging in harmful or threatening behavior, and designate them as a *folk devil* or deviant. Third, *consensus*: a certain, though unspecified, swath of the public shares this concern and feeling of hostility. Fourth, *disproportion*: a measurable disparity exists between concern felt and conveyed (in both talk and action) and the objective threat posed. And fifth: *volatility*: moral panics tend to be outbreaks, temporary episodes of exaggerated concern; they come and go like a fever, although the time span cannot be designated with precision. Some features of the moral panic, such as legislation, may become institutionalized or routinized, but the fever pitch of exaggerated concern cannot be sustained at the same pitch over a long period. As Stanley Cohen says, a moral panic, "by definition, is self-limiting, temporary, and spasmodic, a splutter of rage which burns itself out" (2002: xxx).

## The Origin of the Moral Panic Concept

Where did the notion of the moral panic come from? How did it arise, why did it catch on, and what impelled it on its journey through the corridors of academic and media history? The fertile soil from which the moral panic concept sprang — as Jock Young (2009) himself narrated forty years after the fact — comprised four ingredients: the "new" perspective toward deviance, the notion of resentment and indignation as crucial in judging deviance, the cultural and political upheaval of the 1960s — especially, in Europe, the massive strikes and student protests of 1968 — and the first meeting of a circle of leftish sociologists and criminologists whose organizers baptized themselves the National Deviancy Conference (NDC) (Cohen 1971, Taylor and Taylor 1973: 209–14).

Both historically and contemporaneously, practically all sociologists have paid and continue to pay lip service to the acknowledgement that what is regarded as right and wrong is relative to time and place. Yet, until the 1960s, the principal quest of deviance researchers had been to account for or explain the etiology or causes of non-normative behavior. Traditionally, deviance had been seen as a more or less coherent set of acts, with certain features in common, caused or facilitated by specific, identifiable conditions or factors — such as social disorganization, poverty, anomie, hanging out with the wrong crowd, and inadequate socialization. This "old," explanatory or positivistic perspective toward deviance was *objectivistic* or *essentialistic* in that it regarded categories in the world as having an existence independent of human conceptualization (deviance was regarded as *a kind of behavior*), and *deterministic* in that it sought cause-and-effect explanations between and among variables (deviance was caused by identifiable forces and factors to some degree beyond the actor's control). In the words of Jock Young, the "old" sociology of deviance "deprived" unconventional actions of subjective meaning, attributing them to pathological, undesirable, deterministic factors beyond the actor's agency.

## The "New" Sociology of Deviance

In contrast, the "new" perspective that emerged in the 1960s was constructionist rather than positivist, affirming that deviance was a label rather than a form of behavior, applied *by* certain audiences *to* behavior and enactors, and consequently, the quest for a general explanation of this ephemeral, shifting, contingent, and variable phenomenon was quixotic and unattainable. Perhaps the most often quoted statement to this effect was penned by sociologist Kai T. Erikson (1962: 308, emphasis in original): "Deviance is not a property *inherent in* certain forms of behavior; it is a property *conferred upon* these forms by the audiences which directly or indirectly witness them." Moreover, this "new" approach affirms that efforts to control wrongdoing often backfire, stimulating more deviance rather than less. This perspective shifted the sociologist's attention *away from* the actor and the nature of the act, that is, the person engaged in deviant acts and the acts themselves, *to* the audiences judging, evaluating, and reacting to the actors and the acts designated as deviant (Becker 1963: 8–14). Clearly, the moral panic concept was based on the pivotal idea that the members of the society at large or a sector of the society—including the media, legislators, law enforcement, and social movement activists—feel and express concern toward a threat that is constructed or socially defined as a result of misplaced or exaggerated fear rather than their concern reflecting the amount of overt or objective harm that putative threat can or does objectively visit upon the society. In short, moral panic is only a conceptual baby step away from the "new" sociological definition of deviance.

Admittedly, the distinction between deviant behavior as a form of behavior and deviance as a perceived violation of rules that are themselves "defined, classified, and processed as deviant," is not always easy to make (Cohen 1971: 246). But just as clearly, the two approaches hold sharply contrasting conceptions of deviance and regard their intellectual mission in divergent ways; hence, as with all other distinctions in the social sciences, the difference between them is a matter of degree. Today, when we read the table of contents of a positivistic textbook containing chapters and sections such as "The Criminal Activity of Gangs," "Who Engages in Deviance and Crime?," and "How Much Deviance Is There?" we are impressed by the stark contrast in their orientation with constructionist texts, the chapters of which bear titles such as "The Relativity of Deviance," "Acquiring Deviantness," and "Avoiding Stigma." Arguing that, since deviance and social control are dyadic and interactional, we are unable to detect the difference between the two perspectives that study these domains is nonsensical. The "old" conception of deviance regards it as what it *is*, while the "new" conception sees it as how it is *constructed*, what it is *thought to be*, and how it is *responded to*.

## Indignation, Resentment, and Outrage

Attributions of deviance by definition entail disapproval, censure, and condemnation of actors and acts. In 1938, the Danish sociologist Svend Ranulf, working with ideas formulated a generation or more earlier, argued that moral indignation, or the disinterested tendency to inflict punishment, springs from the self-restraint and repression of hedonism self-imposed by the lower middle class or petite bourgeoisie (1938). Reworking the Ranulf thesis, criminologist Albert K. Cohen (1965: 6–7) argues that one of the cornerstones of the deviance concept is the tendency to stake a claim to one's virtue by condemning deviant others. It could be, Cohen reasons, some audiences feel that certain actors achieved what they have by "cutting corners, cheating, using illegitimate means" (1965: 6). Perhaps these audiences feel that they themselves have exercised "self-restraint, effort, discipline, inhibition" while deviant actors are supposedly "morally undisciplined" and "give themselves up to idleness, self-indulgence" and "forbidden vices" (Cohen 1965: 6). An audience, explains Cohen, may express "righteous puritanical wrath to mete out punishment to the deviants, not so much to stamp out their deviant behavior, as to reaffirm the central importance of conformity as the basis for judging men [and women] and to reassure himself [and herself] and others of his [and her] attachment to goodness" (1965: 7).

Albert K. Cohen's insight that indignation plays a significant role in designations of deviance is clear in the work of both Jock Young and Stanley Cohen. Young (1971a: 95–103), citing the work of Albert K. Cohen, devotes an entire section of *The Drugtakers: The Social Meaning of Drug Use* to the "moral indignation" — hostility and outrage over the use of illicit psychoactive substances for hedonistic purposes by bohemians, hippies, addicts, and other marginal denizens of society — aroused in upright, respectable folk: "For if a person lives by a code of conduct which forbids certain pleasures, which involves the deferring of gratification in certain areas, it is hardly surprising that he will react strongly against those whom he sees to be taking shortcuts" (1971a: 96). Interestingly, in this book, Young makes use of the concepts of "moral indignation" (1971ba: 95–103, 149, 172–4, 223–4) and "moral crusaders" (102–4) — without employing the actual term *moral panic*, which, as we saw, he launched in a different publication the same year (1971b: 50).

In contrast, Stanley Cohen builds his conceptualization of moral indignation not on Albert K. Cohen's reworking of Ranulf's notion but rather on sociologist Joseph R. Gusfield's (1963) analysis of the social origins of alcohol prohibition in the United States. Outrage at the shenanigans of the mods and rockers, said Stanley Cohen, bore a strong resemblance to the temperance movement's efforts to outlaw the sale of alcohol. But Gusfield argued that the motive of most temperance advocates did not spring from their repression of sensuousness, since they themselves did not secretly crave alcohol. And their targets were not members of their own class or community (that is, abstemious, lower middle class, mainly rural, churchgoing, white Anglo-Saxon Protestants) but people who were substantially different from their own kind, either big-city, working-class ethnic Catholics, or upper class and upper middle-class, well-educated Protestants, the members of both of which categories drank (Gusfield 1963: 114). Gusfield's analysis of indignation held that temperance supporters suffered from status panic — the collapse of abstinence as a sign of respectability. Albert K.

Cohen's analysis of indignation as the key ingredient in deviance and Gusfield's analysis of supporters of Prohibition reacting with indignation to a loss in status tie directly in with the moral panic concept. Both authors conclude the reason that actors become riled over minor threats can be traced to moral issues more than material issues, and are more strongly felt in particular social sectors than by the public at large.

## The Sixties

Today, we regard the 1960s as an era of political turmoil and cultural innovation and unconventionality. Recreational drug use, especially of marijuana and LSD, became widespread, and was widely condemned. Rock and roll music exploded, delivering a spirit of rebellion, subversion, intensity, and excitement (along with more than a whiff of marijuana smoke) to a whole generation of teenagers and evoking anger and hostility from their parents' generation. From San Francisco to Berlin, students by the millions protested the war in Vietnam, earning infamy from the conservative mainstream. The massive union strikes of 1968 (the year that Young mentions as being so influential in his and Stanley Cohen's conceptualization of the moral panic) nearly brought down a conservative, nationalist French government. And in August 1968, Soviet tanks crushed a liberal, democratic Czech government. In 1969, patrons of a gay bar in New York City's Greenwich Village rioted in protest against police raids. Feminism achieved widespread recognition and influence as well as hostility from traditional quarters.

Young's designation of the events of 1968 as crucial to his and Stanley Cohen's formulation of the moral panic concept is important to understanding their perspective. Young and Cohen's feeling toward the behavior mainstream society saw as a threat was positive. The Czech regime was vastly more benign than Soviet repression, the music of the Beatles and the Rolling Stones was more exciting and intense than the pap that oozed from the voice and strings of Perry Como and Mantovani, and homosexuality was more beneficent than conventional society's absolute repression of variant sexual expression. It was marijuana as opposed to alcohol, peace versus war, gender equality versus sexism, the reasonable demands of labor versus prevailing low wages and unsafe working conditions. Distinctive about these sixties events and developments was that not only did major sectors of the society overreact to a putative threat; they also greeted these largely positive occurrences negatively, in a hostile fashion. True, these developments seemed to represent the *overturning of a moral order*, but from the point of view of Young, as a man in his twenties during the sixties, the moral order *needed* overturning. Surely, the seed of the moral panic concept could not have been planted in more fertile soil.

The National Deviancy Conference Young mentions the NDC as the fourth of the most significant influences in the genesis of the moral panic concept. The NDC, in the words of its original membership secretary (Taylor 1973: 209) was formed by a small group of sociologists "with a view to widening the nature of

British academic criminology." The organizers regarded the NDC as a kind of "umbrella organization for radicals involved directly in action" in collaboration with activists creating alternatives to incarceration, demanding rights for prisoners, and obtaining shelter and habitation for squatters, and aiding and abetting "revolutionary" social workers and "alternative" psychiatrists (Taylor 1973: 209). The NDC was founded in 1968 and disbanded in 1975. Its conferences produced five published volumes, and the 63 speakers who presented papers at its meetings published, during its active span, 100 books on deviance, crime, and social control (Young 1998: 16).

The conference came together practically spontaneously and without planning. As David Downes explained, the NDC's founding took place, "bang" in the middle of the Third National Criminology Conference at Cambridge.[1] Stanley Cohen asked Downes and several other criminologists if they'd like to get together at a nearby pub and talk about organizing "our own kind of conference," less positivist, less conventional, and less subservient to established interests, those being the Home Office and the criminal justice system. Eventually, the NDC, sorted out between sociologists and criminologists who considered themselves "intellectually radical," who focused on deviance as culture and insurgency, and the "politically radical" wing, those who were concerned with the political economy issues surrounding deviance—in a word, the Marxists. As Jock Young explained the matter, the NDC "was just the right thing at just the right time."[2]

The NDC brought together a group of sociologists and criminologists who pictured the society during the late 1960s and early 1970s as one in which the ruling strata had become increasingly "threatened by a world of pluralism and misbehaviour" (Young 2009: 41) and felt their hegemony more and more precarious and menaced by these sea-changes. In that era, the absolute certainties as to truth and falsity, good and evil, normal and abnormal, was collapsing—an awareness of which the mass of the society became aware. Moral panics develop, NDC participants recognized, when sectors in control lose their grip on the reins of power. It was a time, Young argues, when the authorities stirred up moral panics to reassert their dominance. The concentration of dozens of scholars who shared this view (the first meeting of the NDC attracted between 100 and 200 participants) reported their perspective in several of the National Deviancy Conference proceedings, reaffirmed that perspective in discussions, and broadcast it in book chapters and journal articles, serving to propagate it throughout their respective fields.

## The Trajectory of the Moral Panic Concept

If we take academic attention as a measure of success, the moral panic concept has proven to be a whopping one. With each succeeding decade, the number of books,

---

1    Personal communication.
2    Personal communication.

articles in the mass media and academic journals, and citations and references in the social science literature, substantially increase. It is "safe to say," criminologist Jason Ditton (2007: 1) declares, that the moral panic "has been far and away the most influential sociological concept to have been generated in the second half of the twentieth century." As a concept, the moral panic has proved so valuable and useful that, says sociologist David Garland (2008: 9), if Stanley Cohen had not devised the term, "it would have been necessary for someone else to invent it." At the same time, as we saw, in common with all successful concepts and theories, it has attracted more than its share of criticism (Waddington 1986, Johnson 1997, Ungar 2001, Cornwell and Linders 2002, Waiton 2008), which is to be expected—if no one cared about them, no one would criticize them.

Joel Best (2004: ix–xi) takes the number of articles (as seen in the JSTOR database) containing the word *deviance* published in the *American Journal of Sociology*, the *American Sociological Review*, and *Social Forces* decade by decade from the 1940s to the 1990s as an indication of the degree to which sociologists have found the concept useful in understanding behaviors. Cohen (2002: xxxv) conducted a citation count himself, locating eight citations to moral panics in UK newspapers for 1984, 25 for 1992, 145 for 1993, and an average of 109 from 1994 to 2001—a huge rise from the 1980s to the 1990s, a dip in the 1990s, and a leveling off through the 1990s into the early 2000s.

Similarly, we believe that interest in the moral panic concept can be measured by publications dedicated to or mentioning the topic. And in the academic literature, each decade since the appearance of *Folk Devils and Moral Panics: The Creation of the Mods and Rockers* has witnessed a growing number of publications that refer to or discuss the moral panic. Consider books: we searched Amazon.com, the Library of Congress, and New York University's and Columbia University's catalogues for books with "moral panic" or "moral panics" in their title. During the 1970s, the only book published that contained "moral panics" in its title was Stanley Cohen's original volume. During the 1980s, three appeared (counting the second edition of Cohen's book, which was released in 1980). In the 1990s, there were 11. And in the decade between 2000 and 2009, the number had increased to 16. As we can see from table 1.1, the same is true of journal articles. Two ProQuest searches, an OmniFile Wilson Web search, a Harzing citation search, and a Web of Science/Web of Knowledge search all indicate a substantial growth in scholarly (and popular) attention to the topic of the moral panic since its introduction; only JSTOR indicates a leveling off. Clearly, to judge from productivity and citations, moral panic is vastly more influential than it was in decades past.

**Table 1.1    Use of "Moral Panic" or "Moral Panics" in the Title[3]**

|  | Book Titles | Articles ProQuest Smart Search | Articles ProQuest Central | Articles OmniFile WilsonWeb | Articles Harzing Citation Search | Articles JSTOR | Web of Science/ Web of Knowledge |
|---|---|---|---|---|---|---|---|
| 1971–9 | 1 | 0 | 0 | 0 | 11 | 0 | 3 |
| 1980–9 | 3 | 0 | 3 | 4 | 50 | 2 | 13 |
| 1990–9 | 11 | 32 | 97 | 29 | 236 | 20 | 61 |
| 2000–9 | 16 | 40 | 187 | 53 | 355 | 20 | 137 |

## Summary and Conclusions

In 1964, Stanley Cohen, searching for a dissertation topic, noticed the overblown reaction by the press, the public, law enforcement, and legislators to relatively minor scuffles and acts of vandalism engaged in or committed by two youth groups, the mods and the rockers, which had taken place in a small seaside town. During the incident, the police arrested nearly a hundred young people, and the British press enjoyed a field day of sensationalism. The story had enough media and public interest to go international in scope and enough staying power for tie-in incidents occurring in nearby communities to remain in the news for a couple of years afterward. The episode tapped into larger, deeper resentments felt by the British public that an entire generation had become ungrateful, spoiled, delinquent, violent, hedonistic, and ill-suited for and unwilling to meaningfully participate in the demands of contemporary technological society. At the same time, Jock Young, a fellow sociology graduate student and Cohen's friend, noticed the same discrepancy regarding the relatively minor threat posed by marijuana use and the substantial public, media, and law enforcement concern and indignation that the supposed threat stirred up.

As Chas Critcher (2003: 10) explains, "A whole new social problem had been defined" by the seaside disorders. A year after the Clacton incident, Cohen collected relevant newspaper articles on it and related disturbances, traveled to

---

3    Category "Articles" includes book reviews. Count includes only articles that include the exact phrase "Moral Panic" or "Moral Panics" in the title (or reviews a book with that phrase in its title). The total number of books published in the United States each year remained stable between the mid-1970s and the mid-1990s at roughly 40,000; in 1999, R.R. Bowker, the publisher of *Books in Print*, drastically changed its method of compiling the count and in 2005 the number of recognized published books increased to 157,000. We have not been able to find out what data were included in the count. Clearly, the later count cannot be compared with the earlier ones. But just as clearly, the enterprise of moral panic research and scholarship has expanded—as has social science research and scholarship more generally.

several seaside communities and interviewed journalists, residents, local opinion leaders, and young people, and held discussion groups to understand the discrepancy between the outlandishly exaggerated social reaction he observed and the comparatively trivial nature of the offenses.

Young used the moral panic term to refer to such incidents in a paper at a conference in 1968, published as a chapter in a book in 1971. Cohen (2002) says that both of them "probably" picked up the term from Marshall McLuhan's popular, trendy 1960s essay, *Understanding Media: The Extensions of Man* (1964: xxxv). The notion of a disproportion in social reaction was clearly in the air; it comprised the foundation stone of most of the innovative early sociological theorizing about deviance. The four core chapters of *Outsiders: Studies in the Sociology of Deviance,* sociologist Howard S. Becker's (1963) influential treatise, focused on marijuana smokers and dance musicians, the majority of the chapters in Becker's collection *The Other Side: Perspectives on Deviance* (1964) also dealt with "soft" or nonvictim deviance, and sociologist Kai T. Erikson's monograph *Wayward Puritans: A Study in the Sociology of Deviance* (1966) addressed the topic of witches, a nonexistent form of deviance. The era of the 1960s likewise was one in which outrage over unjust treatment of members of powerless, marginal social categories dominated political discourse and protest; again, we see the parallel with moral panics in its stress on disproportion.

However influential were the politics and culture of the 1960s—the birth of the "new" perspective on deviance, the NDC, and Albert K. Cohen's (and Svend Ranulf's) notion of indignation—to the formulation of moral panics, the concept continues to remain influential. In fact, with each passing decade, the number of academic and mass media mentions, attacks by critics attempting to discount it, and books and articles bearing the phrase in their titles continues to grow. In the 1970s, it was an idea whose time had come. It remains, today, an idea whose utility has proven timeless.

# References

Becker, H.S. 1963. *Outsiders: Studies in the Sociology of Deviance.* New York: Free Press of Glencoe.

Becker, H.S. (ed.). 1964. *The Other Side: Perspectives on Deviance.* New York: Free Press of Glencoe.

Best, J. 2004. *Deviance: Career of a Concept.* Belmont, CA: Wadsworth.

Cohen, A.K. 1965. The sociology of the deviant act: anomie theory and beyond. *American Sociological Review*, 30(1), 5–14.

Cohen, S. (ed.). 1971. *Images of Deviance.* Harmondsworth: Penguin Books.

Cohen, S. 2002 (1972, 1980). *Folk Devils and Moral Panics: The Creation of the Mods and Rockers.* 3rd Edition. London: Routledge.

Cornwell, B. and Linders, A. 2002. The myth of "moral panic": an alternative account of LSD prohibition. *Deviant Behavior*, 23, 307–30.

Ditton, J. 2007. Folk Panics and Moral Devils. Unpublished paper.

Erikson, K.T. 1962. Notes on the sociology of deviance. *Social Problems*, 9(3), 307–14.

Erikson, K.T. 1966. *Wayward Puritans: A Study in the Sociology of Deviance*. New York: John Wiley.

Garland, D. 2008. On the concept of moral panic. *Crime Media Culture*, 4(1), 9–30.

Gusfield, J.R. 1963. *Symbolic Crusade: Status Politics and the American Temperance Movement*. Urbana: University of Illinois Press.

Johnson, N.N. 1997. Review: *Moral Panics: The Social Construction of Deviance*, by E.Goode and N. Ben-Yehuda. Oxford, UK: Blackwell. *Social Forces*, 75(4), 1514–5.

McLuhan, M. 1964. *Understanding Media: The Extensions of Man*. New York: McGraw-Hill.

Ranulf, S. 1964 (1938). *Moral Indignation and Middle Class Psychology*. Copenhagen: Levin and Munsgaard.

Taylor, I. 1973. A note on the National Deviancy Conference, in *Politics and Deviance*, edited by I. Taylor and L. Taylor. Harmondsworth: Penguin Books, 209–10.

Taylor, I. and Taylor, L. (eds). 1973. *Politics and Deviance*. Harmondsworth: Penguin Books.

Ungar, S. 2001. Moral panics versus the risk society: the implications of the changing sites of social anxiety. *British Journal of Sociology*, 52, 271–91.

Waddington, P.A.J. 1986. Mugging as a moral panic: a question of proportion. *British Journal of Sociology*, 37(2), 245–59.

Waiton, S. 2008. *The Politics of Antisocial Behavior: Amoral Panics*. Routledge Advances in Criminology. New York: Routledge.

Walton, P. and Young, J. (eds). 1998. *The New Criminology Revisited*. Houndmills: Palgrave Macmillan.

Young, J. 1971a. *The Drugtakers: The Social Meaning of Drug Use*. London: MacGibbon and Kee.

Young, J. 1971b. The role of the police as amplifiers of deviancy, negotiators of reality and translators of fantasy: some consequences of our present system of drug control as seen in Notting Hill, in *Images of Deviance*, edited by S. Cohen. Harmondsworth: Penguin Books, 27–61.

Young, J. 1998. Breaking windows: situating the new criminology, in *The New Criminology Revisited*, edited by P. Walton and J. Young. Houndmills: Palgrave Macmillan, 14–46.

Young, J. 2009. Moral panic: its origins in resistance, ressentiment and the translation of fantasy into reality. *British Journal of Criminology*, 49(1), 4–16.

# Tracking Moral Panic as a Concept

## Toby Miller

Social scientists anxiously police their own borders at the same time that they disrespect others' frontiers. Perhaps most notoriously, economists claim to understand all forms of social organization, disregarding historians, sociologists, and anthropologists who fail to subscribe to the ratiocinative, desiring, selfish, monadic subject at the heart of the neoclassical belief system. They rarely pay attention to heterodox economic ideas either from within their own elect or as they are incarnated elsewhere (Ruccio 2008).

Sociology, anthropology, literary studies, communication, and cultural studies are similarly imperialistic in their panoramic gaze at the world—but it does not really matter what they say outside college cloisters. Their social and political influence is minimal by contrast with the rational-actor true believers, who have successfully parlayed their precepts into three decades of influence over economic policy, military recruitment, bombing, regulation, the law, medical provision, and so on. Rarely does a concept from socio-cultural theory even begin to penetrate the sciences or the bourgeois media, by contrast.

## Moral Panics

Moral panic is different. It is not just an externally imposed scholarly category that circulates in scholarly space or lands on an unsuspecting and unaware public to organize and pronounce upon their lives from within commercial or governmental bureaucracies. The idea of moral panic has successfully migrated from musty libraries and neglected websites to the public realm. Unusually for sociological and cultural theories, it is frequently used by, for example, the mainstream United Kingdom, Australasian, and Filipino press and the British National Council for Civil Liberties. Even the US media recently caught on (contemporary media references include Dewan 2000, Wilgoren 2002, Hendershott 2003, McLemee 2003, Shea 2003,

Wright and Rosenfeld 2003, Barlow 2004, Muschamp 2004, Surowiecki 2004, Ortiz 2005, Taylor 2011, Sullum 2011, Gilligan 2011).

For some keepers of the academic flame, this development is threatening. It is to be condemned, because it leads to methodological impurity and theoretical impiety. As a consequence of its public popularity, the notion of moral panic has supposedly become too imprecise and easily redeployed to retain scholarly legitimacy absent a rescue mission by accredited *ologists* (Rohloff and Wright 2010, Klocke and Muschert 2010).

In this chapter, I am not greatly interested in occupational loyalty or theoretical purism. Rather, I am concerned to look at the work done by the idea of moral panic—not as it is debated by academics in our journals and halls, but as the concept circulates in the public sphere. Having established its creative provenance in popular culture, I draw on it to investigate the contemporary discourse and material circumstance of young people in the United States. Perhaps perversely, I suggest that the energies of a moral panic be redisposed to help demilitarize yanqui youth, starting with electronic games, which are key recruiters and trainers for their empire. In other words, I go so far as to oppose the moral panic about moral panics, arguing instead for the tactical utility of creating such a force against prevailing imperialist ideology. Moral panics are popular-cultural reactions to limit cases of riskiness, played out in highly exaggerated ways and projected onto scapegoats or folk devils. The term was coined within critical British criminology in the early 1970s to describe media messages that announced an increase in the crime rate, and the subsequent establishment of specialist police units to deal with the alleged problem. Moral panics are usually short-lived spasms that speak of ideological contradictions about economic inequality. They exaggerate a social problem, symbolize it in certain groups, predict its future, then conclude, or change. So, we might summarize them as sudden, frequently brief, but seemingly thoroughgoing anxieties about particular human subjects or practices. Generated by the state or the media, then picked up by interest groups and social movements (or vice versa) their impact is generally disproportionate to the problems they bring into being (Thompson 1998: 7, Barker 1999, Jenkins 1999: 4–5, Goode 2000).

Moral panics are often sustained by activists (known as moral entrepreneurs) who seek to protect a majority they see as feckless and vulnerable. Turncoats, rejects, dissident former insiders, or professional experts can be crucial witnesses (Shaps 1994, Thompson 1998: 3, 12, 91). The dual roles of experts and media critics in the constitution of moral panics see the former testifying to their existence and the latter sensationalizing and diurnalizing them—making the risks attributed to a particular panic seem like a new, terrifying part of everyday life. The cumulative impact of this alliance between specialist and popular knowledge is a heightened, yet curiously normalized sense of risk about and amongst the citizenry (Wagner 1997: 46).

Moral panics tend to function synecdochally: part of society is used to represent (or perhaps distort) a wider problem—youth violence is a suitable case for panic about citizenship, whereas systemic class inequality is not; adolescent behavior and cultural style are questionable, but capitalist degeneracy is not; rap is a problem, the situation of urban youth is not; Islamic violence is problematic, Protestant violence is not. Particular kinds of individuals are labeled as dangerous to social well-being because of their deviance from agreed-upon norms of the general good. Once identified, their life practices are then interpreted from membership of a group and vice versa (Cohen 1973: 9–13, Yúdice 1990, Cohen 1999: 192–3, Wichtel 2002).

Critics of the moral panic process propose that we ask not why people behave like this, but why this conduct is deemed deviant and whose interest does that serve (Cohen 2002: 12–13)? Attempts to retrieve folk devils for progressive politics, historical and contemporary analyses of slaves, crowds, pirates, bandits, audiences, minorities, women, and the working class have utilized archival, ethnographic, and textual methods to emphasize day-to-day noncompliance with authority via practices of consumption that frequently turn into practices of production. For example, British research has lit upon teddy boys, mods, bikers, skinheads, punks, students, teen girls, Rastas, truants, dropouts, and magazine readers as its magical agents of history, that is, groups that deviated from the norms of schooling and the transition to work. Scholar-activists examine the structural underpinnings to collective style, investigating how bricolage subverts the achievement-oriented, materialistic, educationally driven values and appearance of the middle class. The working assumption has often been that subordinate groups adopt and adapt signs and objects of the dominant culture, reorganizing them to manufacture new meanings. Consumption is thought to be the epicenter of such subcultures.

Historically, moral panic discourse was the province of progressive critics: reactionaries at the *British Medical Journal* and the *Daily Mail* have attacked use of the moral panic framework to evaluate science or criticize carceral practices, progressives at *The Lancet* have found moral panic persuasive, and groups such as lesbian-gay-bisexual-transgender coalitions deploy the concept. But it has developed beyond these origins, appealing, *inter alios*, to the true believer libertarians at *Reason*. They love the idea of moral panic as a means of criticizing notions such as public health and occupational safety (Daniels 1998, Barker 1999, Tan 2001, "An Avalanche" 2002, Wichtel 2002, Critcher 2003: 2, 53, Fitzpatrick 2003, Gillespie 2003, Power 2004: 12, Žižek 2005, Gilman 2010, Gilligan 2011, Sullum 2011).

## Risk Society

I think the success of the concept of moral panic is closely tied to what is described by a related idea: risk society. The contemporary world is laden with institutions that seek to protect people from social, political, economic, and individual risks and ensure the time discipline required by capitalism (Beck 1999, 2001, 2002). Risk societies must come to terms with the unintended consequences of modernity, not only via technocrats seeking solutions to problems created by themselves or other technocrats, but also via transparent decision-making systems that encourage public debate, rather than operating in secret or deriding public perceptions as ipso facto erroneous (Beck 1999: 3, 5). If early modernity was organized around producing and distributing goods in a struggle for the most effective and efficient forms of industrialization, with devil take the hindmost and no thought for the environment, today's society is about enumerating and managing those dangers (for example, establishing markets for pollution that send murky industries offshore). It organizes what cannot be organized, embodying and propelling the desires of capital and state to make sense of and respond to problems, whether or not of their own making. Risk is sold, pooled, and redistributed (Power 2004: 10, 17).

Put another way, whereas early modernization was primarily concerned with the establishment of national power and the accumulation and distribution of wealth, developed modernity produces new risks for its members beyond collective security and affluence and provides them with incentives and systems for a carefully calibrated self-management. But such practices often appear of limited value in the face of iatrogenic crises brought on by deliberate policy, for example nuclear energy, genocidal weaponry, biotechnology, and industrial pollution—professional miscalculations and scientific discoveries hurtling out of control (Kitzinger and Reilly 1997: 320). These can lead to a raft of governmental responses. In Western Europe, the last twenty years have seen new consumer-protection legislation to increase safety. In the United States, the response has been more a matter of litigation (Smutniak 2004).

From where I write, the United States is *the* risk society, with 50 percent of the population participating in stock market investments. Far from residing in the hands of professionals, risk is brought into the home as an everyday ritual or an almost blind faith (sometimes disappointed) in mutual funds patrolling retirement income. In 1999, US residents spent US$800 billion on insurance—more than they paid for food and equivalent to 35 percent of the world's total insurance expenditure. The insurance costs alone of September 11, 2001 have been calculated at US$21 billion and the industry's global revenues exceed the gross domestic product of all countries, barring the top three. At one level, this represents a careful calculation of risk, its incorporation into lifelong and posthumous planning—prudence as a way of life. At another level, it is a wager on hopelessness and fear that has since emerged in politics because so many risks that yanquis worry about are *un*insurable. As dangers mount, safeguards diminish. So, whether we are discussing nuclear power plants or genetically modified foods, the respective captains of industry argue that they pose no risks, but insurance companies decline to write policies on them for citizens, precisely because they are so risky. It is significant that Paul Bremer, George Bush Minor's patrón of Iraq after the invasion, quickly established a crisis consulting practice after September 11, 2001. He is part of the emergent category of risk managers who quantify danger and the costs of meeting it—for a fee (Beck 1999: 53, 105, Strange 2000: 127, Martin 2002: 6, 12, Klein 2003, *World Trade* 2003: 2, Zorach 2003, "Covered" 2004).

The contemporary cultural-political agenda is characterized by an actuarial gaze, a visual management of threats and responses, with the media simultaneously a mirror and a site of creation, reflection, policy, and action that bind the everyday to the spectacle and the private to the public (Feldman 2005: 206–7). This is where risk society encounters, or is embedded in, moral panic. The epithet once used to deride local news television in the United States—if it bleeds, it leads—today applies to network news, where the correlation between national crime statistics and coverage of crimes shows no rational linkage. The drive to create human-interest stories from blood has become a key means of generating belief in a risk society, occupying 16 percent of network news in 1997, up from 8 percent in 1977. When ratings are measured, US television news allocates massive space to supposed risks to viewers. The idea is to turn anxiety and sensation into spectatorship and money. Local news in particular is remorselessly dedicated to youth violence (Auletta 2001, Lowry et al. 2003, Hickey 2004, Grossberg 2005: 43, Project for Excellence in Journalism 2005).

Risk society is abetted and indexed by incidents like the media hysteria over anthrax in October 2001—responses that were out of all proportion to reality, given the under-reported plenitude of dangerous industrial chemicals and organisms confronted by US workers every day and the extraordinary hazards posed by chemical plants to literally millions should there be an accidental or deliberate release of their deadly product. Bush Minor's Presidential addresses enunciated this helplessness and risk. Ever ready with a phrase describing or predicting catastrophic, apocalyptic terror, the ratio of negative, pessimistic words to positive, optimistic ones was vastly greater in Minor's lexicon than those of Franklin Roosevelt, Ronald Reagan, George Bush the Elder, Bill Clinton, or Barack Obama. In his first term, the word "evil" appeared over 350 times in formal speeches. The 2004 presidential election testified to the efficacy of this approach: risk of attack was the key issue determining older voters' choices. Clearly, risk is crucial to panic, and governance and the media provide staging grounds for its symbolic work (Brooks 2003, Kellner 2003: 82–3, "Congressional Report" 2005, Feldman 2005, *Trends* 2005: 4).

## The Young

The United States today is a risk society *laden* with such moral panics. For example, when school drug use diminishes, people believe it increases. The basis for such misconceptions is media reportage—so when the number of murders declines, the coverage of murders soars. The classic case is young African-American men in the United States over the past two decades. As rates of violence, homicide, and drug use fall dramatically amongst black men under thirty, press panic about their conduct heads in the opposite direction. The disparity between the imaginary and the symbolic in the public circulation of these men is central, even as they suffer massive material discrimination (Glassner 1999: xi, xxi, 29, Males 2004). While the specifics of this assault on blackness are clearly articulated to slavery and racism, they also derive from a historical discourse of risk and panic aimed at young people in general, as indexed in popular culture.

US popular culture has long been a risky locale for the combustion of moral panics about the young. In the early twentieth century, opera, Shakespeare, and romance fiction were censored for their immodest impact on children (Heins 2002: 23). Such tendencies moved into high gear with the Payne Fund Studies of the 1930s, which inaugurated mass social scientific panic about young people at the cinema (Mitchell 1929, Blumer 1933, Blumer and Hauser 1933, Dale 1933, Forman 1933, May and Shuttleworth 1933). These pioneering scholars boldly set out to gauge youthful emotional reactions to the popular by assessing galvanic skin response (Wartella 1996: 173). That example has led to seven more decades of obsessive attempts to correlate youthful consumption of popular culture with antisocial conduct. The pattern is that whenever new communications technologies emerge, children are immediately identified as both pioneers and victims, simultaneously endowed by manufacturers and critics with immense power and immense vulnerability. This was true of 1920s Radio Boys, seeking out signals from afar, and 1990s Girl Power avatars, seeking out subjectivities from afar. They are held to be the first to know and the last to understand the media—the grand paradox of youth, latterly on display in the digital sublime of technological determinism, but as always with the superadded valence of a future citizenship in peril (Mosco 2004: 80). Youth's grand paradox is to be simultaneously the most silenced population in society and the noisiest (Grossberg 1994: 25).

Complex relations of commodification, governmentality, and conservatism fueled these tendencies. *Popular Science* magazine coined the word *teenager* in 1941, *Seventeen* magazine appeared on newsstands three years later, and by the 1950s the white-picket family and home seemed under threat from a newly enfranchised shopper and worker, whose physiological changes were supposedly exacerbated by the temptations of consumer culture and irresponsibility. In 1957, *Cosmopolitan* gloomily predicted teenagers taking over via a vast determined band of blue-jeaned storm troopers (soon to be among its valued readers, of course) (Griffin 1993: 22, Steinberg and Kincheloe 1997: 1–2, Mazzarella 2003: 230, Grossberg 2005: 3).

Congressional hearings and trade publishers promoted psychiatric denunciations of comic books, for example, as causes of nightmares, juvenile delinquency, and even murder. To elude regulation, publishers developed codes of conduct that embodied respect for parents and honorable behavior in their precepts of self-governance (Heins 2002: 52–4, Park 2004: 114). A decade later, young people lost free speech protection, because the Supreme Court differentiated youthful from adult citizens in permitting state governments to legislate in ways that would be unconstitutional if applied to adults (*Ginsberg v. New York* 390 US 629). Both mass movement and mass market, the right was horrified by this commercial child (Liljeström 1983:144–6, Lewis 1992: 3).

Why? The privatized nuclear household with its male breadwinner, female homemaker, and dependent children shifted from an insurgent ideal of the white middle class in the nineteenth century, to a tentatively achieved, but ideologically naturalized, norm in the twentieth. In the 1950s, 80 percent of children grew up with their married, biological parents. But that was true of just 12 percent of children by the end of the 1980s, and only 7 percent of them lived with an employed father and home-duties mother, while the 2000 census disclosed that married couples with children were just 25 percent of the population (Reeves and Campbell 1994: 186–9, Coltrane 2001: 390). To the horror of evangelical Christianity, these numbers reveal the family to be a contingent form of association, with unstable boundaries and varying structures (Shapiro 2001: 2). At the same time, conservatives adopted a moral panic argument to the effect that state intervention and progressive ideas had melded to create lost generations. A new risk-society prudence and prudery, allied to economic deregulation, would rescue them for sanctity and capital (Grossberg 2005: 37).

These familial crises, understood as failures of ethical principle, have displaced attention from the horrific impact on the young of the cessation of vital social services during the disastrous presidencies of Reagan, the Bushes, Clinton, and Obama. The data on youth welfare demonstrate the centrality of big government to the family solidity that these hegemons rhetorically pined for, but programmatically undermined thanks to massive erosions in expenditure on health care, nutrition programs, foster care, and a whole raft of services for young people. A succession of judicial decisions further disenfranchised them. Conservative justices were contemptuous of privacy rights for children, and the United States repeatedly established new records amongst developed countries for the execution of people under eighteen, with the longstanding support of the Supreme Court, half of whose justices favored killing those aged under fifteen before the 2005 *Roper v. Simmons* decision that executing those who were under 18 when they committed their crimes was unconstitutional (Males 1996: 7, 35, Kaplan 2004: 21). The bizarre *4parents.gov* website (defunct) suggested condoms were ineffective, stigmatized HIV patients as risky young people, ignored queer children—and was the product of a pet Bush Administration nongovernmental organization, the National Physicians Center for Family Resources The outcome of these policies has been that US citizens over forty are the wealthiest group in world history and have the lowest tax payments in the First World. Whereas in the first half of the twentieth century few teenaged children in the United States worked for money, almost half had to do so by its end, and one child in eight has no health coverage. In 1999, at the peak of the New Economy, child poverty was up 17 percent from 1979, 50 percent higher than the national average across all age groups, while the twenty-first century recession was accompanied by reductions in youth employment programs (Ruddick 2003: 337, 348, *State of America's Children* 2004, *2004 Report* 2004, Liebel 2004: 151, Grossberg 2005: 59, 64, Ivins 2005).

Despite this disenfranchisement, the little beasts are prevailed upon to love their country, as per Bush Minor introducing a Lessons of Liberty schools program to ideologize them into militarism. In 2004, 83 percent of US high schools ran community-service programs, up from 27 percent two decades earlier, and some required anti-leftism (Westheimer and Kahne 2004). For all the world a throwback to Soviet era yanqui drills that involved scurrying under school desks to elude radiation, Minor's ("Kids' Role" 2004) Ready for Kids initiative hailed children in emergency responses to terrorism. He announced policies to improve students' knowledge of American history, increase their civic involvement, and deepen their love for our great country, requiring that children learn that America is a force for good in the world, bringing hope and freedom to other people (Westheimer 2004: 231). And Senator Lamar Alexander (Westheimer 2004: 231), a previous head of education and university bureaucrat, sponsored the American History and Civics Education Act so our children can grow up learning what it means to be an American. Meanwhile, progressive political activism by young people led to immediate sanction. In West Virginia, a high school pupil was suspended for inviting her colleagues to join an antiwar club, as were a ninth-grader in Maryland for marching against the invasion of Iraq, and a high schooler in Colorado for posting peace flyers (Westheimer 2004: 232). Wrong knowledge of American history, wrong type of civic involvement.

Meanwhile, social statistics were indexing youth trauma. Thirty thousand people kill themselves in the United States each year, making suicide the eleventh most frequent cause of death, but it is third amongst the young (Romer and Jamieson 2003). Suicide levels fell across the population between 1950 and 1995, but the rate for fifteen- to nineteen-year-olds quadrupled. Key social measures of unhappiness correlate with youth today in a way that they did not up to the mid-1970s, and young people report greater distress than before, beyond even the concerns of the elderly (Putnam 2000: 261–3). The psy-complexes argue that adolescents are ten times more likely to suffer depression than 100 years ago (Gillham and Reivich 2004: 152). Perhaps to cope with their feelings of helplessness, 135,000 teenagers packed a gun with their sandwiches and schoolbooks each day in 1990, while by 2004, eight children and teenagers died by gunshot per day (Lewis 1992: 41, *State of America's Children* 2004). This in turn relates to marketing. With the white male market for firearms saturated, and attempts to sell to women falling short of the desired numbers, manufacturers turned to young people in the 1990s (Glassner 1999: xxi, 55).

Young people clearly incarnate adult terror in the face of the popular. They provide a *tabula rasa* onto which can be placed every manner of anxiety (Hartley 1998: 15). Hence, Clinton announcing in 1997 that "we've got about six years to turn this juvenile crime thing around or our country is going to be living in chaos" and the Senate Judiciary Committee declaring that the facade of our material comfort secretes a national tragedy where children are killing and harming each other—even as youth crime had just dropped by almost 10 percent in a year. In 2000, 70 percent of adults expected a neighborhood school shooting, even though pupils were much more likely to be hit by lightning than by gunfire on campus. When Bush Minor joined the chorus to proclaim a plague of school violence, he went against statistics that clearly show schools to be some of the safest places for children to be. Youth violence is dropping, even as rates of incarceration soar. A child is arrested every twenty seconds, many through violations of municipally imposed curfews. Conversely, while child abuse increases, rates of imprisonment for offending adults remain low (Glassner 1999: xiv, Grossberg 2005: 4, 41–2, 44). The economic deregulation Clinton Minor and Obama presided over, with all its attendant risks, was twinned with a moral reregulation, with all its attendant panics.

Risk and morality have merged, with mutual impact. Moral panics become means of dealing with risk society via appeals to values, a displacement from socio-economic crises and fissures. They both contribute to, and are symptomatic of, risk society. But rather than being mechanisms of functional control that necessarily displace systemic social critique onto particular scapegoats, moral panics have themselves been transformed by the discourse of risk society. Because certain dangers seem ineradicable, moral panics are mobilized to highlight issues in keeping with the tenets of conservative and neoliberal cultural politics (Thompson 1998, Ungar 2001, Critcher 2003, Hier 2003). Religion is a key form of mobilization, with evangelical Protestantism legitimizing neoliberal risk at the same time as it promotes righteous indignation against groups that provide an alternative (leftists, feminists, queers, and foreigners), groups whose very existence brings into question foundational myths of the nation (African Americans), or groups whose fragility indexes the future of the nation (young people).

Iatrogenic risk produces moral panic. Ignorant citizens are ill equipped to understand what is happening around them. The void is filled by religiosity and other forms of superstition and ahistorical politics. The process exemplifies the governance of everyday life at arm's length via a stress on national, personal risk rather than global, collective solidarity. It starts with young people, fetishized as unreliable custodians of a future that may not arrive, due to their amorality. Moral panic has become a crucial tool if we are to comprehend, and mend, this juggernaut of a nation. Hewing to a methodological purism that decries the use of the idea in the public realm is to miss both the value of popular culture and the reincarnation of theory in heterodox ways and *fora*. The concluding segment of this chapter picks up the idea of the moral panic and reverses it: instead of being things to expose and criticize, perhaps moral panics could actually enlighten us if successfully managed.

## Militarism

The US Navy's promotional strategy, comprising a multimedia campaign orchestrated since 2009 around the notion of being "A Global Force for Good™" (as opposed to the previous recruiting technique, which promised young people it would "Accelerate Your Life") has produced such enticements as the following:

> Take the world's most powerful sea, air and land force with you wherever you go with the new America's Navy iPhone app. Read the latest articles. See the newest pics and videos. And learn more about the Navy—from its vessels and weapons to its global activities. You can do it all right on your iPhone—and then share what you like with friends via your favorite social media venues. (*America's Navy*)

Further examples of this newly beneficent if still speedy work are offered in television commercials that show Navy personnel capturing Somali pirates, treating Haitian earthquake survivors, and handing toys to impoverished children. But there is always another side to this notion. An unbridled nationalism rides side-saddle with civil-society mythology. The Navy twins these duties via its trite but revealing slogan "First to Fight, First to Help," and insists that "the strength and status of any nation can be measured in part by the will and might of its navy" ("A Global Force" 2011). Such campaigns rely on a poverty draft and the militarization of everyday life. The military is the nation's premier employer of 17- to 24-year-old workers (Verklin and Kanner 2007). Throughout the country, there is an extraordinary reliance of working class people on military welfare as a source of work, whether through making weaponry—the nation's principal manufacturing export—or via direct employment as servants of the Pentagon, be it in the field, the hospital, or the bureau.

Consider the student body I teach. Located just east of Los Angeles, it is working class economically and diverse culturally. There is no ethnic majority on campus, with white students comprising less than a fifth of the population. Unsurprisingly, many folks serve in the military or have relatives doing so. California has a million-person majority voting for Democrats in presidential elections—and every person, at every moment, is never further than 70 kilometers from a military establishment. That is quite a multiplier effect, both economically and ideologically. Everyday life in this putatively progressive part of the United States is not a site of resistance, as per the romantic wishes of many on the left, but a site of militarization. Similar things could be said across the country, especially in poverty zones (see Goldberg 2010).

To join the US military, it is not necessary to be a citizen—obtaining citizenship is a potential benefit that attracts recruits. Killing and dying are culturally transterritorial, with 38,000 US soldiers being aliens. Neoconservatives even call for the Pentagon to recruit undocumented residents and people who have never been in the United States, under the rubric of a *Freedom Legion*. The reward for service would be citizenship, following similar gifts to anticommunist East Europeans in the 1950s. Plus US military recruiters highlight free or cheap elective plastic surgery for uniformed personnel and their families (with the policy alibi that this permits doctors to practice their art) (Amaya 2007, Fifield 2009, Miller 2007, 2008).

The result? The impact of warfare on young people cannot be overestimated. A weak president like Obama is no counter to this tendency, even if he wanted to be. When that is linked to the horrors of September 11, 2001 and a supine and incompetent news media, the outcome is hardly surprising—it is exactly what Osama bin Mohammed bin Awad bin Laden counted on.

Electronic games are at the core of how the military targets young *yanquis* to enlist and then behave as soldiers et al. Military sites such as those designed and maintained by the US Army (*Downloads* 2011) and the US Air Force (*Videos & More 2011*) offer games that simulate life as both killer and enabler. What follows gives some history to this situation and proposes a strategy for undermining it by creating a moral panic.

The Pentagon worked with Atari in the 1980s to develop *Battlezone*, an arcade game, as a flight simulator for fighter pilots, at the same time that it established a gaming center within the National Defense University (Power 2007: 276). In the early 1990s, the end of Cold War II wrought economic havoc on many corporations involved in the US defense industry. They turned to the games industry as a natural supplement to their principal customer, the military. Today's new geopolitical crisis sees these firms, such as Quantum 3-D, conducting half their games business with the private market and half with the Pentagon (Hall 2006). Players of the commercial title *Doom II* can download *Marine Doom*, a Marine Corps modification of the original that was developed after the Corps commandant issued a directive that games would improve tactics. Sony's *U.S. Navy Seals* website links directly to the Corps' own page. TV commercials have depicted soldiers directly addressing gamers, urging them to show their manliness by volunteering for the real thing and serving abroad to secure US power.[11]

It should come as no surprise, then, that visitors to the Fox News site on May 31, 2004 encountered a *grey zone*. On one side of the page, a US soldier in battle gear prowled the streets of Baghdad. On the other, a *Terror Handbook* promised to facilitate "Understanding and facing the threat to America" under the banner: *"WAR ON TERROR sponsored by* KUMA WAR" (a major gaming company). The *Kuma War* game includes online missions entitled "Fallujah: Operation al Fajr," "Battle in Sadr City," and "Uday and Qusay's Last Stand." Its legitimacy and realism are underwritten by the fact that the firm is run by retired military officers and used as a recruiting tool by their former colleagues. Both sides benefit from the company's website, which invites soldiers to pen their battlefield experiences—a neat way of getting intellectual property *gratis* in the name of the nation (Deck 2004, Power 2007: 272, Turse 2008: 137). The site features "Quotes from Players in the Trenches" and recreates the mission that assassinated Abu Musab al-Zarqawi. It boasts, "Kuma War is a series of playable recreations of real events in the War on Terror. Nearly 100 playable missions bring our soldiers' heroic stories to life, and you can get them all right now, for free. Stop watching the news and get in the game!" Such ideological work became vital because the military-diplomatic-fiscal disasters of the 2001–7 period jeopardized a steady supply of new troops. So at the same time as neophytes were hard to attract to the military due to the perils of war, recruits to militaristic game design stepped forward—nationalistic designers volunteering for service. Their mission, which they appeared to accept with alacrity, was to interpellate the country's youth by situating their bodies and minds to fire the same weapons and face the same issues as on the battlefield (Power 2007: 282, Thompson 2004).

The Naval Postgraduate School's Modeling, Virtual Environments and Simulation Academic Institute developed a game called *Operation Starfighter*, based on the film *The Last Starfighter* (1984). The next step was farmed out to George Lucas's companies, inter alia. *America's Army* (*AA*) was launched, with due symbolism, on July 4, 2002—doubly symbolic in that Independence Day is a key date in Hollywood's summer release of feature films (Phoenix) The military had to bring additional servers into play to handle 400,000 downloads of the game that first day. The *Gamespot* website (Osborne 2002) awarded it a high textual rating and was equally impressed by the *business model*. *AA* takes full advantage of the usual array of cybertarian fantasies about the new media as civil society, across the gamut of community fora, Internet chat, fansites, and virtual competition. And

---

1    *Go Army* [Online]. Formerly available at: http://www.goarmy.courage [accessed: March 17, 2011].

the game is formally commodified through privatization—bought by Ubisoft to be repurposed for games consoles, arcades, and cell phones and turned into figurines by the allegedly edgy independent company, Radioactive Clown. Tournaments are convened, replete with hundreds of thousands of dollars prize money, along with smaller events at military recruiting sites (*America's Army* 2011, Lenoir 2003: 175, Power 2007: 279-80, Turse 2008: 117–18, 123–4, 157).

A decade later, *AA* remains one of the ten most played games online and has millions of registered users. Civilian developers regularly refresh it by consulting with veterans and participating in physical war games, while paratexts provide promotional renewal. With over 40 million downloads, and websites by the thousand, the message of the game has travelled far and wide—an excellent return on the initial public investment of US$19 million and US$5 million for annual updates. Studies of young people who have positive attitudes to the US military indicate that 30 percent formed that view through playing the game—a game that sports a Teen rating, forbids role reversal via modifications (preventing players from experiencing the pain of the other), and is officially ranked number one among the Army's recruiting tools (Craig 2006, Mirrlees 2009, Nieborg 2004, Ottosen 2008, 2009a, 2009b, Shachtman 2002, Thompson 2004).

## Concluding Remarks

Many of us who draw on moral panic discourse criticize media effects studies— from a comfortable distance—as crude, unproven, anti-child, and anti-pleasure. But we need to address, for example, the fact that the American Academy of Pediatrics (2009) denounces the mimetic force of violent electronic games on young people, yet fails to describe how this is preyed upon by the Pentagon. Are we prepared to criticize games that promote death, at the same time as we criticize scientists' neglect of this tendency when it abets empire?

We need to take the next step: creating a moral panic. This can start at home, that is, in the academy, by working to counter the Pentagon's ideological incorporation of untenured faculty, whom it seeks to engage via the "Young Faculty Award," whose goal is "to develop the next generation of academic scientists, engineers and mathematicians in key disciplines who will focus a significant portion of their career on D[epartment]o[f]D[efense] and national security issues" ("Opportunities" 2011). This is an outrage given the horrors perpetrated by militarism around the globe. It should have no place in universities, which should be centers of peaceful inquiry with applications for culture and commerce, not killing.

Faculty must take a stand against military research: make public statements, refuse to publish in journals or visit research centers that are complicit, refuse to publish military-funded studies, require that ethics norms of human subjects research be applied to Pentagon money, and so on. Scholars in other countries should boycott military-endowed US universities and researchers if we fail to contest these murderous paymasters.

The task is massive, and it will require people with progressive politics to collaborate as never before. Far from retrieving game players from the status of folk evils and transforming them into popular heroes, we need to draw public attention to the killing work of empire, to criticize the excessive nationalism that underpins gringo love of violence, and generate a moral panic about the unsustainability of empire. Pretty clearly, the United States is in monumental decline as a global suzerain. Its death throes may be violent. We need to restrain and retrain it. Any and all peaceful tactics are worth trying—why not moral panics?

# References

Amaya, H. 2007. Dying American or the violence of citizenship: Latinos in Iraq. *Latino Studies*, 5, 3–24.

2011. *America's Army* [Online]. Available at: http://beta.americasarmy.com/ [accessed: October 25, 2011].

2011. America's navy iPhone app. *America's Navy: A Global Force for Good* [Online]. Available at: http://www.navy.com/iphone.html [accessed: October 26, 2011].

2002. An avalanche of unnecessary vetting set off by moral panic. The *Independent*, September 7, 18.

Phoenix. 2008. AA: SF Tops 9 Million User Mark. *America's Army* [Online February 10]. Available at: http://beta.americasarmy.com/press/news.php?t=70 [accessed: March 17, 2011].

American Academy of Pediatrics, Council on Communications and Media. 2009. Policy statement: media violence. *Pediatrics*, 124(5), 1495-503.

Auletta, K. 2001. Battle stations. *The New Yorker*, December 10.

Barker, M. 1999. Review. *Sociology*, 33(2), 224–7.

Barlow, R. 2004. Weighing teachings on gluttony. *The Boston Globe*, October 16, B2Beck, U. 1999. *World Risk Society*. Cambridge: Polity Press.

Beck, U. 2001. The fight for a cosmopolitan future. *New Statesman*, November 5.

Beck, U. 2002. *Sobre el Terrorismo y la Guerra*, translate d by R.S. Cabó. Barcelona: Paidós.

Blumer, H. 1933. *Movies and Conduct*. New York: Macmillan.

Blumer, H. and Hauser, P.M. 1933. *Movies, Delinquency and Crime*. New York: Macmillan.

Briggs, A. and Burke, P. 2003. *A Social History of the Media: From Gutenberg to the Internet*. Cambridge: Polity Press.

Brooks, R. 2003. A nation of victims. *The Nation*, June 30, 20–22.

Bush, G.W. 2005. Second inaugural address. *The Washington Post*, January 21, A24.

Center for Information and Research on Civic Learning and Engagement. 2004. *Youth Turnout Up Sharply in 2004*, November 3.

Charland, M. 1986. Technological nationalism. *Canadian Journal of Political and Social Theory*, 10(1), 196–220.

Cohen, P. 1999. *Rethinking the Youth Question: Education, Labor, and Cultural Studies.* Durham: Duke University Press.

Cohen, S. 2002 (1972, 1980). *Folk Devils and Moral Panics: The Creation of the Mods and Rockers.* 3rd Edition. Routledge: London.

Coltrane, S. 2001. Marketing the marriage "solution": Misplaced simplicity in the politics of fatherhood: 2001 presidential address to the Pacific Sociological Association. *Sociological Perspectives,* 44(4), 387–418.

2005. Congressional report uncovers chemical security risks throughout the country. *OMBWatch* [Online, July 11]. Available at: http://www.ombwatch.org/node/2496 [accessed: October 26, 2011].

Craig, K. 2006 Dead in Iraq: it's no game. *Wired* [Online] June 6. Available at: http://www.wired.com/gaming/gamingreviews/news/2006/06/71052 [accessed: March 17, 2011].

Critcher, C. 2003. *Moral Panics and the Media.* Maidenhead: Open University Press.

Dale, E. 1933. *The Content of Motion Pictures.* New York: Macmillan.

Daniels, A.M. 1998. Review. *British Medical Journal,* 7(1), 327.

Dewan, S.K. 2000. Do horror films filter the horrors of history? *The New York Times,* October 14, B9.

2011. *Downloads. U.S. Army* [Online]. Available at: http://www.goarmy.com/downloads/games.html# [accessed: October 26, 2011].

Feldman, A. 2005. On the actuarial gaze: from 9/11 to Abu Ghraib. *Cultural Studies,* 19(2), 203–26.

Fifield, J. 2009. Just war and citizenship: responses to youth violence. *International Journal of Communication,* 3, 668–82.

Fitzpatrick, M. 2004. Doctoring the risk society: choice. *The Lancet,* 36, 668.

Fogel, A. 1993. The prose of populations and the magic of demo-graphy. *Western Humanities Review,* 47(4), 312–37.

2004. Covered for climate change. *Foreign Policy,* November/December, 18.

Forman, H.J. 1933. *Our Movie Made Children.* New York: Macmillan.

2004. *Report: The Foundation for Child Development Index of Child Well-Being (CWI), 1975–2002, with Projections for 2003* [Online]. Durham: Duke University Press. Available at: http://www.soc.duke.edu/~cwi/fcd_cwi_report_04.pdf [accessed: October 26, 2011].

Gillespie, N. 2003. Moral panic buttons. *Reason,* April 4.

Gillham, J. and K. Reivich, 2004. Cultivating optimism in childhood and adolescence. *Annals of the American Academy of Political and Social Science,* 591, 146–63.

Gilligan, A. 2011. East London mosque keeps on lying. *Daily Telegraph,* February 26.

Gilman, S.L. 2010. Moral panics and pandemics. *The Lancet,* 375(9729), 1866–7.

Glassner, B. 1999. *The Culture of Fear: Why Americans Are Afraid of the Wrong Things.* New York: Basic Books.

2011. A global force for good. *America's Navy: A Global Force for Good* [Online]. Available at: http://www.navy.com/about/gffg.html [accessed: October 26, 2011].

Goldberg, D.T. 2010. A conversation with David Theo Goldberg. *CulturalStudies* [Online, August 18]. Available at: http://culturalstudies.podbean.com/2010/08/18/a-conversation-with-david-theo-goldberg [accessed: March 10, 2011].

Goode, E. 2000. No need to panic? A bumper crop of books on moral panics. *Sociological Forum*, 15(3), 543–52.

Griffin, C. 1993. *Representations of Youth: The Study of Youth and Adolescence in Britain and America*. Cambridge: Polity Press.

Grossberg, L. 1994. The political status of youth and youth culture, in *Adolescents and their Music: If It's Too Loud, You're Too Old*, edited by J.S. Epstein. New York: Garland, 25–46.

Grossberg, L. 2005. *Caught in the Crossfire: Kids, Politics, and America's Future*. Boulder: Paradigm Publishers.

Hall, K.J. 2006. Shooters to the left of us, shooters to the right: first person arcade shooter games, the violence debate, and the legacy of militarism. *Reconstruction: Studies in Contemporary Culture* [Online], 6(1). Available at: http://reconstruction.eserver.org/061/hall.shtml [accessed: March 17, 2011].

Hartley, J. 1998. "When your child grows up too fast": juvenation and the boundaries of the social in the news media. *Continuum: Journal of Media and Cultural Studies*, 12(1), 9–30.

Heins, M. 2002. *Not in Front of the Children: Indecency, Censorship, and the Innocence of Youth*. New York: Hill and Wang.

Hendershott, A. 2003. Redefining rape. *San Diego Union-Tribune*, August 15, B7.

Hickey, N. 2004. TV: hype takes a hit. *Columbia Journalism Review*, May/June, 6.

Hier, S.P. 2003. Risk and panic in late modernity: implications of the converging sites of social anxiety. *British Journal of Sociology*, 54(1), 3–20.

Hitchens, P. 2011. A brick in the face of a beautiful girl. *Daily Mail*, February 20.

Ivins, M. 2005. Screw the children. *AlterNet* [Online, February 17]. Available at: http://www.alternet.org/story/21294/screw_the_children/ [accessed: October 26, 2011].

Jenkins, P. 1999. *Synthetic Panics: The Symbolic Politics of Designer Drugs*. New York: New York University Press.

Kaplan, E. 2004. Follow the money. *The Nation*, November 1, 20–23.

Kellner, D. 2003. *From 9/11 to Terror War: The Dangers of the Bush Legacy*. Lanham: Rowman and Littlefield Publishers.

Kitzinger, J. and Reilly, J. 1997. The rise and fall of risk reporting: media coverage of human genetics research: "False Memory Syndrome" and "Mad Cow Disease." *European Journal of Communication*, 12(3), 319–50.

Klein, N. 2003. Downsizing in disguise. *The Nation*, June 23, 10.

Klocke, B.V. and Muschert, G.W. 2010. A hybrid model of moral panics: synthesizing the theory and practice of moral panic research. *Sociology Compass*, 4(5), 295–309.

*The Last Starfighter* (dir. Nick Castle, 1984).

Lawrence, G. and Herbert-Cheshire, L. 2003. *Regional Restructuring, Neoliberalism, Individualisation and Community: The Recent Australian Experience*. Paper to the European Society for Rural Sociology Congress, Sligo, August.

Lewis, J. 1992. *The Road to Romance and Ruin: Teen Films and Youth Culture*. New York: Routledge.

Liebel, M. 2004. *A Will of Their Own: Cross-Cultural Perspectives on Working Children*, translated by C. Boone and J. Rotherburger. London: Zed.

Liljeström, R. 1983. The public child, the commercial child, and our child, in *The Child and Other Cultural Inventions*, edited by F.S. Kessel and A.W. Siegel. New York: Praeger. 124–52.

Lowry, D.T., Nio, T.C.J., and Leitner, D.W. 2003. Setting the public fear agenda: a longitudinal analysis of network TV crime reporting, public perceptions of crime, and FBI crime statistics. *Journal of Communication*, 53, 61–73.

Males, M. 2004. With friends like these. *EXTRA!* January/February, 15–16.

Males, M.A. 1996. *The Scapegoat Generation: America's War on Adolescents*. Monroe: Common Courage Press.

Martin, R. 2002. *Financialization of Daily Life*. Philadelphia: Temple University Press.

May, M.A. and Shuttleworth, F.K. 1933. *The Social Conduct and Attitudes of Movie Fans*. New York: Macmillan.

Mazzarella, S.R. 2003. Constructing youth: media, youth, and the politics of representation, in *A Companion to Media Studies*, edited by A.N. Valdivia. Malden: Blackwell, 227–46.

McLemee, S. 2003. Murder in black and white. *Newsday*, August 31, D29.

Miller, T. 2007. *Cultural Citizenship: Cosmopolitanism, Consumerism, and Television in a Neoliberal Age*. Philadelphia: Temple University Press.

Miller, T. 2008. *Makeover Nation: The United States of Reinvention*. Cleveland: Ohio State University Press.

Mirrlees, T. 2009. Digital militainment by design: producing and playing *SOCOM: U.S. Navy SEALs*. *International Journal of Media and Cultural Politics*, 5(3), 161–81.

Mitchell, A.M. 1929. *Children and the Movies*. Chicago: University of Chicago Press.

Mosco, V. 2004. *The Digital Sublime: Myth, Power, and Cyberspace*. Cambridge: MIT Press.

Muschamp, H. 2004. The new Arcadia. *The New York Times*, August 29, 224.

Nieborg, D.B. 2004 "America's Army: more than a game," in *Transforming Knowledge into Action through Gaming and Simulation*, edited by T. Eberle and W.C. Kriz. Munich: SAGSAGA. CD-ROM.

O'Malley, P. 2004. *Risk, Uncertainty and Government*. London: Glasshouse Press.

2011. Opportunities at DARPA: young faculty award. *DARPA* [Online]. Available at: http://www.darpa.mil/Opportunities/Universities/Young_Faculty.aspx [accessed: October 26, 2011].

Ortiz, J. 2005. Fans hold court on skullcaps. *The Sacramento Bee*, January 29, A1.

Osborne, S. 2002. America's Army review. *Gamespot* [Online, October 23]. Available at: http://www.gamespot.com/americas-army/reviews/americas-army-operations-review-2895424/ [accessed: August 30, 2012].

Ottosen, R. 2008. Targeting the audience: video games as war propaganda in entertainment and news. *Bodhi: An Interdisciplinary Journal*, 2(1), 14–41.

Ottosen, R. 2009a. The military-industrial complex revisited. *Television and New Media*, 10(1), 122–5.

Ottosen, R. 2009b. Targeting the player: computer games as propaganda for the military-industrial complex. *Nordicom Review*, 30(2), 35–51.

Park, D.W. 2004. The couch and the clinic: The cultural authority of popular psychiatry and psychoanalysis. *Cultural Studies*, 18(1), 109–33.

Power, M. 2004. *The Risk Management of Everything: Rethinking the Politics of Uncertainty*. London: Demos.

Project for Excellence in Journalism. 2005. *The State of the News Media: An Annual Report on American Journalism*.

Putnam, R.D. 2000. *Bowling Alone: The Collapse and Revival of American Community*. New York: Simon and Schuster.

Reeves, J.L. and Campbell, R. 1994. *Cracked Coverage: Television News, the Anti-Cocaine Crusade, and the Reagan Legacy*. Durham: Duke University Press.

Rohloff, A. and Wright, S. 2010. Moral panic and social theory. *Current Sociology*, 58(3), 403–19.

Romer, D. and Jamieson, P. 2003. Introduction. *American Behavioral Scientist*, 46(9), 131–6.

Rose, N. 1999. *Powers of Freedom: Reframing Political Thought*. Cambridge: Cambridge University Press.

Ruccio, D.F. (ed.). 2008. *Economic Representations: Academic and Everyday*. Routledge Frontiers of Political Economy. London: Routledge.

Ruddick, S. 2003. The politics of aging: globalization and the restructuring of youth and childhood. *Antipode*, 35(2), 334–62.

Shachtman, N. 2002. Shoot 'em up and join the army. *Wired* [Online], July 4. Available at: http://www.wired.com/gaming/gamingreviews/news/2002/07/53663 [accessed: March 17, 2011].

Shapiro, M.J. 2001. *For Moral Ambiguity: National Culture and the Politics of the Family*. Minneapolis: University of Minnesota Press.

Shaps, S. 1994. When moral panic is the real villain of the piece. The *Independent*, November 5.

Shea, C. 2003. The last prejudice? *The Boston Globe*, July 27, E1.

Smutniak, J. 2004. Living dangerously. *The Economist*, January 24, 3–4.

2004. *The State of America's Children 2004: A Continuing Portrait of Inequality Fifty Years after* Brown v. Board of Education. Washington, DC: Children's Defense Fund.

Steinberg, S.R. and Kincheloe, J.L. 1997. Introduction: no more secrets: kinderculture, information saturation, and the post-modern childhood, in *Kinderculture: The Corporate Construction of Childhood*, edited by S.R. Steinberg and J.L. Kincheloe. Boulder: Westview Press, 1–30.

Strange, S. 2000. *The Retreat of the State: The Diffusion of Power in the World Economy*. Cambridge: Cambridge University Press.

Sullum, J. 2011. It turns out *non*alcoholic energy drinks are *also* an intolerable threat to the youth of America. *Reason* [Online, February 14]. Available at: http://reason.com/blog/2011/02/14/it-turns-out-nonalcoholic-ener [accessed: October 25, 2011].

Surowiecki, J. 2004. The risk society. *The New Yorker*, November 15, 40.

Tan, M.L. 2001. Moral panic. *Philippine Daily Inquirer*, March 27, 8.

Taylor, D.J. 2011. Freedom's just another word for … . The *Independent*, February 6. Ellipsis in original.

Thompson, K. 1998. *Moral Panics*. Key Ideas. Milton Park: Routledge.

Thompson, C. 2004. The making of an X box warrior. *The New York Times Magazine* [Online], August 22. Available at: http://www.nytimes.com/2004/08/22/magazine/the-making-of-an-x-box-warrior.html [accessed: March 17, 2011].

2005. *Trends 2005. PewResearchCenter Publications* [Online, January 20]. Available at: http://pewresearch.org/pubs/206/trends-2005 [accessed: October 26, 2011].

Ungar, S. 2001. Moral panic versus the risk society: the implications of the changing sites of social anxiety. *British Journal of Sociology*, 52(2), 271–91.

2004. Kids' role in securing USA. *USA Today*, August 10.

Verklin, D. and Kanner, B. 2007. Why a killer videogame is the U.S. army's best recruitment tool. *MarketingProfs* [Online] May 29. Available at: http://www.marketingprofs.com/articles/2007/2377/why-a-killer-videogame-is-the-us-armys-best-recruitment-tool [accessed: March 17, 2011].

2011. *Videos & More. U.S. Air Force* [Online]. Available at: http://www.airforce.com/games-and-extras/ [accessed: October 26, 2011].

Wagner, D. 1997. *The New Temperance: The American Obsession with Sin and Vice.* New York: Westview Press.

Wartella, E. 1996. The history reconsidered, in *American Communication Research: The Remembered History*, edited by E.E. Dennis and E. Wartella. Mahwah: Lawrence Erlbaum, 169–80.

Westheimer, J. 2004. Introduction. *PS: Political Science and Politics*, 37(2), 231–4.

Westheimer, J. and Kahne, J. 2004. Educating the "good" citizen: political choices and pedagogical goals. *PS: Political Science and Politics*, 37(2), 241–8.

Wichtel, D. 2002. Music that makes for moral panic. *New Zealand Herald*, December 14.

Wilgoren, J. 2002. Scholar's pedophilia essay stirs outrage and revenge. *The New York Times* [Online], April 30, A18. Available at: http://www.nytimes.com/2002/04/30/us/scholar-s-pedophilia-essay-stirs-outrage-and-revenge.html [accessed: October 30, 2011].

2001. *World Trade Developments in 2001 and Prospects for 2002. World Trade Organization* [Online]. Available at: http://www.wto.org/english/res_e/statis_e/its2002_e/its02_general_overview_e.htm [accessed: October 26, 2011].

Wright, R. and Rosenfeld, R. 2003. We're racing toward moral panic. *St. Louis Post-Dispatch*, January 26, B3.

Yúdice, G. 1990. For a practical aesthetics. *Social Text*, 25–26, 129–45.

Žižek, S. 2005. The empty wheelbarrow. The *Guardian*, February 19, 23.

Zorach, R. 2003. Insurance nation. *The Boston Globe*, March 9, D2.

# Assemblages of Moral Politics: Yesterday and Today

## Alan Hunt

In 1971, Jock Young announced the arrival of moral panics over drugs and drug use. Stanley Cohen (1972) promoted the concept when young men fought on winter beaches. This chapter explores the historical trajectory of moral regulation projects by comparing the characteristics of the forms of moral regulation that were active at the end of the nineteenth century with those found at the beginning of the twenty-first century. At the outset, it might be helpful to state my view on the relationship between moral regulation and moral panic. I treat moral panics as more- or less-intense variants of projects of moral regulation that are generally of short duration. In contrast, moral regulation projects not only may persist over longer periods, but then also tend to recede only to re-emerge at some later point, often in slightly changed form.

Before proceeding further, it is important to draw attention to ambiguity in the way in which the "moral panic" concept has come to be used. A significant number of circumstances that have been classified as moral panics have had little if anything to do with morals or morality. Many controversies that have been labeled "moral panics" have been anxieties associated with risks, in particular with technological or medical risks. Anxieties over AIDS in the 1980s and more recently over SARS and H1N1 (swine flu) are better described as "medical anxieties." These concerns share common considerations about whether the anxiety occasioned is proportionate to the risk involved, but few if any of these risk anxieties or medical anxieties has a directly moral dimension. For this reason, I will focus on episodes that have some discernible moral dimension. I will treat morals as involving all instances in which the values and practices that, irrespective of any consequences that they give rise to, are deemed to be wrong to a degree that justifies condemnation. In this chapter, I will seek to clarify the connection between morals, anxieties, and risks.

First, I will pursue the narrower dimension in order to attend more closely to the specifically moral dimension of moral regulation and moral panics. I treat moral politics as embracing both moral regulation and moral panics and as a form of politics in which some agents act to problematize the conduct, values, or culture of others and seek to act upon them through moralizing discourses, moralizing practices, and regulation. Moralization involves imposing judgments about the rightness or wrongness of the conduct or values of others. Moral politics may involve, but are not reducible to the instrumental interests of their proponents. Thus, moral forms of politics involve the deployment of distinctively moral discourses that construct a moralized subject and an object or target that is acted upon by means of moralizing practices.

I will demonstrate that there have been both continuities and discontinuities in the trajectory of projects of moral politics. I will engage with the significant continuities in the history of moral regulation projects in Western capitalist societies. I will then attend to different forms of discontinuity (for example, when certain projects seem to disappear from the historical record) and identify distinctively new varieties of moral politics. On the basis of this survey, I will consider whether there are any lessons to be drawn. I will argue that while in the past moral politics was focused on a narrowly conceived moral preoccupation, today moral politics is much more heterogeneous. It is often hybrid in the sense that different features are emphasized. These features, I will argue, are best grasped by developing the concept of an assemblage of moral politics.

## Continuities in the Trajectories of Moral Regulation

There have been important continuities in the targets at which moral politics has been directed over a long period. Perhaps the three most important examples are prostitution, obscenity, and alcohol. Projects directed at their suppression and regulation were particularly active in the late nineteenth century. It is significant to note that there were striking geopolitical differences. The campaigns directed against prostitution exhibited significant parallels in Britain and the United States. In contrast, while attacks on alcohol in the name of temperance never entirely disappeared in Britain they had nothing of the breadth and intensity that culminated in Prohibition in the United States.

However, in all three cases, a great variety of specific targets changed over time. These differences were often due to local variations in national or regional circumstances. For example, in Victorian campaigns against prostitution in New York, the primary target was clandestine accommodations. New York State's Raines law (1896) sought to reduce the number of saloons that provided many small rooms frequented by prostitutes and their customers, whereas in London the primary target was street solicitation (McHugh 1980). In addition, a distinctively British preoccupation was the longstanding conflict for and against the state regulation of prostitution through the Contagious Diseases Acts, 1852–69 (Walkowitz 1980). Similarly, while there was a long history of campaigns against obscenity in both America and Britain there were significant differences in the targets of such projects. In the United States, the targets were both nude representations hung in galleries and mass-produced representations, whereas in Britain the targets focused more on novels along with cheap reproductions of obscene images (Beisel 1997, Nead 2000).

The most salient feature of late nineteenth-century moral projects was that the principal agents were middle class reform movements that applied pressure for legislative intervention upon state institutions that were generally wary about intervening, but sometimes found it expedient to respond to political pressure. Of special significance in this period were feminist interventions, significant because, lacking formal political power, these movements spearheaded some of the most significant moral political movements. The unifying feature of moral reform movements was the deployment of discourses that characterized their targets in terms of "sin" and "vice," signifying that the target in itself was to be condemned and needed no other reason for its prohibition. However, it should be noted that considerations of the harm occasioned also played a role. Thus, for example, the campaign waged by the Women's Christian Temperance Union against the evils of alcohol in the United States made strong play on the imagery of the drunken husband who on payday drank his wages in the saloon and had nothing to take home to his wife and children. In the campaigns of the "white slavery" panic that led to the passing in the United States of the Mann Act of 1906 campaign materials made heavy use of images of innocent country girls transported to brothels in distant cities (Langum 1994). But, in contrast, at the high point of the campaign in Britain to raise the age of sexual consent—exemplified in newspaper editor W.T. Stead's onslaught on the "Maiden Tribute to Modern Babylon" in 1885, which featured his attempt to purchase a young virgin—he and his supporters showed little concern for the fate of the Lily, the 13-year-old at the heart of the story (Walkowitz 1992). Discourses of harm that remained mostly marginal in the nineteenth century become central to moral politics in the twentieth century. The nineteenth century's emerging focus on harm was exemplified in J.S. Mill's classic formulation: "The only purpose for which power can be rightfully exercised over any member of a civilized community, against his will, is to prevent harm to others" (Mill 1910:72). The concept of harm occupied center stage for much of the twentieth century, though by the end of the century the discourses of risk had come to predominate.

## Contemporary Moral Politics

Moral movements from the early twentieth century on have exhibited a much greater diversity than earlier moral reform movements. This diversity is manifest in a shift both in the discursive construction of its targets and in the selection of the targets themselves. This shift is evident even in those projects that exhibit degrees of continuity with earlier movements. This is illustrated in two persistent targets of moral regulation, namely, pornography and prostitution. Anti-pornography projects retain some element of the immorality of indecent sexual representations, but much more significant is that indecency is insufficient to sustain anti-pornography campaigns. But even here, we should note that such long-running and influential campaigns as that headed by Mary Whitehouse (1998) and the Viewers and Listeners Association against the BBC placed indecency and bad language at the heart of their message. Yet, the emblematic anti-pornography campaign of the late twentieth century was the one associated with the names of Andrea Dworkin (1981) and Catharine MacKinnon (1993). It avoided talk of indecency and offensiveness and in its place focused on the harm that they claimed pornography did to women.

## Discourses of Harm and Danger

And it is significant that the discourse of harm was bipolar. On one hand were the specific claims of the harms that they claimed were, for example, imposed on performers such as Linda Lovelace (1983). On the other hand, MacKinnon, Dworkin, and others asserted the universal claim that pornography harmed all women: "It is for pornography, and not by the ideas in it, that women are hurt and penetrated. ... Only for pornography are women killed to make a sex movie" (MacKinnon 1993: 15). This contention retained features of the earlier moralistic contention that pornography was intrinsically indecent and obscene. Indeed, this traditional moral objection to pornography has not entirely gone away. Recent English legislation has made it an offense to produce and distribute "extreme pornography" (S.63 *Criminal Justice and Immigration Act* 2008), which seems to imply the paradoxical position that "ordinary" pornography has become so commonplace that it is acceptable. And, a similar shift in the construction of targets is evident in changing constructions of sexual danger. The nineteenth century's focus on immoral conduct is captured in the highly moralized wrong of "seduction" that was significantly organized around a patriarchal discourse in which the victim was not the seduced female but the father or other male guardian of the "victim." In the late twentieth century, patriarchal discourses disappeared, to be replaced by the technological agency of "date-rape drugs" (Valverde and Moore 2001).

A significant extension of claims of harm was occasioned when moral politics seized on the opportunities provided by the increasingly popular and influential rise of the discourses of risk theory. From the late 1980s, risk in particular, through the writings of sociologist Ulrich Beck (1992), became common currency in the social sciences. Risk theory had a particularly significant impact on moral politics for a number of reasons. First, it seemed to remove the assessment of specific risk claims from the contentious normative realm of morals. Moral discourses came to function through the proxy of risk. The moral dimension is not excluded, but becomes subsumed within the discourses of risk, the characteristics of which inhabit a utilitarian guise. The outcome of this interconnection between moral discourse and risk discourse constitutes an instance of hybridity: the combination of two types of discourses so that their characteristics merge into a distinctively new form (Hunt 2003). The most striking feature of the hybridization of morals and risks is the creation of an apparently benign form of moralization in which the boundary between objective hazards and normative judgments becomes blurred.

Perhaps the most common form of hybridization is found in the prevalent medicalization of risk epitomized by the US Surgeon General's warning on wine bottles: "According to the Surgeon General women should not drink alcoholic beverages during pregnancy because of the risks of birth defects." Individuals come to be assessed, and are invited to assess themselves, as being "at risk." A new expansionary cycle of responsibilization sets in. Responsibilization refers to a form of governing that discursively imposes some specific responsibilities on individuals for their own conduct or that of another for whom they are presented as being responsible (Jonas 1984). Much responsibilization is entirely conventional: parents for their children, employers for their employees. But the technique lends itself to expansion. Increasingly, for example, patients are deemed responsible for the management of their own health by adopting healthy practices. It is no longer a matter of taking responsibility for one's own drinking, but, for example, for the guests one entertains. Responsibilization is further compounded by waves of expanding legal liability accompanied by prudential insurance.

## Discourses of Risk

Risk discourses and their uptake into social policy seem to promise a world of increased objectivity and calculability, a world in which risk can be measured and a response can be made. This does not make our world safer or more secure, but declares that we exist in a world transected by dimensions of security and danger. Safety and danger stand in nonlinear relation to security, anxiety, and fear, and discourses of risk play a significant part in the ways that risks are experienced and lived. This promise of the calculability of risk has the significant effect of holding out the possibility of taking command of the future. The goal of achieving future security is dependent on placing ever-greater reliance upon expertise. But this is happening just when expertise itself is becoming increasingly contested. Experts are no longer securely legitimized by virtue of their location in state institutions or traditional professional organizations. Experts are increasingly dispersed across rival institutional sites and disseminate a plethora of incompatible knowledge and advice. The medical field is riven by the competition between opposing bodies of knowledge. Medical controversy is not new, but it is new in that its disagreements are increasingly fought out in public. Experts disagree about what the risks are, how risky they are, how these risks can or should be quantified, and how they, too, are minimized.

The fracturing of expert knowledge has occurred at the same time as massive growth in non-expert expertise. A proliferation of single-issue movements have developed their own expertise, through which they dispute traditional forms of state and professional expertise and act as what may be usefully referred to as "risk-promotion" movements. The significance of such movements is that they not infrequently succeed in effecting the "regulatory capture" of expert systems insofar as it is often easier for them to "go along with," rather than resist, the risk entrepreneurs of such risk-promotion movements. In contests over pertinent knowledge, a new space emerges into which an assemblage of opinion, often grounded in contested claims, enters, with the result that a new domain of moralizing politics has come to inhabit and destabilize such fields as medicine and climatology. The promise held out by the rise of risk analysis of a more objective and predictable world has become an expanded arena of contested moral opinion into which moral politics rush. This is exemplified by the discredited research published by Andrew Wakefield in *The Lancet* in 1998, which suggested a link between a well-tested vaccine and autism, and resulted in hundreds of thousands of children in Britain not receiving the measles, mumps, and rubella (MMR) vaccine (see Durbach 2003).

## Technological Fears and Anxieties

This case serves as a useful introduction to one of the most distinctive features of contemporary moral politics, namely that it is increasingly the results of technological innovation that generates social anxieties and gives rise to moral panics or other forms of moralizing concerns. This does not imply that the behavior of others no longer generates moralizing concerns and interventions; perhaps the most important contemporary moral project is the campaigns against sexual trafficking that have many similarities with the early twentieth century campaigns against the "white slave trade" that focused attention on "innocent" young women victimized by ruthless "traffickers."

In highlighting the recent shift of attention to technological fears and anxieties, it should not be forgotten that these were also present in the nineteenth century. The full story has yet to be written about anxieties induced by the spread of railways. Cultural historian Wolfgang Schivelbusch (1979) tells part of this history of the anxieties induced by the noise and speed of the railways. Schivelbusch (1988) also touches briefly on anxieties induced by electrification. There is consensus that the technological innovations associated with the rise of modernity gave rise to a wide variety of fears, anxieties, and panics. Modernity has increasingly become characterized by "ontological insecurity," a rise in risks and dangers that leads to persistence of "anxiety" (Giddens 1991: 35). Sociologist Anthony Giddens (1991: 52) argues that existence in modernity is characterized by Kierkegaard's (1944) "dread," the prospect of being overwhelmed by anxieties that go to the root of our coherent sense of being in the world. Beck extends this treatment of what he and Giddens (see Beck, Giddens, and Lash 1994) term reflexive modernization. The new technologically created hazards and insecurities induced and introduced by modernization itself are distinguished from the old dangers and fears of industrial and pre-industrial society, the new risks give rise to widespread and shared anxieties. Now that we have lived with the experience of risk society for some decades, it seems pertinent to suggest that we distinguish between the range and types of risk. It is certainly the case that some of the "big" technologically created risks are still very much with us. Global warming has become a more central focus of contemporary politics and personal anxiety. But it is less clear that the shadow of

Chernobyl haunts us so vigorously. And, in passing, it is interesting that one of the earlier meta-risks associated with the mutually assured destruction of the nuclear arms race during the Cold War has, if not vanished, become a much less pressing source of the anxieties of reflexive modernization. Nuclear weapons were my own entry into a long process of politicization, but I have to confess that I no longer lose sleep because of anxieties about nuclear conflagration.

I want to press a distinction between the mega-risks and the much more numerous everyday risks of technological society. These risks come and go. Do we remember the widespread anxiety panic over the millennial "Y2K" 1999, which disappeared on January 1, 2000? Others persist or reappear in new guises. Cell phones have proved a potent source of anxiety. Epidemiologist Devra Davis (2011) traces the history of these anxieties that shift their focus from transmission towers to the phones themselves. Maybe soon there will be more reliable evidence, then cell phones will be as unproblematic as the old-fashioned landline telephones or, alternatively, become subject to stringent regulation. From the 1960s, there was widespread apprehension about radiation from microwave ovens, which seems to have retreated, or perhaps even to have disappeared. One feature of such technological anxieties is that they find expression in specific constituencies of anxiety in which some express deep concerns, while many others remain indifferent. A classic instance has been the regular eruption of controversies over fluoridation of water supplies. It is significant that so many of these sources of anxiety are invisible.

Perhaps even more significant than the characteristic invisibility of risks is the complexity of the chains of causality involved. And it is complexity that is at the heart of probably the most numerous forms of contemporary anxiety that are associated with medical risks where the number of risk conditions that have been reported expand exponentially. One important implication is that it renders the tasks confronting social theorist Nikolas Rose's (1996) neoliberal citizens, who increasingly govern themselves through their choices, increasingly challenging. Today, there are so many health advisories, risks, competing experts and media material that the most that the individual can do is to select a few substances to avoid, practices to renounce and regimes to adopt that they are perhaps best conceptualized as a form of identity politics. I may cut down on salt and saturated fats, but decide to continue drinking coffee and eating red meat. There is an ever-expanding, but contradictory advice generated from a proliferation of experts. For example, the advice to those with elevated blood pressure to rely on a daily low-dose aspirin now seems to be countermanded by cautions against the use of aspirin. Similarly, the longstanding advice to avoid cooking with animal fats and to rely on vegetable oils has recently been countered by warnings against some of the most popular vegetable oils. Faced with conflicting and contradictory expertise, individuals are left with little chance of evaluating the warnings and can do little to make informed decisions.

With the proliferation of health anxieties and warnings, there is a re-emergence of a moralizing range of choice that tends to give priority to moral judgments rather than objective risk assessment. This is evident with respect to wide-ranging controversies over genetically modified foodstuffs. The evidence available to even the well-informed citizen is so complex that the majority will be forming their opinions on what are probably little more than ethical or moral judgments about the desirability of genetic modification. The search for links between diet, lifestyle, environment, and disease is an unending source of anxieties, but it rarely yields any certainty. The consequence of the emphasis on health, and its foundation on a sense of vulnerability to poorly defined risk factors, is that people have become inclined to believe that invisible agents in their environment are affecting their health, and they become increasingly distrustful of expert knowledge.

## The Precautionary Principle

Authorities of every variety when besieged by these multiple anxieties have responded by adopting precautionary responses out of fear of being held responsible and worried about facing legal action should some link between inaction and harm be demonstrable. The widespread adoption of what has come to be called "the precautionary principle" has resulted in the rise of a "culture of precaution" that shifts focus of attention in the face of such anxieties from the activists to governments as the primary agents of precaution. This has resulted in a significant shift of focus of what now constitutes politics; traditional political concerns with the economy and international affairs have become marginalized and attention has shifted to issues of health and environmental risks. The emergence of what may be called a precautionary society is one in which governments and other agencies tend to adopt a precautionary response to marginal risks. For governments not to be seen to be responding to risk, courts danger for them. The precautionary principle takes many forms, but the main idea is that regulators should take steps to protect against potential harms, even if causal chains are unclear and even if we do not know that those harms will come to fruition. Too often people are influenced by "worst case scenarios," where they neglect any serious consideration of probabilities.

A significant shift in the contemporary construction of prominent anxieties is that there is a move away from blaming the individual to focusing both moralization and regulatory interventions on an institutional target. An important focus of current health concerns has been the adverse impact of junk food. While there is an obvious sense in which the high rates of consumption of unhealthy commercially produced food could be laid at the door of the consumers who choose hamburgers and fries over "healthy food," such a response would accord with a "traditional" moralization of the individual who makes bad choices. However, the current construction of health discourses focuses attention on the big producers of junk food, who are not only subject to moral blame but are increasingly likely to be subject to regulation. A similar shift can be detected in the related question of "obesity" politics. In earlier epochs, individuals were blamed for their inability or unwillingness to control their weight. Historian Keith Thomas (1997) demonstrates that from the sixteenth century medical advice books offered a secularized version of the seven deadly sins that was now organized around a condemnation of "excess"

Individuals were blamed for their greed and gluttony. It is interesting to note that while legacies of such moralized discourse are still directed at the obese, in the recent past there has been a shift of emphasis in expert and regulatory discourses to generate a generalized moral panic over a global obesity epidemic that has "fat" threatening society as a whole (Gilman 2010).

Even more significant is a generalized feature of contemporary moral politics found in a focus upon the presence of multiple targets. It is clear that the whole field of smoking is hegemonized by the powerful discourses of health. It should be noted that health has not entirely displaced a more traditional moralization of individual responsibilization; the smoker is still moralized in terms of the weakness of character that is targeted by the ubiquitous slogan, "Just Quit." The moralization of smoking is also evident in the creeping prohibitions of an expanding range of sites: the expulsion of the smoker from traditional locations such as the restaurant, the bar, public buildings, and, the most recent advance, general public spaces. While these prohibitions are encompassed within health discourses, there is a persistent moral aspect to the idea that the smoker needs to be segregated from the virtuous nonsmoker. This moralization is explicit in the degradation ceremonies daily imposed on smokers as they are forced to stand outside their places of work or recreation in order to demonstrate their failings to all who pass by. These prohibitions were given the most profound impetus through the "discovery" of second-hand or passive smoking that transformed the cigarette from an object of pleasure and attraction to a symbol of personal disregard for the health of others and thus a sign of personal weakness (Brandt 1998). To this should be added other moralizing elements, such as the focus on the antisocial odor of the smoker's body and clothes, that link to the powerful injunctions about individual responsibility for personal hygiene (Smith 2007).

The war on smoking is carried forward through a complex set of regulatory interventions that hit a multitude of target by imposing regulatory obligations on them. While the ultimate targets of tobacco regulation are cigarette manufacturers who have become more and more tightly ensnared most visibly by the minutiae of the controls placed on packaging and restrictions on advertising. The regulatory embrace has long reached retailers, who are subject to detailed restrictions on the display of cigarettes. Similar restrictions are placed upon those who run bars and restaurants. Beyond those directly involved in the production and distribution of cigarettes are a complex array of public and private institutions who are participants in the regulation of smoking through the policing of sites and occasions that restrict or prohibit cigarette smoking. The most visible evidence of this multiplicity of sites is the unofficial graffiti of the instantly recognizable "No Smoking" decal (Hermer and Hunt 1996). The official displays have been multiplied by the voluntary spread of this signage to private residences, motor vehicles, and a multitude of other sites. The anti-smoking campaign is perhaps the most significant instance of modern moral politics: its significance lies in the multiplicity of forms, agents, and volunteers that form a complex network.

# Conclusion: The Assemblages of Moral Politics

In tracking the diverse patterns that have marked the trajectory of moral politics over the last century, I started out with the hunch that I might find a shift from one pattern that started out with a traditional focus on sin or immorality to a more "modern" pattern focused on risks and anxieties. But it has not taken such a smooth or evolutionary path. Rather, a picture has emerged of shifting combinations of elements of morals, sin, medical, health, risks, anxieties, and numerous other features. What is needed is a way of conceptualizing these mobile combinations. One possibility that seemed attractive was the idea of a network conceived as a series of distinct connections between a multiplicity of elements. This conceptualization has variously been proposed by sociologist Manuel Castells's (1996) "network society" and Pierre Bourdieu's (1993) notion of "the field" as a network or configuration of objective social relations. But the limitation of the concept of network is that it is pertinent to picture-changing sets of relations between the same group of relations, that is, where the elements remain the same, only the ordering or connections vary. In other words, networks, as is suggested by the imagery associated with the concept, are too linear: the lines of connection diverge but the elements remain the same.

More serviceable for my purpose is the concept of an assemblage. This notion has been used in strands of thought as diverse as those of philosophers Gilles Deleuze and Félix Guattari (1987), of sociologist and anthropologist Bruno Latour as seen in his actor-network theory (2005), and more recently of political scientist Jane Bennett (2010). An assemblage is a grouping of diverse elements, of elements the composition of which varies over time and is not coordinated from any central position, and in which no single element determines the trajectory of the assemblage. There is no agency within an assemblage, but an assemblage does contain a consistent pattern of reappearing elements that are found in persistent association.

I was troubled by the question of how to think about some of the more important themes, in particular, about the relationship between moral regulation and moral panics. Should they be regarded as merely different aspects of the same phenomena? The concept of assemblage provided a solution. It suggests that these important strands are distinguishable relative to the priority of each element within different assemblages of moral politics. Thus, moral panics, because of their linkage to persistent elements of anxiety, form a somewhat different assemblage from that associated with moral regulation because the latter tends to manifest moralizations that are more overt.

The final issue that needs to be considered is whether by naming this assemblage "moral politics," I am violating the disclaimer that assemblages do contain a core or central organizing principle. This violation does not arise because all that is being done is to give a label of convenience that reminds us that the intention is to draw attention to a field in which moral features are a persistent but not necessarily a universal feature. But it does make the strong claim that fields marked by features of risk, medicalization and anxiety frequently have moral dimensions that are located not far below the surface.

This assertion can be illustrated by one last example: my workplace has recently introduced a perfumed products policy under which everyone is urged to desist from using perfumed body products. This is advanced in the form of a medical risk discourse located within a concern for the rapidly expanding discourse of allergies. The policy makes no references to any evidence about the prevalence of allergic reaction to any specific allergens. It is assumed that all perfumed products are capable of causing allergic reaction. So, although framed within a discourse of medical risk, there is a strong moralizing dimension that anyone who is selfish enough to use perfumed products is exhibiting a lack of concern for others and thus manifests an unacceptable degree of responsibility to the abstract community of all who frequent the institution.

The strong conclusion may be drawn that while moralization was a central feature of late nineteenth-century moral politics, today moral politics embraces a complex assemblage of elements within which the moral dimension remains a persistent and pertinent feature.

# References

Beck, U. 1986. *Risk Society: Towards a New Modernity*, translated by M. Titter. London: Sage Publications.

Beck, U., Giddens, A., and Lash, S. 1994. *Reflexive Modernization: Politics, Tradition and Aesthetics in the Modern Social Order*. Cambridge: Polity Press.

Beisel, N.K. 1997. *Imperiled Innocents: Anthony Comstock and Family Reproduction in Victorian America*. Princeton: Princeton University Press.

Bennett, J. 2010. *Vibrant Matter: A Political Ecology of Things*. Duke: Duke University Press.

Bourdieu, P. 1993. *The Field of Cultural Production: Essays on Art and Literature*, edited by R. Johnson. New York: Columbia University Press.

Brandt, A.M. 1998. Blow some my way: passive smoking, risk and American culture, in *Ashes to Ashes: The History of Smoking and Health*, edited by S. Lock, L.A. Reynolds and E.M. Tansey. Amsterdam: Rodopi, 164-87.

Castells, M. 1996. *The Rise of the Network Society*. The Information Age: Economy, Society and Culture, Vol. 1. Oxford: Blackwell.

Cohen, S. 1972. *Folk Devils and Moral Panics: The Creation of the Mods and Rockers*. London: MacGibbon and Kee.

Davis, D. 2011. *Disconnect: The Truth about Cell Phone Radiation*. London: Dutton.

Deleuze, G. and Guattari, F. 1987. *A Thousand Plateaus: Capitalism and Schizophrenia*, translated by B. Massumi. Minneapolis: University of Minnesota Press.

Durbach, N. 2003. *Bodily Matters: The Anti-Vaccination Movement in England, 1853–1907*. Radical Perspectives. Durham: Duke University Press.

Dworkin, A. 1981. *Pornography: Men Possessing Women*. New York: Perigee.

Giddens, A. 1991. *Modernity and Self-Identity: Self and Society in the Late Modern Age*. Cambridge: Cambridge University Press.

Gilman, S.L. 2010. *Obesity: The Biography*. Oxford: Oxford University Press.
Hermer, J. and Hunt, A. 1996. Official graffiti of the everyday. *Law and Society Review*, 30(3), 501–26.
Hunt, A. 2003. Risk and moralization in everyday life, in *Morality and Risk*, edited by R. Ericson and A. Doyle. Toronto: University of Toronto Press, 165–92.
Jonas, H. 1984. *The Imperative of Responsibility*. Chicago: University of Chicago Press.
Kierkegaard, S. 1944 (1844). *Kierkegaard's The Concept of Dread*, translated by W. Lowrie. Princeton: Princeton University Press. Originally published as *Begrebet Angest*.
Langum, D.J. 1994. *Crossing Over the Line: Legislative Morality and the Mann Act*. Chicago: University of Chicago Press.
Latour, B. 2005. *Reassembling the Social: An Introduction to Actor-Network-Theory*. Oxford: Clarendon Press.
Lovelace, L. 1983. *Ordeal*. New York: Berkeley.
McHugh, P.G. 1980. *Prostitution and Victorian Social Reform*. London: Croom Helm.
MacKinnon, C.A. 1993. *Only Words*. Cambridge: Harvard University Press.
Mill, J.S. 1910 (1859). On liberty, in *Utilitarianism, Liberty and Representative Government* [Online].
London: Everyman. Available at: http://www.archive.org/details/PhilosophyAnd Theology [accessed: October 5, 2011]. Originally published as *On Liberty*. London: John W. Parker and Son.
Nead, L. 2000. *Victorian Babylon: People, Streets, and Images in Nineteenth-Century London*. New Haven: Yale University Press.
Rose, N. 1996. Governing "advanced" liberal democracies, in *Foucault and Political Reason: Liberalism, Neo-Liberalism and Rationalities of Government*, edited by A. Barry, T. Osborne and N. Rose, Chicago: University of Chicago Press, 37–64.
S63 *Criminal Justice and Immigration Act* 2008.
Schivelbusch, W. 1979. *The Railway Journey: Trains and Travel in the Nineteenth Century*. New York: Urizen Books.
Schivelbusch, W. 1988. *Disenchanted Night: The Industrialization of Light in the Nineteenth Century*. University of California Press: Berkeley.
Smith, V. 2007. *Clean: A History of Personal Hygiene and Purity*. Oxford: Oxford University Press.
Thomas, K. 1997. Health and morality in early modern England, in *Morality and Health*, edited by A.M. Brandt and P. Rozin. London: Routledge, 15–34.
Valverde, M. and Moore, M. 2001. Maidens at risk: "date rape drugs" and the formation of hybrid risk knowledge. *Economy and Society* 29(4), 514–31.
Walkowitz, J.R. 1980. *Prostitution and Victorian Society: Women, Class and the State*. Cambridge: Cambridge University Press.
Walkowitz, J.R. 1992. *City of Dreadful Delight: Narratives of Sexual Danger in Late-Victorian London*. Chicago: University of Chicago Press.
Whitehouse, M. 1967. *Cleaning Up TV*. London: Blandford Press.
Young, J. 1971. The role of the police as amplifiers of deviancy, negotiators of reality and translators of fantasy: some consequences of our present system of drug control as seen in Notting Hill, in *Images of Deviance*, edited by S. Cohen. Harmondsworth: Penguin Books, 27–61.

# The Problems with Moral Panic:
# The Concept's Limitations

## Joel Best

Sociologists have a difficult time keeping control of their concepts. Typically, an analyst devises a new term and applies it to some striking case. Often, because that case's striking qualities seem self-evident, the analyst is able to skimp on the concept's definition; after all, the example makes what is meant by the term self-evident. If the concept catches on, others adopt the term and extend it to additional cases. Quite often, these cases differ from that initial, striking case, so that the new applications expand the concept's domain, via arguments that the new cases resemble—are analogous to, the equivalent of, or fundamentally like—that original case. Because the original definition lacked precision, it is hard to criticize these new, broader conceptions of the term as illegitimate. As the concept is applied to a wider range of phenomena, its domain stretches, and it becomes a more familiar term, even as its analytic usefulness is thereby diminished. For instance, once nearly every family can be labeled dysfunctional, then the term dysfunctional family becomes little more than another term for family, and whatever power the concept had to identify particular sorts of family interactions is reduced. Not infrequently, as a new concept diffuses, it crosses disciplinary boundaries, which only increases the likelihood that its meaning will morph in unexpected ways as a broader range of scholars apply the term. For instance, as the term *social construction* spread from sociology into, not just other social sciences, but the humanities, the natural sciences, and even into popular discourse, the various people who appropriated the term began using it to mean very different things (Hacking 1999).

Something similar has happened with the term moral panic. It originated within the National Deviancy Conference (NDC), a group of British sociologists that formed in the 1960s. They had been influenced by the rise of labeling theory among American sociologists of deviance. Used by Jock Young in passing in 1971, moral panic became the central concept in the first edition of Stanley Cohen's (2002) *Folk Devils and Moral Panics: The Creation of the Mods and Rockers* in 1972. Cohen's often-quoted, paragraph-long definition of moral panic was vague. The concept had been devised to describe a striking example—the overwrought British press coverage of seaside holiday scuffles between mods and rockers (two rival styles adopted by lower middle-class and working-class youth, respectively). The contrast between these events, which resulted in minor injuries and some modest property damage, and the worried commentaries about youth out of control, gave a sense of what moral panic might involve, without actually specifying what did or did not constitute a moral panic.

Moral panic was not an instant hit as a concept. Cohen's book was hard to come by in the United States until a second edition appeared in 1980. During those initial years, the term's usage was restricted to a few British scholars; most famously, it figured in Hall et al.'s (1978) critique of an anti-mugging campaign, *Policing the Crisis: Mugging, the State, and Law and Order*. It also appeared in one journal article and three book reviews published in the *British Journal of Sociology* and the *British Journal of Criminology*.[1] The next decade (1981–1990) saw a marked increase in the term's appearances in the same two leading journalsat least 16 articles and several more reviews referred to moral panics. The concept soon spread far beyond academia until it became common in Britain's popular media. For instance, during 2001–2010, it often appeared in British newspapers: nearly 100 times in both the *Observer* and *The Times* of London, nearly 200 times in the *Guardian*.

The term took longer to gain a foothold in the United States than it did in Britain. No author writing in the US journal *Social Problems* (the leading forum for sociologists of deviance) used the term until 1990, nearly twenty years after the first edition of Cohen's book. The publication of the first edition of *Moral Panics: The Social Construction of Deviance* in 1994, co-authored by the American Erich Goode and the Israeli Nachman Ben-Yehuda (2009), seems to have done much to encourage not just sociologists, but also scholars in other social sciences and the humanities to use the term. Still, moral panic has made only modest inroads in the American popular press: during 2001–10, *The New York Times* used the term only about 30 times, *The Washington Post* about half as often.

In about 40 years, then, the notion of moral panic has become familiar to a good many people, but this is not necessarily a cause for celebration. Just as in the case of other concepts that have spread far beyond their sociological origins, the meaning of moral panic—never defined in an especially precise manner—has become increasingly uncertain. It is not clear whether the concept remains analytically useful. This chapter seeks to explore these issues by reviewing some key criticisms of the idea of moral panic and considering what the concept contributes to our understanding of public issues. In particular, I draw attention to differences in the ways British and American analysts use the term.

---

1 These figures on usage are derived from searching *JSTOR*'s full-text database for major scholarly journals (such as the *British Journal of Sociology*), or from searching the electronic files for other journals (such as Oxford Journal's *BJC* holdings). Figures for newspapers come from LexisNexis searches (for a more detailed discussion of moral panic's diffusion, see Altheide 2009).

## *Moral* Panics and Moral *Panics*

The concept of moral panic emerged at a particular time and place: Britain in the late 1960s and early 1970s. The British sociologists who belonged to the National Deviancy Conference borrowed the labeling framework developed by Howard S. Becker (1963) and other American sociologists of deviance during the 1960s. Basically, labeling theory had challenged mainstream sociology's assumption that deviants were simply people who violated norms; it was easy for labeling's advocates to show that deviance was not so much a matter of what one did, but rather of how people reacted. Some norm violations were ignored, while other, even minor, offenses could lead to harsh responses. Labeling theorists were fond of illustrating societal reactions to deviance through case studies of victimless crimes, such as homosexuality and marijuana smoking (Best 2004).

The sociologists in the NDC began to apply these ideas to interpreting social life in 1960s Britain—to drug use, soccer hooliganism, hippies, and the like. However, they reinterpreted labeling through a British sensibility. British sociology has long been more overtly political than its American counterpart, more likely to view social problems and social policies as expressions of class interests. In particular, they viewed moral panic in terms of class and politics in a way that the American analysts who later adopted the concept would not.

When Cohen used the concerns about mods and rockers to illustrate the concept of moral panic in 1972, his audience in Britain heard the term as *moral* panic. That is, they understood the reaction to mods and rockers as a moral critique, mounted by conservative, upper- and middle-class authorities, who worried not just about the disorder caused by the minor holiday clashes between the two groups, but also about the larger moral significance of those events. Mods and rockers were stylistic choices for lower middle- and working-class youth who had a bit of disposable income. Both styles implied a troubling independence from and indifference to the adult moral order.[2] Cohen's casual definition of moral panic invoked a lineup of authorities: these usual suspects included "the mass media," "editors, bishops, politicians and other right-thinking people," and "socially accredited experts" (2002: 1). Cohen and his British readers understood that these were *moral* authorities making *moral* judgments.

In contrast, when the term did cross the Atlantic, American audiences tended to hear it as moral *panic*. That is, their emphasis tended to be on the panicky, emotional, irrational nature of the reaction. In this view, moral panic seemed akin to other ill-defined concepts that highlighted irrational fears: terms such as witch-hunt, drug scare, collective delusion, and mass hysteria—all episodes when people seemed to take leave of their senses. This emphasis implied that increased concern about some well-documented threat did not constitute a moral panic, that a moral panic involved overblown or unreasonable fears. Thus, when in 1994 the American-

---

2   This was hardly a new phenomenon in England, where there was a long history of worried commentaries about troubling youth styles: teddy boys, hooligans, scuttlers, and so on (see Pearson 1983).

Israeli team of Goode and Ben-Yehuda sought to specify the characteristics of moral panic, they spoke of "disproportionality": "Public concern is in excess of what is appropriate if concern were directly proportional to objective harm" (2009: 40). Contrast their treatment of the concept with that of the British sociologist Kenneth Thompson (1998: 8, emphasis in original):

> The reason for calling it a *moral* panic is precisely to indicate that the perceived threat is not to something mundane—such as economic output or educational standards—but a threat to the social order itself or an idealized (ideological) conception of some part of it.

For American analysts, the issue of disproportionality was central to identifying a moral panic. This was nicely illustrated in the aftermath of the 2001 terrorist attacks, when a writer for *Reason* magazine asked several American sociologists (including me) whether the concern about terrorism constituted a moral panic— and we all hedged (Walker 2002). It took time for the post-9/11 anxiety to subside, for US analysts to judge the fear of terrorism overblown—to begin labeling it another moral panic (Victor 2006). In contrast, British sociologists struggled to locate moral panic in a changing ideological landscape. Thus, sociologist Stuart Waiton (2008:104) coined the term "amoral panic" to acknowledge that claims to arouse public concern could be grounded in a broad range of ideological and professional worldviews:

> Whereas panics in the past were ... generated by conservatives, today 'panics' come from various sections of society, and cover an ever-wider array of issues, from the MMR vaccine to bird flu, the millennium bug, paedophiles, binge drinkers, sexually transmitted diseases and passive smoking, to name but a few .... Rather than panicking being the preserve of reactionary traditionalists, it seems that to one degree or another we are all in a panic about something.

From the British perspective, if people other than the conservative elite were panicking, it was not a moral panic, and a new term was needed.


## Moral Panic's Problems

Like other sociological concepts before it, the term moral panic was introduced without a clear, precise definition. It caught on and spread from the United Kingdom to the United States and beyond sociology to other academic disciplines, and even into popular discourse. But those who adopted the term did not necessarily mean the same things by it. Nor was this definitional confusion the only issue. More people started using the term moral panic in the 1990s and usage has continued to increase since 2000. While this suggests that the idea has become influential, its spread has revealed some conceptual problems that again derive from the absence of a clear definition. As with other sociological concepts, increased popularity has tended to come at the cost of analytic precision.

## The Idea of Social Construction

One reason that American sociologists may have been slower to adopt the term was the emergence of constructionist studies of social problems in the 1970s (the same decade, remember, when moral panic got its start in Britain). There was a long tradition of American sociologists questioning the value of social problem as a sociological concept: so many different phenomena—ranging from individual actions such as suicide, to global crises such as overpopulation—were labeled social problems that it was difficult to devise a definition of the concept's domain. The 1970s saw efforts by several theorists, most notably sociologists Malcolm Spector and John I. Kitsuse (1977), to redefine the concept: instead of viewing social problems as a type of condition, they proposed understanding social problem as a social process by which troubling issues came to public attention. That is, they called for analysts to focus on the social construction of social problems. Other sociologists adopted this approach and began to conduct case studies of this process of social problems construction.

The constructionist orientation offered a good deal on analytic flexibility. It proved equally useful for analysts who wanted to understand social movements with which they sympathized, as it was for more critical analyses of claims. It permitted a focus on the claims themselves (that is, what rhetoric was chosen to convince audiences that something ought to be considered a social problem), on the advocates making the claims, on the media's treatment of those claims, and so on. There were soon dozens, then hundreds of constructionist analyses, and Goode and Ben-Yehuda (2009) chose a subtitle that linked moral panics to this constructionist literature: *Moral Panics: The Social Construction of Deviance*.

However, the constructionist literature points to some problems with the concept of moral panic. In trying to devise a tighter definition for the term, Goode and Ben-Yehuda identified five features of moral panics, including "disproportionality," that is, moral panics are claims that exaggerate a threat. This is arguably the key criterion (Goode and Ben-Yehuda devote more pages to explaining disproportionality than to any of their other four criteria). Expressing exaggerated, outsized fear is what makes something a moral *panic*, an overreaction.

But social problems construction occurs in a social problems marketplace (Hilgartner and Bosk 1988). At any given moment, there are many advocates seeking to construct one social problem or another; they are making claims and trying to attract the attention of the public, the press, and policymakers. Each is convinced that his or her particular issue is especially important, and each must struggle to be heard amid the cacophony of claims being made in the marketplace. Many of these individuals spend much of their time among people who share their concern, who believe that their issue is especially deserving of attention. It is easy to appreciate that, say, a parent who has had a child killed by a drunk driver is likely to consider drunk driving a terrible problem and, moreover, that associating with other parents who have experienced similar losses is likely to create a sort of hothouse atmosphere in which concern about drunk driving will be intense. Such advocates are unlikely to downplay the seriousness of their issues. Rather, they may understandably favor emotionally intense rhetoric. They are unlikely to think critically about statistical estimates for their problem's size, reasoning that this is a big problem, and here is a big number—so the number must be about right (Best 2001). In other words, exaggeration—disproportionality—is widespread, an element of many—one suspects most—social problems claims. If disproportionate concern defines a moral panic, are most social problems moral panics?

## The Importance of Disapproval

Even those analysts most enthusiastic about the concept of moral panic are unlikely to argue that all exaggerated social problems claims denote moral panics. Again, this would threaten to expand the term's boundaries so far as to make the term useless: if all social problems are moral panics, then moral panic becomes just another word for social problem. And there is another issue: moral panic is an invidious label, assigned by analysts to claims they wish to debunk; analysts are reluctant to apply the concept to causes with which they sympathize.

Recall that the British sociologists who coined the term saw sociology as a left/liberal framework for analyzing social conditions and social policies. They used the label moral panic to challenge, to delegitimize conservative claims about working-class youth, muggings, and so on. A similar, albeit less overt, tendency runs through American sociology. Thus, sociologist Barry Glassner's *The Culture of Fear: Why Americans Are Afraid of the Wrong Things* (1999) criticizes as exaggerated a host of social problems claims made by conservatives and argues that these misdirect attention away from those social problems (constructed in analogous ways, but by liberals) that should concern people. Campaigns with which sociologists are likely to sympathize—for example, claims from feminists, environmentalists, and so on—are unlikely to be labeled moral panics even when they feature claims that can be criticized as disproportionate. In contrast, the claims that US sociologists label moral panics are usually advanced by conservatives (Garland 2008). Similarly, a study of journalists invoking the concept "found only one instance in which a progressive movement/orientation was challenged as promoting a [moral panic]" (Altheide 2009: 90–91).

The ideological underpinnings of moral panic were somewhat less problematic for British sociologists in that their conception of *moral* panics was intended to describe claims advanced by conservatives who saw themselves as defenders of morality. (This is precisely why Waiton argued for a new term to describe campaigns that might be promoted by all sorts of advocates.) The situation posed more problems for American sociologists, who sought to frame their analyses as scientific or at least social scientific, which implied a degree of dispassionate, non-ideological objectivity. Thinking in terms of moral *panics* suggested that these phenomena could be distinguished by an emotional reaction, by behavior that could be characterized as panicky. While it might be pleasant to imagine that only conservatives are subject to these fits of irrationality, and while it is certainly possible to point to examples of red scares and other excessive conservative concerns, it is not difficult to find contrary examples of dubious claims promoted by and inspiring panicky reactions among liberals, ethnic minorities, feminists, environmentalists, and so on.

In particular, environmental movements have given liberals far more access to the public sphere. Although the British sociologists who introduced the term may have viewed the press as a venue where conservative claims received more—and more respectful—coverage, today, at least in the United States, it is conservatives who most often complain about mainstream media bias. My point is not that the media actually display a consistent slant; there are of course parallel literatures by progressives charging that the media fail to question the culture and institutions of the *status quo* and by conservatives insisting that the media constantly legitimize liberal causes. But, in the decades after the civil rights movement's glory days, the media have been far more far more likely to give both liberal and conservative activists a platform for their claims. Alarming, even apocalyptic warnings, have become fairly common. One thinks, for instance, about the series of environmental advocates warning about overpopulation (Paul Ehrlich's *The Population Bomb* projected "massive famines will occur soon, possibly in the early 1970s, certainly by the early 1980s") (1968: 44), the exhaustion of natural resources (*The Limits to Growth* warned, "The great majority of the currently important nonrenewable resources will be extremely costly 100 years from now" and calculated that the planet's supplies of aluminum, copper, gold, lead, and mercury would be exhausted by 2003) (Meadows et al. 1972: 75, 64), and global cooling (in 1975, *Newsweek* forecast, "The drop in food output could begin quite soon, perhaps only 10 years from now") (Gwynne 1975: 64), all of whom received extensive attention in the mainstream press. Clearly, conservatives do not have a monopoly on exaggerated, panicky rhetoric, yet sociologists have been reluctant to characterize such warnings as moral panics.

## Defending Moral Panic as a Concept

Complaints that the criterion of disproportionality is applied unevenly and moral panic is less an analytic concept than an invidious label applied to claims that sociologists wish to discredit are hardly new (Garland 2008). They have inspired two reactions. First, some sociologists have sought to defend the concept, to argue that its critics have misunderstood or misconstrued what is at issue, that moral panic remains a useful concept. In particular, the authors of the key works that launched the concept in both Britain and America continue to mount defenses.

In a recent essay, Jock Young, the first sociologist to use the term in print, in 1971, offers a more theoretically nuanced specification of moral panic's meaning

(2009). He argues that moral panics are expressions of underlying cultural unease: "A moral panic does not occur when hegemony is successful, but rather when it is in crisis" (Young 2009: 13). He deals with the issue of disproportionality by viewing the moral panic as an expression of this emotional crisis:

> What is disproportionate is the reaction to its immediate manifestation. It is proportional to the anxiety, not to the actual event. It is, on the surface of things, a mistake in reason, but it is not, on a more in-depth level, a mistake in emotion. (Young 2009: 14)

Young's response to the critics shifts attention to an underlying emotional order, which raises new questions about what constitutes a proportionate response. He seems comfortable with moral panic as an essentially invidious category, noting that the label "would not, of course, be countenanced in respect of crimes such as rape or racist attack" (Young 2009: 14).

In his introduction to the third edition of *Folk Devils and Moral Panics: The Creation of the Mods and Rockers*, Cohen (2002) acknowledges that related theoretical advances—the rise of social constructionism, cultural studies, and the sociology of risk—have supplanted the labeling position from which the notion of moral panic emerged, yet defends the term. He repeatedly accepts the points made by moral panic's critics, even as he argues that the concept has value: "The term 'panic' has caused unnecessary trouble, [yet] I believe that it still makes some sense as an extended metaphor" (Cohen 2002: xxvi), "the assumption of disproportionality is problematic ... [yet] there are surely many panics where the judgement of proportionality can and should be made" (Cohen 2002: xxvii), and the study of moral panics "is concentrated on (if not reserved for) cases where the moral outrage appears driven by conservative or reactionary forces" (Cohen 2002: xxxi), yet "some disparities are so gross, some claims so exaggerated, some political agendas so tendentious that they can only be called something like, well, 'social injustice'" (Cohen 2002: xxxiv).

Similarly, Goode and Ben-Yehuda's second edition (2009) features a chapter, "The Moral Panic Meets its Critics," in which they dismiss "the chorus of naysayers who contend they have the argumentative wherewithal to delete the concept of moral panic from the current sociological and theoretical lexicon" (74). Rather, they argue that the growing number of analysts who refer to moral panic is proof that the concept is useful. They do offer some guidelines for determining that a reaction is disproportionate, for example "if the figures that are cited to measure the scope of the problem are grossly exaggerated, we may say that the criterion of disproportion has been met" (Goode and Ben-Yehuda 2009: 76). They acknowledge that "it has become increasingly difficult to stir up a traditional moral panic" (Goode and Ben-Yehuda 2009: 86), but insist that the fact that the people use the concept proves its value.

## Revamping the Concept of Moral Panic

Young, Cohen, and Goode and Ben-Yehuda have a stake in the notion of moral panic and we should not be surprised to find them defending the concept. In all cases, they acknowledge the term's critics, but suggest that their critiques are not compelling. A second reaction to criticisms has been pursued by those who seek to retain the term (which, after all, has the virtue of being well known) but want to redefine the concept in some way that might circumvent the critics. For instance, Brian V. Klocke and Glenn W. Muschert (2010: 295) propose a "hybrid model of moral panics." They synthesize the definitions proposed by Cohen and Goode and Ben-Yehuda in terms of a process, a sequence of three stages (cultivation; operation, further subdivided into an initial episode, followed by magnification and regulation; and dissipation). In presenting their hybrid model, they gloss over the definition of moral panic, noting that framing a moral panic "will involve provocative language to describe the deviance or its impacts ... and will declare the level of the threat as high and needing punitive and/or preventive action" (Klocke and Muschert 2010: 300). This model circumvents most of the criticisms of moral panic: it does not ask what constitutes a "panic," it begs the question of proportionality, and it ignores the possibility that moral panic is an invidious term. It does specify that moral panic refers to constructing forms of deviance, as opposed to other sorts of social problems, and anticipates that this will involve provocative language and declarations of high threats—presumably to distinguish moral panics from less emotionally intense constructions of deviance. In effect, Klocke and Muschert argue that the best way to deal with the debates surrounding the concept of moral panic is to ignore them. Their model is designed to sensitize researchers to a sequence of stages rather than definitional issues.

Other analysts propose retaining the term moral panic, but redefining it in terms of moral regulation. Sociologist Sean P. Hier's "Thinking beyond Moral Panic" (2008: 174) argues, "Contemporary moralization finds expression in hybrid configurations of risk and harm." That is, individuals in contemporary societies are bombarded with warnings – the dangers of obesity, the risks of carcinogenic chemicals, threats from immigrants, and so on. These encourage various sorts of responses, ranging from tougher social controls of others, to self-monitoring. This framework conceptualizes moral panics as part of a far broader system for regulating individuals' behaviors. However, Chas Critcher (2009: 24) warns, "The relocation of moral panics into the context of moral regulation is in danger of encompassing potentially any topic within its remit." He seeks to specify moral panics as a particular kind of moral regulation, one that involves a high threat to moral order, is a problem constructed as highly amenable to social control, yet is not deemed as easily controlled through individuals' self-management. In this view, the domain of moral panic remains fairly traditional—Critcher's three examples are child sexual abuse, violent crime, and asylum seeking (all topics that have been treated as moral panics by British analysts)—while suggesting new theoretical criteria for denoting these as moral panics.

Amanda Rohloff and Sarah Wright (2010) offer yet another effort to respecify the concept, this one derived from sociologist Norbert Elias's argument that history has been characterized by a long-term civilizing process (that is, toward society becoming increasingly governed, rationalistic, and so on) that is marked by countervailing, decivilizing processes. They suggest that moral panics can be "conceptualized as *short*-term, partial decivilizing processes that occur within (and partly as a result of) civilizing processes" (Rohloff and Wright 2010: 411, emphasis in original). They suggest that this approach will allow analysts to "*protect* (but not be restrained by) the political underpinnings of the traditional moral panic project as we seek to imagine how the model can be connected to theory" (Rohloff and Wright 2010: 415, emphasis in original). In other words, they hope to relocate moral panic within Elias's theoretical model, by relabeling what earlier analysts viewed as reactionary, disproportionate, or irrational as decivilizing. However, they do not offer illustrations of how this new theoretical language can, in practice, resolve moral panic's conceptual problems.

These efforts to reformulate the concept of moral panic can be seen as attempts to retain a popular concept, but to set it upon a different theoretical foundation that may circumvent some of the problems critics have raised. Neither Klocke and Muschert, nor Hier, nor Critcher, nor Rohloff and Wright try to defend the notion of disproportionality, nor do they want to treat moral panic as simply an invidious label (although they all seem sympathetic with what Rohloff and Wright call "the political project" of using the concept of moral panic to criticize some claims as ideologically wrongheaded).

The problem with these efforts, of course, is that the moral panic literature has grown. As with other imprecisely defined sociological concepts that have diffused broadly, there are now lots of people using the term in lots of ways, many of them trying to keep moral panic in the sociological vocabulary by hooking it to whatever theoretical model is currently fashionable. There are now lots of visions of moral panic being promoted within different literatures. At this point, it is unlikely that analysts will rally around a particular new definition. After all, they have not needed a precise definition, so far … .

## Concluding Remarks: Is Moral Panic a Valuable Concept?

The career of moral panic resembles those of other sociological concepts. A term captures people's imaginations and they begin to use it. Because its definition is vague, there do not seem to be many rules governing its usage, and the concept's domain seems to swell. Critics warn that the idea is becoming less useful, yet there is no consensus about how the concept should or should not be used.

The more people speak of moral panic, the less sure they are what the term means. In the case of moral panic, the words themselves seem ill chosen. Not only is there disagreement about whether the accent belongs on *moral* or on *panic*, people cannot agree on whether all moral panics involve moral concerns or whether they involve any sort of panic. It is hard not to wish that Cohen had given the concept a different name. Still, the term's defenders have a point: the very fact that people know the term seems to give it value. But how best to conceptualize it?

My view is that moral panic is best seen as a specific variety of social problems construction. Sociologists find it useful to talk about crime waves (usually understood as waves of media coverage) or drug scares (constructions of particular drug problems); both concepts denote campaigns to construct particular sorts of social problems – concerns about crimes or drugs. Perhaps moral panics can be conceptualized in an analogous manner. Here, it seems important to get away from the elements that have caused so much theoretical confusion: the meaning of panic and the invidious implications of the term. Rather, we might focus on moral panics as short-lived concerns that emerge largely via media coverage, as opposed to prolonged campaigns by social movements, and that these concerns typically focus on threats to or by young people. This usage fits Cohen's original focus on mods and rockers, as well as successive concerns about hippies, skinheads, goths, missing children, and so on, and it is consistent with the cases many analysts have chosen to study (see, for example, Krinsky 2008). Thus, just as crime waves are about crimes and drug scares about drugs, we may find it useful to conceptualize moral panics as focused on children and youth.

Restricting the use of moral panics in this way may seem to constrain the concept, but unrestrained usage has been the ruin of many sociological concepts. Perhaps it is not too late to salvage moral panics.

# References

Altheide, D.L. 2009. Moral panic: from sociological concept to public discourse. *Crime, Media, Culture*, 5(1), 79–99.

Becker, H.S. 1963. *Outsiders: Studies in the Sociology of Deviance*. New York: Free Press of Glencoe.

Best, J. 2001. *Damned Lies and Statistics: Untangling Numbers from the Media, Politicians, and Activists*. Berkeley: University of California Press.

Best, J. 2004. *Deviance: Career of a Concept*. Belmont: Wadsworth.

Cohen, S. 2002 (1972, 1980). *Folk Devils and Moral Panics: The Creation of the Mods and Rockers*. 3rd Edition. London: Routledge.

Critcher, C. 2009. Widening the focus: moral panics as moral regulation. *British Journal of Criminology*, 49(1), 17–34.

Ehrlich, P.R. 1986. *The Population Bomb*. New York: Ballantine.

Garland, D. 2008. On the concept of moral panic. *Crime, Media, Culture*, 4(1), 9–30.

Glassner, B. 1999. *The Culture of Fear: Why Americans Are Afraid of the Wrong Things*. New York: Basic Books.

Goode, E., and Ben-Yehuda, N. 2009 (1994). *Moral Panics: The Social Construction of Deviance*. 2nd Edition. Malden: Wiley-Blackwell.

Gwynne, P. 1975. The cooling world. *Newsweek*, April 28, 64.

Hacking, I. 1999. *The Social Construction of What?* Cambridge: Harvard University Press.

Hall, S., Critcher, C., Jefferson, T., Clarke, J., and Roberts, B. 1978. *Policing the CrisisMugging, the State, and Law and Order*. Critical Social Studies. Houndmills: Palgrave Macmillan.

Hier, S.P. 2008. Thinking beyond moral panic: risk, responsibility, and the politics of moralization. *Theoretical Criminology*, 12(2), 173–90.

Hilgartner, S. and Bosk, C.L. 1988. The rise and fall of social problems. *American Journal of Sociology*, 94(1), 53–78.

Klocke, B.V. and Muschert, G.W. 2010. A hybrid model of moral panics: synthesizing the theory and practice of moral panic research. *Sociology Compass*, 4(5), 295–309.

Krinsky, C. (ed.). 2008. *Moral Panics over Contemporary Children and Youth*. Aldershot: Ashgate.

Meadows, D.H., Randers, J., and Behrens III, W.W. 1972. *The Limits to Growth*. New York: Signet.

Pearson, G. 1983. *Hooligan: A History of Respectable Fears*. Houndmills: Macmillan.

Rohloff, A. and Wright, S. 2010. Moral panic and social theory: beyond the heuristic. *Current Sociology*, 58(3), 403–19.

Spector, M., and Kitsuse, J.I. 1977. *Constructing Social Problems*. Menlo Park: Cummings.

Thompson, K. 1998. *Moral Panics*. Key Ideas. Milton Park: Routledge.

Victor, J.S. 2006. Why the terrorism scare is a moral panic. *The Humanist*, July–August, 9–13.

Waiton, S. 2008. *The Politics of Antisocial Behaviour: Amoral Panics*. New York: Routledge.

Walker, J. 2002. Panic attacks: drawing the thin line between caution and hysteria after September 11. *Reason*, March, 36–42.

Young, J. 1971. The role of the police as amplifiers of deviancy, negotiators of reality and translators of fantasy: some consequences of our present system of drug control as seen in Notting Hill, in *Images of Deviance*, edited by S. Cohen. Harmondsworth: Penguin Books, 27–61.

Young, J. 2009. Moral panic: its origins in resistance, ressentiment, and the translation of fantasy into reality. *British Journal of Criminology*, 49(1), 4–16.

# PART II
# SEX PANICS

# Overview of Part II

In *Sex, Politics and Society: The Regulation of Sexuality since 1800* (1981), social historian Jeffrey Weeks argues that anxiety over sexuality functions as a central element in moral panics, with supposed sexual deviants frequently acting as folk devils. Weeks (1981: 14) writes,

> The moral panic crystallises widespread fears and anxieties, and often deals with them not by seeking the real causes and conditions which they demonstrate but by displacing them on to 'Folk Devils' in an identified social group (often 'immoral' or 'degenerate'). Sexuality has had a peculiar centrality in such panics, and sexual 'deviants' have been omnipresent scapegoats.

According to Weeks, moral panics revolving around sexual issues commonly lead to three diverging political responses: moral crusaders may initiate social morality campaigns to confirm condoned values and behaviors, reformers may agitate for a relaxing of standards for sexual behaviors, or radicals may promote wholesale changes in sexual values.

In her widely reprinted 1984 essay, "Thinking Sex: Notes for a Radical Theory of the Politics of Sexuality," cultural anthropologist Gayle S. Rubin contends (echoing Hall et al.'s ideas about the workings of such episodes generally) that sex panics delegitimize relatively benign behaviors by linking them, to their detriment, with more troubling activities. She avers,

> Because sexuality in Western societies is so mystified, the wars over it are often fought at oblique angles, aimed at phony targets, conducted with misplaced passions, and are highly, intensely symbolic. Sexual activities often function as signifiers for a moral panic, such fears attach to some unfortunate sexual activity or population. The media become ablaze with indignation, the public behaves like a rabid mob, the police are activated, and the state enacts new laws and regulations. When the furor has passed, some innocent exotic group has been decimated, and the state has extended its power into new areas of erotic behavior.

> The system of sexual stratification provides easy victims who lack the power to defend themselves, and a preexisting apparatus for controlling their movements and curtailing their freedoms. The stigma against sexual dissidents renders them morally defenseless. Every moral panic has consequences on two levels. The target population suffers most, but everyone is affected by the social and legal changes.
>
> Moral panics rarely alleviate any real problem, because they are aimed at chimeras and signifiers. They draw on the pre-existing discursive structure which invents victims in order to justify treating "vices" as crimes. The criminalization of innocuous behaviors such as homosexuality, prostitution, obscenity, or recreational drug use, is rationalized by portraying them as menaces to health and safety, women and children, national security, the family, or civilization itself. Even when activity is acknowledged to be harmless, it may be banned because it is alleged to "lead" to something ostensibly worse (another manifestation of the domino theory). Great and mighty edifices have been built on the basis of such phantasms. Generally, the outbreak of a moral panic is preceded by an intensification of such scapegoating. (Rubin 1994: 25)

Rubin argues that by means of the associations drawn by crusaders and the public between mostly disparate sexual behaviors, the state extends its control over a greater number of activities and individuals, repressive laws and policies can then be enacted, and, though sexual folk devils are especially aggrieved as a result, everyone else suffers, as well.

Writing in *Sexuality and its Discontents: Meanings, Myths, and Modern Sexualities* (1985), after concerns over the spread of AIDS entered the public consciousness, Jeffrey Weeks (1985: 44) re-emphasizes the centrality of sex panics to a host of social conflicts over sexual behaviors as well as to problems that, superficially at least, are not closely related to sexual matters:.

> Sexuality is a fertile source of moral panic, arousing intimate questions about personal identity, and touching on crucial social boundaries. The erotic acts as a crossover point for a number of tensions whose origins are elsewhere: of class, gender, and racial location, of intergenerational conflict, moral acceptability and medical definition. This is what makes sex a particular site of ethical and political concern—and of fear and loathing.
>
> The history of the last two hundred years or so has been punctuated by a series of panics around sexuality—over childhood sexuality, prostitution, homosexuality, public decency, venereal diseases, genital herpes, pornography—which have grown out of or merged into a generalised social anxiety.

Sexual issues offer an especially rich source of moral panics not only because they are in themselves of critical significance in society, but also because, being so important, they can be mobilized as part of a range of episodes expressing "generalised social anxiety."

In 1987, Simon Watney, a historian and theorist of photography, published the first edition of *Policing Desire: Pornography, AIDS and the Media* (1996), in which he applies a moral panic framework to the study of social responses to AIDS. In his book's third chapter, called simply "Moral Panics," Watney (1996: 41, emphasis in original) considers that while the moral panics model might be helpful in explaining moral and social conflicts generally, it is less than completely adequate to explain conflict over sexual morality:

> Whilst such analyses offer a certain descriptive likeness to events, they also reveal many severe limitations, which suggest the inadequacy of the concept to the overall ideological policing of sexuality, especially in matters of representation. To begin with, it may be employed to characterise all conflicts in the public domain where scape-goating takes place. It cannot, however, discriminate between either different orders or degrees of moral panic. Nor can it explain why certain types of events are especially privileged in this way. Above all, it lacks any capacity to explain the endless "overhead" narrative of such phenomena, as one "panic" gives way to another, or one anxiety is displaced across different "panics". Thus one moral panic may have a relatively limited frame of reference, whilst another is heavily over-determined, just as a whole range of panics may share a single core meaning whilst others operate in tandem to construct a larger overall meaning which is only partially present in any one of its individual "motifs".... In other words, the theory of moral panics is unable to conceptualise the mass media as an industry which is intrinsically involved with *excess*, with a voracious appetite and capacity for substitutions, displacements, repetitions and signifying absences.

Like Weeks and Rubin, Watney opines that in moral panics sexual issues tend to merge with or stand in for a host of social problems. He departs from them, however, in criticizing the moral panics model on several crucial counts. Watney argues that the concept gives short shrift to the ongoing narrative of concern and anxiety of which moral panics are episodic expressions, fails to consider that moral panics may be either one of a series or single episodes, and does not account for the extent to which mass media rely on sexual issues, and on sex panics, for their continued existence.

Of the researchers who have repeatedly examined moral panics over sexuality, historian of religion and criminologist Philip Jenkins (1998) has expressed the most drastically changing perspective on the phenomenon. In *Moral Panic: Changing Concepts of the Child Molester in Modern America* (1998: 238), Jenkins finds that the heightened and often misdirected concern and anxiety associated with moral panics over child sexual abuse hinder well-warranted attempts to address an objectively discernible social problem:

> Predators, psychopaths, and pedophiles represent a very minor component of the real sexual issues faced by children, while even sexual threats must be considered alongside many other dangers arising from physical violence, environmental damage, and the myriad effects of pervasive poverty. During the twentieth century, however such dangerous outsiders have attracted a vastly disproportionate share of official attention, precisely because they represent the easiest targets for anyone wishing, however sincerely, to protect children.

Jenkins sees the danger inherent in moral panic as one of one of well-intentioned crusaders overlooking the causes of great and real harm to children in favor of sensationalizing easy targets.

By the time he wrote "Failure to Launch: Why do some Social Issues Fail to Detonate Moral Panics?" (2009), Jenkins's perspective on moral panics over child sex abuse had undergone something of a turnabout. He questions why, with minors' increased presence as subjects of online pornography, no sustained and widespread moral panic has ensued. Jenkins (2009: 7–8, emphasis in original) offers three possible reasons for this absence:

> 1. *Lack of media access.* Child porn represents an unusual legal area, in which journalistic access to original material is entirely forbidden: within the United States, no journalistic exemption applies to very stringent federal laws, and 'just looking' is not possible. Other countries enforced somewhat less strict rules, granting researchers some access under police supervision, but such licensing is granted very sparingly. It is not therefore possible for media to check independently on the nature or scale of illegal material, access to which is entirely controlled through law-enforcement gate-keepers. The kind of study that I was able to do in 1999–2000 is now impossible, as the bulletin boards are now strictly password-protected. The media exert no pressure to change this situation because of
> 2. *The invisibility of the problem.* Child-porn material exists within a relatively self-contained universe that the ordinary user cannot simply 'stumble across'. While accidental contact may occur, it does not suggest the real scale of the issue.
> 3. *Pre-emption by Other Causes and Interest Groups.* Given the lack of appreciation of the child-porn world, the topic can be appropriated in symbolic forms by various pressure groups. Anti-pornography activists, for instance, use generalized concerns about children and the internet to focus on the issue of children being exposed to pornographic materials online. Particularly given the lack of possible media activism in this area, no pressure can be generated to expose

or combat the actual trade. Federal agencies speak mainly in terms of online seduction or paedophiles stalking victims via computers—an area in which police can hope to achieve results. In consequence, the larger problem is merged with other issues, including *cyberstalking*, or predatory individuals who seek to contact and seduce children online; *cyberporn*, or children gaining electronic access to adult pornographic materials; and *child pornography*, or the distribution of obscene or indecent images of under-aged subjects. Serious child pornography trafficking is thus ignored and the problem left unconstructed.

If, then, we are seeking the reasons why the child-porn panic never occurred, we would need primarily to understand the legal and bureaucratic environment, and the means by which news is gathered, processed and interpreted. If claims-makers are absent or few in number, if their understanding of the issue is flawed or limited, then even such a tempting topic will largely escape public gaze.

Significantly (though at this point he does not delve deeply into the matter), Jenkins evidently bases his analysis on the assumption that some social problems concerning sex justify moral panics, in other words, that there can be "good" as well as "bad" moral panics. Here, Jenkins identifies three main reasons why no major moral panic over Internet child pornography has emerged: first, current laws limit media access to child porn just as they do that of private individuals, so that locating the images and information that might trigger public concern are lacking. Second, child pornographers, too, limit access to the images that might evoke moral panic. Finally, because such ills as cyberstalking and cyberporn are easier to access, define, and turn into effective folk devils than child pornography and pornographers, moral panics over those problems have developed instead, leaving the serious problem of trafficking in child pornography unaddressed.

## Sex Panics

As in the works of Weeks, Rubin, Watney, and Jenkins, the research included in part two of this volume shows that sex panics often have considerable impacts on issues not directly or exclusively related to sexuality. In chapter five, "Public Punitiveness, Mediation, and Expertise in Sexual Psychopath Policies," Chrysanthi S. Leon and John J. Brent find that though many commentators have assumed that public support for laws criminalizing homosexual conduct have long reflected, as well as resulted in, punitiveness, case studies of the legal response to criminal sexual conduct in the mid-twentieth century show that the law in action reveal a tension between punitive and rehabilitative impulses. Leon and Brent contend that this tension has created a space for the folk devils not only to talk back, but even to shape t the public perceptions and policies that most affect them. . Sexual psychopath laws may have been passed because of popular punitiveness, but they have been written with rehabilitative priorities, and have had surprising effects on prevailing definitions as well as on treatment of child sex abusers. Rather than serving only to punish and control moral deviants, laws were mediated by frontline workers who focused on the relative harmlessness of homosexual persons and their conduct. In addition, psychiatric experts used LGBT subjects to justify their own expertise and jurisdiction and in so doing enabled networking among LGBT individuals.

In chapter six, "Revelation and Cardinals' Sins: Moral Panic over 'Pedophile Priests' in the United States," Pamela D. Schultz argues that a wide range of cultural factors have coalesced since the mid-1980s to turn the public's attention to the issue of priests' sexual abuse of minors within the US Catholic Church, even though similar incidents occur elsewhere and took place long before that time. These contributing factors include increased controversy over the requirement that priests remain celibate, feminist reinterpretations of child sexual abuse, and the Church's policy of remaining silent concerning allegations of abuse. The moral panic over "pedophile priests" in the Catholic Church expresses a crisis of faith concerning, as well as a loss of trust in, the Church. Churches are viewed as places of sanctuary, places that keep the monsters at bay. The moral panic over child sexual abuse in the Catholic Church reflects the disillusioned recognition that it harbors monsters in its midst.

Chapter seven, "The Demise of the Same Sex Marriage Panic in Massachusetts," by Jaime McCauley, looks for the reasons that the moral panic obstructing legalization of same sex marriage in most US states died a fairly quick death in Massachusetts. Determining factors that averted a potential local episode of the US same sex marriage panic included the state's culture, politics, and the ability of its LGBT community organizers to strategize successfully. For example, Massachusetts has high proportions of workers in the higher education, technology, and service industries, few members of the churches that have fought same sex marriage elsewhere (except for the Catholic Church), a comparatively ethnically and racially diverse population, a strong liberal political tradition, and an open LGBT community with experienced political organizations (which earlier defeated passage of a state DOMA law).

In chapter eight, "Considering the Agency of Folk Devils," Mary deYoung notes that the folk devils of classical moral panic analyses invariably are embodied, already socially marginalized and, quite frankly, rather easy to demonize. However, deYoung's chapter focuses less on re-analyzing the demonization process than on reconceptualizing folk devils as social actors who use whatever personal power, agency, social capital, or capacity for resource mobilization they may possess to resist demonization. The chapter centers on four middle-aged female day care providers accused of horrific sexual crimes against their young charges during the satanic ritual abuse moral panic of the 1980s. The ensuing analysis reveals that when they became folk devils, the day care providers used the social capital they possessed not only to resist demonization and impose control, but also to reframe the notion of threat fuelling the moral panic. These exercises in agency had direct effects on the demonization strategies of moral entrepreneurs, the media and the control culture, and the public reactions to those strategies. The chapter concludes by discussing the agency of folk devils, with the intent of increasing the explanatory power of moral panics models.

# References

Jenkins, P. 1998. *Moral Panic: Changing Concepts of the Child Molester in Modern America*. New Haven: Yale University Press.

Jenkins, P. 2009. Failure to launch: why do some social issues fail to detonate moral panics? *British Journal of Criminology*, 49(1), 35–47.

Rubin, G.S. 1994 (1984). Thinking sex: notes for a radical theory of the politics of sexuality, in *The Lesbian and Gay Studies Reader*, edited by H. Abelove, M.A. Barale, and D.M. Halperin. New York: Routledge. First published in slightly different form in *Pleasure and Danger: Exploring Female Sexuality*, edited by C.S. Vance. Boston: Routledge and Kegan Paul, 267–319.

Watney, S. 1996 (1987, 1989). *Policing Desire: Pornography, AIDS and the Media. Media and Society*. 3rd Edition. Minneapolis: University of Minnesota Press.

Weeks, J. 1981. *Sex, Politics and Society: The Regulation of Sexuality since 1800. Themes in British Social History*. London: Longman.

Weeks, J. 1985. *Sexuality and its Discontents: Meanings, Myths, and Modern Sexualities*. London: Routledge.

# Public Punitiveness, Mediation, and Expertise in Sexual Psychopath Policies

Chrysanthi S. Leon* and John J. Brent

Lesbian, gay, bisexual, and transgender (LGBT) histories have characterized a series of sex crime panics in the United States since the 1930s as crackdowns on queer communities and individuals. Either implicitly or often explicitly, these crackdowns have been condemned as expressions of popular punitiveness that used gay men as vehicles for drawing moral boundaries and deriving political benefit (see, for example, Bottoms 1995). Such accounts reflect anger about public and political support for laws that focused on sexual deviance and certainly reflect the lived experience of many people who were harassed by the police and prosecuted and sentenced under laws criminalizing consensual homosexual conduct. But they also overgeneralize the punitive effects of the new laws as well as the punitive intentions of those who implemented new laws and enforced existing criminal codes.

In contrast, this chapter grounds claims about the "law" and "punitiveness" in implementation data, using official documents and admissions data of prison and sexual psychopath civil commitment institutions in California from 1930–80, snapshots of enforcement and disposition practices, and archival material from the Kinsey Institute for Research in Sex, Gender and Reproduction regarding California and New York. The law in practice had punitive and repressive effects, but it was also constitutive for LGBT communities and psychiatric experts. Further, the generic view of law enforcement actors as participants in crackdowns misses the mediation that took place within precincts and courtrooms, as well as the role the "deviants" themselves played in constructing their experience of sexual psychopath laws.

*     Chrysanthi S. Leon wishes to acknowledge the exceptional research assistance of Michelle Pfaulmer, the generosity of the University of Delaware's Faculty Research Support Grant, the Kinsey Institute for Research in Sex, Gender, and Reproduction for facilitating the use of their library and special collections, as well as New York University Press and the International Association of Law and Mental Health for allowing the use of brief passages from earlier work.

## Moral Panics and Freaks Talking Back

The most developed discussions of the genesis and success of sex offender policies in the twentieth century suggest that they are the result of moral panic, defined as a period or cycle of exaggerated concern over a perceived threat that results in the classifying and targeting of deviants (Goode and Ben-Yehuda 2009). Some of the most influential work in providing a conceptual framework for such panics comes from outside sociology: from journalists (see, for example, Nathan and Snedeker 1995, Miller 2002) and historians (Jenkins 1998). But some sociologists of moral panic might not agree that sustained interest in these laws can be usefully described as a moral panic. Sociologist Jeffrey S. Victor (1998: 543), for example, builds on the social constructionist and symbolic interactionist scholarship to explain the satanic ritual abuse hysteria as a moral panic, but does so with a definition that would not apply to the longer term preoccupation with child molesters that Jenkins and others call "moral panic." Victor (1998: 543) explains,

> A moral panic can be defined as a societal response to beliefs about a threat from newly perceived moral deviants. A moral panic has five distinguishing characteristics. First, the societal reaction shows volatility in the form of a sudden eruption and subsiding of concern about the threat. Second, the concern about the threat is widespread in a society. Third, the purported deviants are regarded as a threat to the basic moral values of the society. Fourth, there is consensus in significant segments of the population that the threat is real. Fifth, concern about the threat is disproportional to empirical measures of harm from the purported deviants.

Evoking the work of early constructionists, threats to a population's moral propriety indicate the presence of boundaries that distinguish "us" from "them" and "acceptable" from "unacceptable." Jock Young (1999) and Pierre Bourdieu (1984), for example, argue that inclusion or exclusion rests delicately on the symbolic meaning of socially constructed boundaries between groups. Of particular importance, however, is the political nature of these demarcations: an attention to which group has the power and resources to define and police boundaries that exclude and marginalize. Sociologist Joshua Gamson, in his efforts to understand gender movements and exclusion, echoes this call: "When and how exclusion takes place, then, is closely tied to the specific conditions under which the collective boundaries are being used politically." He continues, "Those boundaries are, in a sense, cultural resources, communication tools in a specific political struggle" (1997: 192).

Gamson's (1998: 25) later work examining the construction of sexuality on talk shows exposes the political battles over sexual morality, the "implications for the important, dangerous, and necessary changes in the cultural presentation of sex and gender difference." Although talk shows celebrate tension in a "democratic" public forum, Gamson argues that they only expose existing larger conflicts and intensify already established battles. He sums up,

> Where sexual meaning-making, sexual politics, and the redrawing of key social boundaries meet up, are the paradoxes of visibility that talk shows dramatize with such fury: democratization through exploitation, truths wrapped up in lies, normalization through freak show. There is in fact no choice here between manipulative spectacle and democratic forum, only the puzzle of a situation in which one cannot exist without the other, and the challenge of seeing clearly what this means for a society at war with its own sexual diversity. (Gamson 1998: 19)

Instead of reifying the stigmatization of sex and gender nonconformists, Gamson (1998: 242) employs the term "freak" to call attention to, and complicate, this construction that (mis)defines a population. His efforts illuminate "the general dilemma of identity politics," a paradox for sex and gender nonconformists in their self-development (Gamson 1995: 391). The argument proposes that fixed identities can provide the source of both oppression and political power.

On one hand, LGBT people, for instance, have made noteworthy progress in establishing a sense of identity, enabling the LGBT community in becoming a major force. "In this ethnic/essentialist politic," Gamson writes, "clear categories of collective identity are necessary for successful resistance and political gain" (1995: 391). Any collective, on the other hand, is met by a logic that seeks to eliminate socially established boundaries that provide the means for further oppression and social control. Here, Gamson's (1995: 402) paradox becomes clear: "It is as liberating and sensible to demolish a collective identity as it is to establish one." Gamson shows that sex and gender nonconformists are often placed on a contested boundary—between becoming socially normalized and morally vilified. The same event that can normalize or naturalize homosexuality (for example, an appearance on television) can also further marginalize it and reinforce prevailing conditions.

## Legal Change: Fears of the Sexual Psychopath

Bourdieu's concepts of "*doxa*" and "field" as applied to the field of law provide an additional theoretical frame here. *Doxai* are "common assumptions and understandings," which Richard Terdiman (1987: 809), Bourdieu's translator, explains as implying,

> Immediate agreement elicited by that which appears self-evident, transparently normal. Indeed, doxa is a normalcy in which realization of the norm is so complete that the norm itself, as coercion, simply ceases to exist as such.

In other work, Leon describes the *doxai* surrounding sex offenders in three eras, and the contradictory assumptions that were increasingly elided, especially from policy (Leon 2011a, 2011b).

These *doxai*, prevailing understandings about who sex offenders are and how they should be handled, must be understood in terms of the professional and social structures that support them, what Leon (2011a: 198) calls the "sex offender discursive field." Bourdieu (1987: 809) explains that a field is "a structured, socially patterned activity or 'practice'" and is often "the site of struggle, of competition for control." Struggle for control leads to a hierarchical system within the field. For example, the juridical field "is organized around a body of internal protocols and assumptions, characteristic behaviors, and self-sustaining values—what we might informally term a 'legal culture'" (Bourdieu 1987: 806):

> The specific codes of the juridical field—the shaping influence of the social, economic, psychological, and linguistic practices which, while never being explicitly recorded or acknowledged, underlie the law's explicit functioning—have a determining power that must be considered if we are to comprehend how the law really functions in society. (Bourdieu 1987: 807)

The field surrounding sex offender social control is analogous to Bourdieu's juridical field, although it encompasses multiple professional groups who accept segments of the sex offender "problem."

We focus here on the first era, characterized by fears of the "sexual psychopath," that roughly spanned the years 1930 to 1955 (see Freedman 1987). In contrast to subsequent eras, the 1930s, 1940s, and early 1950s were characterized by a diverse and inclusive mix of ideas and strategies that cohered around fears of "the sexual psychopath" or "sex fiend." This fear emerged from the criminological theories of degeneracy and feeblemindedness that dominated at the beginning of the twentieth century (Fass 1993) and were popularized by newspapers seeking readers (Schudson 1978). The dominant public discourse framed sexual psychopaths as deviants with a compulsive sex disorder who were running rampant and must be identified, classified, and captured. Once known, they could be incapacitated, studied, and, by the 1950s, treated.

Several child murders received sustained national news coverage during this period, leading to the description of the era as a sex panic. For example, in 1939 California passed a civil commitment law for sexual psychopaths, inspired by a panic over the murder of young girls attributed to a neighborhood crossing guard in Inglewood named Albert Dyer, who became nationally known as a sexual bogeyman. The *Los Angeles Times* described him as a "dull, stupid man," who was familiar to local children ("Jury Decrees" 1937: 1). When the bodies of three elementary schoolgirls were found, he quickly became the primary suspect despite witnesses' descriptions of a man who did not resemble Dyer (Waters 2008). During the trial, a deputy was brought to tears as he testified about the crime scene ("Dyer's Horror Story" 1937: 4) and a crowd gathered outside the city jail threatening to lynch Dyer (Vanderwood 2004: 18). Dr J. Paul De River (quoted in "Dyer Trial Climax" 1937: 1), the nation's most famous and controversial expert on "sexual psychopathy," provided the explanation for the crimes:

> As he perpetrated each murder by strangling them to death he became more sexually excited and when he had completed his third and last murder before he began his infamous assaults on the victim's bodies, everything turned black to him he was so emotionally overcome.

This could be a voice-over for a cautionary tale. It demonstrates not only the hyperbolic description of a monster among us, but also the foothold gained by psychiatric expertise in the national conversation.

Nonetheless, the legal system and the government avoided some of the more extreme expressions of public concern, funding research and institutions for treatment besides passing new laws to increase punishment. Undeniably, public pressure did determine some policy, as scholars writing during and after the sexual psychopath era have noted (Ploscowe 1951, Sutherland 1950a, 1950b, Freedman 1987, Jenkins 1998). But numerous and competing strategies were available to policymakers, and in places, including California and New York, they generally enacted the less punitive ones.

Fears of sexual psychopaths did lead to the enactment of new civil laws. Under sexual psychopath laws, individuals who demonstrated a mental abnormality that might compel them to commit sexual crimes could be committed to state hospitals (Freedman 1987, 1995). These laws enjoyed support from multiple sources, were briefly implemented in several states (see Lave 2009), and remained in use in California from 1939 to 1979.

The use of civil commitment through the sexual psychopath laws has been criticized as a crackdown on homosexuals and as a potentially dangerous expansion of social control. More broadly, contemporaneous critics of civil commitment and of indeterminate sentencing called the overall medicalization of criminality a veil for increasing social control (see, for example, Szasz 1963). This critical view emphasized the inequality of outcome for different groups of offenders. For example, critics of indeterminate sentences pointed out the systematically longer sentences served by black offenders (see, for example, Mitford 1973), while critics of civil commitment declared that it led to the extensive confinement of nonviolent offenders (Szasz 1961) and was used to express anxieties about particular kinds of threatening deviance (Freedman 1987, Jenkins 1998).

Similarly, Sklansky (2008: 902), summarizing the LGBT scholarship of the 1990s that described specific cities and crackdowns, including those in New York, Atlanta and Iowa, reiterates a typical claim: "The upshot was that the campaign against sexual psychopaths often became, in practice, a campaign against homosexuals." A more systematic examination of data, looking especially at offenses used to charge homosexuals, shows that these "campaigns" were not the norm and rarely had the widespread punitive effects implied by such a statement.

## Panic and Practice: Implementation of Sex Crime Law and Homosexual Subjects

Popular imagery behind the sexual psychopath laws characterized sexual deviants as monstrous offenders. The monster image is something like Bourdieu's *doxa*. The existence of such psychopaths was so unquestioned that often police and the media inferred sexual motivations for crimes that had no supporting evidence other than the identity of the victims (young single women or children) ("Girl Victim" 1947, "Mexico-US Hunt" 1949). Alongside this predominant view, mid-twentieth century America was becoming more interested in ways of thinking about the world provided by the psychiatric field.

Michel Foucault (1975: 15) notes that the nineteenth century ushered in a new order in the scientific inspection of the body, recognizing that medical personnel placed the patient under "perpetual examination." His interest, however, centers on the discourse that produced, maintained, and extended the medical look or "gaze." The "clinic," for Foucault, became an apparatus of examination, a site of knowledge production bound by rules and regulations, an authoritative institution where the individual became the object of scrutiny (Long 1992). His early effort to theorize the role of medicine sheds light on the historical process that sociologist Peter Conrad (2007) and others have described as the "medicalization" of society.

Conrad's use of the term medicalization denotes a process by which nonmedical problems and issues are defined and treated medically, usually as an illness or disorder (2007: 4). Public health scholar Jo C. Phelan (2005) and historian David T. Courtwright (2010) further this notion by discussing the process of "geneticization" and, more specifically, its reshaping of social problems. For these authors, the growing interest in medicine to explain behavior was unavoidable given improved medical instrumentation, new laboratory techniques, substantial monetary grants, and developments in research. Armed with growing support, medical authority, and political backing, the medical paradigm became a major voice within the crime and deviance debate.

Conrad (2007) highlights that the range of behaviors constructed as illness warranting both the perpetual gaze of medical personnel and medicinal treatment has grown since the 1950s. As the medical framework expands and gains authority over social problems, definitions change, different prescriptions are written, and alternative practices are adopted to abate social ills. Conrad and fellow sociologist Joseph W. Schneider (1980) argue that homosexual conduct as a sexual offense also underwent medicalization—being reconstructed as a disorder, a departure from predefined acceptable behavior. Beginning in the late nineteenth century, physicians and psychiatrists started the process of ridding homosexuality of its criminal implication by redefining it as a medical pathology. Specifically, K.M. Benkert (writing as Karoly Maria Kertbeny) in 1869 and Richard Kraft-Ebbing in 1886 argued that sexual deviants should undergo medical treatment instead of becoming objects of punishment under the oppressive legal apparatus of the time (Conrad 2007: 98). Conrad and Schneider contend that securing authority over defining behaviors and persons is central, as when a problem is defined using medical jargon, interpreted through medical frameworks, and treated with medical intervention (1980: 8). Homosexuality as a medical issue, for Conrad (2007), then came, with its inclusion in the *Diagnostic and Statistics Manual Disorders* (DSM) and the World Health Organization's International Classification of Diseases, as a mental disorder. While prior research and scholarly efforts had primed conditions, homosexuality's inclusion into the DSM solidified it as a medical rather than a social pathology.

It follows that examination of scholarship about sexual offending during the mid-twentieth century demonstrates that psychiatric experts prioritized categorization and classification, and therefore differentiates among offenders (Leon 2011a). Psychiatric experts differentiated both by identifying psychiatric and non-psychiatric offenders and by creating typologies within the category of psychiatric offenders. This complemented the criminal justice practice, as actors such as police made judgment calls as part of their daily work. This exercise of bureaucratic discretion leads police to distinguish between offenders who look like good guys and those who look like bad guys, and to figure out how to handle offenders who appear good, even when caught breaking the law (Aaronson, Dienes, and Musheno 1984: viii–ix).

## California

What then was the impact of the public panic, medicalization of homosexuality, and new sexual psychopath laws that used hospitalization to solve sex crime problems? The rate of civil commitment did increase in the late 1940s and early 1950s. However, multiple sources of official and other data show that while the overall civil commitment population increased, homosexual offenders were never committed in large numbers, at any point between 1950 and 1980.[1] For example, a snapshot of California's civil commitment population in 1952 shows only 16 percent sodomy/homosexuality, compared to 52 percent child molesters/pedophilia, 14 percent exhibitionism and 5 percent rape (Lieberman and Siegel 1957). A later criminological evaluation of the program shows even fewer homosexuals, and the studies described below confirm this.

California is used here as a particularly significant case because its correctional and civil commitment programs were the largest nationally. Other scholars have examined offense compositions in sexual psychopath civil commitment programs in other states as well. California's predominant commitment of child molesters and low confinement of sodomy offenders is typical (for the unusual case of Indiana, see Lave 2009, for a full list of state reports on sexual psychopath programs, see Jenkins

---

1    We have not located any data disaggregated by offense/diagnosis prior to 1950. It is possible that the pre-1950 civil commitments were more dominated by homosexual offenders, but even if their relative proportion was high, the population was low — never over 100.

1998). Despite public concerns about homosexuality and the efforts of figures like J. Edgar Hoover to focus generalized crime fears on sexual deviants (Jenkins 1998, Freedman 1987), neither the prison nor the civil commitment populations reflected increased punitiveness directed at homosexual offenders.[2] Exploring the mediation that intervened between public outrage and increased government detention reveals the importance of insulated experts, as well as the constitutive effects of what have been considered purely repressive laws and policies.

## Mediation: Criminal Justice

LGBT histories have documented the repressive effects of police practices that targeted homosexuals, especially the sting operations in bars and toilet stalls that also had notable constitutive effects in galvanizing social movements (Chauncey 1993, 1994, D'Emilio 1998, Eskridge 1997). More recently, Sklansky has suggested that homosexual sting operations were also the secret subtext of some of the Warren Court's major constitutional decisions regarding criminal procedure, in particular *Katz v. United States* (1967, see Sklansky 2008). While the practices of vice squads and other sporadic but systematic attempts to enforce laws against homosexuality have been revealed, little attention has been paid to the general disinclination to seek serious penalties for homosexual offenders.

A series of primary documents provide an "insider" view of homosexual offenders that shows the predominant nuisance view of homosexual conduct. These should be read with the predominant worldview of most law enforcement actors, from police to prosecutors in mind. Typically, good guys are upstanding citizens and bad guys are hoodlums or others with criminal records. Before the 1970s, sex offenses committed by people who otherwise looked like good guys did not make them bad guys. As a result, homosexual cases presented a problem for law enforcement, and more than anything were perceived as nuisances. A thorough project conducted by UCLA law students examined every second felony prosecution and every fifth misdemeanor prosecution for consensual homosexual activity during a single year in Los Angeles County (Gallo et al. 1966c). Their findings show that the criminal justice system quietly sorted the offenders who "deserved" punishment from those who did not appear to be monsters. The California penal code offered wide latitude for selecting arrest charges. Prosecutors and defense attorneys could negotiate a variety of issues before plea. Judges could impose indeterminate sentences to prison, a more determinate term in confinement through civil commitment or, as they did most often, judges could sentence offenders to probation or jail.

---

2     These are well documented in discussions of reactions to the 1948 Kinsey report and need not be repeated here (see, for example, Reumann 2005, Schultz 2005).

This discretion was so pronounced that the UCLA project authors recommended changes to the sex laws that would dramatically restrict discretion at every level. Nevertheless,

> The area of lewd and lascivious conduct is another area where there was a substantial difference between recommendation and disposition. Of those recommended for denial for this offense, 67% were denied and 33% were granted. It may be that some probation departments have a tendency to request a denial in cases that may arouse public controversy, such as lewd and lascivious conduct, while the courts in turn may not feel so dependent upon public acceptance of their actions. (Bureau of Criminal Statistics 1958: 122)

Despite imposed restrictions, the discretion used by judges often moderated the punitive attitudes expressed by the public.

The UCLA study found that the great majority of offenders investigated for sex crimes were convicted of misdemeanors (99 percent), and were often sentenced to probation (Gallo et al. 1966: 673).The researchers explain this fact as largely the result of "judicial evaluation of public consensual homosexual activity as a nuisance rather than as a menace to the community" (Gallo et al. 1966: 738), but also include information about police preferences, which reflect an intermediary position between the punitive views that were reflected in media and the judicial tendency to view homosexuals as nuisances.

This intermediary view is evident in the discussion of police attitudes towards the obligation to register as a sex offender. The authors of the UCLA study explain that police preferred to charge homosexuals with offenses that would require they register, ostensibly because of the belief in escalation of offenses from minor to violent,

> The police are very adamant in their desire to have homosexuals registered and are annoyed when the courts allow defendants to plead to a non-registerable lesser included offense. The reasons for requiring registration of consensual homosexuals are not altogether clear. Some enforcement officials feel that the requirement for registration is itself effective as a deterrent to homosexual activity. ....
> There is disagreement as to whether or not the heinous types of sex crimes involving children or violence are likely to be committed by the average homosexual. Enforcement officials who favor registration do so on the assumption that homosexuals are prone to commit violent crimes and crimes against children. (Gallo et al. 1966a: 737–8)

Out of the 493 felony defendants and 475 misdemeanants they studied, only 17 were referred for civil commitment proceedings (less than 2 percent), and only two were committed (0.2 percent). Few offenders were civilly committed for "sexual perversion" or for consensual homosexual activity among adults, and even for those who were caught in the wider net, the disposition was relatively preferable.[3] As with the UCLA study, a study of three counties in California ten years later also found that when homosexual offenders were charged in the criminal justice system, they almost always received probation rather than commitment or prison sentences (Forst 1978: 114–6).

Simon A. Cole has interpreted longitudinal data from New Jersey's sex offender programs as support for arguments made by historians Estelle B. Freedman and George Chauncey that sexual psychopath laws used violence as a pretext for cracking down on deviants. The Freedman and Chauncey arguments may be right to bring our attention to a limited expansion of social control on the front end, that is, these laws and the underlying fears of escalation may have justified police sting operations, but those offenders were not civilly committed. By the mid-1960s, the belief that homosexuality should be nipped in the bud before turning into homicidal mania was already absent from judicial and psychiatric discourse. The UCLA project in its totality shows the remarkable under-enforcement of consensual sex offenses at the peak period of public support for therapeutic rehabilitation. While we do not have a full longitudinal picture of the typical length of civil commitment, snapshots show that the average commitment was 18 months or less. Compared to the typical time served in prison in the 1950s (between three and four years for both rapists and child molesters), civil commitment was clearly preferable (Leon 2011a). In sum, civil commitment in California, the state with the largest and longest-running sex offender program, was not a mechanism for expanding penal control over homosexuals. Instead, civil commitment focused on nonviolent child molesters and other offenders who would have served short jail terms without the option of civil commitment. (Leon 2011).

## New York

After the publication of Alfred Kinsey's investigations of male and female sexuality, his institute began to look explicitly at the ways that the legal system reflected norms of sexual behavior. Kinsey delegated a research associate, Alice Withrop Field (1951), to conduct an ethnographic study in New York City courts, looking at their processing of homosexual offenses. Although never published, a preliminary progress report dated 1951 describes how criminal justice actors worked around the laws on the books (Field 1951). Field thoroughly combed the criminal codes used to prosecute homosexuals, including disorderly conduct and loitering, as well as the charges with specific reference to the "crime against nature or other lewdness." She complemented this legal research with months of observations of court processing and interviews with many judges, police, and other court personnel.

---

3    Jenkins cites civil commitment snapshots in other states, including New Jersey and Indiana, which included larger proportions of homosexual offenders, but he also notes that the total number of committees was small nationwide, with the exception of California (1998: 86–9).

Unfortunately, Field never gave any specific information about the length or scope of her interviews and observations, but her report contains information on dozens of interviews and many observations of particular cases.

Evidence shows that some judges in New York's lower courts recognized homosexual offenders as an unnecessary drag on their dockets. In 1950, New York City's Chief City Magistrate ordered that all charges for homosexual soliciting and loitering by a railway be sent to felony court rather than charged as misdemeanors. According to Field, this created a drop in homosexual arrests due to the additional burden placed on charging officers and prosecutors, as the magistrate intended. This move also came at the same time that the criminal codes were amended to decriminalize consensual anal or oral sexual activity occurring in private, conduct that had formerly been charged under sodomy. Field also reported in several pieces of correspondence with Kinsey that judges and others in New York attempted to create an entirely separate docket to handle homosexual offenses, a "homosexual court" that could quickly dispose of such nuisance cases.

In addition to her findings about judicial efforts to mediate homosexual prosecutions, Field noted similar police actions. Although officers believed that the law stated that if penetration occurred, they must charge with sodomy, Field (unnamed judge, quoted in 1951: 12) found that "it is so much trouble to take a case through … that unless the partner wants to make a complaint, the police are very careful not to see penetration." Thus, police could also avoid "seeing" what they did not want to see. Although Field's data are from her observations during 1950, another snapshot of New York City's sex crime prosecutions from the 1930s confirms the relatively low proportion of homosexual charges, suggesting that her findings were not unique to the period she studied. In 1939, the city of New York conducted a study to determine whether there had been a sex crime wave between 1937 and 1939, the report on which was entitled *The Problem of Sex Offenses in New York City: A Study of Procedure Affecting 2022 Defendants made by the Staff of the Citizens Committee on the Control of Crime in New York*. To address the question of whether this belief was true, the Committee studied all 2,022 defendants "accused, arrested and brought to arraignment or trial for a sex offense in the boroughs of Manhattan, Brooklyn, the Bronx and Queens" between July 1, 1937 and December 1, 1938 (quoted in Lave 2009: 7). Table 3 included in the report records that 161 of the charges were for sodomy (8 percent of the total) (Lave 2009: 7). Even if a share of the other offense categories that could have included homosexual conduct, indecent exposure, or impairing morals were also used to charge homosexuals, the total share would not even approach 30 percent. Of course, these data exclude people charged under loitering or other charges that were not sex crimes on their face—this is the advantage of the Kinsey and UCLA studies that combined statistics with observations and interviews.

## Mediation and Constitutive Effects

### California

The materials documenting the heyday of Atascadero State Hospital, the flagship for California's sex offender civil commitment program, capitalize on the public's willingness to view some deviant sexual conduct as psychiatric in nature. Just as some police and judicial actors viewed homosexual offenders as significantly less harmful and less prison-worthy than other offenders, experts on the treatment side also helped mediate the punitive sting of public panic. But rather than consistently screening homosexual offenders out, as criminal justice actors did with the criminal justice system, the psychiatric experts involved in civil commitment tended to screen homosexual offenders in when they could, in order to have treatment subjects with whom they would enjoy working. That is, while homosexual offenders were never numerically significant proportions of California's civil commitment regime, statements by the psychiatric experts and others who worked at Atascadero indicate that they were the *preferred* subjects. This is in large part explained by the coming together of the accommodationist strand in California's homophile movement and the rhetoric of citizenship and reform that became a component of public discourse around sex crime in the 1950s and 1960s (D'Emilio 1998).

Atascadero State Hospital's Emotional Security Program focused on normalization. As a 1955 pamphlet, *The New Approach: Sex Offender to Good Citizen*, written and paid for by the participants, explains,

> Sex offenders are of no particular type and are not restricted to a specific occupation, or to a set economic or social level. The majority were respected members of their communities, rearing their families, engaging in gainful occupations, living the average life, apparently as happy, useful citizens.

This passage highlights the patients' attempts to define themselves as "average"—not deviant or monstrous—but as merely suffering from an emotional illness. It also bears striking similarity to other expressions of the homophile movement, such as those promoted by the Mattachine Society (Mattachine Society Project Collection 2008). In fact, it is possible that there was a direct connection— Kinsey's notes reveal that the men who created the Emotional Security program at Atascadero had been transferred from a facility in Southern California, where Mattachine and the homophile movement flourished.

Across the period of legally authorized sex offender civil commitment in California, 1939–1979, psychiatrists and other mental health workers influenced how thousands of sex offenders would serve their time—in a hospital setting or in prison, using a vague determination about "treatment amenability" (Leon 2011a). The standard for amenability was interpreted in practice to address institutional capabilities and the preferences of the penal operatives rather than an individual's diagnosis. This molding of legislative and public intention to the insiders' preferences is described in both published sources and in the notes made by Alfred Kinsey and his colleagues during their visit to Atascadero State Hospital in 1956.[4]

It turns out that treatment amenability meant men to whom the treatment staff could relate. The hope was that the selected men could be taught to control their impulses, and were therefore treatable subjects upon whom the psychiatric experts could prove their value and potential. Thus, the homosexuals who were civilly committed tended to be those whose crimes were described as "situational … resulting from work stresses."[5] Kinsey's interview subjects commonly expressed the belief that the best therapy was "masculinization." This included the practice, officially discouraged but promoted by at least one administrator, of encouraging sexual encounters between the male sexual psychopaths and the female psychiatric patients who were housed in the same hospital. Atascadero also formally sponsored opportunities for heterosexual contact, including dances and card games to which the public was welcomed and regular visits from female volunteers who socialized with the patients. Thus, the bulk of "treatment" for civilly committed sexual deviants consisted of therapeutic recreation, as also including "stamp, astronomy, prospector and dance clubs" as well as music and drama, all intended to "aid the men in … enhancing partially learned or forgotten acceptable leisure time habits" (Leon 2011: 8). "Patients" were also encouraged to interact with outsiders, so young female volunteers from the community were welcomed into the hospital to play cards and lead some of the recreational activities. In addition, "those patients who have responded to treatment and are considered harmless— Peeping Toms, exhibitionists—are given gate passes to attend dances and other functions in nearby towns" ("Convicts' Trysts" 1959: B1, see also Miller 2002). In addition to augmenting the services the understaffed program could provide, these interactions were also about modeling heteronormative relationships.

The preference for homosexual subjects makes sense in light of the psychiatric orthodoxy surrounding other offenders. The psychiatric view saw offenders as rule breakers, not heinous monsters, and as both rational actors and mentally or emotionally abnormal. They are subject to compulsive desires, but because these impulses can be controlled if not cured, choice plays a role along with compulsion. They can be deterred by the threat of further prosecution and they can be treated through behavioral techniques to resist their desires. Other offenders, such as exhibitionists, were viewed, then as now, as far more compulsive and less amenable to any treatment. Rapists tended to be viewed as typically situational, but practically untreatable if they were the rare pathological types. Child molesters spanned the range between the situational alcoholic and the pathological, but violent molesters were sent to prison, not the hospital.[6] In addition to their relative

---

4    1958. Kinsey Notes (unpublished). Box SO1, Folder 1D, Dated: March 28, 1958, accessed through the generosity of the Kinsey Institute on Sex, Gender and Reproduction.

5    These explanations of homosexual conduct as temporary lapses were explicit in three of the psychiatric experts whom Kinsey interviewed.

6    This differentiation by offense type is expressed in the Kinsey notes and further explicated from other sources in Leon 2011a.

treatability, the homosexual offenders tended to be older and more professionally established, and therefore more like the psychiatric experts themselves as well as potentially more eager to return to a publicly heterosexual identity (see Lave 2009). As a result, psychiatric experts preferred the sex offenders who seemed to fit this model, so they screened in homosexual offenders whenever they could, along with the child molesters who had not physically wounded their victims (Leon 2011a).

In addition to the ability to select for treatable subjects to whom they related, and the use of heteronormativity as a treatment method that dovetailed well with the goal of "passing" that some in the homophile movement promoted, homosexual subjects also facilitated the expansion of psychiatric expertise. They could be treated and therefore counted as success: Atascadero boasted a "very low" recidivism rate. These offenders also facilitated psychiatric knowledge production. In the 1930s and 1940s, supporters of the sexual psychopath laws nationwide had touted specialized institutions both for their potential for addressing known sex criminals and as research sites. Commentators like Dr J. Paul De River, who held forth concerning the Albert Dyer case, and J. Edgar Hoover provided a way of thinking about criminals that focused on the sexual aspect of their drive to commit crime—a largely undifferentiated narrative of the monstrous offender. But most psychiatric experts argued for differentiation, chief among them Dr Karl Bowman. Bowman was famous for his evaluations of Nathan Leopold, Jr., and Richard Loeb during their trial for the abduction and murder of Bobby Franks in 1924. Historian Paula Fass (1993) uses this case to document the rising prominence of psychiatric expertise in making sense of childhood, sexuality, and evil. More precisely, she credits Bowman and his co-evaluator, Dr Harold Hulbert, with offering a new way to make sense of criminal deviance:

> First the newspapers, through which the case initially exploded into the public arena, and then other cultural agencies participated in a public discourse that offered Americans the new terms normality and abnormality to understand transgressive behavior. Indeed, the judicial hearing that determined Leopold and Loeb's fate was guided, not by legal questions of responsibility, but by a psychiatrically driven defense that popularized those terms. (Fass 1993: 920)

After his rise to international fame, Bowman directed California's sexual deviation research at the Langley-Porter Neuropathic Institute. This positioned Bowman (1952: 181) to join many others who studied sexual offending in opposing "sexual psychopathy" as a diagnosis, calling the term, "nearly meaningless."

Academically affiliated psychiatric researchers labored against popular assumptions about sexual offending as unique behaviors committed by a particular kind of monstrous offender. Their normalizing discourse was never dominant, but it was available. This normalizing impulse should not be misconstrued as indicating benevolence towards sex offenders on the part of Bowman and all his colleagues. In practice, sex deviation research did not provide a knowledge base to help identify and treat sexual offending, but rather focused on biological markers of homosexuality, and on law enforcement techniques. During this era, police across the country used polygraph testing during investigations to extract information about sex crimes, while the minds and bodies of hospitalized and incarcerated sex offenders also provided sources of knowledge. An unpublished government document suggests that research on sex offenders at Sing Sing in New York may have been part of the Central Intelligence Agency's investigation into the use of truth serum and LSD as tools for coercing confession (on file with the author). Psychedelic research was also conducted in the late 1950s by two doctors associated with Langley-Porter (Watts 1968). Although we do not know if sex offenders were the objects of that study, we do know that accused sex offenders were given LSD as "truth serum" in Iowa (Miller 2002).

But the effects reached further. Alongside the problematic research he conducted, historian Susan Stryker (2008: 40–46) describes the role Bowman played in facilitating networking among transsexuals in the San Francisco Bay Area, possibly even orchestrating gender reassignment surgery for individuals who sought them under the aegis of his state research. Stryker (2008: 41–2) also alleges ominously that Bowman "conducted research" on soldiers being held in psychiatric detention who were exposed as homosexual during their WWII service.

## Concluding Remarks

We do not argue that the police sting operations and the public and political antipathy towards homosexuals in the United States during the mid-twentieth century were not terrible, misguided, or incredibly harmful. Many lives were destroyed by vice squads and by the Lavender Scare that accompanied McCarthyism (Johnson 2004). Nor do we suggest that the majority of judges, police officers, and psychiatric experts were the unlauded heroes of their time. Instead, we point out the need to recognize individual agency in the face of repressive law, often facilitated by psychiatric priorities and the differentiation among offenders that characterizes criminal justice practices. Not only does the genesis of a moral panic depend on social and institutional contexts, but so does its implementation: when repressive law is brought to bear on bodies and minds, it can also have constitutive effects. Public campaigns against homosexuals cost some individuals dearly. But a purely repressive account takes anecdotal and cross-sectional evidence and assumes an impact at the institutional level. This case demonstrates the need for continually more nuanced and empirically grounded, historically comparative accounts of the multiple effects of law as it is implemented, even law that is repressive on its face and has well-known examples of punitive implementation.

# References

Aaronson, D.E., Dienes, C.T., and Musheno, M. 1984. *Public Policy and Police Discretion*. New York: Clark Boardman.

Bottoms, A. 1995. The philosophy and politics of punishment and sentencing, in *The Politics of Sentencing Reform*, edited by C.M.V. Clarkson and R. Morgan. Oxford Monographs on Criminal Law and Criminal Justice. Oxford: Clarendon Press, 17–49.

Bourdieu, P. 1984 (1979). *Distinction: A Social Critique of the Judgment of Taste*. Cambridge: Harvard University Press. Originally published as *La distinction: critique sociale du jugement*. Paris: Editions de Minuit.

Chauncey, G. 1993. The postwar sex crime panic, in *True Stories from the American Past*, edited by W. Graebner. New York: McGraw-Hill, 160–78.

Chauncey, G. 1994. *Gay New York: Gender, Urban Culture, and the Makings of the Gay Male World, 1890–1940*. New York: Basic Books.

Cole, S. 2000. From the sexual psychopath statute to Megan's Law: psychiatric knowledge in the diagnosis, treatment, and adjudication of sex criminals in New Jersey, 1949–1999. *Journal of the History of Medicine and Allied Sciences*, 55(3), 292–314.

Conrad, P. 2007. *The Medicalization of Society: On the Transformation of Human Conditions into Treatable Disorders*. Baltimore: Johns Hopkins University Press.

Conrad, P. 1992. Medicalization and social control. *Annual Review of Sociology*, 18, 209–32.

Conrad, P. and Schneider, J.W. 1980. *Deviance and Medicalization: From Badness to Sickness*. Philadelphia: Temple University Press.

1959. Convicts' trysts with wives seen for future. *Los Angeles Times*, August 11, B1.

Courtwright, D.T. 2010. The NIDA Brain Disease Paradigm: History, Resistance and Spinoffs. *BioSocieties*, 5(1), 137–47.

1937. Crime: three little girls. *Time* [Online], July 12. Available at: http://www.time.com/time/magazine/article/0,9171,788130,00.html [accessed: October 20, 2011].

1937. Dyer's horror story placed before jury. *Los Angeles Times*, August 17, 4.

1937. Dyer trial climax set for Monday. *Los Angeles Times*, August 21, 1.

D'Emilio, J. 1998 (1983). *Sexual Politics, Sexual Communities: The Making of a Homosexual Minority in the United States, 1940–1970*. 2nd Edition. Chicago: University of Chicago Press.

Emotional Security Program: Atascadero State Hospital. 1955. *The New Approach: Sex Offender to Good Citizen*. Sacramento: Atascadero State Hospital.

Eskridge, W.N. 1997. Privacy jurisprudence and the apartheid of the closet, 1946-1961. *Florida State Law Review*, 24(4), 703–811.

Fass, P.S. 1993. Making and remaking an event: the Leopold and Loeb case in American culture. *Journal of American History*, 80(3), 919–51.

Field, A.W. 1951. Homosexual behavior and the law. Unpublished report, on file in the library and special collections of archives of the Kinsey Institute for Research in Sex, Gender, and Reproduction, Indiana University, Bloomington.

Forst, M.L. 1978. *Civil Commitment and Social Control*. Lexington: Lexington Books.

Foucault, M. 1975 (1963). *The Birth of the Clinic: An Archeology of Medical Perception.* New York: Vintage Books. Originally published as *Naissance de la clinique: une archéologie du regard medical.* Paris: Presses Universitaires de France.

Freedman, E.B. 1987. Uncontrolled desires: the response to the sexual psychopath, 1920–1960. *The Journal of American History,* 74(1): 83–106.

Gallo, J.J., Mason, S.M., Meisinger, L.M., Robin, K.D., Stabile, G.D., and Wynne, R.J. 1966. The consenting adult homosexual and the law: an empirical study of enforcement and administration in Los Angeles County. *UCLA Law Review,* 13, 643–792.

Gamson, J. 1995. Must identity movements self-destruct? A queer dilemma. *Social Problems* 42(3), 391–407.

Gamson, J. 1997. Messages of exclusion: gender, movements, and symbolic boundaries. *Gender and Society* 11(2), 178–99.

Gamson, J. 1998. *Freaks Talk Back.* Chicago: University of Chicago Press.

1947. Girl victim of sex fiend found slain. *Los Angeles Times,* January 6, 2.

Goode, E. and Ben-Yehuda, N. 2009 (1994). *Moral Panics: The Social Construction of Deviance.* 2nd Edition. Chichester: Wiley-Blackwell.

Jenkins, P. 1998. *Moral Panic: Changing Concepts of the Child Molester in Modern America.* New Haven: Yale University Press.

Johnson, D.K. 2004. *The Lavender Scare: The Cold War Persecution of Gays and Lesbians in the Federal Government.* Chicago: University of Chicago Press.

1937. Jury decrees Dyer must die for murders. *Los Angeles Times,* August 27, 1.

Lave, T.R. 2009. Only yesterday: the rise and fall of twentieth century sexual psychopath laws. *Louisiana Law Review,* 69(3), 549–91.

Leon, C.S. 2011a. *Sex Fiends, Perverts and Pedophiles: Understanding Sex Crime Policy in America.* New York: New York University Press.

Leon, C.S. 2011b. Sex offender punishment and the persistence of penal harm in the U.S. *International Journal of Law and Psychiatry,* 34, 177–85

Lieberman, D. and Siegel, B. 1957. A program for sexual psychopaths in a state mental hospital. *American Journal of Psychiatry,* 113(9), 801–7.

Long, J.C. 1992. Foucault's clinic. *The Journal of Medical Humanities* 13(3), 119–38.

2008. Mattachine Society Project Collection, Coll2008-016, ONE National Gay and Lesbian Archives, Los Angeles, CA.

1949. Mexico-US hunt on for girl's slayer. *Los Angeles Times,* November 16, 1.

Miller, N. 2002. *Sex-Crime Panic: A Journey to the Paranoid Heart of the 1950s.* Los Angeles: Alyson Books.

Mitford, J. 1973. *Kind and Usual Punishment: The Prison Business.* New York: Alfred A. Knopf.

Nathan, D. and Snedeker, M. 1995. *Satan's Silence: Ritual Abuse and the Making of a Modern American Witch Hunt.* New York: Basic Books.

Phelan, J.C. 2005. Geneticization of deviant behavior and consequences for stigma: the case of mental illness. *Journal of Health and Social Behavior,* 46(4), 307–22.

Ploscowe, M. 1951. *Sex and the Law.* New York: Prentice-Hall.

Schudson, M. 1978. *Discovering the News: A Social History of American Newspapers.* New York: Basic Books.

Schultz, P.D. 2005. *Not Monsters: Analyzing the Stories of Child Molesters*. Lanham: Rowman and Littlefield Publishers.

Sklansky, D.A. 2008. One train may hide another: Katz, Stonewall, and the secret subtext of criminal procedure. *UC Davis Law Review*, 41(3), 875–934.

Stryker, S. 2008. *Transgender History*. Berkeley: Seal Press.

Sutherland, E. 1950a. The diffusion of sexual psychopath laws. *American Journal of Sociology*, 56(2), 142–8.

Sutherland, E. 1950b. The sexual psychopath laws. *Journal of Criminal Law and Criminology*, 40(5), 534–44.

Szasz, T.S. 1961. *The Myth of Mental Illness; Foundations of a Theory of Personal Conduct*. New York: Hoeber-Harper.

Szasz, T. 1963. *Law, Liberty, and Psychiatry: An Inquiry into the Social Uses of Mental Health Practices*. New York: Macmillan.

Terdiman, R. 1987. Translator's introduction: the force of law, toward a sociology of the juridical field, by P. Bourdieu. *Hastings Law Journal*, 38(5), 805–13.

Vanderwood, P.J. 2004. *Juan Soldado: Rapist, Murderer, Martyr, Saint*. American Encounters/Global Interactions. Durham: Duke University Press.

Victor, J.S. 1998. Moral panics and the social construction of deviant behavior: a theory and application to the case of ritual child abuse. *Sociological Perspectives*, 41(3), 541–65.

Waters, Robert A. 2008. Three little girls lost. *Kidnapping, Murder and Mayhem* [Online]. Available at: http://kidnappingmurderandmayhem.blogspot.com/2008/07/three-little-girls-lost.html [accessed: October 21, 2011].

Watts, A. 1968. Psychedelics and religious experience. *California Law Review*, 56(1), 74–85.

Young, J. 1999. *The Exclusive Society: Social Exclusion, Crime and Difference in Late Modernity*. London: Sage Publications.

# Revelation and Cardinals' Sins: Moral Panic over "Pedophile Priests" in the United States

Pamela D. Schultz

The Bible has its horrors: monsters that evoke chaos, terror, and disgust such as Leviathan, Behemoth, and Yam. The Book of Revelation warns of an apocalypse symbolized by a dragon and perpetrated by devils and demons. Like adherents of such other religions as Judaism and Hinduism, Christians stave off the monstrous with the power of faith. Many Christians rely upon symbolically or literally anointed representatives of God to manifest the values and behaviors that pronounce their faith while assuring them a place in heaven. These moral leaders, embodied in ministers, priests, and other clergy, are viewed as divinely inspired role models, counselors, and teachers. When they are not only discovered to be merely human, but are also exposed as troubled or even deviant, the disillusionment can be profound. The moral panic over "pedophile priests" in the Catholic Church reflects an outrage sparked by a crisis of faith as well as a loss of trust. Churches have been viewed as places of sanctuary, places that keep monsters at bay. The moral panic over child sexual abuse in the US Catholic Church reflects the recognition that the Church harbors monsters in its midst.

In *Moral Panics: The Social Construction of Deviance*, Erich Goode and Nachman Ben-Yehuda (2009) discuss five indicators of moral panic. First is *volatility*, which is a sudden explosion of concern about a newly perceived threat from people considered to be moral deviants. Second is *hostility*, where these deviants are depicted as enemies of basic social values and have stereotypically evil behaviors imputed to them. Third is *measurable concern*, meaning that public anxiety about the threat can be objectively measured. Fourth is *consensus*, meaning that consensus exists concerning the the nature of a perceived evil. And fifth is *disproportionality*: the response, in terms both of fear engendered and of actions taken, is greatly out of proportion to measurable facts concerning a possible social danger. This last indicator is perhaps the most potent in regard to present-day moral panics, given that media appear to have become American society's principal educator and shaper of the popular imagination.

The "pedophile priest" crisis in the Catholic Church is representative of media's power to shape and perpetuate a widespread moral panic. While the enormity of the Church's sins in abetting and covering up the sexual abuse of children by its priests and laypersons cannot be disputed, mass-mediated accounts of the crisis have certainly helped fuel the hysteria. Yet, sexual abuse in the Church is nothing new, although the tone of the coverage might make it seem so. Child sexual abuse has been a persistent problem in the Church for decades, even centuries, just as it has been in American society and the rest of the world. The question is, why did the public become so caught up in a fury of fear and panic at this particular point in history?

## Brief Timeline of the Moral Panic

The current sexual abuse scandal in the American Catholic Church seems to have erupted in 1984 when the Reverend Gilbert Gauthe of the Lafayette, Louisiana, diocese pled guilty to molesting 11 boys, while admitting to abusing many more. The Louisiana case acted as the hole in the dike, as more victims across the country began to stream forward with tales of sexual abuse at the hands of priests and clergy. After journalist Jason Berry wrote a story on the scandal for the *National Catholic Reporter*, secular media followed suit. In 1992, Berry expanded his investigation into a book, *Lead Us Not into Temptation: Catholic Priests and the Sexual Abuse of Children*. Berry estimated that by the time of the book's publication—less than a decade after the Gauthe case—400 priests had been accused of sexual abuse, costing the Church in the neighborhood of $400 million. That same year, the US Bishops took their first collective action in addressing the problem of priests and sexual abuse, endorsing a set of principles for handling cases. This step was propitious, given that the next twenty years would bring a steady onslaught of accusations and convictions.

Although the crisis kept building through the rest of the 1990s, the dawn of the twenty-first century brought perhaps the most devastating, high-profile cases of sexual abuse by priests. In 2002, *The Boston Globe* covered the case against defrocked Catholic priest John Geoghan who had been accused of abusing 130 children over a 30-year period while he was actively serving as a priest in the Archdiocese of Boston. Geoghan was convicted of indecent assault and battery, and sentenced to nine-to-ten years in a state prison for groping a 10-year-old boy in a public swimming pool. The year 2002 turned out to be an eventful, unpleasant year for Catholics. In April, Pope John Paul II summoned America's cardinals to the Vatican to discuss the sexual abuse crisis. In June, America's Catholic bishops adopted a policy that would strip abusive clergymen of their authority when accused of sexual abuse but would not automatically oust them from the priesthood. In July, during an outdoor mass concluding World Youth Day in Toronto, some victims of clergy abuse were disappointed when the Pope came short of offering an apology but told the crowd of over 800,000 that "the harm done by some priests and religious to the young and vulnerable fills us all with a deep sense of sadness and shame" (Cohen

2002). In October, victims and advocates were further dismayed when the Vatican rejected the US Roman Catholic Church's new sexual abuse policy, claiming that some of the elements conflicted with universal church law. In November, US Roman Catholic bishops adopted revisions of its policy, including a clause stating that priests should be removed from public ministry after any act of sexual abuse with a minor, but critics viewed this as merely continuing the church's history of sheltering sexual predators. In December, bowing to months of public outrage, Cardinal Bernard Law resigned as Boston archbishop, as the Boston archdiocese faced bankruptcy from lawsuits filed by more than 400 alleged victims.

On July 23, 2003, the Massachusetts Attorney General's Office released a report that estimated that since the 1940s perhaps over one thousand people in the Boston Archdiocese had been victims of sexual abuse. In the report, Attorney General Tom Reilly wrote,

> Eighteen months ago, we began to learn of a tragedy of unimaginable dimensions: According to the Archdiocese's own files, 789 victims have complained of sexual abuse by members of the clergy; the actual number of victims is no doubt higher. The evidence to date also reveals that 250 priests and church workers stand accused of acts of rape or sexual assault of children. This widespread assault has occurred for at least six decades under the administrations of three successive Archbishops; clearly, this massive assault is the responsibility of no one person or administration. (Office of the Attorney General 2003: 1–2)

In August 2003, 68-year-old John Geoghan was murdered in prison by a fellow inmate. That same month, the Roman Catholic Archdiocese of Boston offered $55 million to settle more than 500 clergy sexual abuse lawsuits. Lawyers for the claimants viewed this offer as a good starting point for negotiation. In September, The Boston Archdiocese agreed to pay $85 million to settle the lawsuits; individual victims would receive awards ranging from $80,000 to $300,000.

Following the heavily publicized sins of the Boston archdiocese, archdioceses across the United States were caught up in the sexual abuse crisis, including those in Phoenix, Arizona; Tucson, Arizona; Los Angeles, California; Orange County, California; Philadelphia, Pennsylvania; Portland, Oregon; Galveston-Houston, Texas; and Spokane, Washington. In 2004, facing dozens of pending lawsuits accusing clergy of sexual abuse, the archdiocese of Portland, Oregon, became the first US archdiocese to file for bankruptcy and the Roman Catholic Diocese of Tucson, Arizona, became the second. The settlements made with victims of clergy sexual abuse kept growing steadily. In 2004, the Orange County, California, diocese reached a settlement with 87 victims that was rumored to be bigger than the record $85 million agreement with the Boston archdiocese. In 2007, the Catholic Archdiocese of Los Angeles topped that when it agreed to pay $660 million to hundreds of plaintiffs, a figure that remains the largest of the payouts.

By March 2010, the most recent annual report from the United States Conference of Catholic Bishops claimed that the number of abuse victims, allegations, and offending clergy had dropped in 2009 to their lowest numbers since data started being collected in 2004. The report also showed a decline in the amount of money paid out in settlements ("Catholic Church Clergy" 2010). In February 2011, the Archdiocese of Wilmington agreed to settle 142 claims of sexual abuse by priests for $77 million. By that point in time, Roman Catholic Archdioceses had collectively paid approximately $2.7 billion in settlements to victims since the scandal erupted nearly a decade earlier, and at least eight US archdioceses had filed for bankruptcy protection.

## Sources of the Moral Panic

One of the most influential books to be published in the 1990s about the growing sexual abuse scandal in the Catholic Church was historian of religion Philip Jenkins's *Pedophiles and Priests: Anatomy of a Contemporary Crisis* (1996). Although the book was widely praised for its expansive treatment of the issue, some critics claimed that the book actually perpetuated the Church's evasiveness regarding incidents of sexual abuse among the clergy, which was as much a part of the outrage as the actual sexual assaults on children. In a 2002 article in *The Boston Globe Magazine*, Garry Wills, Professor *Emeritus* of History at Northwestern University, as suggested by the favor it found among conservative Catholics, its veracity might well be questioned. Wills (2002) claims that Jenkins, with his theme of moral panic, focuses too much on the idea of an anti-Catholic conspiracy, and …

> Thus concludes that the pedophile scandal is a tempest in a teapot, an artificial construct fitting his definition of moral panic: "A panic is a sudden manifestation of exaggerated public fear and concern over an apparently novel threat." The sense of dire peril, therefore, is "fatuous." There is some pedophilia, he admits, but not as much as has been claimed and not more than in other professions, and the problem has not grown — only our panicky awareness of it has.

Yet Wills misses the point of Jenkins's book, which is not necessarily to debunk the "pedophile priest" scandal but rather to prove that although a number of factors had been festering over time, inexorably heading for release, the mass-mediated moral panic overshadows the reality of the problem. During his first papal visit to the United States in 2008, Pope Benedict XVI confessed that the sexual abuse scandal involving US clergy had caused "deep shame" and was "gravely immoral behavior" ("Pope Calls Church Sex Abuse a 'Deep Shame'" 2008). Since the United States was not the only country struggling with proof of child sexual abuse in its Catholic archdioceses, Benedict had a great deal of shame to shoulder. Yet, from a historical perspective, cases in which Catholic clergy were accused of sexual abuse were nothing new. As psychologist Thomas G. Plante (2004: xvii) writes in *Sin against the Innocents: Sexual Abuse by Priests and the Role of the Catholic Church*,

> Comments about clergy sexual abuse were recorded hundreds and even well over 1,000 years ago. For example, St. Basil (330–379 C.E.) stated, "A cleric or monk who seduces youths or young boys ... is to be publicly flogged. ... For six months he will languish in prison-like confinement ... and he shall never again associate with youths in private conversation nor in counseling them."

Thomas P. Doyle (2003), a canon lawyer, has with colleagues looked at penitential books (handbooks that describe particular sins and their penances) from two millennia to trace the history of Catholic clerical sexual violations to the present day. Several of these volumes maintain that clerics who abuse young boys and girls should receive up to twelve years of penance. Other books, including the *Book of Gomorrah* (1982, written around 1049), the *Decretum Gratiani* (2011, written 1140), and the *Corpus Juris Canonici* (collected canon laws, including the *Decretum Gratiani*, published in 1582, include references to child sexual abuse and pederasty by clergy. Doyle et al. (2003: 197) comment,

> The historical development of legislation concerning clergy sexual abuse verifies that it has been a serious problem from the earliest years of the Church. ... Such official mention of sexual abuse is clearly an indicator of the existence of the problem. There is no sense of the extent of clergy sexual abuse but one can surmise that the official notification betrays a problem of significant proportion.

Thus, the problem of child sexual abuse by Catholic clergy is deeply entrenched in the Church's history, just as it is in secular society. The issue is why clergy sexual abuse has inflamed public outrage, fear, and disgust at this particular point in time. A simplistic hypothesis might be that the focus on the Catholic Church's problem with child sexual abuse is merely a microcosm of American society's problem with child sexual abuse as a whole. Yet, other factors have contributed to the "pedophile priest" panic, as well, including the controversy over celibacy in the priesthood, feminist reinterpretations of child sexual abuse, the satanic ritual abuse moral panic of the 1970s and 1980s, and the "conspiracy of silence" by which the Church muffled allegations of sexual abuse.

## The Celibacy Issue

The Catholic Church's history concerning sexual abuse of minors is inevitably tied to the celibacy issue that has plagued the Church for so long. Although ostensibly the emphasis on celibacy is to free priests from fleshly pleasures to focus on spiritual enlightenment, to an outsider this seems to create an odd commune of overgrown boy scouts. In general, research suggests that about six percent or fewer of Roman Catholic priests or other male clergy have had a sexual encounter with a minor under age eighteen. In *Pedophiles and Priests: Anatomy of a Contemporary Crisis,* Jenkins estimates that the sexual abuse of a prepubescent child is rare among clergy, affecting only 0.3 to 1.8 percent of the entire population of Catholic clergy. He concludes that the notion that Catholic priests are more likely to abuse children aged thirteen and younger than are other groups of men is a myth. In other research,

> On the high-estimate side, [sociologist and former priest and Benedictine monk A.W. Richard] Sipe (1990, 1995, 1999) states that two percent of priests are pedophiles (i.e., sexual involvement with prepubescent children) and an additional four percent are ephebophiles (i.e., sexual engagement with postpubescent teens). Since there are approximately 46,000 active Catholic priests in the United States [as of 2004], Sipe's figures suggest that approximately 2,700 Catholic priests have been involved with minors. If we include the additional 15,000 retired priests and other male Catholic clergy such as brothers, this figure swells closer to 3,600. (Plante 2004: xix)

In February 2004, a report was released that estimated the total number of allegations of sexual abuse by priests between the years 1950 and 2002 was approximately 11,000. The report, commissioned by the US Conference of Catholic Bishops and undertaken by the John Jay College of Criminal Justice, tallied the total number of priests alleged to have abused children at 4,450, or roughly 4 percent of the nearly 110,000 priests who served during this period. Although most suspected priests were accused of perpertrating a single incident, over 1,000 were accused of two or three incidents and over one hundred were accused of ten or more. As B.A. Robinson (2011) of the grassroots organization, Ontario Consultants on Religious Tolerance, points out, a large percentage of the victims were post-pubertal teens from 14 to 17 years old. Thus, the rate of pedophilia (sexual abuse by adults of prepubertal children) is lower among US clergy than among the general male population. However, rates of hebephilia (sexual preference by adults for children in the early stages of puberty) and ephebophilia (sexual preference by adults for mid- to late-adolescents) have been higher among US clergy than in the general male population (Robinson 2011).

Because most victims of Catholic priests are teenage boys, the offenders are more accurately described as ephebophiles rather than pedophiles (so the current crisis should rightfully be termed the "ephebophile priest panic," which from a media standpoint would be much less catchy). The preponderance of ephebophilia raises the "problem" (as some Catholics perceive it) of homosexuality in the Church. The Vatican claims, "Priestly celibacy is a gift of the Holy Spirit" (Weber 2010). Yet, as researcher A.W. Richard Sipe (2010) comments on a Catholic website,

> Psycho-sexual immaturity predominates in the ranks of the priesthood … the Vatican and American bishops are conducting an orchestrated chorus of reform that involves excluding homosexual candidates

from the ministry, revamping seminaries, reinforcing strict doctrinal orthodoxy, and urging bishops to holiness. The score will never realize a public performance simply because the system intended to welcome maturing men and produce celibate priests is itself largely sexually active. Many of the bishops, rectors of seminaries, and spiritual directors who are entrusted with the responsibility of training priests are themselves sexually active and at times with the men they purport to mentor. The horror of the sexual abuse crisis of minors has demonstrated this disturbing pattern within seminaries and the priesthood generally. Numbers of priest abusers were themselves sexually active with other, sometimes highly placed, priests.

According to Maureen Orth in her 2002 *Vanity Fair* article, "Unholy Communion":

> Father Donald Cozzens, the former Vicar of Priests in Cleveland, writes in *The Changing Face of the Priesthood*: "Our respective diocesan experience revealed that roughly 90 percent of priest abusers target teenage boys as their victims. Relatively little attention has been paid to this phenomenon by Church authorities—perhaps it is feared that it will call attention to the disproportionate number of gay priests."

Orth continues,

> In fact, the issue of homosexuals in the priesthood has become a lightning rod used by both sides in the current controversy. Vatican spokesman Joaquin Navarro Vals declared that gays should not be ordained, whereas the gay Jesuit I spoke with says the vast majority of gay priests are "observant" of celibacy and consider their homosexuality 'a gift' which allows them to be more sensitive to prejudice. He agrees with Cozzens that what is not addressed is the 'enormously high rate. There are a very large percentage of priests who are gay. I think it is acknowledged in the clergy being 70 or 80 percent.... Priests feel open to reveal themselves to other priests, but also feel for personal reasons they can't reveal it publicly—the culture wouldn't be ready for it,' certainly not 'the clerical administrative culture.' (2002, ellipsis in original)

Historically, the Catholic Church has seemed to spend more time on its intolerance of homosexuality than on its horror of child sexual abuse. According to Mary Gail Frawley-O'Dea in *Perversion of Power: Sexual Abuse in the Catholic Church*:

> The Church is particularly certain and stringent about what is morally correct in the area of human sexuality. As the same time that popes and other officials spoke with conviction about how human beings should lead their moral lives, however, they were and still are

presiding over a moral scandal of the worst kind—the sexual abuse of children and young people by priests and the ecclesiastical cover-up of those crimes. The juxtaposition of manifest moral rectitude offset by evidence of underlying moral corruption captures the human imagination. (2007: 7)

So, perhaps because there is no correlation between homosexuality and pedophilia—in fact, most pedophiles are heterosexual in their preferences—ironically, it seems as though it might be preferable for the Vatican to lament the presence of pedophilia in the Church rather than draw attention to ephebophilia.

## Feminist Reinterpretation of Child Sexual Abuse

The current crisis in the Catholic Church is also connected to the feminist reinterpretation of child sexual abuse that occurred in the United States in the 1970s. In 1971, the New York Radical Feminists held its first conference on rape. At this conference, Florence Rush, a former psychiatric social worker at the New York Society for the Prevention of Cruelty to Children, shared her personal story of being molested as a child and urged feminists to make the issue of child sexual abuse part of their framing of rape. This rhetorical revision rejected the conventional psychoanalytic position on child sexual abuse, which affixed blame on the victim's unconscious desires, and reframed the family therapeutic approach, which looked at incest within the family dynamic. A new definition of the abuse victim was crafted in which child sexual abuse was devastating for children because it was most fundamentally a violation of trust:

> Joel Best (1997) outlined this ideology of victimization as it applies to CSA. Firstly, sexual abuse—even no-touch incidents and single, brief instances of fondling—can cause profound and long-lasting psychological after effects of many types, undermining all manner of adult functioning and well-being. Secondly, sexual abuse victimization is not only widespread, but also largely unrecognized, even by victims themselves, who must therefore be taught to recognize their experiences for what they truly represent. Thirdly, all sexual abuse is morally unambiguous. Claims of victimization must always be respected, since anything less would be victim blaming. In this way, CSA is framed as inevitably devastating, widespread, and generally unavoidable. Every child is at risk, and any adult could have experienced sexual abuse as a child and not even know they experienced it until recovering the memories years later. (Schultz 2008: 101)

The paternalistic nature of the Catholic Church is similar to the type of highly patriarchal family structures that feminists claimed contributed to the presence of sexual abuse. The Catholic Church is deeply, strictly, irrevocably hierarchical and patriarchal in its power structures, like that of incestuous families.

Concurrent with the rise of Second Wave feminism:

> Vatican II began to move the Church away from relational grids based on dominance and submission [but] Pope John Paul II, whose papal term (1978-2005) encompassed almost all the years of the contemporary sexual abuse crisis, once again centralized Church power, resuscitating an emphasis on dominance and submission.... Rather than encouraging theologians and lay experts from various disciplines to air, fully delineate, and energetically debate controversial exegeses of Church teachings, especially those related to gender and sexuality, John Paul clamped down on anyone he judged to be in dissent from his view. (Frawley-O'Dea 2007: 47)

Although some consider that John Paul's views on women were a step up from the virgin/whore dichotomy so prevalent in the Catholic Church, exemplified by traditions surrounding the Virgin Mary and Mary Magdalene, the apparent progress remained mostly superficial:

> The pope's gender theory of "equal in dignity but separate in social roles" stamps this new version of gender with just another kind of dualism. It is in fact a regurgitation of historically stereotypical gender roles, [which] have been potentially dangerous for women (and by extension, children) who are rendered unable to say *no* to abuse and oppression. ... Hubris about clerical power over women and children, combined with objectifying attitudes about both, significantly mediated the sexual abuse of minors and, especially, its cover-up. (Frawley-O'Dea: 2007: 71)

"The pope's gender theory" still emphasized the subservient positions of women and children in Catholicism, privileging maleness.


## Satanic Ritual Abuse

After the feminist "discovery" of child sexual abuse in the 1970s, expanding media coverage of child sexual abuse had put the issue forefront in the public's imagination. In 1977 and 1978 alone, "almost every national magazine ran a story highlighting the horror of child sexual abuse" (Schultz 2005: 6). By the 1980s, the fear had built into a full-fledged panic that escalated into the satanic ritual abuse scare. The ritual abuse phenomenon gained prominence in 1983 when a woman alleged her son had been molested at the McMartin Preschool in Manhattan Beach, California. As I wrote elsewhere,

115

> The McMartin case was followed in 1984 by a case in which abuse investigators in Jordan, Minnesota, explored allegations of occult rituals and human sacrifice. Over the next year, a number of similar investigations followed. By the early 1990s, supposed survivors of ritual abuse had a wealth of sources to draw on, including books, magazine articles, and self-help groups such as Survivors of Abusive Rituals (SOAR). (Schultz 208: 102)

According to Mary deYoung (2008: 133), who has examined the ritual abuse panic in detail: "One aspect [of moral panic] that remains under-appreciated is the master narrative of moral panic, that is, its core myth about evil and innocence, right and wrong, and virtue and venality." She claims that the master narrative of the ritual abuse panic was continually repeated by so-called experts who emerged from the McMartin case and spread the word across the lecture circuit, the press, and television talk shows. Their persuasive rhetoric recruited others to the cause, who went on to dig up examples of day care ritual abuse in their own communities. In this manner, the moral panic was self-perpetuating and self-sustaining, driven by dramatic images of innocents betrayed. *Devil Worship: Exposing Satan's Underground*, a TV special hosted by Geraldo Rivera that originally aired on NBC on October 22, 1988, and featured a group interview with "parents of children in the notorious McMartin Preschool," represented perhaps the peak of credulity (although in 1995 Rivera publicly apologized for contributing to public fears about the McMartin case and child sexual abuse) ("Geraldo River: Satanic Ritual Abuse").

The idea that child-molesting satanists had infiltrated the United States titillated conspiracy theorists and gave the Christian right more fodder for its campaign for family values, which it claimed were threatened by increasing numbers of single-parent households and dual working parents (not to mention outspoken feminists). The simple but powerful message of good versus evil was irresistible. This existential struggle is at the heart of Christian belief. Although it certainly ran contrary to the Christian right's earnest attempts to revitalize religion, in this environment it was unavoidable that the image of Catholic priests molesting children under the Church's watchful eye should be swept into the panic. That trusted clergy could perpetrate sexual abuse against the children in their flock fits perfectly into panicky media coverage on the prevalence of child sexual abuse in homes, day care centers, and other places where children were supposed to be protected from harm. One major claim of the movement to uncover child sexual abuse was that child molestation occurred most frequently close to home, given that many abusers were known to their victims and even their victims' families (and oftentimes were members of those families). Catholic priests often create close relationships with members of their flock, as their roles are not merely as conduits for God but as role models and social leaders.

## "Conspiracy of Silence" and Church Cover-Ups

To maintain relational bonds, the Catholic Church has emphasized secrecy. The secrecy that is so indelibly a part of the Church's history abuts the "conspiracy of silence" that has become an integral aspect of the rhetoric we use today to describe the dynamics of child sexual abuse. Media coverage of the Catholic Church's struggles with sexual abuse has highlighted the ways in which the Church appeared to dismiss legitimate claims, cover up for the perpetrators, and silence discussion. In the 2003 Massachusetts Attorney General's Office's report on the Boston Archdiocese, Attorney General Tom Reilly wrote,

> For decades, Cardinals, Bishops, and others in positions of authority within the Archdiocese chose to protect the image and reputation of their institution rather than the safety and well-being of children. They acted with a misguided devotion to secrecy and a mistaken belief that they were accountable only to themselves. (2-3)

These revelations have been perhaps the most disheartening aspects of the sexual abuse crisis.

In 2003, CBS News obtained a confidential Vatican document, written in 1962, that sketched out a church policy on sexual abuse by priests. The document, *Instruction on the Manner of Proceeding in Cases of the Crime of Solicitation* (1962: 1, 2), bearing the seal of Pope John XXIII, mandated absolute secrecy in these cases, threatening anyone who spoke out with expulsion. For example, although the document states that priests who have "tempt[ed] a penitent" should unload their guilty consciences as soon as possible and "take care to introduce, discuss and terminate [these cases] with their proper tribunal," the action recommended is to supervise the priest's activities, to offer "salutary penances, to admonish and correct, and, if the case demands it, to remove him from the ministry." The offender may also be transferred to a different assignment. Even the victims or accusers are exhorted to silence, although they are not subject to the same penalties as clergy: "The accused, however, must be most seriously warned that even he, with all [the others], especially when he observes the secret with his defender, is under the penalty of suspension *a divinis* in case of a transgression to be incurred *ipso facto*" (*Instruction* 1962: 3). If an investigation by the Church determines that an accusation is groundless, all documents associated with the alleged abuse are to be destroyed (*Instruction* 1962: 8).

A lawyer representing alleged victims of clergy sexual abuse declared that the document was significant "because it's a blueprint for deception ... it's an instruction manual on how to deceive and how to protect pedophiles" (Collins 2003). The United States Conference of Catholic Bishops protested that the document was taken out of context, that it only pertained to religious sins, and that the secrecy was meant to protect, not exploit alleged victims as well as the Church. But the Conference's protestations were doomed to be ignored, considering how shrill the sexual abuse scandal had become by then. The public was primed to view any apparent evidence as proof that the Church harbored abusive priests, enabling the abusers to commit their crimes with impunity.

Though it arose in part from stridency, critics' skepticism about the Catholic Church's treatment of abusers was justified. The case of James Porter shows that the Church was capable of casual, even callous disregard for the welfare of victims and their families. In 1963, a mother confronted two priests at St. Mary's in Attleboro, Massachusetts, with the accusation that Porter had molested her twelve-year-old son: "The bishop of Fall River first learned of Porter's predilections in March 1964, when his chancellor—who later became a cardinal and archbishop of Boston—finally informed him that Porter had molested thirty to forty children at St Mary's. Bishop James Connolly sent the priest home to his parents to contemplate and pray" (Bruni and Burkett 2002: 19). After a few more complaints, Porter was transferred to another parish:

> A few months later, after Porter was picked up by New Hampshire State Police for molesting a thirteen-year-old boy … the priest was sent to Wiswall Hospital in Wellesley for treatment, including electroshock therapy. By September 1965, his physician declared that Porter had simmered down and he was transferred to St James parish in New Bedford to work as the chaplain at the local hospital. Within weeks, he was training altar boys in New Bedford. Within weeks, he was abusing them. (Bruni and Burkett 2002: 19–20)

When yet more complaints surfaced, Connolly once again sent Porter home, where he molested again. In 1967, Porter was sent to a retreat center for troubled priests in Jemez Springs, New Mexico. For the next couple of years, he moved between New Mexico and Texas, leaving more victims in his wake. In 1970, he was accused of molesting two boys at his parish in Minnesota. Only then was Porter advised to leave the priesthood by a psychologist. In his 1973 petition for release from his priestly vows, Porter wrote to Pope Paul VI that he "used to hide behind a roman collar, thinking that it would be a shield for me" (Bruni and Burkett 2002: 21). The pope granted that petition, and after fourteen years as a priest—and as many as a child sexual abuser—James Porter lost the right to call himself Father on January 5, 1974 (Bruni and Burkett 2002: 21). When some of James Porter's victims, now adults but still suffering the aftermath of abuse, came forward in the early 1990s to press charges against the former priest, they were angered by what they perceived to be the church's treachery. That the church could protect Porter, over and over, at the expense of children, was mindboggling.

The actions of the Boston Archdiocese also illustrate administrators' willful, even criminal, ignorance when faced with allegations of sexual abuse. The Reverend Paul R. Shanley made his reputation as a Boston "street priest" in the 1960s and 1970s, a crusader for runaways, drug addicts, and teenagers struggling with questions about their sexual identity. But those who turned to Shanley for comfort and guidance often found themselves in the clutches of a sexual predator. Thousands of pages of documents show that church officials knew of numerous sexual abuse allegations against Shanley and that the priest had publicly advocated sex between men and boys. Despite this, Shanley was shuttled from parish to parish in the Boston Archdiocese, and eventually transferred to a California church with a letter of recommendation from one of Cardinal Bernard Law's top deputies. In another case, after the Reverend Bernard J. Lane was accused of raping teenagers in the 1970s at a treatment facility he ran for troubled young males, the Archdiocese of Boston settled at least six sexual abuse cases against Lane yet permitted him to remain in an administrative position. And, of course, there is the case of John Geoghan. Colleagues in the Boston Archdiocese who suspected Geoghan's activities either turned a blind eye to them or half-heartedly offered solace to the victims while avoiding any confrontation with Geoghan. The few times archdiocesan officials were told of incidents of sexual abuse, they failed to summon law enforcement. The prevailing attitude was summed up by Bishop Thomas V. Daily. When asked why he had not acted more decisively in 1980 when he was told a parishioner at St. Thomas Church in Boston's Jamaica Plain area had accused Geoghan of molesting her sons and nephews, he replied, "I am not a policeman; I am a shepherd" (Kurkjian 2002).

Perhaps the public might have been appeased had it seemed that the Church was willing to take responsibility not only for the perpetrators but also for the policies that enabled the abuse and cover-ups to occur. Yet, at the 2002 meeting of the United States Conference of Catholic Bishops in which they passed new norms for diocesan management of sexual abuse in the form of the Charter for the Protection of Children and Young People, they avoided calling for censure for bishops who violated those norms. Some bishops even refused to follow some provisions of the charter and declined to participate in the John Jay study on the prevalence of sexual abuse in the Catholic Church. They argued against any further audits of diocesan compliances with sexual abuse norms, claiming that they could audit themselves. Thus,

> in refusing to accept responsibility for the sexual abuse crisis, many bishops were publicly willing to embrace and claim brotherhood with those who had most disregarded the welfare of children. ... A year later, at the June 2003 USCCB meeting, after [Cardinal Bernard] Law had resigned in disgrace as archbishop of Boston, he was welcomed by his fellow bishops, not one of whom publicly suggested that his presence there was an offense ... in May 2004, Pope John Paul II appointed Law archpriest of St Mary Major basilica in Rome, and he still serves on several Vatican congregations. (Frawley-O'Dea 2007: 11)

Some victims even blamed Pope Benedict for conspiring in the cover-up of child sexual abuse. In 2005, in a Texas civil lawsuit, Joseph Ratzinger (just before becoming Pope Benedict XVI) was accused of conspiring, as head of the Congregation for the Doctrine of the Faith, with the Archdiocese of Galveston-Houston to cover up the abuse of three boys in the mid-1990s. However, the lawsuit was dismissed because Assistant US Attorney General Peter Keisler decided that, as pope, Benedict enjoyed immunity as a head of state and that to allow the lawsuit to proceed would compromise the United States' foreign policy interests.

The fight to break through the silence and secrecy continues. In February 2011, three priests and a Philadelphia Catholic schoolteacher were charged with sexually assaulting two young boys over the course of several years. The grand jury also charged a monsignor with child endangerment for knowingly allowing the abusive priests to continue in roles in which they had access to children. The church launched its own investigation after the release of the grand jury report, which claimed that some 27 priests remained "in active ministry with credible allegations of child sexual abuse" ("Survivors' Advocate" 2011). A former high-ranking church official was accused of transferring problem priests to new parishes without revealing any prior abuse complaints (Loviglio 2011). In March 2011, the Philadelphia archdiocese placed on administrative leave 21 priests named as child molestation suspects (Loviglio 2011). During an Ash Wednesday mass on March 9, 2011, Cardinal Justin Rigali asked "forgiveness of all those whom we have offended in any way … I personally renew my deep sorrow to the victims of sexual abuse in the community of the church and to all others, including so many faithful priests who suffer as a result of this great evil and crime" ("Survivors' Advocate" 2011).

## Concluding Remarks

Expedited by exhaustive media coverage, moral panic over "pedophile priests" signals a crisis of faith among many Catholics as social conflict and change present new challenges to the Church. Such historical moments as feminist reinterpretation of both child sexual abuse and women's role within the Catholic Church, a satanic ritual abuse panic exploited by the Christian right, as well as the Church's inadequate response to charges of abuse made against priests, created moral panic among both Catholics in particular and the American public in general.

Recently, the Church has been moved to respond to, and try to assuage, the heightened anger, fear, and concern over "pedophile priests." In May 2011, the Vatican issued new guidelines aimed at stopping sexual abuse, including doubling the length of time during which the church can prosecute suspected abusers, increasing it from ten to 20 years; making it a church crime for a priest to download child pornography; and allowing the pope to defrock a priest without a formal Vatican trial. However, the guidelines were voluntary and failed to require Bishops to report priests accused of child sexual abuse to the police ("Vatican Abuse Guidelines" 2011).

In the United States, on May 17, 2011, *The New York Times* reported on the publication of a five-year study of child sexual abuse by US priests conducted by researchers at John Jay College of Criminal Justice at a cost of $1.8 million. Commissioned by the United States Conference of Catholic Bishops, *The Causes and Context of Sexual Abuse of Minors by Catholic Priests in the United States, 1950–2002* was roundly criticized for pursuing a "blame Woodstock" strategy, blaming the increased freedom introduced by the Sexual Revolution as the source both for increased numbers of homosexuals in the priesthood and for victims' greater willingness to report abuse (Goodstein 2011).

Then, in June 2011, the United States Conference of Catholic Bishops revised its 2002 charter to coincide with the Vatican's new guidelines. But critics remained unimpressed, claiming that the changes did not go far enough because the guidelines, which, in contrast to those issued by the Vatican, instructed bishops and other religious leaders to "report an allegation of sexual abuse" of a minor to "the public authorities," were not enforced ("U.S. Catholic Bishops" 2011). In the end, as these and other developments within the Church demonstrate, neither the crisis of faith experienced by some Catholics, nor the problem of child sexual abuse by US priests, nor the ensuing moral panic over "pedophile priests" show any signs of abating anytime soon.

# References

Berry, J. 2000. *Lead Us Not into Temptation: Catholic Priests and the Sexual Abuse of Children*. Champaign: University of Illinois Press.

Bruni, F. and Burkett, E. 2002 (1993). *A Gospel of Shame: Children, Sexual Abuse, and the Catholic Church*. 2nd Edition. New York: Perennial.

2010. Catholic Church clergy abuse claims drop. msnbc.com [Online, March 23]. Available at: http://www.msnbc.msn.com/id/36000986/ [accessed: October 22, 2011].

2011. *The Causes and Context of Sexual Abuse of Minors by Catholic Priests in the United States, 1950–2010: A Report Presented to the United States Conference of Catholic Bishops by the John Jay College Research Team* [Online]. Washington, DC: United States Conference of Catholic Bishops. Available at: http://www.scribd.com/doc/55745387/Causes-and-Context-of-Sexual-Abuse-Minors-by-US-Catholic-Priests-1950-201051211 [accessed: October 23, 2011].

Cohen, T. 2002. Pope's sadness over abuse angers victims. *The Independent on Sunday* [Online], July 29. Available at: http://www.independent.co.uk/news/world/americas/popes-sadness-over-abuse-angers-victims-649823.html [accessed: October 22, 2011].

Collins, D. 2003. Sex crimes cover-up by Vatican? [Online, August 6]. Available at: http://www.cbsnews.com/stories/2003/08/06/eveningnews/main566978.shtml [accessed: October 23, 2011].

1582. *Corpus Juris Canonici*. Rome: *Inaedibus Populi Romani*. UCLA Library Digital Collections [Online]. Available at: http://digital.library.ucla.edu/canonlaw/ [accessed: August 31, 2012].

Damian, P. 1982 (*circa* 1049). *Book of Gomorrah: An Eleventh-Century Treatise against Clerical Homosexual Practices*, translated by P.J. Payer. Waterloo: Wilfrid Laurier University Press. Originally called *Liber Gomorrhianus*.

deYoung, M. 2008. Speak of the Devil, in *Moral Panics over Contemporary Children and Youth*, edited by C. Krinsky. Aldershot: Ashgate, 127–41.

*Devil Worship: Exposing Satan's Underground* (starring Geraldo Rivera, 1988).

Doyle, T.P., Sipe, A.W.R., and Wall, P.J. 2006. *Sex, Priests, and Secret Codes: The Catholic Church's 2,000 Year Paper Trail of Sexual Abuse*. London: Volt.

Frawley-O'Dea, M. G. 2007. *Perversion of Power: Sexual Abuse in the Catholic Church*. Nashville: Vanderbilt University Press.

Geraldo Rivera: satanic ritual abuse and recovered memories. *ReligiousTolerance. org* [Online]. Available at: http://www.religioustolerance.org/geraldo.htm [accessed: August 31, 2012].

Goode, E. and Ben-Yehuda, N. 2009 (1994). *Moral Panics: The Social Construction of Deviance*. 2nd Edition. Chichester: Wiley-Blackwell.

Goodstein, L. 2011. Church report cites social tumult in priest scandals. *The New York Times* [Online], May 17. Available at: http://www.nytimes.com/2011/05/18/us/18bishops.html?pagewanted=all [accessed: October 23, 2011].

Gratianus the Canonist. 2011 (*circa* 1140). *Decretum Gratiani*. Charleston: Nabu Press.

1962. *Instruction on the Manner of Proceeding in Cases of the Crime of Solicitation* [Online]. Available at: http://www.cbsnews.com/htdocs/pdf/Criminales.pdf [accessed: October 23, 2011].

Jenkins, P. 1996. *Pedophiles and Priests: Anatomy of a Contemporary Crisis*. New York: Oxford University.

Kurkjian, S. 2002. Officials avoided confronting priest. *The Boston Globe* [Online], January 24. Available at: http://www.boston.com/globe/spotlight/abuse/stories/012402_geoghan.htm [accessed: October 23, 2011].

Loviglio, J. 2011. Twenty-one PA priests suspended before penance period. *Honolulu Star Advertiser* [Online, March 9]. Available at: http://www.staradvertiser.com/news/breaking/20110310_21_Pennsylvania_priests_suspended_before_penance_period.html [accessed: October 23, 2011].

Office of the Attorney General, Commonwealth of Massachusetts. 2003. *The Sexual Abuse of Children in the Roman Catholic Archdiocese of Boston: A Report by the Attorney General* [Online]. Available at: http://www.bishopaccountability.org/downloads/archdiocese.pdf [accessed: October 22, 2011].

Orth, M. 2002. Unholy communion. *Vanity Fair* [Online, August]. Available at: http://www.vanityfair.com/culture/features/2002/08/orth200208 [accessed: October 23, 2011].

Plante, T.G. 2004. *Sin against the Innocents: Sexual Abuse by Priests and the Role of the Catholic Church*. Westport: Praeger.

2008. Pope calls church sex abuse scandal a "deep shame." *CNN U.S.* [Online, April 16]. Available at: http://articles.cnn.com/2008-04-16/us/pope.wed_1_pope-benedict-xvi-abuse-scandal-sexual-abuse?_s=PM:US [accessed: October 22, 2011].

Robinson, B.A. 2011. Sexual and other abuse by Christian clergy and other leaders: a "perfect panic" [Online]. Available at: http://www.religioustolerance.org/clergy_sex.htm. *ReligiousTolerance.org*. [accessed: October 23, 2011].

Schultz, P.D. 2005. *Not Monsters: Analyzing the Stories of Child Molesters*. Lanham: Rowman and Littlefield Publishers.

Schultz, P.D. 2008. "Naming, blaming, and framing: moral panic over child molesters and its implications for public policy, in *Moral Panics over Contemporary Children and Youth*, edited by C. Krinsky. Aldershot: Ashgate, 95–110.

Sipe, A.W.R. 2010. Celibacy is a problem for priests—and laity too! *Catholica* [Online].Available at: http://www.catholica.com.au/gc2/occ/043_occ_020210. php [accessed: October 23, 2011].

2011. Survivors' advocate says apologetic words aren't enough. *CNN* [Online, March 10]. Available at: http://www.cnn.com/2011/CRIME/03/09/pennsylvania. priests/index.html [accessed: October 23, 2011].

2011. US Catholic bishops revise guidelines against sex abuse. *CNN* [Online, June 16]. Available at: http://articles.cnn.com/2011-06-16/us/catholic.sex.abuse_1_child-abuse-sexual-abuse-survivors-network?_s=PM:US [accessed: October 23, 2011].

2011. Vatican abuse guidelines don't require reporting. *SentinelSource.com* [Online, May 16]. Available at: http://www.sentinelsource.com/news/national_world/ vatican-abuse-guidelines-don-t-require-reporting/article_fd8547af-7343-5fb6-941c-1f9662688ae1.html [accessed: October 23, 2011].

Weber, K. 2010. Is celibacy partly to blame for sexual abuse by clergy? *America: The National Catholic Weekly* [Online, March 12]. Available at: http://www. americamagazine.org/blog/entry.cfm?blog_id=2&entry_id=2067 [accessed: October 22, 2011].

Wills, G. 2002. The scourge of celibacy. *The Boston Globe Magazine* [Online], March 24. Available at: http://www.boston.com/globe/spotlight/abuse/stories/032402_ magazine.htm [accessed: October 22, 2011].

# The Demise of the Same Sex
# Marriage Panic in Massachusetts

## Jaime McCauley*

On November 18, 2003, the Massachusetts Supreme Judicial Court issued a 4–3 ruling deciding that the state had "failed to identify a constitutionally adequate reason for denying civil marriage to same sex couples" (*Goodridge v. Department of Public Health* 2003). The decision provoked a near-immediate backlash around the nation as preachers, pundits, and politicians swung into action. The same day, a statement issued by George W. Bush's White House declared, "Marriage is a sacred institution between a man and a woman. Today's decision of the Massachusetts Supreme Court violates this important principle" (quoted in Belluck 2003). With this exchange, the stage was set to re-ignite America's smoldering moral panic over same sex marriage.

As the state legislature battled over how to execute the Massachusetts Supreme Court's ruling, lawmakers across the country scrambled to shore up "traditional marriage" against the new threat out of the Northeast. In his State of the Union address of January 2004, President Bush called on Americans to "defend the institution of marriage" and proposed a federal anti-same sex marriage amendment. By November 2004, nine states amended their constitutions to ban same sex marriage, while similar amendments continued to be added to state constitutions each election cycle through 2009. As recently as November 2010, voters ousted three Iowa Supreme Court Justices for ruling the year before against a state banning same sex marriage, voting that not only reflected the backlash against "activist judges" whom many opponents held responsible for the spread of same sex marriage, but also expressed a nationwide rise in populist sentiment (which would come to be symbolized by the anti-establishment Tea Party).

This was not the first time the United States panicked over same sex marriage. In 1993, the Hawaii Supreme Court decision in *Baehr v. Lewin* favored same sex marriage, thus sparking a legislative flurry and, throughout the 1990s, Defense of Marriage Act (DOMA) statutes were passed at the federal level and in most

* The author would like to thank Barry Adam for his comments on earlier versions of this chapter.

states (Lambda Legal Marriage Equality Timeline 2009). Remarkably, after the Massachusetts decision, even many states that already had DOMA statutes on the books passed anti-same sex marriage constitutional amendments. This chain of events raises two questions: why does same sex marriage drive such fear into the hearts of Americans and how did Massachusetts resist this panic to become the first state with legally recognized same sex marriage?

## Anatomy of a Panic

In *Folk Devils and Moral Panics: The Creation of the Mods and Rockers*, Stanley Cohen (2002: 1) describes a moral panic as a situation in which "a condition, episode, person, or group of persons emerges to become defined as a threat to societal values [and] moral barricades are manned by editors, bishops, politicians, and other right-thinking people." As moral panic is discussed in this chapter, the "homosexual" supposedly represents the threat to social values and norms in the United States and, by extension, same sex marriage represents a fundamental threat to the institutions of marriage and family. Homosexuals are not new subjects of moral panics, though as the moral entrepreneurs behind such panics grow more sophisticated, "rather than attacking individuals as perverse [they] attack the status of homosexuals as a group that deserves legal protection" (Stein 1999: 15).

When a moral panic takes hold, several social processes are taking place. First is a process that Cohen (2002: 59) calls sensitization: a process that "amplifies" behavior considered deviant and leads to "assignment of blame and the direction of control measures towards a specific agent thought to be responsible" for social discord. When significant elements of the public become sensitized, some regulatory response from the "societal control culture" follows (Cohen 2002: 59). Such responses typically include diffusion (when the control culture is diffused beyond the locus of the deviant behavior's initial impact), escalation (when not only the membership, but also the scope and intensity of the control culture are extended), and innovation (characterized by the introduction of new methods of social control) (Cohen 2002: 65–8). This pattern is evident in the successive waves of same sex marriage panic that have swept the United States. In both cases, moral panic began to diffuse from states where the courts were the first to favor same sex marriage (Hawaii in 1993 and Massachusetts in 2003), then escalated as legislators around the country took up increasingly vitriolic rhetoric against "the homosexual agenda" and the threat it posed. Then, innovation occurred with the introduction and passage of Defense of Marriage Act statutes in the 1990s and the numerous state-level marriage amendments passed by voters in the following decade (as well as with the introduction of the Federal Marriage Amendment, notwithstanding the measure's failure to win the support of a majority of lawmakers).

While some agents of social control respond to moral panic out of reasonable concern or even because they have themselves been swept up in the panic, others act from the desire to exploit moral panic for their own gain. Cohen refers to this strategy as ideological exploitation (2002: 115, emphasis in original), which he defines as "the use of the deviant in communication, particularly public, to defend or announce an ideology, for example, religious or political" (2002: 116). In the United States, the religious right has been quite successful in its "appeal to traditional moral values and its ability to create moral panics about sexuality" (di Mauro and Joffe 2009: 47) and its ability to turn these moral panics into political momentum for socially conservative candidates who promise regulatory measures against deviant behavior once in office. Similarly, cultural anthropologist Gilbert Herdt (2009) asserts a connection between the exploitation of same sex marriage panic and the success of the Republican Party in the 2004 elections.

Although it remains unclear whether promises of regulatory action against same sex marriage tipped the 2004 election in favor of Republican candidates overall—perhaps because many Democratic candidates also stated opposition to same sex marriage—it is clear that many voters were motivated by the presence of anti-same sex marriage amendments on state ballots (Camp 2008, Lucas 2008). Because "hurried legislation [in response to moral panic] is typically followed by an abatement of moral fervor" (Adam 2003: 259) we may have witnessed a peak in regulatory activity for same sex marriage for the time being; however the issue does not appear to have lost its effectiveness in mobilizing the base of socially conservative voters (see, for example, Schulte 2010). Examining these factors is useful in identifying a moral panic and locating social responses to it. However, identification of a panic should be the start of an analysis, not its end. Once a moral panic is recognized, we are still left to explain how and why a panic developed, took root, and then declined (Adam 2003, Goode and Ben-Yehuda 1994, McRobbie and Thornton 1995).

## Mobilizing Forces and Moral Entrepreneurs

Multiple factors are responsible for the successful development of the same sex marriage panic in the United States. Perhaps the most significant is the influence of evangelical Protestantism on American culture and politics. Evangelical Protestants remain "the most consistent opponents of equality for lesbians and gay men in US political coalitions, reproducing a cosmology where homosexual people are placed among the 'evil people'" (Adam 2003: 263). This assertion is corroborated in later research by sociologist Bayliss J. Camp (2008) and in polls carried out by the Pew Forum on Religion and Public Life ("U.S. Religious Life" 2008, "Majority Continues to Support" 2009, "Public Opinion" 2009). Evangelicals make up roughly 25 percent of the US population and represent a well-organized group with tremendous voting power. Moreover, Evangelical Christians have an important, though at times "uneasy," relationship with the Republican Party (Adam 2003: 264). Indeed, even if overt homophobia is shrinking to a smaller hard core of the most doctrinaire evangelicals, same sex marriage remains a useful "wedge issue" for the Republican

Party and few Democratic leaders have come forth to offer unequivocal support for the cause (Fetner 2008, Herdt 2009, Lucas 2008, Schwartz and Tatalovich 2009).

Furthermore, countries where same sex marriage is legal tend to have more robust labor movements than is the case in the United States. In Canada, for instance, labor unions and social democratic parties have played important roles in "placing new social issues on the public agenda," and often early gay rights gains like obtaining domestic partner benefits were championed by labor unions in collective bargaining (Adam 2003: 265). The United States boasts neither a labor movement operating at full strength nor any politically viable equivalent to Britain's Labour Party or Canada's New Democratic Party. Tied to this set of circumstances are the ethos of libertarian individualism and the distrust of the state prevalent in the United States, where any collective appeal for "equality rights can be tainted as the refuge of the lazy, the 'special' plea for favoritism among those who can't cut it on their own" (Adam 2003: 272). Opponents of gay rights have been particularly successful at positioning lesbians and gay men as "enemies of common folk" who are "privileged, spoiled, and demanding 'special rights'" for a chosen lifestyle, and a lifestyle considered immoral at that (Adam 2003: 269). This misrepresentation of gay and lesbian people and their quest for equal rights manipulates several important cultural tropes and taps into an underlying cultural malaise concerning America's changing (diminishing?) role on the world stage.

The first wave of the recent same sex marriage panic that has swept over the United States occurred in the 1990s, manifesting a number of social changes that made Americans uneasy. Deindustrialization decimated the market for the manufacturing jobs that supported generations of working class families, rising divorce rates and increasing numbers of children born outside of marriage challenged the "traditional" male breadwinner-female homemaker family model, and these social currents together created dual "crises" of masculinity and the family (McVeigh and Diaz 2009, Stein 2001). Additionally, the close of the Cold War signified the end of an era that had defined America's power and influence over world politics for half a century (Herdt 2009, Terry 1999). After a brief period of rising economic indicators, the 1990s ended with the dot.com bust and the United States ushered in the new millennium with a teetering economy. Shortly after came the terrorist attacks of September 11, 2001 and the country found itself embroiled in fighting along two fronts in the ensuing War on Terror. If Americans were uneasy in 1993, when the Supreme Court of Hawaii at first ruled in favor of same sex marriage, by the time of the Massachusetts Supreme Judicial Court decision in 2003, they were infuriated (Herdt 2009).

Herdt (2009: 261) sees this cultural anger not only as the underlying cause of same sex marriage panic in the United States following the 2003 decision by the Massachusetts Supreme Judicial Court, a phenomenon he describes as "one of the most important and dramatic chapters in the use of cultural anger and moral panics to reduce and restrain the rights of individuals in American history," but also, beginning with the Cold War, as a primary impetus for anti-gay sentiment. During the Cold War, the "accusation of homosexuality was a de facto accusation of communism pure and simple" and both homosexuality and communism were considered "the emasculator of strong warriors" (Herdt 2008: 164). Yet, the end of the Cold War did not lessen the extent to which homosexuals were considered suspect. In fact, "the collapse of the Soviet Union …appears to have shifted neoconservative attitudes about sexuality in the United States toward more 'traditional values' platforms" (Herdt 2008: 165). The post-Cold War 1990s inaugurated an era of conflict that some observers have called the "culture wars," a struggle to "define America" in which homosexuality was increasingly considered to "threaten the most fundamental institution of any society," the "traditional" family, thereby threatening society itself (Hunter 1990: 189–95).

Sociologist Tina Fetner (2008: 102) chronicles the rise in the strength and power of the religious right as a social and political force during the "culture wars," asserting that in the ensuing "contests for the hearts and minds of the American people," the "1990s brought lesbian and gay issues from the margins of political discourse to center." It was in this climate that same sex marriage first became a public issue when Hawaii's *Baehr v. Lewin* case was winding its way through the courts. According to Fetner (2008: 111), while "lesbian and gay activists in the early 1990s might have preferred that this issue not come to the nation's attention…leaders in the religious right considered marriage to be a tipping point for conservatives who had not yet joined the movement." Leaders of the religious right proved adept at marshaling cultural anger over same sex marriage into "a new coalition of sexually conservative/Christian coalition forces that rallied to enact the [federal] Defense of Marriage Act (DOMA) in 1996" and were so successful that "by 2005, forty states had enacted legislation or amendments to their state constitutions banning same-sex marriage" (Herdt 2008: 171).

One hallmark of moral panics is said to be that they "always leave an informal, and often an institutional legacy" (Goode and Ben-Yehuda 1994: 149). Given the upsurge in federal and state legislation against same sex marriage, it is clear that the moral entrepreneurs behind the panic over same sex marriage in the United States were quite successful in this regard. But the participation of potentially effective moral entrepreneurs in itself does not necessarily generate moral panics, which "arise as a consequence of specific forces and dynamics" (Goode and Ben-Yehuda 1994: 151). Therefore, when a panic does emerge, we should examine the particular historical and social contexts from which it arises (Adam 2003, Cohen 2002, Goode and Ben-Yehuda 1994, McRobbie and Thornton 1995). As well, Erich Goode and Nachman Ben-Yehuda (1994: 168) ask that more attention be paid to the demise of moral panics, as that topic has been "virtually neglected."

The reasons for the same sex marriage panic in the United States include the prominence of religious and political affiliations against same sex marriage and the presence of moral entrepreneurs who successfully tapped into cultural anger and other ideologies, combined with historical moments that facilitated acceptance of panicked rhetoric linking "traditional family values" with the strength of the nation (Adam 2003, Camp 2008, Herdt 2008). But the moral panic over same sex marriage did not take off in the same way all over the United States. Regional differences in sexual attitudes exist across the United States and these are reflected in the varying degrees to which the same sex marriage panic took hold in different states. For example, 5 out the 6 states where same sex marriage is currently legal lie in New England, one of the nation's most liberal regions in regard to sexual issues (Laumann, Gagnon, Michael, and Michaels 1994).

## What Made Massachusetts Different?

With a rising tide of moral panic lapping at its shores, how did Massachusetts stay the course toward justice and equality for lesbians and gays? Massachusetts is certainly not immune to moral panic and many Bay Staters did in fact panic over same sex marriage. Several attempts to pass DOMA legislation or constitutional amendments banning same sex marriage were made, and local media coverage revealed the looming fears entertained by many Massachusetts citizens faced with the specter of same sex marriage (Gozemba and Kahn 2007).

However, such moral panic left no institutional legacy in Massachusetts, the explanation for which is twofold. First, when considering cultural and demographic variables associated with anti-same sex marriage sentiment, Massachusetts is an outlier on nearly every single one. When the causal analysis of the same sex marriage panic in the United States is applied to Massachusetts, a far different picture from those of most states emerges. Second, because of the cultural variables that make Massachusetts unique, the state is home to various "interest groups, pressure groups, lobbies, and campaigning experts [who] are mobilized to intervene in moral panics" (McRobbie and Thornton 1995: 556). For example, gay liberation and later LGBT social movement organizations developed early there and were successful in winning rights, including anti-discrimination laws, long before same sex marriage was on the national agenda (Gozemba and Kahn 2007, Rayside 2008, Smith 2008). In the process, alliances were made with supporters in media, politics, grassroots organizations, and religious congregations—groups that were later mobilized against the moral panic over same sex marriage.

When moral panic erupted across the rest of the country, the tactic of casting lesbian and gay couples as scary "folk devils" was met with greater resistance in states like Massachusetts, where lesbians and gays were already relatively less marginalized. British cultural studies scholars Angela McRobbie and Sarah L. Thornton (1995: 566) argue that in cases where the objects of a moral panic "are less marginalized … they find themselves vociferously and articulately supported in the same mass media that castigates them" and "the proliferation of groups… set up to campaign on behalf of 'folk devils' and the skill with which they engage with media is an extremely important development." The extent to which lesbians and gays in Massachusetts were marginalized and organized proved essential in resisting the nationwide moral panic that resulted in DOMAs during the 1990s as well as a key impetus propelling the state toward establishing legally protected same sex marriage in 2003.

## Marginalization

But how did same sex couples in Massachusetts come to be less marginalized than those in other states? Besides the fact that, as sociologists Edward O. Laumann, John H. Gagnon, Robert T. Michael, and Stuart Michaels's (1994) analysis shows, New England has been be one of the most tolerant regions of the United States concerning sexual behaviors, normative or otherwise, several other conditions encouraging greater integration of same sex couples into mainstream culture existed in Massachusetts. First, the state has high concentrations of the demographic groups that are most likely to support LGBT rights including same sex marriage. Bayliss J. Camp (2008) identifies several factors as integral to passing anti-marriage amendments in 2004: religion, education, party affiliation, and type of work were all important indicators of how a person might vote when faced with a ballot initiative against same sex marriage. According to these schematics, Massachusetts, with a low percentage of evangelical voters, a highly educated population largely affiliated with the Democratic Party, and a developed postindustrial economy, would be among the most likely states to support same sex marriage. Massachusetts also has a long history of labor organizing and today retains a level of union affiliation 3.5 percent above the national average (Gavin 2009). As previously suggested, labor has been an important ally for lesbian and gay activists (Adam 2003, Brown and Tager 2000, Rayside 2008).

Anchored by coastal, cosmopolitan Boston and buoyed by university towns that draw students from across the country and around the world, Massachusetts's population is less homogeneous than those in most of the states where full-blown moral panics developed over same sex marriage (Brown and Tager 2000, Peirce 1976). While Massachusetts is predominantly white and Christian, it is also home to foreign-born residents of many races and ethnicities and to practitioners of many different religions, including Reform Jews and (as detailed below) members of progressive Christian denominations that have historically supported advances in lesbian and gay rights (*United States Census* 2000, "U.S. Religious Life" 2008). Massachusetts also scores high on measures of occupational diversity, which means that Bay Staters' participation in the workforce maintains a closer balance between the blue collar and white collar economic sectors than is the case in other states (*United States Census* 2000, "Majority Continues to Support" 2009). Evidence suggests that people who live in areas with greater social diversity feel less uneasy when confronted with a person or group of people who may be identified as "other" and that greater social heterogeneity makes it difficult for any one group to influence unduly legislators or others in positions of power, so that minority challengers have a better chance of influencing policy decisions (Nicholson-Clotty 2006).

That Massachusetts ranks high on measures correlated with support for LGBT issues is a significant factor in the early development of an LGBT rights movement, and this, in turn, encouraged integration of same sex couples into Massachusetts communities. In addition, the early development of an LGBT rights movement in Massachusetts meant that basic anti-discrimination laws and other forward-looking protections, for example the legalization of second parent adoption, were established years before the same sex marriage panic swept the nation (Gozemba and Kahn 2007, Rayside 2008). That their rights were established early on made it easier for lesbians and gays to become visible in their communities, thereby making it difficult for moral entrepreneurs to paint them as shadowy strangers seeking special rights or as folk devils threatening children, families, or even civilization itself (Smith 2008, Stein 1999). When moral entrepreneurs supporting the same sex marriage panic sought to tap into Massachusetts's cultural anger, the tactic was not as successful as in other regions in part because such tropes tend to resonate more deeply with people in economically depressed areas (Adam 2003, Camp 2008, Stein 1999). Massachusetts, with its highly educated citizenry and largely postindustrial economic base, contains a number of residents who are less likely to be convinced by this particular rationale to demonize lesbians and gays or otherwise panic over same sex marriage.

However, Massachusetts is also home to large numbers of socially conservative Roman Catholics, less educated and lower income folks less likely to support LGBT rights, and upper class people who are socially conservative (Adam 2003, Herdt 2008). Besides those who were sensitized to the issue of same sex marriage, there were also many Massachusetts residents who, to use Cohen's (2002: 59) phrase, supported "the direction of control measures toward the specific agent thought to be responsible." In 1998, the first attempt to establish DOMA legislation was filed in Massachusetts. But this took longer than it did in other states (26 states plus the federal government had already enacted DOMA legislation or constitutional amendments against same sex marriage), and, more importantly, DOMA legislation in Massachusetts faced organized resistance the likes of which existed in few other states (Gozemba and Kahn 2007).

In the mid-1990s, as moral panic swelled in other states, stories in two major Massachusetts newspapers, *The Boston Globe* and the *Boston Herald* reflected residents' conflicting views about same sex marriage, but also suggest that the papers did "their duty by providing 'balance' in their reporting," in the process showing that "'folk devils' can and do fight back" (see McRobbie and Thornton 1995: 566). In July 1996, *The Boston Globe* featured an editorial opposing same sex marriage, asserting, "Legal improvements in the status of gay people can be made without redefining this bedrock institution of society." Similarly, in the *Boston Herald* (1996), editors lamented the *Baehr v. Lewin* decision that brought same sex marriage to the fore: "Once more the American people are at risk of being forced into a vast social experiment against their will at the whim of tyrannical judges." Unlike the *Boston Herald*, *The Boston Globe* also published stories sympathetic to gay and lesbian couples wanting the right to marry, including a feature story that proclaimed, "Is Anything Wrong with this Picture? In the South End, a Couple Wants to Seal their Love with Marriage. In Congress, Lawmakers Try to Stop Them" (Sege 1996).

## Organization

The LGBT rights movement in Massachusetts began organizing in the early 1970s. By the time DOMA was on the table in 1998, activists had made significant inroads into the political establishment of the state, developed alliances with religious leaders and other grassroots organizations, and become a significant media presence (Adam 1995, Rayside 2008). Having already established anti-discrimination protections and quelled controversies over foster parenting, adoption rights, and domestic partner benefits, activists in Massachusetts were better positioned than those in most other states to push back a rising tide of panic. In fact, at the same time that the case in Hawaii incited panic across the country, Massachusetts activists formed new groups like the Freedom to Marry Coalition, and leaders of older organizations like Gay and Lesbian Advocates and Defenders (GLAD) began strategizing to bring same sex marriage cases before courts in the New England region (GLAD 2009, Gozemba and Kahn 2007). These early successes were integral to ensuring that the panic in Massachusetts left no institutional legacy.

The attempted DOMA bills introduced in the Massachusetts legislature in the 1990s were so far-reaching that they would not only have banned same sex marriage, but would also have eliminated even the possibility of establishing domestic partner benefits for same sex couples. Legislative attempts to establish a Massachusetts DOMA, starting with House Bill 472, introduced by Democrat John H. Rogers in 1998, floundered in the legislature (Abraham 2001b, Hayward 1999). While no legislative or executive allies explicitly supported same sex marriage rights at the time, the possible elimination of all benefits meant that even the more tepid allies of the LGBT community could be counted on to oppose DOMA bills (Abraham 2001b). For example, Republican governors Bill Weld, Paul Cellucci, and Jane Swift all managed to position themselves against same sex marriage while supporting some expansion of LGBT rights, however small (Abraham 2001c, Crowley 1999, Vaillancourt 1996). Meanwhile, a series of events occurred that increased the level of Bay Staters' sensitization to same sex marriage: the creation of civil unions in Vermont with *Baker v. State* in 1999, the filing of *Goodridge v. Department of Public Health* in Massachusetts in 2001, and the Massachusetts Supreme Judicial Court's 4–3 decision in favor of same sex marriage in 2003 (Lambda Legal Marriage Equality Timeline 2009). As each of these events brought same sex marriage closer to reality for Massachusetts citizens, both formal and informal "agents of social control" responded with renewed fervor and repeated attempts to pass legislation or amend the state constitution to ban same sex marriage, and LGBT social movement organizations and their allies, both new and old, dug in to resist each attempted bill or amendment (Cohen 2002, Gozemba and Kahn 2007, Rayside 2008).

From the moment that *Goodridge v. Department of Public Health* was filed in 2001 until the final legislative vote on same sex marriage in 2007, Massachusetts served as the front line in a culture war battleground as tension escalated between those citizens who panicked over the prospect of same sex marriage and those who celebrated the possibility. Fighting for same sex marriage in Massachusetts meant capitalizing on the extent to which gay and lesbian people in Massachusetts were (1) integrated into Massachusetts's culture, politics, and communities and (2) organized to the extent that they could simultaneously wage a defensive fight against DOMA and an offensive battle for marriage equality. In the course of these campaigns, Massachusetts activists successfully trumped two of the most potent tropes used by moral entrepreneurs in the moral panic over same sex marriage: religion and family values.

Regions where strong religious opposition to LGBT rights already exists are particularly ripe locations for moral panic against same sex marriage (Camp 2008, Fetner 2008). Ohio, for example, where the Evangelical Christian population mirrors the national average of 26 percent, has one of the most stringent anti-same sex marriage laws on the books, a law that goes as far as eliminating domestic partner benefits at private companies (Seigel 2004). And in Arkansas, where Evangelical Christians top 50 percent of the population, not only is same sex marriage outlawed per DOMA and constitutional amendment, but same sex couples are prohibited from fostering and adopting children as well (*Arkansas Code* 1997, *Arkansas Constitution* 2004, Majority Continues 2009, The Task Force 2008). In sharp contrast, Massachusetts contains a greater number of religious denominations that support same sex marriage than other regions in the United States (for example, Unitarian Universalists, United Church of Christ, Reform Jews) and LGBT alliances with these congregations were effectively utilized to fight DOMA (Gozemba and Kahn 2007, Rayside 2008). Most notably, LGBT allies in Massachusetts's religious community amassed public support from religious leaders by forming the Religious Coalition for the Freedom to Marry (RCFM).

Organized during the initial DOMA push in 1998, by the height of the marriage battle in 2006 the RCFM listed "more than 700 clergy, congregations and faith-based organizations from twenty-two faith traditions that support marriage equality for same sex couples" (Religious Coalition for the Freedom to Marry 2006: i). RCFM members testified during statehouse hearings, lobbied legislators, wrote letters to the editor, and spoke to the media. While groups like the Massachusetts Family Institute and the Roman Catholic Church utilized religion as a force in opposition to same sex marriage, the public presence of religious voices in support of same sex marriage was a key factor in pushing back against the same sex marriage panic in Massachusetts (Gozemba and Kahn 2007). While LGBT rights and same sex marriage proponents in other regions have religious allies to be sure, the overall religious composition of those regions makes it difficult to mobilize effectively against deep religious opposition to same sex marriage (Fetner 2008, Rayside and Wilcox 2011). The presence of diverse religious congregations in Massachusetts counteracted moral entrepreneurs using religious rhetoric to inflame a panicked response to same sex marriage.

Along with clergy and religious organizations, families have been in the forefront of the same sex marriage debate since its inception, not least because opponents of same sex marriage vociferously claim that such marriages are harmful to children and "traditional" families (Fetner 2008). In Massachusetts, activists were prepared to turn this argument, also known as the family values frame, to their advantage (Abraham 2001a). Mary Bonauto and GLAD's decision to file a marriage case was informed by the knowledge that "Massachusetts is a state that is committed to equality and it's a state where gay and lesbian families are no stranger at any branch of government, and those things matter" (GLAD 2009). Therefore, when the time came to fight for marriage and opponents attempted to position lesbians and gays as "the 'enemy' of common folk," as had worked successfully for opponents in panic-driven DOMA campaigns across the United States, they were unsuccessful in Massachusetts (Adam 2003: 269). In Massachusetts, gay and lesbian families were already established members of their communities, with the force of law already supporting them in many ways (that is, second parent adoption, de facto parenting rights). In Massachusetts, gay and lesbian people could not be made into the enemies of common folk, because they *were* common folk—a fact repeatedly emphasized by the LGBT movement throughout the struggle for marriage equality.

In Massachusetts, LGBT movement strategies emphasized family from the beginning: the couples represented in *Goodridge v. Department of Public Health* were carefully chosen so that some would have children, couples frequently brought photos of their children to show to legislators while lobbying, and families with children featured prominently in the media campaign for marriage equality. For example, the "It's wrong to vote on rights" campaign, designed by the LGBT rights organization MassEquality, successfully coopted the family values frame by emphasizing the protections that marriage provided for lesbian and gay couples and their children. This campaign featured a series of ads that highlighted lesbian and gay families and sometimes their extended family members. One such ad featured two dads and their daughter. In another, parents of a lesbian reflected on their love for their daughter, her partner, and their child. And another featured the grown son of a lesbian couple who poignantly explained how much it meant to him that his moms were finally able to marry (MassEquality). Each two-minute segment powerfully asserted that that it was wrong to deny the rights and protections of marriage to lesbian and gay families.

This campaign was successful in part because it was developed well after *Goodridge v. Department of Public Health* was decided and lesbian and gay couples had been marrying for nearly a year. These ads brought home the point that passing a law or amendment against same sex marriage now would be taking away rights that already existed. This is the way that Bonauto and the legal team at GLAD had strategized when they filed *Goodridge v. Department of Public Health* in April 2001, believing that if they won marriage equality before their opponents established a DOMA, people would see that same sex marriage was not so scary or threatening after all (Gozemba and Kahn 2007). They were right.

After same sex couples began to marry in May 2004, the panic quieted down remarkably, leaving some to wonder what all the fuss had been about (Walker 2005). A proposed DOMA amendment was still being actively debated in the legislature, but the same factors that had caused public opinion to rise in support of same sex marriage also convinced some legislators to support marriage equality and oppose the DOMA amendment (Phillips 2005). Heading into the decisive vote on the DOMA amendment in June 2007, no one could predict how the vote would turn out, except that it would be close, as indeed it was. The DOMA amendment lost by only one vote in a Constitutional Convention that required 75 percent of the legislature to vote against the amendment for it to be defeated (Gozemba and Kahn 2007). The rationale of some same sex marriage supporters in the legislature directly reflects the family-focused strategy used by LGBT rights organizations. For example, State Senate Minority Leader Richard Tisei, a Republican, summed up his position:

> There are a lot of families out there who have children that are same sex couples and those kids deserve the same sort of rights and protections under the law. I'm glad I was on the right side of history, and I'm glad that our state was, and our legislature. (MassEquality 2009)

That a conservative legislator like Tisei came to support same sex marriage because it protects families and children indicates the demise of the same sex marriage panic in Massachusetts, a demise that occurred at the same time much of the rest of the country was still in the midst of moral panic.


# Conclusion

From the time that a DOMA bill was introduced in the Massachusetts legislature in 1998 to the final vote that eliminated DOMA in 2007, 27 states passed constitutional amendments against same sex marriage. By 2008, only five states in the United States had neither a DOMA statute nor a constitutional amendment against same sex marriage ("Issues by State" 2010). Opponents of LGBT rights had become victorious in other states by mobilizing populist discourses to incite a series of moral panics over the advancement of LGBT rights and same sex marriage in particular. One of these is the "special rights" argument, which casts gay and lesbian individuals and couples as "privileged, spoiled, and demanding 'special rights'" for a "lifestyle" of which many do not approve or may even find dangerous or threatening (Adam 2003: 269). After constructing LGBT rights and same sex marriage this way, opponents then "mobilized a constituency that identified itself as the victims and outcasts of unfeeling liberal elites, including gay people among them" (Adam 2003: 269). Certainly, this strategy was tried by opponents of same sex marriage in Massachusetts, but it failed because political and cultural conditions in Massachusetts differed significantly from those in many other states.

Casting lesbians and gays as a threat to an entire way of life or to a civilization is most likely to succeed in regions where a great deal of social anxiety already exists, especially anxiety over economic and social change, and where suspicion is already high in regard to racial, immigrant, or otherwise categorized "outsiders" (Adam 2003, Smith 2008, Stein 1999, Rayside 2008). Given Massachusetts's status as a wealthy state with a stable economy, a long history of immigration, and considerable social diversity, these arguments—though put forth with fervor by some citizens of the state—are less likely to be successful with a majority of

Massachusetts residents (Camp 2008, Nicholson-Crotty 2006). Additionally, these arguments are often floated with an attachment to religious beliefs about the danger of moral decline, but in Massachusetts a diversity of religious traditions ensures that this moral vision is challenged by religious leaders from many denominations (Gozemba and Kahn 2007). A diversity of religious beliefs works against the uptake of religiously based arguments against same sex marriage that contribute to panic over a "moral decline" that threatens the family and society.

Early rights victories of the Massachusetts LGBT movement meant that Massachusetts citizens had already been confronted with most anti-gay arguments and had seen them defeated. The legacy of these rights is that lesbian and gay couples were increasingly visible in their jobs, places of worship, schools, and neighborhoods. The extent to which same sex couples were integrated into their communities diminished the efficacy of the moral entrepreneurs attempting to position them as the objects of moral panic, and the presence of knowledgeable and experienced rights groups able to intervene successfully when such attempts were made was crucial to overcoming the same sex marriage panic in Massachusetts. In Massachusetts, lesbians and gays are not scary strangers, or outsiders demanding "special rights," images often used in moral panics over LGBT issues (Adam 2003, Herdt 2008, Stein 1999). They are the two dads of your daughter's friend from her soccer team. They are the lesbian moms who drive their son to hockey practice every morning just as you do. They are a married couple who want reassurance that they can visit each other in the hospital should one of them fall ill, a couple who want to know that one will be able to keep the house should the other move into a nursing home. These are the "special rights" of same sex marriage. By utilizing the social integration and political organization of LGBT people in the state to drive home this point, supporters of same sex marriage ensured that an obstructive moral panic met its demise in Massachusetts.

# References

Abraham, Y. 2001a. Gays seek right to marry. *The Boston Globe*, April 12, A1.

Abraham, Y. 2001b. Bill Targets Domestic Partner Benefits. *The Boston Globe*, May 17, B2.

Abraham, Y. 2001c. Swift to Extend Same Sex Benefits. *The Boston Globe*, August 16.

Adam, B.D. 1995. *The Rise of a Gay and Lesbian Movement*. New York: Twayne.

Adam, B.D. 2003. The Defense of Marriage Act and American exceptionalism: the "Gay Marriage" panic in the United States. *Journal of the History of Sexuality*, 12(2), 259–76.

*Arkansas Code § 9-11-109*. 1997 [Online]. Available at: http://www.lambdalegal.org/states-regions/arkansas#quickset-regional_offices_information=2 [accessed: November 20, 2011].

Brown, R.D. and Tager, J. 2000. *Massachusetts: A Concise History*. Amherst: University of Massachusetts Press.

*Baehr v. Lewin*. Supreme Court of Hawaii. 852 P.2d 44 (1993).

*Baker v. State*. Vermont Supreme Court. 744 A.2d 864 (1999).

Belluck, P. 2003. Marriage by gays gains big victory in Massachusetts. *The New York Times LearningNetwork* [Online]. Available at: http://www.nytimes.com/learning/teachers/featured_articles/20031120thursday.html [accessed: October 13, 2011].

Bush, G.W. 2004. *Address Before a Joint Session of the Congress on the State of the Union*, January 20. *The Presidency Project* [Online]. Available at: http://www.presidency.ucsb.edu/ws/index.php?pid=29646#axzz1ainUyw21 [accessed: October 13, 2011].

Camp, B.J. 2008. Mobilizing the base and embarrassing the opposition: defense of marriage referenda and cross-cutting electoral cleavages. *Sociological Perspectives*, 51(4), 713–33.

Cohen, S. 2002 (1973, 1980). *Folk Devils and Moral Panic: The Creation of the Mods and Rockers*. 3rd Edition. New York: Routledge.

2009. *Civil Union to Marriage: Fighting for Equality in New England and Beyond* [Online]. Gay and Lesbian Advocates and Defenders. Available at: http://www.youtube.com/watch?v=NONL829JLOw [accessed: October 16, 2011].

2004. Constitution of the State of Arkansas of 1874. 83rd Amendment [Online]. Available at: http://www.arkleg.state.ar.us/assembly/Summary/Arkansas Constitution1874.pdf [accessed: November 20, 2011].

Crowley, M. 1999. Gay rights bill would face battle in Mass. *The Boston Globe*, December 23, B8.

1996. H.R. 3396–104th Congress: Defense of Marriage Act [Online: 1996]. Available at: http://www.govtrack.us/congress/bills/104/hr3396 [accessed: October 6, 2012].

1996. Editorial: gays and marriage. *The Boston Globe* [Online] July 27, A16. Available at: http://pqasb.pqarchiver.com/boston/access/16210924.html?FMT=ABS&FMTS=ABS:FT&type=current&date=Jul+27%2C+1996&author=&pub=Boston+Globe+%28pre1997+Fulltext%29&edition=&startpage=A.16&desc=Gays+and+marriage [accessed: November 20, 2011].

1996. Editorial: marriage in a democracy. *Boston Herald* [Online], December 5, 41. Available at: https://verify1.newsbank.com/cgi-bin/ncom/BNHB/ec_signin [accessed: November 22, 2011].

Fetner, T. 2008. *How the Religious Right Shaped Lesbian and Gay Activism*. Minneapolis: University of Minnesota Press.

Gavin, R. 2009. Union membership rises in Massachusetts. *The Boston Globe* [Online], January 29. Available at: http://www.boston.com/business/ticker/2009/01/union_membershi_1.html [accessed: October 16, 2011].

Goode, E. and Ben-Yehuda, N. 1994. Moral panics: culture, politics, and social construction. *Annual Review of Sociology*, 20, 149–71.

2007 (2003). *Goodridge v. Department of Public Health*. Massachusetts Supreme Judical Court, reprinted in *Courting Equality: A Documentary History of America's First Legal Same Sex Marriages*, edited by P. Gozemba and K. Kahn. Boston: Beacon Press.

Hayward, E. 1999. Gays take aim at bill outlawing same-sex unions. *Boston Globe*.

Herdt, G. 2009. Gay marriage: the panic and the right, in *Moral Panics, Sex Panics: The Fight Over Sexual Rights*, edited by G. Herdt. New York: New York University Press.

Hunter, J.D. 1991. *Culture Wars: The Struggle to Define America*. New York: Basic Books.

2008. Issue Maps. *National Gay and Lesbian Task Force* [Online]. Available at: http://www.thetaskforce.org/reports_and_research/issue_maps [accessed: November 20, 2011].

2010. Issues by state. *DOMA Watch* [Online]. Available at: http://www.domawatch.org/stateissues/index.html [accessed: May 15, 2010].

2009. Marriage equality timeline. *Lambda Legal* [Online]. Available at: http://www.lambdalegal.org/publications/fs_marriage-equality-timeline [accessed: November 20, 2011].

Laumann, E.O., Gagnon, J.H., Michael, R.T., and Michaels, S. 1994. *The Social Organization of Sexuality: Sexual Practices in the United States*. Chicago: University of Chicago Press.

Lucas, D.L. 2008. Same sex marriage in the 2004 election, in *The Politics of Same-Sex Marriage*, edited by C.A. Rimmerman and C. Wilcox. Chicago: University of Chicago Press.

2009. Majority continues to support civil unions: most still oppose same-sex marriage. *Pew Forum on Religion and Public Life* [Online]. Available at: http://pewforum.org/Gay-Marriage-and-Homosexuality/Majority-Continues-To-Support-Civil-Unions.aspx [accessed: October 16, 2011].

Massachusetts House Bill 472. 1998.

MassEquality. 2009. *Marriage Equality Works* [Online]. Boston. Available at: http://www.massequality.org/content/marriage-equality-works-massachusetts [accessed: August 10, 2011].

di Mauro, D. and Joffe, C. 2009. The religious right and the reshaping of public policy: reproductive rights and sexuality education during the Bush years, in *Moral Panics, Sex Panics: Fear and the Fight Over Sexual Rights*, edited by G. Herdt. New York: New York University Press.

McRobbie, A. and Thornton, S.L. 1995. Rethinking 'moral panic' for multi-mediated social worlds. *British Journal of Sociology*, 46(4), 559–74.

McVeigh, R. and Diaz, M.E. 2009. Voting to ban same-sex marriage: interests, values, and communities. *American Sociological Review*, 74(6), 891–915.

Nicholson-Crotty, S. 2006. Reassessing Madison's diversity hypothesis: the case of same-sex marriage. *Journal of Politics*, 68(4), 922–30.

Ohio Constitution, Article XV, section 11 [Online]. Available at: http://www.legislature.state.oh.us/constitution.cfm?Part=15&Section=11. [accessed: November 20, 2011].

Peirce, N.R. 1976. *The New England States: People, Poltics, and Power in the New England States*. New York: W. W. Norton.

Phillips, F. and Mohl, B. 2005. Bid seen weakening to ban gay marriage. *The Boston Globe* [Online], January 18. Available at: http://www.boston.com/news/specials/

gay_marriage/articles/2005/01/18/bid_seen_weakening_to_ban_gay_marriage/ [accessed: October 16, 2011].

2009. Public opinion on gay marriage: opponents consistently outnumber supporters. *Pew Forum on Religion and Public Life* [Online]. Available at: http:// pewforum.org/Gay-Marriage-and-Homosexuality/Public-opinion-on-gay-marriage-opponents-consistently-outnumber-supporters.aspx [accessed: May 21, 2010].

Rayside, D. and Wilcox, C. 2011. The difference that a border makes: the political intersection of sexuality and religion in Canada and United States, in *Faith, Politics, and Sexual Diversity in Canada and the United States*, edited by D. Rayside and C. Wilcox. Vancouver: UBC Press.

Rayside, D.M. 2008. *Queer Inclusions, Continental Divisions: Public Recognition of Sexual Diversity in Canada and the United States*. Toronto: University of Toronto Press.

Religious Coalition for the Freedom to Marry. 2006. *People of Faith Testimony: Rejoicing in Marriage Equality*. Private Collection of Jaime McCauley.

Schulte, G. 2010. Iowans dismiss three justices. *DesMoinesRegister.com* [Online]. Available at: http://www.desmoinesregister.com/apps/pbcs.dll/article?AID=/ 201011030405/NEWS09/11030390 [accessed: January 11, 2011].

Schwartz, M.A. and Tatalovitch, R. 2009. Cultural and institutional factors affecting political contention over moral issues. *Comparative Sociology*, 8(1), 76–104.

Sege, I. 1996. Is anything wrong with this picture? *The Boston Globe* [Online]. Available at: http://pqasb.pqarchiver.com/boston/access/10253610.html?FMT= ABS&FMTS=ABS&type=current&date=Sep+10%2C+1996&author=Sege%2C+I rene&pub=Boston+Globe&edition=&startpage=D1&desc=Is+anything+wrong+ with+this+picture%3F [accessed: November 20, 2011].

Seigel, J. 2004. Wording of Ohio's gay marriage ban called sweeping. *Cincinnati Enquirer* [Online]. Available at: http://www.enquirer.com/editions/2004/10/09/ loc_gaymarriage09side.html [accessed: November 20, 2011].

Smith, M. 2009. *Political Institutions and Lesbian and Gay Rights in the United States and Canada*. New York: Routledge.

Stein, A. 1999. *The Stranger Next Door: The Story of a Small Community's Battle over Sex, Faith, and Civil Rights*. Boston: Beacon Press.

Terry, J. 1999. *An American Obsession: Science, Medicine, and Homosexuality in Modern Society*. Chicago: University of Chicago Press.

2008. U.S. religious landscape survey. *Pew Forum on Religion and Public Life* [Online]. Available at: http://religions.pewforum.org/affiliations [accessed: June 11, 2011].

2000. *United States Census* [Online]. Available at: http://www.census.gov/ census2000/states/ma.html [accessed: October 16, 2011].

Vaillancourt, M. 1996. Weld: Mass would honor out of state gay unions. *The Boston Globe* [Online], December 5. Available at: http://www.highbeam.com/ publications/the-boston-globe-boston-ma-p2935/dec-5-1996 [accessed: January 29, 2012].

Walker, A. 2005. Calm after the storm. *The Boston Globe* [Online], May 16. Available at: http://www.boston.com/news/specials/gay_marriage/articles/2005/05/16/calm_ after_the_storm/ [accessed: October 16, 2011].

# Considering the Agency of Folk Devils

## Mary deYoung

Moral panic theorists and researchers from a variety of disciplines have been paying a debt of gratitude to Stanley Cohen and Stuart Hall et al. for forty years. It was their innovative analyses of the volatile reactions of moral entrepreneurs, the media, and control culture to norm-violators that not only launched the concept of moral panic, but also made folk devils essential to it. In Cohen's (1972) oft-cited work, of course, the folk devils were the mods and the rockers, factions of two emerging and edgy youth subcultures in Great Britain. It was their altercation in the seaside town of Clacton-on-Sea over the rainy Easter weekend of 1964 that set off a hostile, excessive, and repressive social reaction that Cohen went on to analyze as a moral panic. Hall et al. (1978) laid out the complex process by which the media translated the warning of police and politicians about street crime into a public idiom that gave a discursive reality to the vague fears of the public. They examined the discursive loop by which the public's frightened reactions to media reportage were then fed back to the police and politicians as indicators not just of public opinion, but also of public support for augmenting the control culture by increasing arrest rates for muggers, passing new laws, and raising maximum terms for prison sentences.

While there are substantive theoretical and analytical differences between these two groundbreaking works on moral panic (see Critcher 2003, Thompson 1998), the folk devil is paramount in both. And in both, the folk devils had a certain marginal status *before* they even were nominated as folk devils. The mods and the rockers were straddling the boundaries between convention and deviance, "not quite in their places," as Cohen (1995: 222) puts it, and the muggers of Hall et al.'s analysis were lurking in the shadows of decaying, racially stratified cities across the nation. In both cases, their liminal status targeted them as folk devils and made it easy for moral entrepreneurs, the media, and the agents of social control to reduce them to stereotypes even while they amplified their alleged threat to the social and moral orders.

Indeed, the folk devils of subsequent moral panic analyses have the same threatening, morally sinister air as the youth hooligans and muggers analyzed by

Cohen and Hall et al. There are the coarse women of the witch hunts (Ben-Yehuda 1980), the lazy dole scroungers and dissolute single mothers of the welfare state panics (Ortiz and Briggs 2003, Shepard 2007), the antisocial addicts and pushers of the drug crusades (Armstrong 2007, Goode 1990), the sleazy pornographers, child molesters, and Internet predators of the stranger-danger alarms (Jenkins 1999, Ost 2002, Sandywell 2006) or the shadowy foreigners of the asylum-seeking, illegal immigration, and terrorism scares (Altheide 2006, Rothe and Muzzatti 2004, Welch and Schuster 2005). All of them were cultural strangers—gendered, stigmatized, racialized, criminalized, marginalized as "the Other" (Bauman 2001)—well before they were nominated and then constructed into these moral panics' folk devils.

The very notion of socially marginalized folk devils, hapless victims of the bloated rhetoric of moral entrepreneurs, the stereotypical representations by the media, and the heavy hands of agents of control culture, is so securely ensconced in moral panic analyses, in fact, that it is almost axiomatic. As a consequence, the "otherness" of folk devils is reified by their treatment as objects rather than subjects, as powerless rather than agentic. Thus, what remains under-theorized and under-analyzed is the agency of folk devils, that is, how they expend what social capital they have to resist their demonization and social control, and to what effect on the course and the outcome of a moral panic.

It is the purpose of this chapter to disturb the tranquility of this axiom by considering the agency of folk devils. In so doing, I am proposing that adding "feisty folk devils," as Critcher (2010: 252) so impishly calls them, to the equation of social strains, moral entrepreneurs, discourse, media representation and control culture, will result in a more theoretically nuanced and analytically enriched approach to moral panics.

Although there is no dearth of definitions of social capital, Pierre Bourdieu and Loïc Wacquant (1992: 119) handily describe it as "the sum of the resources, actual or virtual, that accrue to an individual or group by virtue of possessing a durable network of more or less institutionalized relationships of mutual acquaintance and recognition." If accrued by folk devils, these resources, which include wealth, power, reputation, knowledge, interpersonal connections, taste, affiliation, and status, can be mobilized in the agentic action of resisting their demonization and social control (Lin 2001).

The day care ritual abuse moral panic in the United States provides a unique opportunity to analyze feisty folk devils. This pernicious moral panic, spanning the decade of the 1980s, resulted in accusations against more than two hundred day care providers in large cities and small towns across the country for observing or participating in the sexual abuse of their young charges in ghastly satanic rituals that included blood drinking, torture, and infant sacrifice. Like the folk devils of Cohen's and Hall et al.'s classic studies, the day care providers stood in proxy for deeper and unsettling social, economic, political and ideological forces that were radically changing family structure and gender roles during that decade, and thus increasing anxiety about risks to young children posed by care outside of the family home (deYoung 2004). But quite unlike them, most of the accused day care providers were otherwise quite ordinary middle-aged working- or middle-class women who were integrated into their communities and, in every other way, were conforming members of society. More to the point of this chapter, they had varying amounts of social capital to spend in the contest over meaning, moral boundaries, and social control that is part and parcel of any moral panic.

## Analytic Strategy

In 23 high-profile day care satanic ritual abuse cases, 32 women providers were publicly accused, arrested and charged for sexually abusing the young children in their care during the course of satanic rituals (deYoung 2004, 2007, 2008). For analytical purposes, they were placed on a social capital axis dichotomized into low and high. Their placement on the axis was based on the simple coding of the amount, kind and quality of the resources available to them at the time of their arrests, including the relationship, organizational and institutional networks in which they were embedded, their economic resources, social standing and reputation, and the number, kind and quality of advocatory individuals or groups that spoke out or acted on their behalves.

If the social capital of these folk devils of the day care ritual abuse moral panic varied, so did their perceived threat to the social and moral order. On the basis of the allegations against them, therefore, the women day care providers were placed on a threat axis that was dichotomized into "observer" and "participant." A woman provider was classified as an observer if she was accused of orchestrating, watching, filming, or photographing the satanic ritual abuse of the children while it was being performed by others, and as a participant if she was accused of performing one or more sexually intrusive acts, that is, vaginal or rectal penetration, oral-genital contact, or fondling, on the body of one or more children in the context of satanic rituals, whether by herself or in the presence of others.

When the social capital axis then is transected by the threat axis, the result is an orthogonal grid that is not just pleasingly tidy, but also instructive about the resources that the folk devils of the day care ritual abuse moral panic called on *to* resist, and even *what* they needed to resist in the first place. More directly stated, far from being hegemonic and monolithic, the demonization strategies of moral entrepreneurs, the media and the control culture, and the public reactions to those strategies varied according to where the accused women day care providers fell on this grid.

A series of decisions aimed at further facilitating analysis then was made. First, since the accrual of social capital is somewhat dependent upon age, any accused woman provider below the age of 55 was removed from the grid. Second, any woman provider who was accused after 1985 also was removed. This analytical criterion was predicated on the fact that in those early years of the decade-long moral panic, the tone of the reportage of both local and national media tended to be credulous and uncritical of the allegations. In what sometimes is described as a "feeding frenzy," media outlets competed with each other not only to uncover details of the alleged satanic ritual abuse, but also to provide more complex profiles of the accused. Third, any woman provider for whom there were insufficient archival data in the form of published legal decisions, interviews, and court transcripts, investigative reports, newspaper and magazine articles, or radio and television transcripts to assess either her amount and expenditure of social capital or her role in the alleged satanic ritual abuse was removed from the grid. Fourth, when more than one remaining accused woman provider was employed in the same day care center, one was randomly chosen to remain on the grid. Fifth, when more than one remaining accused woman provider occupied one of the four quadrants of the grid, one was randomly chosen to remain on the grid.

From these analytical decisions, four women day care providers emerged as subjects for this analysis of the agency of folk devils: Virginia McMartin, Mary Lou Gallup, Cora Priest, and Frances Ballard. Their positions on the orthogonal grid can be seen in table 8.1.

**Table 8.1    Social Capital and Perceived Threat of Role for Four Women Day Care Providers**

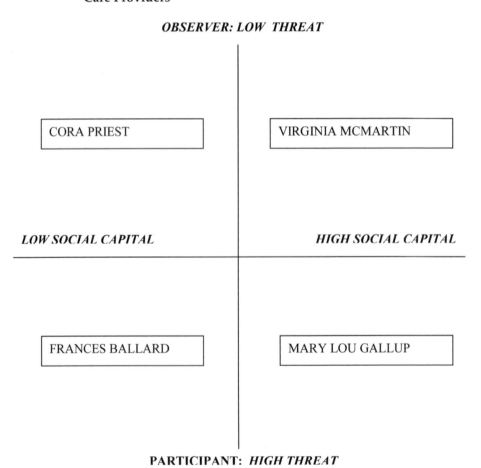

*OBSERVER: LOW THREAT*

| CORA PRIEST | VIRGINIA MCMARTIN |

*LOW SOCIAL CAPITAL*          *HIGH SOCIAL CAPITAL*

| FRANCES BALLARD | MARY LOU GALLUP |

**PARTICIPANT:** *HIGH THREAT*

# Feisty Folk Devils

## Virginia McMartin

Virginia McMartin, the founder of the McMartin Preschool, had accumulated considerable social capital over the 75 years preceding her arrest. She had earned a graduate degree, joined professional organizations, won awards for civic achievement, boasted an annual income well in excess of most day care providers, and had a wide circle of family, friends, and coreligionists. In 1983, the "good life" that she had written about in her unpublished autobiography came to an abrupt end when she and six of her employees, including her daughter and two grandchildren, were arrested for sexually abusing hundreds of their past and current enrollees in satanic rituals that included cannibalism, the disinterment and mutilation of corpses, and infant sacrifice (deYoung 1997). McMartin's arrest not only grabbed national and international headlines, but triggered the day care ritual abuse moral panic as parents, investigators and social workers frantically interrogated the young children enrolled in day care centers across the country to determine if they, too, had been ritually abused by their providers.

Unlike her employees, McMartin was accused of observing, rather than participating in, the satanic ritual abuse of her young charges. In interviews with relentlessly probing interrogators, the accusing children described her as watching from the corner of a room, encouraging her employees as they danced naked or in dark robes around them, and penetrated their vaginas or anuses with knives and swords. In the moral economy of this burgeoning moral panic, her perceived threat to the social and moral order was comparatively less than that of her participating employees.

With high social capital and low threat, McMartin was both an unusual and an unlikely folk devil, therefore the media and the moral entrepreneurs who emerged to lend self-proclaimed expertise to deciphering this baffling crime, were left with the dilemma of how to demonize her. A content analysis of the *Los Angeles Times*, the newspaper that, almost a decade after McMartin's arrest, would win a Pulitzer Prize for its scathing criticism of its own reportage on the case (Shaw 1990a, 1990b, 1990c), finds that it sought safety in mystifying her, that is, in treating her as an enigma even while wallowing in its own bewilderment as to why such a respectable person would watch with apparent pleasure such vile acts, and never intervene to protect the children. To that end, the newspaper quoted at length the incredulous friends, neighbors and even the parents of some of the alleged victims who characterized her as "beloved," "compassionate," and a "wonderful Christian woman" (Rohrlich and Welkos 1984: B4). It offered no speculation as to her motivation and quoted no one who did. It declared her an "enigma" (Arnold and Decker 1984: A18) , and when all charges were dropped against her for lack of evidence, it published an editorial titled, "Begging for Answers," which implored anyone to make sense of the case and the role McMartin allegedly played in it (1986: B4).

The strategy of the media and moral entrepreneurs of mystifying McMartin ironically opened a space for her to expend her social capital. From the moment of her arrest, she met every attempt to demonize her as a folk devil with immediate, public, and ferocious counterclaims. She authored her own biography in interviews with newspapers and magazines and humanized herself in appearances on nationally and locally syndicated television news and talk shows. She publicly mocked moral entrepreneurs, the media, and agents of social control, even loudly proclaiming to the judge overseeing her pretrial hearing that the accusations against her were a "load of bull." She brought suits against the local police for false arrest, the local television news station for libel, and even against the parent of one her alleged victims for slander after he went on a nationally syndicated television show and declared her a satanic ritual abuser. She won that suit. The judge awarded her just $1 in damages, but she claimed a pyrrhic victory: "I got what I wanted—the truth to come out," she told a press conference. "I don't give a snip about the money. I just wanted him to shut-up" (McGraw 1991: B1).

The space also was opened for advocatory activities. Well after it was no longer socially acceptable, or even tolerable, to support the day care providers or, for that matter, to reserve judgment about their guilt or innocence, McMartin still had a coterie of ardent supporters who braved public opprobrium and social ostracism to staunchly work on her behalf and proclaim her innocence.

Long before her death in 1995, just a few years after the only McMartin providers to stand trial were acquitted of all charges, McMartin had already become more of a folk hero than a folk devil. She had traded on that new identity by publicly criticizing the national pursuit of satanic day care providers as a "witch hunt," and by defending accused providers around the country. In apparent acknowledgment of the characteristic that this chapter refers to as the exercise of agency, her very brief obituary in the *Los Angeles Times* simply described her as "feisty" (Oliver 1995: A1).

If the payoff of a folk devil's expenditure of social capital in agentic action is measured only by the halting of a moral panic before it can spread, McMartin received little return. The day care ritual abuse moral panic would go on for the rest of the decade of the 1980s and many more providers, most of them women, would be accused, scores of them would be arrested, some would stand trial and most of those would be found guilty and sentenced to draconian prison terms that would quietly be overturned years later (deYoung 2007, 2008). But if the payoff is measured by the opening up of space for counterdiscourse and contestation, by the recruiting of supporters and advocates with their own social capital to spend, or, even more personally, by the protecting of biography and identity from the unrelenting effects of stereotyping and demonizing, then she indeed achieved significant returns on her expenditure.

## Mary Lou Gallup

Mary Lou Gallup, in contrast, did not. With as much social capital as McMartin, including a graduate degree, a regional reputation as an educator, and a robust network of family, friends, coreligionists, and colleagues, Gallup owned and ran a chain of profitable Christian day care centers in mid-Oregon. In 1987, Gallup's husband and adult son were indicted on sexual abuse charges involving seven different children who alleged they had been fondled or sodomized. Suspecting "another McMartin," investigators and social workers interrogated other enrollees of the centers. Within a matter of months, not only had the number of victims increased to 100, but their allegations had become increasingly bizarre. The children described sexual abuse in satanic ceremonies that included animal sacrifices, murders, and the forced ingestion of "pee punch," a concoction of urine and fruit juice. And they eventually identified Gallup, then 61 years old, as one of their abusers.

Because she was alleged to have participated in the satanic ritual abuse, Gallup's perceived threat to the social and moral order was high. Moral entrepreneurs and the media were well apprised of her social capital since she had already spent a great deal of it in the vigorous and public defense of her husband and son, and she had built up a rather formidable reputation in doing so (Leeson 1989). She had allied herself with an aggressive grassroots organization, Victims of Child Abuse Laws (VOCAL), comprising parents and others who claim they were victims of false allegations of child abuse. Critical of the very kind of investigative and interview techniques of agents of what it referred to as the "child abuse industry" that resulted in Gallup's arrest, VOCAL was gaining momentum as a countermovement to the burgeoning satanic ritual abuse moral panic (Thousand Friends of Gallup).

Gallup was articulate, outspoken and well versed in the critical language of VOCAL, thus to both silence her and undermine her credibility, moral entrepreneurs and the media pathologized her. They discursively transformed her into the sort of figure Watney (1987) would term a "monstrous representation," by continuously repeating the appalling nature of the charges against her, speculating about the number of still unidentified victims, and repeating rumors, which were as abundant in this case as any other, as facts. The local media, in fact, were so single-minded on this strategy of pathologizing that their pretrial coverage of the case forced a change of venue for Gallup's criminal trail (*Oregon v. Gallup* 1991).

Moral entrepreneurs had emerged *en masse* during the McMartin Preschool case and were settling on a vocabulary to make satanic ritual abuse by women providers "culturally intelligible" (Butler 2004: 1). They were cobbling together scraps of information, speculation, rumor, and conjecture to construct profiles of satanic ritually abusive women providers. Through the unrestrained use of such words as "monstrous," "grotesque" and "evil," and the untutored use of such diagnostic terms as "psychopath," "pathological liar" and "pedophile," moral entrepreneurs were fleshing out the monstrous representation in widely cited literature (Finkelhor and Russell 1984, Finkelhor and Williams 1988). In a discursive loop, these terms found their way into media reportage on the Gallup case and then were fed back to moral entrepreneurs as substantiation of their profile, thus reifying the pathological image of women day care providers as satanic ritual abusers, and of Gallup as reflecting it.

Bearing the stigmata of moral and civil discredit, all of Gallup's attempts to recover her reputation, resist her representation, and insist upon her innocence in press conferences and town hall meetings had paradoxical effects. The very possibility that evil had for so long been lurking behind the facade of an otherwise ordinary middle-aged, middle class, devoutly religious woman only made her audiences more fearful and vengeful. Gallup's life was threatened, property she owned was defaced with graffiti that declared her a rapist, and a fire destroyed a vacant home near hers; investigators surmised that the arsonist had mistaken it for her own ("Fire Destroys Vacant House" 1988).

Often the strategy of demonizing via monstrous representation publicly silences supporters and skeptics alike, who fear being tainted by the same brush (Ingebretsen 2001). Organizationally protected by VOCAL, however, Gallup's supporters continued to proclaim her innocence. They wrote letters to the editor of the local newspaper, took out ads in support of Gallup, and filled the courtroom during her trial. All these proclamations of innocence aside, Gallup was convicted of one count of sexual abuse and served one year in prison before her conviction was overturned on a technicality. Because she was never retried on that charge, or any of the others filed against her, she never was afforded the opportunity to challenge her monstrous representation in a court of law.

## Cora Priest

Cora Priest, on the other hand, had low social capital. She was a 62-year-old widow of very modest means, who had been operating her day care center out of her home for years in the small town of Sequim, Washington. Besides caring for young children, as well as the occasional foster child, she also cared for her adult son who had had several run-ins with the law and periods of institutionalization in state mental hospitals. In 1986, Priest and her son were charged with sexually abusing four of the children in her care in bizarre rituals that included slashing animals and infants with knives, and group orgies with strangers in black robes. Despite the serious allegations, Priest, herself, posed a relatively low perceived threat to the social and moral order in that she was accused of being under her mentally ill son's control and therefore unable to stop the satanic ritual abuse, and too frightened to report it (Bizarre Rites 1986).

Priest's case not only challenges conventional notions of agency as active, direct resistance, but also reveals the ways in which even low social capital can be used in agentic action if perceived threat is low. As a widow struggling to make ends meet, embedded in a relationship network that included her family and a small cadre of like-situated friends, and at the mercy of the demands of her mentally ill son, Priest was depicted by moral entrepreneurs, the media, and agents of social control as more victim than observer. This was a representation she either found consistent with her identity or cleverly traded upon to garner widespread support. It opened space for advocacy. Sporting "We Adore Our Cora" buttons, supporters went door-to-door with jam jars to collect money for her defense, and with neither organizational protection nor a vocabulary of counterclaims, such as Gallup had, they awkwardly and somewhat naively questioned the veracity of the allegations and the legitimacy of those making them (Duncan 1987).

Although Priest shied away from opportunities to speak or act on her own behalf, her representation as a victim coupled with naïve grassroots advocacy eventually quieted moral entrepreneurs and agents of social control. It also brought about more restrained and reflexive reportage on her case. News coverage took a dubious turn, dissecting the allegations, criticizing the skills and biases of those who interrogated the children, and quoting experts who were gaining national reputations as skeptics of satanic ritual abuse (Gelernter 1989).

It was that turn from bombastic to cautious claims, from credulity to skepticism that opened more space for contestation and increased the volume of it. In what was taken by both Priest and her supporters as capitulation, all charges against her and her son were dismissed a year after they were filed, and the assistant prosecuting attorney, the most outspoken of the agents of social control, resigned under duress (Duncan 1987). All civil suits against Priest and her son were dismissed years later (*T.T. et al. v. Priest* 1993).

## Frances Ballard

Like Priest, Frances Ballard had low social capital. A visually impaired 55-year-old woman with an eighth-grade education and an annual income at the poverty line, she had a recent history of psychological problems. Although she had never worked outside the home, she took a minimum wage job as an aide at the Georgian Hills Baptist Church day care center in Memphis, Tennessee, when her husband became ill and could no longer work. Unlike Priest, however, Ballard's perceived threat to the social and moral order was high. She was accused of participating in the satanic ritual abuse of children enrolled there, and was arrested in 1984 on multiple counts of aggravated rape. In interviews with police, social workers, and prosecutors, the children alleged that Ballard had sexually abused them in satanic rituals that included baptisms in the name of the devil and the torture of animals. Some of the children alleged that Ballard, who had never even had a driver's license, had flown them to the mountains in a helicopter for orgies with robed and hooded strangers (Berry 1987).

It was a formidable task to demonize such a woman, who was a devout churchgoer, babysitter for neighborhood children, and generous neighbor. Her timidity and reticence, which could easily be mistaken for a lack of intelligence, argued against the kind of diabolical machinations she must have engaged in to perform the acts the children had described. At first, the strategy of moral entrepreneurs, the media, and agents of social control was one of mystifying Ballard, as had been the case with Virginia McMartin. As her trial drew closer, however, and the public demanded answers to why this crime had taken place, they homed in on the single most unflattering aspect of her biography—she had seen a host of doctors over the years for vaginitis and recently had been referred to a psychiatrist who was treating her for depression. This fact, revealed to the news media by an investigator, prompted the strategy of psychologizing Ballard, that is, of finding reasons and motivations for the satanic ritual abuse in what were assumed to be the intrapsychic conflicts and sexual dysfunctions that must have wreaked havoc on her mental stability. That strategy was evident in the prosecutor's opening statement in her trial. "You'll hear children telling you that Frances Ballard talked about needing them to love her because her husband was old and sick," the jury was told. "Ballard has not had normal sexual relations with her husband for more than a year, and by some accounts, six years" (Garrett 1987: A1).

Ballard had her share of defenders; a score of them testified as character witnesses in her trial, but few spoke outside of the courtroom on her behalf. She was convicted in 1987 of one count of sexual abuse and sentenced to five years in prison. But Ballard's case is interesting in that it not only illustrates that *post hoc* advocacy can substitute for the durable network of institutionalized relationships of mutual acquaintance and recognition that are the sum and substance of social capital, but also shows that it can do so without the personal exercise of agency on the part of the folk devil.

In Ballard's case advocacy came after her sentencing and in the form of a series of investigative articles published in the *Commercial Appeal*. The Memphis newspaper had thoroughly and quite credulously covered her case, but in this series, two investigative journalists reported on day care satanic ritual abuse cases across the country. They found that between the McMartin case in 1983 and the Ballard case in 1987, more than a hundred such cases had been investigated, and concluded that in the single-minded pursuit of imaginary satanic ritual abusers, the systems and experts devoted to protecting children had railroaded innocent people and diverted attention and resources from real cases of sexual abuse (Charlier and Downing 1988). It certainly would be an uncommon moral panic that swells and spreads without its share of counterclaims and criticisms such as this (deYoung 2004, McRobbie and Thornton 1995), but the investigative reports illustrate why their impact should not be underestimated or overlooked. On a local level, the reports created a sea change in public opinion about the Ballard case. Citing the reports in its decision, the Appeals Court overturned Ballard's conviction, stating that parents, social workers, investigators and the prosecutor had unduly influenced the nature and content of the children's allegations, and that investigators had improperly destroyed audiotapes of early interviews with some of the children (*State of Tennessee v. Ballard* 1991). On a national level, the investigative reports slowed the day care ritual abuse moral panic; they provided a resource for subsequent reportage on a local level, thus providing a foundation for counterclaims and criticisms (deYoung 2004, Nathan and Snedeker 1995).

## Conclusion

The purpose of this chapter has been to consider the agency of folk devils, and in doing so, to disturb the tranquility of the axiom that folk devils are more acted upon than actors.

It certainly is true that this analysis was facilitated by the fact that the women providers of the day care ritual abuse moral panic were not at the time of their nomination as folk devils, and had never been before, "the Other," that is, the cultural strangers of most moral panic analyses. The fact remains, however, that when their biographies and voices are reclaimed from the hysterically pitched discourse of the moral panic, it is evident that as a group they varied not only in their perceived threat to the social and moral order, but in the amount of social capital they had to expend in the agentic action of resisting their demonization and social control. It is also evident that their exercise of that agency affected the course and outcome of the moral panic, although the effects may have been more local than national in scope.

I proposed at the start of this chapter that if "feisty folk devils" such as these women day care providers were added to the equation of social strains, moral entrepreneurs, media representation, and control culture, the result would be not just be a more analytically enriched approach to moral panic research, but a more nuanced approach to moral panic theory, as well. That assertion is predicated on the fact that the recent renewed interest in moral panics has raised two persistent criticisms about the explanatory power of concepts might be thought of as classical moral panic theory for today's late modern society. While considering the agency of folk devils does not redress these criticisms, it does *address* them and in interesting ways.

First, classical moral panic theory is criticized for its consensual notions of society, notions that by glossing over the "distinctions between the media and the state, the media and public belief, and between the state and other social institutions and groups" (Miller and Kitzinger 1998: 216) almost certainly underestimate the pluralism of late modern society. And it is that pluralism that may open up avenues for folk devils, indeed even already socially marginalized folk devils, to find allies and advocates, build constituencies, and exercise agency. Second, classical moral panic theory is criticized for its determinism, even its *over*-determinism (Critcher 2003). In mapping out the trajectories of moral panics, it is rarely taken into account that the very act of doing so imposes a temporal and logical order that most moral panics never really have. Moral panics ricochet about, lose and gain emotive steam and moral outrage, mutate in response to varying social reactions, achieve some social control ends, and fail to achieve others (deYoung 2004). While much of that erratic trajectory is due to the same features of late modern society that classical moral panic theory often underanalyzes—the conflicting interests, the inconsistent claims, the contradictory media representations, the plurality of social reactions—some of it may well be due to folk devils' expenditures of social capital in agentic actions. That exercise of agency may end up altering the strategies of moral entrepreneurs and the media to demonize them, and may thwart their continuous and concerted efforts to continue demonizing them during the course of the moral panic.

Many critics agree that moral panic theory is "deeply in need of revisiting and revamping" (McRobbie 1994: 198) to retain its explanatory power in late modern society. Considering the agency of folk devils is but one avenue for doing just that.

# References

Altheide, D.L. 2006. *Terrorism and the Politics of Fear*. Lanham: AltaMira Press.

Armstrong, E.G. 2007. Moral panic over meth. *Contemporary Justice Review*, 10(4), 427–42.

Arnold, R. and Decker, C. 1984. McMartin case: a community divided. *Los Angeles Times*, April 29, A1, A3, A17, A18.

Bauman, Z. 2001. *Community: Seeking Safety in an Insecure World*. Cambridge: Polity Press.

Begging for Answers 1986. Editorial, *Los Angeles Times*, January 2, B4.

Ben-Yehuda, N. 1980. The European witch craze of the 14th to 17th centuries: a sociological perspective. *American Journal of Sociology*, 86(1), 1–31.

Berry, M. 1987. Charges dropped in sex abuse trial. *United Press International News Wire*, April 24.

Bizarre rites at day-care center alleged 1986. *Seattle Post-Intelligencer*, September 15, D1.

Bourdieu, P. and Wacquant, L. 1992. *An Invitation to Reflexive Sociology*. Chicago: University of Chicago Press.

Butler, Judith. 2004. *Undoing Gender*. London: Routledge.

Charlier, T. and Downing, S. 1988. Justice abused: a 1980s witch-hunt. Series. *The Commercial Appeal*, January.

Cohen, S. 1972. *Folk Devils and Moral Panics: The Creation of the Mods and Rockers*. London: MacGibbon and Kee.

Critcher, C. 2003. *Moral Panics and the Media*. Issues in Cultural and Media Studies. Buckingham: Open University Press.

Critcher, C. (ed.). 2010 (2006). *Critical Readings: Moral Panics and the Media*. Issues in Cultural and Media Studies. 2nd Edition. Maidenhead: Open University Press.

deYoung, M. 1997. The Devil goes to day care: McMartin and the making of a moral panic. *Journal of American Culture*, 20(1), 19–25.

deYoung, M. 2004. *The Day Care Ritual Abuse Moral Panic*. Jefferson: McFarland.

deYoung, M. 2007. Two decades after McMartin: a follow-up of 22 convicted day care employees. *Journal of Sociology and Social Welfare*, 34(4), 9–33.

deYoung, M. 2008. "The Devil's walking parody": A follow-up of 12 convicted women day care providers. *Contemporary Issues in Criminology and the Social Sciences*, 2(1), 33–59.

Duncan, D. 1987. Mother vows to clear family name. *Seattle Times*, May 3, B1.

Finkelhor, D., and Russell, D.E.H. 1984. Women as perpetrators: Review of the evidence, in *Child Sexual Abuse: New Theory and Research*, edited by D. Finkelhor. Beverly Hills: Sage Publications, 171–87.

Finkelhor, D. and Williams, L. 1988. *Nursery Crimes: Sexual Abuse in Day Care.* Newbury Park: Sage Publications.

1998. Fire destroys vacant house 1988. *United Press International Newswire*, September 23.

Garrett, C. 1987. Love needs called key in sex trial. *Commercial Appeal*, October 29, A1, A8.

Gelernter, C.Q. 1989. A conspiracy of evil? *Seattle Times*, February 19, JI.

Goode, E. 1990. The American drug panic of the 1980s: social construction or objective threat? *International Journal of the Addictions*, 25(9), 1083–98.

Hall, S., Critcher, C., Jefferson, T., Clarke, J., and Robertson, B. 1978. *Policing the Crisis: Mugging, the State and Law and Order*. Critical Social Studies. Houndmills: Palgrave Macmillan.

Ingebretsen, E. 2001. *At Stake: Monsters and the Rhetoric of Fear in Public Culture.* Chicago: University of Chicago Press.

Jenkins, P. 1999. *Synthetic Panic: The Symbolic Politics of Designer Drugs*. New York: New York University Press.

Leeson, F. 1989. Gallup testifies in sex abuse trial. *Oregonian*, October 27, D10.

Lin, N. 2001. *Social Capital: A Theory of Social Structure and Action*. Cambridge: Cambridge University Press.

McGraw, C. 1991. McMartin figure wins $1 in civil trial. *Los Angeles Times*, May 8, B1.

McRobbie, A. 1994. *Postmodernism and Popular Culture*. London: Routledge.

McRobbie, A., and Thornton, S.L. 1995. Re-thinking "moral panic" for multi-mediated social worlds. *British Journal of Sociology*, 46(4), 559–74.

Miller, D. and Kitzinger, J. 1980. AIDS, the policy process and moral panics, in *The Circuit of Mass Communication: Media Strategies, Representation and Audience Reception in the AIDS Crisis*, edited by D. Miller, J. Kitzinger, K. Williams, and P. Beharrell. London: Sage Publications, 200–218.

Nathan, D. and Snedeker, M. 1995. *Satan's Silence: Ritual Abuse and the Making of Modern American Witch Hunt*. New York: Basic Books.

Oliver, M. 1995. Preschool founder Virginia McMartin dies. *Los Angeles Times*, December 19, A1.

*Oregon v. Gallup* 108 Ore. App. 508; 816 P.2d 669; 1991 Ore App. LEXIS 1266.

Ortiz, A.T. and Briggs, L. 2003. The culture of poverty, crack babies, and welfare cheats: the making of the healthy white baby crisis. *Social Text*, 21(3), 39–57.

Ost, S. 2002. Children at risk: legal and social perceptions of the potential threat that possession of child pornography poses to society. *Journal of Law and Society*, 29(3), 436–60.

Rohrlich, T. and Welkos, R. 1984. Shock follows McMartin arrest. *Los Angeles Times*, March 28, B1, B4.

Rothe, D.L. and Muzzatti, S. 2004. Enemies everywhere: terrorism, moral panic, and US civil society. *Critical Criminology*, 12(3), 327–50.

Sandywell, B. 2006. Monsters in cyberspace: cyberphobia and cultural panic in the information age. *Information, Communication and Society*, 9(1), 39–61.

Shaw, D. 1990a. Where was the skepticism in the media? Pack journalism and hysteria marked early coverage of the McMartin case. *Los Angeles Times*, January 19, A1, A20–A21.

Shaw, D. 1990b. Reporter's early exclusive triggered a media frenzy. *Los Angeles Times*, January 20, A1.

Shaw, D. 1990c. McMartin coverage was biased, critics charge. *Los Angeles Times*, January 22, A1, A20.

Shepard, B. 2007. Sex panic and the welfare state. *Journal of Sociology and Social Welfare*, 34(1), 155–71.

*State of Tennessee vs Frances Lucindy Ballard*. 1991 Tenn. Crim. App. LEXIS 116.

Thompson, K. 1998. *Moral Panics*. Key Ideas. Milton Park: Routledge.

Thousand Friends of Gallup. *Open Letter*. Private Collection of Mary deYoung.

*T.R. et al. v. Priest* 1993. Court of Appeals of Washington 69 Wn App 106; 847 P 2d 33; 1993.

Watney, S. 1987. *Policing Desire: Pornography, AIDS, and the Media*. London: Methuen.

Welch, M. and Schuster, L. 2005. Detention of asylum-seekers in the US, UK, France, Germany, and Italy. *Criminology and Criminal Justice*, 5(4), 331–55.

# PART III
# MEDIA PANICS

# Overview of Part III

Upon their introduction to the public, new entertainment and information media have repeatedly been met with moral panics over their corrupting influences on their first widely recognized audiences as well as on their disruptive consequences for society. In late modern societies, the working class, criminals and individuals broadly classified as delinquent or deviant, women, immigrants, members of racial and ethnic minorities, and especially children and youth have acted as folk devils, symbolic victims, or sometimes both during moral panics over new media.

Commenting on the alarmist discourses that alerted the public to the widely predicted harmful effects of VCR and videos on print media, children and youth, and whole societies when it made its commercial debut in industrialized countries in the early 1980s, media studies scholar Kristen Drotner (1992) coined the term "media panic" to describe this phenomenon. In her essay, "Modernity and Media Panics," originally published in the edited collection, *Media Cultures: Reappraising Transnational Media*, Drotner writes,

> The reaction to video has clear historical antecedents. From the advent of mass-circulation fiction and magazines to film and television, comics and cartoons, the introduction of a new mass medium causes strong public reactions whose repetitiveness is as predictable as the fervour with which they are brought forward. Adult experts—teachers and social workers, cultural critics and politicians—define the new mass medium as a social, psychological, or moral threat to the young (or mixtures of the three), and appoint themselves as public trouble shooters. Legal and educational measures are then imposed, and the interest lessens—until the advent of a new mass medium reopens public discussion. That spiralling motion characterizes a *media panic*. (Drotner 1992: 43, emphasis in original)

Drotner emphasizes the repetitive character of media panics. New media are seen by adults as undermining established institutions for the education of children. Expert discourses warn of the threat posed and new legal and educational measures are imposed. Adult control is extended over children's use of the new medium, and the medium itself is integrated into mainstream discourses. Then, a new medium is introduced and the next media panic begins.

Historian John Springhall's *Youth, Popular Culture, and Moral Panics: Penny Gaffs to Gangsta-Rap* (1998) reminds us that all media once began as new media. He remarks that in the United States and Britain, the introduction of a new, cheap cultural medium has repeatedly been greeted with a moral panic over its corrupting influence on the young. He writes,

> Socially, media panics attempt to re-establish the generational *status quo*, culturally they act to prevent the undermining of the cultural elite as a critical force, hence their advocacy by librarians, teachers and literary critics. Media panics have been called 'cultural seismographs' that reveal the broader problems of modernity, acting as a tacit or explicit social regulation through cultural enlightenment of the young, who are panic targets because they represent experiences and emotions irrevocably lost to adults… .
>
> At least since the 1830s, if not before, each time British or American society has found itself in confusion or crisis, often because of perceived rises in juvenile crime, there have been attempts to shift blame for social breakdown onto the entertainment forms of the age: penny theatres, 'penny dreadfuls', dime novels, gangster films, 'horror comics', television, 'video nasties', and now video games have each in turn played the role of 'folk devils' which *must* be causing delinquency. A belief that the young can somehow be weaned away from the newest media craze on offer suffers from a profound historical amnesia. Media or moral panics often tell us a great deal more about adult anxieties—fear of the future, of technological change, and the erosion of moral absolutes—than about the nature of juvenile misbehavior. Attacks on the influence of the media thereby act to conceal social uncertainties, such as a fear of the new technology that amuses the young but is beyond our adult capacity to comprehend ('computer games have not lodged themselves in the affections of the older generation'). (160–61, emphasis in original)

Like Drotner, Springhall highlights the repetitive nature of media panics, though he goes much further in detailing the shared and individual aspects of each new episode. For Springhall, moral panics over new media's effects on the young express adults' concerns about the future, technological advancements, and moral decline, which become centered on young people, who seem to understand new media better than their elders and can therefore amuse themselves outside adults' capacity to surveil and regulate their activities.

In "Dangerous Media? Panic Discourses and the Dilemmas of Modernity" (1999), Kristen Drotner returns to the subject of media panics, contending that the children and youth who are supposedly victimized by new media provide a symbolic battlefield for adults' negotiation of the conflict between individualism and social norms, and between continuity and change, inherent in the competitive capitalism of modernity. Drotner (611–12) relates,

Children and young people are continuously defined as objects—and often vulnerable victims—in the panics. This leads to the ... assumption that deals with the relation between culture and social psychology. According to this assumption, cultural development and human development are aspects of one and the same process. Children's cultural edification is part of, indeed proof of, their social elevation. Therefore their cultural fare must be guarded, watched over and protected because its composition is vital for their mental growth. Following this logic, if adults watch *Oprah Winfrey* or *Melrose Place* every week, then their humaneness is gradually undermined. But if children watch the same programmes every week, then they never even get a chance to develop this humaneness. Culture is seen as a civilizing force for better or worse... . Historically, this fusion of cultural and mental development is shaped by the fundamental importance played by general character formation in the development of modernity.

Modernisation is a dynamic process founded on a capitalist competition for profit. The economic and social upheavals of secularisation, industrialisation and urbanisation have as their corollary profound transformations of cultural symbols, experiences and expressions, transformations that together may be termed modernity. Some traditions and qualifications are rendered obsolete, others become increasingly important, and people are constantly engaged in interpreting this complex constellation of continuity and change. While actual experiences naturally vary according to age and gender, ethnicity and region, everybody must learn the fundamental lesson of modernity: to live with the possibility of social, cultural, and psychological change—to face the possibility of difference from others and from previous manners and mores. Modernity fosters individuality as a social norm.

To adults, young audiences for new media seem able to change in order to keep pace with the future in a way no longer possible for most adults. Freer to diverge from pre-existing moral norms, youth, in their relationships to new media, seem able to evolve into the individuals among other, but similar individuals nurtured by modernity, and thus outpace adults in feeling at ease in the world of the future. Importantly, Drotner points out the common assumption that "cultural development and human development are aspects of one and the same process," that is, that children and youth are widely seen as constructed by new media. Media panics, then, seek to control new media in order to control children's development as embodiments of modernization, of the endurance of capitalism, and of the future.

## Media Panics

Sharing significant concerns with Drotner and Springhall, the authors of the three succeeding chapters examine media panics in relation to the construction of social identities as well as that of communities and societies. In chapter nine, "From Nickel Madness to the House of Dreams: Moral Panic and the Emergence of American Cinema," Charles Krinsky takes a look back at the dawn of American movie history and finds that the film industry's responses to moral panics over the new medium helped make motion pictures and moviegoing a central element in the nation's daily life. To defend themselves against the condemnations of clergy, progressive reformers, and other crusaders, to distinguish themselves from other cheap forms of entertainment then under attack (for example, saloons and cheap vaudeville houses), and to compete with imported films that seemed risqué to some observers, movie executives supported a measure of outside regulation of movie content, created films intended for family audiences, and produced motion pictures with religious, historical, and recognizably American themes. As a result, a new medium at the center of a series of moral panics became a widely accepted form of popular entertainment.

Chapter ten, "Sexual Predators, Internet Addiction, and Other Media Myths: Moral Panic and the Disappearance of Brandon Crisp," by Patricia Molloy, examines the media-fueled moral panic that occurred in fall 2008 because of a rumor that a sexual predator lured away Brandon Crisp, a teenager in Ontario, Canada, following an argument between the boy and his parents about the time he was spending on the Internet playing *Call of Duty 4*. The chapter suggests that a perpetual discourse of danger governs both mass mediated and parental understandings of young people, envisioning them as particularly vulnerable to the supposed harm wrought by exposure to media, popular culture and technology. Specifically, the moral panic over the disappearance and subsequent death of Brandon Crisp was fueled simultaneously by two popular discourses, one of addiction and one of fear of sexual predation, both of which are also disseminated without reference to media consumption,, but which intensify when they become associated with young people's use of media and Internet technologies.

Besides examining mass media accounts of the Brandon Crisp tragedy, Molloy looks at responses to the events leading up to his disappearance within the online gaming community. Underpinning each account is a metadiscourse of blame about the ultimate cause of Crisp's death and who should be responsible for preventing further tragedies. While notions of negative media effects still hold sway in popular discourses, particularly those about the effects of violent content on young psyches, Molloy finds an absence in such discourses of any consideration of the culture of militarized masculinity within which first-person shooter games such as *Call of Duty* were developed and continue to thrive.

In chapter 11, "My Moral Panic: Adolescents, Social Networking, and Child Sex Crime Panic," authors Samantha A. Smith and Simon A. Cole describe the social networking moral panic that erupted for a brief time during the middle of the first decade of the twenty-first century. This moral panic expressed concern that the skyrocketing popularity of social networking technology among teenagers facilitated the activities of pedophilic sexual predators. The chapter argues that this was not an independent moral panic, but a technological strand of the larger child sex crime panic noted by a number of researchers, a strand that the authors call the "emerging technology child sex crime panic." The chapter goes on to address the divergent responses to the panic of two major online social networks, MySpace and Facebook. It suggests that Facebook offered the more adept response from a public relations viewpoint and even benefited from the moral panics, gaining market share. The chapter concludes with the finding that the short-lived social networking moral panic was superseded by concerns over newer practices, such as sexting and tweeting, facilitated by teenagers' use of smartphones.

# References

Drotner, K. 1992. Modernity and media panics, in *Media Cultures: Reappraising Transnational Media*, edited by M. Skovmand and K.M. Schrøder. London: Routledge, 42–64.

Drotner, K. 1999. Dangerous media? Panic discourses and the dilemmas of modernity. *Paedagogica Historica*, 35(3), 593–619.

Springhall, J. 1998. *Youth, Popular Culture, and Moral Panics: Penny Gaffs to Gangsta-Rap, 1830–1996*. New York: St. Martin's Press.

# From Nickel Madness to the House of Dreams: Moral Panic and the Emergence of American Cinema

## Charles Krinsky

Anyone coming to the subject for the first time might be forgiven for concluding that, at least in the United States, the silent movie era consisted of an unbroken series of moral panics over motion pictures' supposedly harmful effects on audiences, communities, and the nation. Indeed, the story of moral panics' influence on American cinema reaches all the way back to the prehistory of the medium. If only because they were so frequent, studying moral panics over early movies can provide significant insight into the construction and evolution of moral panics in general. Moreover, because their impact was often decisive, researching such episodes can add sizably to existing knowledge about social, cultural, and state influences on the content of early motion pictures and the structure of the emerging film industry.

## And There Was Light

On April 23, 1896 the first technologically and commercially successful projection of motion pictures onto a canvas screen took place as part of a vaudeville show at Koster and Bial's Music Hall in Manhattan. The next day, *The New York Times* announced, "Edison's Vitascope Cheered" (Musser 2002: 25 n.12). In reality, despite the credit given the famed inventor, the projector used was the creation of Charles Francis Jenkins and Thomas Armat, working entirely independently of Edison. After buying out Jenkins (who went on to become an inventor of mechanical television), Armat and his backers, Norman Raff and Frank Gammon, reached an agreement with Edison to market the invention as "Edison's Vitascope" (Musser

2002: 14). Armat served as projectionist for the first public movie screening (Musser 2002: 14). The large audience was treated to six views, lasting about 20 seconds each, including a humorous boxing match from Ivan Caryll and Gustave Kerker's successful burlesque, *Little Christopher*, and an excerpt from Charles H. Hoyt's hit musical farce comedy, *A Milk White Flag*. (Musser 2002: 15–16).

This enthusiastically received exhibition of projected motion pictures was not, however, the earliest successful public showing of filmed moving images. The kinetoscope, invented by Thomas Edison and members of his staff including W.K.L. (William Kennedy Laurie) Dickson and William Heise, was designed so that scenes could be viewed by individuals looking through a peephole located near the top of the cabinet that housed the invention's workings (Musser 2002: 13). The device's commercial debut took place when the Holland Brothers' kinetoscope parlor opened its doors on April 14 1894 at 1155 Broadway in Manhattan (Hendricks 1966: 56–7). The premises featured ten kinetoscope machines, each showing a different film, arranged in two rows of five machines each. Customers could view all the films in one row for 25 cents and for 50 cents could watch every one in both rows. Interestingly, before their involvement with the Vitascope, Raff and Gammon gained experience in the movie business as pioneering marketers of Edison's kinetoscope machines and views (Musser 1990: 81).

In an episode that adumbrated moral panics soon to emerge, about three months after the Holland Brothers' establishment debuted, *The Newark Evening News* of July 17 1894 reported on a visit paid by State Senator James A. Bradley and Asbury Park Mayor Franklin L. Ten Broeck (both Republican) to a kinetoscope parlor in New Jersey on its opening day:

> Founder Bradley [who, besides being a state senator, was also the developer of Asbury Park, the seaside resort town where Ten Broeck served as mayor] said he would have to look at the pictures to see if they were proper views for the people sojourning in the twin cities by the sea to witness without causing blushes to mount to their cheeks. ... on the night of the day Founder Bradley and Mayor Ten Broeck went to the pavilion and proceeded to pass judgement on the pictures that Inventor Edison had so carefully prepared. The first picture shown the Senator and Mayor was that of the barroom and fight, and it was decided that the supremacy of the law over the rougher element had a good moral tone ... . (quoted in Hendricks 1966: 77, ellipsis in original)

If the senator was satisfied that the barroom brawl scene emphasized the triumph of good over evil, the next picture that he saw elicited a strikingly different reaction:

> The view was that of Carmencita in her famous butterfly dance, and the Senator watched the graceful gyrations of the lovely Spanish dancer with interest that was ill-concealed. But near the end of the series of pictures the Spanish beauty gives the least little bit of a kick,

which raises her silken draperies so her well-turned ankles peep out
and there is a background of white lace.
That kick settled it. (quoted in Hendricks 1966: 77–8)

Bradley informed the unnamed exhibitor that he must substitute a different scene
for Carmencita's dance, a decision with which Ten Broeck predictably concurred.
The exhibitor hurriedly replaced Carmencita with *The Boxing Cats (Prof. Welton's)*,
which starred two felines wearing tiny boxing gloves and scrapping with
one another (with their manager "Prof." Henry Welton egging them on in the
background). Assumedly, for some customers images of two cats forced to stand
unsteadily on their hind legs flailing at one another were far more disquieting than
Carmencita's decorous dance. Bradley's and Ten Broeck's tolerance of a bar fight
and disapproval of Carmencita's movements suggest that, as would so often be the
case in the future, violence was from the first more palatable to censors than sex.

# The Nickelodeon Boom

On June 19 1905 Harry Davis, Pittsburgh, Pennsylvania's leading operator of
vaudeville theaters, opened a storefront venue for movie exhibition on Smithfield
Street, calling it the Nickelodeon (not yet a generic term) (Musser 1990: 418). As
film historian Charles Musser (1990) states, "The significance of this theater was
not that it was some official 'first' but that it was to some degree responsible for the
rapid proliferation of theaters across the United States" (418). Later the same year,
Davis opened the first movie theater in Philadelphia. Early in 1906, he opened the
first one in Rochester, New York, as well. Davis went on to open movie theaters
in Buffalo, New York, Cleveland, Ohio, and Toledo, Ohio. By March 1907, Davis's
growing nickelodeon circuit comprised about 24 theaters in various cities (Musser
1990: 421, Abel 1999: 50, 214 n.16).

Earlier, projected motion pictures had been exhibited, often as accompaniment
to live presentations, in a wide variety of locations, including lecture halls, burlesque
houses, penny arcades, beer halls, civic opera houses and auditoriums, and dime
museums as well as storefront theaters. After Davis's early success (he was to suffer
business setbacks), new storefront theaters showing continuous bills of movies and
song slides for five or ten cents sprouted with unprecedented speed (Musser 1990:
418, 421). In May 1907, an article published in the weekly trade paper *The Moving
Picture World* estimated that there were between 2,500 and 3,000 nickelodeons in
the United States (Abel 1999: 50, 214n18). In January 1908, a story in *Views and
Films Index*, another trade weekly, boasted that as of the previous spring the motion
picture industry had attained record prosperity (Abel 1999: 50, 213 n.14).

That nickelodeons hugely boosted the popularity of movies caught the attention
of civic leaders as well as the film industry. Facing the knowledge that "the cinema
was rapidly becoming a site of mass entertainment and mass consumption"
(Musser 1990: 433):

> Established community leaders didn't know what to think about the
> change except to know that they did not control it. Some thought it
> should be abolished, others were more laissez-faire. A few embraced
> it, but many thought it needed to be reformed. Film fires proved
> that they were dangerous, but there was even more concern with the
> way the collective though intimate experience of the screen could
> change—and from a certain viewpoint corrupt—the consciousness
> of its devotees. The nickelodeons inaugurated an era in which the
> "movies," as they came to be called, were seen in a new light. (Musser
> 1990: 447)

As they proliferated, flourishing outside their sphere of influence, some community
leaders welcomed, but many more disparaged nickelodeons. Not least among the
dangers that reformers associated with nickel theaters was the power of movies
and moviegoing to create new (and, as many thought, corrupt) shared identities.
As a result of the increased popularity, attention, and concern brought about by
nickelodeons, movies had come to occupy a central and contentious place in the
public imagination.


## Moral Panic

Early remarked upon in print by Jock Young in 1971 and gaining wider currency
with the publication of Stanley Cohen's *Folk Devils and Moral Panics: The Creation of
the Mods and Rockers* the next year, moral panic would in time become an influential
but highly contentious concept in academic fields ranging from media studies to the
sociology of childhood. Cohen's (2002: 1) book begins with the thought-provoking
definition:

> Societies appear to be subject, every now and then, to periods of moral
> panic. A condition, episode, person or group of persons emerges to
> become defined as a threat to societal values and interests; its nature
> is presented in a stylized and stereotypical fashion by the mass media;
> the moral barricades are manned by editors, bishops, politicians and
> other right-thinking people; socially accredited experts pronounce
> their diagnoses and solutions; ways of coping are evolved or (more
> often) resorted to; the condition then disappears, submerges or
> deteriorates and becomes more visible.

Often expedited by sensationalized media coverage, a group, event, or behavior
thought to pose a threat to social order comes to the public's attention. Acknowledged
experts issue pronouncements and sometimes initiate laws and policies designed
both to define and to combat the menace. As a moral panic abates, the deeper social
problems that it obscures can come into focus.

In 1978, the concept of moral panic was further developed in *Policing the Crisis: Mugging, the State, and Law and Order*, written by British sociologists Stuart Hall, Chas Critcher, Tony Jefferson, John Clarke, and Brian Roberts. Besides being a painstaking study of a British moral panic over mugging (allegedly only recently imported to Britain from the United States), this work amounts to a book-length anatomization of the idea. Building on Cohen's definition, Hall et al. (1978: 16, emphasis in original) offer a concise guide to recognizing when one might be under way:

> When the official reaction to a person, groups of persons or series of events is *out of all proportion* to the actual threat offered, when 'experts,' in the form of police chiefs, the judiciary, politicians and editors *perceive* the threat in all but identical terms, and appear to talk 'with one voice' of rates, prognoses and solutions, when the media representations universally stress 'sudden and dramatic' increases (in numbers involved or events) and 'novelty', above and beyond that which a sober, realistic appraisal could sustain, then we believe it is appropriate to speak of the beginnings of a *moral panic*.

Media, state agencies, and community institutions act as one to identify and fight an apparent social menace. Exaggerating its perils, and sharing a single perspective, experts declare that an unexampled and unpredicted menace threatens social order.

While contending that they were especially prominent in moral panics of the early 1960s, Hall et al. point out several elements that also structured moral panics over early films. They observe,

> There is a tendency, in the early years of our period, for there to develop a succession of 'moral panics' around certain key topics of controversial public concern. In this early period, the panics tend to be centred on social and moral rather than political issues (youth, permissiveness, crime). Their typical form is that of a dramatic event which focuses and triggers a local response and public disquiet. Often as a result of local organising and moral entrepreneurship, the wider powers of the control culture are both alerted (the media play a crucial role here) and mobilised (the police, the courts). This issue is seen as 'symptomatic' of wider, more troubling but less concrete themes. (Hall et al. 1978: 221)

Hall et al. describe a series of localized moral panics arising from heightened civic concern, likely prompted by a specific event, over a perceived social or moral problem rather than over laws or public policies. Frequently, community activism, abetted by sensationalistic media coverage, widens the scope of the moral panic, mobilizing powerful elites to identify, combat, and control the ostensible menace. Experts, government officials, grassroots organizers, and the public all view the particular issue arousing their fears as but one manifestation of a pervasive, terrifying, and inscrutable problem.

## Moral Panic in Chicago

### The Uplift 5 Cent Theater

In 1889, Jane Addams and her friend and probable lover Ellen Gates Starr cofounded Chicago's Hull-House, the first settlement house in the United States. Like other progressive social reformers, Addams viewed delinquency and criminality as the products of environment rather than heredity. According to film historian J.A. Lindstrom (1999: 94, see also Addams 1909: 6), referencing Addams's biographer Daniel Levine, "Addams and other Hull House residents 'implicitly assumed that crime, like poverty, was a symptom of a misconstructed environment, not of individual character weakness.' One aspect of this 'misconstructed environment' was 'organizing work and failing to organize play.'"

Among Addams's notable efforts in organizing play was hosting a five-cent theater at Hull-House, an experiment undertaken in a spirit of reform that both accepted the arrival of moving pictures and sought to raise their moral stature. According to an article entitled "A Clean Nickelodeon" published in *The Moving Picture World* of June 1, 1907, the same day that the Hull-House nickel theater opened:

> We observe that Chicago reformers, headed by Miss Jane Addams, are going to show the proprietors of nickelodeons how to give a clean exhibition. The whole plan was outlined at a meeting of the City Club, the object being to purify and elevate the five-cent theater, which one of the speakers declared "was an institution come to stay." "It is all right and all it needs is to be regulated." The project received the blessings of the Bench and the Church. We will watch the progress of the venture and wish it all success. But the pity of the whole matter is, that a great and growing industry like this needs such an example and so severe a public reprimand as the above action is, and hope the lesson will not be lost, although we think to make it effective the new venture should keep the Sunday exhibitions out of its programme. (198)

The author of the article pointedly characterizes the reformers' attempt to "purify and elevate the five-cent theater" as a "reprimand," one that it would be well to reinforce by keeping "the Sunday exhibitions out of its programme." Parenthetically, it may have been a bit premeditated that "the blessings of the Bench and the Church" were sought and received on the premises of the City Club, a Chicago civic organization that was then in the process of investigating "conditions in that city, relating to the penny arcade and the cheap theater," as well as movie exhibition, examining their effects on the lives of men and boys ("Trade Notes" 1907a: 263).

Three thousand invitations went out to members of the various Hull-House clubs announcing the new venture, with the movie shows running from 3:00 pm to 10:00 pm daily including Sundays, regardless of *The Moving Picture World*'s expressed desire ("Hull-House 5-Cent Theatre" 1907: 35). The moving picture theater operated under the supervision of Dr. Gertrude Howe Britton, who, besides being a longtime member and sometime resident of Hull-House, served as superintendent of a local nonprofit organization called the Juvenile Court Committee, which was conducting investigations of Chicago movie houses at the time (Lindstrom 1999: 99). The projector was a gift of William Selig's Selig Polyscope Company, while the films were donated by Selig's competitor, Carl Laemmle, of the Independent Moving Picture Company (IMP), a charitable gesture that Laemmle lauded in his own advertising (Lindstrom 1999: 95). Hull-House staff chose the films to be shown, making their decisions with an eye to both entertaining and educating their audiences. As the 1906–7 *Hull-House Yearbook* recounts,

> The management were able to select films of fairy stories which delighted the children; foreign scenes which filled our Italian and Greek neighbors with homely reminiscences, dramatizations of great moral lessons contained in such stories as Uncle Tom's Cabin and Jean Val Jean, modern heroism as portrayed by the firemen and the life-saving corps, as well as that multitude of simpler domestic scenes which fascinate the spectator through their very familiarity because they reveal an inner beauty he has not suspected before. (35)

Revealingly, staffers were not above promoting the "great moral lessons" on view in their movie theater with old-fashioned plugging just outside its doors. As *The Moving Picture World* reported, "Early in the evening, while Halstead street was crowded with Sunday evening sightseers, a leather lunged 'barker', a negro, stepped out in front of the uplift 5 cent theater and began to describe the wonders of 'Uncle Tom's Cabin' as set forth in motion pictures" ("Trade Notes" 1907b: 278). The wording used by *The Moving Picture World* is suggestive, "uplift" being a favored term for Progressive Era reformers (see, for example, "Trade Notes" 1907c, "More about 'Uplift'" 1909).

Because of hot weather, the Hull-House movie theater closed a little more than two weeks after it opened. While the level of popularity it enjoyed in the meantime remains an open question (see McCarthy 1976, Lindstrom 1999), Hull-House staffers clearly counted the endeavor a success. The 1906–7 *Hull-House Year Book*'s (35, also quoted in Lindstrom 1999: 95) report on the experiment closed with this prediction:

> It is unfortunate that the Five-Cent Theatre has become associated in the public mind with the lurid and unworthy. Our experience at Hull-House has left no doubt in our minds that in time moving pictures will be utilized quite as the stereopticon is at present, for all purposes of entertainment and education, and that schools and churches will count the films as among their most valuable equipment.

Their experience with moving picture exhibition had convinced the theater's management that the movies offered both entertainment and instruction, would be useful to church and school, and were certain to become a universal cultural medium. While the *Year Book*'s forecast for the new medium was rosy, however, it offered a prophecy of future advancements more than an assessment of present accomplishments, and the presumption remained that motion pictures were yet to fulfill their calling.

## Municipal Censorship

In November 1907, just months after the Hull-House experiment ended and only about two years after Chicago's first nickel theater opened for business, the City Council passed an ordinance requiring permits for the exhibition of movies (McCarthy 1976: 45). Film historian Garth S. Jowett (1989: 63) states,

> On 4 November 1907, after continued pressure from reformers, and the press, the Chicago City Council passed a movie censorship ordinance to be effective November 19th of that year. The ordinance empowered the General Superintendent of Police to issue permits for the exhibition of motion pictures, with the right of appeal to the Mayor, whose final decision was binding. Permits could be refused if in the Superintendent's judgment a film was 'immoral or obscene, or portrays depravity, criminality or lack of virtue of citizens of any race, color, creed or religion and exposes them to contempt, derision or obloquy, or tends to produce a breach of the peace or riots, or purports to represent any hanging, lynching or burning of a human being'.

A local episode of heightened concern over movie morality touched off by reformers and sustained by the press swiftly resulted in changes in municipal policy and law. In practical terms, the new ordinance vested Chicago's superintendent of police, advised by a police board, with authority subordinate only to that of the mayor to ban any movie judged offensive even before its release (McCarthy 1976: 44, Jowett 1989: 63).

The fledgling movie industry promptly mounted a counter-assault that included a lawsuit, *Block v. Chicago*, that came before the Illinois Supreme Court in 1909. The Superintendent of Police had refused to issue permits for two movies, *The James Boys* and *The Night Riders*. Lawyers for the local exhibitor of the films argued that the ordinance was discriminatory (it applied only to movie houses, not the legitimate theater), that it effectively delegated legislative power to the Superintendent of Police, and that it deprived him of his property without due process. Ruling against the exhibitor, the Court decided controlling "obscene and immoral" materials fell within police powers and that the exhibitor held no legitimate property rights in such items (Jowett 1989: 64). The Court also rejected the plaintiff's contention that the ordinance discriminated unfairly against movie exhibitors. On behalf of the Court, Chief Justice James A. Cartwright (quoted in Jowett 1989: 64) declared that the ordinance applied exclusively to movie theaters for good reason, explaining,

> Five and ten cent theaters … on account of the low price of admission, are frequented and patronized by a large number of children, as well as those of limited means who do not attend the productions of plays and dramas given in the regular theatres. The audience includes classes whose age, education and situation in life specially entitle them to protection against an evil influence of obscene and immoral representations.

In the Court's view, nickelodeons represented a special case, distinct from other entertainments, because their audiences, comprising large numbers of children, the poor, and the uneducated attracted by low entrance fees, needed extra protection from evil influences. In 1915, the US Supreme Court upheld the Illinois high court's decision (McCarthy 1976: 45) The 1907 ordinance was not repealed until 1961 (Jowett 1989: 63).

## The House of Dreams

Though mention of the Hull-House movie theater can be found nowhere in its pages, the same conflicting attitude toward motion pictures that accompanied that experiment also informs Addams's "The House of Dreams," a chapter in her *The Spirit of Youth and the City Streets* (1909) dedicated to a discussion of urban youth's involvement with the new medium. Perhaps signaling her recognition that nickelodeons were already a fixture of American city life or, just as likely, implying that both amusements were of equally dubious social value, throughout the chapter Addams treats movies and live drama of the cheaper variety as essentially one medium. In any case, and regardless of Addams's ambivalence concerning pictures' social and moral value, "The House of Dreams" begins on a decidedly positive note. Early in the chapter, Addams (1909: 75–6) declares,

> 'Going to the show' for thousands of young people in every industrial city is the only possible road to the realms of mystery and romance; the theater is the only place where they can satisfy that craving for a conception of life higher than that which the actual world offers them. In a very real sense the drama and the drama alone performs for them the office of art as is clearly revealed in their blundering demand stated in many forms for 'a play unlike life'." The theater becomes to them a 'veritable house of dreams' infinitely more real than the noisy streets and the crowded factories.

Addams describes plays and movies as almost literally transporting urban youth from the industrial cities that would otherwise condemn them to futures of crime and delinquency to, through movie fantasies, a glimpse of a better life.

As the chapter progresses, though, Addams (1909: 86) determines that the dreams on offer at nickel theaters are for the most part uninspiring:

> The room which contains the mimic stage is small and cozy, and less formal than the regular theater, and there is much more gossip and social life as if the foyer and pit were mingled. The very darkness of the room, necessary for an exhibition of the films, is an added attraction to many young people, for whom the space is filled with the glamour of love making.
>
> Hundreds of young people attend these five-cent theaters every evening in the week, including Sunday, and what is seen and heard there becomes the sole topic of conversation, forming the ground pattern of their social life. That mutual understanding which in another social circle is provided by books, travel and all the arts, is here compressed into the topics suggested by the play.

Even the interior architecture of nickelodeons encourages young moviegoers to remain focused on gossip, pleasure, and lovemaking. Unlike literature, travel, or the fine arts, moving pictures limit rather than expand young people's imaginations, inspiring them to dwell solely on the dreams on offer at nickelodeons. In case her rundown of the social and spiritual ills associated with movies should prove inadequate in itself, and ignoring the policies followed by the Hull-House five-cent theater, Addams also takes a glancing shot at nickelodeon operators for conducting business on Sundays.

Despite her many doubts, in the end Addams gives the movies her (provisional) blessing. She predicts hopefully that, stimulated by the dreams formed in movie houses, the children of today's immigrants, will grow up to compose a culturally varied and vibrant urban America:

> Many Chicago citizens who attended the first annual meeting of the National Playground Association of America, will never forget the long summer day in the large playing field filled during the morning with hundreds of little children romping through the kindergarten games, in the afternoon with the young men and girls contending in athletic sports; and the evening light made gay by the bright colored garments of Italians, Lithuanians, Norwegians, and a dozen other nationalities, reproducing their old dances and festivals for the pleasure of the more stolid Americans....
>
> ... To insist that young people shall forecast their rose-colored future only in a house of dreams, is to deprive the real world of that warmth and reassurance which it so sorely needs and to which it is justly entitled; furthermore, we are left outside with a sense

of dreariness, in company with that shadow which already lurks only around the corner for most of us—a skepticism of life's value. (Addams 1909: 102–3)

Throughout "The House of Dreams," Addams alternates precipitously between deprecating movies' limitations and extolling their capacity to delight and inspire. Still, the chapter's optimistic first pages set the tone for much that follows and finally Addams proposes that movies can play a beneficial role in young people's lives, inspiring their dreams and aspirations, provided that their influence can be managed and cultivated through more structured recreations.

## Moral Panic in New York City

### Bishops Man the Barricades

Concerning Progressive Era campaigns against nickelodeons, Garth S. Jowett (1989: 59) opines that for some reformers, motion pictures symbolized unwelcome changes in American politics, society, and religion, which they feared they would be unable to prevent:

> The motion picture controversy was much more than a fight between reformers and a morally suspect group of filmmakers. For the long-dominant Protestant segment, the new entertainment medium was, in reality, a dramatic and highly visible symbol of those social and political changes in turn-of-the-century America which they seemed powerless to prevent, and which threatened to inexorably alter the face of the nation.

In fall 1906, Canon William Sheafe Chase of Christ Progressive Episcopal Church and Rev. Dr F.M. Foster founded the Interdenominational Committee for the Suppression of Sunday Vaudeville. While local blue laws had long been on the books, they were enforced only intermittently, and Chase and Foster sought to ensure that New York City's nickelodeons as well as its vaudeville theaters would observe the Christian Sabbath. In April 1907, Police Commissioner Theodore A. Bingham had police captains create lists of all public amusements, especially cheap amusements, in their precincts. In July, after the lists were completed, Bingham recommended to Democratic Mayor George B. McClellan (son of the Civil War general), who had appointed him police commissioner, that the mayor revoke the licenses of all New York City nickelodeons, penny arcades, and cheap vaudeville theaters because they admitted children unaccompanied by adults, showed obscene films, and violated building codes and fire regulations, a recommendation that the mayor did not at this time follow (Czitrom 1992: 532).

In the meantime, in June 1907, New York City's besieged movie exhibitors had organized the Motion Picture Exhibitors Association (MPEA) to protect their interests (Czitrom 1992: 533). Cultural studies scholars Angela McRobbie and Sarah L. Thornton (1995: 567) have discussed this sort of counter-strategy on the part of groups under fire from moral crusaders in the context of the rise of niche media in the 1990s:

> The effectiveness of these groups and in particular their skills at working with the media and providing highly professional 'soundbites' more or less on cue make them an invaluable resource to media machinery working to tight schedules and with increasingly small budgets. They allow the media to be seen to be doing their duty by providing 'balance' in their reporting. At the same time, they show how 'folk devils' can and do 'fight back'.

That folk devils, or at least those with a large stake in a booming new media industry, could and did fight back the better part of a century before McRobbie and Thornton wrote is borne out by the series of events that transpired in New York City during the latter half of 1907. With Bingham's agreement, the Interdenominational Committee brought a test case against William Hammerstein's large-capacity Victoria vaudeville house, located in the Broadway theatrical district. On December 3, Supreme Court Justice Thomas A. O'Gorman, citing an 1860 law banning Sunday entertainment, revoked the Victoria's license. For two Sundays, all the city's theaters, including penny arcades and foreign-language live theaters, remained closed, with the exception of William Fox's nine nickelodeons, for which Rogers, Fox's friend and business partner as well as the MPEA's counsel, succeeded in obtaining an injunction letting them remain open (Czitrom 1994: 533–5).

Then, in December 1907, Alderman Reginald Doull proposed a somewhat ambiguously worded ordinance officially exempting movie and vaudeville houses from blue laws. To rally support for Sunday closures, Chase issued a statement in which he neatly conflated devoutness, patriotism, honest government, economic generosity, the interests of labor (organized labor had opposed the Sunday closings), and the common good. It read in part,

> We are relying upon all patriotic citizens who want decent concerts on Sunday to let their Alderman and the President of the Board of Aldermen know what they think about this matter before next Tuesday [Christmas Eve]. We want to save the day from business greed and compulsory labor. In this battle, graft is arrayed against godliness. Graft has able, legal, cunning and astute politicians in its employ, but the laboring people and the general public is not so easily deceived as in former years. ("The Sunday Trouble" 1907: 704)

Despite the efforts of Chase and other foes of the nickelodeons, however, before the year was out the Board of Alderman passed and McClellan signed the ordinance,

Rogers (acting on behalf of the MPEA) obtained injunctions exempting nickelodeons from older blue laws, and New York City's nickelodeons were again allowed to remain open on Sundays (Czitrom 1994: 534–5, "The Sunday Trouble" 1907: 704).

## The Nickel Madness

As early as August 1907, just over a year after the nickelodeon boom began, and while the battle over Sunday movie shows in New York City was still in progress, moral crusades against the moving picture were enough in evidence to become the subject of a ruminative essay published in *Harper's Weekly*. Popular novelist and progressive journalist Barton W. Currie (1907), who authored the piece, entitled "The Nickel Madness," found that Americans' rising enthusiasm for nickelodeons presented no extraordinary or even unfamiliar dangers for either audiences or society:

> The very fact that we derive pleasure from certain amusements, wrote [nineteenth century historian Edward Hartpole] Lecky, creates a kind of humiliation. [Moral reformer] Anthony Comstock and Police-Commissioner Bingham have spoken eloquently on the moral aspect of the five-cent theatre, drawing far more strenuous conclusions than that of the great historian. But both the general and the purity commissioner generalized too freely from particulars. They saw only the harsher aspects of the nickel madness, whereas it has many innocent and harmless phases.

Currie argues that crusaders Comstock and Bingham draw conclusions about nickelodeons' capacity for degrading audiences out of proportion to the actual dangers revealed by objective inquiry. Their public condemnations overstate the threat that nickel theaters pose to society, ignoring the fact that all forms of amusement share an element of "humiliation" and disregarding the many "innocent and harmless phases" of moviegoing.

For his part, Currie (1907) reassures his readers that movies offer a host of valuable lessons filmed in picturesque locations, instructing and elevating rather than corrupting audiences:

> But if you happen to be an outlaw you may learn many moral lessons from these brief moving-picture performances, for most of the slides offer you a quick flash of melodrama in which the villain and criminal are getting the worst of it. Pursuits of malefactors are by far the most popular of all nickel deliriums. You may see snatch-purses, burglars, and an infinite variety of criminals hunted by the police and the mob in almost any nickelet you have the curiosity to visit. The scenes of these thrilling chases occur in every quarter of the globe, from Cape Town to Medicine Hat.

A man of mark in his time, Currie's endorsement of crime dramas because of the moral lessons imparted echoes Senator Bradley and Mayor Ten Broeck's approval, a decade or so earlier, of a kinetoscope view of a bar-room fight that, in their opinion, retained "a good moral tone" (Hendricks 1966: 77).

Continuing his commentary, Currie (1907) concedes that nickelodeon operators pander to the public's prurience in order to draw customers, but claims that in the end they steer well clear of satisfying such tastes:

> Of course the proprietors of the nickelets and nickelodeons make as much capital out of suggestiveness as possible, but it rarely goes beyond a hint or a lure. For instance, you will come to a little hole in the wall before which there is an ornate sign bearing the legend:
>
> FRESH FROM PARIS
>
> Very Naughty
>
> Should this catch the eye of a Comstock he would immediately enter the place to gather evidence. But he would never apply for a warrant. He would find a "very naughty" boy playing pranks on a Paris street — annoying blind men, tripping up gendarmes, and amusing himself by every antic the ingenuity of the Paris street gamin can conceive.

French libertinism remains a promotional gimmick for nickel theaters rather than a characteristic of the films themselves. By the time a customer leaves a nickelodeon, the promise of Parisian promiscuity will have become the reality of harmless fun. Currie concludes, "And after all it [the nickel madness] is an innocent amusement and a rather wholesome delirium" (1907).

## Closing (and Reopening) the Nickelodeons

On December 23, 1908, almost exactly a year after he had signed an ordinance allowing the city's nickelodeons and vaudeville houses to remain open Sundays, Mayor McClellan conducted a five-hour hearing at City Hall on the future of New York City's nickelodeons. As historian Daniel Czitrom (1984, 1992) recounts, clerics speaking against the movies concentrated on their perceived ability to corrupt youth. F.M. Foster, Chairman of the Interdenominational Committee, wanted to know, "Is a man at liberty to make money from the morals of people? Is he to profit from the corruption of the minds of children?" Answering his own question, Foster (quoted in Czitrom 1992: 543) continued, "The man who profits from such things is doomed to double damnation. To show indecent pictures is a violation of the statutes and the removal of such shows from the city is clearly justifiable."

Defending the movies, Charles Sprague Smith, Director of the People's Institute, a progressive civic organization associated with the Cooper Union, ventured, "Years ago, the man was in the rum shop on a Sunday night. Where do you find him now? Side by side with his children witnessing a moving picture show" (quoted in Czitrom 1992: 543, see Rosenbloom 1987: 309). Gustavus A. Rogers (quoted in Czitrom 1992: 544), representing 200 local exhibitors, referred to recent developments in Chicago: "If this is a practical suggestion or solution, we are willing to accede to it."

The next day, Mayor McClellan finally rescinded the licenses of all nickel movie theaters in New York City, directing the chief of the Bureau of Licenses to inspect each one personally before deciding on whether to grant it a new license (Jowett 1989: 65, Czitrom 1992: 545). While a statement the mayor issued concerning the hearing also noted fire hazards and safety issues, it paid due attention to objections raised by clergy:

> Because of the serious opposition presented by the rectors and pastors of practically all the Christian denominations in the city, and because of the further objections of the Society for the Prevention of Cruelty to Children and the Society for the Prevention of Crime, I have decided that licenses for moving picture shows shall only be issued hereafter on the written agreement that the licensee will not operate the same on Sunday. And I do further declare that I will revoke any of these moving picture show licenses on evidence that pictures have been exhibited by the licensees which tend to degrade or injure the morals of the community. (quoted in Czitrom 544)

On Christmas Day, a group made up of "the proprietors of the five-cent places, manufacturers and distributors of the films, and some of the 10-cent men," including William Fox and Marcus A. Loew, met, with Gustavus Rogers's assistance, to organize to fight the mayor's decision ("Picture-Show Men" 1908). On December 26, William J. Gaynor, Justice of Appellate Division of the Supreme Court of New York (actually an intermediary appeals court) granted the movie men an injunction against the closings, which in the end lasted just one full day (Rosenbloom 1987: 313, Jowett 1989: 65).

## The National Board of Censorship

In March 1909, just a few months after New York City exhibitors' victory, Rogers, acting on behalf of the MPEA, and John Collier, executive secretary of the People's Institute, organized the National Board of Censorship, with Collier as its general secretary as well as chairman of its Executive Committee (Czitrom 1984: 4, Rosenbloom 1987: 309). Initially, all major movie production companies, including members of the recently (1908) organized moving picture trust, the Motion Picture Patents Company (MPPC), agreed to submit their productions to the Board for review prior to release, assumedly because without certificates of approval, their movies would not be shown by members of the MPEA (Jowett 1989: 65). Financed by licensing fees paid by moviemakers and staffed largely by social workers, the

Board represented a compromise between the freedom of speech desired by the movie industry and the regulation of film content sought by reformers (Jowett 1989: 65–6).

Having no direct power of enforcement, the Board relied on "moral coercion" to regulate film content (Jowett 1989: 65). Though it reviewed about 85 percent of films exhibited in the United States, it had no jurisdiction over pictures produced by small, evanescent companies (Jowett 1989: 65). Yet, despite such drawbacks, the Board managed to achieve a degree of effectiveness. According to the *Report of the Board of Censorship to the Gentlemen of the Motion Picture Patents Company*, issued in 1909, in its first year the board's censorship committee rejected motion pictures for depicting "the criminal passion and rough handling of a white girl by Negroes," adultery, and suicide, as well as for holding the insane up to ridicule (quoted in Rosenbloom 1987: 311). Sometimes, instead of refusing a certificate outright, the committee asked for specific changes in a film's content. For example, it requested that scenes showing a drunken woman, a boy tossing a banana peel on the ground, and burglary be removed from various films (Rosenbloom 1987: 311).

# The Drive for Respectability

## Devout and Reverent

Around 1907–8, in response to reformers' attacks, some moviemakers initiated a defense strategy that media scholars William Uricchio and Roberta E. Pearson dub, "The film industry's drive for respectability" (1993: 41). The drive for respectability meant that besides such gambits as turning to the courts or introducing voluntary censorship, the American film industry raised movies' aesthetic quality and moral tone in accordance with prevailing standards of taste and decorum. Historian Kathleen D. McCarthy (1976: 49) identifies some of the reasons that moviemakers sought respectability:

> Several factors lay behind the film producers' willingness to comply with the reformers' demands: fear of censorship, the quest for respectability, and the desire to elicit highly coveted endorsements.
>
> Moviemakers consciously began to seek out and promote films with educational value in order to achieve these ends.

American movie studios produced historical, religious, or otherwise instructional films with several goals in mind: as well as heading off calls for censorship and regulation, by integrating condoned ideas and themes into select motion pictures, leaders of the film industry hoped to attract middle-class audiences and secure the support of reformers.

Keenly aware of the benefits that might accrue, industry members were quick to produce, import, exhibit, and promote movies that provided uplift. On April 10, 1907, the *Chicago Tribune* published a letter from George Kleine of the Kleine Optical Company, a Chicago film rental exchange, responding to an editorial (one in a series) that was strongly critical of the movies (and MPPC member). Kleine (1907: 101) enthuses,

> We quote verbatim from the *Tribune* editorial: 'Most of them (the five cent theaters) are evil in their nature, without a single redeeming feature to warrant their existence. ... They manufacture criminals to infest the streets of the city. Not a single thing connected with them has influence for good.' ...
>
> We state the following facts to prove the inaccuracy of these assertions.... . Taking the list of pictures issued during the month of March by the various factories, both foreign and domestic, as shown on the enclosed printed list, your attention is called to the most conspicuous subject of the month, a new Passion Play which requires one hour for projections, and which is one of the most elaborate and expensive products of its kind ever made. This Passion Play reproduced in moving pictures was shown in several five cent theaters in Chicago with all solemnity to as devout and reverent audiences as could be found in any church.

It was perhaps not entirely coincidental that Kleine was a US agent for Pathé Frères, the French studio responsible for *The Passion Play*, the production he references as a recent example of spiritual purity and lavish artistry in films (Abel 1999: 88). This "new Passion Play" was in fact a rerelease, under several different titles, of Pathé's *La vie et la Passion de Jésus-Christ, N.S. [Notre Seigneur]*, originally released in various versions with somewhat differing content in 1902–3 and again in 1905. In 1907 as in 1905, the film depicted 31 scenes in the life of Christ and had an exceptionally long running time of 44 minutes. For *The Passion Play*'s 1907 release, all scenes were enhanced with tinting produced by the recently developed Pathécolor stenciling process, a mechanized but still labor-intensive method adapted from a procedure used for coloring postcards (Abel 1999: 60, Coe 1981: 113–15). *The Passion Play* was likely both Pathé's most popular production of the 1907–8 season and the most widely seen film in the United States during those two years (Abel 1999: 59, 61).

## Family Theater

For the American film industry, achieving respectability necessitated differentiating movies from other cheap amusements also under attack for corrupting patrons. As Uricchio and Pearson (1993: 41–2) put it,

> Taking its lead from those investigating cheap amusements, the industry attempted to distinguish itself from these entertainments while at the same time claiming to serve as an active agent in the downfall, inasmuch as the moving picture habit could substitute for the vastly more offensive saloon, dance hall, or penny arcade habit.

Responding to reformers' criticisms of cheap amusements, including but not limited to nickelodeons, supporters of the industry promoted movies and illustrated slides as a clean and safe alternative to a host of unsavory entertainments, one perhaps popular enough to put an end to such amusements.

In 1908, not long before he joined the National Board of Censorship, the People's Institute's John Collier contributed a brief piece entitled "Cheap Amusements" to *Charity and Commons*, a trade journal for settlement house administrators (reprinted in Jowett 1989: 65–76). In the article, which summarizes a field investigation of Manhattan's cheap amusements conducted by a joint committee of the Woman's Municipal League and the People's Institute, Collier (1908, quoted in Abel 1999: 65) extols the nickelodeon as an ever more moral and decent entertainment:

> Five years ago the nickelodeon was neither better nor worse than many other cheap amusements are at present. It was often a carnival of vulgarity, suggestiveness and violence, the fit subject for police regulation. It gained a deservedly bad name, and although no longer deserved, that name still clings to it. During the present investigation a visit to more than two hundred nickelodeons has not detected one immoral or indecent picture, or one indecent feature of any sort, much as there has been in other respects to call for improvement. But more than this: in the nickelodeon one sees history, travel, the reproduction of industries. He sees farce-comedy which at worst is relaxing, innocuous, rather monotonously confined to horseplay, and at best is distinctly humanizing, laughing with and not at the subject. Some real drama: delightful curtain-raisers, in perfect pantomime, from France, and in the judgment of most people rather an excess of mere melodrama, and in rare cases even of sheer murderous violence…. In addition to the moving-picture, the nickelodeon as a rule has singing, and almost invariably the audience joins in the chorus with a good will. Thus has the moving-picture show elevated itself. But the penny arcade has not elevated itself, and the cheap vaudeville, if anything, has grown worse.
>
> The nickelodeon is a family theater, and is almost the creation of the child, and it has discovered a new and healthy cheap amusement public.

Like Addams a little later, Collier portrays movies as a gateway to the wider world. Despite admitting that motion pictures sometimes descend to "sheer murderous violence" (which seems more rhetorical flourish than sincere criticism), Collier represents the movie house as an antidote to, and an enemy of, the less respectable penny arcade and cheap vaudeville theater.

On October 1, 1910, *The New York Times* published a letter from Walter Storey, General Secretary of the National Board of Censorship, itemizing the benefits that regulation by his organization had brought to the film industry. In closing, Storey (1910: 12) proclaims,

Finally, it has been the general verdict of social workers expressed in numerous reports made on different occasions in different parts of the country that motion pictures are on the whole a cleaner, a more moral, and a more intellectually versatile form of dramatics than any other form of the cheap theatre now extant. This is so because the audience of motion — picture shows is in the main an audience of wage-earners and of families whose standards are not base and whose craving for education is genuine and deep.

In news media as in trade journals for the settlement house movement and the film industry, reformers' attacks were defused by crediting nickelodeons with saving women, children, working men, and immigrants from the debasing influence of cheap vaudeville, stage melodrama, the penny arcade, and the saloon.

## The Red Rooster Scare

From fall 1905 (soon after the start of the nickelodeon boom) to summer 1908 or later, motion pictures imported from France's Pathé were probably the most popular and prestigious films seen in the United States (Abel 1999: 48). For several years more, the prominence of films produced by Pathé (and, beginning in 1910, of movies made in Jersey City, New Jersey by its US subsidiary, Pathé Cinematograph) meant that the company held sway as a leading player in the American movie business. Countering Pathé and other French firms such as Gaumont and Urban-Eclipse, boosters of American movie companies diverted moral panics over nickelodeons toward films associated with French culture. In *The Red Rooster Scare: Making Cinema American, 1900–1910*, Richard Abel (1999: 87), a historian of early cinema in the United States and France, describes the initial inspiration for the scare:

> By stimulating and then exploiting the nickelodeon boom in the United States, Pathé sharply defined the issue of who would exercise control over the cinema market, and how. Once that struggle for control is framed in terms of American interests versus perceived foreign interests, as it was during the period from 1907 to 1909, the threatening 'foreign body' of 'red rooster' films indeed looms large.

During the years 1907–9, competition between American companies and Pathé for control of the US market for films was recast as a clash between national interests. To some, Pathé's growing presence in the United States seemed like a first assault in a foreign invasion.

In the same vein, the anonymous author of "The Inadmissible Subject," a feature story published in *The Moving Picture World* on January 22, 1910, displayed a marked tendency to construe any new French film as additional proof that the questionable qualities of that people were imperiling the American character, complaining,

> The newspapers the other day published a French cablegram telling of a use of the moving picture camera that we desire to write of. The love of the morbid in the French nature, as everybody knows. In Paris, the morgue, where you may inspect the bodies of suicides, is a common thing, and one of the attractions to tourists. Even in their judicial trials, as one read of in the case of Mme. Steinheil, the alleged murderess of President Faure, the love of the morbid is carried down to the minutest detail of fact and conjecture.
>
> It was apparently the same national trait which recently dictated the use of the moving picture camera in the execution of a criminal. Films were made both immediately before and immediately after the poor wretch had been killed. And they were talked of for public exhibition! Fortunately, humanity stepped in and the films were stopped and another slur kept off the fair reputation of motion picture photography. (83)

Dismayed and indignant because of an unconfirmed report that unreleased films came close to showing (even though they never included images of) the execution of a convicted criminal in France, the writer intimates that Americans have barely avoided being contaminated by "the love of the morbid in the French nature," obviously to blame for the nonexistent but nevertheless dangerous footage.

Later in his book, Abel (1999: 118) isolates some of the concerns that underlay the intense aversion to French films and movie companies that he calls the Red Rooster Scare after Pathé's trademark. He discovers,

> What made Pathé's very presence, let alone its influence, especially undesirable at this historical moment [about 1907–10], I would argue, was a conjunction of concerns about what and who were being constructed as 'American'. Of all those who constituted the nickelodeon's mass audience (and variations, of course, existed from one region or city to another), several groups especially attracted attention. One was the disproportionate number of recent immigrants from eastern and southern Europe, concentrated in urban centers throughout the Northeast and the upper Midwest.... The other group was hardly mutually exclusive, consisting of women and children who, according to most accounts (however self-serving), made up the greater portion of nickelodeon audiences across the country.

Abel maintains that Pathé drew especially harsh criticism because of rising distress about rapidly evolving conceptions of the American national character. Nickelodeons appealed to a mass audience, but attracted a "disproportionate number of recent immigrants" living in the cities of the Northeast and northern Midwest. It was also commonly reported that most moviegoers across the nation were women and children. During the Red Rooster Scare, doubts and anxieties about the assimilability of these groups found expression in intensified hostility toward a French movie company, its films, and their perceived foreignness.

In January 1910, *The Moving Picture World* published an anonymously authored article entitled "What Is an American Subject?" that examined the possible qualities that would make a film distinctively American. At one point, the unnamed author takes strong exception to the prevalence of foreign motion pictures in American movie theaters:

> Let us look at the moving picture field. Out of about forty films commented upon in the last number of THE MOVING PICTURE WORLD, exactly one-half are foreign subjects and were made abroad. Of those that were made in this country, not more than ten are of American themes, that is, themes "racy of the soil" and distinctly American characterization, scenery and surroundings. The other subjects were such as might have been made in Europe. In the licensed releases for the week ending January 15, out of about 31 movies, 11 are foreign subjects; of the remaining 20 only 6 are clearly American. The remainder are, if we may so put it, nondescript. ("What Is an American Subject?" 1910: 82)

Significantly, the article mentions neither the wholesome fun that Barton W. Currie discovered nor the artistic merit that George Kleine defended in French movie fare in 1907. Its author contends that to be demonstrably American, a film not only needs to be made in the United States, but must also express peculiarly American concerns or, in other words, convey themes "racy with the soil" (ironically, a phrase coined by the Irish poet Padraic Colum).

In the next paragraph, the article's author discusses at some length the constitutive elements of a truly American subject:

> It will be seen from this, that the American subject, even after a year's plugging away [by US movie companies], does not seem to have secured a predominant part in the film program of the moving picture theaters of the United States. It is permissible to inquire whether this is because the makers are unable to keep up the supply of purely American subjects, or because the tastes of the public are many and varied and have to be catered for accordingly? We incline to the latter view. There seems to be amongst exhibitors, among whom we have made the inquiry, a strong and increasing demand for Indian and Western subjects, and here probably we get the most satisfactory answer to our own question. Indian and Western subjects may fairly be considered American, because they deal with the aboriginal or original life of the pioneers of the country. ("What Is an American Subject?" 1910: 82)

Tellingly, in attempting to pinpoint typically American subjects, the writer looks at genres already proven popular with movie audiences. The article also proffers having "secured a predominant part in the film program of the moving picture theaters of the United States" as the true measure of American subjects' viability. Seemingly, the drive for respectability encompassed the closely intertwined goals of ideological and commercial dominance.

The drive for respectability and related efforts produced considerable changes in motion picture content. According to Uricchio and Pearson: "The heaviest American production of quality films coincides with the transitional years of 1907 to 1913" (50). As film companies transitioned toward respectability, they rapidly increased their production of "quality films" such as historical epics, biblical stories, and literary adaptations (all genres of proven popularity). Edison moved from producing or licensing titles like *Jack the Kisser* (1907), *Cohen's Fire Sale* (1907), and *Jamaica Negroes Doing a Two-Step* (1907) to concentrating on more prestigious offerings, including *Frankenstein* (1910) and *Michael Strogoff* (1910). Similarly, Biograph went from producing *Dream of a Racetrack Fiend* (1906), *The Model's Ma* (1907), *The Tired Tailor's Dream* (1907), and the like to making *A Corner in Wheat* (1909), based on an incident in American writer Frank Norris's 1903 novel *The Pit*, and *Enoch Arden: Parts I and II* (1911).

In an effort to transform movie shows into family theater, Biograph switched from offering such risqué items as *From Show Girl to Burlesque Queen* (1903) and *A Fire in a Burlesque Theatre* (1904) to family-oriented films like *The Sunbeam* (1912), which featured child actors, and *What Shall We Do with our Old?* (1911). Abel details American movie studios' production of Westerns: with Selig and the Lubin Manufacturing Company among the earliest and most prolific, US movie companies began featuring cowboys-and-Indians stories that presented spectacular locations in the American West and frequently racist and xenophobic views, as well. Movies depicting white heroes and Indian villains included *The Renegade* (1908), produced by the Kalem Company (cofounded by George Kleine the previous year), in which a white soldier rescues a white girl captured by Indians, and Lubin's transparently entitled *The White Chief* (1908), in which a white man saves an Indian girl from the clutches of a Mexican man, afterward becoming the white chief of her Indian tribe (Abel 1999: 160).

## Concluding Remarks

While they met with only mixed success in the short term, localized moral panics over nickelodeons were to have long-lasting and wide-ranging social and cultural effects. With the nickelodeon boom, reformers, clergy, police, the courts, and politicians quickly mobilized, sometimes defending, but far more often condemning the movies. By participating in public controversies over movies and movie theaters, reformers and crusaders could extend their influence over popular perceptions and government policies regarding social problems ranging from state censorship to education, public recreation, urban poverty, and citizenship. Moral panics over nickelodeons provided a public forum for conflict and negotiation concerning the meanings of nationality, race, religion, class, gender, and age.

Within the film industry, producers, distributors, and exhibitors responded to their critics and pursued middle-class audiences by introducing industrial self-censorship, creating morally instructive narratives, presenting professedly high-quality motion pictures, and producing stories intended to celebrate the American national character. Defenders of the nickelodeon made use of moral panic to placate reformers and compete with other cheap amusements for customers' nickels and dimes. Promoters of American movie companies turned moral panic to their advantage to challenge the ascendancy of Pathé and French films in the United States.

American cinema emerged amid a series moral panics. Initially distrusted as a licentious, disreputable, or dangerous amusement, in the wake of moral panic motion pictures became a widely accepted (though not universally welcomed) part of American life.

# References

1907. Editorial. *The Moving Picture World*, April 20, 100.

1907. Letter to the editor: the five cent theaters. *The Moving Picture World*, April 20, 101–2.

Abel, R. 1999. *The Red Rooster Scare: Making Cinema American, 1900–1910*. Berkeley: University of California Press.

Addams, J. 1909. *The Spirit of Youth and the City Streets*. New York: Macmillan.

Armour, R.A. 1990. Effects of censorship pressure on the New York nickelodeon market, 1907–1909. *Film History*, 4(2), 113–21.

*The Boxing Cats (Prof. Welton's)* (dir. W.K.L. Dickson and William Heise, 1894).

*Carmencita* (dir. W.K.L. Dickson, 1894).

1907. A clean nickelodeon. *The Moving Picture World*, June 1, 198.

Cohen, S. 2002 (1972, 1980). *Folk Devils and Moral Panics: The Creation of the Mods and Rockers*. 3rd Edition. London: Routledge.

Coe, B. 1981. *The History of Movie Photography*. Westfield: Eastview Editions.

Collier, J. 1908. Cheap amusements. *Charities and Commons*, April 11, reprinted in *The Red Rooster Scare: Making Cinema American, 1900–1910*, R. Abel, Berkeley: University of California Press, 73–7.

Currie, B.W. 1907. The nickel madness. *Harper's Weekly* [Online], August 24, 1246–7. Available at: http://www.cinemaweb.com/silentfilm/bookshelf/17_hw_1.htm [accessed: October 10, 2011].

Czitrom, D. 1984. The redemption of leisure: the National Board of Censorship and the rise of motion pictures, 1900–1920. *Studies in Visual Communication*, 10(4), 2–6.

Czitrom, D. 1992. The politics of performance: from theater licensing to movie censorship in turn-of-the-century New York. *American Quarterly*, 44(4), 525–53.

1896. Edison's Vitascope cheered. *The New York Times* [Online], April 24, 5. Available at: http://query.nytimes.com/mem/archive-free/pdf?res=9B05E2DF1331E033A2 5757C2A9629C94679ED7CF [accessed: October 10, 2011].

Grieveson, L. 2004. *Policing Cinema: Movies and Censorship in Early Twentieth-Century America*. Berkeley: University of California Press.

Hall, S., Critcher, C., Jefferson, T., Clarke, J., and Roberts, B. 1978. *Policing the Crisis: Mugging, the State, and Law and Order*. Critical Social Studies. Houndmills: Palgrave Macmillan.

Hendricks, G. 1966. *The Kinetoscope: America's First Commercially Successful Motion Picture Exhibitor*. The Beginnings of the American Film. New York: GPO 2552.

Historical note. People's Institute Records, 1883–1933, Manuscripts and Archives Division, The New York Public Library. *New York Public Library Digital Library Collections* [Online]. Available at: http://digilib.nypl.org/dynaweb/ead/human/ msspeopl/@Generic__BookTextView/206;pt=206 [accessed: October 10, 2011].

1907. Hull-House five cent theatre, in *Hull-House Year Book*, 1906–7. Chicago: Hull-House, 39. Reprinted in J.A. Lindstrom. 1999. "Almost worse than the restrictive measures": Chicago reformers and the nickelodeons. *Cinema Journal*, 39(1), 96.

1910. The inadmissible subject. *The Moving Picture World*, January 22, 83.

Jackson, W.H. 1910. The moving picture "world," *The Moving Picture World*, June 4, 932–3.

Jowett, G.S. 1989. "A capacity for evil": the 1915 Supreme Court *Mutual* Decision. *Historical Journal of Film, Radio and Television*, 9(1), 59–78.

Jowett, G.S. 1990. Moral responsibility and commercial entertainment: social control in the United States film industry, 1907–1968. *Historical Journal of Film, Radio and Television*, 10(1), 3–31.

Kleine, G. 1907. A clarion note. *The Moving Picture World*, April 20, 101.

Kleine, G. 1907. Copy of Mr. Kleine's letter to the *Chicago Tribune*. *The Moving Picture World*, 101–2.

Lindstrom, J.A. 1999. "Almost worse than the restrictive measures": Chicago reformers and the nickelodeons. *Cinema Journal*, 39(1), 90–112.

McCarthy, Kathleen D. 1976. "Nickel vice and virtue: movie censorship in Chicago, 1907–1915. *Journal of Popular Film*, 5(1), 37–55.

McKeever, W.A. 1910. The moving picture: a primary school for criminals. *Good Housekeeping*, August 10, 184–6.

McRobbie, A. and Thornton S.L. 1995. Rethinking 'moral panic' for multi-mediated social worlds. *British Journal of Sociology*, 46(4), 559–74.

1909. More about "uplift." *The Moving Picture World*, April 24, 508.

Musser, C. 1990. *The Emergence of Cinema: The American Screen to 1907*. History of the American Cinema. Volume 1. Berkeley: University of California Press.

Musser, C. 2002. Introducing cinema to the American public: the Vitascope in the United States, 1896–7, in *Moviegoing in America*, edited by G.A. Waller. Malden: Blackwell, 13–26.

*The Passion Play* [*La vie et la Passion de Jésus-Christ, N.S.*] (dir. Lucien Nonguet and Ferdinand Zecca, 1907 [1902–3, 1905]).

1908. Picture-show men organize to fight. *The New York Times* [Online], December 26. Available at: http://query.nytimes.com/mem/archive-free/pdf?res=F50610FB 3A5A17738DDDAF0A94DA415B888CF1D3 [accessed: October 10, 2011].

Rosenbloom, N.J. 1987. Between reform and regulation: the struggle over film censorship in progressive America, 1909–1922. *Film History*, 1, 307–25.

Storey, W. 1910. Limits of censorship. *The New York Times* [Online], October 1, 12. Available at: http://query.nytimes.com/mem/archivefree/pdf?res=F20910F9395 D11738DDDA80894D8415B808DF1D3 [accessed: October 10, 2011].

1907. The Sunday trouble. *The Moving Picture World*, December 28, 703–6.

1907a. Trade notes. *The Moving Picture World*, June 29, 261–4.

1907b. Trade notes. *The Moving Picture World*, July 6, 277–8.

1907c. Trade notes. *The Moving Picture World*, December 21, 683–4.

Uricchio, W. and Pearson, R.E. 1993. *Reframing Culture: The Case of Vitagraph Quality Films*. Princeton: Princeton University Press.

1910. What is an American subject? *The Moving Picture World*, January 22, 82.

Young, J. 1971b. The role of the police as amplifiers of deviancy, negotiators of reality and translators of fantasy: some consequences of our present system of drug control as seen in Notting Hill, in *Images of Deviance*, edited by S. Cohen. Harmondsworth: Penguin Books, 27–61.

# Sexual Predators, Internet Addiction, and Other Media Myths: Moral Panic and the Disappearance of Brandon Crisp

## Patricia Molloy*

On October 13, 2008, Brandon Crisp, a 15-year-old boy from the rural community of Barrie, Ontario, ran away from home following a dispute with his parents, who had confiscated his Xbox 360 due to the inordinate amount of time he had been spending playing *Call of Duty 4: Modern Warfare*—to the extent of falling grades and skipping school. Steve Crisp, Brandon's father, who had himself run away from home as a teenager, initially called his bluff and even helped pack his son's knapsack, thinking "he would come home the next day with his tail tucked between his legs" (Boyle 2008). When Brandon did not in fact return home the next day, his parents reported him missing to local police authorities, who began an intensive area search using heat-sensitive cameras and a canine unit on October 18, which two weeks later broadened into a national missing person's case.

As with any case of a missing (white) child, Brandon's disappearance sparked extensive media coverage throughout Ontario, including Toronto-based news outlets such as *The Toronto Star*, the *Toronto Sun*, and City TV, receiving as well, significant coverage on national news networks including the Canadian Television Network (CTV), the Canadian Broadcasting Corporation (CBC), and national newspapers such as the *National Post* and *The Globe and Mail*, and eventually spilling into the United States with reports on Fox News and CNN. Indeed, with headlines such as "family fears boy lured by gamers" (Boyle 2008), the media coverage of the disappearance of Brandon Crisp constituted a moral panic that did not wane with the discovery of his body on November 5, 2008, despite the pronouncement that

* The author would like to thank Greig de Peuter for his invaluable suggestions regarding this chapter.

the boy had not been the victim of foul play as largely speculated but had, rather, died of natural causes after falling from a tree just a few miles from his home.

A perpetual discourse of danger governs both mass mediated and parental understandings of young people as particularly "vulnerable" and "at risk" to the supposed harm wrought by exposure to and prolonged engagement with the vicissitudes of media, popular culture and technology. More specifically, the moral panic over the disappearance of Brandon Crisp was fueled both by popular discourses about addiction and by those related to fear of sexual predation. Fearful discourses about sexual predation often circulate independently of notions about media consumption, but intensify when directed toward young people's use of the Internet and other media. Underpinning responses within the gaming community concerning the events leading up to Brandon Crisp's disappearance has been a metadiscourse of blame centering on what ultimately "caused" Brandon's death and who should be responsible for preventing further tragedies. As we shall see, while facile notions of negative media effects still hold much currency in popular discourse, particularly the "effects" of violent content on the young psyche, with gaming apologists taking an (understandably) oppositional stance, what is lacking is any consideration of a culture of militarized masculinity, within which first-person shooter games such as *Call of Duty* have developed and continue to thrive.

## "Teenagers: Freedom or License?"

As I have argued elsewhere, moral panics are best located within an existing discourses of danger that affirms and renews political identity. Insofar as we identify who we are in comparison to whom we are not and, more importantly, whom we fear, communities erect and maintain boundaries that demarcate the "safe and secure" from the "dangerous and insecure." What this means is that in the perpetual quest for security and cohesion, communities *require* a consistent supply of threats. And if none exists, they have to be invented (Molloy 2002). Importantly, the same discourse of danger that separates "us" (self) from "them" (other) locates youth as "other:" dangerous by design. As well-noted by Stanley Cohen (2002) in the first edition of his seminal work *Folk Devils and Moral Panics: The Creation of the Mods and Rockers* in 1972, moral panics have historically been disproportionately directed at young people and serve to influence the making of public policy. Public perceptions and media representations of dangerous youth who need to be kept in check are, then, a time-honored tradition. In October 1949, for example, CBC radio broadcast an episode of its weekly *Citizens' Forum* called "Teenagers: Freedom or Licence? Have Today's Parents Enough Authority?," in which guest panelist Dr S.R. Laycock proclaimed that "even primitive man had trouble with teenagers."

Sociologist Bernard Schissel (2008) argues that a North American public antipathy toward youth is only increasing with time. Because of a widespread perception that young people are "more disrespectful now than in the past," they are consequently considered to be "more dangerous" (Schissel 2008: 15)

Schissel (2008) cites a 2005 poll that found that 63 percent of Canadians believed that sentences meted out to criminals, young offenders included, were not severe enough. Schissel (2008: 15) writes:

> Politicians, in concert with lobby groups (often organized by families of victims), argue that the epidemic of adolescent misbehavior is the result of poor parenting, dysfunctional families inhabiting certain geographical areas and class positions, and, most importantly, a lenient justice system. The conservative mantra decrying inadequate law and order is fraught with simplistic arguments that young people are getting away with murder.

As a result of such "simplistic arguments," with the Youth Criminal Justice Act replacing the Young Offenders Act in 2002, the Canadian government lowered the age at which a child can be considered a young offender from 12 to ten and the age at which a young offender can be tried and sentenced as an adult from 16 to 14, even though Canadian youth are no more dangerous or criminal today than in the past. Moreover, Canada "locks up more young offenders than any other jurisdiction in the industrialized world" to the extent that "proportionately more youth are incarcerated per capita than are adults despite the fact that adult crimes far surpass youth crimes in gravity and in number" (Schissel 2008: 15). But the new Act includes a provision that allows some youth to bypass adult criminal justice institutions for "restorative community-based alternatives." The effect is paradoxical: while the Act contains harsh provisions for supposedly dangerous youth, it is presented in a context of restorative justice and diversion programs.

Schissel (2008) attributes Canada's penchant for criminalizing its youth to the marginal positioning of children and youth in our socio-economic system. He (Schissel 2008: 16) argues that "moral panics over school shootings, inner city gang activities, schoolyard bullying, and child and youth killers are part of a larger cultural and economic environment in which children and youth are prolific consumers and a source of cheap, obedient, and disposable labor for multinational food and clothing industries," and thus fundamental to the very survival of global capital. Despite current Western political rhetoric of appreciation for the rights of a "diversity of citizens," children and youth are left out of the equation of rights and freedoms. Targeted as "threats to the common good," the scapegoating of children and youth through a punitive justice system "and attendant sensationalist media" serve to benefit the interests of those in positions of power (Schissel 2008: 16).

## The Anxiety of Influence

The discourse of danger that succeeds in marginalizing and criminalizing young people also constructs them as "at risk" and in need of protection *from* the same sensationalist media and cultural channels that perceive them as dangerous. To be sure, young people's consumption of media and popular culture has long carried a warning label. As media scholar and educationist David Buckingham (1993) points out, even Plato had reservations about the influence of poets on youth in classical Greece, suggesting they be banned from his ideal of a republic. It was not just the content of dramatic poetry that made Plato anxious, but also the possibility of *mimesis*—the imitation or copying involved in artistic representation and the emotions to which it gives rise. Poetry, according to Plato, might indeed serve as the primary means of moral training, but "it also held the dangers of 'luxury' and 'indulgence' in the emotions. Like sex, access to it should be rigorously controlled, and the temptations of 'frenzy' and 'excessive pleasure' avoided at all costs" (Buckingham 1993: 2–3). Contemporary moral panics about video violence and computer games are thus part of a continuum that has seen campaigns waged against horror comics in the 1950s, moves to regulate cinema in the 1920s and 1930s, and anxieties about popular literature in the Victorian era (Buckingham 1993: 4).

Fears of the "harmful" influence of mass media and popular culture on children owe much to the perception of young people as "other" than adult or even *lesser* than adult. Indeed, young people are often seen as "too immature or simply too feeble-minded to resist the negative influence of the media" (Buckingham 1993: 4). Empirical research on the so-called "negative effects" of mass media, influenced by Frankfurt School concerns over fascist propaganda in Europe in the 1930s and American functionalist sociology in the 1940s and 1950s, has largely fallen out of scholarly favor as theoretical advances in the humanities and British cultural studies refocused the terms of the debate away from an all-powerful "mass media" to culture, ideology and the politics of representation. While the sort of controlled laboratory "stimulus and response" experiments of the 1960s have been found faulty on methodological grounds (from the contexts in which experiments were conducted and the types of media used to the kinds of responses that were elicited or perhaps encouraged), effects research also neglects the fundamental issue of meaning itself. Writes Buckingham (1993: 7),

> The question of what 'violence› means, both to those who watch it and to those who perpetrate it (or indeed are victims of it) in real life, has often been answered in highly simplistic terms. Meaning is said to be inherent in the 'message,› and to be transmitted directly into the mind and thence the behaviour of the viewer. As a result, it becomes unnecessary to investigate what viewers themselves define as violent, or the different ways in which they make sense of what they watch.

While the issue of the "harmful effects" of media and particularly the notion that violence in television content "causes" violent behavior in viewers continue to hold popular appeal for teachers, parents, and the public, the moral panic today, with the advent of video games and the Internet, "is not only about the passive adoption of violent tendencies. It also addresses the risks of audiences enacting their fantasies with interactive technology preparatory to the real world" (Miller 2002: 1). And again, when that audience is youthful, the risk seems to escalate. For literary scholar Robert Payne (2008: 33), the Internet produces social and moral anxiety due to its "layers of unknowing and unknowability," which he describes as an "aproportionality." It is not so much that the continuous expansion of information and materials available on the Internet and the increasing complexity of relationships are out of proportion to "material reality" as it is that they are unknowable in proportional terms, if knowable at all (Payne 2008: 33).

What happens with moral panics over children and the Internet is a "process of escalation" as negative attention and fear of "emerging problems" shifts from one target to the next. Drawing on historian of religion and criminologist Philip Jenkins's work on moral panic and online child pornography, Payne writes, "Interest groups move their stigmatizing focus from issues on which political ground has been lost to easier targets, such as from pornography to child pornography" (2008: 33). Thus, perceived threats to children become "symbolic politics" (Jenkins, quoted in Payne 2008: 33), an existing social threat escalates to an even higher threshold of victimization when transferred from adult to child, "thus posing an even greater threat to the social order" (Payne 2008: 33). We can observe a similar symbolic politics and escalation of threat with the moral panic of children being "lured" by "sexual predators" on the Internet, regardless of its likelihood. Indeed, when Brandon Crisp first disappeared, his father was reported as fearing his son met someone online while playing *Call of Duty 4* (CoD4) on his Xbox 360 Live. "Pedophiles can stalk kids through these games," Steve Crisp said in an interview with *The Toronto Star* on October 19, six days after Brandon ran away. In addition to the possibility of being stalked by a sexual predator, Brandon's father felt that his son might have fallen victim to someone involved in organized crime or Internet gambling (Morrow 2008), while his mother, Angelika Crisp, was convinced Brandon was "taken" by a fellow CoD4 player "who may be participating in a bizarre video game that has somehow crossed over into reality" (Cops Organize Big Search" 2008), a sentiment that was widely repeated in the mainstream media.

On October 25, 2008, the Ontario Provincial Police announced that their cybercrimes unit was working with Microsoft Corporation in examining Brandon's Xbox in order to identify members of the boy's gaming CoD4 clan. Not only did Microsoft agree to breach its privacy protocols in releasing personal information of its subscribers, but the company also contributed $25,000 towards a reward for information concerning the missing teen (Dabrowski 2008). Meanwhile, in cyberspace, countless bloggers weighed in: a website "findbrandoncrisp.com" was launched and students at Brandon's high school began a Facebook group, "Where is Brandon Crisp," which grew to 22,000 members before being taken down by its moderator for abusive comments being posted. And on Monday, October 20, 2008, *GamePolitics.com*, a website self-described as "where politics and video games collide," began to chronicle Brandon's disappearance, posting daily updates of mainstream media coverage and their own analysis of both the coverage and the issues surrounding the case. For *GamePolitics.com*, while acknowledging that there are documented cases of sexual predators using video games to stalk young victims, the possibility that Brandon could have been abducted by someone involved in organized crime or Internet gambling was decidedly far-fetched, as was the likelihood that he had run away to join a professional gaming league, which was also widely speculated on within the mass media. Fueling the fear over abduction, whether by a pedophile or another gamer, and of much more concern to posters and managers of *GamePolitics.com* was the discourse of Internet addiction, which, as discussed above, seems to be overtaking violent content as the most "harmful effect" of video games. All these "risks" are interrelated: in common parlance, the more time a child spends online, the greater the likelihood of either falling prey to a pedophile or developing antisocial and possibly violent behaviors.

## Addiction Panic

A decade ago, Canadian parents were far more likely to restrict their children's television viewing than their video game playing. To be sure, a study conducted by communication and media scholar Stephen Kline in 1997 found that less than 25 percent of teens had experienced parental restrictions with regard to video games while 43 percent had television restrictions. Kline (1999) argues that given the degree of industry promotional publicity, it "is not surprising that many parents adopt an uncritical attitude towards video game play," seeing it, rather, as promoting computer literacy. And when restrictions were in place, they tended to be concerning homework, the lateness of playing time and duration of the play, more than the content of the games. Notably, "heavy players were no more likely to experience censorship than light players" (Kline 1999). Following the tragedy of Brandon Crisp, however, Toronto's Centre for Addiction and Mental Health initiated a pilot project to treat problem gaming, gambling and Internet addiction, joining a growing increase in government-sponsored programs worldwide (Caron 2002). According to a clinical director with an American Center for Online Addiction, warning signs of Internet addiction include playing for increasing periods of time, thinking about gaming during other activities, gaming to escape "real life" problems and anxieties, lying to friends and family about the extent of one's gaming habits, and "feeling irritable" when trying to cut down on gaming (Caron 2002). Nonetheless, neither the Canadian Medical Association nor the American Medical Association has yet to recognize or acknowledge Internet addiction as a medical condition.

While Kline himself resists the discourse of addiction, his research subjects do not: 50 percent use the word to describe a friend's gaming behavior (Tournemille 2008). In his 1998 study of 650 youth aged 11 to 18, Kline found that 93 percent had played video games and 24 percent were heavy players (playing more than one hour per day). In a more recent survey of 1500 teenagers, 25 percent showed signs of compulsive gaming (Tournemille 2008). At issue for many gamers, however, is not merely whether obsessive or compulsive game play should be considered an addiction, but the broader implications of the discourse. A November 26, 2008, posting on *GamePolitics.com*, three weeks after the discovery of Brandon Crisp's body, cites a BBC interview with Keith Bakker, founder of the Smith and Jones Centre in Amsterdam, Europe's first (and apparently only) clinic to treat game addiction, in which Bakker maintained that 90 percent of compulsive gamers are not, in fact, addicts and that compulsive gaming is a social problem rather than a psychological one. Bakker bases his conclusions on two years of treating compulsive gamers, during the course of which his thinking shifted on what constitutes addiction. While kids came to the clinic showing symptoms "similar to addictions and chemical dependencies," Bakker soon recognized that 80 percent had been bullied at school and felt isolated. Continuing to think of gamers' behavior as addiction "takes away the element of choice these people have." In accordance, his clinic altered its treatment program to focus on "activity-based social and communication skills to help them rejoin society." Ultimately, for Bakker, clinics such as his would no longer be needed if "parents and adults in the community took more responsibility for the habits of their children" ("Journalist Reflects" 2008)

Brandon Crisp's parents repeatedly stressed that, while frustrated with failed attempts to limit the amount of time their son was spending with his Xbox (which they had taken from him several times before), they had little idea just what gaming meant to him. As Steve Crisp said to *MacLean's*, "When I took his Xbox away, I took away his identity" (Campbell and Gatehouse 2008). For *GamePolitics. com*, irritated by the "constant theme" of Internet addiction running throughout the investigation of Brandon's disappearance, not written about was "the fact that Brandon was experiencing the same issues that plague many adolescents: difficulty in finding one's place and conflicts with parents." According to *GamePolitics.com*, commenting on CBC journalist Jesse Brown's December 2008 podcast (in which he described *Call of Duty 4* as a "sad place"): "What Brown doesn't get is that CoD4 may have become for Brandon a place where he could fit in, have fun and enjoy a sense of community and accomplishment" ("Journalist Reflects" 2008).

In addition to Brown's podcast, two pieces of mainstream journalism on the various dangers of video games drew the ire of the gaming community, including a *MacLean's* article of October 30, 2008 entitled "What Happened to Brandon?" and subtitled "The Disappearance of the Teen has Sparked an Outcry over Video Game Addictions." For Andy Chalk, writing for the online gaming journal, *The Escapist*, while the article does attempt balance by citing Entertainment Consumer Association President Hal Hilpin on how the larger issue of "media addiction" has been politicized down to "game addiction" at the expense of all other forms of mass media entertainment, *MacLean's* chose to ignore assessments that video game addiction "doesn't necessarily exist at all" (Chalk 2008). Nor does it mention that the American Psychiatric Association changed its mind on recommending it be adopted as a diagnosis. For Chalk, the Canadian news magazine is just the most recent example of "the games made him do it" coverage that plagues mainstream journalism. As Chalk sees it, the disappearance of Brandon Crisp highlights one of the biggest problems facing the video game industry today: the sensationalism of the mass media.

*GamePolitics.com* also took issue with the *MacLean's* article, citing excerpts from and a link to Chalk's article. The last Crisp-related posting on the site, however, was on March 6, 2009, alerting readers of an investigative report that was to air on CBC's *The Fifth Estate* that night, with its opening line reading, "If preliminary reports are any indication, video games are in for a media beatdown on Canadian TV network CBC tonight." The posting cites two such reports: from the national newspaper, *The Globe and Mail*, and the tabloid *Toronto Sun*. For *The Globe and Mail*'s columnist Andrew Ryan (quoted in "CBC to Air" 2009):

> Some kids get hooked on Guitar Hero, but the vast majority of gamers today spend more money—and time—on shockingly graphic search-and-destroy video games. Turning every violent teen male fantasy into reality, these games have a simple primal theme: kill, and kill again. And then keep killing.

The excerpt from *The Globe and Mail* article cites *The Fifth Estate*'s Gillian Findlay, who relayed how shocked she was, as a parent, by how little she knew about "this world" (quoted in "CBC to Air" 2009). For Findlay, "The violence of these games is so real and beauty of the graphics is almost overwhelming. You can see how seductive these games can be to teenage players" (quoted in "CBC to Air" 2009). While for Ryan, *The Fifth Estate*'s piece (entitled "Top Gun") was "typically objective" though likely to "rattle some viewers" (particularly parents of kids who might already be "addicted"), for *GamePolitics.com* the show "sounds like a cheap media manipulation" (quoted in "CBC to Air" 2009). For example, when recalling an interview with players from a Canadian professional gaming league, Findlay remarks that it was conducted with large monitors playing video game footage in the background, which, Findlay remembers, the players could not take their eyes off. *GamePolitics.com* (quoted in "CBC to Air" 2009) asks,

> Did the reporter *really* conduct this interview in front of large monitors and then blame some kind of video game effect for the subjects' eyes wandering? Would it have been any different if a hockey game or House was running on those monitors? Maybe that's why most reporters don't conduct interviews with their subjects facing TV screens. They're, you know, distracting.

*GamePolitics.com* also cites Steve Tilley, for whom the CBC's piece is "lazy, cheap and disappointingly one-sided" ("CBC to Air" 2009). At issue for Tilley, who covers video games for the *Toronto Sun*, is Findlay's "lack of journalistic responsibility" to educate herself adequately on the topic that she was investigating (quoted in "CBC to Air" 2009). Her approach rather was to treat "teenaged gamers like slack-jawed addicts obsessed with virtual mass murder. It's demeaning not only to the majority of gamers for whom this is harmless recreation, but to the nongaming viewing audience who might not know better" (quoted in "CBC to Air" 2009). For gaming enthusiasts and industry apologists, *The Fifth Estate*'s "Top Gun" was certainly bound to offend, as were headlines such as Ryan's "A training ground for killing machines" in *The Globe and Mail* (quoted in "CBC to Air" 2009). I would here, then, like to revisit the debate over violent content, not just concerning the issues Findlay addressed, but also in regard to, overlooked in her analysis, the allure of violent, specifically war-themed video games for young males.

Airing months after Brandon Crisp's death, *The Fifth Estate*'s "Top Gun" made no mention of the earlier speculations that he had been lured to his death by a cyber-predator, even though the show included initial interviews with Brandon's parents conducted while their son was still missing. Nor did Findlay discuss the role Microsoft played in the investigation. Rather, the focus of the report, which Findlay also wrote, was on video game addiction, violent content, and who should bear responsibility for safeguarding minors from a lucrative and increasingly powerful global industry. Using a standard documentary format, "Top Gun" highlighted the Brandon Crisp tragedy as an entry point into the larger issue of the video game industry, moving from the personal to the political if you will.

By naming the program "Top Gun," the CBC could be seen as invoking an ironic nostalgia for a time when war-themed mass entertainment was "harmless," before the advent of first-person shooter video games with corporate-sponsored tournaments for professional "e-athletes." One of the top grossing Hollywood films of the 1980s, Tony Scott's 1986 *Top Gun* was at the same time acknowledged by its producer to be a recruitment ad for the US Navy (David 2004: 181), ushering in a new era of "technofetishism" refiguring "public interest in the military from the axis of ideology to the axis of technology" (Stahl 2010: 28). Findlay's report did discuss the popularity of war-themed games and their graphic intensity and featured interviews with young male gamers discussing the thrill of the kill, the sense of achievement as one moves up to a higher skill (kill) level, as well as the (largely homophobic and misogynist) "trash talk" they encounter playing with clans online (for example, "shut up, you faggot," "check the size of your dick," "you shit bitch"). Also interviewed was the CEO for Modern League Gaming, who acknowledged that there are 100 million gamers in the United States alone, of whom 96 percent are males under the age of 30, thus a valuable target for advertisers. What Findlay's "Top Gun" did not do, however, was state the obvious: that it is not merely *teenagers* who are "seduced" by the "promises of fame and fortune for those who can kill their way to the top," as per her preamble to the show, but *boys*. While the show did well to contextualize the Crisp tragedy within a political economy of a highly profitable gaming industry that seemingly bears no accountability, it presumes that that industry is autonomous rather than a cultural product of militarized masculinity. If, for the moment, we want to remain within the discourse of addiction, perhaps we should follow Chris Hedges (2002: 3) and name war as the drug.

## War Games and Boy Gamers

Video games were certainly not the first entertainment form to engage in the romance and romantic fictions of war and warfare. Even before Hollywood action films, the *Iliad* and *Beowulf* testify that "as long we've been consuming narrative entertainment, we've thrilled to the exploits of blood-streaked warriors who hack limbs off their opponents" (Herz 1997: 194, cited in Kline et al. 2003: 248). Hollywood itself emerged out of World War I; as renowned screenwriter Anita Loos put it, "World War one was the reason for Hollywood" (Virilio 1984: 38). Thus it is perhaps not surprising that in 1929 the first Academy Award for best motion picture went to the combat film *Wings* (1927) which was (and still is) praised for the technical mastery of its aerial dogfight sequences. Lauded for its "groundbreaking realism," the film's director, writer, and stars all had military flight experience, which was especially crucial for the stars "who were sent aloft solo to play their scenes into automatic cameras welded to the cockpits of their biplanes" (Burr 1999: 130), a precursor to both *Top Gun* of 1986 and watching the 1991 Persian Gulf War on television through the lens of the bomber pilot. More than 70 years after *Wings*, Steven Spielberg's *Saving Private Ryan* (1998) was heralded as the most "realistic" combat film to date, scoring heavily both with critics and at the box office, not to mention the US Department of Defense, which awarded Spielberg a Medal for Distinguished Service for helping to "reconnect the American public with its military men and women, while rekindling a deep sense of gratitude for the daily sacrifices they make on the front lines of our Nation's defenses" (Hozic 2001: 140–41, 202). This gave a needed boost to Spielberg's financially beleaguered multimedia entertainment company, DreamWorks SKG. Founded in 1994, DreamWorks (boasting the first motion picture studio built in Los Angeles in over 50 years) is one of 875 entertainment-related companies that dot the LA landscape, employing some 14,000 of the more than 50,000 people on the Hollywood payroll. Surpassing the air and space industries, the entertainment industry is now Southern California's largest employer, wooing former defense contractors to boot. Alongside the conversion of old military bases into studio lots, computer companies such as Silicon Graphics, which were formerly dependent upon the Department of Defense, are increasingly turning to Hollywood for research projects and funding (Hozic 1999).

This is not to say that the entertainment industry has come to replace the military-industrial complex outright. Rather, initiatives in the 1990s such as the Clinton administration's Technology Reinvestment Project, which promotes the development of products having both a military and civilian use, Hollywood is a prime economic and strategic asset to the Pentagon (Hozic 1999). Thus, we see flight simulators used in amusement parks, the technology used for submarine detection making its way into recording studios, and the image generation technology used for missile "rehearsal" incorporated into the software for computer games. However,

> the state-initiated conversion has done little to increase the transparency of military financing or to open it to public debate; rather, it has created a novel form of commercial-military alliance in which even the state's monopoly over violence now depends on global consumption of entertainment, communication and transportation. (Hozic 1999: 298)

This alliance has thus gone beyond even what Dwight D. Eisenhower cautioned against in 1961 as the military-industrial complex. Adding media and entertainment industries to the mix amounts to what James Der Derian (2001: xi–xix) describes as a "military-industrial-media-entertainment network" (or MIME-NET) wherein simulation technologies create a fidelity between the representation and "reality" of war, and the human faculties for entertainment join forces with cyborg programs for killing. Video games, war-themed games in particular, are firmly located within this network although—as with the pre-cinematic war narratives mentioned above—the history of war gaming extends further than its digitization in the 1980s, think only of Chess (Deterding 2010: 23). Kline et al. argue that interactive video games initially "flowed from military infrastructures into subcultures of hacker play, sci fi speculation and cybernetic simulation" ever since what is regarded by many as the very first video game, *Spacewar*, inspired by the "real" war in space over the Sputnik launch in 1957, was developed in 1962 at MIT (Kline, Dyer-Witherford and de Peuter 2003: 85–90, Halter 2006: 74–8). It is significant that *Spacewar* evolved from an academic setting rather than the toy business or electronics industry, for before the advent of personal computers in the 1970s, the most advanced electronics and computer research was being conducted by "Big Science," which was itself "created and fostered for military purposes" (Halter 2006: 78).

In the early years of the video game industry, the role of the Pentagon was largely as financier, backing only a few select projects, but evolved into a more active game producer as the military-entertainment industry continued to accelerate in the 1980s and 1990s, generating "texts that blur the line between entertainment and militarism" (Huntman and Payne 2010: 5). Atari's *Battlezone* is an early indication of the dissolution of that line. Developed in 1980 as an arcade game, it was the first three-dimensional game in a first-person perspective as seen through a periscope positioned in a simulated tank. Accordingly, it caught the attention of the US Army Training Support Center, who recognized its potential as a simulation training tool (Kline et al. 2003: 96, 100). Thus began an increasingly synergistic dynamic between the military and video game industries:

> As in all symbiotic relationships, the benefits flowed both ways: the relationship between military research and video gaming, although at first a classic case of civilian spin-offs from war preparations, was also becoming a sophisticated way of getting the entertainment sector to subsidize the costs of military innovation and training. (Kline et al. 2003: 101)

Still, the cozy alliance between the US military and the video game industry is not in itself sufficient to explain the role violent games play in the gaming industry. After all, alongside war games, the beginnings of the industry also saw the emergence of more benign, and enormously popular, fare like *Pong* and *Pac-Man* (Kline et al. 2003: 248). The escalation of virtual violence, as Kline et al. argue, was due to a confluence of factors, from maturing consumers to improved technology, but especially because of increasingly specialized and competitive marketing. As they explain, following Atari's crash in the 1980s, Nintendo seized the opportunity to expand into the home console market by conducting research monitoring the tastes, preferences and buying power of core customers, which confirmed that the principal players were males between eight and seventeen years of age: "Once the action-adventure, sports, racing, fighting, and shooting genres adapted from the arcade proved popular with this youthful male audience, the company had strong economic incentive to continue to amplify the genres, rather than risk breaking ground with new content" (Kline et al. 2003: 249). From here on, it was a matter of successive gaming manufacturers upping the ante with more, and more intensive, violence, including products such as Sega's *Mortal Kombat* and id Software's *Doom* and *Quake* in the mid-1990s. Given that first-person shooter games essentially share the same formula, the only way for developers to differentiate products from their competitors is by "elaborating and intensifying speed and violence" (Kline et al. 2003: 251). Violent games are also a way of minimizing production costs. As with film and television producers, game developers realize that violence requires a minimum of creative scripting and design: "From the point of view of marketers, violence is a cultural idiom that requires no translation within increasingly transnational entertainment markets" (Kline et al. 2003: 251).

None of this was lost on the military. Given that video game companies and Army recruiters often target the same demographic (primarily young males), when in 1999 recruitment figures reached their lowest point in thirty years, US Congress increased the Army's recruitment budget to 2.2 billion dollars, which proved a catalyst to develop *America's Army*, designed (by the Naval Postgraduate School's Modeling, Virtual Environment and Simulation Institute) to give players a sense of what army life is like (Nichols 2010). Aiming at "realism," game designers draw on actual military ordinance, training locations, and even actual military campaigns and combat scenarios. Widely criticized as a "government-sanctioned" first-person shooter game that teaches combat skills to middle- and high school children, *America's Army* is also highly popular and profitable with more than 500,000 downloads within the first month of the game's release and more than 8.5 million registered users around the world by October 2007. Some 20 percent of cadets entering West Point and 40 percent of new Army recruits said that they had played it and, moreover, more than 30 percent of Americans admit that their knowledge of the US Army came from the game (Nichols 2010). Considered relatively mild on the violence scale to ensure a Teen (T) rating (players who are killed hear no sound and are shown only a small red circle marking their virtual death), in the first section of the two-part game characters are taught the virtues and values of US Army life. In order to advance, players must score in areas of "loyalty, duty, respect, selflessness, service, and honor" (Nichols 2010: 41). In selling American military values and strategic goals both at home and abroad, for David Nieborg (2010: 58), *America's Army* is thus a public relations tool for the War on Terror specifically and an example of what Nye has defined as "soft power" (cultural power) by "tapping into and affecting popular culture by becoming culturally popular."

Nieborg considers *Call of Duty 4: Modern Warfare* among the examples of first-person shooter games that serve as propaganda for the US-led War on Terror (although in contrast to *America's Army*, players of CoD4 are not restricted to the vantage point of the US soldier and can thus play from "enemy" positions). Perhaps not surprisingly, the September 11 terror attacks and the resultant invasions of Afghanistan and Iraq saw a boom in sales of war-themed video games that exude "the pure experience of battle" by avoiding any alternative narrative (Stahl 2010: 98). As communication scholar Roger Stahl (2010: 98) describes,

> Games tended to avoid legal, ethical, moral, or ideological considerations, including any other criteria used to measure the wisdom of war. Indeed, if there is a dominant 'ideology⊚ expressed in these game narratives, it is a marked disdain for diplomacy and preference for force consistent with the rhetoric of the war on terror (as in President Bush's mantra, 'We will not negotiate with terrorists⊚).

When Microsoft released its fourth instalment of *Call of Duty* in 2007, it marked a departure from its prior history of producing World War II scenarios, instead featuring conflicts in the Middle East, as well as a "growing rivalry," named Russia – and became the top selling game worldwide (Stahl 2010: 101). In one level of the game, "Death from Above," the player controls an AC-130 Spectre gunship (a plane armed with a large calibre machine gun and mounted cannon), which received significant public exposure during the invasions of Iraq and Afghanistan as the Pentagon periodically released images of infrared gun sight footage to television networks (which inevitably ended up on YouTube). Voices instruct players how to feel, celebrating successful strikes with "Good kill, see lots of little pieces down there." In other words, the game permits the player to replay what they had seen on television and YouTube. So striking is the verisimilitude that one player posted scenes from the game on YouTube in pretence that it was the "real thing" and drew the ire of other users. As one user commented, "Stop putting videos of your gameplay of COD4 like its real life. damn. when i want to look up a real AC-130 bombing the crap out of towel heads i don't want to see some kid play a game that 2 million people have already beat. Ok!" Tellingly, also on YouTube, a real AC-130 video bore the caption: "Note: This is not Call of Duty 4" (Stahl 2010: 103)!

## Militarized Masculinity

None of this suggests that video gamers cannot distinguish between the real and the fake in "real life." Players know full well that they are not killing "real people" when immersed in the fictive world of the game. Gaming apologists continually argue that video games are a healthy means of channeling rather than performing aggression. And on one level, one could indeed argue that playing war-themed video games is a safe alternative to engaging in actual warfare. But whether Brandon Crisp had aspirations to join the Canadian Armed Forces or a professional gaming league is beside the point. Building on political economist Robin Luckham's 1984 work on "armament culture," and setting aside his tendency to assume a wholly passive consumer, Matthew Payne (2010: 207) considers that cultural products such as war-themed videos "agree with a military logic even when there are no discernible ties linking toys or games with government or defense firms, even when leisure pursuits ... do not take place within obviously militarized contexts." We can see this logic at work with the above YouTube comment on "bombing the crap out of towel heads" and in the homophobic and misogynist "trash talk" observed in players in *The Fifth Estate*'s "Top Gun," discussed above.

For Payne, Luckham's analysis of armament culture grants too much power to military-inflected culture (1984) and not enough to consumers' actual practices. In conducting an enthnographic study of "ludic war," which he defines as "the activity of playing war or military-themed video games alone or with others," Payne observes a number of trends amongst players of *Call of Duty 4* that warrant attention as they pertain to militarized masculinity (2010: 207). Ludic wars, he emphasizes, may be fictional but are nonetheless played in real-world spaces and in specific technological and social configurations. One lesson that Payne learned while immersed in a LAN environment was the degree of technology fetishism, with players preoccupied with understanding weapons technologies and team tactics, which then extends from the virtual battlefield to having the requisite PC technologies and skill. Uncritically celebrating the latest and greatest gadgetry, Payne argues, reflects deeper cultural issues: "Not unlike the military-themed games' basic play logics, this unreflective adulation of newer and 'better' consumer wares suggests that for every problem there is a technological solution" (Payne 2010: 213). That such techno-rationality is highly gendered, and racialized, should not go without saying. Indeed, the Persian Gulf War of 1991 has been widely commented on as the moment in which American political identity was reconfigured through a specifically techno-masculinized military to counter the "impotence" brought on by the humiliation of defeat in Vietnam. For feminist scholar Christina Masters (2005: 118), the Gulf War's "rebirth" of the American military was contingent upon the "re-production of hegemonic militarized masculinity," which by necessity rendered Iraq and Iraqis as wholly "other." She explains,

> The testing of American 'manhood', the flexing of military phallic muscle, visions of the American 'warrior' and all types of phallic representations reconstituted the American military discourse and simultaneously reconstituted American soldiers. Throughout the Gulf War, it did not seem to matter than many soldiers (combat and non-combat) were women, racial, and ethnic and sexual minorities. It did not seem to matter because central to representations of the American self during the war was the constitution of the Middle Eastern 'other' which posited and privileged American identity as white, western, heterosexual and masculine with the definitive purpose of defeating the non-white non-western, Middle Eastern emasculated other. (Masters 2005: 118)

This constructing of an emasculated other is readily apparent in Payne's (2010: 216) account of a discourse of domination running throughout the gaming space, LANopolis. With women, girls, and people of color notably absent (with no more than six female players present at any one time during his entire period of study), players' comments were rife with "braggadocio, machismo, sexism, racism and homophobia." These include the type of "trash talk" noted previously but also the flaming of games that were not considered "masculine enough," for example, talk of playing Nintendo would be derided as for "babies and sissies" (Payne 2010: 217). One comment in particular encapsulates both the technology fetishism and discourse of domination that together demonstrate a militarized masculinity of first-person shooter game culture. During an all-night gaming session, one player, having taken a break to fetch a drink, took a loud slurp and, joking to the gamer next to him, said "I like my C4 (an explosive device popular in many combat games) like I like my women.... I like them in small, tight packages that are ready to blow," as he used his hands to mimic a mushroom cloud explosion (Payne 2010: 219).

## Concluding Remarks

In concluding, I would like to refer briefly again to *The Fifth Estate*'s "Top Gun" which, as noted, failed adequately to address the inherently gendered nature of violent video games. The militarized masculinity that pervades war-themed games, as Kline et al. (2003: 257) suggest, is bound up with the medium's gender bias; from the structuring of the industry and "testosterone marketing" schematics to the ways that women and girls are represented within video games, perpetually appearing in limited and stereotypical roles. In their words: "Such a culture seems to provide boys with (yet another) vivid source of instruction in how to ignore, objectify, or even abuse women, while unmistakably informing girls that digital space is not for them" (Kline et al. 2003: 257). The moral panic that accompanies young peoples' use of popular culture and Internet technologies, focusing as it does on a discourse of addiction and copycat violence, does little to address this imbalance. Present in some, but absent in most mainstream media accounts of Brandon Crisp's disappearance is the fact that he was of slight stature and build. As his parents recall on *The Fifth Estate*, he was an avid hockey player, a star goalie in fact, yet his "small size left him sitting on the bench" and at the age of twelve, he was pulled. As many observed, the online game world was one where he could fit in, find a sense of community and personal accomplishment and, I would add, recuperate and assert his masculinity.

As with any form of popular culture, there exist moments of resistance and possibilities for subversion within video game culture. Some gamers have turned to making short films and videos, which oppose military game culture by exposing its pleasures of death and destruction (see Chien 2010). And *America's Army* has itself been transformed into a site of anti-war protest by performance artist Joseph Delappe, who entered the game in March 2006 on the third anniversary of the invasion of Iraq. Using an avatar named "dead-in-iraq," Delappe began typing in the name, age, service branch, and date of death of each American soldier killed in Iraq in an ongoing project that, he says, will continue until the war is over (Chan 2010). For real.

# References

2008. Addiction specialist: 90% of compulsive gamers are not addicts. *GamePolitics.com* [Online]. Available at: http://www.gamepolitics.com/category/topics/brandon-crisp [accessed: September 24, 2011].

Boyle, T. 2008. Family fears boy lured by gamers. *The Toronto Star* [Online, October 22].

Available at: http://www.thestar.com/news/article/521731 [accessed: September 24, 2011].

Buckingham, D. (ed.) 1993. *Reading Audiences: Young People and the Media*. New York: Manchester University Press.

Burr, T. 1999. Top guns. *Entertainment Weekly*, March 1, 130.

Campbell, C. and Gatehouse, G. 2008. What happened to Brandon? *MacLean's* [Online, October 30]. Available at: http://www.macleans.ca/culture/lifestyle/article.jsp?content=20081030_22084_22084 [accessed: September 25, 2011].

Caron, N. 2008. Experts reflect on video game addictions. *gamefwd* [Online, November 13]. Available at: http://gamefwd.org/index.php?option=com_cont ent&view=article&id=37:experts-reflect-on-video-game-addictions&catid=10:h ealth&Itemid=8 [accessed: September 24, 2011].

2009. CBC to air investigative report into Brandon Crisp case tonight. *GamePolitics. com* [Online, March 6]. Available at: http://www.gamepolitics.com/category/topics/brandon-crisp [accessed: September 25, 2011].

Chalk, A. 2008. The stigma of normal. *The Escapist* [Online, November 5]. Available at: http://www.escapistmagazine.com/articles/view/columns/the-needles/5446-The-Stigma-of-Normal [accessed: September 25, 2011].

Chan, D. 2010. *Dead-in-iraq*: The spatial politics of digital game art activism and in-game protest, in *Joystick Soldiers: The Politics of Play in Military Video Games*, edited by N.B. Huntemann and M.T. Payne. New York: Routledge, 272–86.

Chien, I. 2010. Playing against the grain: machinima and military gaming, in *Joystick Soldiers: The Politics of Play in Military Video Games*, edited by N.B. Huntemann and M.T. Payne. New York: Routledge, 239–51.

Cohen, S. 2002 (1972, 1980). *Folk Devils and Moral Panics: The Creation of the Mods and Rockers*. 3rd Edition. London: Routledge.

2008. Cops organize big search for missing gamer; mom clings to CoD4 theory. *GamePolitics.com* [Online, October 24]. Available at: http://www.gamepolitics. com/2008/10/24/cops-organize-big-search-missing-gamer-mom-clings-cod4-theory [accessed: January 29, 2012].

Dabrowski, W. 2008. "Microsoft matches reward for missing Canadian teen. *Reuters* [Online, October 27]. Available at: http://www.reuters.com/assets/print?aid=USTRE49Q5N320081027 [accessed: September 25, 2011].

Der Derian, J. 2001. *Virtuous War: Mapping the Military-Industrial-Media-Entertainment-Network*. Boulder: Westview.

Deterding, S. 2010. Living room wars: remediation, boardgames, and the early history of video wargaming, in *Joystick Soldiers: The Politics of Play in Military Video Games*, edited by N.B. Huntemann and M.T. Payne. New York: Routledge, 21–38.

Halter, E. 2006. *From Sun Tzu to Xbox: War and Video Games*. New York: Thunder House.

Hedges, C. 2002. *War Is a Force That Gives Us Meaning*. New York: Public Affairs.

Hozic, A. 1999. Uncle Sam goes to Siliwood: of landscapes, Spielberg and hegemony. *Review of International Political Economy*, 6(3), 289–312.

Hozic, A. 2001. *Hollyworld: Space, Power, and Fantasy in the American Economy*. Ithaca: Cornell University Press.

2008. Journalist reflects on Brandon Crisp case, terms CoD4 multiplayer "a sad place." *GamePolitics.com* [Online, December 18]. Available at: http://www.gamepolitics.com/category/topics/brandon-crisp [accessed: September 25, 2011].

Kline, S. 1999. Moral panics and video games [Online]. Available at: http://www.sfu.ca/media- lab/research/mediaed/Moral%20Panics%20Video%20Games.pdf [accessed: September 25, 2011].

Kline S., Dyer-Witheford, N., and de Peuter, G. 2003. *Digital Play: The Interaction of Technology, Culture, and Marketing*. Montreal: McGill-Queen's University Press.

Luckham, R. 1984. Armament culture. *Alternatives*, 10(1), 1–44.

2008. Magazine profile of missing gamer focuses on game addiction. *GamePolitics.com* [Online, November 5]. Available at: http://www.gamepolitics.com/category/topics/brandon-crisp [accessed: September 25, 2011].

Masters, C. 2005. Bodies of technology: cyborg soldiers and militarised masculinities. *International Feminist Journal of Politics*, 7(1), 112–32.

Miller, T. (ed.) 2002. *Television Studies*. London: British Film Institute.

2008. Missing gamer found dead. *GamePolitics.com* [Online, November 5]. Available at: http://www.gamepolitics.com/category/topics/brandon-crisp [accessed: September 25, 2011].

Molloy, P. 2002. Moral spaces and moral panics: high schools, war zones and other dangerous Places. *Culture Machine* [Online]. Available at: http://culturemachine.tees.ac.uk/Articles/molloy.htm [accessed: August 9, 2011].

Morrow, A. 2008. No leads yet in Barrie teen's disappearance. *The Toronto Star* [Online, October 19]. Available at: http://www.thestar.com/News/Ontario/article/520251 [accessed: January 28, 2012].

Nieborg, D.B. 2010. Training recruits and conditioning youth: the soft power of military games, in *Joystick Soldiers: The Politics of Play in Military Video Games*, edited by N.B. Huntemann and M.T. Payne. New York: Routledge, 53–66.

Payne, M.T. 2010. "F*ck you, Noob Tube!" Learning the art of ludic LAN war, in *Joystick Soldiers: The Politics of Play in Military Video Games*, edited by N.B. Huntemann and M.T. Payne. New York: Routledge, 206–22.

Payne, R. 2008. Virtual panic: children online and the transmission of harm, in *Moral Panics over Contemporary Children and Youth*, edited by C. Krinsky. Aldershot: Ashgate, 31–46.

Robb, D. 2004. *Operation Hollywood: How the Pentagon Shapes and Censors the Movies*. New York: Prometheus Books.

*Saving Private Ryan* (dir. Steven Spielberg, 1998).

Schissel, B. 2008. Justice undone: public panic and the condemnation of children and youth, in *Moral Panics over Contemporary Children and Youth*, edited by C. Krinsky. Farnham: Ashgate, 15–29.

Stahl, R. 2010. *Militainment, Inc. War, Media, and Popular Culture*. New York: Routledge. *Top Gun* (dir. Tony Scott, 1986).

1949. Teenagers: freedom or licence? Have today's parents enough authority? *Citizens' Forum. Canadian Broadcasting Corporation* [Online, April 4, 2008], October 27. Available at: http://archives.cbc.ca/society/youth/clips/14470/ [accessed: September 25, 2011].

Top gun. 2009. *The Fifth Estate. CBC.ca* [Online], March 6. Available at: http://www.cbc.ca/fifth/content/2009/03/top-gun.html [accessed: September 25, 2011].

Tournemille, D. 2002. First-person shooter: the video gamer's addiction. *CTV News* [Online, August 28]. Available at: http://www.ctv.ca/CTVNews/ExclusivesSciTech/20020828/game_addiction_020823/ [accessed: September 25, 2011].

Virilio, P. 1989. *War and Cinema: The Logistics of Perception*. London: Verso.

*Wings* (dir. William Wellman, 1927).

# MyMoralPanic: Adolescents, Social Networking, and Child Sex Crime Panic

### Samantha A. Smith and Simon A. Cole*

In April 2006, 19-year-old-Pete Solis of Travis County, Texas, came across a profile on MySpace that caught his attention. The information on the MySpace profile of "Julie Doe" identified her as a 14-year-old first year high school student, and Solis had no reason to doubt she was who she said she was. Solis's own MySpace page said that he was an 18-year-old high school senior and football star. The two had numerous interactions via MySpace and over the phone before agreeing to meet in real life for a date; in each of these instances, neither Solis nor Doe told the other that their MySpace profiles were not entirely accurate.

According to Solis, the two went to dinner and a movie, followed by some sexual activity not including intercourse (Hylton 2006a). The following day, Julie's mother "Jane" called the police and reported the sexual assault of her daughter. In Texas, it is a felony for anyone over the age of 18 to engage in a sexual act with someone under the age of seventeen, though a defendant has an affirmative defense if he is less than three years older than a victim who is at least 14 years old (Texas§ 22. 011). Solis faced potential criminal charges for statutory rape and violated MySpace's terms of service policy by intentionally providing false information. It turned out that Julie Doe was actually 13 years old and thus also in violation of MySpace's terms. Her mother filed a lawsuit against MySpace seeking $30 million in damages, alleging, "MySpace actively and passively encourages young underage children to join MySpace, and then directs them to communicate and socialize with complete strangers" (*Doe v. MySpace* 2006: 13). As such, the complaint continued, MySpace and its parent company News Corp, as well as Pete Solis, were guilty of negligence,

---

\*    The authors are grateful to James Hess for his comments on an earlier draft of this chapter. The chapter is partially based on work supported by the National Science Foundation under grant no. IIS-0527729. Any opinions, findings, and conclusions or recommendations expressed in this material are those of the authors and do not necessarily reflect the views of the National Science Foundation.

gross negligence, fraud, fraud by nondisclosure, negligent misrepresentation, sexual assault, and intentional infliction of emotional distress.

In essence, the Does accused MySpace and its owner, Rupert Murdoch's News Corp, of exaggerating the extent of the measures taken to prevent children under fourteen from using the site. The lawsuit alleged that MySpace tacitly encouraged underage kids to use it, pretending to protect them from online predators, while in actuality doing nothing. The lawsuit charged that MySpace and News Corp should be held responsible for the sexual assault of Julie Doe because without MySpace facilitating her communication with Solis the assault would have never occurred. In 2007, a federal judge in Austin, Texas ruled in favor of MySpace and that ruling was upheld by the Fifth Circuit Court of Appeals in 2008 (Kunzelman 2008).

In this chapter, we suggest that *Doe v. MySpace* may be treated as a convenient temporal marker of the beginning of a moral panic about adolescents, sex crime, and social networking technology, a "social networking moral panic." We argue that this was not a distinct moral panic but rather should be seen as a phase of an emerging technology child sex crime panic that has evolved in concert with changing technology and is itself the intersection of at least three larger moral panics. This moral panic is a portent and example of a new breed of techno-scientific moral panics that historian of religion Philip Jenkins (2009: 46) suggests will emerge "as social issues focus more on scientific areas that demand substantial background—in information technology and biotechnology, to name just two." We argue that this panic did not end, but rather transitioned to a new suite of technologies: away from social networking and toward mobile devices. We also argue that the moral panic created risks and opportunities for technology providers. In the case of the social networking the moral panic played a role in shifting the balance of power between the two titans of the industry, MySpace and Facebook. Facebook's more adept response to the moral panic, a response which may not necessarily have entailed actual technological superiority but merely superior public relations, may have played in a role in its seemingly permanent displacement of its erstwhile competitor.

## Intersecting Moral Panics

Moral panics result from a collective response to the behavior of a few that is seen as deviant, immoral, and a threat to society. As Goode and Ben-Yehuda (1994: 13) explain, "The moral panic ... is characterized by the feeling, held by a substantial number of the members of a given society, that evildoers pose a threat to the society and the moral order as a consequence of their behavior." To this definition, other scholars add that moral panics tend to erupt suddenly, with a multitude of voices speaking as a consensus and media representations emphasizing sudden and dramatic increases in numbers and incidences far beyond a logical evaluation of the facts would support (Jenkins 1998, Hall et al. 1978). Of paramount importance in moral panics is a collective sense of being wronged, that an accepted boundary has been crossed, and someone or something fundamentally evil is to be held accountable. The sources of these evildoers, these folk devils (Cohen 1972), do not appear overnight. Rather, they consist of "some existing and recognizable elements" (Goode and Ben-Yehuda 1994: 28). As the name implies, a moral panic involves some uproar along a moral boundary, a fear of change or invasion by some sort of known yet mysterious evil, and a collective response to this perceived transgression.

An occurrence we will call the "social networking moral panic" may be viewed as merely one moment in a continuous panic that we call the emerging technology child sex crime panic. This panic is itself merely one of many moral panics over children and youth. As a number of commentators have noted, children and youth are especially prone to becoming the subject of moral panics (Buckingham 2000: 1–3, Krinsky 2008: 1).The social networking panic may also be viewed as a sort of braided rope composed of at least three strands of moral panics: a child sex crime panic, an Internet sex crime panic, and a larger panic over the effect of computer technology on young people.

The episodic child sex crime panics that have occurred over the course of the twentieth century are among the most studied of American moral panics (Chauncey 1993, Fass 1997, Freedman, 1987, Grometstein 2008, Jenkins 1998, Kincaid 1998). As long ago as 1998, Jenkins observed that, while historically child sex crime panics had waxed and waned periodically due to political, social, and ideological shifts, the contemporaneous panic over child sex crimes, which had begun around 1980, showed no sign of abating. The subsequent decade has done little to cast doubt on Jenkins's assessment. A number of scholars have explored the contours of the current child sex crime panic (see, for example, Corrigan 2006, Pratt 2005, Simon 1998, 2000, Zimring 2004). Jenkins (1998) notes that it is an accepted "fact" in America that children face a pervasive and grave threat of molestation or sexual abuse, especially by some unknown predator. However, in the contemporary sex crime panic, scholars have noted that sexual predators have been particularly associated with computer technology and the Internet, giving rise to the notion of the "cyber-predator" (Barak 2005: 80–81, Jenkins 1998, Lynch 2002, Schultz 2008).

The development of computer technologies inexpensive enough for mass consumption and the internetworking of these technologies, transforming them into communication devices, provoked social anxiety about sex for adult users: a "cyberpanic" (for example, Aycock and Buchignani 1995, Sandywell 2006). The notion that communication tools such as online communities and chat sites might be used to experiment with different sexual identities through cybersex produced both euphoria and anxiety (see, for example, Shaw 1997, Stone 1995). The proliferation of pornography and adult services on the Internet provoked further anxiety (Sandywell 2006: 50, Kuipers 2006). Online dating was seen as novel and risky. Early anxieties focused on rape in text-based online communities and multi-user domains and whether the idea was even plausible (Dibbell 1993, MacKinnon 1997a, 1997b, Mnookin 1996). There were worries that the Internet facilitated sexual harassment (Barak 2005) and fostered "anonymity and amorality in everyday life and incivility in public discourse" (Sandywell 2006: 49).

A third converging moral panic involves anxieties about the effects of computer technology on young people in general. While techno-optimists have seen computer technology as a potentially empowering educational tool for young people, techno-pessimists have seen a wealth of threats in the increasing availability of computer technology to young people, including vision problems, bad posture, decline of physical activity, failure to develop social skills, isolation and antisociality, exposure to violence, pornography, and content promoting seemingly destructive behaviors like self-harm, cyberbullying," reinforcement of gender stereotypes, and obesity (see, for example, Attewell, Suazo-Garcia, and Battle 2003, Boyd, Ryan, and Leavitt 2011, Buckingham 2000, Livingstone and Helsper 2010). The Internet is often portrayed in the media as fraught with "dangers" for "the digital generation," which is viewed as "vulnerable, at risk from new information and communication technologies" (Livingstone 2003).

And some scholars agree. Media scholar Sherry Turkle (2011), for example, found that many teenagers reported feeling anxious and that they had to maintain a particular image in regard to their online profiles. Other teens discussed the pressure they felt in creating online profiles and reported that they often feel completely tethered to their technology. Turkle ponders the potential long-term effects on teens who grew up with the Internet and are unable to set boundaries or even to arrange much-needed "alone time." Turkle considers what the possible long-term effects will be for a generation that has grown up posting every kind of information online, where it might be accessible forever.

These three strands of panic, we suggest, combine to form an especially potent emerging technology child sex crime panic. This panic itself may be seen as passing through various stages as information technology evolves at the blistering pace to which we have become accustomed in contemporary culture. Journalist Emily Bazelon (2011) observes that the moral panic in the 1940s over the pernicious influence of comic books on youth was eerily similar to of the contemporary morla panic over the influence of social networking and mobile technology. In the early 1990s, concerns about computers, youth, and sex crimes focused on technologies that would today be regarded as quaint artifacts of the prehistory of computer networking (and social networking), such as MUDs. There was concern about the increasing availability of "cyberporn" and about the even more serious concern that child pornography was being spread through file-sharing technologies like Usenet and bulletin boards that today might be viewed as obsolete (Jenkins 1998, 2009, Potter and Potter 2000).

The media scare over the Chamberlain case in 1996, precisely a decade prior to *Doe v. MySpace*, illustrates that certain themes have persisted despite changes in technology. A scare erupted over the activities of George Chamberlain, a prison inmate serving time for murder in Minnesota. Chamberlain, "a murderer known even outside the prison as a computer genius," worked while incarcerated as "manager of computer operations" for Insight, a company that essentially insourced computer and telemarketing work to cheap labor in American prisons. Using the Internet connection provided by this work assignment, Chamberlain had collected child pornography. But something seemingly both more innocuous and more "sinister" caused the scare: a database of children's names, ages, and addresses compiled from local newspapers, which had—with trustfulness that seems like naivety—run features with photographs of local children with titles like "Citizens of Tomorrow." Media coverage described the incident "as a case study on the cusp of a new information culture, at the shadowy crossroads of technology and criminal justice." It described "hamlets in northern Minnesota, places born of the railroad in the last century and bypassed by the highway in this one" which "now ... stand at the threshold of a new information age." It described the list as "a kind of nightmare mutation of data-base marketing" and said it "demonstrates how easily information can lose its innocence," a remarkable turn of phrase, "in the era of the Internet" (Bernstein 1996). Although the technology seems anachronistic, the discourse seems prescient. In subsequent years, similar scares emerged about chat rooms as facilitators of sexual predators seeking children (Potter and Potter 2001: 38, Sandywell 2006: 48).

## Social Networking

By 2006, there was little worry about chat rooms. Social networking sites (and especially the two most popular sites, MySpace and Facebook) were now the online locations where youth were vulnerable to being preyed upon by sexual predators (Grimmelmann 2009: 1190). Privacy concerns, particularly over the redistribution and accessibility of underage users' personal information, were a major source of criticism for both Facebook and MySpace. In 2006, MySpace's "Terms of Use Agreement" (*About Us*) dictated that in order to create a profile, one must be at least 14 years old, promise not to post false information knowingly, and agree not to post identifying information such as phone numbers, street addresses, last names, or emails (*About Us* 2006). However, since MySpace did not require verification of a user's age, for example, by having users submit photocopies of drivers' licenses, there was no way to ensure that user-generated information was accurate. Additionally, research shows that Internet users routinely lie about identity, gender, and physical attributes (Donath 1999, Lenhart and Madden 2000). As a result, it is not surprising that MySpace's rules about honesty, self-report information, and age were broken often, with little reprimanding from other users or the company.

In 2006, MySpace (*About Us* 2006) described itself in this way:

**MySpace is for everyone:**

- Friends who want to talk Online
- Single people who want to meet other Singles
- Matchmakers who want to connect their friends with other friends
- Families who want to keep in touch – map your Family Tree
- Business people and co-workers interested in networking
- Classmates and study partners
- Anyone looking for long lost friends!

MySpace promoted itself as the premier social networking site. MySpace used virtual space in order to facilitate and keep track of real-time interactions and relationships. MySpace was marketed primarily as a place to keep in touch with people one already knew. Nevertheless, with a multitude of search options available to users, it was perhaps easier to make new acquaintances than to reconnect with old friends.

On the other hand, Facebook represented itself as a place to connect with more people: friends, colleagues, and classmates. In its original conception, Facebook only allowed college students with valid college email addresses to join. Over time, Facebook's policy on membership became more inclusive and by 2006 anyone with a valid email could join (Thomas 2007). Facebook was similar to MySpace in that its terms of service restricted users under the age of 14 from creating a profile and banned registered sex offenders from joining. Further, Facebook's terms mandated that each person only create one personal profile and that one could not provide any false personal information (Boyd et al. 2011). Facebook also nominally required that contact information be current and correct and the site encouraged users to stay aware of changing privacy policies (*Terms* 2011). With all the insistence on truthfulness and accurate self-representation, Facebook appeared to be a place to both reconnect with friends and make new ones.

Despite these terms of service, both sites were accessed by users who failed to abide by all the terms. But MySpace and Facebook had little incentive to prioritize enforcement of their terms, as a more rigorously policed sign-up processes would discourage users from joining their networks. If the purpose of social networking sites was to connect with known friends, why did people routinely connect with strangers, and in particular, why was there so much concern about interacting with strangers online? The media hype surrounding social networking sites, Facebook and MySpace in particular, underscored the perception that such sites facilitated oversharing of private information, especially by adolescents. The panic surrounding social networks is part of a wider concern that youth have developed a culture of oversharing, supported by advances in technology, including smartphones and other mobile devices. Adolescents today have more opportunities to overshare, and these opportunities proliferate in step with technology.

In tandem with this culture of oversharing, much attention was given to the presence of sexual predators online, and how information shared not only by adolescent users themselves but also by their schools and community clubs could be gathered and used by lurking predators online, echoing similar concerns expressed with older technology in the Chamberlain case. This phantom predator then, was often portrayed as using social networking sites in order to prey upon adolescents online, though some research indicated that the rise of social networking had actually been accompanied by a *decrease* in sexual soliciting of minors online (Mann 2009: 262).

## The Social Networking Panic

Solis was not the only man accused of meeting his victim on a social networking site. The *Doe v. MySpace* (2006: 6–9) lawsuit catalogued 13 instances of an underage girl being sexually attacked or solicited by a man over 18 through MySpace. Another story, out of Chicago, was the court case of a 15-year-old girl who was gang raped and left unconscious in an alley after meeting two high school seniors who contacted her through MySpace (Sherriff 2006). Yet another online meeting to end in tragedy was that of Ashleigh Hall, a 17-year-old British female who left one night in October 2009 to meet a boy she had corresponded with on Facebook. However, instead of the teenage boy she had expected, she met a 32-year-old sex offender who raped and murdered her (Handley 2010).

Along with public concern about the online presence of sexual predators, significant social anxiety also existed concerning a problem that was, in a sense, its mirror image: young people oversharing accurate identifying information about themselves. The fear of oversharing online was often fueled by cases of offline victimization that frequently began with an online meeting, as with the case of Pete Solis and MySpace. For example, in 2006, 13-year-old Missouri resident Megan Meier committed suicide after receiving negative correspondence via MySpace from a boy named Josh Evans, whom she had met on the site. As it turned out, Josh Evans did not exist. His profile was created by Lori Drew, the mother of a classmate of Meier. Drew claimed that she created the account as part of plan to uncover whether Meier had been spreading malicious rumors about her 13-year-old daughter, Sarah. The plot then evolved to include embarrassing Meier at school by printing out correspondences with Josh—and showing them to classmates (Glover 2008). Masquerading as Josh Evans, Drew befriended Meier, and after gaining her trust, began sending her hurtful messages. The final blow allegedly came in a message from Evans that told Meier "the world would be a better place without you" (Zavis 2009).

Though Drew tried to conceal her involvement in Meier's suicide by deleting the account, she was indicted in federal court in Los Angeles on felony charges usually applied to hackers who steal government information ("More Thoughts" 2008). Local officials in Missouri had tried to find a way to charge Drew, but could not find any legal statutes under which her activities fell, a lacuna that, to many, demonstrated that the law was falling behind technology (see Carbonell 2010 on a similar case in Australia). Because MySpace's head offices were located in Los Angeles, prosecutors believed (apparently incorrectly) that they found a way to charge Drew with felony violation of the terms of service in order to use MySpace illegally to access information about Meier ("More Thoughts" 2008). Drew was acquitted of felony charges associated with violating MySpace's terms of service agreements, and the judge questioned whether the charges were an appropriate use of the statute. If Drew had been convicted of a felony crime for violating MySpace's terms of service, it would have made anyone who provided false information on the website (intentionally or not) guilty of committing a crime (Zavis 2009). The case then became widely read as an example of prosecutorial overreaching (see, for example, Jones 2011).

But moral panics are less about actual dangers than perceived threats. The notion that social networking sites posed unique and insidious dangers to young people was repeatedly featured in newspaper and online articles during this period. For example, articles in the *New York Times* included headlines such as "MySpace Draws a Questionable Crowd" (Gordon 2006), "New Scrutiny for Facebook over Predators" (Stone 2007b), "States Fault MySpace on Predator Issue" (Stone 2007a), "Teens Who Tell Too Much" (Downes 2006), and "Don't Talk to Invisible Strangers" (Bahney 2006). Articles in *Time* magazine included "How Safe is MySpace" (Hylton 2006b), "The Internet: Safe for Kids?" (Cruz 2009), "Teens Behaving Badly" (Stephey 2009), and "Should Facebook Have a 'Panic Button'" (Handley 2010)? *Newsweek* ran stories like "Predator's Playground" (Schrobsdorff 2006), and "A Towering Danger to Kids" (Braiker 2007). Articles from other news sites included headlines such as "MySpace, Facebook Attract Online Predators" (Williams 2006), "MySpace: Your Kids' Danger?" (Kreiser 2009), and "Thousands of MySpace Sex Offender Refugees Found on Facebook" (Schonfeld 2009).

These articles (along with hundreds of similar ones) reflected a picture of social networking sites as safe havens, even playgrounds, for sexual predators. Though numerous articles were written about potential online threats for adults, considerably more space was dedicated to the specific threat of online sexual predators to children and young adults, and in far more inflammatory language. For example, *The New York Times* (Stone 2007a) reported, "Some of the country's top law enforcement officials are charging that the online social network MySpace has discovered thousands of known sex offenders using its service, but has failed to act on the information." Here, MySpace was accused of failing to act to remove thousands of sex offenders that were known to be using the site, and this claim was supported by statements from the country's top law enforcement officials. This assertion highlighted the fear not only that social networking sites were full of predators, but also that those running the websites did nothing about it: "MySpace is in the spotlight today because it revealed that 90,000 registered sex offenders have been kicked off its site in the past two years. But where did all of those sex offenders go? Some evidence suggests that a portion of them are now on Facebook" (Schonfeld 2009). This statement reiterated the claim that social networking sites were full of sex offenders, who traveled from one site to another. Tens of thousands of sex offenders were removed from one site, and a portion of them moved to another. The size of the portion did not matter; what mattered was that sex offenders flocked to social networking sites in droves, while the sites failed to defuse the threat, either because they did not try or because they were unable to do so.

"Police and school officials nationwide urge parents to remind their children that when they post their private thoughts online, strangers are definitely watching," one online news article cautioned (Williams 2006). Again, the dangers online were from the unknown stranger who stalked children's profiles. Parents were bombarded with images of lurking predators gathering information posted by youth enveloped in the culture of oversharing. The confusing realm of social networking sites required even more vigilance than prior threats. According to *Time*: "For parents who have only a passing knowledge of MySpace, let alone the ever multiplying horde of competitors like Xanga, Facebook and Bebo, it may be hard to understand why kids flock to these sites and how they can be more dangerous than old-school chat rooms" (Hylton 2006b). Social networking sites were not only dangerous, but were even more dangerous than earlier subjects of concern like the dreaded online chat rooms. Monique Nelson (quoted in Schrobsdorff 2006), an Internet safety expert who co-founded the *Web Wise Kids* site in 2000, warned, "These networking sites are a perfect predator's playground. Predators don't have to go to chat rooms, they can troll through and look for pretty faces that they like and get all the information they want." Social networking sites were easier to access than chat rooms. Instead of predators hunting for victims in chat rooms, on social networking sites teenagers put themselves on display. These media reports alluded to imagery typically associated with childhood innocence, and social networking sites were portrayed as an open door to pursuing children. This fear of online predation was legitimated through cases like those of Solis and Drew despite the stark difference between the fear (online sexual predators) and the reality (deception in identity and cyberbullying by a known person).

The Solis and Drew cases highlighted the complex social, political, and legal issues that comprise a moral panic. In the end, the cases functioned less to prosecute individual offenders than to alert the public to the supposed dangers of social networking. Though these cases attracted media attention, both MySpace and Facebook remained incredibly popular and highly visited sites. Further, these cases illustrate, yet again, the persistent pattern that child sex crime panics focus on strangers even though the actual threat to children from known, trusted individuals is far greater. In particular, with the Megan Meier case, it was a classmate's mother, not a sex offender, who stalked and tormented her. When it comes to social networking sites, it really is all about whom one knows, and "friends" can be far more dangerous than strangers.

## Privacy Protection as Opportunity

Moral panic did not successfully bring down social networking; however, it may have had unforeseen effects on the competition between social networking providers. At the time of the outbreak of the social networking panic, around 2006, MySpace was the dominant social networking site, ranked sixth in overall web traffic with more than triple the number of Facebook's unique US visitors (Dwyer, Hiltz, and Passerini 2007). Today, of course, Facebook is the dominant social networking site, having vanquished both MySpace and the earliest such site, Friendster (Grimmelmann 2009: 1144, "Global Swap Shops" 2010). Today, MySpace is primarily a niche site focusing on music, with a vaguely sordid and thoroughly youth culture-ish reputation. MySpace's status in the social networking hierarchy was further delegitimized in the summer of 2011, when News Corp sold the site for $35 million, 6 percent of the price for which it had purchased the site in 2005 ("MySpace Sold" 2011). Facebook's fortune and status have continued to escalate, however, as evidenced by its $50 billion valuation from Goldman Sachs. This figure represents fifty times its value in 2007 (Craig and Sorkin 2011).

In sharp contrast to MySpace, Facebook is perceived as thoroughly respectable, as well as potentially a key portal to the Internet, as evidenced by its stratospheric market value and omnipresence in commerce. Today, Facebook is thoroughly corporate and mainstream: advertisements for consumer products regularly refer consumers to the vendor's Facebook page. At one time, the difference between perceptions of the sites was perhaps due to the fact that Facebook was initially exclusive and collegiate, whereas MySpace was democratic (Grimmelmann 2009: 1148). Even when Facebook opened to everyone, it retained its classier image. In 2007, Dwyer et al. found that MySpace had a poor reputation in terms of members' trust, among users, while "Facebook's association with physical entities, i.e., universities, helps vouch for the authenticity of its members." Perhaps because of this, Facebook users tended to reveal *more* personal information than MySpace users (Dwyer et al. 2007).

While MySpace made little effort to address concerns about the protection of its users' information, Facebook rolled out a sophisticated campaign to address, or at least appear to address, such issues. Facebook's effort was headed by its Chief Privacy Officer, Chris Kelly, a Harvard Law School graduate, veteran of the *Harvard Journal of Law and Technology*, where he would have been exposed to various perspectives on technology and privacy, and future candidate for Attorney General of California. The issue was less the efficacy of Facebook's privacy policy, which has been roundly criticized, than the fact that Facebook, contrary to MySpace, *had* a privacy policy at all. Kelly unapologetically addressed Congress about Facebook's privacy policies, and he was able to declare, "From the founding of the company in a dorm room in 2004 to today, Facebook's privacy settings have given users control over who has access to their personal information by allowing them to choose the friends they accept and networks they join" (Kelly 2008).

Paradoxically, concerns about the privacy issues surrounding social networking today focus on Facebook, not MySpace (Boyd 2008, Grimmelmann 2009). But that is because Facebook has rendered MySpace largely irrelevant. Moreover, the privacy concerns about Facebook primarily involve such matters as damage to reputations, exploitation by corporate advertisers and so on (Boyd, 2008, Grimmelmann, 200, Mayer-Schönberger 2009). Even the privacy debates surrounding Facebook have mainly escaped the sorts of concerns about outright violence and criminal behavior—such as provoked suicides and statutory rapes— associated with MySpace and the social networking panic, though there have been some homicides associated with such activities as updating of Facebook status (Grimmelmann 2009: 1174).

Surprisingly, Facebook emerged from the social networking panic with an enhanced reputation. Its chief rival, meanwhile, has largely been eliminated from serious competition and appears to have had its reputation permanently tarnished. Even though Facebook's privacy policies have been widely criticized, teenagers continue to use Facebook, and little has been done to prevent its use as a platform for predatory behavior (Boyd 2008, Grimmelmann 2009, Mann 2009).

## Conclusion: After Social Networking

Since 2010, there has been a shift in the controversy surrounding social networking sites. Greater emphasis has been placed on the culture of oversharing, the changing definition of privacy, and the real danger that people known to users might pose. An emerging trend in online oversharing is location-based applications, which post users' locations on their social networking profiles in real time, leaving them vulnerable to victimization by someone in their network (Efrati and Valentino-DeVries, 2011). Another trend garnering both media and academic attention is that of mobile technologies and youth culture (see Turkle, 2011, Lewin 2010).

A study released in early 2010 revealed some surprising statistics about who actually uses social networking sites. According to the study, social networking users are older than generally believed, especially on Facebook: social networking is no longer a youth culture phenomenon. The primary users of social networking sites are adults, not children. In fact, users under the age of 18 make up only about 15 percent of social networking site users ("Study" 2010). MySpace now markets itself as "a leading social entertainment destination powered by the passions of fans. Aimed at a Gen Y audience, MySpace drives social interaction by providing a highly personalized experience around entertainment and connecting people to the music, celebrities, TV, movies, and games that they love" (*About Us* 2011). Through this re-imaging, MySpace is appealing to the original users of social networking sites, now in their thirties, by appealing to their music and entertainment interests. But Facebook remains the premier social networking site, describing itself as a place "giving people the power to share and make the world more open and connected" (*Information* 2011). As the statistics and the site's own self-descriptions indicate, the focus of social networking has evolved to an older audience and moral panic over youth and oversharing is becoming obsolescent.

While both Facebook and MySpace remain a focus for discussions of privacy and the potential harm of posting things on the Internet, where they remain forever, Mark Zuckerberg stated in January 2010 that "people have really gotten comfortable not only sharing more information and different kinds, but more openly and with more people. That social norm is just something that is evolved over time. We view it as our role in the system to constantly be innovating and be updating what our system is to reflect what the current social norms are" (quoted in Paul 2010). Zuckerberg here portrays the discourse surrounding decreased user control of privacy on Facebook as a reflection of evolving social norms, and thus, what the public wants. But the issue he elides is the power wielded by Facebook, as the "default" social networking site, in constructing those norms.

Does this mean that the emerging technology child sex crime panic has abated? We argue that, rather than abating, the panic has shifted to new technologies. Panic about predators on social networking sites has almost become passé, as social networking sites themselves have come to be viewed more as mainstream tools used by all sectors of society, including corporations and adults, and less cutting-edge, youth-oriented technologies. While young people still use social networking sites, they have shifted their primary modes of communication to new technologies, notably Twitter and smart mobile devices. Indeed, the rapid proliferation of smart mobile devices has prompted yet another phase in this ongoing moral panic, over issues like sexting and "digital dating abuse," a new form of cyberbullying (Boyd et al. 2011, Hoffman 2011, "Digital Dating Abuse" 2011). This drifting of the moral panic across technological platforms may be seen as analogous to the sort of drifting of moral panics across youth culture "fads, crazes, and fashions" observed by Cohen (1972: 201). Indeed, today technologies increasingly *are* fashions, fads, and crazes. It has become progressively more difficult to determine whether young people's choices of communication platforms are guided by technology or fashion (or even to distinguish between the two). In this context, it is important to note that the child sex abuse panic discussed here displays a characteristic that Jenkins (1998: 189), writing well before the rise of social networking, called "the protean quality of the child abuse idea and its ability to adapt to changing political and technological environments." While it is difficult to make firm predictions about how the next phase of the child sex crime panic will play out, one prediction we can make with confidence is that it will shift to yet another emerging technology before long.

# References

2006. *About Us*. MySpace [Online]. Available at: http://www.myspace.com/index. cfm?fuseaction=misc.aboutus [accessed: August 6, 2006].

2011. *About Us*. MySpace [Online]. Available at: http://www.myspace.com/Help/ AboutUs [accessed: July 1, 2011].

Attewell, P., Suazo-Garcia, B., and Battle, J. 2003. Computers and young children: social benefit or social problem? *Social Forces*, 82(1), 277–96.

Aycock, A. and Buchignani, N. 1995. The e-mail murders: reflections on "dead letters," in *Cybersociety: Computer-Mediated Communication and Community*, edited by S.G. Jones. Thousand Oaks: Sage Publications, 184–231.

Bahney, A. 2006. Don't talk to invisible strangers. *The New York Times* [Online, March 9]. Available at http://www.nytimes.com/2006/03/09/fashion/thursdaystyles/ 09parents.html [accessed: July 1, 2011].

Barak, A. 2005. Sexual harassment on the Internet. *Social Science Computer Review*, 23(1), 77–92.

Bazelon, E. 2011. The ninny state. *The New York Times Magazine*, June 24.

Bernstein, N. 1996. The list: a special report. *The New York Times*, November 18, A1.

Bijker, W.E. 1995. *Of Bicycles, Bakelites, and Bulbs: Toward a Theory of Sociotechnical Change*. Cambridge: MIT Press.

Boyd, D., Ryan, J., and Leavitt, A. 2011. Pro-self-harm and the visibility of youth-generated problematic content. *I/S: A Journal of Law and Policy for the Information Society* [Online], 7(1), 1–32. Available at: http://www.danah.org/papers/2011/IS-ProSelfHarm.pdf [accessed: October 27, 2011].

Braiker, B. 2007. A towering danger to kids. *Newsweek* [Online, January 19]. Available at http://www.newsweek.com/2007/01/18/a-towering-danger-to-kids. html [accessed: July 1, 2011].

Buckingham, D. 2000. *After the Death of Childhood: Growing Up in the Age of Electronic Media*. Cambridge: Polity Press.

Carbonell, R. 2010. Law falling behind cyber bullying trend. *The World Today*, April 9. ABC News [Australia]. Radio.

Chauncey, G. 1993. The postwar sex crime panic, in *True Stories from the American Past*, edited by W. Graebner. New York: McGraw-Hill, 160–78.

Cheever, C. 2008. Thoughts on privacy. *Developer Blog. Facebook* [Online, May 15] Available at: http://www.facebook.com/news.php?blog=1&story=111. [accessed: 18 May 2008].

2011. Digital dating abuse. *CNN* [Online, February 4]. Available at: http://www.cnn.com/video/#/video/tech/2011/02/03/teens.digital.dating.abuse. cnn?iref=allsearch [accessed: July 13, 2011].

Cohen, S. 1972. *Folk Devils and Moral Panics: The Creation of the Mods and Rockers*. London: MacGibbon and Kee.

Corrigan, R. 2006. Making meaning of Megan's Law. *Law and Social Inquiry* [Online], 31(2), 267–312. Available at: http://rmcorrigan.files.wordpress.com/2009/08/lsi-making-meaning-of-ml.pdf [accessed: February 4, 2012].

Craig, S. and Sorkin, A.R. 2011. Goldman invests in Facebook at $50 billion valuation. *The New York Times* [Online, January 2]. Available at: http://dealbook. nytimes.com/2011/01/02/goldman-invests-in-facebook-at-50-billion-valuation/ [accessed: March 23, 2011].

Cruz, G. 2009. "The Internet: safe for kids?" *Time* [Online, January 15]. Available at: http://www.time.com/time/nation/article/0,8599,1871664,00.html [accessed: July 1, 2011].

Dibbell, J. 1993. A rape in cyberspace. *The Village Voice*, December 21, 36–42. Available at: http://www.juliandibbell.com/texts/bungle.html [accessed: December 6, 2006].

Donath, J.S. 1998. Identity and deception in the virtual community, in *Communities in Cyberspace*, edited by P. Kollock and M. Smith. London: Routledge, 27–58.

Downes, S. 2006. Teens who tell too much. *The New York Times* [Online, January 15]. Available at: http://www.nytimes.com/2006/01/15/opinion/ nyregionopinions/15LIdownes.html [accessed: July 1, 2011].

Dwyer, C., Hiltz, S.R., and Passerini, K. 2007. *Trust and Privacy Concern within Social Networking Sites: A Comparison of Facebook and MySpace*. Paper to XIII Americas Conference on Information Systems, Keystone, CO, August 9–12.

Efrati, A. and Valentino-Devries, J. 2011. Computers, too, can give away location. *The Wall Street Journal*, April 27, B1–B2.

Fass, P.S. 1997. *Kidnapped: Child Abduction in America*. Cambridge: Harvard University Press.

Freedman, E.B. 1987. "Uncontrolled desires": the response to the sexual psychopath. *Journal of American History*, 74(1), 83–106.

2010. Global swap shops. *The Economist* [Online], January 28. Available at: http://www.economist.com/node/15350972 [accessed: October 27, 2011].

Glover, S. 2008. Cyber-bully verdict is mixed. *Los Angeles Times* [Online, November 27]. Available at http://articles.latimes.com/2008/nov/27/local/me-myspace-trial-verdict27 [accessed: July 1, 2011].

Glover, S. and Huffstutter, P.J. 2008. "Cyber-bully" charges filed in L.A. *Los Angeles Times* [Online, May 16]. Available at: http://articles.latimes.com/2008/may/16/local/me-myspace16 [accessed: September 4, 2010].

Goode, E. and Ben-Yehuda, N. 1994. *Moral Panics*. Oxford: Blackwell.

Gordon, J. 2006. MySpace draws a questionable crowd. *The New York Times* [online, February 26]. Available at: http://www.nytimes.com/2006/02/26/nyregion/nyregionspecial2/26ctspace.html [accessed: July 1, 2011].

Grometstein, R. 2008. Wrongful conviction and moral panic: national and international perspectives on organized child sexual abuse, in *Wrongful Conviction: International Perspectives on Miscarriages of Justice*, edited by C.R. Huff and M. Killias. Philadelphia: Temple University Press, 11–32.

Hall, S., Critcher, C., Jefferson, T., Clarke, J., and Roberts, B. 1978. *Policing the Crisis-Mugging, the State, and Law and Order*. Critical Social Studies. Houndmills: Palgrave Macmillan.

Handley, M. 2010. Should Facebook have a "panic button?" *Time* [Online, April 14]. Available at http://www.time.com/time/business/article/0,8599,1981975,00.html [accessed: July 1, 2011].

Hoffman, J. 2011. A girl's nude photo, and altered lives. *The New York Times*. March 26, A1.

Hylton, H. 2006a. Another suit in the MySpace case? *Time* [Online, June 22]. Available at: http://www.time.com/time/nation/article/0,8599,1207043,00.html [accessed: September 10, 2006].

Hylton, H. 2006b. How safe is MySpace? *Time* [Online, June 26]. Available at: http://www.time.com/time/magazine/article/0,9171,1207808,00.html [accessed: July 1, 2011].

2011. *Information. Facebook* [Online]. Available at: https://www.facebook.com/facebook?sk=info [accessed: March 23, 2011].

*Jane Doe, Individually and as Next Friend of Julie Doe v. MySpace, Inc., and News Corporation.* 2006. Travis County, Texas.

Jenkins, P. 2009. Failure to launch: why do some social issues fail to detonate moral panics? *British Journal of Criminology*, 49(1), 35–47.

Jones, C.G. 2011. Computer hackers on the cul-de-sac: MySpace suicide indictment under the computer fraud and abuse act sets dangerous precedent. *Widener Law Review*, 17, 261–87.

Kincaid, J.R. 1998. *Erotic Innocence: The Culture of Child Molesting*. Durham, Duke University Press.

Kelly, C. 2008. *Testimony: Privacy Implications of Online Advertising: United States Senate Committee on Commerce, Science, and Transportation* [Online]. Available at: http://www.insidefacebook.com/wp-content/uploads/2008/07/chriskellyfacebookonlineprivacytestimony.pdf [accessed: October 27, 201].

Kreiser, J. 2009. MySpace: your kids' danger? *CBS News* [Online, February 11]. Available at: http://www.cbsnews.com/stories/2006/02/06/eveningnews/main1286130.shtml [accessed: July 1, 2011].

Krinsky, C. 2008. Introduction, in *Moral Panics over Contemporary Children and Youth*, edited by C. Krinsky. Aldershot: Ashgate, 1–6.

Kuipers, G. 2006. The social construction of digital danger: debating, defusing and inflating the moral dangers of online humor and pornography in the Netherlands and the United States. *New Media and Society*, 8(3), 379–400.

Kunzleman, M. 2008. "Court sides with MySpace in suit over sexual assault. *USA Weekly* [Online, May 17]. Available at: http://www.usatoday.com/news/nation/2008-05-16-2507382976_x.htm [accessed: July 1, 2011].

Lenhart, A. and Madden, M. 2007. Social networking websites and teens: an overview. *Pew Internet and American Life Project* [Online, January 7]. Available at http://www.pewinternet.org/PPF/r/198/report_display.asp [accessed: May 18, 2008].

Livingstone, S. 2003. Children's use of the Internet: reflections on the emerging research agenda. *New Media and Society*, 5(2), 147–66.

Livingstone, S. and Helsper, E. 2010. Balancing opportunities and risks in teenagers' use of the Internet: the role of online skills and Internet self-efficacy. *New Media and Society*, 12(2), 309–29.

Lynch, M. 2002. Pedophiles and cyber-predators as contaminating forces: the language of disgust, pollution, and boundary invasion in federal debates on sex offender legislation. *Law and Social Inquiry*, 27(3), 529–66.

Mackinnon, R. 1997a. Punishing the persona: correctional strategies for the virtual offender, in *Virtual Culture: Identity and Communication in Cybersociety*, edited by S.G. Jones. London: Sage Publications, 206–35.

Mackinnon, R. 1997b. Virtual rape. *Journal of Computer-Mediated Communication*, 2(4), 432–42.

Mnookin, J. L. 1996. Virtual(ly) law: the emergence of law in LambdaMOO. *Journal of Computer-Mediated Communication* [Online], 2(1) Available at: http://jcmc.indiana.edu/vol2/issue1/lambda.html [accessed: October 27, 2011].

2008. More Thoughts on the Lori Drew Case. *Los Angeles Times* [Online, December 4]. Available at:http://opinion.latimes.com/opinionla/2008/12/lori-drew-myspa.html [accessed: September 4, 2010].

2011. MySpace sold to Orange County-based ad network. *Los Angeles Times* [Online, June 29]. Available at: http://latimesblogs.latimes.com/entertainmentnewsbuzz/2011/06/myspace-sold-to-orange-county-based-ad-network.html [accessed: July 1, 2011].

Paul, I. 2010. Facebook CEO challenges the social norm of privacy. *PC World* [Online, January 11]. Available at: http://www.pcworld.com/article/186584/facebook_ceo_challenges_the_social_norm_of_privacy.html [accessed: September 4, 2010].

Potter, R.H. and Potter, L.A. 2001. The Internet, cyberporn, and sexual exploitation of children: media moral Panics and urban myths for middle-class parents? *Sexuality and Culture*, 5(3), 31–48.

Pratt, J. 2005. Child sexual abuse: purity and danger in an age of anxiety. *Crime, Law and Social Change*, 43(4–5), 263–87.

Ritchel, M. 2006. "MySpace.com moves to keep sex offenders off its site. *The New York Times* [Online, December 6]. Available at: http://www.nytimes.com/2006/12/06/technology/06myspace.html?_r=1&scp=3&sq=matt+richtel&st=nyt&oref=slogin [accessed: December 6, 2006].

Schonfeld, E. 2009. Thousands of MySpace sex offender refugees found on Facebook. *Tech Crunch* [Online, February 3]. Available at http://techcrunch.com/2009/02/03/thousands-of-myspace-sex-offender-refugees-found-on-facebook/ [accessed: July 1, 2011].

Schrobsdorff, S. 2006. Predator's Playground. *Newsweek* [Online, January 27]. Available at: http://www.newsweek.com/2006/01/26/predator-s-playground.html [accessed: July 1, 2011].

Schultz, P.D. 2008 Naming, blaming, and framing: moral panic over child molesters and its implications for public policy, in *Moral Panics over Contemporary Children and Youth*, edited by C. Krinsky. Aldershot: Ashgate, 95–110.

Shaw, D.F. 1997 Gay men and computer communication: a discourse of sex and identity in cyberspace, in *Virtual Culture: Identity and Communication in Cybersociety*, edited by S.G. Jones. London: Sage Publications, 133–45.

Sherriff, L. 2006. "Girl raped after MySpace meeting, court hears. *The Register* [Online, August 16]. Available at: http://www.theregister.co.uk/2006/08/16/myspace_meeting_rape/ [accessed: September 10, 2006].

Simon, J. 1998. Managing the monstrous: sex offenders and the new penology. *Psychology, Public Policy, and Law*, 4(1–2), 452–67.

Simon, J. 2000. Megan's Law: crime and democracy in late modern America. *Law and Social Inquiry*, 25(4), 1111–50.

Stephey, M.J. 2009. Teens behaving badly. *Time* [Online, January 7]. Available at: http://www.time.com/time/health/article/0,8599,1870045,00.html [accessed: July 1, 2011].

Stone, A.R. 1995. *The War of Desire and Technology at the Close of the Mechanical Age*. Cambridge: MIT Press.

Stone, B. 2007a. "States fault MySpace on predator issue. *The New York Times* [Online, May 15]. Available at: http://www.nytimes.com/2007/05/15/technology/15myspace.html [accessed: July 1, 2011].

Stone, B. 2007b. New scrutiny for Facebook over predators. *The New York Times* [Online, July 30]. Available at: http://www.nytimes.com/2007/07/30/business/media/30facebook.html [accessed: July 1, 2011].

2010. Study: ages of social network users. *Pingdom* [Online, February 16]. Available at: http://royal.pingdom.com/2010/02/16/study-ages-of-social-network-users/ [accessed: September 4, 2010].

Texas Penal Code. Title 5, § 22.011

2011. *Terms. Facebook*. Available at http://www.facebook.com/terms.php [accessed: 23 March 2011].

Thomas, O. 2007. Facebook: a brief history of Mark Zuckerberg's legal woes. *Gawker* [Online, July 20]. Available at: http://valleywag.com/tech/facebook/a-brief-history-of-mark-zuckerbergs-legal-woes-280901.php [accessed: May 18, 2008].

Williams, P. 2006. "MySpace, Facebook attract predators. *MSNBC* [Online, February 23). Available at http://www.msnbc.msn.com/id/11165576/ns/nightly_news/t/myspace-facebook-attract-online-predators/ [accessed: July 1, 2011].

Yadav, S. 2006. Facebook: the complete biography. *Mashable* [Online, August 25]. Available at: http://mashable.com/2006/08/25/facebook-profile/ [accessed: December 6, 2006].

Zavis, A. 2009. Judge tentatively dismisses case in MySpace hoax that led to teenage girl's suicide. *Los Angeles Times* [Online, July 2]. Available at: http://latimesblogs.latimes.com/lanow/2009/07/myspace-sentencing.html [accessed: September 4, 2010].

Zimring, F.E. 2004. *An American Travesty: Legal Responses to Adolescent Sexual Offending*. Chicago: University of Chicago Press.

# PART IV
# MORAL PANICS OVER CHILDREN AND YOUTH

# Overview of Part IV

Whether viewed as closely related but distinct, types of occurrence or regarded as essentially a single phenomenon, moral panics over children, youth, or both have excited the interest of researchers with notable regularity. Concerning moral panics over children, in *Intimate Enemies: Moral Panics in Contemporary Great Britain*, religious studies scholar and criminologist Philip Jenkins (1992: 73) makes the perhaps obvious but crucial observation, "Childhood is a socially constructed phenomenon, the definition and limits of which vary greatly in different epochs and societies." According to Jenkins, moral panics calling on society to safeguard children from sexual abuse and allegedly related dangers such as homosexuality and murder not only set the accepted limits of childhood, but even create children's social identities, doing so quite differently in various times and places.

In *After the Death of Childhood: Growing Up in the Age of Electronic Media* (2000), educationist David Buckingham discusses a series of moral panics over a range of perceived threats to children that took place in the United Kingdom beginning in the 1980s. In doing so, he endeavors to shed light on the nature of adults' shared assumptions about childhood, which, he asserts, also underlie recent moral panics and public debates over the effects of media violence on young children (his book's primary concern). Buckingham (2000: 125–6) reflects,

> In the 1980s, Britain saw the emergence of a series of interdependent moral panics about perceived threats to children; serial murder, child pornography, abductions by paedophiles and satanic ritual abuse were frequently claimed to be reaching epidemic proportions. … These issues provided a powerful focus for the activities of quite diverse interest groups, and indeed for alliances between them. The issue of children's access to media violence has served as a vehicle for similar campaigns, and the same 'moral entrepreneurs' have repeatedly featured in them. Here, too, the specific emphasis on children has served as a powerful means of commanding support for much broader campaigns; the intrusion of the state into the private sphere become significantly more palatable when proposed in the name of children. …

It is possible to detect some contradictory constructions of childhood in these debates. On the one hand, most obviously, there is a post-Romantic notion of the child as innocent and vulnerable, as requiring protection from the unnatural influences of the adult world. Underlying this, however, is a much older view of the child as the bearer of original sin. From this perspective, children are 'natural' not in a positive sense, but in a negative one: they possess drives towards violence, sexuality and anti-social behaviour which are only barely kept under control and which 'irrational' influences like the media are seen to have the power to release.

Crusaders benefit from their involvement in moral panics involving children because, since so many social problems seem intimately related to the question of children's safety, they can then gather support for their other campaigns. Moral panics and related public debates centering on children demonstrate not only the predictable assumption that children are far more natural and innocent than adults and therefore readily preyed upon by them, but also the even more deep-seated supposition that their inherent tendencies toward violence, sexuality, and destruction must be restrained. Unsupervised interaction between children and uncondoned adults may encourage children's antisocial tendencies.

Like Buckingham, in "In the Name of 'Childhood Innocence': A Discursive Exploration of the Moral Panic Associated with Childhood and Sexuality," sociologist Kerry H. Robinson (2008: 115–16) finds that adults' attribution of innocence to children, which makes children frequent and protean symbolic victims for moral panics, also carries with it serious conceptual conflicts and contradictions:

> The notion of childhood innocence has continued unabated to define the child and its place in the world today. Any challenge to the sacrosanct concept of childhood innocence generally leads to a heightened level of concern in society.
>
> The notion of childhood innocence has been inherently enshrined within traditional theories of human development, which have also constituted understandings of sexuality. In terms of hegemonic discourses of sexuality, physiological sexual maturity is constructed as a distinguishing point between adulthood and childhood. Sexuality is generally represented as beginning at puberty and maturing in adulthood, correlating with developmentalist theories of the human, which reinforce biologically determined understandings of childhood and sexuality. Children's sexuality within this discourse is read as nonexistent or immature at the most. Thus, sexual immaturity is equated with 'innocence' — considered inherent in the child.

For Robinson as for Buckingham, the moral panics that call on adult society to protect children (in this case, to keep them safe from sexual abuse) both consent to and produce notions about their innocence that, besides its impacts on adult society, define and constrain children themselves.

In his *Moral Panics*, Kenneth Thompson (1998: 43) draws careful distinctions between the constructions of children evident in moral panics and those of older "youth":

> No age group is more associated with risk in the public imagination than that of 'youth'. Of course, imagined risks to children also lie behind many moral panics, especially those concerning the alleged breakdown of the family, but apart from the relatively rare cases of children who commit murder (such as the Bulger murder), children are not usually regarded as a source of risk. Youth may be regarded as both at risk and a source of risk in many moral panics. This is not surprising in view of the transitional status of this age group, occupying a position between childhood and adulthood. It is this very marginality and ambiguity of status that exacerbates the regulation and the reproduction of the social order. But the relationship between the generations and generational cultures is also problematical for young people themselves, and youth cultures and subcultures can be read or decoded as responses and attempted solutions to those strains. (Thompson 1998: 43)

While Buckingham's (2000) insights cast some doubt on his assertion that children are less widely associated with risks than youth, Thompson's perceptions about the variety of uses moral panics make of "youth" remain persuasive. He argues that, while both children and youth seem particularly vulnerable to unexpected dangers and therefore exceptionally in need of society's protection, youth present an additionally transitional figure, even to themselves. Standing on the threshold of adulthood, youth occupy the borderlands of society, and are equally able to trigger moral panics as either symbolic victims or folk devils. Youth culture itself (a concept exceedingly difficult to define, it might be added) can be seen as expressing young people's own responses to their equivocal position in relation to adult society.

Perhaps more than Thompson, who focuses on scholarly interpretations of the moral panic concept, in "The Dangerousness of Youth-at-Risk: The Possibilities of Surveillance and Intervention in Uncertain Times," social theorist and researcher Peter Kelly (2000) examines the potential impacts that the conceptualizations carried out via moral panics may have on the daily lives of youth. Kelly cautions,

> Cultural and policy contexts which are framed by uncertainty, fear and anxiety provoke dangerous possibilities in the regulation and surveillance of young people. In such contexts, the promise of safety, security, order and certainty which frames many of these surveillance and management practices can only be delivered via more sophisticated and powerful techniques of regulation and intervention. It is not possible to conceive of unregulated spaces. It is possible, however,

that some forms of regulation, even those framed by concerns for the safety and wellbeing of young people, require school, local and national communities to give up more than is promised in the name of certainty, order and safety. In contemporary settings of uncertainty and fear, there is a strong warrant for popular, political and intellectual practices which foreground the dangerous possibilities provoked by a widespread concern to regulate the behaviors and dispositions of young people via the mobilization of more sophisticated techniques of intervention and surveillance. (Kelly 2000: 473)

Kelly warns that, though few adults would want youth to remain entirely outside adult supervision, public policy meant to keep them from harm may have the unintended effect of extending adult regulation, intervention, and surveillance to a degree that would unnecessarily and destructively constrain and encumber them.

## Moral Panics over Children and Youth

In chapter 12 of *The Ashgate Research Companion to Moral Panics*, entitled "Moral Panics and the Young: The James Bulger Murder, 1993," Máire Messenger Davies looks closely at the moral panic (briefly referenced by Kenneth Thompson above) that followed the murder in Liverpool of two-year-old James Bulger by two ten-year-old boys, Robert Thompson and Jon Venables. She discusses the various conceptualizations of children and childhood presented in the public discourses associated with the murder, including those apparent in scholarly research on the case. Messenger Davies concludes that to Stanley Cohen's (1972) six-stage processual model of moral panics, a seventh stage should be added, that of academic analysis of all the previous stages.

Chapter 13, Magdalena Rek-Woźniak and Wojciech Woźniak's "Children Pushed Aside: Moral Panic over the Family and the State in Contemporary Poland," describes a moral panic that emerged around 2008–10 opposing an eventually successful effort to change Polish law to deter domestic violence against children. The authors show that, for reasons including the importance of the Catholic Church in Poland and the country's lack of independent statehood throughout much of the last two centuries, a potential moral panic over domestic violence against children centered instead on allegedly unwarranted state intrusion into the family. Utilizing Klocke and Muschert's (2010) hybrid model of moral panics, Rek-Woźniak and Woźniak track the course of this short-lived episode to its conclusion.

In chapter 14, "Moral Panics versus Youth Problem Debates: Three Conceptual Insights from the Study of Japanese Youth," Tuukka Toivonen examines recent controversies in Japan over NEETs (15- to 34-year-olds, disproportionately male, classified as "not in education, employment, or training"). In this chapter, Toivonen presents three important insights about the moral panic concept and youth problem debates: (1) moral panics over youth may be more accurately seen as components of longer-lasting youth problem debates, (2) opposing political and social agendas merge and interact in youth problem debates, and (3) a kind of "double-disproportionality" may be detected when, as in Japanese debates over NEETs, a relatively small group receives a great deal of media attention but little consideration in terms of public policy (both media coverage and policy impact being therefore out of proportion to the possible threat posed).

# References

Buckingham, D. 2000. After the Death of Childhood: Growing Up in the Age of Electronic Media. Cambridge: Polity Press.

Cohen, S. 1972. *Folk Devils and Moral Panics: The Creation of the Mods and Rockers*. New York: St. Martin's Press.

Jenkins, P. 1992. *Intimate Enemies: Moral Panics in Contemporary Great Britain*. *Social Problems and Social Issues*. Piscataway: Aldine Transaction.

Kelly, P. 2000. The dangerousness of youth-at-risk: the possibilities of surveillance and intervention in uncertain times. *Journal of Adolescence*, 23(4), 463–76.

Klocke, B.V. and Muschert, G.W. 2010. A hybrid model of moral panics: synthesizing the theory and practice of moral panic research. *Sociology Compass*, 4(5), 295–309.

Robinson, K.H. 2008. In the name of 'childhood innocence': a discursive exploration of the moral panic associated with childhood and sexuality. *Cultural Studies Review*, 14(2), 113–29.

Roman, L.G. 1996. Spectacle in the dark: youth as transgression, display, and repression. *Educational Theory*, 46(1), 1–22.

Thompson, K. 1998. *Moral Panics*. *Key Ideas*. Milton Park: Routledge.

# Moral Panics and the Young: The James Bulger Murder, 1993

## Máire Messenger Davies

The 1993 murder of James Bulger in Liverpool in the United Kingdom involved three children: the two-year-old victim and the two ten-year-old perpetrators, Robert Thompson and Jon Venables. At the time of the murder, it was alleged (inaccurately, it appears) that the perpetrators were influenced by seeing the movie *Child's Play 3*. The suggestion that media influences were somehow implicated in the crime generated a large number of books, articles, and academic commentaries — and continues to do so. Many of these publications discuss not so much the horrific nature of the crime itself, but the possible threat to free speech posed by attempts to censor media violence driven by moral panic over this murder of a child by other children. Relating scholarship on moral panics to media reports of this case can help shed light on such issues as competing constructions of childhood and the contentious concept of childhood innocence. It also raises the question of academic authority, of who is deemed legitimately qualified, or not, to comment on the issues presented by the case.

## Moral Panic

In brief, Stanley Cohen's (2002: 1) influential processual model defines moral panic thus:

1. A condition or person is defined as a threat to societal values.
2. It is presented in stylized stereotypical fashion by mass media.
3. The moral barricades are manned by editors, bishops, etc.
4. Socially accredited experts pronounce diagnoses and solutions.
5. Ways of coping are evolved.
6. The condition disappears, then becomes more visible.

Today, it might be suggested that a further step be added to this model:

7. Academic controversy debating the previous six steps emerges.

The Bulger case and its continuing sad aftermath, for instance the media response to the conviction of one of the murderers, Jon Venables, on a charge of accessing child pornography in 2010, when he was 27 years old, have provoked a great deal of academic discussion, arguably contributing to the amplification of the moral panic process (see illustration 12.1).

Historian John Springhall (1998: 8), himself a valuable contributor to moral panic scholarship, has commented on the prevailing view of the phenomenon among academics:

> 'Moral panic' is one of those deflating phrases used by allegedly impartial sociologists and historians to condescend to excitements among the general populace .... The academic's message is a reassuring one, 'do not worry, we have been here before, your concerns are an ersatz compound manufactured by the media, a few odd bishops, strident voices from the left and the right, moralists and nostalgists of all kinds'.

Springhall argues that newspaper readers can be right to panic over, for example, rising crime levels. But he distinguishes between this more justifiable public anxiety and "the sales-driven incentive to frighten newspaper and magazine readers with exaggerated reports about the effects on their children's behaviour of 'sensational and violent amusements'" (1998: 8). Springhall points out that both sorts of amusements, as well as public alarm about them, "have been with us for some considerable time" (Springhall 1998: 8). Although he himself provides a detailed, critical, and sometimes "deflating" historical review of panics around different forms of popular culture—penny dreadfuls, gangster films, horror comics—he is careful to note that "there is a danger of minimizing the contemporary sense of worry and crisis ... by an account of its repetitious and historically relative character" (Springhall 1998: 8). The Bulger murder was such an exceptional and troubling event, with such a widespread public impact not only on "ersatz compounds" and tabloids that an exceptional vocabulary was always going to be required to deal with it. As Springhall notes, for the historian and social analyst, careful evidence will always be required and distinctions need to be drawn between genuinely worrying phenomena like child murders and exaggerated fusses about relatively trivial phenomena, such as pop songs.

## The James Bulger Murder Case

The abduction, torture, and murder of two-year-old James Bulger, by two ten-year-olds, Jon Venables and Robert Thompson, in Liverpool in 1993, apart from being a deeply tragic and distressing event for the parties concerned, has become a

Illustration 12.1    *Sunday Mirror*, "Bulger Killer Jailed Over Child Porn,"
March 7, 2010

defining event in academic discussions about (a) childhood and (b) media effects. At the time, as I commented in my *'Dear BBC': Children, Television Storytelling and the Public Sphere* (2001), quite an academic industry grew up around the reporting of the case and the issues raised by it, including educationist David Buckingham's (1996) *Moving Images: Understanding Children's Responses to Television* and media scholars Martin Barker and Julian Petley's edited collection *Ill Effects: The Media/Violence Debate* (1997), the latter a response to child psychologist Elizabeth Newson's 1994 report on "Video Violence and the Protection of Children." Additionally, Springhall's *Youth, Popular Culture and Moral Panics: Penny Gaffs to Gangsta Rap, 1830–1996* (1998: 1) began with an account of the "sensational reporting" of the Bulger case and John Major's comments as UK Prime Minister about the "relentless diet of violence" and its "serious effects on the young."

The case is frequently referenced in academic literature on the subject of moral panics and the media: Kenneth Thompson (1998: 2) flags it at the start of his book, *Moral Panics*, as does Chas Critcher (2003: 2) at the start of *his* book, *Moral Panics and the Media*. The case is also cited by many of the authors in Critcher's collection, *Critical Readings: Moral Panics and the Media* (2010). The sheer number of these citations hints at stage one of Cohen's "processual model": "A condition or person is defined as a threat to societal values." Looking at the academic discussion of this case, the exact subject of the "panic," or, to put it less emotively, of academic concern is debatable. Is it the actual horror of ten-year-olds torturing and killing a two-year-old? Or, is it the emotive coverage of the case by the media, particularly the popular press? Or, is it the political and legal developments threatening freedom of speech arising from such horror and emotion?

One of the first academic comments on the case came from Elizabeth Newson, whose concern was overtly the welfare of children, but who made the mistake of straying into the media effects debate. She was asked to produce a discussion paper (often referred to simply as The Newson Report) by Liverpool MP David Alton, who was proposing an amendment to the Criminal Justice Act to tighten British Board of Film Classification requirements of video material. Newson's (1994) paper, "Video violence and the protection of children" (reprinted in *The Psychologist*, the journal of the British Psychological Society, June 1994: 273), discussed the extreme savagery of the James Bulger murder, and queried what could have prompted it:

> What then can be seen as the 'different' factor that has entered the lives of countless children and adolescents in recent years? This has to be recognized as the easy availability to children of gross images of violence on video... It now seems that professionals in child health and psychology underestimated the degree of brutality and sustained sadism that film makers were capable of inventing ... let alone the special effects technologies which would support such images; and we certainly underestimated how easy would be children's access to them.

Newson's paper, signed by 36 other health and education professionals concerned with children, was publicly circulated by Alton, resulting in a great deal of press comment, including a sensational headline: "U Turn over Video Nasties: 'Naïve' Experts Admit Link with Real Life Violence," in the London *Evening Standard*. This led to a shocked reaction from Newson who, publishing an article headed "Ordeal by Media" in *The Psychologist*, exemplified a classic stage in the media moral panics process: "Almost all the papers copied the inaccuracies of the *Evening Standard*: the U turn (when only about three of us had ever spoken publicly about the topic before)" (1994: 276). In the large postbag she received as a result of this publicity was a short paper signed by 22 media academics "rubbishing me for knowing nothing about the media; oddly, this paper quoted simplistic statements that I had already rejected as too simplistic, and dealt only with adults not children" (1994: 276).

These 22 media scholars formed the basis of the group that in 1997 produced a collection of essays, *Ill Effects: The Media/Violence Debate*, to combat the views expressed in the Newson report. Firstly, this book challenged the empirical validity of the report. In the words of one of its editors, Martin Barker (1997: 1), the Newson Report "had not a single fact to its name, good or bad. It was a thin tissue of claims whose only virtue was that they were what every politician and newspaper wanted to hear." This objection to lack of evidence has become a key ingredient in academic moral panic discourse: an indignation at the media's failure to consult the relevant academic expertise and evidence in discussions about media impacts.

## Redefining Moral Panic

Chas Critcher (2010: 2) describes moral panics thus: "Moral panics are by definition disproportionate reactions to perceived threats." Critcher argues that studying "moral panics" is important for the academic community because of what they reveal about the workings of power—his "five powerful Ps of moral panics" (2003: 4). These "Ps" are the press and broadcasting, pressure groups and claims makers, politicians and government, police and law enforcement agencies, and public opinion. Critcher argues that entering this debate is a socially necessary form of academic engagement because moral panics "are around us all the time" and, he argues, they have increasing political importance in Britain.

Cohen's classic case study centered on the press coverage given to the fights between mods and rockers (who quickly became folk devils) that took place in resort towns on England's south coast in 1964. The concept of folk devils has been an attractive one in discussing moral panics and, more recently, has come to be applied not to groups or individuals but to mass media, as in Springhall's historical survey running from penny gaffs (cheap working-class music halls and theaters popular in Victorian England) to gangsta raps, all of them meeting the criteria of folk devildom. In an essay originally published in 1997 about the massacre of 35 people in Australia in 1996, media scholar Stephen Stockwell (2010: 131) points out the "implications for moral panic theory" that moral panics "no longer need the focus of deviant lower class males as folk devils" as Cohen suggests. He argues that the focus of moral panic theory has now moved towards "objects not people," that is, media products or, as in the Australian massacre case he writes about, guns. This, says Stockwell (2010: 131), reflects the shift of moral panic theory out of sociology and into media theory, away from "the sociology of deviance," towards a sociology of media.

## Childhood Innocence?

Much academic writing referencing the Bulger murder has found it necessary to examine the supposed "innocence" of childhood, with a tendency to suggest that, seen in the light of this case, children are actually not innocent at all. In a chapter called "Myth Appropriation: The Childhood Theme," Critcher (2010: 155) explores the academic literature addressing the "myth" of childhood innocence. He cites feminist scholars Stevi Jackson and Sue Scott (1995: 5): "The degree of anxiety generated by risks to children is associated with a particular construction of childhood as an age of innocence and vulnerability which adults have a duty to protect." Whether the duty of adults to protect children is simply "a particular construction" or something more tangible will be discussed later in this essay. Critcher also cites David Buckingham's (2000: 3) dystopic *After the Death of Childhood*, in which Buckingham argues, "In recent years debates about childhood have become invested with a growing sense of anxiety and panic." Buckingham cites press reports about child murders, "home alone kids," abduction by pedophiles, sex tourism, child crime, drug taking, and teenage pregnancy, moral panics about the influence of "video nasties," pornography on the Internet, and the "authoritarian and punitive" responses of politicians and policymakers to all these concerns. Sociologist of childhood Chris Jenks (1996: 124) is also quoted by Critcher on the topic: "A dominant modern discourse of childhood continues to mark out 'the child' as innately innocent, confirming its cultural identity as a passive and unknowing dependent." The quotation marks around "the child" in this passage suggest some nervousness on the part of the writer about using the term in a literal sense, as if he can only contemplate the phenomenon of "child" as mythical construction. The use of "it" rather than "him" or "her" to signify "child" reinforces this impression.

Critcher goes on to discuss children as *victims* of Cohen's model of folk devils, rather than as folk devils themselves. In much moral panic discourse, children are indeed seen as innocent victims, as, for example, in the case of educationist Neil Selwyn's (2003, quoted in Critcher 2010: 363) innocent computer user inundated by "filth." However, the idea of the child as innocent victim is not sustained in the discourse surrounding the Bulger case, in which ten-year-old Venables and Thompson were themselves constructed as Cohenesque monstrous folk devils—"freaks of nature," as the *Daily Mirror* called them at the time (quoted in McNutt 2010).

Discussions of moral panics have mostly neglected the assumptions manifest in official international definitions of "The Child," as evidenced in the 54 detailed articles of the UN *Convention on The Rights of the Child* (1989). These rights are invoked in a variety of institutional and discursive modes around the world, including, for example, children's right of access to media. For instance, in Article 17, "the child" is not defined as a mythical construction:

> States Parties recognize the important function performed by the mass media and shall ensure that the child has access to information and material from a diversity of national and international sources, especially those aimed at the promotion of his or her social, spiritual and moral well-being and physical and mental health.
>
> To this end, States Parties shall:
>
> (a) Encourage the mass media to disseminate information and material of social and cultural benefit to the child and in accordance with the spirit of article 29;
> (b) Encourage international co-operation in the production, exchange and dissemination of such information and material from a diversity of cultural, national and international sources;
> (c) Encourage the production and dissemination of children's books;
> (d) Encourage the mass media to have particular regard to the linguistic needs of the child who belongs to a minority group or who is indigenous;
> (e) Encourage the development of appropriate guidelines for the protection of the child from information and material injurious to his or her well-being, bearing in mind the provisions of articles 13 and 18. (*Convention* 1989)

Here, the child is treated as a person for whom specific and concrete legal and social arrangements are expected to be made by member states.

Of particular interest in discussions about childhood innocence (or lack of innocence) are the proceedings of the Office of the Secretary General for Children and Armed Conflict. Children, including (or, for this UN office, especially) children who have taken part in brutal acts of violence and aggression, are constructed unambiguously as victims, and deserving of protection, because, unlike adults, "Children suffer disproportionately in times of war. They therefore have the highest stake in peace" (Otunnu 2000). This includes a major concern of the office: child soldiers.

In UN documents, the age of criminal responsibility is discussed as follows:

> The age of criminal responsibility should be that of the legal minimum age for recruitment into armed forces or groups [in most countries, this is the late teens at the earliest, in some, the early twenties]. Consistency between the age of criminal responsibility and the legal minimum age of recruitment is essential to avoid the deliberate use of children in the

commission of Crimes, due to their de jure immunity from prosecution by the Court. ("Secretary-General's Special Representative" 1998)

In the United Kingdom, the age of criminal responsibility is ten, exceptionally low by international standards. Jon Venables and Robert Thompson were tried in adult court and the anonymity usually given to children involved in criminal cases, although given at the time of the trial, was denied to them later, "in the public interest." Since their release in 2000, they have lived under assumed identities, but Jon Venables's arrest for possessing child pornography in 2010 was discussed under his own name in the media. At their trial in 1993, not only were Venables and Thompson deemed legally responsible for their actions, but, as discussed, they were also demonized in the media as "monsters." The paradox of this media treatment was that they were seen to be particularly "monstrous" precisely because they *were* children, not adults.

From a child development perspective, it could be argued that even if children of ten really were "monsters," it could not be assumed that they would forever stay in the same state. Ten-year-olds can be constructed as "innocent," in the word's more limited sense of "inexperienced," because all ten-year-olds, monsters or not, have much less knowledge and much less experience than adults, simply by virtue of being only ten. They may also lack fully developed moral subtlety and the empathy expected of adults, and indeed may be capable of cruel and antisocial behavior precisely because of this lack. They are pre-adolescent, pre-pubescent, and, whatever their behavior or experience as children, are all going to change in the years ahead. They inevitably have a considerable amount of development, physical, social, and experiential, ahead of them. A developmental, humanistic construction of "the child" at ten would imply, as poet, novelist, and journalist Blake Morrison does in an article headlined, "Jon Venables Is Not Yet beyond Redemption," published in the *Guardian* on July 26, 2010:

> The tabloid script requires this image of irredeemable evil … so that it can continue to vilify the Bulger killers: whether in prison or not, they will always serve a life sentence in the media. But the picture of Venables that emerged last week doesn't suggest a Iago or Macbeth but a sad loner, immature and out of his depth, struggling to cope with adult life…. he was the more volatile and damaged of the two …. When the psychologist Susan Bailey came to his secure unit before the trial, she found a boy deep in denial—he had lined his bed with furry animals 'to keep the bad things away'.

The humanistic belief that children who do "bad things" are redeemable lies behind the United Nations Office for Children and Armed Conflict's recommendations on the treatment of children involved in war:

> Apart from the reestablishment of security and the consolidation of peace, perhaps the most daunting challenge a country faces after

war is the 'crisis of the young people'—the desperate conditions of young children and adolescents. The prospects for recovery in many countries therefore depend very much on rehabilitating these young people and restoring to them a sense of renewed hope. (Otunnu 2000)

The same could be said of children in trouble in the criminal justice system, and the United Nations provision for the age of criminal responsibility to be the same as the age at which a person is deemed mature enough for military service explicitly links the two.

## Child's Play 3: The Media and Media Effects

Springhall writes, "Whenever the introduction of a new mass medium is defined as a threat to the young, we can expect a campaign by adults to regulate, ban or censor, followed by a lessening of interest until the appearance of a new medium reopens public debate" (1998:7). In the Bulger case, the campaign to "regulate, ban or censor" focused on the film *Child's Play 3* (1991), which the killers were (wrongly) assumed to have seen.

In a chapter in *Ill Effects: The Media/Violence Debate* about the "demonic" representation of childhood popular at the end of the twentieth century (in contrast to the innocent images favored by the Victorians), Patricia Holland (1997: 53) points out that contemporary cultural representations of children/childhood say much about adults' anxieties about how to manage, control, and ensure the survival of their young. Holland discusses the dangerousness of the concept of play as echoed in the titles of *Child's Play* series of films:

> The horror comes when play merges into reality. In this discourse it is also the margin between the experience of being a child and that of being an adult which is at stake. Jon Thompson and Robert Venables acted out those confusions in their most horrific form when they murdered James Bulger.

Stockwell (2010: 129) discusses this movie almost as if it were itself configured as a victim. He mentions the accusations against *Child's Play 3* related to the Bulger case and suggests that the film was "an acceptable target for moral panic" in the media because it was "the product of young writers and directors with little studio support." In *Ill Effects: The Media/Violence Debate*, Martin Barker calls it a moral film, and in a chapter in the same volume, David Buckingham downplays its seriousness by noting that the children with whom he spoke thought it was funny. In other words, there is a certain degree of academic disagreement about the worth or value of the film as a film, despite some consensus that it should not be blamed for having any effect on the perpetrators of the Bulger murder, particularly in view of the lack of evidence that the boys had seen it. However, if they had seen it (and there was evidence that they had seen other violent movies), a further argument would be required to demonstrate that, in fact, it had had no effect on them. It is in this case that academics skilled in interpreting children's behavior, such as child psychiatrists, would be needed.

Blake Morrison (2010) interviewed child psychiatrist Arnon Bentovim and asked if sexual abuse could have been a cause of Jon Venables's childhood crime and conviction as an adult for possessing child pornography. "Not necessarily," said Bentovim, who had carried out research in this area while working at Great Ormond Street Hospital for Sick Children. Bentovim told Morrison,

> Studies of sexually inappropriate behaviour in adolescents and adults have shown that exposure to violence during childhood is a key factor… . It's a complex business. There are genetic factors, too. But the overriding story is that exposure to violence will have a significant impact on behaviour and mental health.

Bentovim does not suggest that media violence be included in this damaging exposure, as did Elizabeth Newson and many other commentators on the Bulger case, including the trial judge. It is the suggestion that media violence, as well as actual violence, can lead to delinquent behavior that results in what I have suggested is a seventh step in the moral panic process: the indignant denial by media scholars that exposure to media representations of violence will have "a significant impact on behaviour and mental health." As Martin Barker and Julian Petley complain in their introduction to *Ill Effects: The Media/Violence Debate*: "When Elizabeth Newson (1997: 3) issued her report, the press, radio and television, were lining up to cover it. When we tried to state the opposite case, no one wanted to hear."

Stephen Stockwell (2010: 129) does not exempt all media from having a possible copycat effect on criminal behavior. In his discussion of *Child's Play 3*, he draws attention to the well-documented, amplification role of the *print* media in generating public anxiety, possibly even generating further harmful effects, "The news media avoided any stigma of their own coverage of the mass murder at Dunblane [Scotland] which friends of Bryant suggested may have been a trigger." So, from Stockwell there is a measure of acknowledgement of the Newson view that some media might have harmful effects on psychopathic, unbalanced, or—as in the case of Venables and Thompson—immature and damaged people.[1]

---

1    Most of the moral panic literature reviewed here predates new social media: Internet sites such as Twitter and Facebook. In the 2011 riots in English cities, it was suggested that instant communication facilitated riotous behavior. It also, of course, facilitated a great deal of prosocial behavior such as volunteer clean-up operations. However, there was no denying the sense of panic, and the spread of often-inaccurate rumors, in the thousands of tweets and messages incorporated into 24-hour rolling TV news commenting on the riots.

# Disproportionality and Volatility

In the introduction to the third edition of his classic *Folk Devils and Moral Panics: The Creation of the Mods and Rockers* (2002), Stanley Cohen discusses the criteria by which "media-driven narratives" can be "easily recognised as moral panics": drama, emergency and crisis, exaggeration, cherished values threatened, an object of concern, anxiety and hostility, evil forces. These characteristics can be summarized in the two characteristics identified by Kenneth Thompson (1998:9) as essential ingredients of moral panics: "disproportionality" (exaggeration, dramatization) and "volatility" (concern, anxiety, hostility.) "Volatility" means that moral panics appear suddenly and are short lived. Says Thompson, "'Disproportionality'" refers to "an implicit assumption on the part of someone who uses the term 'moral panic' that the threat or danger is more substantial than is warranted by a realistic appraisal" (1998: 9). The problem with discussing the Bulger case is that, because of its exceptional nature, exaggeration in describing it seems hardly possible. The facts of the case are harrowing enough, so any amplification of them is automatically in danger of seeming emotionally disproportional. Blake Morrison (2010) points out the disturbing nature of some of the evidence, "The murder, it's sometimes forgotten, did have a sexual component.... . details skimmed over at the trial in order to spare the Bulger family further suffering."

Academic discourse on the subject sometimes conforms to moral panic criteria by suggesting "serious threats to societal [in this case, academic] values" (Cohen 2002). An example is the fear of "a wider ideological package which its [censorship's] proponents would like to impose on us" (Barker and Petley 1997: 4). The sheer frequency of citation of the Bulger murder also creates an accumulative impression of urgency. The anxiety on the part of these expert commentators is that freedom of expression is gravely at risk. Like Elizabeth Newson, Julian Petley (1997: 2) experienced emotional disturbance: "What I read [about the academic U-turn over video nasties] both calmed and worried me." In *Ill Effects: The Media/Violence Debate*, Petley and Martin Barker (1997: 2) even identified something that sounds like a "folk devil." They blamed the attention given to the Newson Report on the efforts of a group "lurking" in the background of Alton's amendment, the Movement for Christian Democracy, which had "a quite specific moral agenda which, in its own words, used the Bill as a means of "coming of age politically." In his indignation at the press coverage given to the Newson Report, Martin Barker (1990) offers an example of "othering"—the depersonalizing of those who disagree with us—by frequent use of the word "them." Like those he criticizes, Barker (1990: 2) uses militaristic language to counterattack "them" (in this case, the Christian-right enemy and its allies):

> There is now an urgent need to counter attack; and our part as critical researchers and academics is to pull together what is known and to press this agenda that will cut away the ground from under them [that is, from under anti-media campaigners]. They hide their nonsense in a fog of their own making but also of our unquestioning.

This is a call to arms of a kind different from that of the tabloids railing against the ten-year-old "monsters," but it certainly shares some of the characteristics of moral panic discourse. I would suggest that (sympathetic as I am to the viewpoint) it falls into the category of disproportionality. Many "critical researchers and academics" would have less urgent desire to "attack" this unnamed "them" or to defend horror movies than to argue for children's rights or legal reform of the age of criminal responsibility.

Speaking for myself, and given inevitable limitations on time and energy, I do not want to spend any spare moral indignation defending media products — whether horror films, comic books, tabloids, reality TV shows, or operas — that I do not particularly like, or dislike. This is not to say that I want to launch a campaign to ban them. It is simply that, for me, they do not warrant the kind of heightened *language* that Barker uses, whereas the demonization of children *is* something that "disturbs and worries me," in Petley's words, and justifies the worried language of Elizabeth Newson. Her concern was to understand "the long drawn-out and merciless" attack on James Bulger, committed by two children who in her professional view were neither "freaks" nor psychopaths, with "little evidence of extremes of abuse or neglect" in their backgrounds. Newson's conclusion that "perhaps we should consider future Roberts and Jons and how far society should accept some responsibility for children who, at least in some sense, are its victims themselves," stands as a humane and reasonable position.

With regard to discourse, it seems appropriate and proportionate to be shocked and disturbed by the torture and murder of a two-year-old by two ten-year-olds, and even to be moved to highly emotive language on the subject. It does not seem similarly appropriate and proportionate to be shocked and disturbed by attacks on a B-movie. As Stephen Stockwell (2010: 125) comments about another disturbing crime, "It is very difficult to prescribe the correct manner of dealing with such a large, complex and emotive event." In such circumstances, language often fails.

## Reaction and Action

Stanley Cohen identifies two forms of public reaction to moral panic-type events: under-reaction (apathy, denial, and indifference) or over-reaction (exaggeration, hysteria, prejudice, and panic). But a third form of reaction also exists: doing something about a moral panic and its aftermath or about the problem at its center. In extreme cases of murder and public disturbance, appropriately equipped government agencies or non-profit organizations have to step in to pick up the pieces. And this was just as true on Bank Holiday Monday in Brighton in 1964, after the mods and rockers departed, as it is today. The views of these "sweepers-up" (who, in the case of damaged children, include child psychologists such as Newson and Bentovim) need to be part of the processual account.

Regarding the Bulger murder, something had to be done with Venables and Thompson, and the appropriateness and effectiveness, or otherwise, of the reaction is still being discussed (as in Blake Morrison's article). Something also had to be done—and still has to be done—to support James Bulger's family. Many commentators, including Julian Petley (1997) in a humane discussion of the Gulbenkian Foundation's 1995 *Report on Children and Violence* included near the end of *Ill Effects: The Media/Violence Debate*, agree that reforming action is necessary. Petley deplores the fact that the report's reasoned proposals such as "consistent disavowal of all forms of inter-personal violence" provoked further tabloid moral panic, including the *Daily Express*'s "fury at call to ban smacking" (1995).

*Ill Effects: The Media/Violence Debate* concludes with a constructive essay from psychologist Ann Hagell and criminologist Tim Newburn (1997: 151) about handling the media when publicizing research on such controversial issues as young people's relationships with the media:

> Learn to be clear and positive about what the research showed and to speak in media-talk [that is, short, connected colloquial sentences] ... grit your academic teeth and get the help of professionals.

To put it another way, keep calm and don't panic.


## Concluding Remarks

In *'Dear BBC': Children, Television Storytelling and the Public Sphere* (2001: 245), a study of children's attitudes to television drama (and incorporating their views on much else besides), I point out that "through the processes of collaboration and debate, determined by the children themselves ... a consistent bias towards social responsibility was produced":

> What these data [based on children's own proposals for a television service for children] suggest, is that, when it comes to cultural constructions of childhood, the constructs of 'children as spokespersons for other children' employed by the children in our study, are very far from being the focus of 'anxiety and panic' described in Buckingham's account [2000]. As such, the children's constructs of childhood and its public characteristics and needs, were divergent from current adult constructs.

I describe further evidence for this divergence in an exercise I carried out with teachers, which asked media educationists to role-play nine-year-old children carrying out the same tasks that children of about that age had been given. Unlike the children in the study, the teachers pretended to be "naughty" and when asked to work in groups to construct a children's schedule, they primarily chose entertainment programming such as cartoons. The 9- to 14-year-old children in the study did not do so; they negotiated with each other to reach consensus, they considered the audience as a whole, and they chose a varied schedule.

An assumption existed on the part of these role-playing adults that children would be self-oriented, unable to accept the needs, rights, and tastes of others. This was not the case, nor was it the case in any of the research I conducted over the years with children about their media consumption and their opinions about media controversies. In debates about moral panic discourse, particularly those concerned with children, childhood, media, and violence and antisocial behaviors, we should bear in mind that amid the sound and fury of grown-up indignation, sometimes the still, small voice of reason comes most eloquently from children themselves.

# References

Barker, M. 1997. The Newson Report: a case study in "common sense," in *Ill Effects: The Media/Violence Debate*, edited by M. Barker and J. Petley. London: Routledge, 12–31.

Buckingham, D. 1996. *Moving Images: Understanding Children's Responses to Television*. Manchester: Manchester University Press.

Buckingham, D. 1997. "Electronic child abuse," in *Ill Effects: The Media/Violence Debate*, edited by M. Barker and J. Petley. London: Routledge, 32–47.

Buckingham, D. 2000. *After the Death of Childhood*. Cambridge: Polity Press. *Child's Play 3* (dir. Jack Bender, 1991).

Cohen, S. 2002 (1972, 1980). *Folk Devils and Moral Panics: The Creation of Mods and Rockers*. 3rd Edition. London: Routledge.

1989. *Convention on the Rights of the Child. Office of the United Nations High Commissioner for Human Rights* [Online]. Available at: http://www2.ohchr.org/english/law/crc.htm [accessed: October 19, 2011].

Critcher, C. 2003. *Moral Panics and the Media*. Issues in Cultural and Media Studies. Buckingham: Open University Press.

Critcher, C. (ed.). 2010 (2006). *Critical Readings: Moral Panics and the Media*. Issues in Cultural and Media Studies. 2nd Edition. Maidenhead: Open University Press.

1995. Fury at call to ban smacking. *Daily Express*, November 10, 1.

Hagell, A. and Newburn, T. 1997. Going public with young offenders and the media, in *Ill Effects: The Media/Violence Debate*, edited by M. Barker and J. Petley. London: Routledge, 147–51.

Holland, P. 1997. Living for libido; or *Child's Play IV*, the imagery of childhood and the call for censorship, in *Ill Effects: The Media/Violence Debate*, edited by M. Barker and J. Petley. London: Routledge, 48–56.

Jackson, S. and Scott, S. 1999. Risk anxiety and the social construction of childhood," in *Risk and Socio-cultural Theory*, edited by D. Lupton. Cambridge: Cambridge University Press, 86–107.

Jenks, C. 1996. *Childhood*. London: Routledge.

McNutt, H. 2010. Tainted by the James Bulger legacy. *The Guardian* [Online, March 2], March 2, SocietyGuardian 1 Available at: http://www.guardian. co.uk/society/2010/mar/03/james-bulger-legacy-disturbed-children [accessed: October 28, 2011].

Messenger Davies, M. 2001. *'Dear BBC': Children, Television Storytelling and the Public Sphere*. Cambridge: Cambridge University Press.

Morrison, B. 2010. Blake Morrison: Jon Venables is not yet beyond redemption. The *Guardian* [Online, July 27], July 26, G2 10. Available at: http://www.guardian. co.uk/uk/2010/jul/27/blake-morrison-jon-venables [accessed: October 19, 2011].

Newson, E. 1994. "Video violence and the protection of children," *The Psychologist*, June, 273–75.

Otunnu, O. A. 2000. Statement of Olara A. Otunnu, Under-Secretary-General, Special Representative of the Secretary-General for Children and Armed Conflict to the Commission on Human Rights. *Office of the Special Representative of the Secretary-General for Children and Armed Conflict* [Online]. Available at: http://www.un.org/children/conflict/spanish/11april2000state.html [accessed: October 19, 2011].

Petley, J. 1997. Going public with children and violence, in *Ill Effects: The Media/ Violence Debate*, edited by M. Barker and J. Petley. London: Routledge, 152–5.

1998. Secretary-General's special representative calls for maximum protection for children in statute of international criminal court. *Office of the Special Representative to the Secretary-General for Children and Armed Conflict* [Online]. "Reissued as received from Office of Special Representative." Available at: http://www.un.org/children/conflict/english/pr/1998-06-1659.html [accessed: October 19, 2011].

Selwyn, N. 2003. Doing IT for the kids: re-examining children, computers and the "Information Society." *Media, Culture and Society* [Online], 25(3), 351–78. Available at: http://rcirib.ir/articles/pdfs/cd1%5CIngenta_Sage_Articles_on_194_225_11_89/ Ingenta901.pdf [accessed: October 19, 2011].

Springhall, J. 1998. *Youth, Popular Culture and Moral Panics: Penny Gaffs to Gangsta Rap, 1830–1996*. Houndmills: Macmillan.

Stockwell, S. 2010 (2006). Panic at the port, in *Critical Readings: Moral Panic and the Media*. 2nd Edition, edited by C. Critcher. Maidenhead: Open University Press, 124–34.

Thompson, K. 1998. *Moral Panics*. Key Ideas. Milton Park: Routledge.

Utting, W. (chair). 1995. *Children and Violence: Report of the Gulbenkian Foundation Commission*. London: Calouste Gulbenkian Foundation.

# Children Pushed Aside:
# Moral Panic over the Family and
# the State in Contemporary Poland

Magdalena Rek-Woźniak and Wojciech Woźniak

Public discourses revolving around issues of child abuse are currently among the most common topics analyzed by scholars using a moral panic framework. Besides scholars' own interests in these two issues, the regularity with which they are chosen as research topics reflects the increasing attention paid by media and politicians to substantial structural changes in the West regarding family models, parental roles, sexual identities, perceptions of childhood, recognition of children's rights and status, gender relations, and women's rights. Moral panics triggered by public discourses regarding children's well-being have often expanded to encompass multidimensional transformations in axiological systems, encompassing changing demographic trends on a global scale, increasing individualism, and conservative and progressive political ideologies.

In Poland, a nascent moral panic over child abuse within the family quickly metamorphosed into a moral panic centering on the family itself, perceived by many to be an endangered social institution. In other words, the moral panic provoked by parliamentary action regarding the law against domestic abuse can more accurately be defined as an episode of heightened concern not over children, but about the integrity of the family (in its patriarchal form). Indeed, remarkably little thoughtful discussion of child abuse was evident in the eventual moral panic over the family, even when dramatic cases of children abuse and family violence were in the news. The role of folk devil was played by the state (or its agents: social workers and other civil servants) rather than those child abusers. Perceptively, Kenneth Thompson (1998: 2) identifies a growing tendency for moral panics to encompass numerous and diverse social problems:

> Earlier panics tended to be focused on a single group—teenagers
> who went to coffee bars, drug addicts or young black muggers.
> Contemporary panics seem to catch many more people in their net.
> For example, panics about child abuse seem to call into question the

very institution of the family and especially physical relations between fathers and their children, perhaps reflecting a general unease about masculinity and the role of the father. Just as an incident of 'home alone' children raises questions about the 'maternal instinct' and the independent woman.

According to Thompson (1998: 20), certain changes in predominant moral values (and as a result in laws as well) have falsified old arguments, creating a need for new conceptualizations.

In this chapter, we analyze public discourses produced and disseminated between February 2009 and August 2010 concerning a revision of the law on domestic violence. Notably, in Poland, moral panic recently triggered by concerns over children's welfare proceeded over several years by way of distinct stages. In researching our sources, we have kept in mind that changes in modern societies, including the evolution of media landscapes, have redefined moral panic: "As a result, moral panics can no longer be seen as discrete events, having definite beginnings and ends, in which media promote and society enforces a uniform viewpoint" (Krinsky 2008: 3). In tracking the ongoing progress of moral panic in Poland, we have looked at such media texts as press releases, television programs, public opinion polls, and websites maintained by interest groups.

# Models of Moral Panics

## Stanley Cohen

Empirical applications of the moral panic concept may be said mainly to follow two approaches. One, the processual model, founded on Stanley Cohen's (2002: 1) research and conceptualization beginning in 1972, focuses on analyzing the dynamics of moral panic: its causes, consequences, and agents:

> Societies appear to be subject, every now and then, to periods of moral panic. A condition, episode, person or group of persons emerges to become defined as a threat to societal values and interests; its nature is presented in a stylized and stereotypical fashion by the mass media; the moral barricades are manned by editors, bishops, politicians and other right-thinking people; socially accredited experts pronounce their diagnoses and solutions; ways of coping are evolved or (more often) resorted to; the condition then disappears, submerges or deteriorates and becomes more visible. Sometimes the object of the panic is quite novel and at other times it is something which has been in existence long enough, but suddenly appears in the limelight. Sometimes the panic passes over and is forgotten, except in folk-lore and collective memory; at other times it has more serious and long-

lasting repercussions and might produce such changes as those in legal and social policy or even in the way the society conceives itself.

Key agents of moral panic include media (which deliver images of deviance and deviants as folk devils), "moral entrepreneurs" (representatives of interest groups who urge elimination of the "threat"), the societal control culture (representatives of public institutions such as courts, police, and politicians), and public opinion.

## Erich Goode and Nachman Ben-Yehuda

Besides Cohen's processual model, the attributional model, inspired by work done by Erich Goode and Nachman Ben-Yehuda (2009: 37–43, emphasis in original), focuses on the structural criteria that define moral panic:

> First, there must be a heightened level of *concern* over the behavior of certain group or category and the consequences that that behavior presumably causes for one or more sectors of the society. Such concern can be engendered by a range of factors, including the media, but if it's felt, we can feel confident that we have a moral panic in our hands.... Second, there must be an increased level of *hostility* toward the group or category regarded as engaging in the behavior or causing the condition in question. Members of this category are collectively designated as the enemy.... Third, to qualify as moral panic, we must have substantial or widespread *agreement* or *consensus*—that is, at least a certain minimal measure of consensus or agreement, either in the society as a whole or in designated segments of the society-that the threat is real, serious, and caused by the wrongdoing group members and their behavior.... Fourth [disproportionality], there is the implicit assumption in the use of the term moral panic that there is a sense on the part of many members of the society that a more sizeable number of individuals are engaged in the behavior in question than actually are.... And fifth, by their nature, moral panics are *volatile*; they erupt fairly suddenly (although they may lie dormant or latent for long periods of time, and may reappear from time to time).

Despite sharing significant similarities, the differences between the two models, as Chas Critcher points out, run deep (2008: 1134–5). In Cohen's processual model, the role played by media in creating moral panics is of critical concern. This approach also stresses the roles played by politicians and public institutions in provoking moral panics. In contrast, the attributive model centers on the mesostructure of civil society, particularly on interest groups (see Thompson 1998). In terms of the discourses they examine, researchers using the attributive model often focus on "claim-making rhetoric" (Critcher 2008: 1135), while the processual model emphasizes the relation between moral panic and larger ideological discourses (see also Cornwell and Linders 2002, deYoung 2004, Ungar 2001).

### Brian V. Klocke and Glenn W. Muschert

Here, we apply to moral panics over children the hybrid model developed by Brian V. Klocke and Glenn W. Muschert (2010). Klocke and Muschert (2010: 301) combine Cohen's approach with that of Goode and Ben-Yehuda, taking into account critical commentaries that have emerged concerning the concept of moral panic:

> The hybrid model and our suggestions for applying the model to MPs research attempt to account for the indeterminacy and volatility of contemporary MPs phenomena, and the capacity of folk devils to resist, while acknowledging the disproportionality of social and institutionalized power. Our model also recognizes the ability of ideological and discursive patterns and structures to cultivate future MPs and to have lasting cultural and institutional outcomes.

This chapter is structured according to the guidelines regarding methodology with which Klocke and Muschert supplement their model, namely their recommendation that in examining moral panic, researchers are well advised to follow three critical stages in the development of moral panics: cultivation (genesis and evolution), operation (climax and consequences), and dissipation (deceleration and dissolution).

# The Case of Poland: An Application of Klocke and Muschert's Moral Panics Model

Historian of religion Philip Jenkins's remark concerning a moral panic over the supposedly imminent destruction of the family in the United Kingdom holds equally true for many other countries, including Poland: "For right-wing critics, the chief folk devil was the interfering social worker, sometimes cast as a rabid left-wing feminist, determined to shatter the family unit" (1992: 16–17). In a number of countries, the process of opening the family to scrutiny and regulation as an institution that is no longer entirely private and undisclosed has been expedited by a growing recognition of children's rights, as well as by the assigning of responsibility for protecting those rights to the state. Nevertheless, state intervention in family life has remained a highly contentious issue, both politically and as a subject of sociological inquiry. Sociologist Jennifer A. Reich (2008: 904–5), who has analyzed historical perspectives on state intervention in the family, sees a need for careful consideration of competing rights and interests:

At a time when sociologists are voicing great concern about the increasing amount of surveillance individuals and families face, inadequate attention has been paid to the child welfare system .... The complexities and contradictions of the child welfare system require meticulous research and theorizing with nuance and compassion. This work must go beyond program evaluation to an interrogation of the very meanings of system process. This is a dynamic system with historical trends that represent shifting cultural ideologies about children, gender, and family life. Heavy-handed interventions are easy to criticize, as are the myriad problems with normalization of parents. However, we also must recognize the successes of the system, the way new families are sometimes made or existing families, defined more broadly than ever before, are supported. This is a complex system that reflects many of our cultural struggles, values, and intentions. It is ready for conscientious examination.

The main and most provocative point here is that since children as individuals lack legal and economic autonomy, law and society should treat them as a unique group with its own particular needs.

## Cultivation

According to Klocke and Muschert (2010: 301), the cultivation phase begins in advance of a moral panic, when:

There needs to be a conflict between two or more competing moral universes that is articulated by moral entrepreneurs who have been busy in creating a public perception of the problem, setting the stage for the possible development of MP.

It requires:

The emergence of conditions, actors, and discourses that make the growth of a MP more likely, such as the following: Conflict among competing moral universes and/or rapid social change, economic or political crisis, media attention/public concern about related social problems. (Klocke and Muschert 2010: 301)

In using the term "possible development," Klocke and Muschert suggest that cultivation should not be defined as a situation immediately leading to moral panic, but rather as a social, economic, or political climate that could enable or enforce such an episode now or in the future. In April 2003, in Łódź, Poland's second largest city, a police officer searching an apartment in a decrepit inner city tenement discovered in a wardrobe two blue plastic barrels of the sort usually used for pickling cabbage. Instead of cabbage, the barrels contained the mummifying corpses of two infants and two 5-year-old twin brothers. It turned out that their mother had murdered the children four years earlier. The family (which, besides the four victims, included two parents and two children still living) had for years been supervised by Łódź municipal social services. Then, a few months after this discovery, a similarly macabre incident also came to light. The bodies of five infants were found in a barrel secreted in the cellar of a house in Lublin Province in southeastern Poland. Their mother, having drowned the infants, first hid the bodies in a freezer, but, moving to a house provided by social services, took them with her in the barrel.

The public and media debates roused by these events were brief and inconclusive. Media and other public discourses featured such themes as:

- Pathological and demoralized families for whom poverty has exacerbated individuals' preexisting deadly potential. In one article, a psychologist was quoted as claiming,

  > Jolanta K. is a clinical example of a psycho acting as an intelligent serial killer…. She has chosen the easiest solution. Now she tries to defend herself by showing repentance, but it seems to me a learned behavior. Childhood, the death of her mother, had some effect on her, but not a decisive one. She was just born like that.

  The same article quotes a priest as saying, "How could you be that much afraid of your husband to kill children? Mothers should be ready to lay down their life for children. I see no mitigating circumstances for her" (Reszka 2008: 10).
- Mistakes or negligence on the part of social services. Although it was noted that the average social worker supervised more than 100 families, making individual oversight impossible, the social workers in question were publicly named and punished. Their complicity was emphasized even in accounts of the trial that centered on the failures of state institutions: "Police confirmed they made mistakes. But it was also court and probation officers who made mistakes. A defense attorney claimed, 'What were a probation officer, social workers, police doing? Nothing. They were making notes, sending letters, but they should have paid more attention and maybe the tragedy would not have happened. … A few dozen people lived on that block and they paid no attention, they were isolated from that family'" (Torański 2004: 3).
- Impoverished neighborhoods supposedly lacking in strong social ties and moral values. In Łódź, neighbors and relatives had assumed that the twins had left home to live with their stepfamily.
- The alleged ineffectiveness of social welfare programs. Especially in regard to the murders in Łódź, media reaction was reminiscent of a debate concerning ghettoes and the underclass that had been part of public discourses since

the beginning of the seventies, which to some extent had paved the way for cutbacks in social welfare programs.

The media covered the twin tragedies as scandalous crimes, and only for a short time at that, without discussing such issues as a child's rights as a citizen *in spe*. One article summarizing the murderers' trial, published in the most popular Polish newspaper, *Gazeta Wyborcza*, was titled "Doomed to Hell" (Markowska 2004: 1). Another news story, published in the tabloid *Super Express* and titled "Shocking Testimony of 12-yearold Monika: 'I saw my Dad Killing [my Siblings],'" included detailed information about the means by which two parents committed murder (Kucharski and Marczyńska 2004: 1). The subheading for a passage focusing on the parents cried, "Monsters" (Kucharski and Marczyńska 2004: 1). The possibility of underlying social or economic causes was ignored and informed political debate failed to take place. Seemingly, no one sought to identify social structural reasons for the tragedies. In parliament, no legal measures or even informal policies to prevent similar tragedies in the future were implemented.

Given the lack of public or state response to news of the tragedies, it seems reasonable to conclude that, at least in the near future, no case of child abuse will likely be drastic enough to draw much political attention. Nevertheless, by 2005, some left-wing politicians had begun pushing for parliamentary action to protect children from domestic abuse. It would seem that giving children legal protection that recognizes their specific situation would hardly lead to controversy. Yet, discord eventually did follow, though it failed to center on children for long. Public discussion concerning an amendment to the law on domestic violence soon left the topic of children's rights behind, centering instead on the state's proper relation to the family. Despite sensationalism, mainstream media's treatment of the topic touched on at least two questions that had been the subjects of heated debated since the collapse of communism in 1989: the relative social value of the modern family versus the "traditional" model and, tied to this, the Roman Catholic Church's power to impose norms and values concerning family life.

Amending the law was justified by the figures. In 2009, 132,000 cases of family violence were reported to the police, with 81,000 women, 40,000 children, and 11,000 men reported as victims.[1] Moreover, by 2005, the public debates over the propriety of corporal punishment within families that had long been present in Western Europe had reached Poland. Approval of corporal punishment is relatively high in Polish society. While beating children is generally held to be unacceptable, "smacking" (slapping or striking) is still widely tolerated as a means of tuition. Thus, in 2008, half of adult Poles opposed introducing a ban on striking children. Opinions did not differ significantly by class or political orientation (see opinion polls "Bicie Dzieci" 2005, "Raport z Badania" 2008, *Społeczne* 2008). In 2009, a survey reported that two thirds of Poles acknowledged having disciplined their children by striking them (Sajkowska 2009: 14).

---

1    See http://www.statystyka.policja.pl/.

## Operation

In Klocke and Muschert's (2010: 302) model, the operation phase comprises the "exact" moral panic, that is, the stage at which the moral panic itself is in motion, rather than growing or subsiding. This phase consists of several substages and is usually stirred up by sensationalized media coverage of some shocking event or events. Unusually, however, rather than being ignited by a discreet event, this moral panic resulted from a long process of often-provocative public debate about whether Polish families needed protection from domestic abuse. A rightist and individualist political climate paved the way for heightened fear and concern regarding a change in the law. To some extent, one might say this was a moral panic *a rebours*, with the family presented as the supposed victim, and with the state, its representatives, and even sometimes children themselves playing the role of folk devil. *Rzeczpospolita* (*The Republic*), one of the most important broadsheets in the nation, played a crucial role in framing the limits of the debate. Co-owned by the Ministry of the Treasury and a British firm, the Mecom Group, *Rzeczpospolita* is strongly right wing, regularly engaging in moral crusades against liberal or modernizing social measures, including gay rights, *in vitro* fertilization and contraceptive use, sex education, and placing limits on the Roman Catholic Church's political involvement.

In February 2009, the government proposed amending the law against domestic violence along the same lines earlier recommended by left-wing members of parliament. From the first, the most controversial aspects of the proposed changes involved article 12A, which mandated that in case of a direct threat to the life or health of a child, especially when the legal guardian was inebriated, a social worker could place the child with a foster family or in institutional care:

- In the case of a direct threat to the life or health of a child, especially when a legal guardian is in a state of intoxication, a social worker has the right to remove the child from the family, to be placed with a foster family or in an around-the-clock care institution.
- When removing a child from the family, a social worker must be accompanied by a physician, EMT, nurse, or police officer.
- A social worker must inform the guardianship court as soon as possible, but not more than 24 hours later, that the child has been removed from the family and placed with a foster family or in an around-the-clock care institution.

Despite receiving some support, a ban on corporal punishment was not included. Augmenting the amendment, Minister of Labour and Social Policy Jolanta Fedak issued a decree that starting in 2011 social workers would be required to satisfy new professional requirements in order to guarantee their competence.[2]

---

2    See http://orka.sejm.gov.pl/Druki6ka.nsf/0/E7D206E9D4B5292AC125756100371248/$file/1698.pdf.

After the proposed changes were announced, debates engaged mainstream media, politicians (especially those of the conservative opposition Law and Justice Party, who fought against changing the law), journalists, and recognized experts on social questions. Using Klocke and Muschert's terminology, this substage of the operation phase is identified with "magnification": perceived dangers are magnified in the public imagination. They undergo "distortion," that is, they are exaggerated or misrepresented, and there is a "prediction" of greater harm to come. *Rzeczpospolita* published incendiary articles that indicated the direction much of the public debate was to take, for example "Will there be Family Police? (Domagalski and Zalewski 2009), "Smacking Is Not Abuse" (Rafałowicz 2009), "Family: Victim of the Omnipotent State" (Wojciechowski 2009), and "The State Haunts Families" (Szymański 2009).

Stanley Cohen notes that while the folk devil in moral panics is usually an individual or group in some sense recognizable even when distorted, it can sometimes be more abstract. Here, the folk devil embodied the state imagined as a loosely defined, yet infinitely powerful bureaucratic mechanism seeking only to increase its control over citizens' lives, with social workers serving as its advance guard. Cohen (2002: xv) suggests that during some moral panics, social workers are likely to be seen as

> either gullible wimps, or else storm troopers of the nanny state, either uncaring, coldhearted bureaucrats, not intervening in time to protect the victim, or else over-zealous, do-gooding meddlers intervening groundlessly and invading privacy.

Early in the debate over changing the law, *Rzeczpospolita* (Wildstein 2009) described social workers in military terms: "If the government's project of changing the law on domestic violence succeeds, an army of 15,000 state social workers will be able to decide whether a child should be taken from its family. The idea makes your hair stand on end."

By the start of 2010, the debate heated up again (especially on the part of opponents) when it became known that in February amendments to the law against domestic violence, having been modified by a parliamentary Committee on Social Policy and Family, would be submitted to parliament for debate and possible revision. Experts on law, theology, and human psychology, as well as representatives of various organizations, were quoted in mainstream media, a phase that Klocke and Muschert (2010: 302) call "officiation." The Council for Family Affairs of the Conference of the Polish Episcopate formally expressed its opposition to a law that would supposedly interfere with the integrity of the family and parents' right to raise children in accordance with their worldview: "Passage of the law will result in mass control over families, even against their will and without justification, hampering the raising of children and weakening familial bonds" (Górny 2010). In May, the Council published another official statement, titled "Ensnaring Families by Law" (Górny and Rębacz 2010), which argued that present laws protected "the legitimate need to counteract violence." The statement predicted that "scientifically unjustified" legislation would lead to "surveillance of families" (Górny and Rębacz 2010). Addressing the *ratio legis*, the statement referenced research showing that striking children was widely accepted in Poland. Though the new law stated clearly that only serious cases of domestic violence would be subject to intervention, the statement suggested that it would lead to prosecutions against about half of Polish families (a prediction also made by many other opponents of the law). Children's rights were mentioned only once in the entire document: "At the same time, we want to emphasize that parents divorcing and killing children constitute the greatest aggression." The reference to killing children co-opted keywords used by pro-life forces in Poland and elsewhere.

Typical of opponents' rhetorical strategies was *Tomasz Lis na żywo* (*Tomasz Lis Live*), a popular prime time news and commentary program broadcast weekly on TVP1. In a studio discussion involving, in support of the new law, Katarzyna Piekarska (a member of parliament, of the left-wing Democratic Left Alliance), Dorota Zawadzka (psychologist and TV celebrity known as the Polish supernanny), and, for the opposition, Tomasz Terlikowski (a conservative Catholic journalist) and Karolina Elbanowska (representing an organization called "Spokesman for Parents' Rights" and an initiator of opposition to the new law). Acting as a supposedly objective moderator, Lis introduced the topic:

> According to this measure, a social worker will ... as a matter of course ... immediately take a child from parents if he is convinced that either they mistreat this child, or they are unable to bear the cost of the child's upbringing. ... There is an argument from the Council of the Episcopate, from ... various associations, and above all, from parents that this is an outrage by state against families.

In fact, a proponent of the law, left-wing politician Katarzyna Piekarska, favored stricter standards for social workers:

> Because of your viewpoint, they [social workers] will not intervene, because they are frightened. And I really prefer a situation where someone maybe once makes mistake and the court says—give the child back—than to find a child's body.

Such statements presented a concept of the family strikingly different from that held by opponents, who see the family as a single entity or individual potentially in need of help from state institutions. According to Magdalena Środa (2010), a professor of ethics, feminist activist, and columnist for *Gazeta Wyborcza* (the centrist *Electoral Gazette*, Poland's bestselling non-tabloid newspaper):

> Even a theologian ... should know that the modern democratic state is based on the concept that human rights are granted to individuals, not to families or local communities. These are the rights to security, physical integrity, to autonomy, happiness, etc., and one of the most

important obligations of the state is to defend these rights, sometimes against the family and against the Bible.

This statement highlights the fact that rather than protecting children, or even protecting the family, this moral panic concerned opposing views of the individual's relationship to the state and social welfare.

Coverage of the problem in the centrist press mostly reiterated opponents' spins and arguments, which can be put in a nutshell:

- It increases the omnipotence of the state; Orwellian.
- It gives too much power to social workers.
- It destroys the traditional family.
- It is a result of moral panic inflamed by the ruling party and liberal elite.
- It was imported from the laic West, infected by the "civilization of death" (a term coined by Pope John Paul II to describe the self-destructive aspects of permissive, laic Western culture).
- It would lead to greater excesses.

When discussing the issue of corporal punishment in the home, *Rzeczpospolita* frequently referenced Ruby Harrold-Claesson, the leader of The Nordic Committee for Human Rights, a Scandinavian nongovernmental organization claiming to defend family rights against the oppression of the welfare state (an interview with her was titled "Dictatorship of the Social Workers") (Nowacka-Isaksson 2010). Harrold-Claesson's foremost scientific authority on abuse has been Dr Laura Schlesinger, as cited in Harrold-Claesson's article, "Smacking Children Is Not Harmful" (2006). In May 2010, Harrold-Claesson was invited to Poland by civil organizations opposed to the law and spoke to senators as an expert on the family.


## Dissipation

The dissipation phase is the period when a moral panic recedes from public attention (Klocke and Muschert 2010: 302, 304–5). In Poland, the moral panic dissipated unusually rapidly because another newsworthy event diverted the public's attention. It might even be said that this moral panic began to dissipate even before it reached the climax of the operation stage. On April 10, 2010, the Polish president Lech Kaczyński, his wife, and 94 other people died when the plane on which they were traveling crashed in Russia. The timing of this tragedy probably also significantly contributed to the fact that the process of passing the law through parliament, which took place between May and August 2010, went rather smoothly. On May 6, the law was passed by the lower chamber of parliament, on May 31 by the upper chamber, and on June 18 it was signed by the new President, Bronisław Komorowski. After *vacatio legis*, the law came into force on August 12. The new president held more liberal views than his predecessor had done. Most probably, the act would have been vetoed by Kaczyński, as his party, Law and Justice, was the main political opponent of the amendment.

Unsurprisingly, there were some rearguard efforts to fight the new law. Its opponents kept on creating catastrophic visions of the future, seeing Article 12A as a portent of state abuse:

> Orwell called the secret services 'the Ministry of Love'. This is the way our government is heading now. ... Totalitarian experiment in Sweden lasts for 30 years. Civil servants snatch more than 10 thousand children per year. Children are depraved, they snitch and use violence against parents, peers and teachers. Love and trust in families have been destroyed. (Wojciechowski 2010)

In the same article, the significance of "moral" arguments was reinforced by referring to "objective" facts and "pragmatic" reasoning that the "demographic condition of Poland is terrible. Now, there is one more reason to avoid having children" (Wojciechowski 2010).

An online interest group called Spokesman for Parents' Rights continued to make its voice heard. The organization's founders, Karolina and Tomasz Elbanowski (2010: 2), wrote an article for the hard-copy edition of the bestselling Polish tabloid newspaper *Fakt*, commenting,

> Altering [the law] will result in stalking 'parental misbehavior' like grounding children, criticizing or shaming them, it is all defined as violence. They say that smacking children will not be punished, because the amendment itself will change the attitudes and habits. Crime without punishment? Not really. Smacking is now equal to hitting adult person, which is punishable. Before long, we will be witnessing social workers interfering in any attempt to nurture a child, like in Norway and Sweden, there will be a huge wave of denunciations ... . What will be the result of all this? Probably we will see children taken away from parents who are considered not clever enough or even overly protective, the way it is in Germany, Scandinavia, or England.

The online protest was intended to justify challenging the law in court, which in the end failed to happen. The Spokesman for Parents' Rights site reminded visitors about the objections raised by the Conference of the Polish Episcopate and some experts. Despite continuing protests from the Spokesman for Parental Rights, critics of the new law were left without political support.

# Conclusion

In studies devoted to the phenomenon, moral panics are often presented as spirals of irrational, exaggerated reactions, motivated by fear and resulting in short-term action and inadequate or even counterproductive solutions implemented without proper diagnosis and aimed rather at gaining public support than dealing with actual problems. While we shy away from making wholesale generalizations, it seems likely that the fact that Polish society is neither unreservedly secular nor wholeheartedly capitalist helped make the course of the moral panic over the state's proper relation to the family unusual in being remarkably short-lived and even, in a sense, tepid.

The dominance of Roman Catholicism in the symbolic sphere and the cultural triumph of neoliberal ideology lend support to the common belief that social problems are in fact individual failures or (moral) deficiencies on the part of specific social groups. Claim-making rhetoric was deeply embedded in a generalized, historically formed mistrust of the state as the provider of support for the weakest members of the society. It was not without reason that the representatives of the state who served as folk devils in the debate remained voiceless.

What makes Polish discourses about child abuse exceptional is that no moral panic over this social problem has ever been triggered by even the most drastic cases. Even in the debate over a law intended to protect and nurture children, opponents of the new legislation completely ignored data documenting the real and significant problem of mistreatment of children within families, disregarded the issue of human dignity, and paid no attention to constitutional rights. It is also worth noting the lack of pluralism in the Polish media market, caused by prevailing conservatism, the Church, and more: no mainstream media speak for those at the bottom of the social structure. Public media are weak and subject to partisan conflicts, whereas private media present a strictly pro-market economy perspective that translates as praise of welfare retrenchment and individualism.

Yet, this moral panic testifies to the extent to which a pro-"traditional" family ideology is deeply and firmly embedded in Polish society, prescribed by the Church, and reinforced by neoliberal rhetoric. In the words of Michał Wojciechowski, a theology professor at the University of Warmia and Mazury in Olsztyn, in an article he published in *Rzeczpospolita*: "Always and everywhere, the family is the basis of human community, while the state is a secondary phenomenon typical of civilizations more developed in material terms" (2010). Poland's moral panic over state intervention into family life reinforced the prevailing conviction that the family is a naturally occurring unit that, in terms of morality, carries more weight than either individual rights or state institutions.

# References

Cohen, S. 2002 (1972, 1980). *Folk Devils and Moral Panics: The Creation of the Mods and Rockers*. 3rd Edition. London: Routledge.

Cornwell, B. and Linders, A. 2002. The myth of moral panic: an alternative account of LSD prohibition. *Deviant Behavior*. 23(4), 307–30.

Critcher, C. 2008. Moral panic analysis: past, present and future. *Sociology Compass*, 2(4), 1127–44.

deYoung, M. 2004. *The Day Care Ritual Abuse Moral Panic*. Jefferson: McFarland.

Domagalski, M. and Zalewski, T. 2009. Czy powstanie policja rodzinna [Will there be family police]. Rzeczpospolita, January 29.

Elbanowska, K. and Elbanowski, T. 2010. Polska dyskryminuje rodziców [Poland discriminates against parents]. Fakt [Online, August 14]. Available at: http://www.fakt.pl/Polska-dyskryminuje-rodzicow,artykuly,79760,1.html [accessed: July 17, 2011].

Górny, K. 2010. Oświadczenie Rady Konferencji Episkopatu Polski ds. Rodziny [Statement of the Council of the Conference of Polish Episcopate for the Family Affairs]. Konferencji Episkopatu Polski [Online]. Available at: http://www.episkopat.pl/?a=dokumentyKEP&doc=201031_0 [accessed: August 25, 2011]

Górny, K. and Rębacz A. 2010, Ustawowe osaczanie rodziny [Entrapping Families by Law].

Konferencji Episkopatu Polski [Online]. Available at: http://www.episkopat.pl/?a=dokumentyKEP&doc=2010519_0 [accessed: August 25, 2011]

Goode, E. and Ben-Yehuda, N. 2002 (1994). Moral Panics. The Social Construction of Deviance. 2nd Edition. Chichester: Wiley-Blackwell

Harrold-Claesson, R. 2006. Smacking children is not harmful. Scoop, October 15. Available at: http://www.scoop.co.nz/stories/PO0610/S00150.htm [accessed: July 17, 2011].

Klocke, B.V. and Muschert, G.W. 2010. A hybrid model of moral panics: synthesizing the theory and practice of moral panic research. *Sociology Compass*, 4(5), 295–309.

Krinsky C. 2008. *Introduction, in Moral Panics over Contemporary Children and Youth*, edited by C. Krinsky. Aldershot: Ashgate, 1–6.

Kucharski, D. and Marczyńska, M. 2004. Wstrząsające zeznania 12-letniej Moniki: Widziałam, jak tata mordował [Shocking testimony of 12-year-old Monika: I saw my dad killing]. Super Express, June 4, 1.

Markowska, A. 2004. Skazani na piekło [Doomed to hell]. Gazeta Wyborcza, June 22, 1.

McRobbie, A. and Thornton, S. 1995. Rethinking 'moral panic' for multi-mediated social worlds. *British Journal of Sociology*, 46 (4), 559–74.

Nowacka-Isaksson, A. 2010. Dyktatura urzędników socjalnych: wywiad z R. Harrold-Claesson [Dictatorship of the social workers: interview with R. Harrold-Claesson. Rzeczpospolita, May 17. Available at: http://www.rp.pl/artykul/480850.html [accessed: July 17, 2011].

Rafałowicz, M. 2009. Klaps to nie znęcanie się [Smacking is not abuse]. Rzeczpospolita, March 31.

Reich, J.R. 2008. The child welfare system and state intervention in families: from historical patterns to future questions. *Sociology Compass*, 2(3), 888–909.

Reszka, P.P. 2008. I przestałam być człowiekiem [And I stopped being human]. Gazeta Wyborcza, September 1, 6,10.

Sajkowska, M. 2009. Raport z badań: Bicie dzieci: Postawy i doświadczenia dorosłych Polaków. [Research Report: Smacking Children: Attitudes and Experiences of Adult Poles]. Fundacja Dzieci Niczyje [Online]. Available at:http://www.dziecinstwobezprzemocy. pl/repository/media/raport_Bicie_dzieci.pdf [accessed: July 12, 2011].

2008. Społeczne przyzwolenie na bicie dzieci [Social Acceptance for Smacking Children]. Centrum Badania Opinii Społe Cznej [Online]. Available at: http://www.cbos.pl/SPISKOM.POL/2008/K_106_08.PDF [accessed: June 15, 2011].

Szymański, A. 2009. Państwo osacza rodzinę [The state haunts families]. Rzeczpospolita, December 27.

Środa, M. 2010, Barbarzyństwo trzyma się dobrze [Barbarity is alive and well]. Gazeta Wyborcza [Online, August 4]. Available at: http://wyborcza.pl/1,80322 ,8209845,Barbarzynstwo_trzyma_sie_dobrze.html#ixzz1W8XcNfVc [accessed: August 25, 2011].

Torański, B. 2004. Nie potrafili kochać [They couldn't love]. Rzeczpospolita, June 22.

Thompson, K. 1998. *Moral Panics. Key Ideas*. Milton Park: Routledge.

TNS OBOP. 2005. Bicie dzieci w rodzinie polskiej [Smacking children in Polish families]. TNS OBOP [Online]. Available at: http://www.tnsglobal.pl/archive-report/id/4296 [accessed: June 15, 2011].

2008. Raport z badania TNS OBOP dla Ministerstwa Pracy i Polityki Społecznej: badanie dotyczące zjawiska przemocy w rodzinie wobec dzieci [TNS OBOP report for the Ministry of Labour and Social Affairs: research on the phenomenon of domestic violence against children]. TNS OBOP [Online]. Available at: http://www.niebieskalinia.org/download/Badania/TNS_OBOP_II_2008.pdf [accessed: June 15, 2011].

Ungar, S. 2001. Moral panic versus the risk society: the implications of the changing sites of social anxiety. *British Journal of Sociology*, 52(2), 271–91.

Wildstein, B. 2009. O czym zapomnieli państwowi uszczęśliwiacze [What have the state-pleasers forgotten]? Rzeczpospolita [Online, January 28]. Available at: http://www.rp.pl/artykul/255109.html [accessed: July 12, 2011]

Wojciechowski, M. 2009. Rodzina: ofiara wszechmocnego państwa [Family: victim of the omnipotent state]. Rzeczpospolita, June 10.

Wojciechowski, M. 2010. Ustawa przeciwko rodzinie [Law against family]. Rzeczpospolita [Online, July 29]. Available at: http://www.rp.pl/artykul/515559. html?p=4 [accessed: July 12, 2011].

# Moral Panics versus Youth Problem Debates: Three Conceptual Insights from the Study of Japanese Youth

## Tuukka Toivonen\*

There can be little doubt that though most of the relevant literature focuses on Europe and North America, non-Western societies with modern media apparatuses are similarly susceptible to episodes of moral panic.\*\* In the case of East Asia, even an outside observer without fluency in the local languages has nowadays little difficulty locating examples of heated controversy over topics such as Internet addiction, anorexia, or excessive gaming in places like mainland China, Hong Kong, and South Korea (see, respectively, Technology 2009, Watters 2009, "South Korea Cracks Down" 2010). The most salient of such *domestic* debates are almost routinely (and now even more frequently, as China increases its global stature) taken up by transnational media and diffused *internationally*.

Japan, the society at the center of my own sociological and social policy-oriented empirical inquiry, is no exception. Indeed, a particularly colorful list of public, morally charged controversies filled the Japanese media between the 1980s and the 2000s. To mention just a few, the 1980s saw growing worries about the misuses of corporal punishment as well as concerns over a crisis of the family as more younger women chose to work outside the home instead of becoming *sengyō shufu* (professional housewives) and caring for elderly family members. Along with anxiety over the burst of the economic bubble and the problem of bad loans, the 1990s began with the so-called "1.57 shock," raising alarm over the fact that Japan's Total Fertility Rate had sunk to its lowest level in recorded history.

---

\*    The author wishes to express his gratitude to all those who assisted in his fieldwork.
\*\*   Portions of this chapter were adapted from Tuukka Toivonen (2011) "'Don't Let Your Child Become a NEET': The Strategic Foundations of a Japanese Youth Scare," *Japan Forum*, 23(3), 407–29.

The demographic future of Japanese society has since been a recurrent cause of national trepidation and the theme of successive social problem debates. The 2000s, meanwhile, ushered in renewed concerns about the deteriorating academic performances of Japanese students vis-à-vis international standards and worries over the sharp polarization of Japan's population into haves and have-nots (the *kakusa shakai* debate).

Recognizing this striking and possibly intensifying tendency of Japanese society to produce provocative media-led public scares, I recently collaborated with a group of critical sociologists and anthropologists (all fluent in Japanese) leading to the publication of *A Sociology of Japanese Youth: From Returnees to NEETs* (Goodman, Imoto, and Toivonen 2012). As the title suggests, we noted at the outset of our undertaking that the most controversial and definitive social problem debates in Japan in fact focused on young people. *Parasite singles* (twenty-somethings, usually women, who still live with their parents and engage in luxury consumption), futōkō (children who continually miss school),hikikomori (socially withdrawn youth), and *freeters* freeters (part-time working youth who reject, or fail to enter, the long-term employment system) are the focus some of the best-known recent debates wherein young people's perceived deviance from established gender, education, and work norms have been problematized. Regardless of their high media visibility, however, the underlying sociological logic of these and their many successor issues has not yet been well understood. We thus decided to examine this logic through eight in-depth case studies explicated using a social constructionist framework informed by the classic work of sociologists Malcolm Spector and John I. Kitsuse (1977). Instead of viewing them as objective social facts, these authors redefined social problems as "the activities of individuals or groups making assertions of grievances and claims with respect to some putative conditions" (Spector and Kitsuse 1977: 75). Contesting the view that social problems somehow emerge "naturally" from an amorphous "society," this definition prompted us to analyze instead the concrete strategies and utterances of identifiable actors. This allowed us to demystify even problems that had been framed in the international media as idiosyncratically Japanese.

What is the relevance, it might be asked at this point, of moral panic as another social scientific lens for the study of the many controversies over Japanese young people? Have scholars actively utilized this concept in their investigations of youth in Japan? They have indeed: at least since visual culture scholar Sharon Kinsella's (1998) well-known inquiry into Japanese young people'sotaku and manga subcultures of the 1990s (first brought to public attention in Japan after four little girls perished at the hands of a comics fan), native and non-native analysts alike have quite frequently applied (or at least cited) this concept. Political scientist David Leheny's (2006) critique of the teenage prostitution (enjo kōsai) discourse is also relevant example here. Cultural anthropologist Anne Allison's (2009) account of Japanese youth embracing new flexible forms of sociality while being criticized for their changed lifestyles also highlights several current moral panics over young people. In fact, in terms of English-language scholarship on Japanese young people, it is now harder to locate scholarly accounts that *do not* allude to moral panic in one way or another than it is to find accounts that do.

My goals in this chapter are threefold: first, I will briefly return to our recent research project on Japanese youth and elaborate on the role that we believe moral panics play within the—typically more prolonged—careers of individual youth problems. This section sets out my first conceptual argument which I hope will have relevance for the study of moral panics and youth issues in any late modern setting. I will then examine, as one extended example that illustrates my conceptual arguments, the controversy over the jobless NEETs that erupted in Japan in the mid-2000s and that remains relevant as I write this account in late 2011. For Japanese commentators, the term NEET denotes 15- to 34-year-old "lazy" young adults who are classified as being "not in education, employment, or training" and who therefore controvert Japanese norms of work and gender.[1]

The third main section of the chapter extracts, from the specific case of NEETs (albeit with the above-mentioned book-length investigation in mind), two further implications for the literature on moral panics that is associated with the works of Stanley Cohen (1972) and Erich Goode and Nachman Ben-Yehuda (2009). The first of these is that "progressive" and "conservative" elements often mingle in youth debates to such a degree that it would be wrong to view moral panics over young people as processes dominated by socially conservative actors. This contrasts with strong assumptions that moral panics are usually produced by conservative forces that view a given phenomenon as a threat to the social order itself (see, for example, Thompson 1998) only to propose conservatively oriented countermeasures. The second point is that a type of "double-disproportionality"—related to the phenomenon of disproportionality that some leading authors argue centrally characterizes moral panics (Goode and Ben-Yehuda 2009)—seems to operate in debates on young people whenever a demographically tiny, clearly delineated group receives considerable media attention but only a negligible amount of *policy* attention. This suggests a useful alternative view of disproportionality as a feature of moral panics and of the relationship between moral panics and policymaking outcomes.

## Moral Panics as a Key Component of Youth Problem Debates

What exactly is the role or the function of moral panics in mainstream youth debates such as the controversy in Japan over NEET or the recent American debates on "boomerang kids" and "mean girls?" In his ethnographically grounded works, cultural anthropologist Roger Goodman implies that moral outrage is to some extent always an element in the discovery of various social problems surrounding children and youth in Japan (1990, 2000). However, it is useful to clarify further

---

1    See Toivonen (2012) regarding the labor market shifts that paralleled the social constuction of NEETs in the 2000s as Japan increasingly became a "postindustrial" society.

this relationship, based on an understanding that moral panics over (presumably deviant) youth and youth problems are *not* one and the same thing and that these terms should therefore not be conflated lest their analytical value become obscured.

Two theoretical propositions set out in recent work in which I have participated have bearing here. The first of these posits that, observed over the long term, individual youth problems proceed as waves of collective attention that are characterized by relatively short episodes of moral panic as well as by longer two- to three-year policy cycles (see Toivonen and Imoto 2012: 17–18). Subsequently, some issues wane while others survive under the public radar only to re-emerge later. There is recognition here that moral panics feature centrally within youth problem debates yet should be viewed as intense but brief episodes within larger policy-making cycles. In other words, this basic conceptualization suggests that moral panics are a key *component* of youth problem debates without being their only important ingredient. However, this amounts to little more than a descriptive statement on the possible role of moral panics in relation to youth controversies. How can we better explain their operational significance within the overall careers of youth problems?

Another of our six propositions offers new hope on this count: interestingly, mainstream youth problem debates can be conceptualized as comprising several coherent *subdiscourses*, as shown in table 14.1, some of which are channelled into the media arena by agile claims makers who may be viewed as "translators" owing to their role in synthesizing subdiscourses into an appealing general-language discourse. By definition, these subdiscourses need to be positioned as existing prior to the initial emergence of a given mainstream youth discourse. For instance, *otaku* (nerds) was a term generated by young manga hobbyists before being picked up by the national media, while NEET (jobless youth), as we shall see, was very much an academic and government policy discourse prior to being raised as a general public concern.

What powers the movement or transfer of particular subdiscourses, mediated by the efforts of skilled claims makers, into the center of national media attention? In the cases of the *kikokushijo* (returnee schoolchildren), the otaku, and the hikikomori, it seems that shocking incidents involving violent acts played a role in pushing these issues into the public consciousness. As Goodman recounts, when a 19-year-old boy killed his aunt and uncle with a baseball bat in December 1982, most of the media concentrated on the fact that he had spent 11 years in the United States before returning to Japan, and was therefore a so-called *kikokushijo* (2012b: 30). In 1989, when a man named Miyazaki Tsutomu was convicted of murdering four girls aged between four and seven, the press framed the perpetrator as an otaku after stacks of manga and pornographic anime films were found in his room, making this label known across Japan. Three incidents in late 1999 and early 2000, one of which involved the hijacking of a bus and the stabbing of a passenger in southern Japan by a 17-year-old boy who had stopped attending high school, became associated with the phenomenon of social withdrawal, or hikikomori, in a highly similar process (Horiguchi 2012: 127). The issue of child abuse, moreover, became far more central in the Japanese media after two intense periods of reporting on child beatings, torture, and dumping in May 2001 and then again in late June and early July 2001 (Goodman 2012a: 111).

**Table 14.1    Breaking-Down Youth Problem Debates into Different Types of Discourses**

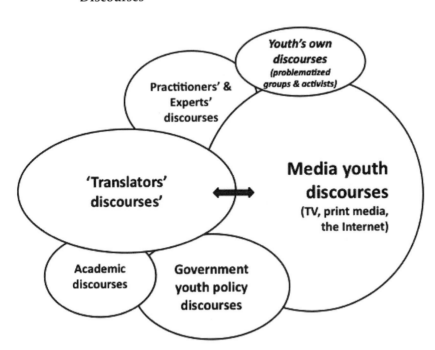

*Source*: Reprinted from: Toivonen, T. and Imoto, Y. 2012. Making sense of youth problems, in *A Sociology of Japanese Youth: From Returnees to NEETs*, edited by R. Goodman, Y. Imoto, and T. Toivonen. Abingdon: Routledge, 20 figure 1.6.

It seems clear, then, that disturbing incidents may contribute to the transformation of more delimited, pre-existing youth discourses into full-blown national media concerns. Yet, it may be more to the point to say that rather than such incidents per se, it is the press and featured experts that construct all-important associations between cases of youth-related violence and certain youth labels: *it is these associations and interpretations that ultimately produce the episodes of moral panic that sometimes ensue and that researchers typically pick up on.* Here, what matters most centrally is whether a moral panic is produced or not, as this regulates the movement of a given youth discourse to the mainstream media arena. High-profile incidents are hence not themselves the indispensable element here, though they can certainly add force to claims around specific youth problems. The case of NEETs, reviewed below, is one example of an explosive youth panic that emerged without support from major incidents.

# The Policy Category NEET: A Progressive Youth Agenda

The category NEET, denoting disengagement from formal education, employment, and training, originates in the United Kingdom where it has been used, starting with Blair's New Labour government in the late 1990s, to discuss the social exclusion of a growing group of 16- to 18-year-olds (Social Exclusion Unit 1999). How did this catchy but rather curious category traverse the vast geographical and cultural distance eastwards to Japan in the mid-2000s? Who were responsible for importing this new label? What were their objectives and what was their relationship to the new moral panic that soon ensued?

A handful of leading labor economists and policy experts were the first authors to write about NEET in Japanese in 2003 (see Kosugi 2003, Kosugi and Hori 2003). The two pivotal reports where this term initially featured had been officially commissioned by the Occupational Skill Development Bureau of the Ministry of Health, Labour and Welfare (MHLW) with the purpose of generating new knowledge to bolster fresh policy initiatives. This took place in a context where jolted by the discovery in 2002 of two million *freeter* (temporary workers aged 15 to 34), a figure that in relation to long-term employment conventions seemed highly alarming (Kosugi 2008), labor bureaucrats within the MHLW began to turn their attention from "restructured" middle-aged workers to youth employment problems.[2]

Importantly, Kosugi Reiko and Hori Yukie of the Japan Institute for Labour Policy and Training, a bureau of the MHLW, found that the proportion of Japanese young people who were *NEETs* had grown dramatically in the preceding years (2003). Drawing on the *Kokusei chōsa* (National Census), they calculated that in the year 2000 there had been as many as 760,000 15- to 34-year-olds who "expressed no will to work," leading the authors to argue that appropriate countermeasures were needed. By excluding those non-employed youth—overwhelmingly female—who were reportedly engaged in *kaji* (housework), Kosugi and Hori had effectively produced a formulation of "Japanese-style NEETs" that would become the standard definition over subsequent years and therefore also the basis for episodes of moral panic over jobless youth.

Before discussing the motives and interests of key actors behind the construction of NEET in Japan, it is worth pointing out that there was a striking lack of agreement between 2003 and 2006 on the prevalence of non-employment among Japanese youth despite the basic definition established by Kosugi and Hori. Table 14.2 shows that salient figures ranged from 400,000 to 2.5 million. That these numbers drew on at least seven different surveys partly accounts for this diversity, but equally consequential were the intricate battles over finer definitional points fought in the background.

---

2    Interview with the former chief of the Career Development Office, July 4, 2007.

**Table 14.2   Competing Figures for NEETs Put Forth in 2003–6**

| Number | Explanations and data sources |
| --- | --- |
| 760,000 | 15–34 year olds who were "NEET" (*excluding* those who did housework) in 2000 (Kosugi and Hori 2003). Data source: National Census (Ministry of General Affairs). |
| 2.5 million | 15–34 year olds who were "NEET" (*including* women who did housework or cared for children) in 2002 (Genda 2004). Data source: Special Labour Force Survey and Basic School Survey. |
| 400,000 | 15–24 year olds who were "NEET" and expressed *no desire* to work or study in 2003 (Genda and Maganuma 2004). Data source: Labour Force Survey Detailed Results. |
| 640,000 | 15–34 year olds who were non-employed and not in education (*excluding* those who did housework) in 2003 (Kosugi Reiko; interviewed in *Asahi Shinbun*, October 2, 2004). Data source: *Health* 2004 |
| 1 million | A projection of the number of "NEETs" in 2010 (Dai-ichi Seimei Research Center, quoted in *Asahi Shinbun*, October 22, 2004). |
| 520,000 | 15–34 year old "NEETs" in 2003 (*excluding* those who did housework; MHLW, quoted in *Asahi Shinbun*, March 6, 2005). Data source: *Health* 2004 |
| 847,000 | 15–34 year olds who were "NEET" (*including* those who did housework) in 2002 (Cabinet Office; cited in *Asahi Shinbun*, March 24, 2005). Source: Employment Structure Basic Survey. |
| 640,000 | 15–34 year olds who were "NEET" (*excluding* those who did housework) in 2002–2006 (MHLW, numerous articles and publications in 2004–2006). **The most widely accepted and cited figure since 2005.** Source: Labour Force Survey. |

One lingering conflict revolved around the issue of gender roles: were unmarried, formally non-employed women who reportedly engaged in housework (kaji) to be counted as NEETs or not? The answer of labor economist Genda Yuji, a central claims maker, was "yes," based on the contention that many female survey respondents preferred to say they were "engaged in housework" when they really were out of work (2007). The MHLW, however, disagreed, preferring to take the housework category at face value and thus keeping to Kosugi's original definition. Since the Cabinet Office nevertheless adopted Genda's definition, this meant that an intra-government conflict emerged over who should be considered a NEET. Eventually though, it was the MHLW that appeared to have won the feud as its figures—producing an annual number of 640,000 NEETs between 2002 and 2006—became the most widely cited ones since the mid-2000s (see table 14.3). This was significant as the MHLW was the government organ directly in charge of developing new social programs for non-employed youth.

Table 14.3   The number of NEETs by age group between 1993 and 2006 according to the Japanese Ministry of Health, Labour and Welfare

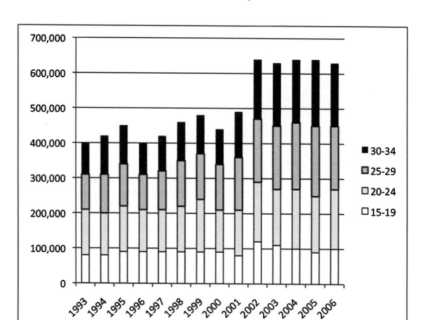

If we take a step back from these definitional and statistical debates and focus on the larger process of youth problem construction itself, we find that it was a select group of *progressive* policy actors who initially introduced NEET to Japan and then went on to call for new measures to tackle this problem. We also see that the process of defining and counting NEETs was characterized by some disagreement between actors who were in the position—in other words, who had the power—to participate in the definitional process. All the centrally involved actors were in any case sympathetic towards Japanese young adults and, most critically, they were all in favor of enacting new policy interventions. At this stage little emphasis was put on the potentially moral dimensions of youth inactivity: the main argument was that an increase in non-employed youth was a legitimate problem from a rational economic and social security perspective and that it should be countered with new policies backed by sufficient funding. In this sense, the central academic claims makers insisted that NEETs were different from the socially withdrawn *hikikomori*—another "inactive" group that had just a few years earlier become framed as a mental health and family issue—and therefore more deserving of employment support. This argument made strategic sense in a conservative public policy context where "economic" issues had more legitimacy compared to "welfare" matters.

The organizational affiliations, self-interests, and objectives of the central claims makers—an important element of youth problem processes (Goodman 1990, 2000, 2012a, 2012b)—were consistent with their progressive youth policy agenda, which concentrated on bringing in a novel camp-based work training program as well as a multifunction counselling center (Toivonen 2011). Once again, since their goal was to produce tangible policy responses instead of educational campaigns, these operatives had little intrinsic interest in problematizing young people's morals *per se*. Rather, in line with the well-known argument advanced earlier by Genda (2006), they were all more or less in agreement that *structural* rather than moral changes largely accounted for the changed labor market behavior of young adults. They viewed those in their late teens and twenties as facing an increasingly risky labor market environment compared to their parents' generation, with many finding themselves unemployed or underemployed due to lower overall labor demand and a sharper polarization into labor market insiders and outsiders. Yet to advance their goals, it was ultimately necessary for the progressive operatives to raise the salience of their policy agenda, and it was for this simple reason that constructing a moral panic soon became an attractive option for this cast of actors. It needs to be stressed, in any case, that key developments unfolded prior to any public panic over NEETs ever emerged, which accords with the conceptualizations offered above and reminds us that the careers of youth problems are longer and broader than the fleeting lifespans of moral panics.

## The Social Category *Niito*: A Conservative Moral Panic

Two brief quotations suggest the high level of anxiety felt by some Japanese observers concerning NEETs:

> NEETs do not have confidence in themselves. One out of two NEETs feels inferior in terms of sociability, initiative and communication skills compared to other people of their age.
>
> (Genda 2004: 165)

> *Niito* are ravaging the wealth and pensions of the state and parents.
>
> (Asai and Morimoto 2005: 15)

As it transformed from a dry, mundane policy term into an almost universally known, even fashionable social category, NEET took on provocative symbolic meanings with significant consequences. While the definitional process of the policy category had been all but monopolized by labor researchers, its colloquial mirror image was crafted through a slightly less centralized process in the mass media between 2004 and 2006. It was through this process that NEET became associated with episodes of moral panic in the classic sense of the term where "a condition, episode, person or group of persons emerges to become defined as a

273

threat to social values and interests" and where "its nature is presented in a stylized and stereotypical fashion by the mass media" (Cohen 1972: 1).

The beginnings of this flow of events can, nevertheless, be traced back to the efforts of Genda Yuji, a leading labor economist at Tokyo University. He first publicly engaged with the issue of non-employed youth in the February 2004 issue of *Chuo Koron*, a magazine that prints in-depth essays on policy-related topics, drawing attention to a layer of young people who were "not fortunate enough to even become *freeters* or formally unemployed and who hence fell into the curious category of NEET" (Genda 2004). The trend-setting scholar argued it was high time to consider support measures for this group which had been hitherto all but ignored by mainstream society as well as public policy.

Citing the results of a small Internet survey, Genda first constructed NEETs as "lacking in communication skills and confidence." This representation of the problems of jobless youth soon became a dominant theme in the discourses of various official government publications (see, for example, the MHLW White Papers for 2005 and 2006), sympathetic academics and youth workers, though not in the mainstream media. By spelling the name of this category not in the Roman alphabet but in Japanese katakana script as *niito*, Genda facilitated the indigenization of this category as he injected it from the narrow realm of labor market policy into that of the general public debate.

Although Kosugi Reiko also helped popularize *NEET* by interpreting the issue for the media, the defining publication of the debate was without doubt *Niito: Neither Freeter nor Unemployed*, written by Genda with freelance author Maganuma Mie and published in July 2004. Intended as a general interest rather than an academic volume, the book draws on a mix of statistical data and journalistic interviews to explore the vexing puzzle of NEETs. It was in this volume that academic and *moral* discourses around jobless youth began to converge, with significant consequences to the framing of the entire issue.

Concretely, by drawing a strict line between the new category of NEETs (those who did not actively seek jobs at the time of surveying) and the pre-existing category of the officially unemployed (that is, unemployed job-seekers), and by portraying the youth whom Maganuma had interviewed as "adult children," the book aroused outrage over "lazy" youth who challenged established work norms. These emergent characterizations had clear elements of a moral underclass discourse. To be sure, Genda himself emphasized that it was not that NEETs did not want to work; they simply *could not*, for one reason or another. Yet, as a whole, the book *Niito: Neither Freeter nor Unemployed* conveyed a highly mixed message regarding the nature of non-employed young adults, stirring controversy while at the same time trying to temper criticisms regarding the personal failings of presumably unmotivated youth.

This discursive balancing act was all but doomed to fail for two specific reasons. First, the prevailing political and media environment being dominated by middle-aged and older men with a deep commitment to long-term employment and stringent work norms, non-working youth were met with a fiercely conservative reaction which drew attention to their presumed shortcomings and lack of morals.

Little time was spent discussing the changed labor market environment as older generations of middle-class males, for ideological reasons and based on their personal career experiences, assumed that all who put in the effort could easily land a good job. Second, with Japan possessing a colorful youth problems pedigree (Toivonen and Imoto 2012) in which various youth labels have consistently and over several decades been problematized from a conservative standpoint, it was only to be expected that any new youth categories would come to be debated in highly similar ways. While not all Japanese youth labels are introduced by policy experts—*otaku*, for example, originated in communities of amateur *manga* fans as pointed out above—mainstream media has, time and again, used them to highlight youth's presumed deviance from "appropriate" social norms and their "insufficient" level of social integration. With previous categories such as those of *adult children*, the socially withdrawn *hikikomori* and the part-time working *freeters* having been used to highlight a lack of masculinity, work motivation and maturity among young men in particular, it was predictable that the same symbolic meanings would come to be ascribed to NEETs.

Indeed, the bulk of Japanese mass media all but competed to sensationalize NEETs and play up the controversy around "rapidly proliferating" workless youth. This tendency was manifest all the way from respectable broadsheets such as *Sankei Shinbun* and *Yomiuri Shinbun* to perhaps less respectable weekly magazines. It was aggressively and consistently asserted that non-working youth were not just lazy or unmotivated, but even essentially worthless, and by implication undeserving of any beneficial public support. This fierce reaction to *niito*—most glaringly expressed in TV talk/variety shows that brought in young men to pose as defiantly work-resistant idlers—contributed to the rapid diffusion of the term across the general Japanese population.

There were some exceptions to this treatment of *niito*: the *Asahi Shinbun* (the *Asahi Times*), Japan's leading left-leaning national newspaper, was one institution to take a relatively constructive attitude to non-employed youth. Indeed, this newspaper frequently featured comments by key policy experts such as Kosugi, Genda, Kudo Kei, as well as Kudo Sadatsugu, and even called on society to provide more support to youth on their way to independence (Wakamono no jiritsu 2005). The *Asahi Shinbun* can thus be viewed as a close ally of the central claims makers in their campaign to lift a novel youth problem and associated policies onto the national agenda.

Regardless of such exceptions, the Japanese debate on NEETs came overwhelmingly to resemble a moral panic as negative, provocative images of young adults too lazy, uninterested, and unmotivated to look for work filtered into the public consciousness. It is indeed highly unlikely that NEET could have been successfully constructed as a social problem without this strongly stirring moral element, suggesting that episodes of moral panic—unfolding with greatest energy between mid-2004, when Genda and Maganuma published their book, and 2006—were an indispensable element of its career. Table 14.4 charts the evolution of the controversy around NEETs by tracing the number of articles published in two leading Japanese broadsheets between 2002 and 2008. Though this figure hides shorter intense episodes of moral panic, it reveals an unusually sharp burst of attention around NEETs, an example of what I have elsewhere called a "youth problem wave," that was powered by bouts of morally provocative books, articles, online postings, as well as TV programs (Toivonen and Imoto 2012: 17–18).

Table 14.4    Annual number of articles that feature "NEET" published in the *Asahi Shinbun* (the *Asahi Times*) and the *Nihon Keizai Shinbun* (the *Japan Economic Times*), 2002–8

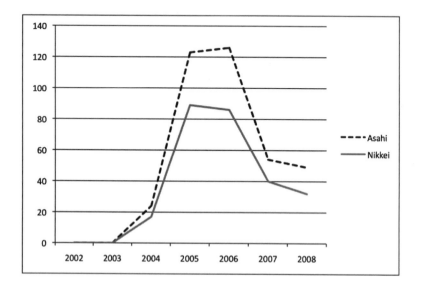

*Note*: All the counted articles contain the acronym NEET, the word *niito*, or both.

To sum up, there is no doubt that the NEET issue was initially put forth by progressive policy actors who were cognizant of the structural drivers of youth non-employment, but neither is there doubt that it soon morphed into a socially conservative youth problem debate through episodes of moral panic. Advocates of novel youth support programs can be said to have benefited from the enormous public attention these episodes generated, but their agenda also suffered substantial setbacks as a result.

## Policy Outputs and Double-Disproportionality

What were some of the main outputs of the Japanese NEET debate? In other words, if this debate was the publicly visible side of a campaign with certain strategic objectives, what did it produce beyond new categories and discourses? The short answer is: Japan's first tangible support programs to integrate into society young people who engage in neither study nor employment and lie beyond the reach of pre-existing employment services such as Hello Work or the Job Cafe. These fresh programs made up the Youth Independence Camp (2005), a residential work and life skills training program, and the Youth Support Station (2006), a drop-in counseling center with diverse career and psychological counselling functions (Toivonen 2008). NEETs were positioned as the foremost target group for these two unprecedented measures, although the actual target group was somewhat narrower.

The progressive campaign behind the NEET label may hence be deemed a success – after all, it bred two concrete interventions for nonworking youth between the ages 15 and 34. However, at a closer look we find that these interventions emerged only in a severely compromised form: only 20 Youth Independence Camps could be opened instead of the planned 40, and program participants were required to pay a considerable fee out of their own pockets. Neither program was coupled with income-support schemes as is typical in Europe and Canada, greatly decreasing their relevance to youth from deprived backgrounds. Limited PR activities meant that both initiatives were unknown, even after several years had elapsed from their launch, to the majority of the citizenry.

Most importantly perhaps, the programs received only modest budgets, 900 million yen (11 million dollars at December 2011 rates) in the case of the Youth Independence Camp in 2005—shrinking to 600 million in 2008—and 470 million yen (6 million dollars) in the case of the Youth Support Station, growing, significantly, to 1,800 million yen, or 23 million dollars, in 2008.[3] Strikingly, the budget that the Youth Support Station received from the national government in 2008 (with nearly 100 centers in operation across Japan at this point) amounted to *just 6.6 percent of the government's total youth employment policy budget* in this year. The total youth employment policy budget itself amounted to *less than 0.2 percent* of the total social spending of the MHLW in the same year. The number of actual users of new programs for NEETs, moreover, did not rise beyond a few thousand per year in the 2000s. One therefore observes a disparity between the enormous degree of public *media* attention afforded to the NEET issue in mid-2000s Japan and the amount of *policy* attention directed at this concern thereafter. If we also consider that the extent of media panic over the problem of non-employed youth was disproportionate with the objective scale of the problem to begin with (640,000 inactive youth in a country of 127 million, or about 2.5 percent of all 15- to 34-year-olds, most of whom were anyhow active at home or studying for exams (see Honda et al. 2006), what we end up with is a case of double-disproportionality. In other words, we observe a pattern where a demographically small issue grows into a large social problem, but ultimately results in a tiny policy response. What could be some of the case-specific and more general sociological factors that produce such an outcome?

---

3    All figures reported here are based on data handed directly to the author by MHLW officials and budget figures reported annually on the MHLW website.

Four particular factors can be inferred from the above and from fieldwork data reported in Toivonen (2009):

1. From the start of the NEET campaign, the central policy actors had in mind not new policies for *all* non-employed youth in Japan, but programs for a more delimited sub-group of NEETs.
2. Key actors used statistics to exaggerate the number of non-employed youth and quite willingly allowed episodes of moral panic to unfold since these tactics helped to maximize social concern over NEETs.
3. Crucially, heavy restrictions were imposed by sections of the government on the proposed youth programs and their budgets owing to the negative, strongly *undeserving* image of NEETs. This is in line with the theoretical schema on the relationship between target group constructions and policy benefits proposed by political scientists Anne Schneider and Helen Ingram (1993).
4. Additionally, the Japanese welfare system being biased in favor of permanent workers (that is, standard employees) and the aged, it was structurally and politically difficult to redirect resources to youth who had no record of social insurance payments.

Of these, points one to three may be relevant to youth problem processes that involve episodes of moral panic in other national contexts also. Indeed, we can quite confidently predict that this kind of a double-disproportionality is likely to emerge whenever a moral panic materializes around a particular, well-defined youth type (or folk devil) such as NEETs in Japan, "mean girls" in the United States, or "hoodies" in the United Kingdom that comes to be constructed in predominantly negative terms, as undeserving. It is precisely the undeserving status of a given target group that makes it highly probable that only modest resources will be channeled to it and that any programs that follow are severely compromised or punitive in character, casting serious doubt on their effectiveness. In sum, although further insights could be gleaned from a deeper examination of the works of Schneider and Ingram (1993) in particular, these observations go some way towards explaining why fantastical moral panics can and do often lead to fantastically modest, ineffective policy responses.

## Conclusion

Beyond demonstrating the relevance of the concept of moral panic to the study of East Asian societies, this chapter articulates three conceptual propositions of wide applicability. Each proposition concerns the relationship between moral panic ideas and youth problem ideas. The first substantive section of the chapter argues that moral panics over youth are best seen as an *important component* of broader youth problem debates that endure much longer than particular episodes of panic. While various other significant processes are also at play, moral panics tend to function as the stage at which pre-existing youth problem ideas are rapidly and energetically introduced into the mainstream public discussion by the media and strategically positioned translators. The case of NEETs precisely illustrates this dynamic.

The second argument is that to a surprising degree progressive and conservative agendas merge and interact in mainstream youth problem debates. The sections on the NEET issue trace the emergence of this debate back to a progressive team of policy actors sympathetic to young adults' difficulties in the post-industrial labor markets and cognizant of political and social structural changes. Paradoxically, this progressive campaign contributed directly to the explosion of a conservative moral panic over non-employed youth and perceived deficiencies in their attitudes toward work. In an important sense, then, it was through the intermingling of progressive and conservative forces that the controversy over NEETs was produced and new policies were enacted. The leading proponents of novel youth interventions benefited from the heightened public attention that episodes of moral panic generated, but their agenda was also severely compromised as a result.[64] This dynamic is intriguing and to an extent contradicts the entrenched tendency, especially in UK scholarship, to view moral panics over young people as primarily the creations of conservative political and media actors.

The third and last suggestion concerns the phenomenon that I dub double-disproportionately. This phenomenon is intimately linked with youth problems' emergence through the interaction of progressive and conservative influences, but appears to derive more directly from the *undeserving status* that moral panics assign to target groups (whenever concrete target groups rather than more ambiguous risks or anxieties are central to the moral panic). Considering related policy outputs may provide a productive avenue for further expanding the moral panic research agenda, while still bearing in mind the concept's limitations, by positioning it as a *component* of the longer careers of various social problems.

Before concluding this account, a few additional comments are in order. Am I suggesting that moral panics play a highly similar role in youth problem debates everywhere or should the findings of this chapter be interpreted as applying primarily to Japan and possibly to a few other culturally proximate countries such as South Korea, Taiwan, and China? In fact, I am trying to strike a more subtle balance with my claims. I believe that while great heterogeneity in the particular ways that issues surrounding youth and young adults are debated exists across national boundaries, the key mechanisms that underlie these debates remain essentially the same. The strong tendency to construct specific labels for "problem youth" groups characterizes relevant debates in Japan, but happens less often (though it is not entirely absent) in places like the Scandinavian countries where young victims and the risks that youth are said to face receive more attention. Plenty of scope exists for carrying out explicitly *comparative* studies to test whether the conceptual distinctions and assumptions put forth in this account hold up in contrasting contexts or need to be modified.

# References

Allison, A. 2009. The cool brand, affective activism, and Japanese youth. *Theory, Culture and Society*, 26(2–3), 89–111.

Asai, J. and Morimoto, W. 2005. *Niito to Iwareru Hitobito: Jibun no Kodomo wo Niito ni Sasenai Hōhō* [*People Called Niito: The Way to Prevent Your Child from Becoming a Niito*]. Tokyo: Takarajima-sha.

Cohen, S. 1972. *Folk Devils and Moral Panics: The Creation of the Mods and Rockers*. New York: St Martin's Press.

Genda, Y. 2004. 14-sai ni "ii otona" to deawaseyou. *Chuo Koron*, 162–9.

Genda, Y. 2006. *A Nagging Sense of Job Insecurity: The New Reality Facing Japanese Youth*, translated by J.C. Hoff. Tokyo: International House Press.

Genda, Y. and Maganuma, M. 2004. *NEET: Furītā demo naku, Shitsugyōsha demo naku* [*NEET: Neither Freeter nor Unemployed*]. Tokyo: Gentōsha.

Goode, E. and Ben-Yehuda, N. 2009 (1994). *Moral Panics: The Social Construction of Deviance*. 2nd Edition. Malden: Wiley-Blackwell.

Goodman, R. 1990. *Japan's 'International Youth': The Emergence of a New Class of Schoolchildren*. Oxford: Clarendon Press.

Goodman, R. 2000. *Children of the Japanese State: The Changing Role of Child Protection Institutions in Contemporary Japan*. Oxford: Oxford University Press.

Goodman, R. 2012a. The 'discovery' and 'rediscovery' of child abuse (*jidō gyakutai*) in Japan, in *A Sociology of Japanese Youth: From Returnees to NEETs*, edited by R. Goodman, Y. Imoto, and T. Toivonen. Abingdon: Routledge, 98–121.

Goodman, R. 2012b. From pitiful to privileged? The fifty-year story of the changing perception and status of Japan's returnee children (*kikokushijo*), in *A Sociology of Japanese Youth: From Returnees to NEETs*, edited by R. Goodman, Y. Imoto, and T. Toivonen. Abingdon: Routledge, 30–53.

Hamai, K. 2004. Nihon no chian akka shinwa wa ikani tsukurareta ka: Chian akka no jittai to haikei youin (moraru panikku wo koete) [How the myth of collapsing public safety was created in Japan: the current situation with public safety and background factors (beyond the moral panic)]. *Japanese Journal of Sociological Criminology*, 29, 10–26.

2005. *Health, Labour and Welfare White Paper*. Tokyo: Ministry of Health, Labour and Welfare, the Government of Japan.

2006. *Health, Labour and Welfare White Paper*. Tokyo: Ministry of Health, Labour and Welfare, the Government of Japan.

2007. *Heisei 19-nen-ban Rodo Keizai Bunseki*. Tokyo: Ministry of Health, Labour and Welfare, the Government of Japan.

Honda, Y., Naitou, A., and Gotou, K. 2006. *Niito te Iu na* [*Don't You Dare Use the Word NEET*]. Tokyo: Koubunsha.

Horiguchi, S. 2012. *Hikikomori*: how private isolation caught the public eye, in *A Sociology of Japanese Youth: From Returnees to NEETs*, edited by R. Goodman, Y. Imoto, and T. Toivonen. Abingdon: Routledge, 122–38.

Kinsella, S. 1998. Japanese subculture in the 1990s: otaku and the amateur manga movement. *Journal of Japanese Studies*, 24(2), 289–316.

Kosugi, R. (ed.) 2003. *Shogaikoku no Wakamono Shūgyo Shien Seisaku no Tenkai: Igirisu to Suweeden wo Chūshin ni [Developments in Youth Employment Support Policy in Foreign Countries: A Focus on the UK and Sweden]*. Tokyo: Japan Institute for Labour Policy and Training.

Kosugi, R. (ed.) 2005. *Freeter to NEET*. Tokyo: Keisoo Shoboo.

Kosugi, R. 2008. *Escape from Work: Freelancing Youth and the Challenge to Corporate Japan*. Melbourne: Trans Pacific Press.

Kosugi, R. and Hori, Y. 2003. *Gakkō kara Shokugyō e no Ikō wo Shien Suru Shokikan e no Hiaringu Chōsa Kekka: Nihon ni okeru NEET Mondai no Shozai to Taiō [Results from a Survey of Institutions that Support the School-to-Work Transition: The Nature of the NEET Problem in Japan and Relevant Response]*. Tokyo: Japan Institute for Labour Policy and Training.

Leheny, D. 2006. *Think Global, Fear Local: Sex, Violence, and Anxiety in Contemporary Japan*. Ithaca: Cornell University Press.

Schneider, A. and Ingram, H. 1993. Social construction of target populations: implications for politics and policy. *American Political Science Review*, 87(2), 334–47.

Social Exclusion Unit. 1999. *Bridging the Gap: New Opportunities for 16–18 Year Olds Not in Education, Employment or Training*. London: Cabinet Office, the Government of the United Kingdom.

2010. South Korea cracks down on gaming addiction. *Time* [Online, April 20]. Available at: http://www.time.com/time/world/article/0,8599,1983234,00.html [accessed: January 3, 2012].

Spector, M., and Kitsuse, J.I. 1977. *Constructing Social Problems*. Menlo Park: Cummings.

2009. Technology: "Web addict" death investigated. *BBC News* [Online, August 6]. Available at: http://news.bbc.co.uk/2/hi/technology/8185412.stm [accessed: January 29, 2012].

Thompson, K. 1998. *Moral Panics*. Key Ideas. Milton Park: Routledge.

Toivonen, T. 2008. Introducing the Youth Independence Camp: how a new social policy is reconfiguring the public-private boundaries of social provision in Japan. Sociologos, 32, 40–57.

Toivonen, T. 2009. *Explaining Social Inclusion and Activation Policy for Youth in Twenty-First Century Japan*. A University of Oxford Ph.D Thesis.

Toivonen, T. 2011. "Don't let your child become a NEET": the strategic foundations of a Japanese youth scare. *Japan Forum*, 23(3), 407–29.

Toivonen, T. 2012. *Japan's Emerging Youth Policy: Getting Young Adults Back to Work*. Abingdon: Routledge.

Toivonen, T. and Imoto, Y. 2012. Making sense of youth problems, in *A Sociology of Japanese Youth: From Returnees to NEETs*, edited by R. Goodman, Y. Imoto, and T. Toivonen. Abingdon: Routledge, 1–29.

2005. *Wakamono no Jiritsu: Saisho no Ippo wo Sasaeyō* [Let's support youth in their first steps toward independence]. *Asahi Shinbun*, August 5.

Watters, E. 2009. *Crazy Like Us: The Globalization of the American Psyche*. New York: Free Press.

# PART V
# MORAL PANICS AND GOVERNANCE

# Overview of Part V

In *Policing the Crisis: Mugging, the State, and Law and Order* (1978), Hall et al. describe the emergence of a new kind of moral panic in the United Kingdom and the United States, one in which state officials initiated an organized campaign against an intangible folk devil:

> There is indeed in the later stages [of the crisis of capitalism] a 'mapping together' of moral panics into a *general panic* about social order; and such a spiral has tended, not only in Britain, to culminate in what we call a 'law-and-order' campaign, of the kind which the Heath Shadow Cabinet constructed on the eve of the 1970 election, and which powered Nixon and Agnew into the White House in 1968. This coalescence into a concerted campaign marks a significant shift in the panic process, for the tendency to panic is now lodged at the heart of the state's political complex itself; and from that vantage-point, all dissensual breaks in the society can be more effectively designated as a 'general threat to law and order itself', and thus as subverting the general interest (which the state represents and protects). (Hall et al. 1978: 222, emphasis in original)

By the late 1960s, moral panics were developing into a constitutive element of the state in both Britain and the United States. Taking aim at such vague but durable targets as threats to law and order, moral panics become longer lasting and more enveloping than in the past. As moral panics became more comprehensive, any significant dissent from prevailing or condoned views could easily be associated with one or another ill-defined threat and hence derogated as "subverting the general interest."

Hall et al. (1978: 338) examine in detail British politicians' exploitation of a nationwide moral panic over mugging, allegedly newly introduced from the United States:

> 'Mugging' is now unquestioningly identified with a specific class fraction or category of labour (black youth) and with a specific kind of area: the inner-ring zones of multiple deprivation. In this localising movement, the social and economic aspects of 'black crime' become visible, even for the crime-control agencies. The zones which are

> specified are the classic urban 'trouble spots', presenting problems of welfare support, of crime prevention control—but also of social discipline and public order... . They are where Mrs Thatcher's 'welfare scroungers' and Sir Keith Joseph's 'single mothers' dwell in ever increasing numbers.

Conservative politicians played on public concerns and anxieties to draw a rhetorical link between black youth and street crime, rousing popular support for abandoning social welfare programs in favor of enforcing "social discipline and public order." Their divisive tactics obscured the economic determinants of poverty and crime, transforming complex social problems into personalized and localized dangers directly traceable to such convenient culprits as "black youth," "welfare scroungers," and "single mothers."

In the decades following publication of *Policing the Crisis: Mugging, the State, and Law and Order*, a number of scholars have explored and assessed later developments in the system of governance that Hall et al. decried from the outset.[1] For example, in *Making Crime Pay: Law and Order in Contemporary American Politics* (1999: 44–5), sociologist and criminologist Katherine Beckett argues that during the 1980s politicians from both major parties attempted to turn the public's concerns about crime to their advantage:

> The salience of the crime and drug issues declined dramatically following President Richard Nixon's departure from office. Neither President Gerald Ford nor President Jimmy Carter mentioned crime-related issues in their State of the Union addresses or took much legislative action on those issues. During and after the 1980 election campaign, however, the crime issue once again assumed a central place on the national political agenda. Like conservatives before him, candidate and President Ronald Reagan paid particular attention to the problem of street crime and promised to enhance the federal government's role in combating it. Once in office, however, the institutional difficulties associated with this project led the Reagan administration to shift its attention from street crime to street drugs. Political and public concern about the drug program increased throughout the 1980s; by August 1989 President George Bush characterized drug use as 'the most pressing problem facing the nation.' ...
>
> Like crime, drug use was defined in political discourse as a social control rather than a public health or socioeconomic problem. And as the decade progressed, the public became more likely to support enhanced law enforcement efforts, harsher sentences, and the contraction of civil rights as appropriate solutions to the problem of

---

1    Regarding Hall et al.'s continuing impact on research concerning the governmental uses of fear, particularly on Beckett (1999) and Simon (2007), see Brown 2008.

drugs. This shift was part of a more general trend toward toughness that began in the 1960s .... This time, however, not only conservatives played a leading role in the campaign to get tough: many Democratic policymakers attempted to wrest control of the crime and drug issues from the Republicans by advocating stricter anticrime and antidrug laws. (44–5)

Ronald Reagan revived a pre-existing moral panic over street crime and drug use, but unable to control street crime directly as president, pointed public attention toward drug use in particular. Beckett proposes that Reagan, in inciting public fears, and George Bush, in prolonging them, redefined the social problems of street crime and especially drug use to gain public support for federal policy that favored punishment over health education or social welfare programs.

In *The Culture of Control: Crime and Social Order in Contemporary Society* (2007), sociologist David Garland finds that in the 1970s and 1980s, criminal justice institutions in the United States and Britain began to identify fear of crime as a distinct social problem not wholly interdependent with the problem of crime control:

> In the late 1970s and early 1980s, when crime-reduction efforts appeared conspicuously unsuccessful, a number of studies suggested that public fear of crime is a measurable phenomenon that is to some degree independent of crime and victimization rates. When a series of police research studies suggested that some measures might fail to reduce actual crime rates but nevertheless succeed in reducing the reported levels of fear and insecurity, the way was opened for a new policy aim. From the 1980s onwards, police departments and government authorities in the USA and the UK began to develop mission-statements and practices that took the reduction of fear as a distinct, self-standing policy goal. (2007: 122)

Garland follows his discussion of the new policy aim of controlling fear of crime independently of combating crime itself with a consideration of coinciding transformations in the prevailing system of governance:

> The attempt to extend the reach of state agencies by linking them up with practices of actors in the 'private sector' and 'the community' might be described as a *responsibilization strategy...* . It involves a way of thinking and a variety of techniques designed to change the manner in which governments act upon crime. Instead of addressing crime in a direct fashion by means of the police, the courts and the prisons, this approach promotes a new kind of indirect action, in which state agencies activate action by non-state organizations and actors. The intended result is an enhanced network of more or less directed, more or less informal crime control, complementing and extending the

> formal controls of the criminal justice state. Instead of imagining they can monopolize crime control, or exercising their sovereign powers in complete disregard of the powers of other actors, state agencies now adopt a strategic relation to other forces of social control. They seek to build broader alliances, enlisting the 'governmental' powers of private actors, and shaping them to the ends of crime control. (Garland: 124, emphasis in original)

Garland describes an intentional program of enlisting the public as informal agents of state control of crime, extending the system of governance beyond the state itself, making offenders seem personally responsible for crime rates, and leading many individuals to take responsibility not only for eschewing criminal behaviors themselves, but also for overseeing others' behaviors.

In *Governing Through Crime: How the War on Crime Transformed American Democracy and Created a Culture of Fear* (2007), legal scholar Jonathan Simon examines the social, cultural, and political reasonswhy inciting public fears about crime presented an exceptionally useful tool for achieving political power in the United States during the 1960s and 1970s. Simon (2007: 24–5) asks,

> But why was crime so much more successful than other emerging hazards in the 1960s and 1970s that might have become the anchor for retooling the New Deal model for a postindustrial age? Competitors included cancer (and other environmental hazards); consumer safety; violence and mental health.... Politicians began to turn to crime as a vehicle for constructing a new political order before the crime boom was recognized. Some, especially white southern politicians, found crime a convenient line of retreat from explicit support for legal racial segregation in education and other public accommodations ... Others, like Bobby Kennedy, were liberals looking for social problems against which to form innovative government strategies that would be less tied to centralized bureaucracies than traditional New Deal governance.

Simon shows that exploiting public fears about crime allowed US politicians to restructure the prevailing model of effective governance while steering clear of the sort of comprehensive social intervention represented by the New Deal. While crime rates were indeed on the rise, politicians of various stripes (including some who wished to camouflage their support of racial segregation) adopted strong anticrime stances in the 1960s and 1970s mostly out of self-interest. Turning their attention to the problem of crime meant that they could determine public policy without encountering unyielding opposition or unmanageable controversy.

Continuing, Simon identifies two main reasons why crusading against crime served politicians of the time as an especially attractive means of furthering their chosen aims:

Indeed, it was the crisis of the New Deal political order, both politically and in its capacity to exercise power effectively, that forms the actual problem to which the crime 'problem' was, in a sense, a solution. In turning to crime to redefine the style and ambitions of government, political leaders were able to take advantage of existing cultural preference in America for political narratives emphasizing personal responsibility and will over social context and structural constraints on freedom, and narratives that could be enacted without fundamental changes to the status quo of wealth and power ... . These advantages, however, are less determinative than the fact that crime, for a variety of reasons, was far less disabled as a pathway for government innovation than most of the available competing programs, especially those that could address the new risks and new social movements at work in the 1960s. (25–6)

Besides seeking a practical path to changing the structure of government, like the Thatcherites, US politicians homed in on the problem of crime in order to dictate the scope of political debates. Tapping into time-honored beliefs about American individualism, they were able to define crime as the consequence of offenders' personal choices rather than the result of pervasive social or economic problems.

## Moral Panics and Governance

Each of the chapters included in part five of *The Ashgate Research Companion to Moral Panics* explores the role of moral panics over crime or other controversial matters in expanding the scope of governance and regulation beyond state institutions to encompass individuals' daily lives. In chapter 15, "Governing Through Moral Panic: The Governmental Uses of Fear," Willem Schinkel analyzes the strategies used by both state and nonstate actors to construct such social problems as crime, safety, and security. Examining the phenomenon through the lens of Michel Foucault's concept of governmentality, Schinkel shows that certain moral panics arise from the combined efforts of heterogeneous agents pursuing shared ends regarding governance by producing and magnifying public fears. To illustrate his conclusions, Schinkel revisits a moral panic over "senseless violence" that emerged in the Netherlands in the late 1990s.

In chapter 16, "Hidden in Plain Sight: Moral Panics and the *Favelas* of Rio de Janeiro," Natália De' Carli and Mariano Pérez ask why, over the past century, the poorest urban areas of Latin America have been stigmatized as dangerous and uncontrolled places. Films, advertisements, and countless news reports have generated moral panics over urban areas of poverty seen as frightening places filled with dangers. Focusing on public perceptions of the *favelas* of Rio de Janeiro, De' Carli and Pérez conclude that moral panics have produced divided cities: media depictions of crime and violence in *favelas* have led the public to define social control and police actions as necessary responses to the problems of the *favelas*, a perspective that deepens already profound economic, political, and social inequalities.

Employing a metatextual framework, in chapter 17, "Intermedia Agenda Setting and the Construction of Moral Panics: On the Media and Policy Influence of Steven Soderbergh's *Traffic*," Bryan E. Denham shows that, in the United States, the film and media and governmental responses to it helped set a comprehensive public policy agenda concerning illicit drug use. Denham argues that *Traffic* (2000) initiated a brief moral panic over drugs that, in precipitating the *Drug Abuse Education, Prevention, and Treatment Act* of 2001 (S.304) as well as a Senate hearing, led to the extension of treatment options for nonviolent offenders.

Chapter 18, Grazyna Zajdow's "I Vote and I Tote: Moral Panics, Resistance, and the Failure of Quiet Regulation," examines a case in which potential folk devils instead became, in a sense, moral crusaders, making highly sophisticated use of media to influence public opinion and reverse public policy. In 2010, the government of the Australian state of Victoria, responding to growing public concern over alcohol-related violence and nuisance, decided to impose new risk-based licensing fees on late-night music venues in order to limit consumption rather than confront the alcohol industry directly. However, when licensees of Melbourne's Tote pub (which offered live music) announced they could not afford to pay the new licensing fees, supporters undercut the government's attempt at quiet regulation by, in effect, transforming themselves from potential folk devils into moral crusaders against the fee hike.

In chapter 19, "Is This One It? Viral Moral Panics," Sheldon Ungar examines the tendency on the part of governmental agencies in the United States and Canada, as well as of the World Health Organization, to instigate moral panics over new and emerging viral outbreaks. He traces the antecedents of viral moral panics back to a chain of developments that includes intrusions into previously secluded viral reservoirs, enhanced surveillance, rapid genetic sequencing, a mutation-contagion interpretative package, prospective vaccines that compel rapid decisions, limited treatments in short supply, and deficient public health systems. Focusing on public reception in Toronto of official pronouncements concerning 2009H1N1, Unger finds that previous wild predictions of epidemics had accumulated in the collective memory so that the newest emerging scare met with skepticism and suspicion. As events unfolded, guardians of public safety lost control over the moral panic they themselves fomented and so encountered a range of dissenting viewpoints that converged in opposition to the 2009H1N1 vaccine.

# References

Beckett, K. 1997. *Making Crime Pay: Law and Order in Contemporary American Politics. Studies in Crime and Public Policy.* New York: Oxford University Press.

Brown, M. 2008. 'Aftermath: living with the crisis': from PTC to Governing Through Crime. *Crime, Media, Culture*, 4(1), 131–6.

Garland, D. 2002. *The Culture of Control: Crime and Social Order in Contemporary Society*. Chicago: University of Chicago Press.

Hall, S., Critcher, C., Jefferson, T., Clarke, J., and Roberts, B. 1978. Policing the Crisis: Mugging, the State, and Law and Order. *Critical Social Studies*. Houndmills: Palgrave Macmillan.

2001. S. 304-107th Congress: Drug Abuse Education, Prevention, and Treatment Act of 2001 [Online: 2001]. Available at: http://www.govtrack.us/congress/bills/107/s304 [accessed: May 25, 2012]

Simon, J. 2007. *Governing Through Crime: How the War on Crime Transformed American Democracy and Created a Culture of Fear*. Studies in Crime and Public Policy. New York: Oxford University Press.

*Traffic* (dir. Steven Soderbergh, 2000).

# Governing Through Moral Panic: The Governmental Uses of Fear

## Willem Schinkel

When Stanley Cohen (2002: 1) popularized the concept of moral panic for the social sciences in 1972, he described the phenomenon as follows:

> A condition, episode, person or group of persons emerges to become defined as a threat to societal values and interests; its nature is presented in a stylized and stereotypical fashion by the mass media; the moral barricades are manned by editors, bishops, politicians and other right-thinking people; socially accredited experts pronounce their diagnoses and solutions; ways of coping are evolved or (more often) resorted to; the condition then disappears, submerges or deteriorates and becomes more visible.

Cohen depicts here an extraordinary cooperative effort. Although the mass media are clearly the main actors for Cohen, they are flanked by a variety of actors coming from different fields. One might discern religion ("bishops") as well as politics and science ("socially accredited experts"). These actors do not consciously work together to produce a moral panic, and yet their cooperation or simultaneous activities add up to forming and sustaining a moral panic. In the language of modern administrative science, their activities might be a prime example of the "governance of social problems." These actors all contribute to political agenda setting, to policy action and to changed practices and policy frames. Among the many ways to look at moral panics, I wish to highlight such "episodes," as Cohen calls them, from the perspective of governing. I will do so from a perspective that allows the description of strategies of problematization in policy by an assemblage of state and nonstate actors ("governance"). This perspective is inspired by Michel Foucault's work on "governmentality," and by the school of "governmentality studies" that has emerged in its wake.

One might say that Cohen's emphasis was on the mass media, because all the actors involved in a moral panic only become visible through their appearance in media. In itself, this does not necessarily mean that media are the most important context of study in moral panics, as "whatever we know about our society, or indeed about the world in which we live, we know through the mass media" (Luhmann 2000: 1). Cohen's study can be regarded as directing attention to the most obvious aspects of moral panics in a media world where public salience of the image of crime trumps that of crime itself. But, there are other aspects to moral panics, one being the element of governing. Indeed, Cohen explored the concept of moral panic with his colleague, Jock Young, who used it primarily to highlight the strategic role of the police in amplifying "deviancy" (1971). A broad recognition exists among scholars of a program that one might call the "uses of moral panic." As sociologists Angela McRobbie and Sarah Thornton (1995: 560) state,

> Moral panics have become the way in which daily events are brought to the attention of the public. They are a standard response, a familiar, sometimes weary, even ridiculous rhetoric rather than an exceptional emergency intervention. Used by politicians to orchestrate consent, by business to promote sales in certain niche markets, and by media to make home and social affairs newsworthy, moral panics are constructed on a daily basis.

Rather than assuming such rational strategies on the part of the agents involved, I believe it to be more instructive to look at the processes through which moral panics actually function as an instrument of governing.

## Moral Panics from the Perspective of Governmentality Studies

The study of processes of governmentality was initially undertaken by Michel Foucault. Especially in his later work at the Collège de France, Foucault was interested in an issue he called "rationalities of governing." To that end, he coined the concept of governmentality (*gouvernementalité*). Foucault (1991: 102) conceptualized governmentality in various ways, one of the best known being

> the ensemble formed by the institutions, procedures, analyses and reflections, the calculations and tactics that allow the exercise of this very specific albeit complex form of power, which has as its target population, as its principal form of knowledge political economy, and as its essential technical means apparatuses of security.

In the wake of Foucault's analyses, a strand of "governmentality studies" emerged in which a variety of processes of governing, from neoliberal forms of governance to Third Way appeals to community, have been researched (for example, Dean 1999, Rose 1999, Miller and Rose 2008, Schinkel and van Houdt 2010). Political scientist Nikolas Rose, legal scholar Pat O'Malley, and criminologist Mariana Valverde (2006: 83), discussing the development of governmentality studies, have described the perspective as a "way of analyzing the emergence, nature, and consequences of the arts of government." From a governmentality perspective, the central question concerns the "how of governing": it asks questions concerned with how we govern and how we are governed, and with the relation between the government of ourselves, the government of others, and the government of the state (Dean 1999: 2).

In using the concept of governmentality, Foucault explicitly meant to analyze processes of governing beyond the sovereign state-centered perspective that political science usually deploys. He thus analyzed the ways in which state- and non-state agencies became enmeshed in an institutional field in which individual citizens can also become agents, for instance through processes of "responsibilization" (Schinkel and van Houdt 2010). At one point in his classic *Folk Devils and Moral Panics: The Creation of the Mods and Rockers* (1972), Cohen comes very close to conceptualizing moral panics in terms of governmentality. Discussing the emergence of, as he calls it, an "exclusive control culture" (Cohen 2002: 66), he speaks of the role of courts and of the police. And he emphasizes that a proper analysis of this "control culture," a concept that sociologist David Garland (1996) recoined and reconceptualized as "culture of control," means broadening the scope beyond official state institutions: "Social control is much broader in scope, including as it does informal mechanisms such as public opinion on the one hand, and highly formalized institutions of the state on the other" (Cohen 2002: 90). However, Cohen's analysis of the state institutions involved is limited to the police and the courts. On the other hand, the concept of "folk devil" is a form of Foucault's practical object or object of "problematization" (1985: 10).

Rationalities of governing proceed by a variety of strategies, political programs, and techniques (Schinkel and van Houdt 2010). Strategies can be regarded as rationalities of governing at the most abstract level. These strategies are embedded in political programs targeted at the governing of specific objects such as deviants, "folk devils," or criminals. Techniques are the actual ways in which these objects of problematization are targeted by policies and other forms of action. From the governmentality perspective, discourses are important because they frame objects of problematization.

When the governmentality perspective is applied to moral panics, we can regard them as *episodes, emerging out of the combined efforts of a variety of heterogeneous agents, in which certain governing objectives are furthered by way of a governing through fear.* As Thomas Hobbes recognized in *Leviathan*, fear is a highly effective element of governing. And I believe it is possible to regard moral panics as instances when governing goals and limits are uprooted and shifted by an assemblage of institutions that extends beyond the Hobbesian sovereign state. In order to assess the value of this conceptualization, it is important to consider the concept of fear implied in the notion of moral panic. The concept of fear that Cohen used is, as Garland has recently remarked, actually a commonsensical notion (2008).

Garland himself earlier argued that fear of crime is a typical reaction in the context of high crime rates as a "normal social fact" (1996: 446). Yet, the strength of the concept of moral panic lies in its recognition that there need not be any connection between the actual crime rate and the emotional response to specific instances of crime. Crime rates are abstractions anyway: it is the visibility of individual cases that triggers emotional response. And the paradox is that individual instances are indeed incidences. So quite apart from the "militarization" that in some places has been a response to high crime rates (Davis 1990: 121), a moral panic is a focused way of mobilizing public energies that has no direct connection to the development of crime but that serve, for instance, to circumscribe normative contours (Cohen 2002: 162).

Governmentality, having the population as its object, thus fares well by means of sentiments of fear and anxiety, since fear helps different actors align to further similar objectives and helps co-opt the segments of the population to be managed. For the elite, fear and anxiety are ways of "acting at a distance," that is, typical governmental forms of indirect rule (Miller and Rose 2008: 33). Articulating policy goals with references to fear gives the goals a context of legitimacy, since communicated anxiety is always experienced as real and honest by an observer (Luhmann 1986). Whoever fears must face a real danger and whoever is concerned about other people has to be honest: "It is impossible to reply 'you are wrong' to someone saying she is afraid" (Luhmann 1988: 33). Fear mobilizes and, in a sense, the mobilization of fear as a way of mobilizing consent is equivalent to a threat of crime made by the state or, more broadly, by the institutions enmeshed in a governmental assemblage.

## A Case of "Senseless Violence"

To show a typical case, I present research involving so-called "senseless violence" in the Netherlands (Schinkel 2008, 2010). In the context of the United States, this concept most closely resembles a notion that has been called "random violence" (Best 1999). "Senseless violence" refers to apparently random instances of violence in the public sphere that do not take place for the sake of some extrinsic motive (see Schinkel 2004). Looking at "senseless violence" from the perspective of governmentality means undertaking a program that Mitchell Dean has called "analytics of government," which he understands as "a type of study concerned with an analysis of the specific conditions under which particular entities emerge, exist and change" (Dean 1999: 20). The entity I am concerned with here is a "moral panic" over "senseless violence," and the first step in ascertaining the origins of the moral panic is to investigate the public coinage of this term. When the way it first became articulated is scrutinized, it appears to fit well with a conception of moral panics as a form of governing through fear. Its first use in the Netherlands can be dated to 1997, when a local police commissioner used the term on the radio, calling for civil action against a problem he called "acts of senseless violence."

## The Production of a Moral Panic

The moral panic over violence took off with the construction of the category of "senseless violence" in 1997. The violent death of Meindert Tjoelker in Leeuwarden in 1997 can be seen as the trigger for a marked increase in media coverage of interpersonal violence. After his death and the attention devoted to it, a victim of similar violence of the year before, Joes Kloppenburg, was honored with a silent march a year after his death. The death of Meindert Tjoelker thus led to the construction of the category "senseless violence" that could then be applied *ex post facto* to cases that were, *qua* violence, similar but were now seen in a different light. Kloppenburg's death in 1997 now came to be seen as "senseless violence" in a sense *avant la lettre*. Similarly, an even older case came to be classified as "senseless violence." This was the death of Kerwin Duinmijer in 1983, a black 15-year-old boy beaten and stabbed severely by skinheads with racist motives, who died as a consequence of his injuries. In the early eighties, his death was predominantly seen as a racist incident, as racism was a major public issue in those days. After 1997, his case was, in a sense, recoded as "senseless violence" and come to provide one of the earliest examples of a phenomenon that could now be given a history and be seen as having significantly increased in scale since those early cases. This leads to the paradoxical situation that, in the first instance, the emergence of the category of "senseless violence" suggests a qualitative growth in violence, which then becomes so popular that it starts to absorb other categories of violence to the extent that it usurps them altogether. Racist violence and domestic violence tend to become recoded by the label of "senseless violence." When media coverage of "senseless violence" is considered, it is seen to include a Turkish case of honor revenge, physical violence in traffic and public transport, and a schizophrenic vagabond stabbing a man to death in a library "just like that." One of the main civil action sites against "senseless violence" posed the question, "Have you ever been a perpetrator of senseless violence (bullying, aggression, physical violence)"?[1] Thus, the concept seems to be turning reflexive: while it initially involved acts no sane person would commit, it now appears that anyone may have been at some point a perpetrator of "senseless violence." This can be justified by invoking the pacifist idea that *all* violence is "senseless," which becomes apparent for instance in the deliberate equation between "violence" and "senseless violence" by the *Foundation Stop Senseless Violence*.

Regarding the take-off of a moral panic, Erich Goode and Nachman Ben-Yehuda (2009) have distinguished among three possible paths: a first path is instigation by an interest group, the second the elite-engineered moral panic, and the third a grassroots-produced moral panic. In the case of ("senseless") violence in the Netherlands, a combination of interest group, in this case a police commissioner, and grassroots instigation appears to be at stake. The term "senseless violence" was introduced in the sense referred to here by police commissioner Bangma,

---

1    The site (www.zinloosgeweld.nl) does not exist as such anymore, but has changed to a new format no longer using the concept of "senseless violence."

who published an article using it in the *Leeuwarder Courant*, a regional newspaper, following the violent death of Meindert Tjoelker on September 13, 1997. Bangma called upon the people of Leeuwarden, where the incident took place, to observe one minute of silence. As such, attention to "senseless violence" was spurred by a state representative who was soon joined by others. A massive response followed, which set an example for other cities. Relatively soon, silence, perhaps several minutes of silence or a silent march, became a trademark response to "senseless violence." Silence was also indicative of an important characteristic of this moral panic, which is that there are no "folk devils." Crucially, the moral panic over "senseless violence" is characterized by the conspicuous absence of moral deviants. From the perspective of governmentality, this makes the moral panic over "senseless violence" all the more flexible in problematizing issues of safety and normative decay in general.

## The Institutionalization of a Moral Panic

Several kinds of therapeutic action have been undertaken in light of the disapproval of senseless violence and the supposed general proliferation of violence in society. This has resulted in an *institutionalization of anxiety* in the sense that many civil actions against "senseless violence" have led to the formation of formal organizations. In Bergen op Zoom, for instance, all babies born from 2003 to 2006 received a bib from the mayor of the town that reads, "Bergen op Zoom against senseless violence." The bibs, furthermore, carried printed ladybirds, the official logo of the Dutch *Landelijke Stichting Tegen Zinloos Geweld* (National Foundation against Senseless Violence), which no longer exists as such. According to the foundation's website, the ladybird is a "symbol against senseless violence." The foundation seeks prevention of violence, since "everybody sees that violence and aggression are used too easily." Its founding member is "fed up" with "beastly attacks out of nothing." It hopes to accomplish by its actions a "structural change of mentality."

Alternative foundations and groups organized around the theme of violence include *Foundation Stappen tegen Geweld* (now defunct), Action Front Against Senseless Violence (possibly defunct), Foundation Day against Violence, Action Committee Art Against Violence, Foundation Gorcum against Violence, Association Parents of a Murdered Child, Foundation Tolerance Unlimited, Foundation Vlaardingen against Senseless Violence, Foundation Groningen Safe, Foundation for Active Nonviolence, Foundation *Kappen nou!*, Foundation from Senseless Violence to Sensible Behavior, Foundation *Aandacht doet spreken*, Foundation Wall against Violence (currently part of the Association for Safety, Respect and Solidarity), Foundation Stop Senseless Violence, Foundation Report Violence, Foundation Victims of Violence, and the governmental National Platform against Violence in the Streets (possibly dissolved). In 2000, 19 such organizations started working together under the general heading of the National Organization for Safety and Respect (LOVR). In addition, several websites exist apart from the organizations mentioned above. Some examples are: *Twenthe tegen Geweld*, (which is part of *Tegen geweld*), *De Trucker Tegen Zinloos Geweld* (defunct), *Slachtoffers van Geweld* (defunct), *Zinloos Geweld Forum, Kids against Violence, No More Violence* (a web forum), and *Tilburgers tegen Zinloos Geweld*.

In line with neoliberal communitarian governmentality (Schinkel and van Houdt 2010), a variety of civil society organizations thus emerged that worked in line with state institutions to foster goals of eradicating "senseless violence" and of a normative revival of Dutch society. The visibility of such organizations and such cooperation between state and nonstate actors has been high. There are, for instance, a number of monuments in memory of victims of such "senseless violence." Amsterdam has a plaque and a tile, Leeuwarden a boulder, Sleeuwijk has a golden tear, The Hague has a traffic sign against senseless violence, Vlaardingen has a memorial monument as do (to name a few) Tilburg, the village of Vinkel, and Arnhem, which hosts the national monument for victims of senseless violence (a plaque with ladybirds). Other actions of a therapeutic nature include a pillow fight involving 400 children in Amsterdam, unrolling an almost 4-mile-long banner against senseless violence in Breda (which, due to lack of public interest, only 50 people showed up, was unfurled only about 300 yards of its length), singing against "senseless violence," and the release of a protest CD against it. There has been DJing against senseless violence. There is still partying against "senseless violence," for which prominent DJs can be booked. There has been rapping against senseless violence, pills against senseless violence have been sold at a dance festival, there have been more music festivals and survival runs, and there has even been a boxing match against senseless violence between an ex-professional fighter and a Protestant minister in a church in Grevenbicht. Besides all this, and besides the occasional "noise march" against violence, "silent marches" have become the most common expression of public disapproval after cases of so-called "senseless violence." These have taken place for instance in Amsterdam, Rotterdam, Zoetermeer, Kerkrade, Leeuwarden, Vlaardingen, Noordwijk, Venlo, Almere, Den Haag and Gorinchem. Boutellier (2000) counted 20 marches in roughly four years (1996–2000), one of which was attended by an estimated 20,000 people. Local support groups against violence exist throughout the Netherlands. In 2000, schoolchildren regarded "senseless violence" as the primary news topic of the previous year. In the same year, the increase in "senseless violence" on the street was polled as the greatest concern of the Dutch (with 65 percent of respondents choosing it), leaving the deterioration of the environment and the rift between rich and poor at second and third. Clearly, there exists a certain anxiety concerning violence, and a concern that violence is growing is present in all the reactions to occasions of "senseless violence" mentioned here. Most common are the silent marches, in which at times a few thousand people participated (Boutellier 2000). While measurements of fear of violent crime did not show an increase during the nineties, several forms of civil action do indicate a high level of concern and anxiety over so-called "senseless violence."

To track the institutionalization of the moral panic in the media, I counted the number of newspaper and magazine articles mentioning "senseless violence" during the period 1990–2010. I have used a more comprehensive search than in my

2008 article (Schinkel 2008). The results, presented in table 15.1 below, evidence the birth of the moral panic in 1997, as well as its subsequent development, when it peaked around 2004–2005, and then gradually dwindled.

Table 15.1   Number of Newspaper and Magazine Articles Mentioning "Senseless Violence," 1990–2010. Hits not pertaining to the phenomenon "senseless violence" deleted.

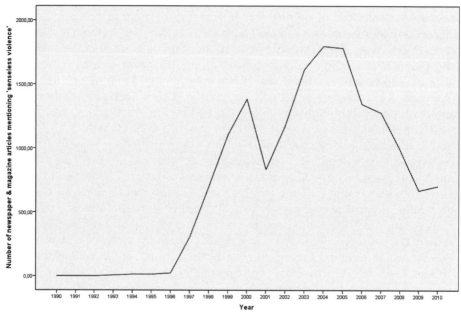

*Source*: LexisNexis Academic.

# Conclusion: Governing through Fear: Violence and the Moral Fiber of Society

It is important to dwell for a bit on the *conspicuous absence of moral deviants* in the moral panic over "senseless violence" in the Netherlands. News reports about "senseless violence" were quite often about *violence in general*, not concerning specific experiences. Althoff, for instance, quotes a train conductor who says, "It should happen to you, to be grabbed in the crotch or to get a knife against your throat." The newspaper article adds, "Not that such things happens often. The worst he [the train conductor] encountered was being spat at" (Althoff 2002: 271). Another example of prediction can be found on the website of the National Foundation against Senseless Violence, whose founder wrote on the occasion of the inception of the organization in 1997:

One minute of silence is not enough.

Another victim of senseless violence. Newspapers were full of it. Everyone on the radio and on television talked about it. But the day after the noise had half died away and the next day all was quiet. It was no longer news for the masses, only for one or two individuals. First, another victim has to fall. Then we will observe another minute of silence. And then everyone will talk about it again. Until the rumor dies away again.

Thus, "victims" figure as part of a larger phenomenon that will occur again unless action is undertaken. For the initiator of the Foundation against Senseless Violence, the "disruption of society" caused by "senseless violence" was the main reason for founding the organization. While "senseless violence" is frequently associated with the issue of "norms and values"— as, for instance, becomes clear from the references made by various civil organizations against "senseless violence" to "norms and values,"—no moral deviants, no perpetrators of "senseless violence" are publicly exposed. Cases of "senseless violence" are remembered by the names of the victims, while the names of perpetrators fail to live on in public memory (some perpetrators' names have never been made public at all). No *category* of perpetrators of "senseless violence" has been discerned and identified as "folk devils." The problem has survived in the absence of perpetrators, as a threat that regularly rains down upon highly publicized *victims*, but remains abstract, unknown, but certain to resurface, therefore all the more fearsome and effective.

In his new introduction to the third edition of *Folk Devils and Moral Panics: The Creation of the Mods and Rockers*, Cohen (2002) does offer some tools for understanding moral panics without "folk devils." He analyzes some recent moral panics, as well as a near-moral panic, and stresses the importance of (1) a suitable enemy, (2) a suitable victim, and (3) "a consensus that the beliefs or action being denounced were not insulated entities ('it's not only this') but integral parts of the society or else could (and would) be unless 'something was done'" (Cohen 2002: xi). The first condition, the suitable enemy, is absent if a particular group or category is referenced here. But, when Cohen defines moral panics (as quoted above) as something in which "an episode, condition, person or group of persons" is "defined as a threat to societal values and interests," the crucial issue is not the folk devil but rather the "threat to society." It is such "threats to society" that Foucault analyzed as prime legitimizations in modern rationalities of rule (2003). In this case, the "violent condition" of society is the enemy. Perpetrators are not the targets of scandal; people's outrage is directed at the condition of violence growing in society. On the other hand, this is only successful when the second condition is satisfied, that is, when "suitable victims" are present. And they are, since most victims of "senseless violence" are white middle-class young men. In fact, these victims are part of the same category that perpetrates acts labeled as "senseless violence," although this fact is not recollected in regard to "senseless violence" (WODC 2006, compare Best 1999). (The third condition, consensus that "it's not only this," is illustrated by the matter of "senseless violence" discussed above.)

The moral panic over "senseless violence" in the Netherlands offers an illustration of the ways that moral panics can involve a governmental assemblage of institutions. In this case, the moral panic was directly instigated by an executive branch of government (the police), and silent marches have been frequently organized in cooperation with local government. The absence of "folk devils" generalizes the effectiveness of governing through fear, since the impossibility of locating the threat is indicative of its generalized presence, which, from the perspective of the governing of populations it helps enable, means as much as a generalized effectiveness. The governing of "senseless violence" can thus be seen as state/nonstate cooperation furthering a moral reinvigoration in general. "Senseless violence" functions as a technique of mobilization: by focusing emotional and moral energy, the neoliberal communitarian goals of moral reinvigoration through activating citizens and individual responsibility are furthered, and all the while a moral justification for the policy priority of crime and safety is provided. Crime and safety became a number-one priority on the national political agenda (Downes and van Swaaningen 2007). From the perspective of governmentality, this process might be interpreted as furthering governing through fear. The institutional orchestration of a moral indignation over "senseless violence" provides an effective (and affective) frame for the heightened problematization of issues of crime and safety in general, as took place in the second half of the 1990s and the first years of the new millennium. Thus, in nine out of 20 silent marches reported by Boutellier (2000), empathy was mentioned as a motive for marching (other motives were anger and powerlessness). Much mentioned were contemplative motives pertaining to questions of norms and values, to the question whether violence can make or have "sense" at all, as well as to respect, tolerance, and the like (Boutellier 2000: 325–6).

In conclusion, I would like to offer an important caveat concerning the social science of moral panics. From a sociological perspective, it is warranted, and even preferable, to regard fear as attributive. That is to say, one must usually assume fear to be a (self-)description that need not correlate (even in self-report survey research) to actual fear and all the consequences for action it might entail. Fear should be regarded as an element placed in a governing assemblage, and as a possible instrument of legitimation. In other words, just as the connection between fear and crime is famously nonlinear, so is the connection between mass mediated fear and actual fear. What matters is *the idea* (the "social construction," one might say) that many are afraid and a "panic" exists. In this sense, fear and anxiety are to be treated as *attributions*, and social scientists investigating moral panics might just as well be included in the governing assemblage because their assumption that fear actually is widespread (implied in the use of a commonsensical concept of fear) contributes to the legitimacy of a moral panic. In particular, analyses of moral panics ratify the idea that panic exists in the first place. Despite conceiving of moral panics as "exaggerations" (Goode and Ben-Yehuda 2009: 208), researchers assent to the idea that fear does exist to an unexaggerated degree. When moral panics take place, social scientists are apt to reify and ratify the fear involved therein. One might, then, wonder whether scholars involved in research on moral panics in fact avoid aligning themselves with the governmental chains that impel governing through fear.

# References

Althoff, M. 2002. "Zinloos geweld" als thema in de media: wijzen van presenteren, verklaren en betekenisgeving. *Tijdschrift voor Criminologie*, 44(3), 262–81.

Boutellier, J.C.J. 2000. Het geluid van de stille marsen. *Tijdschrift voor Criminologie*, 42(4), 317–32.

Cohen, S. 2002 (1972, 1980). *Folk Devils and Moral Panics: The Creation of the Mods and Rockers*. 3rd Edition. London: Routledge.

Davis, M. 1990. *City of Quartz: Excavating the Future in Los Angeles*. London: Verso.

Dean, M. 1999. *Governmentality: Power and Rule in Modern Society*. Los Angeles: Sage.

Downes, D. and van Swaaningen, R. 2007. The road to dystopia? changes in the penal climate of the Netherlands, in *Crime and Justice in the Netherlands*, edited by M. Tonry and C. Bijleveld. Crime and Justice: A Review of Research, Vol. 35. Chicago: University of Chicago Press, 31–71.

Foucault, M. 1985 (1984). *The History of Sexuality, Vol. 2: The Use of Pleasure*, translated by R. Hurley. New York: Pantheon Books. Originally published as *Histoire de la sexualité 2: l'usage des plaisirs*. Paris: Editions Gallimard.

Foucault, M. 1991. "Governmentality," in *The Foucault Effect: Studies in Governmentality*, edited by G. Burchell, C. Gordon, and P. Miller. Chicago: University of Chicago Press, 87–104.

Foucault, M. 2003 (1997). *"Society Must Be Defended": Lectures at the Collège de France, 1975–1976*, translated by D. Macey. New York: Picador. Originally published as *Il faut défendre la société. Cours au Collège de France, 1976*. Paris: Seuil/Gallimard.

Garland, D. 1996. The limits of the sovereign state: strategies of crime control in contemporary society. *British Journal of Criminology*, 36(4), 445–71.

Garland, D. 2008. On the concept of moral panic. *Crime Media Culture*, 4(1), 9–30.

Goode, E. and Ben-Yehuda, N. 2009 (1994). *Moral Panics: The Social Construction of Deviance*. 2nd Edition. Chichester: Wiley-Blackwell.

Hobbes, T. 1996 (1651). *Leviathan*, introduction and edited by J.C.A. Gaskin. Oxford World's Classics. Oxford: Oxford University Press. Originally published as *Leviathan or the Matter, Forme and Power of a Common Wealth Ecclesiasticall and Civil*. London: Andrew Crooke.

Luhmann, N. 2000. *The Reality of the Mass Media*. Palo Alto: Stanford University Press.

Miller, P. and Rose, N. 2008. *Governing the Present: Administering Economic, Social and Personal Life*. Cambridge: Polity Press.

Rose, N. 1999. *Powers of Freedom: Reframing Political Thought*, Cambridge: Cambridge University Press.

Rose, N., O'Malley, P., and Valverde, M. 2006. Governmentality. *Annual Review of Law and Social Science*, 29, 83–104.

Schinkel, W. 2004. The will to violence. *Theoretical Criminology*, 8(1), 5–32.

Schinkel, W. 2008. Contexts of anxiety: the moral panic over "senseless violence" in the Netherlands. *Current Sociology*, 56(5), 735–56

Schinkel, W. 2010. *Aspects of Violence: A Critical Theory*. Houndmills: Palgrave Macmillan.

Schinkel, W. and van Houdt, F. 2010. The double helix of cultural assimilationism and neoliberalism: citizenship in contemporary governmentality. *British Journal of Sociology*, 61(4), 696–715.

WODC. 2006. *Aanpak criminaliteit: uitgaansgeweld—daders* [Online]. Available at: http://www.wodc.nl/publicatie/aanpakcriminaliteit/criminaliteitsproblemen/ uitgaansgeweld/basisfeiten/daders/ [accessed: October 10, 2011].

Young, J. 1971b. The role of the police as amplifiers of deviancy, negotiators of reality and translators of fantasy: some consequences of our present system of drug control as seen in Notting Hill, in *Images of Deviance*, edited by S. Cohen. Harmondsworth: Penguin Books, 27–61.

# Hidden in Plain Sight:
# Moral Panics and the *Favelas*
# of Rio de Janeiro

Natália De' Carli and Mariano Pérez Humanes*

"Leaving aside charity, the police remain." With this ironic phrase, Uruguayan novelist and journalist Eduardo Galeano concluded his reflections on possible responses to the spread of poverty in Latin American cities. But we do not accept the inevitability of this result. Nor will we become engulfed by the prevailing fear of life in marginalized urban areas that makes such a response possible. It is evident that ...

> in our countries the terror industry pays dearly, like any other, for foreign "know-how." U.S. repression technology, tested at the four corners of the earth, is bought and applied. But it would be unjust not to credit Latin America's ruling classes with a certain creative capacity in this field. (Galeano 2005: 360)

To understand even a little the role that fear and terror play in enforcing poverty in Latin America, we would do well to consider the phenomenon known as moral panic.

To speak of moral panic is to speak of a threat that spreads like an uncontainable flood across the entire social field, a threat of which, it seems, we do not know the cause or origin. This concept is similar to cultural theorist Jean Baudrillard's (2004: 42) notion of "terror" because, like moral panic, terror follows no logic, has no end, and extends beyond violence. For Baudrillard (2004: 42):

> Terror is not violence. It is not real, specific, historical violence, the kind that has a cause and a goal. Terror has no goal, it is an extreme phenomenon, that is, that in a way it is beyond its goal: it is more

---

* Natália De' Carli and Mariano Pérez Humanes wish to thank Zita Thompson for her translation of this chapter.

violent than violence. Today, we know that. Any traditional violence renews the system provided that it has meaning. The only real threat to the system is symbolic violence, the kind that has no meaning and provides no ideological alternative whatsoever.

Both moral panic and terror are extreme phenomena, which can only be known by their effects, where the field of danger has been localized and the threatening group remains hidden, never really visible from any angle. In a sense, the entire manner in which moral panic occurs reminds us of the phenomenon of an epidemic, as defined by novelist and nonfiction writer Elías Canetti in *Crowds and Power* (1962). In an epidemic, Canetti (1962: 274) states, "The enemy is hidden; he is nowhere to be seen and cannot be hit. One can only wait to be hit by him. In this battle only the enemy is active; he strikes where he likes and strikes down so many that one soon comes to fear that no-one will escape." Paradoxically, despite their hidden natures, these phenomena are closely related to the concept of the public sphere, because the threat appears thanks to one of the principles that characterize public space: the principle of publicity.

In many cases, it may seem that the threat at the center of a moral panic is a new occurrence, but moral panics almost always come in response to pre-existing situations that suddenly come to the public's attention. Already at the beginning of the 1970s, Galeano (2005: 322) warned us that a quarter of the population of Latin American cities lived in "settlements that escape the modern rules of urban construction." This was the extended euphemism that the United Nations *Comisión Económica para América Latina y el Caribe* (CEPAL) used to "designate the hovels known as *favelas* in Rio de Janeiro, *callampas* in Santiago de Chile, *jacales* in Mexico, *barrios* in Caracas and *barriadas* in Lima, *villas miseria* in Buenos Aires, and *cantegriles* in Montevideo" (Galeano 2005: 322). But a rich and varied vocabulary cannot hide a reality, born in large cities, that expresses the marginality and poverty of a population that arrived, sometimes to suburbs or other difficult-to-access areas such as the hills of Rio de Janeiro, trying to survive.

Many are the researchers who have studied the processes by which the population of Latin American cities swells, engrossed by industrialization that is as accelerated as it is dependent on developed countries. As Galeano (2005: 363) explains, "Underdevelopment is not a step on the road to development. It is a consequence. Underdevelopment in Latin America arises from external development, and continues to feed it." As technological advances have slowed industrialization, the inhabitants of ghettos, largely composed of migrants who have moved from rural areas, have been forced to become part of an informal subsistence economy linked to the service sector: they work as street vendors, household staff, shoe cleaners and in some cases resort to drug dealing and prostitution (See Muñoz, De Oliveira, and Stern 1973, De' Carli and Pérez Humanes 2010b). But we will not linger on the genealogies of these settlements, which in some cases go back as far as the beginning of the twentieth century. Instead, we will focus on their progressive construction as stigmatized places, which has transformed the way we see them: marginalized community settlements suffering typical poverty-related problems have become hyper-ghettos of crime and terror. The first thing we ask ourselves is how it is possible for these urban areas in Latin America to have remained under the radar of public concern for politicians, law officers, intellectuals, and religion, among other social figures of renowned morality. We must also ask ourselves what role the media play in establishing public agendas regarding safety and violence, as well as in creating the increasingly repressive social control policies of which such agendas are a part.

The enormous media coverage dedicated to crime and delinquency suggests that society is threatened by a small group of wrongdoers, an example of the media construction of, in Stanley Cohen's (1980) words, "folk devils," its own scapegoats onto which the public projects its fears and fantasies. In Latin America, the increase in criminality and the consequent media interest in crime and delinquency reaffirm social consensus by emphasizing the threat posed by the figure, stigmatized and made deviant, of the criminal after a sophisticated process in which moral panic, already installed in the media, has itself created that figure. By selecting newsworthy stories and discursive strategies, the media are forging a stereotyped criminal subject. The position of an individual in society plays a crucial role in this primary construction of the criminal subject as an enemy that evokes and makes sense of our fears. Individuals become identifiable with their poor financial state and sordid living conditions, the marginalized status of their social or ethnic groups, and, above all, the exceptionalism, barrenness, and peculiarity of their position in the city.

## Creating Prejudice, Dividing Spaces: The Effects of Moral Panic

The proliferation of precarious settlements as alternative housing for the poorest members of the population represents one of the greatest urban problems of the twentieth and twenty-first centuries in Latin America. In the case of Rio de Janeiro, 5.5 million homes are located in precarious settlements spread all over the city (Segre 2004). Contrary to conventional urban schemas, where the rich and the poor inhabit separate areas, the *favelas* of Rio de Janeiro are built on the city's central hills, close to the elegant areas by the sea. We are looking at a split city, a divided one: hill and asphalt, two cities that fear one another, though they depend on one another more than we might think. Colloquially, these are the bynames given to the two opposed urban areas: the hill, the poor city of the *favelas* situated on the hills, versus the asphalt, the recognized city in the lowlands. Instead of showing a geographical opposition, the contrasting names refer to the material underpinnings that the other side lacks. And which name represents urban civilization? Asphalt, which implies an underlying cultural as well as material difference, built civilization versus raw barbarism.

## Favelas

Turning to the discourses surrounding the *favelas* of Rio de Janeiro, we now address the images and representations, whether transparent or misleading, created around these urban settings, and which are becoming inseparable from the propagation of anxiety, fear, and panic. As Löic Wacquant (2007: 195) observes,

> In the end, little does it matter if these places are ruined or dangerous, whether their population is or is not composed essentially of poor people, minorities or foreigners: the prejudiced belief that they are is enough to trigger socially harmful consequences.

Every day, the media tirelessly deluge the public with terrifying news. The headlines and images shown on television transmit the public event of violent conflicts that take place in the *favelas*, thus increasing the sense of threat, leading the viewer towards a certain reasoning that, generally, demonizes the world of the *favelas* and the individuals that inhabit those lands with a predominantly condemning media discourse (Filho 2004: 139).

Regarding photography, art critic John Berger and photographer Jean Mohr caution, "As soon as photographs are used with words, they produce together an effect of certainty, even of dogmatic assertion" (1982: 91). Both images and discourse gather and reconstruct the most violent events that take place in these settlements: violent stories are told, narrated, and recounted, but, above all, produced and reproduced. Newspapers and news alerts on television and radio, by almost exclusively emphasizing armed conflicts and police involvement in the *favelas*, have ended up generating a discourse that promotes the isolation from, and progressive confrontation of, the *favelas* against the recognized city, which often supports perversely violent and repressive actions by the government (Paiva and Ramos 2007: 48). To some extent, the news communicates a hegemonic representation of the split city, the hill and the asphalt, where the favela plays the role of the "other," an "other" feared and to be avoided at all costs.

In the public imagination, the emphasis, repetition, and frequency of such images construct the favela as a peripheral and criminal place. A news photo by Pablo Jacob taken on November 26, 2010 provides an example (see illustration 16.1). The picture, which appeared in *Extra*, the Sunday magazine of Rio de Janeiro's *O Globo* newspaper, depicts five heavily armed men fending off federal police on Estrada de Iteraré in the city's Complexo do Alemão *favela*. The men, all of whom are dark-skinned, defend an underpass doing service as a sort of barricade or bunker. Their weapons include four rifles and a pistol. Three of the men, two of whom are wearing dark woolen masks that allow their eyes but little else to be seen, look, and aim their guns directly at the camera. The fifth man, apparently running for cover, moves toward the underpass. In this image of a favela, no relations among neighbors, ties of family and friendship, or working lives are at all visible Pictures like this one foster the perception that criminality is an inherent character trait of all inhabitants of the city outskirts and *favelas*. They ostensibly lend credence to the

Figure 16.1   *Extra*. Photographer's Caption: "Provocation in Rio de Janeiro.
Bandits Top of Hill. They Scream and Show their Weapons
to Federal Police, Who Are in Estrada de Iteraré, One of the
Entrances to Complexo do Alemão," Pablo Jacob/Agência O Globo,
November 26, 2010.

notion that the poor themselves are the cause of urban violence and danger (see
Bentes 2003).

Cohen (1980: 17) states that the media are particularly important during the
beginning stages of moral panics since they produce "encoded and processed
images" of deviance and those who exhibit deviant behaviors. In this case, the
symbolic associations produced by this and similar news photos, in tandem with
a widespread process of exaggeration, distortion, and symbolization end up not
only designating the people of the favela as Public Enemy Number One, but also
producing unfeeling constructions of their behaviors and of the dangers those
behaviors allegedly pose to society. To this end, and as fuel for moral panic, the
media focus on those events and individuals that destabilize social order and,
by using certain "deductive structures," subtly suggest particular explanations
concerning the nature of constructive versus antisocial behaviors (Cohen 1971: 17).
Thus, they help news media identify those who transgress social boundaries and
propose a "moral" explanation of why such things happen.

Urban and regional planner Janice E. Perlman (1977: 23) points up the fearful public illusions surrounding *favelas*, which derive from events as depicted in the media and envelop the *favelas* in a "culture of fear" that regards its inhabitants as "dangerous groups" within society. Perlman (1977: 23) observes that both the criticism and the defense of the *favelas* and their inhabitants are premised on shared stigmatizing characterizations: "The favela as a pathological agglomeration," a place of thieves, drug addicts, drunkards, prostitutes and tramps, "the favela as a community in search of improvement," a place of dynamic, honest, able, and happy people, and "the favela as an inevitable calamity," a natural and tragic consequence of urban growth, dependent on paternalistic intervention.

The emphasis that the media place on the criminal events that occur in these marginalized places in effect maps a geographical distribution of urban delinquency that creates clear boundaries between safe and unsafe areas of the city. According to sociologist Patrick Champagne (1999: 53–4):

> What is called an "event" is never in the end anything but the result of mobilization – either spontaneous or caused – of the media around something that, during a certain amount of time, they consider an event. When the object of the press' attention are poor or underprivileged groups, the effects of the media are far from what these social groups might hope because, in these cases, the press yields a particularly important power of constitution, and the creation of the event escapes these people almost completely.

Although we cannot state that the stigma ascribed to these territories is the greatest problem facing the population of the *favelas*, it is important to recognize that without this media-created image, the *favelas* would not be what they are today. Stigmatization has become such an apparently natural phenomenon that to excise this image linked to crime, fear, and violence has become almost impossible. This is so to such an extent that the very victims of stigmatization end up accepting their imposed condition as inevitable. And, as Champagne (1999: 59) states,

> The truth is that most of them, mainly because they lack cultural resources, make this vision of themselves their own. An image produced by *voyeur*-like spectators with interests, who are necessarily journalists ('This is a ghetto,' 'We are not considered,' and so on).

The broad visibility of the violence associated with these settlements, enhanced by the media, does not distinguish the poor from bandits or honest police officers from corrupt police officers. Emphasizing the image of the hyper-ghetto leads to an accelerated process of partition of social groups and homogenizes the diverse inhabitants of each territory. Media control of bodies, events, and conditions in relation to the *favelas* transforms them into threats against the values and interests of society.

## Violent Crime

Beyond moral panic and its effects, countless investigations show that the number of violent crimes committed in Rio de Janeiro has decreased over the last few years. According to the Brazilian Institute of Geography and Statistics, in 2010 as compared to 2004 the homicide rate in the State of Rio de Janeiro had decreased from 50.8 to 41.5 deaths for every 100,000 inhabitants. Nevertheless, the rate remained well above the Latin American average of 27.5 homicides for every 100,000 inhabitants. For sociologist Luiz Antonio Machado da Silva, the fact that the "problem of the *favelas*" comes before the "problem of safety" within the city leads politicians to focus their attention on protecting the divided physical areas, which generates demands for isolation enforced by police repression. On one side of the divide are the drug dealers situated in and around the *favelas* and on the other side are the police organizations that promote the "redefinition of the *favelas* as territorial 'complexes' that should be fought against and confined" (da Silva 2010: 287). This is a battle where there can be no possible winner without the stigmatization and isolation of innocent people. But, the predominant discourse of the media explains, almost naturalizes, violence in the *favelas*. Using the "metaphor of war" and the creation of "myths" associated with it, it is considered normal for the inhabitants of the *favelas* to be dangerous, violent, and delinquent criminals. And these myths support the interpretive pattern that structures both the problem of violence in Rio de Janeiro and the proposals put forward to control and reduce the violence.

In this crossfire of power between the government and drug traffickers, *favela* dwellers have watched 30 years go by without finding a dignified way out. More specifically, as of 1999, elected governments have suggested a serious process of transforming the urban reality of the *favelas* in Rio de Janeiro. So was born the *Favela-Bairro* program, an initiative created by the city to turn the *favelas* into formal neighborhoods. Since then, the slow but sure construction of infrastructure and *public* service facilities, along with other strategies such as implementing educational programs or the ever-difficult task of distributing titles to real property, have aimed to stop the process of separation between those areas of the city. In spite of efforts to normalize their inhabitants' lives and integrate these places into the recognized city, the situation is not being solved, particularly in the larger *favelas*, where conflicts and terror undergo constant growth. In 2009, the Rio de Janeiro government informed the public of the construction of a wall, known as the eco-limit, surrounding 11 *favelas* in the south of Rio de Janeiro, a wall that separates the area recognized as part of the city from the unrecognized side (see De' Carli and Pérez Humanes 2011).

## UPPs

Faced with the problem of violence and bearing in mind the huge events that will take place in the city of Rio de Janeiro—the 2014 World Cup and the 2016 Olympic Games—the government has declared war on these poverty-stricken areas. To this end, it will rely on the Pacifying Police Units (UPPs) as its greatest ally. The Military Police of the State of Rio de Janeiro (PMERJ) offer the following definition of the UPPs, a specialized armed intervention force trained to fight against groups of drug dealers operating within these territories:

> The Pacifying Police Unit is a new model of Public Safety and police that aims to draw police and inhabitants closer, and is allied with the strengthening of social policies within the community. By recovering territories that were occupied by drug dealers for decades, the UPPs bring peace to the community. (*UPP Repórter*)

The pacifying processes have been enforced in more than ten *favelas* in Rio de Janeiro since December 2008, when the first UPP was opened in the favela Santa Marta, to the south of the city of Rio de Janeiro.

Clearly, it is too soon to draw conclusions about their social and structural effects on the city but, as cultural geographer Marcelo Lopes de Souza (2010: 12) argues, the efficiency of the UPPs barely represents a "notch" in the fight against drug dealing. Although it has managed to rid the drug dealers of their territories in some *favelas*, the UPP's strategy, "regardless of its other limitations (and possible perversities), is basically unrepeatable on a greater scale" (Souza 2010: 12). However, and in spite of this distinctly warlike attack, it has become more and more frequent in the media to hear the concern of a middle class that fears a possible "migration" of violence towards the formal city, that demands the police pursue and exclude any person who may appear to belong to the favelas from the asphalt. It is clear that, for them, the only solution is the *policization* of social policies.

One news story that exemplifies the image of *favelas* as territories foreign to the formal city of the asphalt appeared in the *Guardian* online in April 2010. According to the article (accompanied by a headline blaring, "Rio de Janeiro Police Occupy Slums as City Fights Back against Drug Gangs," and subtitled, "Polls Suggest 'Pacification' Project Welcome in Favelas despite Reports of Draconian Tactics"):

> Seven of Rio's 1,000-odd *favelas* have been occupied in the last 18 months as part of the pacification scheme, among them the City of God favela that gained international notoriety in Fernando Meirelles' hit film.
>
> By the end of 2010 authorities say 59 favelas will have benefited from the fledgling pacification units, freeing an estimated 210,000 people from the rule of Rio's gangs. Between now and 2016, when Rio hosts the Olympics, dozens more occupations are planned.
>
> 'Once we have filled the first 40 I think we will have achieved a very large reduction in violence in Rio,' said Allan Turnowski, head of Rio's civil police. 'It's like attacking the main cell—you weaken all the smaller ones around it.' (Phillips 2010)

Instead of depicting police as protecting inhabitants from crime, the article imagines the *favela* as itself analogous to a foreign body invading an otherwise healthy organism.

To stop treating the *favelas* as foreign territory and their inhabitants as threatening subjects would mean admitting new possibilities for the future, not defined by the media or hierarchies of power and control. Additionally, providing them with citizenship would allow these individuals to produce their own history and their own representation. This is no easy task when we see that a single narrative, spreading moral panic throughout the population, prevails. Nevertheless, it is precisely that one insistent story that has made us question the power of that discourse. We have already mentioned the sophisticated level of elaboration in media discourse, that is, the fact that no means are spared to criminalize the chosen enemy. But if those images, backed up by words, end up producing an almost feral reaction to the people of the *favelas*, it is also true that they arouse a certain empathy in most mortals, making us partners in their misfortune. Sociologist Ulrich Beck (2003) refers to humans' ability and disposition to put ourselves into the victim's shoes as "globalization of emotions" and states that this development is largely due to the media. It might be said, then, that the ability to view residents of the *favelas* as victims may be traced to the same media that present them as murderers and criminals. Here, it is relevant to mention the documentary *Halcón: Los chicos del narcotráfico* (*Hawk: The Boys of the Drug Traffic*) in which, of the 16 youths interviewed, 15 had already died by the time the piece was aired in 2006 as part of the *Fantástico* series on Brazil's TV Globo. Despite such occasional peeks into the reality of life in *favelas*, however, official speeches often take refuge in the quarrels between gangs to justify the death tolls. This is what Pablo Ordaz tells us about the Mexican authorities, whose official version of fatalities among the urban poor "holds that the great majority of those fallen since 2007 are hired killers that kill one another" (2011).

Politically engaged portrayals offer an alternative to the spectacular depictions of poverty that are invading the world's media spaces, becoming a part of everyday imagery. Besides the nonfiction *Halcón*, among the better-known fiction films to focus on the *favelas* of Rio de Janeiro in the past decade were *Cidade de Deus* (*City of God*, 2002), *Uma onda no ar* (*Something in the Air*, 2002), *Tropa de elite* (*Elite Squad*, 2007), and *Tropa de elite 2: O inimigo agora é outro* (*Elite Squad II: The Enemy Within*, 2010). But perhaps we should prefer images of events in these marginalized areas in the cities of Latin America that are, in a sense, less clear, less certain. Maybe if the images were half-blurred by our tears, they would bring us closer to the *favelas'* inhabitants:

> Tears, Derrida argued, are the most exalted form of blindness: 'If the eyes of all animals are destined for sight, and perhaps by means of this for the scopic knowledge of the animal rationale, only man knows how to go beyond seeing and knowing, because only he knows how to weep. ... Only he knows that tears are the essence of the eye and not sight. ... Revelatory blindness, apocalyptic blindness, that which

reveals the very truth of the eyes, this would be the gaze veiled by tears.' (1993: 523)

Perhaps we should start by becoming emotional and crying in order finally to ask ourselves about the fate of the people living in slums. Historian Martin Jay writes, "Eyes that cry implore rather than see; they invite the question from the other: whence the pain" (1993: 523)? On the other hand, political theorist Hannah Arendt states, "Tyrannies are doomed because they destroy the togetherness of men: by isolating men from one another they aim to destroy human plurality" (2005: 69). And the public safety measures applied by the government of the State of Rio de Janeiro during mega-events have everything in common with tyrannical behavior, with infliction of real pain. That is why, when faced with separation and exclusion enforced by the horrors of police security policies, imagining strategies to promote access and permeability, integration and comprehension may require a clear-eyed view of the *favelas* as places of social integration and construction rather than as regions stigmatized by fear or terror.

## Conclusion: (A)Moral Panic? From the Cannibalization of Poverty to Informative Ethics

We come to a final question: what is the aim of the media, including our own as investigators, when dealing with situations of fear and terror? As sociologist Zygmunt Bauman (quoted in Pinillos 1997: 322) says, moral intention is irrational "in the sense that it must precede the practical calculation of losses and gains that may derive from carrying it out and, therefore, does not fit the means-end schema of modern reason." And this is what we do not see in much of the available information regarding events in Rio de Janeiro. Or, rather, it is the exact opposite of what we see in the media: when criminalization is intensified and nourished as it is in most media in Rio de Janeiro, something tells us that the means-end schema of modern reason is present and that the *favelas* have become yet another post-capitalist business.[2]

But Bauman demands one more condition of our modern ethics, one that we do not perceive in those who encourage and spread moral panic over the favelas. For this sociologist of liquid modernity, morality comes before society. That is, "The moral responsibility of being 'for the other' precedes being 'with the other'" (quoted

---

2    Further evidence of capitalist exploitation of the *favelas'* squalor is provided by the guided tours of the Favelatour phenomenon, which moves hundreds of thousands of dollars in Rio de Janeiro and has spread to other Latin American cities. See the research of sociologist Bianca Freire Medeiros (2009), "The Favela and its Touristic Transits," and that of De' Carli and Pérez Humanes (2010a), "What is Shown and What Is Hidden: Favelatour and the Aesthetic Dimension of Poverty."

in Pinillos 1997: 323). But in the media of Rio de Janeiro, we also catch a glimpse of "with whom" and "why." As we have said, in a search for safety and order, it seems necessary to stigmatize the *favelas* and their inhabitants first, and then the only option is to fight ruthlessly against them. This is opposed to primary morality, which tends towards others, whatever their background or status. Here, prejudice is obvious right from the start: the inhabitants of the *favelas* are beleaguered and have no rights as citizens because they have chosen their circumstances.

Therefore, we may need to talk of a moral panic in the *favelas*, a kind of moral panic that grows ever-more profitable, the more inhumane and terrible the situation of the individuals who suffer it becomes. The fact that life in the *favelas* is being cannibalized is appalling, and trying to convince us that it is done morally is even more terrible. As cultural studies scholar Ivana Bentes (2003: 85) concludes, "The danger is that people transform poverty into folklore or a cultural genre." Therefore, it seems necessary to specify whether there are possible alternatives to this situation, or whether we must continue to accept these conditions created by moral panic, where the domination of social control, law, and order appears to be the only way out of such violent and terrifying conditions. Slavoj Žižek (2008: 11) suggests that we make violence visible in its full complexity, that is, that we turn from unitary perspectives based on subjective perceptions of violence and move towards

> the complex interaction of the three modes of violence: subjective, objective, and symbolic. The lesson is thus that one should resist the fascination of subjective violence, of violence enacted by social agents, evil individuals, disciplined repressive apparatuses, fanatical crowds: subjective violence is just the most visible of the three.

Žižek's proposal contains an active resistance against subjective violence, the most visible and spectacular sort, but also demands a more complete resistance, because this is not the only kind of violence that generates and reinforces moral panic. There are other kinds of violence that present themselves as "subtle forms of coercion that sustain relations of domination and exploitation, including the threat of violence" (Žižek 2008: 9).

In the poor urban areas of Latin America, the accelerated and automated process of image production and its relation to crime and violence resulting from moral panic have become part of a spectacular game. In this game, we both hide and show certain inhabitants and certain ways of life that seem inevitably linked to those cursed settlements, which have now become true areas of exception. During this process of spectacularization, those in power have constantly joined forces with the media and, in a way, moral panic has been roused due to collusion between the media and the government. However, resistance and alternatives to established power have in recent years been assisted by advances in technology, a development of which "free radio," stations offering dissenting perspectives and information, provides an example. In regard to Rio de Janeiro's *favelas*, in 2002, Tião Santos began organizing community radio stations into a satellite Internet network called

*Radio Viva Favela*. By 2005, *Radio Viva Favela* included 150 community radio stations in the State of Rio de Janeiro, freely circulating programs between them (see Sá Rego Costa and Hermann 2007). For now, the phenomenon of *Radio Viva Favela* and the efforts of various free radio and television stations remain the most significant examples of progress in this area, although the gradual introduction of the Internet into the population promises a different, contrasting kind of information, which may reduce the effects of moral panic.

In 1996, Giorgio Agamben (79) stated,

> The extreme form of this expropriation of the Common is the spectacle, that is, the politics we live in. But this also means that in the spectacle our own linguistic nature comes back to us inverted. This is why (precisely because what is being expropriated is the very possibility of common good) the violence of the spectacle is so destructive; but for the same reason the spectacle remains something like a positive possibility that can be used against it.

Destroy appearances from inside the spectacle, Agamben suggested some 15 years ago. Perhaps the time has come to reinterpret and reappropriate the images produced by moral panic.

# References

Agamben, G. 1996. Violencia y esperanza en el último espectáculo [Violence and hope in the ultimate spectacle], in *Situacionistas: Arte, política, urbanismo* [*Situationists Art, Politics, Urbanism*], by X. Costa, L. Andreotti, M. Bandini, T.Levin, T. McDonough, and G. Agamben. Barcelona: Museu d'Art Contemporani, 73–81.

Agamben, G. 2006. *Che cos`è un dispositivo* [*What Is an Apparatus*]? Roma: Nottetempo.

Arendt, H. 2005. *The Promise of Politics*. New York: Schocken.

Baudrillard, J. 2004. La violencia de lo mundial [The violence of the global], in *La violencia del mundo* [*The violence of the world*], edited by J. Baudrillard and E. Morin. Barcelona: Paidós, 11–43.

Beck, U. 2003. La cuestión de la identidad [The question of identity]. *El País* [Online], November 11, 13–14. Available at: http://www.scribd.com/doc/18653838/Beck-Ulrich-La-Cuestion-de-La-Identidad [accessed: October 29, 2011].

Bentes, I. 2003. O copyright da miséria e os discursos sobre a exclusã [The copyright on the discourse of poverty and exclusion]. *Lugar Común*, 17, 85–95.

Beriain, J. 2007. Chivo expiatorio-mártir, héroe nacional y suicida-bomba: las metamorfosis sin fin de la violencia colectiva [Scapegoat-martyr, national hero and suicide bomber: the endless metamorphosis of collective violence], *Papers*, 84, 99–128.

Berger, J. and Mohr, J. 1982. *Another Way of Telling*. New York: Pantheon.

Canetti, Elías. 1962 (1960). *Crowds and Power*. London: Victor Gollancz. Originally published as *Masse und Macht*. Hamburg: Claassen Verlag.

Castoriadis, C. 1998. *El ascenso de la insignificancia* [*The Rise of Insignificance*]. Madrid: Cátedra.

Champagne, Patrick. 1999. La visión mediática [The view from the media], in *La miseria del mundo* [*The Weight of the World*], edited by P. Bourdieu. Madrid: Akal, 51-63.

*Ciudad de Deus* [*City of God*] (dir. Fernando Meirelles and Kátia Lund, 2002).

Cohen, S. (ed.). 1971. *Images of Deviance*. Harmondsworth: Penguin Books.

Cohen, S. 1980 (1972). *Folk Devils and Moral Panics: The Creation of the Mods and Rockers*. 3rd Edition. Oxford: Blackwell.

Da Silva, L.A.M. 2010. "Violência urbana": segurança pública e favelas: O caso do Rio de Janeiro atual ["Urban violence": public safety, and slums: the case of Rio de Janeiro today]. *Caderno CRH* [*CRH Notebook*] [Online], 23(59), 283–300. Available at: http://www.scielo.br/scielo.php?script=sci_arttext&pid=S0103-49792010000200006&lng=en&nrm=iso [accessed: October 6, 2011].

De' Carli, N. and Pérez Humanes, M. 2010a. *What Is Shown and What Is Hidden: Favelatour and the Aesthetic Dimension of Poverty*. Paper to Destination Slum: The Production and Consumption of Poverty in Travel and Tourism, University of Bristol, December 9–11.

De' Carli, N. and Pérez Humanes, M. 2010b. *Nuevos viejos trabajos de la marginalidad urbana: Creatividad informal y espontaneidad en el espacio público Brasileño* [*New Outsider Art in Marginalized Urban Areas: Informal and Spontaneous Creativity in Brazilian Public Spaces*]. Paper to Repensando la Metrópolis: Prácticas Experimentales en torno a la Construcción de Nuevos Derechos Urbanos. Centro de Estudios Andaluces, Málaga, July 8–9.

De' Carli, N. and Pérez Humanes, M. 2011. An inhuman eco-limit: fear and social-spatial segregation," in *Fear within Melting Boundaries*. Oxford: Inter-Disciplinary Press, 169–79.

De Souza, M.L. 2010. A "reconquista do território", ou: um novo capítulo na militarização da questão urbana ["Reconquering territory," or: a new chapter in the militarization of the urban. *Pasa Palavra* [*Pass the Word*] [Online]. Available at: http://passapalavra.info/?p=32598 [accessed: October 6, 2011].

Filho, J.F., Herschmann, M., and Paiva, R. 2004. Rio de Janeiro: esteriótipos e representaçoes midiáticas [Rio de Janeiro: Stereotypes and Media Representations]. *E-compos: revista da Associaçao Nacional de Pós-Graduaçao em Comunicaçao* [Online]. Available at: http://www.compos.org.br/seer/index.php/e-compos/article/viewFile/1/2 [accessed: October 6, 2011].

Galeano, E. 2005. *Las venas abiertas de América Latina* [*Open Veins of Latin America*]. Madrid: Siglo XXI.

*Halcón: Los chicos del narcotráfico* [*Hawk: The Boys of the Drug Traffic*] (writers, M.V. Bill and Celso Athayde, 2006).

Jay, M. 1993. *Downcast Eyes: The Denigration of Vision in Twentieth-Century French Thought*. A Centennial Book. Berkeley: University of California Press.

Muñoz, H., de Oliveira, O., and Stern, C. 1973. Migración y marginalidad ocupacional en la Ciudad de México [Migration and occupational marginality in Mexico City], in *Imperialismo y urbanización en América Latina [Imperialism and Urbanization in Latin America]*, edited by M. Castells. Barcelona: Gustavo Gili, 183–210.

Ordaz, P. 2011. Son mexicanos, son valientes [Mexicans, the brave ones]. *El País*, June 19, 2–5.

Paiva, A. and Ramos, S. 2007. *Mídia e violência: Novas tendências na cobertura de criminalidade e segurança no Brasil [Media and Violence: New Trends in the Coverage of Crime and Safety in Brazil]*. CESeC: Rio de Janeiro.

Perlman, J.E. 1977. *O mito da marginalidade: Favelas e a política no Rio de Janeiro. [The Myth of Marginality: Urban Poverty and Politics in Rio De Janeiro]*. Rio de Janeiro: Paz e Terra.

Phillips, T. 2010. [Rio de Janeiro police occupy slums as city fights back against drug gangs]. *The Guardian* [Online, April 12], April 12, 23. Available at: http://www.guardian.co.uk/world/2010/apr/12/rio-de-janeiro-police-occupy-slums [accessed: January 23, 2011].

Pinillos, J.L. 1997. *El corazón del laberinto: crónica del fin de una* época [*The Heart of the Labyrinth: A Chronicle of the End of an Era*]. Madrid: Espasa.

2010. Rio favela violence. The *Guardian* [Online, November 28]. Available at: http://www.guardian.co.uk/world/gallery/2010/nov/28/brazil-drugs-trade#/?picture=369131081&index=2 [accessed: January 23, 2011].

Sá Rego Costa, M. and Hermann, W. Jr., 2007. Radios Livres, Radios comunitárias: outras formas de fazer radio y política [Free radio, community radio: another way to do radio and politics], in *Lugar Común*, 17, 97–107.

Segre, R. 2004. Rio de Janeiro metropolitano: saudades da "Ciodade maravilhosa" [Metropolitan Rio de Janeiro: longing for the "Marvelous City"]. *Vitruvius/ Arquitexto* [Online], 46(1). Available at: http://www.vitruvius.com.br/arquitextos/arq046/arq046_01.asp [accessed: October 6, 2011].

*Tropa de elite [Elite Squad]* (dir. José Padilha, 2007).

*Tropa de elite II: O inimigo agora é outro [Elite Squad II: The Enemy Within]* (dir. José Padilha, 2010).

*Uma onda no ar [Something in the Air]* (dir. Helvecio Ratton, 2002).

*UPP Repórter* [Online]. Available at: http://upprj.com/wp/ [accessed: October 6, 2011].

Wacquant, L. 2007. La estigmatización territorial en la edad de la marginalidad Avanzada [Territorial Stigma in the Age of Marginality]. *Ciencias Sociais Unisinos*, 43(3), 193–9.

Žižek, S. 2008. *Violence: Six Sideways Reflections*. New York: Picador.

# Intermedia Agenda Setting and the Construction of Moral Panics: On the Media and Policy Influence of Steven Soderbergh's *Traffic*

Bryan E. Denham

Building on previous scholarship addressing the role of mass communication in the amplification of deviant behavior and the construction of moral panics (see Cohen 1980, Critcher 2003, 2010, Denham 2008, Hunt 1997, McRobbie and Thornton 1995, Wilkins 1964, Young 1971, 1973), this chapter examines the influence of the film *Traffic* (2001) on both media and policy agendas surrounding illicit drug use in the United States. The analysis explores the influence of *Traffic* on newspaper, magazine, and broadcast news reports and its role in precipitating the Drug Abuse Education, Prevention, and Treatment Act of 2001 (S.304). Conceptually, the chapter draws on agenda-setting theory (McCombs 2004) to demonstrate that one medium stands to transfer issue salience to other media (see, for example, Breen 1997, Soroka 2000). Additionally, the chapter shows that a link between motion picture content, mainstream news coverage, and the formation of public policy informs processes of agenda building (Cobb and Elder 1971, Denham 2010), that is, processes that political scientists call policy agenda setting (Bakir 2006).

*Traffic* premiered in December 2000 and within weeks (a) *Newsweek* published a "Special Report" on the problems associated with drug addiction, beginning the article with a discussion of the film, and (b) Ted Koppel of ABC News devoted five consecutive episodes of *Nightline* to the drug trade, titling the series "Traffic," and (c) the Senate Committee on the Judiciary conducted a hearing addressing the need for more drug education, prevention, and treatment programs. Additionally, experts such as former drug czar William Bennett (2001) and editorial writers including A.M. Rosenthal (2001) weighed in through editorial columns, with crime reporters and drug enforcement officials comparing the film to actual events (see

Leen 2001, Marshall 2001). Collectively, media reports helped call greater attention to illicit drug use even though, from an empirical standpoint, little about drug use or drug trafficking in the United States had changed.

## Conceptual Framework

As an academic construct, the term moral panic characterizes a process in which the response to an alleged social problem appears exaggerated, that is, disproportionate to the actual threat posed (Cohen 1980, Garland 2008). Erich Goode and Nachman Ben-Yehuda (1994) identify five characteristics of a moral panic, beginning with a heightened level of *concern* about an issue or event. Heightened concern results in *hostility* toward a certain (that is, deviant) group, and a *consensus* in society regards the threat as legitimate, even though reaction may be *disproportionate* to the problem. Lastly, moral panics are *volatile*, arising and fading quickly. A key concept in research addressing moral panics is *deviance amplification* (Young 1971), which occurs when mass media draw attention to deviant behaviors and, through continuing coverage, amplify those behaviors before media audiences. As sociologist David Garland (2008: 15) notes, media play a key role in validating the existence of deviant behaviors and profit from the coverage, "since the sensation they create—a kind of collective effervescence—sells papers, entertains readers, and generates further news and commentary as the story unfolds, the spokesmen take sides, and the deviant phenomenon develops."

As a theory of mass communication, agenda setting (McCombs 2004) suggests that while mass media may not tell readers, viewers, and listeners exactly what to think, media do tell people what to think *about* when the issues at hand do not otherwise obtrude into their lives. Such a process involves the transfer of issue salience, or importance, from media to mass audiences. Regarding illicit drugs, historian of religion Philip Jenkins (1999) argues that mass media create moral panics periodically, bringing to light an alleged "skyrocketing" in the use of certain substances. Exploring a feature film's engendering of broader (and dramatic) media coverage of drug issues, the present chapter examines processes of intermedia agenda setting (McCombs 2004: 113–17, Reese and Danielian 1989). Examples of research in this area include political scientist Stuart N. Soroka's (2000) investigation of intermedia processes as part of his study of the effect of *Schindler's List* (1993) on press coverage of the Holocaust. In another context, Denham (2004) shows that a 2002 *Sports Illustrated* exposé addressing drug use in major league baseball led not only to significant increases in newspaper coverage, but also to policy hearings held in Washington, DC.

Customarily, media-driven policy conversations have been examined through processes of agenda building (Denham 2004) and policy agenda setting (Bakir 2006), with terminology varying across disciplines. Agenda building and policy agenda setting processes focus on reciprocity and interchange among policymakers, media actors, and mass publics (Denham 2010, Lang and Lang 1983). In regard to *Traffic*, a major film triggered widespread media attention, with media actors seeking feedback from public officials who, as a partial result of heightened press coverage, called a congressional hearing. These reciprocal influences resemble the "collective effervescence" to which Garland refers in his description of moral panics.

## Traffic

Scholars have discussed the potential of films to affect people's perceptions of social reality (Jowett and Linton 1989, Nimmo and Combs 1990). The case of *Traffic* demonstrates that motion pictures can help construct moral panics. Based loosely on *Traffik*, a 1989 British television series (see Boyd 2002, Shaw 2005), *Traffic* received immediate and widespread praise in both the United States and in other nations for its critical assessment of the war on drugs. Reporting from Mexico City, Andrea Mandel-Campbell (2001) wrote in *US News and World Report* that Mexican moviegoers had found the picture highly accurate in its depiction of institutional corruption there. In *Time*, Jess Cagle (2001) described the film as "visually eclectic and alternately jarring and sentimental," while in *Rolling Stone*, Travers (2000) characterized *Traffic* as "a real cannonball, a hardass drama about the drug trade that Steven Soderbergh directs like a thriller—it comes out blazing." In the *Dallas Morning News*, Chris Vognar (2001: 1C) characterized *Traffic* as "a landmark look at an eternally explosive issue," and in *The Christian Science Monitor*, Brad Knickerbocker (2001: 2) considered the potential effectiveness of shifting "from sticks to carrots" in the US drug war.

Prior to the release of *Traffic*, few motion pictures had focused specifically on the drug war, most films featuring drug use and drug trafficking doing so primarily to inform character development (see Boyd 2008, Shapiro 2003, Starks 1982, Stevenson 2000). Unlike other pictures, *Traffic* offers no clear-cut precision in distinguishing right from wrong, explaining, in part, why many studios passed on the project (Mitchell 2001). Hollywood had long assisted government agencies by dramatizing the evils of narcotics (Marez 2004), but *Traffic*, in contrast, affords audiences little sense of closure. In one of three intertwining stories, Michael Douglas plays Robert Wakefield, an incoming drug czar who discovers that his daughter Caroline, played by Erika Christensen, is an addict prostituting herself for drug money. As the film proceeds, Wakefield becomes increasingly aware of the difficulties faced by law-enforcement personnel and, based on the struggles of his own daughter, he realizes that drug agents and border checkpoints will not rid society of illicit substances: education, prevention, and treatment will need to be incorporated if success is to be realized. But Wakefield also recognizes the challenge of abandoning traditional drug-enforcement approaches when he asks his staff to "think outside the box," perplexed by the request, no one says a word.

Whereas the first story examines the US drug war from the perspective of an incoming drug czar, the second one explores the drug trade from the vantage point of a Mexican police officer. Benicio Del Toro won an Oscar for his portrayal of

Javier Rodriguez, a cop forced to rely on his experience and steady temperament when he learns that a military official with whom he must work is involved in the drug trade. Although Rodriguez will survive the ordeal—an ordeal that bears some resemblance to the real-life revelation that Mexican General Jesus Gutierrez Rebollo had been working on behalf of drug cartels (see Weiner 2001)—few moments of glory emerge in his world. Film audiences are left to consider why honest men and women would choose to work in an environment replete with corruption – one in which human life has little value and cold-blooded executions are commonplace. In the film, Rodriguez must attempt to save the life of his partner, who has been "made" by one of the drug traffickers. Failing in this attempt, Rodriguez must remain quiet while his partner is executed in the desert and left to the elements.

In the third story, Catherine Zeta-Jones plays Helena Ayala, a well-heeled wife and mother who learns that her posh lifestyle has been financed by narcotics trafficking. When US agents raid her home and arrest her husband, a major player in the drug trade, a pregnant Ayala does not cower in fear, but takes over the family business, arranging for a key witness against her husband to be assassinated. This story considers discrepancies in the US justice system, which appears to be proficient at incarcerating low-level drug peddlers, but less successful in jailing those who employ small-timers. After the key witness has been eliminated, the husband goes home to a party that celebrates the return to business as usual. *Traffic* thus comments on social class and the extent to which money can resolve legal problems in the United States.

## Constructing a Moral Panic

Holding that moral panics vary in length and intensity (Garland 2008), the present chapter argues that *Traffic* created a moral panic concerning drug use in the United States, which characterized the US war on drugs as a failure and suggested that new approaches needed to be taken at once. *Traffic* examined the problems with treating drug abuse as a criminal issue instead of a health problem, and in transferring that concern to other media outlets, the film served as an intermedia agenda setter. Had *Traffic* simply incorporated drugs into a broader, melodramatic narrative, it may not have received the media reaction it did. As political scientist David F. Prindle (1993: 33) explained, formulaic melodramas are commonplace in film because major studios, as "large corporations responsible to impatient stockholders, tend to be cautious in their artistic decisions. They like stars, sequels and series." In other words, Hollywood studios seek predictability and relative political safety, and *Traffic* moved in the opposite direction; it took on the drug war instead of endorsing it. *Traffic* also triggered widespread press coverage of the war on drugs and led to a Congressional hearing about US drug policy.

Regarding intermedia agenda setting, a February 2001 *Newsweek* "Special Report" titled "The Hell of Addiction" (Greenberg 2001) draws heavily on *Traffic* in calling for new approaches to the drug problem. The *Newsweek* cover story (Greenberg 2001: 52) begins,

> In the new U.S. thriller 'Traffic,' just opening on international screens, Michael Douglas plays Ohio judge Robert Wakefield, a Scotch-drinking conservative who is named the new US drug czar. During an information-gathering trip to the Mexican border, he begins to see how complex and intractable the illegal-drug trade really is. Local honest cops like Javier Rodriguez (Benicio Del Toro) might be able to withstand the temptation of taking bribes, but they are powerless to stop corruption among those around—and above—them.

The lead paragraph recounts Wakefield's realization that his own daughter is an addict and the war on drugs had been waged in futility. The article's author, Susan H. Greenberg (2001: 52), also includes perhaps the most poignant line from the movie, when Wakefield remarks, I don't see how you wage war on your own family." Actor Robert Downey, Jr., whose struggles with drugs were widely known, appears on the cover, drawing attention to a report suggesting, "Drug addiction is increasingly being viewed more as a disease than as a crime" (Greenberg 2001: 52). Alter (2001) previously observed in *Newsweek* that outgoing drug czar Barry McCaffrey had changed his rhetoric from militaristic terms to health-related descriptors, characterizing drug abuse as a "cancer" on society (see also Ansen 2001, Buckley 2001). In her article, Greenberg (2001: 52) posits that the use of amphetamines and ecstasy were "growing rapidly in America"—that is, the cancer was "metastasizing"—and that "In most places, drug users are getting younger and younger." Rapidly progressing diseases and threats to the well-being of young people are familiar tropes in the onset of moral panics, and because few people have expert knowledge of statistics, exaggerated news reports may become accepted as factual based on sheer repetition.

Reviewing *Traffic* for *The New York Times*, Stephen Holden (2000: E1) characterizes the film as "a tragic cinematic mural of a war being fought and lost." A subsequent *Times* feature (Cowan and Wren 2001) examined the film through the perspectives of nine individuals the newspaper had invited to a screening. A recovering addict named Debra Walcott attended the event, stating that she could identify with the Caroline Wakefield character, whom Hunter (2001), writing in *The Washington Post*, considered the "most disturbing" of all. In the *San Francisco Chronicle*, Edward Guthmann (2001: C1) opined that Erika Christensen conveyed the look of a "fallen angel," observing that "When she blisses out on drugs and gets a woozy, ethereal look in her eyes, she's every parent's nightmare come vividly to life." In the *Los Angeles Times*, Carla Rivera (2001) confirmed that the drugs Caroline Wakefield used were readily available in suburban schools and that trips to the inner city as depicted in *Traffic* were not necessary, hard drugs could be obtained with little effort. Finally, Donnie R. Marshall (2001: A19), administrator of the Drug Enforcement Administration, said he did not agree with every detail in *Traffic*, but the first few sentences of an op-ed piece he wrote for *The Washington Post* captured the tone of the US drug war and summed up the significance of *Traffic* as a representation and criticism of it:

> The movie 'Traffic' is the most realistic portrayal of drug law enforcement and the ravages of drugs on American families that I've ever seen. It accurately shows the complexity of the drug trade— from its origins in foreign countries to its terminal point on our streets— and how predatory traffickers victimize young, weak and vulnerable people in our society

Part of the realism to which Marshall refers came from the experiences of screenwriter Stephen Gaghan, a recovering addict. Gaghan had consumed large quantities of heroin and cocaine throughout his adult life, running foul of the law, spending excessive amounts of time locked in bathrooms (not unlike the Caroline Wakefield character), and heading toward death at a young age. As Rick Lyman (2001: E1) notes in a feature story for *The New York Times*, "There were seizures, bouts of incontinence, a long, slow steady descent into mental and physical squalor." Treatment brought Gaghan back from that squalor, and *Traffic* encouraged policymakers to consider new approaches to reducing the extent of drug abuse.

Many newspaper reports praised the movie for is contribution to drug policy debates: "Movies rarely lead to public-policy debates," Manuel Mendoza (2001: 1C) observed in the *Dallas Morning News*. "It's one of the factors distinguishing *Traffic*, the war-on-drugs film that won Oscars on Sunday for director Steven Soderbergh and screenwriter Stephen Gaghan." Writing in the *Miami Herald*, Juan O. Tamayo (2001) noted that *Traffic*, "Has stirred up the Washington policy debate on narcotics trafficking and consumption as never before," while in *The Philadelphia Inquirer*, Steven Rea (2001: W3, see also Adams 2001, Davies 2001, Thompson 2001) credited Soderbergh with conveying the "absolute futility" of the war on drugs. As Claudia Puig (2001: 5E) recounted in *USA Today*, Soderbergh believed that "a complete overhaul of drug policies is needed," and in the *St Petersburg Times*, Steve Persall (2001: 5W) observed, "Too many people have been behind the curve too long with regard to narcotics trafficking and abuse." In *The Christian Science Monitor*, Sara Terry (2000: 1) referenced the significance of *Traffic* in suggesting that "a deeper national conversation does seem to be underway in households, churches, and newspaper columns."

One of the most significant influences of *Traffic* on media characterizations of drug issues became apparent in late March 2001, when *Nightline with Ted Koppel* aired a five-part series on the international drug trade, aptly titled "Traffic" (Barron 2001). As the following segment titles suggest, much of the series' content was apparently consistent with dominant themes in the movie, although *Nightline* focused on drug trafficking more than drug use or treatment:

> Part 1 (3/19/2001) – "Traffic, border war; drug dealers are winning drug war because they have more money to spend."
> Part 2 (3/20/2001) – "Traffic, the players; Arellano-Felix family has become largest, most powerful drug cartel in Mexico."

Part 3 (3/21/2001) – "Traffic, living in fear; once people cross a cartel, their lives change forever, and bodyguards, bulletproof vests, and looking over their shoulder become a way of life."

Part 4 (3/22/2001) – "Traffic, having to answer 'silver or lead?' In Mexico, [Vicente] Fox administration vows to fight corruption that has become standard business practice there."

Part 5 (3/23/2001) – "Traffic, looking for the fix; key to winning drug war lies is reducing demand for drugs."

Each of the five *Nightline* segments features clips from *Traffic*, and each helps amplify the perceived threat of narcotics. As an example, just moments into the first episode, Koppel states, "Drug trafficking is a brutal, enormously profitable industry that eventually sullies or destroys almost everyone it touches." Using imagery from the film, Koppel reports on the risks that drug "mules" take in attempting to move narcotics through the border-patrol checkpoint near Tijuana, Mexico and into the United States. Perhaps seeking to add a degree of authenticity to his film, Soderbergh opted to cast actual US Customs personnel, such as Rudy Comacho, director of field operations for Southern California. In a scene involving the inspection of a vehicle thought to contain narcotics, Comacho adlibs with actor Michael Douglas, as Camacho might have done with a reporter such as Ted Koppel.

As the first broadcast draws to a close, Koppel plays a voice-over from reporter Deborah Amos, taken from a segment that would appear the following evening. The audio clip exposes *Nightline* viewers to the brutality of the drug trade, with Amos recounting that the most violent drug cartel in Mexico had hired a man to seduce the wife of a rival drug dealer: "The man eventually killed her, cut off her head, and sent it in a box to their rival. He took the children to Ecuador, threw them off a bridge, videotaped it, and sent it to him in the mail. That's the kind of message they are willing to send." With the horror of those actions brought to the attention of viewers, Koppel closes, "That's part two of Traffic tomorrow on *Nightline*."

As promised, the second episode describes the ascent of the Arellano-Felix drug cartel, beginning with a forthright statement from Koppel: "Their trademarks are corruption, assassination and torture." The episode includes a voiceover from Amos, setting the tone for additional reporting on the drug trade and its corruptive influence in effect taking over Tijuana. Amos tells the story of Mexican General Jesus Gutierrez Rebollo, whom US drug czar Barry McCaffrey once praised for his integrity in combating the flow of narcotics. McCaffrey later learned that Rebollo had been gathering information on behalf of drug cartels.

In the early moments of the third broadcast, Koppel acknowledges that *Traffic* had inspired the five-part *Nightline* series, and like his counterparts in the print media he appears to have been influenced by the film's central thesis: "Drugs are, first and foremost, a problem of demand. If we in the United States weren't creating such enormous demand for illegal drugs, the producers and the traffickers wouldn't be risking their lives or their liberty getting those drugs to us." But, if demand was indeed the problem when the episode aired in March 2001, one might question why the war on drugs in the United States focused on supply for more than three decades. How many billions of dollars had been spent on interdiction efforts in foreign nations, and why had "first and foremost" concerns not been addressed?

By March 2001, drug cartels had spent millions of dollars corrupting public officials in Mexico, and the question "Silver or lead?" had come to reflect a fundamental choice: accept a payoff or receive a bullet. Amos reports during the fourth episode, "In Tijuana, two police chiefs got the visit and paid the price. The most recent, Alfredo de la Torre, was murdered last year in an ambush on a Tijuana highway." The episode goes on to say that members of drug cartels have crushed people's heads by using a hydraulic press

In "Looking for the Fix," the fifth and final episode of the series, Koppel focuses more on adolescent drug use than on graphic descriptions of executions. Commenting on *Traffic*, Koppel explains that "the reality that this Hollywood production rams down America's throat more effectively perhaps than we in journalism have done, the reality is that drugs recognize no boundaries, nor do they recognize age or race, wealth or status." *Traffic* indeed heightened awareness of adolescent drug use, but that issue-amplification could have come at any time and been just as appropriate. In other words, nothing apart from the film led Koppel to devote five episodes of *Nightline* to issues surrounding drug use and drug trafficking. Actual use statistics had not changed to any appreciable degree, but a dramatic film nevertheless triggered a great deal of press coverage about the dangers of substance abuse.

## Policy Impact

On Wednesday, March 14, 2001, less than three months after *Traffic* premiered, US Senator Orrin Hatch (R-Utah), chair of the Senate Committee on the Judiciary, presided over a hearing on Treatment, Education, and Prevention: Adding to the Arsenal in the War on Drugs. The hearing had been called consequent to a legislative proposal, the *Drug Education, Prevention, and Treatment Act of 2001* (S.304), formulated by Hatch and senators Patrick Leahy (D-Vermont), Mike DeWine (R-Ohio), Joseph Biden (D-Delaware), and Strom Thurmond (R-South Carolina). To remove the "scourge" of drugs from society, Hatch argued, a "holistic" approach— one that would combine law enforcement efforts with drug education, prevention, and treatment programs—needed to be developed, law enforcement alone would not get the job done ("Treatment" 2001: 1, 10). The Senator had appeared briefly in *Traffic*, as had other legislators such as senators Barbara Boxer (D-California) and Harry Reid (D-Nevada). At the hearing, Hatch praised the movie for showing the "real depths of degradation" ("Treatment" 2001: 31) associated with drug use (see Lancaster 2001).

Like Hatch, Patrick Leahy argued that law enforcement alone could not solve the drug problem. In his remarks, Leahy stated that he was struck by a scene in *Traffic*, when Robert Wakefield, the incoming drug czar, questions the lack of emphasis on drug treatment in efforts to reduce substance abuse. A co-sponsor of the Drug Education, Prevention, and Treatment Act of 2001, Leahy noted "No community is immune from the ravages of drug abuse" ("Treatment" 2001: 6). Suggesting that drug traffickers sought to lure young people into prostitution, he explained that the prospective legislation called for the Sentencing Commission to review its guidelines for individuals caught selling drugs to minors. Leahy also submitted for the record a March 13, 2001 *Washington Post* op-ed piece written by Joseph Califano of the National Center on Addiction and Substance Abuse at Columbia University. Califano (2001: A21) had submitted a lengthy statement in support of the legislation, and in his op-ed piece, published one day before the hearing, he wrote that *Traffic* "vividly captures the crude corruption that undermines law enforcement attempts to curb illegal drug distribution and sales" and that law enforcement needed assistance in the form of drug prevention and treatment of the addicted.

Following opening remarks at the Senate hearing, the first panel of witnesses to testify included Donnie Marshall, administrator of the Drug Enforcement Administration (DEA), Paul Warner, US Attorney for the state of Utah, and Alan Leshner, director of the National Institute on Drug Abuse (NIDA). Marshall noted the fundamental charge of the DEA: "To enforce the controlled substances laws and to bring to justice the people responsible for poisoning the citizens of our country" ("Treatment" 2001: 10), but he also spoke to the relative merits of a "holistic" approach to drug control. Similarly, although against the legalization of drugs, Warner conceded that an "interdisciplinary" approach stood to be the most effective strategy, contending "both the carrot and the stick are necessary for an effective drug reduction program" ("Treatment" 2001: 13). In the last of the panelists' opening statements, Leshner advocated preventive treatment, citing its capacity to help alleviate social problems such as crime and delinquency ("Treatment" 2001: 13). Later, Marshall, of the DEA, praised *Traffic* for pulling few metaphorical punches in this regard:

> I thought it was a very realistic movie, and I thought it did a wonderful job of framing many of the issues about the drug problem … I took my own 15-year-old and 16-year-old sons to see this movie, and they had a similar reaction. They said that they didn't realize how vulgar and how gritty and how violent the drug world was, and the consequences that drug abuse has for young people. ("Treatment" 2001: 32)

Thus, the first panel of witnesses, each of whom worked for the US government, lent credence to policymakers seeking to pass a timely piece of drug legislation. References to *Traffic* helped demonstrate (and dramatize) the need for funding, as called for in the *Drug Education, Prevention, and Treatment Act* of 2001. Yet, each witness also stressed the importance of law-enforcement efforts in combating drug abuse, thus reifying the importance of their respective agencies. *Traffic* had portrayed law-enforcement personnel in a favorable manner, but the film had also made the point that treatment options for the addicted needed to be expanded.

The second panel to testify at the March 14, 2001 hearing included Robert DuPont, the first director of NIDA and drug czar for US presidents Nixon and Ford, Edyie Hewitt, former director of the Vermont Federation of Families for Children's Mental Health, Jim Walton, commissioner of the Department of Public Safety in Waterbury, Vermont, Debra Walcott, a former drug user who had been offered (and accepted) a drug treatment program instead of a jail sentence, and Carroll O'Connor, a television star whose son Hugh abused drugs before committing suicide in 1995. Carroll O'Connor spoke emotionally about the loss of his son and supported the proposed legislation for "directing serious attention to the care of the wounded and dying" ("Treatment" 2001: 37). Whereas outgoing drug czar Barry McCaffrey had shifted from military metaphors to health-related descriptors, O'Connor opted to remain with the former:

> This is a good bill. This war against the drug empire is a good war, and except for some who call it a lost war who would legalize drugs and turn the country over to the invader, the American people are not clamoring to withdraw from this war. This war is raging in the streets around them. ("Treatment" 2001: 37)

Few public officials, even if opposed to legislation or certain clauses within it, will openly scrutinize the testimony of individuals who have suffered the loss of loved ones. In fact, that is precisely why officials who hold government hearings typically invite both recognized experts as well as individuals who have been personally affected by an issue. Individuals who have experienced the loss of a child or who have compromised their own health help to create a sense of urgency while making it appear irresponsible for lawmakers *not* to pass a certain bill.

O'Connor called on parents to take a more active, and responsible, role in educating their children about drugs:

> They have to understand and the parents have to understand that the use of these drugs changes the cells in the brain. It just changes people. You go on with this and you are a new person. The kid that shot himself in the head was not my son. That was an entirely different person, a new personality. He had taken leave of his conscience, he had taken leave of love. He could talk about all these things and mouth all these things, but they didn't mean anything to him. 'Yes, I love you Pop,' and so forth and so on. He didn't anymore; he was another person. He wasn't my kid. ("Treatment" 2001: 57)

In his review of *Traffic* for the *San Francisco Chronicle*, Edward Guthmann (2001: C1) wrote that the Caroline Wakefield character represented "every parent's nightmare come vividly to life," O'Connor brought that nightmare before the March 2001 Congressional hearing.

In her own testimony, witness Debra Walcott, a recovering addict and subject of a prior news report in *The New York Times* (Cowan and Wren 2001), stated that substance abuse destroyed her relationships with family members and that she had come in contact with the criminal justice system as a consequence of her drug habit. Similarly, Edyie Hewitt, former director of the Vermont Federation of Families for Children's Mental Health, testified as the mother of three sons who had become addicted to drugs. In her remarks, which focused primarily on two of the three, she recounted that both had been arrested for selling heroin, which they did as a means of supporting their own drug use. Hewitt stated that, although ten years had passed since the arrests, virtually no progress had been made toward the treatment of addicts. In many respects, her experiences resembled those of *Traffic*'s Robert Wakefield, especially in that the discovery of an addict within the family often leads individuals to shift from indifference to advocacy. Jim Walton, commissioner of Public Safety in Vermont, echoed the sentiments of Hewitt, positing that "heroin is a poison that not only destroys the individual who is addicted, but does serious damage to family, friends, and community" ("Treatment" 2001: 44). Again, warnings against threats to the well-being of young people are perhaps the most common types of appeals made at drug-related policy hearings, primarily because few would argue with the need to protect "our youth" from those who would harm them. A familiar cast of characters tends to testify at such hearings, with individuals who have been personally affected by drug abuse speaking alongside scientists and medical professionals. Collectively, their testimony reinforces the need for action, although in many, perhaps most cases the proposed legislation fails to become law. Still, policymakers appear engaged in issues of the day, taking an interest in the welfare of young people.

## Concluding Remarks

This chapter has examined concepts such as agenda setting and agenda building in relation to processes of deviance amplification and moral panics. It has been shown that *Traffic* increased and transferred drug-issue salience to print and broadcast media and that the film and the press coverage it triggered precipitated a Congressional hearing and the introduction of S.304, the *Drug Abuse Education, Prevention and Treatment Act* of 2001. S.304 became part of a broader piece of legislation, the *21st Century Department of Justice Authorization Act* (H.R. 2215). Consistent with S.304, H.R. 2215 extended treatment options for nonviolent individuals addicted to drugs, and in that respect, one can reasonably conclude that the dramatization of the war on drugs presented in *Traffic* influenced at least one dimension of public policy.

The processes that have been described in the chapter reflect the type of short-term moral panic that Jenkins (1999) described in reference to drug concerns. For Congress to continue funding a cause that has apparently been lost, new threats must appear periodically, with policymakers acting on media reports by holding hearings and introducing legislation. Even when they are short lived, drug-related moral panics sell newspapers and increase television ratings while also allowing public officials to demonstrate initiative before constituents. While much of their initiative is symbolic and tends to fade quickly, it nevertheless serves their political interests. Meanwhile, the deviant behavior in question generally continues as it did prior to, during, and after the exaggerated response of moral panic.

# References

Adams, D. 2001. "Traffic" has D.C. all abuzz. *St Petersburg Times*, March 24, 1A.

Alter, J. 2001. A well-timed "Traffic" signal. *Newsweek*, January 15, 29.

Ansen, D. 2001. Soderbergh keeps his streak alive. *Newsweek*, January, 8, 62.

Bakir, V. 2006. Policy agenda setting and risk communication: Greenpeace, Shell, and issues of trust. *Harvard International Journal of Press/Politics*, 11(3), 67–88.

Barron, J. 2001. "Nightline" to devote full week to drugs. *The New York Times*, March 19, C11.

Ben-Yehuda, N. 1990. *The Politics and Morality of Deviance*. Albany: State University of New York Press.

Bennett, W. J. 2001. The real lessons from "Traffic." *The Washington Post*, February 18, B7.

Boyd, S. 2002. Media constructions of illegal drugs, users, and sellers: a closer look at *Traffic*. *International Journal of Drug Policy*, 13(5), 397–407.

Boyd, S. 2008. *Hooked: Drug War Films in Britain, Canada, and the United States*. London: Routledge.

Breen, M.J. 1997. A cook, a cardinal, his priests, and the press: Deviance as a trigger for intermedia agenda setting. *Journalism and Mass Communication Quarterly*, 74(2), 348–56.

Buckley, W.F., Jr. 2001. High on drug warring. *National Review*, February 19, 59.

Cagle, J. 2001. Cinema: Soderbergh's choice. *Time* [Online], January 8. Available at: www.time.com/time/magazine/article/0,9171,998920,00.html [accessed: October 3, 2011].

Califano, J. A., Jr. 2001. A turning point on drugs. *The Washington Post*, March 13, A21.

Cobb, R. W. and Elder, C. D. 1971. The politics of agenda-building: An alternative perspective for modern democratic theory. *Journal of Politics*, 33(4), 892–915.

Cohen, S. 1980 (1972). *Folk Devils and Moral Panics: The Creation of the Mods and Rockers*. 2nd Edition. New York: St Martin's Press.

Cowen, A.L. and Wren, C.S. 2001. Dealing in reality: A film's depiction of drugs. *The New York Times*, January 18, E1.

Critcher, C. 2003. *Moral Panics and the Media*. Issues in Cultural and Media Studies. Maidenhead: Open University Press.

Critcher, C. 2010 (2006). Introduction: more questions than answers, in *Critical Readings: Moral Panics and the Media*. 2nd Edition, edited by C. Critcher. Maidenhead: Open University Press, 1–24.

Davies, F. 2001. "Traffic" is driving Washington's drug debate. *The Philadelphia Inquirer*, March 25, H7.

Denham, B.E. 2004. *Sports Illustrated*, the mainstream press, and the enactment of drug policy in major league baseball: a study in agenda building theory. *Journalism*, 5(1), 51–68.

Denham, B.E. 2008. Folk devils, news icons and the construction of moral panics: Heroin chic and the amplification of drug threats in contemporary society. *Journalism Studies*, 9(6), 945–61.

Denham, B.E. 2010. Toward conceptual consistency in studies of agenda-building processes: A scholarly review. *Review of Communication* [Online, September 28], 10(4), 306–23. Available at: http://www.tandfonline.com/toc/rroc20/10/4 [accessed: January 29, 2012].

Garland, D. 2008. On the concept of moral panic. *Crime, Media, Culture*, 4(1), 9–30.

Goode, E. and Ben-Yehuda, N. 1994. *Moral Panics: The Social Construction of Deviance*. Oxford: Blackwell.

Greenberg, S.H. 2001. The hell of addiction. *Newsweek*, February 12, 52.

Guthmann, E. 2001. Soderbergh's riveting thriller lays open America's anti-drug campaign. *San Francisco Chronicle*, January 5, C1.

Hall, S., Critcher, C., Jefferson, T., Clarke, J., and Roberts, B. 1978. *Policing the Crisis: Mugging, the State, and Law and Order*. Critical Social Studies. Houndmills: Macmillan.

Hunt, A. 1997. 'Moral panic' and moral language in the media. *British Journal of Sociology*, 48(4), 629–48.

Holden, S. 2000. Teeming mural of a war fought and lost. *The New York Times*, December 27, E1.

H.R. 2215-107th Congress: *21st Century Department of Justice Appropriations Authorization Act* [Online], 2001. Available at: http://www.govtrack.us/congress/bills/107/hr2215 [accessed: May 25, 2012].

Hunter, S. 2001. The enemy within. *The Washington Post*, January 5, C1.

Jenkins, P. 1999. *Synthetic Panics: The Symbolic Politics of Designer Drugs*. New York: New York University Press.

Jenkins, P. 2009. Failure to launch: why do some social issues fail to detonate moral panics? *British Journal of Criminology*, 49(1), 35–47.

Jowett, G. and Linton, J.M. 1989. *Movies as Mass Communication*. Newbury Park: Sage Publications.

Knickerbocker, B. 2001. Tactics in drug war take hits. *The Christian Science Monitor*, March 7, 2.

Lancaster, J. 2001. In Senate debate on drugs, "Traffic" moves minds. *The Washington Post*, March 15, A10.

Lang, G. E. and Lang, K. 1983. *The Battle for Public Opinion: The President, the Press, and the Polls during Watergate*. New York: Columbia University Press.

Leen, J. 2001. The straight dope on "Traffic": film gets drug war (mostly) right. *The Washington Post*, January 6, C1.

Lyman, R. 2001. Gritty portrayal of the abyss from a survivor; the screenwriter for "Traffic" says he drew on his past. *The New York Times*, February 5, E1.

Mandel-Campbell, A. 2001. Life on the big screen. *US News and World Report*, April 2, 34.

Marez, C. 2004. *Drug Wars: The Political Economy of Narcotics*. Minneapolis: University of Minnesota Press.

Marshall, D.R. 2001. How real is "Traffic?" *The Washington Post*, April 21, A19.

McCombs, M.E. 2004. *Setting the Agenda: The Mass Media and Public Opinion*. Cambridge: Polity.

McRobbie, A. and Thornton, S.L. 1995. Rethinking "moral panic" for multi-mediated social worlds. *British Journal of Sociology*, 46(4), 559–74.

Mendoza, M. 2001. Differences go beyond spelling in British "Traffic." *The Dallas Morning News*, March 30, 1C.

Mitchell, S. 2001. Protesting another misguided war. *Los Angeles Times* [Online], January 7. Available at: http://articles.latimes.com/2001/jan/07/entertainment/ca-9204 [accessed: October 3, 2011].

Nimmo, D. and Combs, J.E. 1990. *Mediated Political Realities*. New York: Longman.

Persall, S. 2001. In the coils of the drug trade. *St. Petersburg Times*, January 4, 5W.

Prindle, D.F. 1993. *Risky Business: The Political Economy of Hollywood*. Boulder: Westview.

Puig, C. 2001. Real-life drug issues flow through "Traffic." *USA Today*, January 5, 5E.

Rea, S. 2001. Personal skirmishes in the drug war provocative and powerful. *Philadelphia Inquirer*, January 5, W3.

Reese, S.D. and Danielian, L.H. 1989. Intermedia influence and the drug issue: converging on cocaine, in *Communication Campaigns about Drugs: Government, Media, and the Public*, edited by P. J. Shoemaker. Hillsdale: Erlbaum, 29–45.

Rivera, C. 2001. Recovering teenagers see themselves in realistic drug movie. *Los Angeles Times* [Online], February 13. Available at: http://articles.latimes.com/2001/feb/13/news/cl-24601 [accessed: October 3, 2011].

Rosenthal, A.M. 2001. Undermining the war against illegal drugs. *The Washington Times*, March 12, A13.

S. 304–107th Congress: *Drug Abuse Education, Prevention, and Treatment Act of 2001* [Online], 2001. Available at: http://www.govtrack.us/congress/bills/107/s304 [accessed: May 25, 2012].

Shapiro, H. 2003. *Shooting Stars: Drugs, Hollywood and the Movies*. London: Serpent's Tail.

Shaw, D. 2005. 'You are alright, but …': individual and collective representations of Mexicans, Latinos, Anglo-Americans and Africans in Steven Soderbergh's *Traffic*. *Quarterly Review of Film and Video*, 22, 211–23.

Soroka, S.N. 2000. *Schindler's List*'s intermedia influence: Exploring the role of entertainment in media agenda-setting. *Canadian Journal of Communication*, 25(2), 211–30.

Starks, M. 1982. *Cocaine Fiends and Reefer Madness: An Illustrated History of Drugs in the Movies*. New York: Cornwall Books.

Stevenson, J. 2000. Introduction, in *Addicted: The Myth and Menace of Drugs in Film*, edited by J. Stevenson. New York: Creation Books, 5–8.

Tamayo, J.O. 2001. For Colombians, drug movie is mostly the same old story. *The Miami Herald*, March 17. Gale document number: CJ121189923.

Terry, S. 2000. America wavers on get-tough drug sentences. *The Christian Science Monitor*, December 27, 1.

Thompson, G. 2001. "Traffic" goes with the drug flow. *Philadelphia Daily News*, January 15, 52.

*Traffic* (dir. Steven Soderbergh, 2000).

Travers, P. 2000. *Traffic*. *Rolling Stone* [Online], December 18. Available at: http://www.rollingstone.com/movies/reviews/8550/51535 [accessed: October 3, 2011].

2001. Treatment, Education, and Prevention: Adding to the Arsenal in the War on Drugs [Online]. Hearing before the Committee on the Judiciary of the United States Senate, 107th Congress, 1st session. Serial No. J-107-6. Washington: US Government Printing Office. Available at: http://www.eric.ed.gov/PDFS/ED463482.pdf [accessed: February 18, 2012].

Vognar, C. 2001. Soderbergh's can of worms proves popular. *The Dallas Morning News*, January 7, 1C.

Weiner, T. 2001. Mexico's new anti-drug team wins the trust of U.S. officials. *The New York Times*, July 18, A1. Wilkins, L. 1964. *Social Deviance*. London: Tavistock.

Young, J. 1971. The role of the police as amplifiers of deviancy, negotiators of reality and translators of fantasy: some consequences of our present system of drug control as seen in Notting Hill, in *Images of Deviance*, edited by S. Cohen. Harmondsworth: Penguin Books, 27–61.

Young, J. 1973. The myth of the drug taker in the mass media, in *The Manufacture of News: Deviance, Social Problems and the Mass Media*, edited by S. Cohen and J. Young. London: Constable, 314–22.

Young, J. 2009. Moral panic: its origins in resistance, ressentiment and the translation of fantasy into reality. *British Journal of Criminology*, 49(1), 4–16.

# I Vote and I Tote: Moral Panics, Resistance, and the Failure of Quiet Regulation

Grazyna Zajdow

The term moral panic has entered the media-and-popular-culture lexicon, but retains a particular meaning for sociologists. This chapter expands on existing models of moral panics and outlines a case study that illustrates that folk devils have fought back in recent years, using technologies such as social media to present their arguments (in this instance, turning a local political controversy in Melbourne, in the Australian State of Victoria, to their advantage). The battle began over a classic law-and-order issue, that is, the problem of alcohol-related violence, especially as it involves young people. However, the conflict took an unexpected turn when the folk devils successfully used the media to prosecute their case and force the state government's hand.

## The Success of Moral Panics Models

Moral panics models provide a way of understanding cultural conflicts and the resulting moral crusades. According to Stanley Cohen (2002), moral panics occur as a result of anxiety over social norms, and rely on moral crusaders using the media to whip up anger over relatively minor infractions by groups of disenfranchised or deviant individuals. As defined by Cohen (2002: 1), a moral panic exists when

> a condition, episode, person or group emerges to become defined as a threat to societal values and interests; its nature is presented in a stylized ... fashion ... by the mass media ... moral barricades are manned. ... socially accredited experts pronounce their diagnoses and solutions ... the condition then disappears, submerges or deteriorates and becomes more visible.

This model emphasizes alarm, exaggeration, public anxiety, and excessive reaction. Normative groups (often led by the moral entrepreneurs who use the media to engage in conflict) perceive a group of deviants, "folk devils" in Cohen's terms, dangerous. As sociologist David Garland (2008: 11) points out, two elements are often omitted in later iterations of the model: moral dimensions inherent (though not always overtly claimed) in the social reaction and "the idea that the deviant conduct in question is somehow *symptomatic*" of some greater social anxiety.

Sociologists Angela McRobbie and Sarah L. Thornton (1995) argue that the very success of Cohen's moral panics model has become its weakness in a multi-mediated, globalized universe. Folk devils have begun to fight back by using the newest forms of media to resist and produce new narratives, or stigma contests (Schur 1980). In other words (Dotter 2004: 47), "in the scenario, deviance shifts back and forth between biographical images and the broader context of cultural meaning framed in [the deviant] master status." The discourse of moral panic produces resistance in the subjects it attempts to dominate and pull into its orbit.

Sociologist Steven J. Tepper (2009) writes that public dramas played out in the media lie at the center of moral panic studies. Tepper (2009: 282) articulates the move away from moralizing discourses to amoral risk management: "The outcome of regulation will depend precisely on how an issue is framed and the schemas that come to dominate discussion and debate." He suggests that scholars study sites of quiet regulation because they are likely to become more common. This is because of policies of risk management and governance through risk, alongside the greater neoliberal policies of cities that rely on night-time economies for survival. But Tepper (2009) also considers that modern politics demands that rhetorical discourses of inclusivity mean that the traditional folk devils, such as young people, cannot be stigmatized as they have been in the past. Young people have become "a less politically viable target of moral crusaders" (Tepper 2009: 284).

A study of heroin overdoses in Australia in the late 1990s (Zajdow 2008) illustrates both Tepper's (2009) and McRobbie and Thornton's (1995) points. In an effort to change government policy and the low public opinion of heroin users that, as they believed, contribute to heroin overdose deaths, various actors used the media in a filmic and directed way. They used grieving parents, passionate advocates, determined professionals, weary former police, and eloquent victims to warn of the impending holocaust of heroin deaths. This was a period of rising heroin use, falling heroin prices, and increasing heroin overdose deaths. However, in classic moral panic fashion, the moral entrepreneurs exaggerated the number of likely deaths in the future and accused policymakers and politicians of killing the youth of Australia. For example, in an op-ed piece in a major newspaper, one researcher and medical practitioner (quoted in Zajdow 2008: 653) wrote, "Our drug policies are inhuman, ineffective in achieving their stated goals ... They are enormously costly and corrupting ... We ... lack the heart, and the will to care for our young people."

It could be argued, and indeed sociologist Henry Yeomans (2009) has done so, that moral panics over alcohol are endemic rather than exceptional, and the history of alcohol and illicit drugs panics in the twentieth and twenty-first centuries bears this out. Actually, the first real moral panic might be said to be the Gin Craze of the 1730s and 1740s in England (Borsay 2010), and moral panics over alcohol have been a feature of Australian society since the European invasion (Zajdow 2011). But in this instance, the Victorian state government tried to deal with a moral panic over young people and binge drinking through quiet regulation. The attempt backfired spectacularly.

## The Battle over the Tote

The Tote, also known as the Tote Hotel, is a small pub housed in a building formerly operated as a hotel located in Collingwood, an inner city suburb of Melbourne. The Tote has hosted live music in the form of rock and roll (including punk, grunge, and other amplified music) since the 1980s. It has held out against the tide of closures in the inner city that began in the 1990s. However, in 2010, Bruce Milne, with his brother James one of the Tote's two licensees, made a public statement that he could no longer stay open if he were forced to pay for increased security and higher license fees as demanded by the Director of Liquor Licensing Victoria, Sue Maclellan.

The timeline of subsequent events as played out in the print media is outlined below. It should be noted that Melbourne has only two daily newspapers and that the campaign was most prominent in the daily broadsheet, *The Age*. I analyzed all the articles in the local press published from January 15, 2010 until October 2010 that referred to alcohol licensing and the local live music scene. This amounted to 31 in total. I considered doing a systematic analysis of the articles around themes and the number of times they appeared, but on reading the articles, it became immediately apparent that there was no need. With one exception, they were all critical of the new licensing regime and the effect it was about to have on business. *The Age*, in particular, succumbed to the crusade, but there was no opposition to it from the daily tabloid the *Herald Sun* either. However, the *Herald Sun* did not carry nearly as many articles on the topic as *The Age*. The *Herald Sun* published just four in all, while *The Age* published 25 between January 2010 and October 2010, when the accord between the parties was signed. The overwhelming share of these articles was published between January 2010 and May 2010.

The battle over the Tote and small live music venues in Melbourne can only be understood in relation to the night-time economy and the production of a post-industrial economy in many cities in the West. These cities have instituted specific laws and regulations to use space for new ways of producing revenue and labor. Cities such as Melbourne and Newcastle in Australia, Manchester in the United Kingdom, and Baltimore, Maryland in the United States opened up their moribund central cities to 24-hour drinking and entertainment, thus transforming formerly dead or dying hearts into vibrant commercial precincts. However, a corollary to this transformation was a rise in violence and nuisance related to the consumption of alcohol (Hadfield 2006, Hobbs et al. 2003). Most cities dealt with this unwanted consequence by tinkering with licensing laws and regulations in an effort to confine the problems without confronting the alcohol industry directly or restricting the general availability of alcohol. Such was the case in Melbourne (Zajdow 2011).

## Battles in the Night-time Economy

In late 2007 and early 2008, reports of drunken young people, violence, and nuisance in the inner areas of major cities in Australia became prominent in the print and electronic media of Australia. For example, in its main television current affairs program, *The 7.30 Report* of March 10 2008, ABC Television (part of the government-funded Australian Broadcasting Corporation) provided a graphic account of the problems in central Newcastle, a city in New South Wales, with young people and late-night partying in its 15 pubs and clubs, open until 5:00 A.M. on weekends. On this episode, one city councillor claims that Newcastle has the highest assault rate in New South Wales and certainly the visuals used do not look pretty: young people vomiting in the streets and being chased by police, police cars screaming through the streets, young women drunk and crying. A local resident states,

> Most of the residents live in the city, they're 55 and over and they won't come out after dark and they don't leave their environment because they're scared … I know people now who drive four blocks to go to the movies because they won't come out of the cinema late at night for fear of bashings or assaults. (*The 7.30 Report* 2008)

For the opposing side, two young women argue that it is a restriction of their right to drink to consider earlier closing times and a publican claims that the answer is not to restrict his ability to trade but to photograph all patrons and effectively ban those who cause trouble from all the venues. One says,

> If you're asking me, is a curfew or a restriction of trade the answer, absolutely not. It is wrong, it will not address the issue in any way shape, or form …. If there are people who are the cause of antisocial behavior we have manners in which they can have [sic] identified and removed from the system. So should the other 20,000 people who visit Newcastle be punished because of the actions of a few? (*The 7.30 Report* 2008)

A similar argument was proceeding at about the same time in central Melbourne's Queen Street, where 13 bars and clubs jostled for customers within a two-block radius. Like Newcastle, the assault rate in central Melbourne had risen quite steeply, up 17.5 percent in 12 months (Rood 2007). In this area, the licensed capacity was about 10,000, while it was estimated that 300,000 people visited the central business district at night every weekend. Long articles in the daily newspapers described vivid scenes of uncontrolled drunkenness, mostly by young people (for example,

Houston, Austin, and Johnston 2008). The answer suggested by authorities was more policing and surveillance of young people by the state and its proxies. To pay for this, the Victorian government decided to introduce a risk-based fee structure to control the market for alcohol rather than limit the market directly.

In Newcastle, the New South Wales Liquor Administration Board was persuaded to impose earlier closing times for all clubs and bars (Moore 2008). A subsequent study found substantial drops in violent incidents in the area and no displacement of problems into adjoining areas, which its opponents always claimed would be the inevitable result (Jones et al. 2009). In Melbourne, the situation was much more complex partly because of the way that alcohol licensing is controlled in Victoria, as well as a historical ideological commitment to the night-time economy (Zajdow 2011). Initially, Maclellan attempted to impose a 2:00 A.M. lockout on all licensed premises in the central city precinct, but this was opposed by the licensees and their arguments were upheld in the courts (Houston 2008).[1] The state government decided to suspend awarding any new 24-hour licenses in many inner city areas, but problems continued, and the media spotlight did not extinguish itself. Subsequently, Maclellan was given greater enforcement powers, more undercover police, and the Directorate was moved from the Department of Consumer Affairs to the Department of Justice. However, continuing the state's interest in controlling problems by licensing and risk-management rather than direct state control of availability, Maclellan also decided to impose license fees based on perceived risk categories, and in many instances rigorously impose already existing licensing regulations such as mandatory security, as well. A consultant's report (Allen Consulting 2009, see table 18.1) suggested that four risk categories should exist for licensing purposes—low, low-medium, high, and very high—based on venue size and type, opening hours, and previous license violations.

Thus, large, late-opening venues that had gaming machines would be charged substantially more for their licenses than small, laneway bars that closed before 1:00 A.M. For example, under the old regime, a large pub with gaming machines and open until 4:00 A.M. paid a license fee of about $6,000. Under the new rules, this would rise to over $25,000 because of the risk factors attached, while a small restaurant that stayed open only until 11:00 P.M. would have its license fee reduced by over $1,000 (*Liquor Control Reform* 2009). Risk was being managed down as comprehensively as possible and the government was hoping popular opposition would also be managed downwards. Thus, in the effort to combat public perceptions of danger and risk associated with venues, but with "quiet regulation" (Tepper 2009) to undermine resistance, the state brought in Maclellan to do her work. The commercial effects of license fee impositions were immediately felt by some small inner city venues that regularly hosted live music.

---

1    A lockout is a situation where patrons are not allowed to enter or reenter premises after a certain time, in this case 2:00 A.M., although those inside can keep buying drinks until the official closing, in this case 5:00 A.M. or 7:00 A.M.

**Table 18.1    Risk Relativities**

| RISK RELATIVITIES |
| --- |
| **LOW RISK** |
| Licensed premises with none of the specified risk factors |
| **LOW-MEDIUM** |
| Licensed premises with club gaming facilities |
| Licensed premises that close between 11:01 P.M. and 1:00 A.M. |
| **MEDIUM RISK** |
| Licensed premises that close between 1:01 A.M. and 3:00 A.M. |
| Licensed premises with one to two infringements |
| Licensed premises with hotel gaming facilities |
| **HIGH RISK** |
| Licensed premises that close after 3:00 A.M. (not including premises with hotel gaming) |
| Licensed premises with three or more infringements |
| **VERY HIGH RISK** |
| Licensed premises that close after 1:00 A.M. and that also have one or more infringements |

Based on data gathered from (2009) Alcohol-Related Harm and the Operation of Licensed Premises. The Allen Consulting Group [Online]. Available at: http://www.allenconsult.com.au/publications/download.php?id=340&type=pdf&file=1.

# Fighting Back

On January 15 2010, an article entitled "Time Called on Tote in Blow to Melbourne's Music Scene," written by Andrew Murfett, appeared in *The Age*. In it, the Tote's licensees claimed that, because of changes to licensing fees, they could no longer remain in business. Originally, the venue stayed open until 3:00 A.M. to cater to musicians who played elsewhere and who wanted to finish their nights socializing after work. The licensees stated that the hours between 1:00 A.M. and 3:00 A.M. had been the most profitable, but since opening hours after 1:00 A.M. were now classified as high risk, the higher fees made it impossible to stay open past that time. Once the pub started closing at 1:00 A.M., and Maclellan enforced minimum-security arrangements, the venue had become unprofitable, so it was forced to close its doors. The article (Murfett 2010) also noted that a Facebook site had begun that night that called on its members to protest in two days' time (Sunday night) on the final night of gigs. The next day, *The Age* published four letters criticizing the new licensing requirements and their effects on the Melbourne live music scene.

The Tote's final night, Sunday, January 17, saw about 2,000 people protest outside the hotel. The police closed off the street, and the protest was genial and nonviolent. On Tuesday, January 19, a lengthy article appeared in the comments pages of *The Age*, written by one of its senior writers, Jo Roberts (2010), describing the protest and the crowd (including Roberts, who brought along her three-year-old son). Resistance to quiet regulation had begun.

On Thursday, January 21, the leader in *The Age* discussed the unintended consequences of the new licensing regime that had been introduced to counter perceived violence and late night venues in the city and inner city precincts. The writer quotes Robert K. Merton:

> Once again, government regulation has had unintended consequences, despite the lessons of centuries of economic and sociological observation. In 1936, American sociologist Robert K. Merton wrote an influential analysis identifying five sources of unanticipated consequences, with the first two, ignorance and error, the most common. The third he called 'imperious immediacy of interest' when someone wants the intended consequence of an action so much that potential unintended effects are ignored. All three factors arguably contributed to the Tote's closure. ("Liquor Crackdown" 2010: 16)

It is rare, extremely rare, for an Australian leader writer to quote a sociologist, particularly one who wrote in 1936! However, it did indicate a certain dramatic feeling among sections of the population.

By January 22, the Australian Labor Party state government had already signaled its intention to change the way the regulations were being enforced to undercut the criticisms leveled against it (Donovan 2010a). This backdown had as much to do with local Victorian or rather inner city Melbourne politics as it did with live rock and roll. The state government was heading into an election year and two of its most vulnerable seats were in the area at the center of the fight. The previous Monday, Victoria's Consumer Affairs Minister Tony Robinson had claimed that strict licensing regulations were necessary, but by Thursday, the state's Premier John Brumby went on FM radio to say that the regulations would be fine-tuned. As *The Age* reported, "They [political analysts] believe the Government has yielded to pressure from young potential voters in Melbourne's artistic inner north who could punish Labor at the November poll" (Stark and Craig 2010: 4). The same article pointed out that by this time 20,000 people had signed an Internet petition against the regulations and a demonstration had been called for February 23 (Stark and Craig 2010).

The government set up a meeting made up of members of parliament, representatives of the music industry, and bureaucrats to review the regulations and make recommendations for an accord between the various parties, essentially to hose down the antipathy that had developed. However, the meeting did not include Director of Liquor Licensing Sue Maclellan, whose contract was coming up for renewal, and who was unlikely to have another term offered her. In a hyperbolic gesture, Michael Gudinski, a well-known music promoter, "slammed his fist on the table and said, 'You know, it's not rocket science, it's rock 'n' roll'" (Priest 2010: 5). This was certainly an example of folk devils resisting and using the media for their own purposes.

The finale of this local dramatic symphony was played on February 23, the thirty-fourth anniversary of the making of a music video for local band AC/DC's "It's a Long Way to the Top (If You Wanna Rock 'n' Roll)" on Swanston Street, Melbourne's main street. The video shows the band performing on a moving flatbed truck. Most pedestrians blandly walk by, but a few young people start following the truck, dancing. One young woman holds up a joint, apparently offering it to the band. AC/DC's lead singer, Bon Scott (who was to die in 1980), plays a set of bagpipes, which feature prominently the video. (Even more famously, almost anyone who was over 50 by 2010 claimed to have been on the street at the time!) In 2010, up to 2,000 people turned up outside the State Library on Swanston Street to watch musicians play and hear stirring speeches made. To make political capital out of the government's embarrassment over the issue, opposition (center-right) Liberal Party of Australia politicians stood in front of the crowd on the steps of parliament with signs proclaiming, "Liberals love live music." Writer, producer, and comedian Brian Nankervis, one of the event's organizers, claimed, "That's one of the weirder sights I've seen, but we're in this together" (Donovan 2010b: 1). People held up signs and banners proclaiming, "Music does not cause violence" and "I vote and I Tote." Many children were present in the crowd, along with variously outfitted young people as well as middle-aged and (rather grey) older people. In other words, there was little to scare the horses.

By mid-April, the Tote reopened under new management and a number of live music venues had their licensing requirements changed to lessen their financial burdens (Donovan 2010d). In early May, former Small Business Commissioner Mark Brennan was named as the new Director of Liquor Licensing. Brennan was a lawyer who was part of the legal team that in the 1980s drew up the licensing laws that allowed Melbourne's licensed venues to remain open 24 hours if desired.[2] Maclellan was treated as a scapegoat and did not even bother reapplying for her position. The denouement was the signing of the final accord on October 8. One of the people who signed it was journalist Patrick Donovan, chief music critic of *The Age*, who was crucial in the campaign and who subsequently became CEO of a government-funded organization called Music Victoria, set up to act as a lobbying group for the live music scene.

---

2    It was a deliberate policy at the time to produce a night-time economy. See Zajdow (2011) for an account and analysis of this program.

# What Actually Happened?

The fight over the Tote illustrates that the state attempted to transform the moral panic over young people's drinking and violence in the central city into a bureaucratic regulation in order to take the heat and passion out of the issue. It failed, however. This was partly due to particular political circumstances in that the government was under pressure in those inner city seats that housed many of the small venues affected. The enforcement of the regulations also produced a community that may not have existed before and representatives who became the new moral entrepreneurs. These included journalists such as Donovan, the venue operators who had been minor players in the city's night-time economy previously, and previously unknown pressure groups called Save Live Australian Music (SLAM) and Fair Go for Live Music (FG4LM), which came into existence through social media. These new moral entrepreneurs in effect produced an informal media campaign, stressing themes that could be characterized as (1) denying the link between live music and violence by distancing live music from alcohol consumption, (2) drawing a link between the Melbourne live music scene and the community of inner city Melbourne, and (3) producing a politically aware community, thus threatening the state government just prior to a state election.

## Violence? What Violence?

The first and one of the major lines of argument presented by those involved in the campaign was to deny strenuously the link between the live music venues and violence. The licensees of the Tote were specific: violence was not a problem. They claimed that in the nine years they had run it, there had been no violence and that the local police supported them (Murfett 2010). It was deemed essential to reiterate that while it was important to deal with the problem of alcohol-related violence, live music venues did not contribute to it, and thus their inclusion as high-risk venues was unwarranted. Letters to the editors echoed this argument. For example, on January 16, one correspondent wrote in *The Age*, "The prevention of alcohol-fueled violence is a serious and important issue, but one that has nothing to do with the Tote Hotel," while another agreed, "These venues are simply not high risk. I have attended dozens of local and international gigs at the Tote over two decades and never once seen or experienced any violence" ("Knuckle-Headed Decisions" 2010: 6). To emphasize the safety of the venue, one journalist wrote of the peacefulness of the demonstration outside the venue when its closure was first announced. The venue was so safe and pacific that she could take her three-year-old child to the demonstration without fear:

> 'The police are our friends', said Milne (the licensee), to cheers from the crowd, the same 'high-risk' crowd including myself and my three-year-old son who duly dispersed as asked once the speeches

were over, saying hello and thanks to the police officers as we passed. (Roberts 2010: 9)

The correspondent further wrote that she considered herself a good parent who would never put her child in harm's way, so clearly the Tote was a safe and nonviolent place:

> Does the head of liquor licensing believe parents would take our children to afternoon shows in a 'high-risk' venue, especially after reading of other parents who have had to switch off their own child's life support, or nurse a permanently disabled child following violence at other inner-city venues? (Roberts 2010: 9)

Many inner city venues as well as car windows boasted stickers proclaiming, "Music does not cause violence," and, "Attack alcohol, not music." These proclamations did evince a certain historical amnesia related to the pub music scene in Australia since the 1970s. Only one article in this period pointed out the close relationship between live rock and roll in pubs and heavy drinking. When pubs were allowed to open after 6:00 P.M.. in the 1970s, many hotel licensees began offering live music to fill their often-large public bars: "Alcohol and rock music … it was a perfect match. The concept rapidly took off around the suburbs. Pub owners loved it. Pub gigs were cheap to stage, they attracted large numbers of patrons and alcohol sales were high" (Patterson 2010: 92).[3] This journalist (from the tabloid *Herald Sun*, not the broadsheet *The Age*) also pointed out that there were many contributing factors to the loss of music venues. He noted that rent increases, council noise restrictions and the introduction of poker machines were more important to the loss of live music outlets than the new license restrictions. He also noted the way that licensees often exploited young bands by paying them next to nothing: "And let's face it. Some live music venues are unfriendly and unclean. Some patrons have clearly had enough" (Patterson 2010: 92). But his was a lonely voice.

## We Are the Community

This campaign was a geographically limited one, in that its emphasis was the inner city ring of suburbs, particularly the inner northern suburbs of Melbourne. This could be characterized as bohemian but gentrifying. Many pubs had already been forced to stop presenting live amplified music because of noise complaints (as noted above), but this issue was ignored by the Tote campaigners. Instead, they emphasized the centrality of the music scene to these communities and the importance of the pubs and venues for the cultural life of Melbourne. Paul Kelly

---

3    Licensing laws in Victoria and New South Wales limited hotel bar opening hours to 6:00 P.M. during the 50 years between World War I and the late 1960s (Zajdow 2011).

(quoted in Fyfe 2010: 4), a well-known Australian musician, compared the venues to community art centers:

> They are the venues that people go to hear home-grown music. Places where people look out for each other, where musician and songwriters learn their craft, where ideas are exchanged. You might say they are community art centres. Melbourne's music scene has a worldwide reputation, as rich diverse and fertile.... Don't destroy what makes Melbourne unique.

Quincy McLean of SLAM commented, "It's the whole community's problem, not just music's." (Donovan 2010c: 8).

### The Government Caves In

The campaign was so sudden and ferocious that the government gave in almost immediately.[44] This was a long-term government (over ten years old) that was becoming increasingly unpopular and faced an election later in the year. Its inner Melbourne seats were particularly vulnerable to young, educated voters moving their allegiances to other left-wing and green parties. The journalists who took up the cause made this point time and again. From the first small demonstration outside the Tote itself, the shout of "I Tote, I vote" became a rallying cry. Two of *The Age*'s political journalists, Jill Stark and Natalie Craig (2010: 4), made the point in a January 24 piece: "The message to the government was simple 'ignore live music fans at your peril.'" In the *Herald Sun*, music writer Mikey Cahill (2010: 58) concluded an article describing the demonstration with the words, "The pressure must be maintained .... Remember: you Tote, you vote!"

# Concluding Remarks

Did this campaign against risk-based licensing fees amount to moral panic? It could be argued that it was disproportionate to the perceived danger posed by a pre-existing moral panic over violence and venues, a disproportionality apparent, for example, in the media circus that proclaimed the death of live music in

---

4    In October, a final agreement was signed between the state government and representatives of the live music industry. It included paragraphs that stated, "live music makes a significant contribution to the cultural well being of Victorians," "Live music does not cause violence," and most importantly, "The Government will amend the Liquor Control Reform Regulations 2009 to establish a dedicated cost-free procedure for live music venues" (*Agreement* 2010). This was a complete back down on the government's part.

Melbourne. If it was moral panic, the folk devils fought back using the same tools as the moral crusaders, employing new social media such as Facebook to drum up virtual support that turned into real-time support at the demonstration. They were able to convince agenda setters and moral entrepreneurs to involve themselves in the episode on their behalf, in the process becoming agenda setters and moral entrepreneurs themselves.

McRobbie and Thornton (1996) outline the methods that early dance music producers used to engineer a moral panic that paradoxically gave the breath of life to a new media phenomenon. The outrage they produced gave them the free advertising they needed to find a new audience. While there is no evidence suggesting that the leaders of the anti-fee campaign deliberately engineered the closing down of the Tote to give their efforts the momentum they needed, they certainly used the media well. The music journalists in the main newspapers supported the campaign, and one went on to a paid position in a government-funded advocacy group.

Whether moral panic or not, the anti-fee campaign undermined the government's effort to impose quiet regulation, that is, its move to "demoralize" regulation, and thus undercut any attempts at resistance by groups that might mobilize support in the form of moral panic (Tepper 2009). The Victorian state government tried to respond to a possible moral panic over alcohol-driven violence in the night-time economy, and avoid setting off a new moral panic over regulating the alcohol industry, by risk management and risk-based license fees. In this case, the folk devils of the initial moral panic (if that's what it was) fought back, remaking themselves as community-minded citizens, in effect placing themselves at the center of a city that considers itself the cultural capital of Australia, tolerant and inclusive.

# References

2010. Agreement Regarding Live Music Venues [Online]. Available at: http://www.slamrally.org/wp-content/uploads/2010/10/Live_Music_Agreement_5-10-1.pdf [accessed: November 22, 2010].

2009. Alcohol-Related Harm and the Operation of Licensed Premises [Online]. The Allen Consulting Group. Available at: http://www.allenconsult.com.au/publications/download.php?id=340&type=pdf&file=1 [accessed: October 13, 2011].

Borsay, P. 2010. Binge Drinking and Moral Panics: Historical Parallels? *History and Policy* [Online]. Available at: http://www.historyandpolicy.org/papers/policy-paper-62.html [accessed: February 16, 2010].

Cahill, M. 2010. Strike accord. *Herald Sun*, February 25, 58.

Cohen, S. 2002 (1972, 1980). *Folk Devils and Moral Panics: The Creation of Mods and Rockers*. 3rd Edition. London: Routledge.

Davoren, S. 2010. Who cleans up after the boozers go home? *The Age*, January 25, 7.

Donovan, P. 2010a. Rule change for the Tote. *The Age*, January 22, 4.

Donovan, P. 2010b. Marching to the top because they want their rock 'n' roll. *The Age*, February 24, 1.

Donovan, P. 2010c. Tote gets a lifeline. *The Age*, April 16, 8.

Dotter, D. 2004. *Creating Deviance: An Interactionist Approach*. Walnut Creek: Altamira Press.

Fyfe, M. 2010. Icons lead in chorus in battle for live music. *The Age*, February 14, 4.

Garland, D. 2008. On the concept of moral panic. *Culture, Media, Society*, 4(1) 9–30.

Hadfield, P. 2006. *Bar Wars: Contesting the Night in Contemporary British Cities*. Oxford: Oxford University Press.

Hawthorne, M. 2010. Big Day Out festival signs big liquor sponsor. *The Age* [Online], January 21. Available at: http://www.theage.com.au/national/big-day-out-festival-signs-big-liquor-sponsor-20100120-mls1.html [accessed: October 13, 2011].

Hobbs, D., Hadfield, P., Lister, S., and Winlow, S. 2003. Bouncers: Violence and Governance in the Night-time Economy. *Clarendon Studies in Criminology*. Oxford: Oxford University Press.

Houston, C. 2008. Brumby warned of lock out risk. *The Age*, July 22, 7.

Houston, C., Johnston, C., and Austin, P. 2008. This is Melbourne at night. *The Age*, February 23, 1.

Jones, C., Kypri, K., Moffatt, S., Borzycki, C., and Price, B. 2009. *The Impact of Restricted Availability on Alcohol-Related Violence in Newcastle, NSW*. Sydney: NSW Bureau of Crime Statistics and Research.

2010. Knuckle-headed decisions. *The Age*, January 16, 6.

2009. Liquor Control Reform Regulations: Regulatory Impact Statement [Online] Department of Justice. Available at: http://www.justice.vic.gov.au/wps/wcm/connect/DOJ+Internet/Home/Alcohol/About+Liquor+Licensing/JUSTICE+-+Alcohol+-+Regulatory+Impact+Statement+-+Liquor+Control+Reform+Regulations+%28PDF%29 [accessed: September 15, 2009].

2010. Liquor crackdown hits jarring note. *The Age*, January 21, 16.

Massey, J. 2007. Young people and the "right" to the city. *The International Journal of Diversity in Organisations, Communities and Nations*, 7(3), 241–51.

McRobbie, A. and Thornton, S. L. 1995. Rethinking 'moral panic' for multi-mediated social worlds. *British Journal of Sociology*, 46(4), 559–74.

Mihelakos, M. 2010. Bands and booze: sticky carpet. *The Age*, September 24, 8.

Moore, M. 2008. Closing time: courts uphold hotel decision. *Sydney Morning Herald*, March 21, 4.

Murfett, A. 2010. Time called on Tote in blow to Melbourne's music scene. *The Age*, January 15, 3.

Patterson, B. 2010. Silence as pubs shut doors. Sunday Herald Sun, January 24, 92.

Priest, A. 2010. Musos bail up Brumby. *Lilydale and Yarra Valley Leader*, February 15, 5.

Roberts, J. 2010. The Tote: a case of liquor licensing downing one too many. *The Age*, January 19, 9.

Rood, D. 2007. Tough laws aim at CBD violence: nightclubs face on-the-spot closure. *The Age*, August 31, 5.

Schur, E. M. 1980. *The Politics of Deviance: Stigma Contests and the Uses of Power*. Englewood Cliffs: Prentice-Hall.

2008. *The 7.30 Report*. Australian Broadcasting Corporation, March 10.

Stark, J. and Craig, N. 2010. Spring Street tap dances, fearing the Tote could rock the vote. *The Age*, January 24, 4.

Tepper, S. J. 2009. Stop the beat: quiet regulation and cultural conflict. *Sociological Forum*, 24(2), 276–306.

Yeomans, H. 2009. Revisiting a moral panic: ascetic Protestantism, attitudes to alcohol and the implementation of the Licensing Act 2003. *Sociological Research Online* [Online], 14(2). Available at: http://www.socresonline.org.uk/14/2/6.html [accessed: October 13, 2011].

Zajdow, G. 2006. The Narrative of Evaluations. *Contemporary Drug Problems*, 33(3), 399–426.

Zajdow, G. 2008. Moral panics: the old and the new. *Deviant Behavior*, 29(7), 640–64.

Zajdow, G. 2011. Producing the market for alcohol: the Victorian example. *Journal of Australian Studies*, 35(1), 83–98.

# Is This One It? Viral Moral Panics

## Sheldon Ungar

As infectious diseases retreated in the first half of the twentieth century because of a combination of medical and socio-economic factors, the US Surgeon General informed Congress in 1969 that it was conceivable to "close the book on infectious disease" (Garrett 1994). Perhaps the gods were riled by such hubris, as these diseases have resurfaced and become a major source of social anxiety. While penicillin seemed to provide a magical jab, new forms of resistant gonorrhea, followed by herpes and then AIDS revived the threat of sexually transmitted diseases. Tuberculosis made a comeback in a multi-drug resistant form and other bacteria, such as MRSA, also evolved in ways that rendered them exceedingly difficult to treat. Swine flu Fort Dix, Ebola, mad cow or CJD, West Nile, SARS, avian flu, and swine flu *redux* or 2009 H1N1 have all engendered dire warnings of runaway outbreaks and prompted concerted societal efforts to contain them.

While prediction (especially of the future) is always difficult, it is evident that none of the above-mentioned apocalyptic forecasts materialized. These recurring exaggerations seem to fit, at least with hindsight, the disproportionality criterion central to moral panics (Goode and Ben-Yehuda 2009). Applying the concept of moral panic, this chapter seeks to retrodict the abiding tendency to treat every new and emerging viral outbreak other than the seasonal flu as if it portended an all-but-unprecedented catastrophe. Since volatile discourses have become routine reactions to viral upsurges, it aims to show that there are converging and reinforcing conditions and processes that promote sensational claims making. The deep structure of fear generation is linked to enhanced contagion monitoring and associated technological innovations that render organized responses feasible and thereby create a moral incumbency on political and medical authorities—the "guardians of public safety"—to respond in a timely way.

Whereas the sensational claims made by these guardians of public safety have generally provoked corresponding reactions by the media and local health providers, there are signs of attenuated effects in the public realm. Compared to conventional moral panics, which are often localized epiphenomena with impacts more symbolic than real, viral moral panics typically involve efforts to use morality to regulate public behaviors. Principled obligations include calls to stay at home when symptomatic, to conform to applicable quarantine regulations, and to be vaccinated. As the target of widespread attention, fears, and social engineering, viral moral panics also tend to become constituents of the collective memory and hence fabled resources with metaphorical import. Ebola, for example, has become *the* touchstone of terrifying and deadly exotic diseases. Swine flu Fort Dix is recalled as a fiasco, with an ill-fated vaccination program for an epidemic that never happened. Wild predictions about West Nile, SARS, avian flu, and the recent outbreak of swine flu have also accumulated in collective memory, and the reception of the last in Toronto revealed elements of distrust and resistance that seemingly recall this record of overblown scares. As events unfolded, guardians of public safety lost control over the moral panic they fomented and were confronted by a range of disagreements that converged in opposition to the vaccine.

## Moral Panic in Flux

Moral panic is approaching its fortieth anniversary, but that has done nothing to slow down its development. Indeed, we are witnessing a variety of efforts to redefine and refocus the concept. These can be seen in the publication of a Special Issue of the *British Journal of Criminology* (2009), as well as the substantially revised second edition of the well-known book by Erich Goode and Nachman Ben-Yehuda (2009). In its totality, this work pries open virtually every aspect of the concept, from its definition to whether it retains any value. Sociologist Sean P. Hier (2008), for example, seeks to subsume moral panic in a broader conception of the moralization of everyday life. Chas Critcher (2009) finds the idea of moral regulation problematic, concluding that it obscures the very idea of moral panic. Taking a heretical position, sociologist Stuart Waiton proffers "a new framework of *amoral panics*" (2008: 104, emphasis in original). At the same time, Goode and Ben-Yehuda (2009) update their fairly conventional model and mount a spirited defense against revisionists. All this activity can be seen as either a sign of renewal or an indication that the concept has lost its footing.

This chapter does not address these conceptual developments directly but rather examines the use and value of moral panic in understanding societal reactions to viral outbreaks. Work on moral panic has largely developed around deviance and youth (for example, Krinsky 2008). In this context, the focus has been on disproportionality. Whether we move from Stanley Cohen's (2002) first detailed description of the concept in 1972 through his subsequent statements, review the bulk of the empirical research, or examine the media use of the concept to confront politicians for trying to "incite" panics (McRobbie and Thornton 1995), the common element is a perception that expressed fears and hostilities are out of proportion to the actual threat. Such exaggeration encapsulates the political agenda motivating this research domain: specifically, the power of moral entrepreneurs to exercise social control by amplifying deviance and orchestrating social reactions. Disproportionality is also a *leitmotif* among social constructionists. They are keen on showing that social reactions are largely determined by the activities of claims makers rather than the objective standing of the condition (Ungar 1998a). An ideal constructionist research paper reveals that a condition is improving even as claims makers successful foment a moral panic about it.

Critics of disproportionality focus on the problem of measuring and specifying the seriousness of the objective threat (Critcher 2009, Hier 2008). Thus, Hier (2008: 178) observes that we are "short of some reliable indication of what constitutes a realistic level of concern, anxiety, or alarm." He further notes that researchers commonly belittle reactions to the putative threat, viewing them as "irrational" (Hier 2008: 180). Goode and Ben-Yehuda (2009: 40–41) acknowledge that determining and assessing the objective dimension is often a tricky proposition. They go to great lengths to salvage disproportionality, observing, "We must be cautious, modest, and tentative about making statements concerning what is real and true about events in the social world." To be fairly confident that some statements are more likely to be true than others, they list "inventions," "fabrications" and "irrationalities" as indicators of disproportionality (Goode and Ben-Yehuda 2009: 40–41). Hier (2008: 174) substitutes instead the idea of the "volatility of moralizations," suggesting that moral panic discourse tends to be "sensational, inflammatory and spectacular." These criteria are presumably less problematic to identify than exaggerations of a threat that goes well beyond what any "realistic appraisal" of the "objective condition" could uphold.

These alternative formulations are thrown into relief when applied to infectious diseases. Goode and Ben-Yehuda (2009: 42) make some rather curious assertions in this regard:

> There are some supposedly threatening, dangerous or risky conditions which qualify according to the criterion of disproportion but lack the 'folk devil' element: nuclear energy, swine flu, bird flu, e coli, global warming, the shrinking ozone layer, diseases of every description, accidents, the 'military industrial complex,' and so on.

Their contention that the flu and other diseases lack 'folk devils' or the element of hostility is baffling. AIDS was initially termed a "gay plague" and the association between germs and the "stranger" (Jews, immigrants) is both ancient and still potent, as seen in the reaction to SARS in Toronto (Keil and Harris 2008).

But their assertion that diseases of every description qualify according to the criterion of disproportionality is even more puzzling. In viral outbreaks, scientists constantly declare and emphasize that it is impossible to predict how a particular virus will mutate and hence the future course or virulence of an outbreak (Mehta 2009). The media duly reiterate the impossibility of determining the nature of the objective threat. So, unless Goode and Ben Yehuda know things that virologists do not know, it is clear that claims about disproportionality cannot be warranted in the context of such roulette dynamics. It is only *after* the outbreak has subsided that such claims can be *somewhat* justified. The qualification stems from the possibility that, to take one example, the bird flu could reappear, again with an unpredictable virulence.

Without prior knowledge about how an outbreak will evolve, the question of how to characterize the threat of a new or emerging virus is central, unavoidable and invariably problematic. Yet, for each of the recent outbreaks listed in the introduction to this chapter, the most prominent and powerful guardians of public safety—The World Health Organization (WHO), the US Centers for Disease Control, and other national health and regulatory authorities, as well as health ministers and associated government officials—made *extremely* alarming claims, especially during the early stages of each viral threat (Ungar 2008). These were, in Hier's terms, volatile discourses that managed to be sensational, spectacular, and inflammatory. This repeated pattern of volatile claims making can hardly be regarded as indiscriminate slipups. Rather, the next section of this chapter draws on a range of factors and processes to retrodict what can be regarded as the expectable use of moral panic in the public staging of viral outbreaks. Building on this, the subsequent section suggests that viral moral panics are neither discrete nor vanishing events. Rather, the accumulation of volatile claims and moralizations has the unintended effect of generating mistrust and reactance, as the "errors" accumulate and engender a sense of *déjà vu*.

## The Embeddedness of Volatile Viral Claims

It is abundantly clear that new viral outbreaks in the past few decades have been accompanied by sensational and spectacular claims that typically give rise to concerted personal and social measures to protect against the purported threat. Consider a few examples. In the case of swine flu Fort Dix, F. David Mathews (quoted in Di Justo 2009), the US Secretary of Health, Education, and Welfare, declared, "There is evidence there will be a major flu epidemic this coming fall. The indication is that we will see a return of the 1918 flu virus that is the most virulent form of the flu. In 1918 a half million Americans died. The projections are that this virus will kill one million Americans in 1976." The fear was sufficient to inaugurate a national vaccination program, with immunizations starting about six months after the virus was discovered. While this flu caused one death and then mysteriously disappeared, the vaccine came to be associated with Guillain-Barré syndrome. About 500 people were affected, and more than 30 died, leading to the cancellation of the program. This vaccination fiasco has become a memorable resource in subsequent viral discourses.

Ebola Zaire was designated a "disease that could threaten the world" and the "symbol of the biological apocalypse" (Ungar 1998b: 46). With exquisite timing, the Ebola outbreak was announced by the WHO only a few weeks after the release of the hit movie, *Outbreak*. A frenzy of international media coverage from the *hot zone* created the image of a monster virus on a rampage. This all dissipated quickly as the outbreak remained localized and was contained fairly quickly. The metaphor persists.

West Nile disease has consumed considerable media attention, extending from reportage of cases and surveillance of dead birds, to dire warnings and attendant advice on how to avoid mosquito bites. Interest has waned as the number of annual cases has fallen significantly, indicating that relatively few people actually react to the virus.

SARS has been pointedly examined as a health scare, with the WHO predicting up to one hundred million deaths (see, for example, Hooker 2008). The recent swine flu is discussed in the next section. These two bracket the most extraordinary viral moral panic: avian flu. Perhaps the details are getting fuzzy with the passage of time, so it is worth recalling that a well-regarded journal like the *New Scientist*, echoing various medical authorities, asserted that a mutated avian virus could cause *billions* of deaths (Ungar 2008). Such numbers are beyond history. Yet, they were further sensationalized by assertions that the spread of bird flu among humans was all but certain; the question was no longer *if*, but *when*. Dr. David Nabarro (quoted in Ungar 2008: 11), the senior United Nations coordinator for human and avian flu, warned, "It is like a combination of global warming and HIV AIDS."

The alarmed and volatile discourses that follow the discovery of each of the aforementioned viral outbreaks cannot be dismissed as random errors. Presumably, there is some logic to these experts getting it so wrong so regularly. The ensuing analysis aims to pry open the deep structure of fear generation that renders such all-but-apocalyptic claims making about novel viral outbreaks routine and expectable. This deep structure derives from a number of converging and reinforcing conditions and processes. At the bottom-most level, enhanced contagion monitoring has been allied to technological innovations and new theoretical insights that afford a more revealing picture of viral mutations and their attendant risks. Superimposed on these basal developments are altered expectations about the efficacy of public health responses. As new technologies and understandings have developed, there is a greater incumbency on guardians of public safety to plan and prepare for fresh outbreaks. Failure to respond in an adequate and timely way is apt to create a furore over issues related to accountability.

Just as scientists studying the physical world use webs of sensors to take repeated real-time measurements of numerous variables of interest (Broad 2005), disease monitoring teams and networks are constantly seeking to spot new outbreaks or "spores" at their earliest recognizable stages. This is relatively new, and includes organizations like Promed and Global Viral Forecasting Initiative. Promed, for example, depending as it does on worldwide informants with access to computers and the Internet, has been tracking global disease occurrences online since 1994. These efforts can be seen as first order monitoring, "listening posts" for "viral chatter" that serve to unearth localized outbreaks that might otherwise go unnoticed.[11] A second order of monitoring is conducted by national and international disease prevention and control centers that seek to cull those outbreaks that portend novel or large-scale risks. At a third level, mass media

---

1    Jones et al. (2008) find a significant increase in the incidence of infectious diseases between 1940 and 2004, at least part of which was due to better viral surveillance.

outlets selectively disseminate information about worrying developments that threaten to spread to their areas of reporting or herald a global import.

It must be supposed that this enhanced disease-monitoring spawns a heightened sense of a world at risk. Regular scanning of Promed and the websites of second-order disease control centers (for example, the WHO) is instructive *and* startling. There is a veritable plethora of viruses knocking at the gates. Most of these emerge in less developed countries, where it is easier to find a backdoor. If such disease occurrences are generally unknown, on occasion they do get publicized by public medical authorities and the media. Thus, Ebola would hardly have been recognized without teams of Western medical experts and the media descending on Zaire. This outbreak was *news*. However, the disease was not new and would probably have been contained by local, indigenous actions, as apparently happened in the past (Ungar 1998b: 48). Coming at the end of World War I, the 1918 Spanish flu has been termed the "forgotten pandemic" because it quickly faded from public memory. It was not revived as the most fearsome of all pandemics until the late 1990s, when isolated cases of the spread of bird flu to humans were detected (Crosby 2003). Through censorship, China was able effectively to hide the advent of SARS, at least until it spread to neighboring countries.

When coupled with new technologies, monitoring that exposes viruses that are obscure or percolating at the spore stage has a further essential aspect, specifically, the capacity to conduct full genetic sequencing of microorganisms and hence rapidly to identify their genetic phylogeny (or genealogy) and track subsequent mutations. While the first bacterial genome was sequenced in 1977, it was in the 2000s that leading laboratories realized the practice termed "virtuosic" and "ultra-deep" sequencing (Gould 2007). Research reveals that genetic mutations leading to differences in just a single amino-acid component of a protein can make a virus unrecognizable by the immune system, even if the victim was previously immune. This recently revealed capacity of viruses to skirt the immune system renders them far more volatile and fearsome than previously thought. Tracking mutations that often occur at a rapid rate feeds into the fear-generating models that virologists and associated experts draw upon.

To pick up on the last point, flu specialists seem to occupy a world of simmering anxieties, one never far from boiling over. Apprehension can be considered an occupational hazard, both in theoretical and practical ways. The constant surveillance and analysis of viral spores, with the occasional all-nighter central to the disease-hunter archetype, are buttressed by, and simultaneously give credence to, the "mutation-contagion" interpretative package prevalent in the field (Ungar 1998b), a package that entails a rhetoric of endangerment. The complex of images and metaphors it covers include the following: "microbes are on a rampage," "microbes are cleverer than us," they "know no boundaries," and we are just "waiting for the next plague" (Ungar 1998b: 43–5). Mutation-contagion is partially based on the unintended creation of new viral pathways connecting humanity together, as roads and the like have been cut into rain forests and other previously secluded environments. At the same time, mutation-contagion is consistent with a radical shift in evolutionary theory over the last few decades. Specifically, gradualism in evolution has been displaced to a great extent by a model of explosive change (Gould 2007). There can be few assurances when even relatively benign viruses that have accommodated to their hosts can suddenly transmute through a process of antigenic shift and become lethal. For virologists at least, the tiny objects of their studies represent the single biggest threat to our continued dominance on the planet.

Mutation-contagion is more than a metaphor in this context. Virologists, both in recognizing the types of threats that they seek to contain and in selling these to everyone else, use the 1918 Spanish flu as their archetype. That pandemic, which is believed to have come in two waves, killed quickly (often in less than 24 hours) and efficiently, with estimates ranging from 50 to 100 million dead in one year. Unlike the seasonal flu, it targeted young adults. Samples of this influenza were recovered in 1998 from a victim buried in Alaskan permafrost. The virus was sequenced in 2005 (Brown 2005). It has been proposed that its origin was an avian flu. Sequencing of the recent swine flu, that is, H1N1, indicates that it is a descendant or subtype of the 1918 Spanish flu. Viruses are not hoarders or isolates, but efficiently exchange and share bits of DNA, allowing for surprises.

If our perceived vulnerability to a runaway pandemic is stoked by constant disease surveillance coupled with revealing new technologies and theoretical understandings, the encampment with the 1918 Spanish flu exploits a worst-case scenario that is certainly sensational, inflammatory and spectacular. We may be just "waiting for" novel outbreaks, but unpredictability hardly guarantees that it will be plague-like in its impacts or that we are "due" for the big one. There is considerable backward blindness in evaluating past outbreaks. However, from 1700 onwards (and probably from 1500), for which assorted records and proxies are available, it is clear that the Spanish flu is an extreme outlier, with no earlier or subsequent pandemic being nearly as lethal (Jones et al. 2008). The twentieth century witnessed two other pandemics: the 1957–58 Asian flu, with an estimated 1.5 to 2 million deaths, and the 1968–69 Hong Kong flu, with an estimated 1 million deaths. The temporal proximity of these two pandemics seemingly violates the twice a century/every 50 years rule of thumb common in pandemic claims making.

All these developments have a practical side. In the discovery of a novel (read, unpredictable) viral outbreak, medical and political officials are likely to feel that they are acting "under the gun" and do not want to be caught holding the "hot potato" should it turn out to be particularly lethal. The cost of over-reacting, of using positions of oversight to stoke moral panic, is a seemingly less costly option for guardians of public safety than to be rendered the targets of moral outrage for vacillating and not doing enough to prepare for the threat. Uncertainty and unpredictability appear to provide a workable justification for sensationalizing the threat; but they hardly justify inaction should events spiral out of control. In other words, after-the-fact recriminations are more likely to set off a witch-hunt than precautionary actions. The failure to act, whether due to disregard or incompetence, readily shades into a sense of moral and criminal negligence, especially when the consequences are grave. In Walkerton, Ontario, the failure of town authorities to treat and test drinking water adequately, coupled with their subsequent failure to advise people about E. coli contamination, resulted in at least ten deaths and over 2,000 ill (Ungar 2001). The ensuing hunt for "folk devils" stalked water managers, town officials, and even the Ministry of the Environment, which terminated their water testing in favor of privatization. These failures, in light of the ensuing catastrophe, were seen as transcending incompetence and entailing reckless and immoral neglect, and indeed turpitude.

Responding, if it is to entail more than issuing dire warnings, depends on having the capacity to act in a timely and efficacious way. The medical developments outlined above have improved treatment options. In the 1968 pandemic, vaccine became available in limited amounts one month after the outbreaks peaked in the United States. Better monitoring and sequencing resulted in the availability of vaccine before the second wave of 2009 H1N1 was expected to hit.[22]In contrast to the medical helplessness during the 1918 outbreak, doctors now have some methods to treat the infected. Full genetic sequencing of viruses abetted the development of antiviral drugs, most notably Tamiflu, which has been available since 1999 (Watson 2006). 2009 H1N1 deaths were mostly due to respiratory failure, including secondary bacterial infections (pneumonia), which can lead to a systemic inflammatory response (*2009 H1N1* 2010). Ventilators and, in the last resort, cardiac bypass machines have been useful in treating many (though not all) victims.

Though these new technologies have improved medical treatment, their efficacy is limited by shortages, especially in large outbreaks, when medical systems can be overwhelmed. As a result of the medical successes that led to the misplaced hubris of the US Surgeon General in 1969, there were severe cutbacks to the public health systems in most advanced nations. Hence, it is not surprising that from the alarmed reaction to Ebola Zaire through the cascading scares engendered by the avian flu, a lack of preparedness has been stressed by health officials and others. And while, as elaborated later in this chapter, there can be some cynicism regarding efforts by medical officials to command greater resources, it is also the case that the relatively small outbreak of SARS brought the health system in Toronto to the point of breakdown (Hooker 2008).

The extended chain connecting mysterious viral spores to an easily infected humanity — intrusions into hitherto isolated viral reservoirs, enhanced monitoring, rapid genetic sequencing, a mutation-contagion interpretative package linking back to the Spanish flu, prospective vaccines that make immediate decisions imperative, limited treatments in short supply, and deficient public health systems — constitutes the deep structure of fear generation. Not only have an astonishing array of viruses been unearthed, but there is also an uneasy realization of just how unpredictable they are as they traverse evermore convenient pathways of infection. The medical arsenal for countering such seemingly dangerous developments is limited, and virologists are compelled to operate under acute time constraints. Intensive public health preparations and responses are costly and often intrusive, and there

---

2    The production of vaccine was the main holdup in the context of these other innovations. Vaccine is still grown in eggs, and accelerating the production process may depend on learning to assemble molecules through synthetic biology.

is a pressing need to surmount political and public ignorance and indifference, especially when threats do not have the immediacy of a hot crisis.[33] Given such chains of contingency, it is hardly surprising that guardians of public safety rev up the doomsday machine when novel outbreaks with possibly lethal impacts are discovered. Apocalyptic claims not only command considerable public attention, but also facilitate medical and other institutional preparations that in turn provide a degree of reassurance to offset the fearful claims.

## Responses to 2009 H1N1: Complications Set In

2009 H1N1, following soon after SARS and the bird flu, was the third major viral scare of the twenty-first century. As with its predecessors, its alarmed discovery in March and April 2009 was attended by the expected use of sensational claims and occurrences. The H1N1 virus emerged in Mexico, where it spread rapidly and caused a number of deaths, especially among the young. Schools and universities were closed, and public events such as soccer matches cancelled. The virus was quickly deemed "non-stoppable" by the WHO, which warned of up to two billion cases worldwide and from two to ten million deaths (Hellerman 2009). By June, the WHO classified it as a phase 6 outbreak, or pandemic. While 2009 H1N1 was termed the first pandemic of the twentieth century (indeed, the first since 1958), the distinction between an epidemic and a pandemic was often blurred in public discourse. The latter has to do with how widely a virus has spread, not how dangerous it is. However, pandemic was all too often associated with a deadly disease. Since it is impossible even to begin to examine worldwide coverage of a pandemic, the focus here is on Toronto, both because the author resides there and the fact that Toronto was the only city outside South Asia to have had a SARS outbreak. The ensuing discussion is derived from two sources: a daily Google alert for "swine flu" and coverage in the four Toronto newspapers. Perusal of these sources was commenced in June just prior to the pandemic announcement.

The outbreak slowed during the summer in North America but still occasioned a range of volatile claims. While the evidence to this point suggested that 2009 H1N1 was actually milder than the seasonal flu, the threat of a second and far more virulent wave in the coming winter was sounded so frequently that it almost became a mantra. In August, there were warnings about a severe new strain that directly attacked the lungs of otherwise healthy young people. This was often associated with the lung infections that are believed to have rendered the 1918 pandemic so

---

3    As long as the bird flu remained localized in South Asia, dire warnings about this very deadly virus had little impact in Europe (Ungar 2008). National planning, which was often more show than reality, did not begin until the virus was found to have migrated to places like Turkey. The United States, with its greater geographic buffer, was slower to plan than Europe. People are, of course, accustomed to the seasonal flu, and it takes some effort to pierce their apathy.

lethal. It was further observed that 2009 H1N1 spreads at alarming rates, much faster than most viruses (Jameson 2009). Hence, the start of the school year provided ideal conditions for contagion, exacerbated by the concern that there would not be sufficient respirators for those developing severe lung infections. Effectively, a race for life and death was being fashioned, with a dangerous virus piggybacking on the cold pitted against all-out efforts to produce a life-saving vaccine.

Viral moral panics have been exceptional in mobilizing public responses. Unrelenting publicity about the apocalyptic potential of the bird flu not only lead to the wholesale slaughter of countless millions of fowl, but compelled European governments to make and publicize plans for dealing with a looming outbreak. Planning included stockpiling antiviral drugs, making preparations for the production of a vaccine, developing rapid reaction plans for hospitals, arranging for alternative treatment facilities (even if only tents), and preparing to alter social patterns, from the closing of schools to banning public events, hospital visits and so on (Ungar 2008). The sensational claims made about 2009 H1N1 also triggered a number of costly and intrusive plans and programs. The most significant of these was the swift production of a vaccine, coupled with administrative plans to inoculate as much of the population as possible. So grave was the looming threat of a second wave that governments, businesses, and schools and universities were encouraged to set up "task forces" and "epidemic action plans" to prepare for the worst. In Toronto, there was broad compliance with planning requests, and city residents were inundated with warnings and information. Hand sanitizer pumps seemed to pop up everywhere. Universities made contingency plans to continue courses online and waived requirements for doctors' notes for exams missed due to illness (University of Toronto 2009). Plans were also made to create "isolation wards" in student residences, and doorknobs and similar surfaces were wiped down as often as every 45 minutes.

While the WHO's fearful perspective prevailed through summer and the start of the school year, by sometime between mid-October and early November, it became apparent, at least in public discourse, that the second wave was relatively mild. This transition in perceptions is not abrupt, but extends over several weeks in a zigzag pattern. As a whirlwind of overlapping and compressed events branch off in disparate directions, authorities lose control of the problem. First the flu itself, followed by the vaccine, and then the role and interests of the leading guardians of public safety become sites of contestation.

The start of the school year did bring a significant increase in the number of reported cases, but these were generally mild. Medical authorities kept warning that the number of hospitalizations remained high, that potentially dangerous mutations were found in several countries (for example, Ukraine), and that resistance to Tamiflu was occurring (Jameson 2009). But these remained distant and abstract threats. The events that counted were mainly local. Thus, in Toronto, the October 27 death of a teen without any pre-existing medical conditions resurrected the fear, as parents worried about how to protect their children (Vallis 2009). Intense coverage that seemed to amount to a public memorial for the young victim continued for more than a week. People were once again wary, but in the absence of additional deaths anxieties soon dissipated. In this regard, evidence indicates that the public wants an absolute yes/no answer to questions about risk (Ali 1999). Repeated exposure to seasonal flues is an unavoidable part of everyone's experience, and 2009 H1N1 was tamed as it came to be regarded as akin to a seasonal flu.

As fear of 2009 H1N1 began to subside, space opened up in the public realm for disparate voices. Dissident scientists found a number of reasons for challenging the WHO scare scenario, including the generally mild nature of 2009 H1N1, the mild second wave observed in the Australian winter, and the prospect, now given more media attention, that a second wave can be less threatening as many people develop immunity in the first wave. The head of the CDC had questioned the more extreme predictions about 2009 H1N1 in late August, though he was largely ignored (Schapiro 2009). But by early November these isolated rebuttals had become commonplace. In a striking inversion, this ostensibly dangerous outbreak is now broadly perceived as less threatening than the seasonal flu. Over the next few weeks, the pandemic is memorably dubbed a "dud" and sometimes called a "fake" (Jordans 2010).

Considerable attention and hope was initially invested in the impending vaccine. It was estimated that inoculating 70 percent of the population would stop the outbreak. Vaccine became available toward the end of October in Toronto. At the outset, it was reserved for those deemed most at risk, including children and pregnant women. In terms of timing, the vaccine comes on stream as the transition in the public perception of the danger of H1N1 is getting underway. Hence, the initial demand is high (most understandably for those deemed high risk) and remains high for several weeks as vaccinations are being made available to everyone. Then a series of difficulties attend the vaccination program. By the fourth week of the program, there are acute shortages of vaccine and line-ups are cut off (CTV.ca News Staff 2009). The sense of bungling officials became a staple of news coverage, and was made worse by the confusion created by sudden shifts in vaccine requirements. Just as shortages became an issue, officials, citing the WHO, suggested that one dose was sufficient for children less than ten years old. Health Canada originally stipulated that children receive two shots, 21 days apart.

The sense that officials were unprepared and disorganized was perhaps excusable given the unprecedented nature of the vaccine program (McComas 2004). But subsequent errors, which overlapped with shortages, entailed what were perceived to be inexcusable moral oversights. Hockey players, members of hospital boards (not frontline health workers), and selected others were able to jump queues and get vaccines now in short supply. There were numerous reports in Toronto of the "privileged few" buying their way to the front of the line. This set off a storm of protests, with the advantaged mounting various justifications for not having to wait (Valpy 2009). Political and medical authorities, including the head of the vaccination program, asserted that everybody should wait their turn. But this was rather disingenuous, as politicians frequently jumped to the head of the line, as well. Significantly, objections to this preferential treatment seemed to be predominately framed around fairness, rather than who might live or die.

As fear of H1N1 continued to subside, fear of the vaccine came to the fore. Shortages of vaccine were abruptly replaced by shortages of customers. That people opined with their feet is clearly seen in the closure of a number of clinics in Toronto and the absence of waiting times in others. Opposition, which migrated onto the Internet and talk radio, focused on claims that the vaccine was not safe, that it had been produced too quickly and without sufficient testing (Mustafa 2009). Recalling the swine flu vaccine fiasco of 1976 and drawing on such disparate phenomena as the belief that the MMR vaccine is responsible for autism, up to 40 percent of polled Americans said they would not get the vaccine for their children. Far more reported that they would not themselves be vaccinated (McNeil 2010). With the Internet functioning as an echo chamber, fear of an unsafe vaccine merged with sundry mythologies about vaccines and the fear of both big government and big business (see Griffin et al. 2008). Both Glenn Beck and Rush Limbaugh questioned the Obama administration's recommendation that Americans get vaccinated. Limbaugh objected to the "pig flu vaccine" and suggested people would be healthier if they did the opposite of what the government advised (Maugh 2009). Latent antagonisms and anxieties could now be directed at officials who had overblown the threat of 2009 H1N1.

The gap between the public demise of the pandemic and the concerns of leading medical authorities is particularly visible in the New Year. Michael Osterholm, director of the Center for Infectious Disease Research and Policy at the University of Minnesota, said he "was not surprised" by how few received shots: "But that could all change overnight if we get a third wave in late February—and we still could," he added. "That would make this half-time data, not end-of-the-game data" (Bowron 2010). By this point, however, scientific credibility about the issue had been forfeited and the WHO and other medical actors were starting to be cast as "folk devils" who were trying to create panic in order to morally regulate public behavior for their own ends. Harking back continually to the speciously apocalyptic claims made about the bird flu and the medical preparations that followed, the doubling of these errors with 2009 H1N1 led to charges that scientists had inappropriate links with drug companies. Generating fear was seen as a way of generating massive orders for vaccines and antiviral drugs. Besides the financial motivations, health authorities were also maligned for perceived empire building, for trying to command more resources and getting more decision-making powers. The WHO authorities were accused of seeking to impose their own vision of global social justice by efforts to transfer resources from the rich to the poor. Such was the new reality that it became incumbent on the WHO and associated bodies to defend the notion that the pandemic was "real" (Jordans 2010).

## Conclusion

After asserting that "a whole industry is waiting for a pandemic," a European epidemiologist contended that the WHO, public health officials, virologists, and pharmaceutical companies "built this machine around the impending pandemic. And there's a lot of money involved, and influence, and careers, and entire institutions! And all it took was one of these influenza viruses to mutate to start the machine grinding" ("Interview" 2009). In contrast to the elements of conspiracy intimated in this statement, this paper aimed to uncover the deep structure of fear generation. Volatile viral moral panics are traced back to a chain of developments connecting intrusions into previously secluded viral reservoirs, enhanced surveillance, rapid genetic sequencing, a mutation-contagion interpretative package, prospective vaccines that compel rapid decisions, limited treatments in short supply, and deficient public health systems. The guardians of public safety who are linked up to this chain inhabit an outlier's world of fearsome possibilities. The latter give rise to moral and practical imperatives to react, and guardians are wont to employ claims that are sensational, inflammatory and spectacular as a way of mobilizing concerted social responses. Of course, it is only after the fact that their assertions can be deemed to have been disproportionate. Still, we have suggested that they may be (unintentionally) stoking a worst-case model by relying so heavily on the atypical 1918 pandemic.

Social responses to viral moral panic claims making activities reveal that the latter do tap into and stoke genuine public concerns. None of the major outbreaks sensationalized by virologists were greeted with complacency. Indeed, they generated concerted social responses. Perhaps viral claims making has been too successful, for it became apparent in Toronto that significant costs are associated with outbreaks that do not occur or are far less lethal than predicted. From SARS through the bird flu and then 2009 H1N1, the frightful outcomes predicted by virologists went unrealized. While virologists conclude that we have been lucky in dodging the worst of it, public discourse focuses on their errors and the associated tendency to blow risks out of proportion. What are ostensibly prudent precautions when taken singly undermine, as the mispredictions accumulate, confidence in authorities. Indeed, the skepticism and indifference that built up around 2009 H1N1 appears to have carried over and led to a significant reduction in the number of persons getting vaccinated in Ontario for the 2010 seasonal flu (Artuso and Blizzard 2011). At the extreme, these unrealized threats open a deep chasm of distrust, lending credence to opposing moral panics conjuring a world of conspiracies wrought by governments, business, scientists and international organizations. Regardless, with the explosive growth of Twitter and other social media, officials have surrendered considerable control over the message and will need to adjust to two-way communication. They are less and less able to exercise social control and orchestrate social responses in the ways envisioned in the classical model of moral panics.

# References

2009. Academic planning for H1N1. *University of Toronto* [Online]. Available at: http://www.provost.utoronto.ca/public/pdadc/200910/8.htm [accessed: October 14, 2009].

Ali, H. 1999. The search for a landfill site in a risk society. *Canadian Review of Sociology and Anthropology*, 36, 1–19.

Artuso, A and Blizzard, C. 2011. Fewer Ontarians getting flu vaccinations. *Toronto Sun* [Online]. Available at: http://www.torontosun.com/news/canada/2011/01/05/16774641.html [accessed: January 5, 2011].

Bowron, C. 2010. Is a third wave of H1N1 coming our way? *MinnPost.com* [Online]. Available at: http://www.minnpost.com/craigbowron/2010/01/08/14785/is_a_third_wave_of_h1n1_coming_our_way [accessed: January 9, 2011].

Broad, W. 2005. Web of sensors: Taking earth's pulse. *The New York Times* [Online]. http://www.nytimes.com/2005/05/10/science/earth/10wire.html?_r=1&scp=1&sq=a%20web%20of%20sensors&st=cse [accessed: January 12, 2006].

Brown, D. 2005. Resurrecting 1918 flu virus took many turns. *The Washington Post* [Online]. Available at: http://www.washingtonpost.com/wpdyn/content/article/2005/10/09/AR2005100900932.html [accessed: December 9, 2010].

2010. *2009 H1N1 Flu ("Swine Flu") and You. Centers for Disease Control and Prevention* [Online, February 10]. Available at: http://www.cdc.gov/h1n1flu/qa.htm [accessed: March 3, 2010].

Cohen, S. 2002 (1972, 1980). *Folk Devils and Moral Panics: The Creation of the Mods and Rockers*. 3rd Edition. London: MacGibbon and Kee.

Critcher, C. 2009. Widening the focus: moral panics as moral regulation. *British Journal of Sociology*, 49(1), 17–34.

Crosby, A. 2003 (1989). *America's Forgotten Pandemic: The Influenza of 1918*. 2nd Edition. Cambridge: Cambridge University Press.

CTV.ca News Staff. 2009. H1N1 vaccine hits speed bump, shortages likely. *CTVNews* [Online, October 30]. Available at: http://www.ctv.ca/CTVNews/TopStories/20091030/Swine_Vaccine_091030/ [accessed: October 10, 2010].

Di Justo, P. 2009. The last great swine flu epidemic. *Salon* [Online, April 28]. Available at: http://www.salon.com/news/environment/feature/2009/04/28/1976_swine_flu [accessed: December 12, 2009].

Garrett, L. 1994. *The Coming Plague: Newly Emerging Diseases in a World Out of Balance*. New York: Farrar, Straus, and Giroux.

2011. *Global Viral Forecast Initiative* [Online]. Available at: http://www.gvfi.org/ [accessed: October 24, 2011].

Goode, E. and Ben-Yehuda, N. 2009 (1994). *Moral Panics: The Social Construction of Deviance*. 2nd Edition. Chichester: Wiley-Blackwell.

Gould, S. 2007. *Punctuated Equilibrium*. Boston: Belknap Press.

Griffin, R., Yang, Z, ter Huurne, E., Boerner, F, Ortiz, S., and Dunwoody, S. 2008. After the flood: anger, attribution, and the seeking of information. *Science Communication*, 29(3), 285–315.

Hellerman, C. 2009. Swine flu "not stoppable," World Health Organization says. *CNN* [Online, June 11]. Available at:http://edition.cnn.com/2009/HEALTH/06/11/swine.flu.who/index.html [accessed: December 15, 2009].

Hier, S.P. 2008. Thinking beyond moral panic: risk, responsibility and the politics of moralization. *Theoretical Criminology*, 12(2), 173–90.

Hooker, C. 2008. SARS as a health scare, in *Networked Disease: Emerging Infections in the Global City*, edited by A. Harris and R. Keil. Chichester: Wiley-Blackwell, 123–37.

2009. Interview with epidemiologist Tom Jefferson: "A whole industry is waiting for a pandemic." *Der Spiegel* [Online, July 21]. Available at: http://www.spiegel.de/international/world/0,1518,637119,00.html [accessed: July 24, 2009].

Jameson, M. 2009. WHO: Swine flu spreading at unbelievable rate – and the young and healthy particularly at risk. *Examiner* [Online, August 30]. Available at: http://www.examiner.com/family-health-in-denver/who-swine-flu-spreading-at-unbelievable-rate-and-the-young-and-healthy-particularly-at-risk [accessed: December 15, 2009].

Jones, K., Patel, N., Levy, M., Storeygard, A, Balk, D, Gittleman, J., and Daszak, P. 2008. Global trends in emerging infectious diseases. *Nature*, 451, 990–993. Available at: http://www.nature.com/nature/journal/v451/n7181/abs/nature06536.html [accessed: January 12, 2010].

Jordans, F. 2010. "Fake" swine flu pandemic? WHO slams charges. *MSNBC* [Online]. Available at: http://www.msnbc.msn.com/id/35057450/ns/health-cold_and_flu/ [accessed: January 25, 2010].

Keil, R. and Harris, A. 2008 "Racism as a weapon of mass destruction:" SARS and the social fabric of urban multiculturalism, in *Networked Disease: Emerging Infections in the Global City*, edited by A. Harris and R. Keil. Chichester: Wiley-Blackwell, 152–66.

Krinsky, C (ed.). 2008. *Moral Panics over Contemporary Children and Youth*. Aldershot: Ashgate.

Maugh, T., 11. 2009. Beck and Limbaugh weigh in on swine flu. *Los Angeles Times* [Online, October 8]. Available at: http://latimesblogs.latimes.com/booster_shots/2009/10/08 [accessed: December 10, 2009].

McComas, K. 2004. Even the "best laid" plans go wrong: Strategic risk communication for new and emerging risks. *EMBO Reports*, 5, S61–S65.

McNeil, D., Jr. 2010. Most Americans think swine flu pandemic is over, a Harvard poll finds. *The New York Times* [Online]. Available at: http://www.nytimes.com/2010/02/06/health/06flu.html?_r=1&partner=rss&emc=rss [accessed: February 6, 2010].

McRobbie, A. and Thornton, S.L. 1995. Rethinking "moral panic" for multi-mediated social worlds. *British Journal of Sociology*, 46(4), 559–74.

Mehta, A. 2009. Flu outbreak shows how hard they are to predict. *Dana Foundation* [Online: April 29]. Available at: http://www.dana.org/news/features/detail.aspx?id=21374 [accessed: December 10, 2009].

Mustafa, N. 2009. The vaccination debate: to be jabbed or not. *CBC* [Online]. Available at: http://www.cbc.ca/canada/story/2009/10/28/f-vaccination-debate. html [accessed: January 5, 2010].

1994. *ProMed* [Online]. Available at: http://www.promedmail.org/pls/apex/f?p= 2400:1000 [accessed: October 24, 2011].

Schapiro, R. 2009. Head of the CDC, Dr Thomas Frieden, disputes White House swine flu report. *NYDailyNews.com Daily News* [Online, August 27]. Available at: http://www.nydailynews.com/ny_local/2009/08/27/2009-08-27_head_of_ the_cdc_dr_thomas_frieden_disputes_white_house_swine_flu_report.html [accessed: August 28, 2009]

Ungar, S. 1998a. Bringing the issue back in: comparing the marketability of the ozone hole and global warming. *Social Problems*, 45(4), 510–27.

Ungar, S. 1998b. Hot crises and media reassurance: a comparison of emerging diseases and Ebola Zaire. *British Journal of Sociology*, 49(1), 36–56.

Ungar, S. 2001. Moral panic versus the risk society: the implications of the changing sites of social anxiety. *British Journal of Sociology*, 52(2), 271–91.

Ungar, S. 2008. Global bird flu communication: Hot crisis and media assurance. *Science Communication*, 29, 472–97.

Vallis, M. 2009. Thirteen-year-old hockey player dies of swine flu. *National Post* [Online, October 27]. Available at: http://www.nationalpost.com/sports/year+h ockey+player+dies+swine/2149855/story.html [accessed: October 27, 2009].

Valpy, M. 2009. What are the ethics of jumping the queue to avoid the flu? *Globe and Mail* [Online, November 5]. Available at: http://www.theglobeandmail.com/life/ health/h1n1-swine-flu/what-are-the-ethics-of-jumping-the-queue-to-avoid-the-flu/article1353139/ [accessed: November 6, 2009].

Waiton, S. 2008. *The Politics of Antisocial Behavior: Amoral Panics*. Routledge Advances in Criminology. New York: Routledge.

Watson, S. 2006. How Tamiflu works. *Discovery Health* [Online, February 23]. Available at: http://health.howstuffworks.com/medicine/medication/tamiflu. htm [accessed: January 22, 2009].

# PART VI
# THE FUTURE OF THE MORAL
# PANIC CONCEPT

# Overview of Part VI

Among the various researchers who in recent years have advocated rethinking and revising the moral panic concept, a number have advised their colleagues to engage with scholarship not commonly referenced on the topic as an important step in this direction. For example, in "Moral Panic and Social Theory: Beyond the Heuristic," Amanda Rohloff and criminologist Sarah Wright (2010) propose that drawing on sociologist Norbert Elias's (2000) ideas about "the civilizing process" can increase the explanatory power of the moral panics model, moving it beyond its informative but limited applicability as a framework for social inquiry. Rohloff and Wright (2010: 412–13) find that besides having numerous other advantages for researchers, utilizing Elias's insights can, for at least two crucial reasons, shed considerable light on the relationship between individual moral panics and ongoing social currents or conflicts:

> Firstly, … moral panics occur partly as the outcome of civilizing processes — where processes of civilization contribute to decivilization. One example is the long-term civilization trend towards increased specialization and 'expertization' of knowledge (that is, increased division of labour). This process, along with the technicization of the dissemination of knowledge, has increasingly enabled the exaggeration and distortion of events … as well as the deamplification of events …
> Second, to attend to the problem of temporality with specific empirical examples, we can then explore how the specific panic (or panics) are affected by wider social processes specific to the given example under investigation … . The following questions could be asked of the relationship of short-term panics and long-term processes: how do particular social problems come to be defined as such, and develop into moral panics; how do particular groups of people come to be the foci of processes of 'disidentification'?

Rohloff and Wright assert that Elias's ideas can clarify moral panics' role in the civilizing process, which includes managing and manipulating the conflicts that arise when decivilizing countercurrents accompany civilizing trends, when, for example, technology, specialization, and democratization bring social disruptions such as those related to a greater division of labor. Moreover, applying Elias's work to the study of specific moral panics can help researchers answer such questions as why particular social problems lead to episodes and how particular groups become folk devils.

Sociologist Sean P. Hier (2011: 524) suggests that attending to works of moral regulation scholarship, such as *The Great Arch: English State Formation as a Cultural Revolution* (1985) by sociologist Philip Corrigan and historian Derek Sayer, can help researchers' address the extent to which an episode of moral panic constitutes a "volatile short-term manifestation of long-term moral regulation processes." In "Tightening the Focus: Moral Panic, Moral Regulation and Liberal Government," Hier (2011: 538–9) explains,

> It is at the disjuncture of the realization and limitations of liberal freedom (i.e., one's right to choose) that we find the potential for moral panic. In one sense, the limits of contemporary liberal governance are indexed to the harm that one person's exercise of freedom poses to another person's right to pursue their own freedom free of harm caused by others. The imperatives of liberal government are not only about 'individualizing' calculation and prediction but also 'totalizing' responsibility. In plain terms, it is, theoretically, one's liberal right to harm oneself but not to harm others; liberal government encourages individuals to manage themselves and to consider the consequences to others.
>
> Hence, responsibility functions as a counter-tendency to contemporary liberal individualism by socializing individual choice (e.g., risk management techniques). It does so by instilling an ethical content that directs individual liberal freedoms to calculate self-interest in a manner that is self-limiting and socially ramified … The ethics of responsibility fuses individual and collective forms of political action. From this it follows that the government of unfreedom — various forms of authoritarian intervention — is not antithetical to individual liberal freedoms but rather is its corollary … . The normative commitment to individual liberty is not only oriented towards recognizing the capacity of individual autonomous action but also towards addressing those individuals who are judged unable or unwilling to exercise that capacity — folk devils. In one sense, then, the deployment of liberal rights functions as a proxy for moralization, and one central, shared liberal moral value in an age of apparent moral relativism is to ensure one's right to freedom from harm. This does not signify consolidation of the amoral society … but rather the political and moral articulation of risk, harm, and personal responsibility. (2011: 538–9)

Hier shares Rohloff and Wright's conviction that moral panics result from long-term social trends characteristic of late modern societies, but whereas they describe episodes as, in a sense, rearguard actions intended to contain social disruption (endeavors tied to the decivilizing trends associated with the civilizing process), he sees them as constituting an integrated element of liberalization. According to Hier, the liberalizing trend toward greater individual freedom necessitates controlling not only one's own behaviors based on shared moral standards, but also those of individuals deemed unwilling to do so for themselves, who become the folk devils identified in moral panics.

## The Future of the Moral Panic Concept

Like Rohloff and Wright and Hier, in chapter 20, "A Missing Dimension: The Social Psychology of Moral Panics," Chas Critcher and Julia Pearce recommend that researchers call on largely untapped scholarly sources to consolidate and expand the moral panics model. Critcher and Pearce argue that the models and terminology of moral panic research imply the existence of social psychological processes that cannot be captured by primarily sociological perspectives. In their view, social psychological processes are particularly instrument in relationships within elites and between elites and the public. Elites in moral panics comprise media managers, moral entrepreneurs, nominated experts, politicians, and state functionaries whose selection of the social problems deserving of moral campaigning may be politically motivated, but is often psychologically grounded as well.

In chapter 21, "Cultural Trauma and Moral Panic: 9/11 and the Mosque at Ground Zero Affair," Kenneth Thompson examines the moral panic over the planned construction of a mosque near the former site of the World Trade Center in light of the sociology of deviance and social control, scholarship on cultural trauma, and research on the social meanings of ritual. The chapter, which includes careful analysis of pertinent scholarship, presents Critcher's argument that the emergence of a new moral panic almost a decade after 9/11 was made possible by prevailing cultural construction of the remembrance of those events, including its signification as a cultural trauma of a specifically ritualized form. Besides explaining a particular episode, the chapter implicitly offers strategic options for future moral panic research.

Amanda Rohloff's "Moral Panics over the Environment? 'Climate Crisis' and the Moral Panics Model," chapter 22, draws on Norbert Elias's work to explore social responses to the problem of climate change and, in doing so, questions several core assumptions held by scholars about moral panics. Addressing the issue of whether heightened reactions to climate change can be accurately defined as moral panics about the environment, Rohloff examines three crucial elements of moral panic scholarship: the notions of "moral," "panic," and the "folk devil." She revises the idea of "disproportionality" to counter the claim that moral panic research centering on climate change itself constitutes a form of denial concerning an environmental crisis.

Chapter 23, "Practicing Moral Panic Research: A Hybrid Model with Guidelines for its Application," delineates Brian V. Klocke and Glenn W. Muschert's development of a hybrid moral panics model oriented to research practice.

Utilizing elements of Stanley Cohen's (2002) processual model and Erich Goode and Nachman Ben-Yehuda's (2009) attributional model, Klocke and Muschert combine two leading approaches to the moral panic concept in an effort to devise a more comprehensive and protean template. Importantly, Klocke and Muschert include detailed suggestions for the application of their innovative model to moral panic research.

# References

Cohen, S. 2002 (1972, 1980). *Folk Devils and Moral Panics: The Creation of the Mods and Rockers*. 3rd Edition. London: Routledge.

Corrigan, P. and Sayer, D. 1985. *The Great Arch: English State Formation as a Cultural Revolution*. Oxford: Blackwell.

Elias, N. 2000 (1939). *The Civilizing Process: Sociogenetic and Psychogenetic Investigations*. 2nd Edition. Oxford: Blackwell.

Goode, E. and Ben-Yehuda, N. 2009 (1994). *Moral Panics: The Social Construction of Deviance*. 2nd Edition. Chichester: Wiley-Blackwell.

Hier, S.P. 2011. Tightening the focus: moral panic, moral regulation and liberal government. *British Journal of Sociology*, 62(3), 523–41.

Rohloff, A. and Wright, S. 2010. Moral panic and social theory: beyond the heuristic. *Current Sociology*, 58(3), 403–19.

# A Missing Dimension: The Social Psychology of Moral Panics

## Chas Critcher and Julia Pearce

The premise of this chapter is that the models and terminology of moral panic imply the existence of social psychological processes that cannot be captured by primarily sociological perspectives. Such processes affect especially relationships within elites and between them and the public. Elites in moral panics comprise media managers, moral entrepreneurs, nominated experts, politicians, and state functionaries. The choice of which issues are selected for moral campaigning may be politically motivated, but is often psychologically grounded. For example, the protection of children has both an ideological base, in the construction of innocent victims, and a psychological dimension, in the emotional reaction to exploitation of children in need of protection. Such collective emotional dynamics are often ignored or taken for granted in moral panic analysis. A related psychological dimension is campaigns' roles in solidifying the elite as morally unified. Otherwise divided by function or political allegiance, their identity and legitimacy as a group can be symbolically realized by moral panics. Such psychological factors require explanation just as much as the activities of claims makers or the machinations of the mass media.

Parallel psychological mechanisms are involved in public reactions to moral panics. Some panics have clear emotional appeal (immigration, pedophilia, street crime), but others attract lukewarm support (recreational drugs), while elsewhere reaction may be indifferent (sex and violence in the media). The identity of the public as an entity may be confirmed by antipathy towards immigrants/asylum seekers, pedophiles, or muggers. Who "we" are may be constructed and confirmed by defining, and acting against, who we clearly are not.

In the classic moral panic, elite and public views reinforce one another. The power of the resulting consensus is not simply political; it is also emotional, one reason that it is often impossible to find any rational grounds for counter-argument at the height of a moral panic. The intensity of feeling—outrage, the need to expel evil—is too great. The contributions that social psychological factors make to moral panics are too rarely recognized. This chapter has four objectives. First, it reviews previous writers' discussions of this issue by examining two classic studies (Cohen

2002, Goode and Ben Yehuda 2009). Second, it explores psychological aspects of major writings on the "culture of fear." Third, it summarizes a PhD recently completed by one of the authors to show that a social psychological perspective can inform empirical research on moral panics. Fourth, it outlines an equivalent debate about the role of social psychology within British work on fear of crime. The overall effort is to suggest that social psychological elements might be integrated into future work on moral panics.

# Social Psychology in Two Classic Moral Panic Studies

## Cohen

Stanley Cohen's original formulation of moral panic was informed by a social psychological dimension frequently lost in subsequent work. The opening chapter of *Folk Devils and Moral Panics: The Construction of the Mods and Rockers* (2002), first published in 1972, reviews the explanatory resources available. He sought to supplement interactionism with other perspectives. One, collective behavior, provided "detailed accounts of cases of mass hysteria, delusion and panics" (Cohen 2002: 3).This theory had two uses. First, it helped explain the behavior of the crowds of young people milling about the holiday resorts. Second, its functionalist concepts of ambiguity and strain in the social system were used to explain both youthful deviance and social reaction. However, Cohen saw social reaction less as a form of crowd behavior and more as analogous to "how societies cope with the sudden threat or disorder caused by physical disasters" (Cohen 2002: 3). He discovered late the potential of disaster research "for considering the reaction of the social system to something stressful, disturbing or threatening" (Cohen 2002: 12). The alleged behavior of mods and rockers was not a disaster in the conventional sense, but the same mechanisms operated. Hence, Cohen employed as the framework of the book the seven-stage sequential model of disaster research: warning, threat, impact, inventory, rescue, remedy, recovery.

A related social psychological concern was the impact of mass media on their audiences. Cohen used explicitly psychological language to explore how "one perceives and selects according to certain orientations already in existence and then, what is perceived is shaped and absorbed into more enduring clusters of attitudes" (2002: 36).This does not remain an individual process because media images "later encounter reinforcement or resistance in the group setting" (Cohen 2002: 36). Overall, "information is accepted or rejected and finally coded in terms of a plurality of needs, values, membership and reference groups" (Cohen 2002: 36).

Cohen's audience study (nearly 200 informal interviews, opportunistically sampled) explored how far they accepted media images of the disturbances. The audience "coded these (media) images in such a way as to tone down their more extreme implications" so were "better informed about the phenomenon than the media or the moral entrepreneurs whom the media quoted" (Cohen 2002: 49). Views of media coverage, especially its sensationalist elements, ranged from skepticism to hostility. Lacking alternative sources of information, audiences had to work with the material the media provided: "The mainstream of reaction expressed in the mass media—putative deviance, punitiveness, the creation of new folk devils—entered into the public imagery" (Cohen 2002: 53).

Disaster research and audience decodings fade from view in the final part of the book, which is concerned with sociological explanations of the causes and consequences of youthful deviance. Cohen discusses youth subcultures in wholly sociological terms. The symbolic boundaries between mods and rockers and between youth and adult society are explored without reference to the psychology of groups. Thus, a social psychological perspective is unevenly present in the thesis as whole. At crucial points, Cohen recognizes that he needs psychological tools but the theoretical implications are not pursued.

In the introduction to the third edition of his book, Cohen reflects on 30 years of moral panic analysis, emphasizing contributions from social constructionism and cultural and media studies. Social psychology is not a major concern but is never far below the surface. Deviancy amplification needs more exploration using a psychological language that rejects positivistic terms of "triggering off, contagion and suggestibility" (Cohen 2002: xxiv). There are alternative models: "For those who define and those who are defined, sensitization becomes a matter of cognitive framing and moral thresholds" (Cohen 2002: xxiv). Elsewhere, he identifies the "internal trajectory" of moral panics as "a microphysics of outrage—which, however, is initiated and sustained by wider social and political forces" (Cohen 2002: xxxi). Psychology could easily have displaced microphysics. Had it done so, then the brief would have been set for this chapter: to investigate the relationship between the psychological, the social, and the political in moral panics.

## Goode and Ben-Yehuda

Erich Goode and Nachman Ben-Yehuda's (2009: 28) essentially pluralist view of moral panics easily accommodates social psychological factors in the "disparate areas" it reviews: "Deviance, crime, collective behavior, social problems and social movements." Moral panics register emotional states "much like a fever: heightened emotion, fear, dread, anxiety, hostility, and a strong feeling of righteousness" (Goode and Ben-Yehuda 2009: 35).

Goode and Ben-Yehuda's (2009: 130) book, *Moral Panics: The Social Construction of Deviance*, first published in 1994, contains a discrete chapter on collective behavior defined as "relatively spontaneous, volatile, evanescent, emergent, extra-institutional, and short-lived" that "emerges or operates" where "mainstream culture" offers no guidance. The field has four subtopics: rumor, contemporary or urban legends, mass hysteria, and disasters. The discussion of each, though couched in sociological language, highlights processes that are essentially social psychological. Rumor, for example, has amongst its facilitating factors "a state of anxiety or apprehensiveness," presented as "both a personal and a structural variable" (Goode and Ben-Yehuda 2009: 132). Some people are more anxiety prone than others but social conditions may raise everyone's anxiety levels. The terms of social psychology are used but the discipline remains unacknowledged: "Often, rumor affirms in-group membership, virtue and victimization, and out-group exploitation and wickedness" (Goode and Ben-Yehuda 2009: 133). In their review of other aspects of collective behavior, fear looms large. Contemporary or urban legends "often infuse the everyday, mundane world with shock, apprehension, wonderment, and fear" (Goode and Ben-Yehuda 2009: 134). A moral panic can be seen as "a kind of mass hysteria," since both are rooted in "exaggerated fear" (Goode and Ben-Yehuda 2009: 137).

A primarily sociological perspective identifies the irrational fears, genuine anxieties, and group solidarities that shape the courses and focuses of moral panics. Such factors might otherwise be located in the domain of social psychology. Collective behavior has few other proponents as an explanation of the role of emotion in moral panics. Writers on the culture of fear, for example, have not used it to explain contemporary anxieties underlying moral panics. They have, implicitly or explicitly, adopted a different model, one of psychological projection.

## Social Psychology and the Culture of Fear

Here, we briefly review the psychological models implicit in the sociological work of three writers on the culture of fear: sociologists Barry Glassner (2009), David L. Altheide (2002), and Zygmunt Bauman (2006, 2007). One of the earliest writers on the subject, sociologist Frank Furedi (2006) has not been considered because his intellectual orientation precludes psychological questions.

### Glassner

Glassner's (2009: xxvii) project is explicit: "I will try to answer two questions: Why are Americans so fearful lately, and why are our fears so often misplaced?" Our "collective irrationality" needs explaining "from a psychological point of view extreme fear and outrage are often projections" (Glassner 2009: xxviii, xxxiv).

Glassner systematically finds real problems from which fear diverts attention. Fear of youth spirals "in proportion to our unacknowledged guilt." Youth services are cut back but "rather than face up to our collective responsibility we project our violence onto young people themselves, and onto strangers we imagine will attack them" (Glassner 2009: 72). Similarly, panics over teen mums divert attention away from the plight of single parents. Panics over black men disguise enduring racial inequalities. Panics over drugs expel a whole category of citizens from mainstream society.

None of this happens automatically. Some seek to make it happen for their own political or economic ends. They have identifiable strategies, including "statements of alarm," "glorification of wannabe experts," "the use of poignant anecdotes," the "christening of isolated incidents as trends" and "depictions of entire categories of people as innately dangerous" (Glassner 2009: 208). Yet, such strategies can only succeed if they tap the well of public fear.

The argument is consistent and wide-ranging but crucially depends upon the existence of collective psychological mechanisms—displacement and projection— that it never quite names and about which it can only speculate. In a journal article, Glassner specifies the gap between individual and collective fears:

> Neither the things that people do to protect themselves individually and collectively, nor what they report and believe they are protecting themselves from, necessarily reveal their true fears. That fact provides, amongst other things, a basis for seeking out connections between the large-scale, socially constructed fears—what some sociologists call moral panics—and fear within interpersonal relationships. It is hardly surprising that those two spaces (mediatized environments within which people receive and interpret messages and meanings) largely are kept separate in social and cultural analyses. Sociology and allied disciplines have been built, after all, on dualities such as micro versus macro, psychological versus sociological, agency versus structure, and hegemony versus resistance. Still, connections can be made. (1999: 302)

His connections remain those of projection, with fear and its consequences acting to "allow people to ignore, avoid or pretend away, other fears that are uncomfortably close at hand" (Glassner 1999: 302).

## Altheide

Altheide (2002: ix) defines the culture of fear as primarily a discursive formation: "The pervasive communications, symbolic awareness and expectation that danger and risk are all around us." This discourse of fear has been constructed and is sustained by the mass media and popular culture employing "expansive entertainment-oriented media logic, particularly the use of the problem frame that promotes risk and danger as fear" (Altheide 2002: 188).

The audience cannot resist a continuous stream of fear-saturated messages, making fear normal and pervasive in public and private domains. Exactly how the audience interprets media messages remains unclear, as the example of crime illustrates. Altheide cites familiar findings that the (US) media and popular culture are replete with images of fear and crime while separate measures of public opinion suggest a widespread perception of ubiquitous danger. Yet, the causal relationship is problematic. Since his book contains much material on the media and popular culture but little on audiences, his solution to the problem has to be theoretical and speculative. In part, he reiterates the saturation model; this flow cannot but affect its audience so that "the routine display of numerous statements, images and anticipations of fear provides a cultural and cognitive baseline of experience for more and more society members" (Altheide 2002: 40).

More elaborately, Altheide evokes symbolic interactionism, of all sociological theories the most social psychological. Media audiences should be understood as speech communities "which define appropriate identities, roles, language, and styles for members ... they are reflexive of previous role performances, yet directive of future identity affirmations" (Altheide 2002: 8). The media message of fear is so powerful because it "provides both an identity and definition of the situation" (Altheide 2002: 9). Thus the crucial "effect" of the media on the audience may be to define the situation as one of fear and offer an identity of the fearful: "Social fears are related to personal fears in complex ways. Unraveling the relationships for specific fears is an avowedly psychoanalytic task that has been largely neglected, thus opening up another opportunity for social researchers" (Altheide 2002: 195).

Altheide does not share Glassner's preference for displacement and projection as the mechanisms that account for the public endorsing the distortion of social problems by the prism of fear. Saturation and symbolic identity provide partial answers but emotional intensity has yet to be explained. Both writers agree that sociological perspectives alone do not explain the relationship between a public culture of fear and private endorsements of it. The social psychological conundrum persists.

## Bauman

Bauman approaches fear as a cultural product of economic and political forces. A combination of the economic—negative globalization—and the political—the abdication of the state from welfare—have destabilized public and private life. We now live a "liquid" life "experienced as a relentless and inescapable change" that "portends nothing but continuous crisis and strain and forbids a moment of rest" (Bauman 2007: 10). The consequence is a pervasive "existential uncertainty" (Bauman 2007: 93), extending to our most intimate networks. Since "human relations are no longer sites of certainty, tranquility and spiritual comfort," they "become instead a prolific source of anxiety" (Bauman 2006: 69).

Such anxiety needs to find an outlet. Those responsible for economic and political destabilization are invisible, unavailable as targets. We therefore project our resentment onto more visible and available targets. This process, in essence psychological though not termed as such, involves "the *decoupling* of fear-inspired actions from the existential tremors that generated the fears that inspired them; the *displacement* of fears ... to the areas of life largely *irrelevant* to the genuine source of anxiety but instead—consolingly—within sight and reach" (Bauman 2006: 134, emphasis in original).

Of Bauman's many examples, two are especially germane. One is fear of crime. Citing comparative research across Europe, Bauman concludes that exaggerated fear of crime reflects the anxiety induced by economic and political destabilization.

So does antagonism towards the asylum seeker, literally an outsider, often culturally alien, portrayed as exploiting the goodwill of those already disoriented by uncontrolled and ceaseless change. Asylum seekers have, Bauman (2007: 43) suggests, "now replaced the evil-eyed witches and other unrepentant evil-doers, the malignant spooks and hob goblins of former urban legends."

However, projection onto convenient targets is self-defeating since the discharge of hostility cannot alleviate the real sources of anxiety. As long as economic and political forces fail to offer stability or inculcate trust, the cycle of anxiety generation and displacement will continue. Bauman's is perhaps the crudest solution to the problem of accounting for psychological processes underlying the culture of fear, but the asylum seeker example is one we wish to pursue further.

Lest it be thought that this review is too easy an exercise in point-scoring, one of the present authors' own work has consistently failed to recognize any social psychological dimension (Critcher 2003). The crucial role attributed to elites in moral panics has not involved any consideration of group identity formation. The equally important process of media representation has been analyzed without reference to the nature of audience understandings. Social psychological questions are omitted from a later review of the key questions facing moral panic analysis (Critcher 2006). If anything, that work has paid less attention to social psychological factors than all the other writers reviewed here. It is time to rectify this omission. Assistance comes from a recently completed PhD (Pearce 2010), which both recognizes and evaluates the potential contribution to moral panic analysis of social psychological perspectives.

## Towards a Social Psychological Model of Moral Panics

### Theoretical Framework

Attempting to explain the reasons why the public is receptive to moral panic discourse, sociological models inevitably operate at the societal level and do not consider psychological aspects of group dynamics. Explaining such problems as the public's apparent predisposition to "panic" would benefit from considering motivational aspects of group behavior integral to social psychology. Social Psychology focuses on the interaction between the individual and the social with a view to understanding how societies function. It is distinguished from Sociology and Psychology by its focus on the dialectical relationship between the individual and society (Howarth 2001). By exploring group level responses as well as their psychological impact, a social psychological analysis avoids reducing explanation to either an individual or a societal level. From a social psychological perspective, the intergroup relationship between the community doing the "panicking" and the group that it is panicking about is key to understanding the cause and impact of a moral panic. In reconfirming moral boundaries, moral panics define and label what society finds acceptable, determining who does or does not belong (Critcher

2006). Consequently, moral panics help define the social identity of both the group producing the panic and those at whom it is directed. One theoretical framework influential in exploring intergroup relationships is Social Identity Theory.

Social Identity Theory recognizes that group behavior differs from interpersonal behavior because of people's self-conception as group members. It seeks to identify the social psychological processes leading to intergroup conflict, explore the psychological consequences for members of groups of different social statuses and elaborate on strategies for dealing with the resulting challenges (Tajfel 1981). A model of moral panics that incorporates Social Identity Theory therefore has the potential to theorize public receptivity to moral panic discourse. It can also identify the strategies adopted by "folk devils" to negotiate a positive social identity for themselves, an aspect of moral panic that remains largely unexamined (St Cyr 2003). This is important because moral panics focus on what Cohen (2002: viii) describes as "social identity clusters" — such as youth groups, drug users, and single mothers — who lack power or access to cultural capital. The moral panic process stigmatizes these groups, influencing their social identity as "folk devils," with significant consequences for intergroup relations and individual behavior. Social Identity Theory thus has the potential to enhance current models of moral panics through theorizing their underlying processes. However, it is unable to provide an analysis of the content of moral panics.

Moral panics are embedded in particular socio-cultural circumstances that trigger these responses. A moral panic needs to be contextualized within ongoing representational systems and the power dynamics that construct and reproduce cultural knowledge. A relevant approach here is the theory of social representations. In his seminal work on psychoanalysis, Serge Moscovici (2008, originally published 1961) adapted the sociological concept of collective representations to produce a more dynamic version applicable to modern societies and accessible to social psychological inquiry. Moscovici (1973: xiii) defines social representations as "a system of values, ideas and practices" that provide a framework to allow individuals to make sense of their social and material world and act as a classification code enabling communication between members of a community. The primary focus of Social Representations Theory is social knowledge as expressed in language and communication.

Although Social Identity Theory and Social Representations Theory have distinctive perspectives, they have been successfully combined to account for both the content and process of social identity (see Howarth, 2002, 2004, Jovchelovitch 1996). Their epistemological positions are compatible since both recognize the importance of socio-cognitive processes. In adopting a "weak" — or in Goode and Ben Yehuda's terms, a "contextual" — approach to social constructionism, a social representations approach to social identity is highly compatible with moral panic analysis. Recognizing that representations are constructed in relation to the "brute facts" of the world (Bauer and Gaskell 1999: 169), distinctions can be made between more and less adequate representations. This allows judgments to be made of the accuracy of claims about an issue, key to identifying disproportionality in moral panics.

## Empirical Focus and Findings: Social Representations

Pearce (2010) applied such a social psychological model of moral panics to the topic of asylum seekers. This study was based on data from three sources: one hundred and twenty UK national newspaper articles, eight group interviews with 36 members of the "host community" and 25 individual interviews with people seeking asylum in the United Kingdom (all names have been changed to preserve anonymity). Social representations were explored using thematic analysis (as described by Braun and Clarke 2006). A coding frame was developed, initially using an inductive approach. Subsequently, thematic connections highlighted social representations. Each data set was analyzed separately and then synthesized to examine the commonalities and differences between and within them. This facilitated the examination of the spread and transformation of moral panic discourse as communicated in the media and understood by the public, as well as by the "folk devils" themselves.

Six core representations were identified: *bad people* versus *good people, threatening* versus *threatened* and *legitimate* versus *illegitimate*. Each representation appeared in all data sources, although there were differences in peripheral elements, and group and individual interviewees varied in their awareness or assimilation of them. Representations identified in the media sample and "host" group interviews were predominantly negative and remarkably similar, in both basic content and the balance of positive and negative elements. Both media coverage and group interviewees focused on the economic impact of asylum seekers and on "pull" rather than "push" factors as the key motivation for individuals seeking asylum. It is likely that these representations originated in the media as they were reproduced by group interviewees with no direct experience of asylum seekers or access to alternative sources of information. Predictably, group interviewees produced more negative and fewer positive representations than asylum seekers did themselves. More notably, negative representations produced by the media, group interviewees and individual interviewees were remarkably similar, reproducible even by those who rejected them. Asylum seekers were represented as "criminal," "spongers" and "undesirable migrants" in all data sources. Minority representations of asylum seekers as "hardworking" and "law abiding" were formulated as a response to these hegemonic negative representations. This provides further evidence that the media facilitate, proliferate, and disseminate moral panic discourse.

Using Social Representations Theory to examine moral panic discourse proved useful. In addition to identifying the diffusion of moral panic discourse about asylum seekers, it highlighted the resistance of social representations to change. For example, one group interviewee (Sharon, from London) looked up "asylum seekers" on the Internet the evening before the interview because "I know my opinions but it's also nice to know a bit of facts" and discovered that asylum seekers were not allowed to work whilst their applications were being processed. This countered her belief that asylum seekers were "spongers" who did not want to work. However, instead of threatening the core representation of asylum seekers as "bad people," this new information was interpreted as an explanation for asylum seekers being "criminals" (since they are not allowed to work, they need the money). Thus, contradictory information was assimilated through the adjustment of peripheral elements without threatening the core negative representation.

Other knowledge was transformed in the process of being communicated, with the content of the representations of asylum seekers as *threatening* and *illegitimate* elaborated from media to public discourse. In the media sample, asylum seekers were represented as an economic threat, costing the UK taxpayer money and gaining unfair access to scarce resources. These themes also appeared in group interviews but personalized, participants perceiving asylum seekers as "taking our jobs." The prevalence of this representation in group interviews demonstrates the transformation of knowledge once it enters the public domain.

## Empirical Focus and Findings: Social Identity

Group and individual interviews were qualitatively re-analyzed to examine whether, as predicted by Social Identity Theory, intergroup processes underpin host community responses to asylum seekers, and the coping strategies of the "folk devils." According to Social Identity Theory, in-group bias is a function of three variables: relative status positions (high or low), perceptions about status differences (legitimate or stable), and perceptions of group boundaries (permeable or impermeable). Members of high status groups are expected to be threatened by the activities of lower status groups and exhibit high levels of discrimination when they perceive boundaries to be legitimate but unstable (Reynolds and Turner 2001). Minority group members are also expected to adopt strategies in order to challenge stigmatized social identity. If boundaries are considered to be permeable (that is, there is a social mobility belief structure), individual "exit" strategies will be followed, whereas if an individual's fate is perceived to be tied to group membership (that is, there is a social change belief structure) collective action is more likely (Tajfel 1978).

Social mobility requires assimilation, when individuals dissociate themselves from the subordinate group and show preference for the superior out-group. By contrast, where there is a social change belief structure, the only way for individuals to improve their circumstances is for conditions to be changed for the group as a whole, which requires collective rather than individual action. The strategy employed depends on whether status differences between groups are considered legitimate or stable. The first, social creativity, involves redefining the comparative situation and occurs when asymmetries between groups are perceived as legitimate and stable, making radical change more difficult. The second, social competition, occurs when status differences are considered illegitimate and when the social system is insecure so that it is possible to conceive of group relationships becoming more equitable. This leads to attempts to improve the opportunities and status of the group whilst retaining its distinct identity.

The study identified both social categorization and social comparison processes amongst group interviewees. Asylum seekers were categorized as an out-group with evidence for the selective accentuation of intergroup differences favoring the in-group. For example, Dennis (Birmingham group interviewee), argued, "Whatever they do in their country, in this country we keep things tidy ... so if they're going to come to this country they must actually act like we do, keeping places tidy and live like we do instead of like they want to live in their own country." Concern about the allegedly negative impact of asylum seekers on British identity and culture played a central role in responses, with a particular focus on religion and the perception that asylum seekers do not want to abide by British laws and values. Group interviewees clearly associated asylum seekers with radical Islam and terrorism. This overlap with negative representations of "Muslims" amplified hostility to asylum seekers.

This supports predictions about intergroup dynamics underlying host receptivity to moral panic discourse, but concern and hostility were not solely attributable to perceptions of negative group characteristics. Concern about the economic impact of asylum seekers and perceptions regarding unfair distribution of resources were also important factors. For example, Gary (Basildon group interviewee) expressed concern over "how limited our resources are in the country anyway ... the fact that they're maybe taking our jobs, maybe taking our houses, they may be taking resources away from National Health." Both material and psychological factors contributed to the perception of threat. However, whilst there was some evidence that competition for resources played a part in the host response to asylum seekers, particularly amongst those who were on benefits or worked in industries that have been affected by foreign labor, the majority of participants had no direct experience of asylum seekers and provided no evidence that they were adversely economically affected by asylum seekers living in the United Kingdom. Furthermore, discussion of culture and values featured frequently in group interviews, in particular concerns about the impact of asylum seekers on British identity and the perceived threat they pose to the in-group's dominant position. Therefore, whilst the desire to protect the financially privileged position of the in-group was clearly an important issue for these participants, identity concerns also suffused host receptivity to moral panic discourse.

These findings highlight some limitations in applying Social Identity Theory to moral panics. Contrary to the predictions of Social Identity Theory, perceptions of the legitimacy and stability of group boundaries did not distinguish between those who were hostile towards asylum seekers and those who were more sympathetic. Although the majority of group interviewees indicated that they considered the maintenance of inequitable intergroup relationships to be acceptable—in fact, the perception that asylum seekers were receiving the same privileges as members of the host community was an important factor in hostility—there did not seem to be a desire for boundaries to be rigidly maintained. In contrast, the perception that asylum seekers are culturally inflexible and unwilling to adopt "British" cultural practices and assimilate into the host community's "way of doing things" was a key factor in the experience of threat. Furthermore, group interviewees indicated that they wanted boundaries to be initially impermeable: they did not want newcomers to the United Kingdom to have immediate access to the same privileges that they enjoyed. Nevertheless, if asylum applicants were successful, then they felt that they should assimilate into the cultural practices and values of the host community, eventually becoming part of the in-group. This suggests that the dichotomous characterization of boundaries as permeable or impermeable may be a simplistic conceptualization of the ways that groups operate.

Evidence from individual interviews with asylum seekers suggested equally complex understandings of group boundaries as permeable in some contexts, but not others. Several interviewees agreed that they considered themselves British because they felt accepted in the United Kingdom. However, elsewhere these same interviewees suggested that it was not possible for them to be British owing to their ethnicity. Bako (a male from Niger), initially responded, "I know the British before and I am friends with them and we just mix, that's me, that's it, I'm also British now." Yet, he went on to say he could not be British because "normally even the color show you are not British." Other asylum seekers stressed the importance of time, arguing that barriers that were initially impermeable might become permeable if they lived in the United Kingdom long enough. The whole notion of group boundaries in Social Identity Theory therefore requires more stringent examination.

Nevertheless, Social Identity Theory did help identify strategies for coping with stigmatized group membership. Both social mobility and social change strategies were identified, with social mobility adopted by those able to integrate successfully with the host community and social change by those who felt that this was not possible or desirable. One participant, Ndulu (a male from Nigeria), commented, "I don't care what they say about asylum seekers because I know that I'm different," whereas another, Lilith (a female from Iran), said, "I think we shouldn't insist on being integrated you know, because I have my kind of food and you have your kind of food ... so it's just mutual respect and peaceful coexistence with other groups." Both strategies were severely limited by negative host community responses. Social mobility strategies necessitated participants concealing their identity as "asylum seekers" and social change strategies were restricted by difficulties in challenging the negative hegemonic representations of "asylum seekers."

## Conceptual Evaluation

Social psychological processes emerge as significant factors in host receptivity to moral panic. The representational environment plays an important role in delimiting the strategies that "folk devils" may adopt in response to stigmatized group membership. However, there remain some limitations. One of these is that the focus on intergroup processes means it would not make sense to apply this model to moral panics that have no "folk devil." Furthermore, the development of a model of moral panics that focuses on the impact of stigmatized identity on "folk devils" raises questions regarding the legitimacy of stigma: the construction of pedophiles as a group is likely to vary markedly from that of asylum seekers.

Despite these problems, this study demonstrated the potential of social psychological theory for moral panic analysis. Social Identity Theory indicates that the maintenance of intergroup boundaries can encourage hostility towards defined outsiders who then have to renegotiate their own damaged identities. Social Representations Theory identifies the mediation of individual and collective understandings of intergroup hostility and conflict by the images and assumptions circulating in the culture. The courses of moral panics depend on such social psychological mechanisms.

## Conclusion

This kind of assessment of social psychology is also emerging in cognate areas, notably the complex British debate about fear of crime. Research over the past 40 years has consistently come to the same conclusions. Fear of crime increases even when the crime rate is falling. It is highest amongst those least likely to become victims of crime and lowest amongst the most likely (young and male) victims. Elderly women are the most fearful. Yet, plotting the level of fear against socio-demographic variables seems to have reached saturation point. It has not delivered any satisfactory explanation of the possible motivation for the fear of crime.

One approach to incorporating a psychological perspective into fear of crime studies has been to examine how far it is affected by personal anxiety induced by specific situations or by predispositions to anxiety (Chadee, Virgil, and Ditton 2009). But the authors admit neither variable has any great measurable influence. In a series of articles with co-authors (Hollway and Jefferson 1997, Jefferson and Hollway 2000, Gadd and Jefferson 2009), Jefferson has argued for a psychoanalytic approach where fear of crime is not a rational assessment of the risk of victimization, but an expression of anxiety and defense against anxiety. People who appear to be frightened of crime are actually finding ways to ward off felt threats to their sense of identity. Displacement and projection are the crucial psychological mechanisms. An individual's fear of crime is a product of their level of exposure to risk and their degree of anxiety. The whole approach depends upon "a psychoanalytic concept of anxiety involving unconscious, often interpsychic, defences" (Jefferson and Hollway 2000: 47).

Other authors argue for a more orthodox social psychological approach either to the fear of crime in general (Farrall et al. 2000, Farrall and Lee 2009, Jackson 2009) or to audience understandings of media representations (Ditton et al. 2004). The fullest exploration of the implications of such an approach comes in an online journal article seeking to offer fear of crime as a case study in risk perception. Research in risk perception and fear of crime both reveal the same dilemma of connecting individuals' assessments of their own vulnerability with more generalized discourses from public culture. The solution they suggest is "a framework that integrates psychological and sociological analysis" that "reaches across traditional disciplinary boundaries" (Jackson, Allum, and Gaskell 2006: 1).

Linking the individual to the social, there is crime as a catalyst for articulating ideas about society and the role of groups within it. Crime perception is an evaluative activity locating people and their activities in relation to key ideas about social existence: deviance and order, control and discipline, consensus and cohesion. Crime provokes an emotional response because it threatens cherished values of the social order "our deep-seated sense of fairness and cooperation, the value we place on the sanctity of property and liberty, our desire to censure those who defect" (Jackson, Allum, and Gaskell 2006: 62). Transgressors must be punished to uphold the moral integrity of the community. The maintenance of moral boundaries serves simultaneously to confirm group identity.

Indeed, designating as criminal and dangerous an individual or group, a behavior or a set of norms, or a community and its conditions, may itself be a semi-moral act. The identification of dangerous individuals may operate to establish "moral communities" by locating "immoral communities." It may also reinforce the identity and boundaries of a given community by identifying what that community is against, for example certain troublesome individuals or particular groups defined by social class or ethnicity. Social psychology shows that the identification of an out-group operates to strengthen solidarity within the in-group (Jackson, Allum, and Gaskell 2006: 63).

There are clear connections here to our project. We reviewed implicit and explicit psychological concerns in two classic studies of moral panic. We then considered the manifestation of such concerns in the debate about the culture of fear. Finally, we recounted the exploration in Pearce's thesis of the potential for theories of social representations and social identity to occupy the psychological territory within the moral panic domain. It has not been our intention to suggest that we are anywhere near discovering mechanisms to connect individual and social constructions of fear in general or fear of crime in particular, much less the complex constructions of asylum seekers or other deviant groups as "folk devils." But there are indications that social psychology can deliver models and concepts of a type that is essential if moral panic analysis and cognate fields are to find ways to interrelate individual perceptions and collective representations. They offer our best hope of adding a dimension missing in our current knowledge.

# References

Altheide, D.L. 2002. *Creating Fear: News and the Construction of Crisis*. New York: Aldine de Gruyter.

Bauer, M.W. and Gaskell, G. 1999. Towards a paradigm for research on Social Representations. *Journal for the Theory of Social Behaviour*, 29(2), 163–86.

Bauman, Z. 2006. *Liquid Fear*. Cambridge: Polity.

Bauman, Z. 2007. *Liquid Times: Living in an Age of Uncertainty*. Cambridge: Polity.

Braun, V. and Clarke, V. 2006. Using thematic analysis in psychology. *Qualitative Research in Psychology*, 3(2), 77–101.

Chadee, D.A., Virgil, N.J., and Ditton, J. 2008. State-trait anxiety and fear of crime: a social psychological perspective, in *Fear of Crime: Critical Voices in an Age of Anxiety*, edited by M. Lee and S. Farrall. Milton Park: Routledge-Cavendish, 168–87.

Cohen, S. 2002 (1972, 1980). *Folk Devils and Moral Panics: The Creation of the Mods and Rockers*. 3rd Edition. London: Routledge.

Cohen, S. 2002. Introduction to the third edition: moral panics as cultural politics, in *Folk Devils and Moral Panics: The Creation of Mods and Rockers*. 3rd Edition. London: Routledge, vii-xxxvii.

Critcher, C. 2006. Introduction: more questions than answers, in *Critical Readings: Moral Panics and the Media*, edited by C. Critcher. Maidenhead: Open University Press, 1–24.

Critcher, C. 2009. Widening the focus: moral panics as moral regulation. *British Journal of Criminology*, 49(1), 17–35.

Critcher, C. 2011. Drunken antics: the gin craze, binge drinking and the political economy of moral regulation, in *Moral Panic and the Politics of Anxiety*, edited by S.P. Hier. London: Routledge, 171–89.

Ditton, J., Chadee, D., Farrall, S., Gilchrist, E., and Bannister, J. 2004. From imitation to intimidation: a note on the curious and changing relationship between the media, crime and fear of crime. *British Journal of Criminology*, 44(4), 595–610.

Farrall, S., Bannister, J., Ditton, J., and Gilchrist, E. 2000. Social psychology and the fear of crime. *British Journal of Criminology*, 40(3), 399–413.

Farrall, S. and Lee, M. 2008. Critical voices in an age of anxiety: a reintroduction to the fear of crime, in *Fear of Crime: Critical Voices in an Age of Anxiety*, edited by M. Lee and S. Farrall. Milton Park: Routledge-Cavendish, 108–24.

Furedi, F. 2006 (1997). *The Culture of Fear Revisited*. 2nd Edition. London: Continuum.

Gadd, D. and Jefferson, T. 2008. Anxiety, defensiveness and the fear of crime, in *Fear of Crime: Critical Voices in an Age of Anxiety*, edited by M. Lee and S. Farrall. Milton Park: Routledge-Cavendish, 125–42.

Glassner, B. 1999. The construction of fear. *Qualitative Sociology*, 22(4): 310–19.

Glassner, B. 2009. *The Culture of Fear: Why Americans Are Afraid of the Wrong Things: Crime, Drugs, Minorities, Teen Moms, Killer Kids, Mutant Microbes, Plane Crashes, Road Rage, and so much more*. 2nd Edition. New York: Basic Books.

Goode, E. and Ben-Yehuda, N. 2009 (1994). *Moral Panics: The Social Construction of Deviance*. 2nd Edition. Chichester: Wiley-Blackwell.

Hollway, W. and Jefferson, T. 1997. The risk society in an age of anxiety: situating fear of crime. *British Journal of Sociology*, 38(2), 283–98.

Howarth, C. 2001. Towards a social psychology of community: a social representations perspective. *Journal for the Theory of Social Behaviour*, 31(2), 223–38.

Howarth, C. 2002. Identity in whose eyes? The role of representations in identity construction. *Journal of the Theory of Social Behaviour*, 32(2), 145–62.

Howarth, C. 2004. Re-presentation and resistance in the context of school exclusion: reasons to be critical. *Journal of Community and Applied Social Psychology*, 14(5), 356–77.

Jackson, J., Allum, N., and Gaskell, G. 2006. Bridging levels of analysis in risk perception research: the case of the fear of crime. Forum Qualitative Sozialforschun/Forum: *Qualitative Social Research* [Online], 7(1), Art 20. Available at: http://nbn-resolving.de/urn:nbn:de:0114-fqs0601202 [accessed: March 23, 2011].

Jackson, J. 2008. Bridging the social and the psychological in the fear of crime, in *Fear of Crime: Critical Voices in an Age of Anxiety*, edited by M. Lee and S. Farrall. Milton Park: Routledge-Cavendish, 143–67.

Jefferson, T., and Hollway, W. 2000. The role of anxiety in fear of crime, in *Crime, Risk and Insecurity*, edited by T. Hope and R. Sparks. London: Routledge, 31–49.

Jovchelovitch, S. 1996. In defence of representations. *Journal for the Theory of Social Behaviour*, 26 (2), 121–35.

Moscovici, S. 2008 (1961). *Psychoanalysis: Its Image and its Public*, edited by G. Duveen, translated by D. Macey. Cambridge: Polity Press.

Moscovici, S. 1973. Foreword. *Health and Illness: A Social Psychological Analysis*, edited by C. Herzlich, translated by D. Graham. London: Academic Press, ix–xiv.

Pearce, J. 2010. Asylum Seekers in the United Kingdom: A Social Psychological Understanding of a Moral Panic. Unpublished PhD thesis: London Metropolitan University. Supervisor: Dr Elizabeth Charman.

Reynolds, K.J. and Turner, J.C. 2001. Prejudice as a group process: the role of social identity, in *Understanding Prejudice, Racism and Social Conflict*, edited by M. Augoustinos and K.J. Reynolds. London: Sage Publications, 159–78.

St Cyr, J. 2003. The folk devil reacts: gangs and moral panics. *Criminal Justice Review*, 28(1), 26–46.

Tajfel, H. 1978. *The Social Psychology of Minorities*. London: Minority Rights Group.

Tajfel, H. 1981. *Human Groups and Social Categories: Studies in Social Psychology*. Cambridge: Cambridge University Press.

# Cultural Trauma and Moral Panic: 9/11 and the Mosque at Ground Zero Affair

Kenneth Thompson

The effects of the terrible attack of 9/11/2001 on the Twin Towers of the World Trade Center and the Pentagon have been analyzed in many ways, including as cultural trauma (Smelser 2004b, Breithaupt 2003) and as moral panic (Rothe and Muzzatti 2004, Victor 2006). It might have been expected that, with the passage of time, the natural healing process would have eroded the impact of those events on the national consciousness. However, nearly a decade after the event, there was fresh controversy over what was (inaccurately) described as a proposal to build a mosque at Ground Zero (the Associated Press, serving 1,500 newspapers and websites, began using the shorthand term on May 25, 2010, see Calderone 2010). It will be argued that this fresh controversy could lead to a moral panic only because of the ways in which 9/11 and its memorializing had been culturally construed, including bearing the marks of a cultural trauma of a particular—ritualized—form.

In seeking to revive the concept of moral panic in the 1990s (Thompson 1998), it was argued that it was necessary to move this theoretical framework beyond that of deviancy and social constructionism, where it had originally been located in Cohen's (1972) analysis of reactions to youth subcultures. An attempt was made to relate the concept to other theoretical developments such as risk society, discourse analysis and moral regulation (Thompson 1997, 1998). More recently, in the foreword to a collection of new articles on moral panics, it was suggested that the outcry against the proposed Islamic community center near Ground Zero was poised between turning into either a moral panic or another battle in the culture wars (Thompson 2011). In other words, this may be another example where the moral panic concept cannot stand alone and needs to be related to other relevant concepts and theories, such as neo-Durkheimian concepts of "collective effervescence," the sacred, "social solidarity" (Tiryakian 2005), and "cultural trauma" (Alexander et al. 2004).

## Cultural Trauma

The concept of cultural trauma was developed in the course of a year-long dialogue between visiting fellows at the Stanford University Center for Advanced Studies in the Behavioral Sciences in the academic year 1998–1999 (to which the present author was an occasional contributor), culminating in the volume *Cultural Trauma and Collective Identity* (Alexander et al. 2004). In the first chapter, "Toward a Theory of Cultural Trauma," the director of the project, Jeffrey Alexander (2004: 1), stated that, "Cultural trauma occurs when members of a collectivity feel they have been subjected to a horrendous event that leaves indelible marks upon their group consciousness, marking their memories forever and changing their future identity in fundamental and irrevocable ways."

In contrast to other theorists of trauma, including those following psychoanalytic approaches, these cultural trauma theorists adopted a social constructionist approach, rejecting the "naturalistic fallacy" that events in and of themselves create trauma. They claimed that it is how they are "imagined" and represented that matters for the sociologist. It is through the imaginative process of representation that actors make sense of experience. The idea of the "imagined" adopted here, according to Alexander, is more like what Durkheim (1915) meant in *The Elementary Forms of the Religious Life* when he wrote of the "religious imagination." Imagination is intrinsic to the process of representation, seizing upon an inchoate experience and forming it through association, condensation, and aesthetic creation, into some specific shape (Alexander 2004: 9). The persons who compose collectivities broadcast symbolic representations of ongoing social events, past, present and future. These group representations can be seen as "claims" upon the shape of social reality, its causes, and the responsibilities for action entailed. "The cultural construction of trauma begins with such a claim" (Alexander 2004: 11, referencing Thompson's 1998 discussion of moral panics):

> It is a claim to some fundamental injury, an exclamation of the terrifying profanation of some sacred value, a narrative about a horribly destructive social process, and a demand for emotional, instrumental, and symbolic reparation and reconstitution. (Alexander 2004: 11)

Little did the Stanford research group imagine, as they finished their theoretical development of the concept of cultural trauma, that their conceptual imaginings were about to receive their most definitive exemplification in the events of 9/11, 2001. Fortunately, because of the slow process of academic publication, Neil Smelser (2004b) was able to add to the book an epilogue on those events, viewed in terms of cultural trauma. As Smelser puts it in the opening sentence of his epilogue: "If the screen industry's most talented scriptwriter had been asked to draft a scenario for a quintessential cultural trauma, that script could not have surpassed the actual drama that occurred on September 11, 2001" (2004b: 264). Furthermore, the imaginary scriptwriter could not have created two more symbolically perfect targets than the World Trade Center and the Pentagon—"the single most visible symbol of American-dominated global capitalism and the single most visible symbol of American military domination .... Immediately elevated to near-sacred status, those symbols themselves were an integral part of what made the events so traumatic" (Smelser 2004b: 264–5).

Smelser hastened to make the point that, despite the apparent natural disaster character of the events of 9/11, they could not be adequately understood without reference to the particular cultural context in which they occurred. In looking at the American reaction, he (Smelser 2004b: 270) felt there was "a certain old-fashioned quality to it; a reassertion of the virtues of nation and community; unashamed flag-waving patriotism; a feeling that we, as Americans, under attack, were one again; and a feeling of pride in the American way of life, its values, its culture, and its democracy." There is an obvious similarity to the precedent of the unprovoked Japanese attack on Pearl Harbor, together with the characteristics of the American response. He notes, in passing, that we should not forget that such episodes of extreme national fear and unity have always had their darker potential—"for the muting of political opposition, sometimes self-imposed; for scapegoat of internal minority groups thought to be dangerous or somehow linked to the danger, and for the compromise of civil liberties in the name of vigilance and security" (Smelser 2004b: 270). After Pearl Harbor there was also the search for scapegoats, which led to the incarceration of Japanese Americans in camps and a questioning of their loyalty to America.

Granted that 9/11 was a disaster on a grand scale, the way in which it was "imagined" and constantly "re-imagined" drew on the most totemic cultural symbols. In Durkheimian terms, these entailed polarizations of the pure and the impure/polluted, and a sacred site at which ritualized memorial celebrations of solidarity could engender "collective effervescence." Smelser, drawing on Robin Murphy Williams's (1951) classic book on American values, emphasizes the moral orientation of American culture, permeating not just popular entertainment, such as the western film, but also such political crises as Watergate and the effort to impeach President Clinton. He finds it unsurprising that the national reaction to the threats of terrorism should have taken on not only a moral but also a dualistic cast. He cites President Bush's use of the language of good versus evil symbolism, and his framing of the national response as a moral crusade against a "sacred evil" (Smelser 2004b: 277). Another of the American cultural values singled out by Williams, and reiterated by Smelser, is the type of nationalism and patriotism, which is characterized by a sense of American society as "chosen" (deriving from the religious heritage), involving a sense of moral superiority over other peoples. This leads to a strong sense of what it is to be "American" or "un-American," which has sometimes led to the paradoxical legitimation of attacks on citizens considered "un-American." The final set of values taken from Williams are those of "efficiency and practicality," which are a product of the values of individualism, activism, and mastery of the environment, as well as the evolved mythology of the conquest of frontiers (Smelser 2004b: 278). In the case of the response to 9/11, this led to a hyper-active search for ways of eradicating the threat of terrorism, even if this entailed attacking sources of terrorism abroad and at home—hence the wars in Afghanistan and Iraq, and internal surveillance (Smelser 2004: 279).

Like many other sociological concepts that have nonsociological precursors (for example, "social evolution" in nineteenth century sociology drew on the theory of evolution), cultural trauma theory draws on pre-existing sources, in this case psychological theories of trauma, whilst being differentiated in significant ways. Smelser's (2004a) essay on "Psychological Trauma and Cultural Trauma" spells out the similarities and differences between psychological trauma and cultural trauma. Obviously, the main differences stem from the fact that the former is concerned with the individual person, whereas the latter involves collectivities, particularly the nation. He notes that national cultures in complex societies are typically problematic with respect to unity and coherence. It follows that a claim of traumatic cultural change must be established by deliberate efforts on the part of cultural carriers—"cultural specialists such as priests, politicians, intellectuals, journalists, moral entrepreneurs, and leaders of social movements" (Smelser 2004a: 38). Furthermore, once a historical memory is established, its status as a trauma has to be continually sustained and reproduced:

> These features mean that a cultural trauma differs greatly from a psychological trauma in terms of the mechanisms that establish and sustain it. The mechanisms associated with psychological trauma are the intrapersonal dynamics of defence, adaptation, coping, and working through; the mechanism at the cultural level are mainly those of social agents and contending groups. (Smelser 2004a: 38)

On the basis of these comparisons, Smelser (2004a: 38) advances to a formal definition of cultural trauma:

> A memory accepted and publicly given credence by a relevant membership group and evoking an event or situation which is (a) laden with negative affect, (b) represented as indelible, and (c) regarded as threatening a society's existence or violating one or more of its fundamental cultural presuppositions.

The psychological mechanisms involved in responses to trauma have some parallels in cultural trauma. For example, Smelser points out the tendency to attribute blame and to seek a scapegoat often occurs in responses to cultural trauma. Citing Thompson (1998), he (Smelser 2004a: 52) notes that this is a "regular feature of moral panics—collective hysteria in response to uncertainty and threat—in which some inimical agent is identified as attacking something held sacred." Similarly, the dualistic response of attraction and repulsion has an analogy at the socio-cultural level. There may be a dual tendency—efforts to downplay an event or "put it behind us," but also a compulsive preoccupation with it and an effort to keep the memory alive in the public consciousness. A closely related defense mechanism in coping with trauma is to convert a negative event into a positive one. Like psychological ambivalence, its manifestation at the socio-cultural level may be observed in a compulsive examining and re-examining, bringing up new aspects of the trauma, reinterpreting and re-evaluating, and battling over symbolic significance: "These are the ingredients of what might variously be called cultural play, cultural fussing, even culture wars" (Smelser 2004a: 54).

It is by paying attention to these mechanisms and the links between cultural trauma and moral panic (and the broader culture wars), that we can begin to make sense of the connections between the cultural trauma of 9/11, 2001, and the controversy a decade later over the proposed Moslem building near Ground Zero.

## Imagining 9/11 as Cultural Trauma

According to the principle put forward by theorists of cultural trauma, it is not possible to derive the nature of a traumatic response from the *external* characteristics of the traumatizing event itself; the character of the traumatic response must be found in the cultural *context* in which it comes to be embedded (Smelser 2004b: 271). It would be tempting to modify this principle in the case of the events of 9/11; such was their scope and intensity. However, an analysis of the ways in which the perception of the events was shaped by the particular national socio-cultural context, especially media representations, could facilitate a better understanding of why the mosque at Ground Zero affair threatened to develop into a moral panic.

Because academic publication and dissemination are such slow processes compared with mass media publishing, it was possible for the authors of *Cultural Trauma and Collective Identity* (Alexander et al. 2004) to include an epilogue on 9/11 after the rest of the book was finished, but too late to refer to the other most relevant study — Germanic studies scholar Fritz Breithaupt's (2003) "Rituals of Trauma: How the Media Fabricated September 11." Whereas Smelser focuses on certain American values and their functioning in the trauma, Breithaupt emphasizes the role of the media in framing the event as trauma. Breithaupt hastens to explain the somewhat provocative title by stating that in speaking of the fabrication of trauma he did not mean to imply that there had not been an enormous amount of suffering involved, but that he wanted to draw attention to how the media's staging of trauma does not so much record the human suffering as it serves as the central axis of organizing the diverse material in such a way as to bring about the said response in the audience: "In short, the media themselves responded to the attack by creating that which they perceived as the outcome of the attacks: a trauma" (Breithaupt 2003: 67). At the same time, the media recommended themselves as therapist and agent of national healing. But this staging of therapy offered something other than an effective therapeutic mechanism, but rather a "ritualistic practice with its specific mandate, totem and taboo" (Breithaupt 2003: 67). According to Breithaupt's (2003: 68) definition of trauma (drawing on Leys 2000): "Trauma is a memory disorder that prevents an individual from processing events in such a way that they become 'past' events." He adds, "Similarly, the media bring about a heightened present in which the storing of the past *as past* does not and cannot take place" (Breithaupt 2003: 68). In other words, it is suggested, there is a functional similarity between the concept of "trauma" and the culture of the modern mass media. The media are the apparatus that make possible the repetition of events, that amplify the magnitude of events, that offer events as an experience to those who were not present, and that bridge spatial and temporal orders (such as the past and the present). To the extent that media representations are successful in attracting and persuading an audience the result may be to blur the distinctions between who experiences and who does not, and the temporal order between past and present.

In a sense, Breithaupt and Smelser are making the same point when portraying 9/11 as cultural trauma. But Breithaupt (2003: 69) is more specific in pointing out the productive nature of the concept "trauma" in the cultural sphere of the media and its ideological effects:

> For the media, "trauma" is an organizing device, that is, a concept. This is why the word "trauma" appears in quotation marks in this text. Concepts "grasp" reality by offering a clear vision of otherwise complex situations. As a concept, "trauma" is not a diagnosis of existing medical conditions, but rather a prescription for arranging the scenario of an event. Concepts guide the perception of reality. We see (perceive) what we already (conceptually) know; concepts prepare for future situations. In the world of concepts, there are always competing concepts. Indeed, instead of "trauma," there are numerous other concepts that could have guided the media: "anxiety," "anger," "vengeance," "tragedy," "sobriety," "mourning," "disbelief," "dialogue"—all of which do structure some responses to September 11, whether they are named or not. Choosing between concepts always involves making decisions that are not guided by the actual material. This is why concepts imply ideologies; concepts are applied to situations rather than derived from them. For reasons to be examined, "trauma" seems to have been the prime concept (or at least one of the prime concepts) governing the organization of the information involving the attacks on the Twin Towers.

Viewed in the light of the possible alternatives, it might seem curious that the media picked on "trauma" to such an extent when organizing these events. It has been suggested that "sobriety" might have been a realistic alternative—a sober assessment of continuing international tensions and an end to the idealistic beliefs of the post-Cold War 1990s. But the particular appeal of "trauma" is that it emphasizes the innocence of the victims or the collective victim—as exemplified in the most obvious cases, such as rape, domestic violence, genocide, and slavery. It was certainly the case that the individuals killed in the Twin Trade Towers and the Pentagon were innocent victims, but a sober analysis might have drawn more attention to the symbolic significance of these buildings in relation to the actions in the Middle East of American corporations and political-military agencies. In fact, the television coverage provided little analysis of the motives of the attackers other than to repeat the Bush administration's line that it was an attack on American values and its way of life. To have given prominence to such a debate would have called into question the equating of individual innocent victims with America as innocent collective victim. This is not to suggest that television media ideologically colluded with politicians in a propagandist way, but rather that the media were inclined to "let the pictures speak for themselves" in the first instance because they seemed to offer the sense of directly sharing in the "shock and awe" of the experience. The event was presented as a trauma in which the viewers themselves shared and by which they were positioned as members of the collective victim (America), but also as survivors. The structural affinity between mass media and the trauma experience was heightened by the repetition of the same shocking film clips in the first few hours. This was not interrupted or balanced by any strong narrative or neutral voice to accompany the images and to give order to the chaotic material or present opinions with which one could agree or disagree.[1]

After the first few hours of presenting raw images of the "unthinkable," news coverage shifted from responding to uncertain events to imposing form and meaning on them. As media analyst William Uricchio (2001) described it,

> Graphic form, rhythmic form (the footage of the jet smashing into the second tower repeated up to 30 times per hour), and increasingly, narrative form—all gave coherence to events that were still difficult to comprehend. As if a story set in Batman's Gotham, a simple narrative of good versus evil emerged, and as in Batman's universe, evil could be embodied in only a limited number of characters. Bin Laden quickly (and perhaps appropriately—but at the time it was anything but clear) helped to complete the narrative, providing evil with a face and name. The quick transformation of unpredictable live events into familiar narrative patterns, it can be argued, produces a certain comfort; but it also frames the event, establishing specific ways of thinking about the situation, together with an inclination toward narrative resolution.

---

1    Media experts have produced various explanations for the fascination with this kind of spectacular television coverage of a disaster. One suggestion is that the answer lies in the fascination we have as a species for the "sublime," in the sense given by Edmund Burke's 1757 treatise, *A Philosophical Enquiry into the Origin of our Ideas of the Sublime and the Beautiful*, which describes the sublime as the opposite of the beautiful: that which both terrifies and astonishes. Great natural forces, such as volcanic eruptions and tsunamis, have that effect, as do human catastrophic spectacles like those of 9/11 (Weigel 2001). Another possible reason that people willingly watched the images of 9/11 over and over again may lie in the phenomenon of the "pathological public sphere," in which onlookers at a disaster are drawn into a shared identity around "shock, trauma, and the wound" (Weigel 2001). In a public sphere such as that of the modern nation-state where diversity makes national identity problematic, it may be that the pathological condition of watching the unfolding of a horrific disaster enables people to participate in a civic process based on shared terror.

The framing of the story as an "Attack on America" and the insistence upon almost exclusively domestic coverage was a choice. It precluded other sorts of framing such as "an attack on the West" that might have appeared had we seen the spontaneous street demonstrations of shocked and saddened people in Berlin, Copenhagen, Paris, London, and other parts of the world. The "world" part of the WTC accounted for over 1000 now missing "foreigners," and the functions of the businesses within it were emphatically global. But ours was an American story. And the choice of an antagonist who embodies the antithesis of our values (a multi-millionaire who has rejected consumerism, a terrorist who seems deeply religious) helped to mute the complexity of the 18 or so terrorists who destroyed themselves along with their helpless victims. Bin Laden's casting helped to keep narrative causality elegantly simple: evil. While I am not in a position to dispute this attribution, the point I want to make is that this sort of narrative inscription comes easily to our culture's use of television, and it brings with it a simplicity (or is it clarity?) of narrative logic that is muddled, even spoiled by complex questions about history, foreign policy, or representation that yield real insight. By September 15, news coverage carried the graphic "America at War" accompanied by subdued martial theme music (an element conspicuously absent for the first two days or so). And although we are being prepared for a long and difficult war, the image of finding 'em, smoking 'em out of their holes, and running 'em down has the same elegantly simple appeal as the original framing of the story.

By day three, the television narrative had become a "therapeutic one":

> It was about picking up the pieces. In that story, survivors and relatives, the immediate victims of the attacks, were featured and profiled. Their human faces of tragedy were connections to emotional expression for viewers groping to make meaning out of the extraordinary events, and the implied promise of victim-by-victim coverage—which held a voyeuristic pleasure in itself—was that emphatic participation in grief and trauma was the road to recovery. The updates on blood drives, charities, and the celebrity telethon were tools to turn grief into action, to liberate the will to do something to help... In the U.S. in this crisis, network newsmakers assumed a therapeutic role as grief counselor for the nation's inner child, nurturing insecure viewers who had been stripped of their adult self-assurance by the shock of the attacks. (Aufderheide 2001)

The problem is that the therapy offered by television was not one of rational understanding of the complex events linking past, present and future, but rather a ritualistic repetition of static and now totemic images—the destruction, the flag, the heroic firefighters and police, the evil Osama bin Laden, the victims and mourners, and the now sacred and memorialized site of Ground Zero itself. To put it in terms of a movement between key concepts, it is as though we move from trauma, to therapy, and next to ritual and the sacred. The media construction of "trauma" is based on static images that act as a reflective shield, which only formally mimics therapy, and instead sets up a ritual. This can be expressed in terms of Emile Durkheim's study of ritual, the sacred, and the symbolic, presented in *The Elementary Forms of the Religious Life* (1915), in which ritual is that which unites people by bringing about the consciousness of society as such—in this case, America:

> First, there is loss (sacrificial animal, the loss of lives, the firefighters, and Americans who died), then there is the higher unity of identifying with the totem (the flag), the higher being (America), and thus the generation of society. The totem images of the flag and the American firefighter are first seen in the ashes, lost in debris, and then they become the means by which one can achieve the union with this higher being America. The flag on top of the ruins is the totem that solidifies "trauma" as a ritual. (Breithaupt 2003: 77)

Others have written in these Durkheimian terms about the sense of collective effervescence and heightened solidarity brought about in America by the media's representation of 9/11 and the accompanying rituals and symbols reaffirming the sacredness of the collectivity (Tiryakian 2005). They have also referred to the "dark side" of this solidarity or "we-ness," which is the exclusion and fear of the evil "other," in this case militant Moslems/terrorists and their sympathizers. The more strongly 9/11 became ritualized and sacralized, the more powerful was the corresponding taboo on any communication or empathy with the evil other. The White House was quick to brand the terrorists and their sympathizers as evil and "cowardly," with Press Secretary Ari Fleischer warning the rare media commentators who questioned this, such as Bill Maher of *Politically Incorrect*, that they "should watch what they say, watch what they do" (Breithaupt 2003: 79). President Bush (*Public Papers* 2001) made it clear that it was a simple dichotomy of Good versus Evil, about which there was no need for further reasoning about motives and interests: "The people who did this act on America, and who may be planning further acts, are evil people. They don't represent an ideology; they don't represent a legitimate political group of people. They're flat evil. That's all they can think about, is evil."

The president's performance in the days after 9/11, as communicated through television, was crucial in defining the event in the stark terms of good versus evil, America as innocent victim at the hands of an evil terrorist entity. He was able to use visual symbols and oral rhetoric in a way that seemed authentic and natural in binding together government, nation, heroes and victims, in a sacred bond. This was demonstrated on his visit to Ground Zero for the first time only two days after the terrorist attack. Speaking from atop a crushed fire-truck amid the building rubble, with his arm around a firefighter, and using a bullhorn, his opening statement adopted a religious tone: "I want you all to know, that America today is on bended knee in prayer for the people whose lives were lost here, for the workers who work here, for the families who mourn. This nation stands with the good people of New York City, and New Jersey, and Connecticut as we mourn the loss of thousands of our citizens" (the speech and a discussion of its rhetorical form can be found online at *American Rhetoric*). The religious connotations of the opening statement (and the closing statement—"God bless America") and the impromptu ceremony itself, bind together those present, the victims, and the nation, into a sacred whole. The simple, but effective, oratory creates a "collective effervescence," just as in Durkheim's description of the elementary forms of the religious life through which the idealized society was rendered sacred and divine. This sacred entity is defined even more clearly by contrast with the profane other that threatens and could pollute it. And so, when a member of the crowd calls out that he cannot hear, the President replies loudly, "I can hear you! I can hear you, the rest of the world can hear you, and the people who knocked these buildings down will hear all of us soon" (quoted in Broughton 2001). This is clearly a not so coded threat to the evil other, the terrorists and their sympathizers. The crowd begins chanting in patriotic fervor: "USA, USA, USA, USA" (quoted in Broughton 2001). Therapeutic patriotism (Aufderheide 2001) was to be one possible way of healing the trauma, in addition to the rituals of commemoration and mourning at Ground Zero itself and as represented on television.

But in addition to trauma and its therapeutic treatment, the media representation of 9/11 and its aftermath can also be analyzed in terms of the concept "moral panic" (Rothe and Muzzatti 2004, Victor 2006). The overlap with what has been covered in the discussion of cultural trauma lies chiefly in three key characteristics of moral panic. The first is that it relates to a threat to the fundamental moral basis of society — evil threatens the good. The second characteristic is that the alleged perpetrators of the threat are regarded as evil "folk devils." The third characteristic is that the threat is rapidly magnified or escalates from one or more incidents to a widespread fear about a more general and insidious danger. In the case of 9/11, the actions of a small group of terrorists attacking the World Trade Center and the Pentagon rapidly escalates into a global War on Terrorism with constant alarms about imminent threats. The model of the stages of development of a moral panic, as first analyzed by Cohen (1972: 9, Thompson 1998: 8), also focuses on the role of key actors, such as moral entrepreneurs of various sorts (including politicians, policing agencies, and media pundits)—some of the same claims makers as those involved in the construction of cultural traumas. A further overlap between cultural traumas and moral panics is to be found in theories that focus on the anxiety-inducing contextual factors of a socio-cultural kind, such as those featured in theories of risk society and studies of the media's combination of discourses that can produce an amplification spiral leading to panic (Thompson 1998: 61). In the case of the cultural trauma of 9/11, the evil folk devils are Islamic terrorists who threaten America and its values and the dominant discourse becomes that of terror and the need to keep it at a distance, whether that terror is located abroad or in the homeland. The president's use of the term "crusade" to describe the war against terror evoked memories of the medieval crusades of Christians against Moslems, which led some Moslems to believe that they themselves were under suspicion (President Bush referred to "this crusade, this war on terrorism" in an impromptu remark on September 16, 2001, see Lyons 2001). The number of hate crimes against Moslems jumped considerably and there was concern about a growing Islamophobia (*Uniform Crime Reports* 2002).

## Moral Panic and the "Mosque at Ground Zero"

The controversy about a planned "mosque at Ground Zero" provides a classic example of a developing moral panic, in which what originally seemed to be a relatively local incident rapidly went through an amplification spiral as media and claims makers summoned up the trauma-laden discourses of 9/11. The proposal to build a 13-story Moslem community center to be located two blocks from the World Trade Center site in lower Manhattan, at a location already in use for Moslem worship, was reported by *The New York Times* in December 2009 (Blumenthal and Sharaf 2009). Early response to the project was not pronounced and some commentators provided positive coverage, until protests were sparked by a campaign launched by conservative bloggers Pamela Geller and Robert Spencer, founders of the group, "Stop Islamization of America," who dubbed the project the "Ground Zero Mosque" ("Park51" 2011). Much of the mass media took up this abbreviated and inaccurate designation (although some ran with it and then subsequently italicized it; see, for example, Calderone 2010) and this gave the project widespread and controversial coverage, tapping into the collective memory of the earlier trauma and moral panic. There are many elements of the symbolic code from the earlier episode that recur in response to the new stimulus. Perhaps the most telling is that of the threat of evil pollution of the sacred site. Members of a group of victims' relatives, 9/11 Families for a Safe and Strong America (quoted in "The Moment an Angry Crowd" 2010), gave frequent expression to this fear:

> Sally Regenhard, whose son was a firefighter who was killed in the attacks, and who testified before Congress on 9/11, said that the center would be "sacrilege on sacred ground." Rosemary Cain, whose son was killed, said, "I think it's despicable. That's sacred ground." Dov Shefi, whose son Haggai was killed, said: "the establishment of a mosque in this place ... is like bringing a pig into the Holy Temple." Similarly, politicians used the same language to voice their opposition. New York City Council Member Dan Halloran described Ground Zero as "sacred ground to New Yorkers." He was echoed by Democratic Representative Tim Bishop of New York's First District: "As a New Yorker, I believe Ground Zero is sacred ground and should unite us." It was reported in the New York Daily News and other newspapers that a grassroots movement was gaining momentum on the internet, recruiting construction workers at Ground Zero to take a Hard Hat Pledge to boycott work on the project, and quoting Dave

Kaiser, a blaster: "It's a very touchy thing because they want to do this on sacred ground."

Of course, there were voices on the other side of the controversy arguing that the project was a test of American values of tolerance and religious freedom (including President Obama and the Mayor of New York), but the majority of those polled were against it ("Park51" 2011). The strength and depth of the links between the discourse and symbols of the earlier cultural trauma and those surrounding the mosque project were too strong. Even the academic debates failed to break free of the dominant discourse; as in the case of the debate staged by the Council on Foreign Relations where, of the five distinguished participants, two contributors made references to trauma and the sacred. Daniel Senor ("Expert Roundup" 2010)., Adjunct Senior Fellow for Middle Eastern Studies, Council on Foreign Relations, stated, "Many understandably see the area as sacred ground." And Richard Land, President, Ethics and Religious Liberty Commission, Southern Baptist Convention, argued that the mosque "symbolizes that the trauma of 9/11 is still a raw and unhealed emotional wound in American society" and "Ground Zero is hallowed ground consecrated by the nearly three thousand people who died there" ("Expert Roundup" 2010).

## Concluding Remarks

The question that Stanley Cohen (1972) set out to answer with his systematic development of the concept of moral panic was: how and why did a localized incident involving youth gangs fighting on the beach escalate, via an amplification spiral in the mass media and various influential claims makers, so that it became a crisis about a threat to national values and to the collective identity of the nation? It might seem inappropriate and even indecent to pose the same question about 9/11 in view of the magnitude of the tragedy. However, despite the larger scale and greater severity of the original incident in this case, which involved nearly 3,000 deaths, it is still possible to analyze the cultural construction of the event and the form taken by its legacy in the collective consciousness. Commentators have questioned whether the event would have had the same impact if it had not been captured live on television in such a spectacular fashion and then constructed in a particular narrative form as a national cultural trauma. The difference this made only gradually became evident in the case of the proposal for a Moslem cultural center with prayer facilities, located two blocks away from Ground Zero, which did not seem to pose any threat when first seen by the planning authorities. But the amplification spiral took off when the media and claims makers revived central symbols and discourses of the earlier cultural trauma, especially those in which all that was held most sacred was under threat from an alien evil force.

Research on 9/11 and its effects is already very extensive and the controversy surrounding the proposed mosque shows that there are still issues in play. Sociological concepts such as cultural trauma and moral panic are just two suggestive approaches for analyzing this phenomenon. This chapter has sketched out some of the reasons why the two concepts might be fruitfully combined to advance understanding. Each of them taken alone has yielded useful insights, but it has been argued that their combination is heuristically beneficial and theoretically valid.

# References

Alexander, J. 2004. Toward a theory of cultural trauma, in *Cultural Trauma andCollective Identity*, edited by J.C. Alexander, R. Eyerman, B. Giesen, N.J. Smelser, and P. Sztompka. Berkeley: University of California Press, 196–263

Alexander, J.C., Eyerman, R., Giesen, B., Smelser, N.J., and Sztompka, P. (eds.). 2004. *Cultural Trauma and Collective Identity*, Berkeley: University of California Press.

Aufderheide, P. 2001. *Therapeutic Patriotism and Beyond* [Online]. Available at: http://www.nyu.edu/fas/projects/vcb/case_911/resources/essay_aufderheidethera.html [accessed: October 23, 2011].

Blumenthal, R. and Sharaf, M. 2009. Muslim prayers and renewal near Ground Zero. *The New York Times* [Online, December 8]. Available at: http://www.nytimes.com/2009/12/09/nyregion/09mosque.html?_r=1&sq=mosque%20ground%20zero&st=nyt&scp=1&pagewanted=all [accessed: October 23, 2011].

Breithaupt, F. 2003. Rituals of trauma: how the media fabricated September 11, in *Media Representations of September 11*, edited by S. Chermak, F.Y. Bailey, and M. Brown. Westport: Praeger, 67–81.

Broughton, P.D. 2001. "The rest of the world hears you." *The Telegraph* [Online, September 15]. Available at: http://www.telegraph.co.uk/news/worldnews/northamerica/usa/1340612/The-rest-of-the-world-hears-you.html [accessed: October 23, 2011].

Bush, G.W. 2001. *Bullhorn Address to Ground Zero Rescue Workers*, September 14. *Rhetoric of 9-11. American Rhetoric* [Online]. Available at: http://www.americanrhetoric.com/speeches/gwbush911groundzerobullhorn.htm [accessed: June 4, 2011].

Calderone, M. 2010. News outlets split in describing mosque. *Yahoo! News* [Online, August 16]. Available at: http://news.yahoo.com/blogs/upshot/news-outlets-split-describing-mosque.html [accessed: December 3, 2010].

Cohen, S. 1972. *Folk Devils and Moral Panics: The Creation of the Mods and Rockers*. London: MacGibbon and Kee.

Durkheim, E. 1915 (1912). *The Elementary Forms of the Religious Life*, translated by J. W. Swain. London: Allen and Unwin. Originally published as *Les formes élémentaires de la vie religieuse*.

Johnson, T. 2010. Expert roundup: is a mosque near Ground Zero a bad idea? *Council on Foreign Relations* [Online, August 23]. Available at: http://www.cfr.org/religion/mosque-near-ground-zero-bad-idea/p22830 [accessed: January 19, 2011].

Leys, R. 2000. *Trauma: A Genealogy*. Chicago: University of Chicago Press.

Lyons, J. 2001. *Bush Enters Mideast's Rhetorical Minefield* [Online, September 21]. Available at: http://greenspun.com/bboard/q-and-a-fetch-msg.tcl?msg_id=006SM3 [accessed: October 23, 2011].

2010. The moment an angry crowd protesting against Ground Zero mosque turns on man in a skullcap … because they think he is a Muslim [ellipsis in original]. *Mail Foreign Service. MailOnline.com* [Online, August 24]. Available at: http://www.dailymail.co.uk/news/article-1305255/Ground-Zero-mosque-protest-The-moment-angry-crowd-turns-man-skull-cap--think-Muslim.html [accessed: October 23, 2011].

2011. Park51. *Wikipedia* [Online]. Available at: http://en.wikipedia.org/wiki/Park51 [accessed: March 22, 2011].

2001. *Public Papers of the Presidents of the United States: George W. Bush.* Book I: July 1 to December 31. September 28. *GPO Access* [Online]. Available at: http://www.gpoaccess.gov/pubpapers/gwbush.html [accessed: October 23, 2011].

Rothe, D. and Muzzatti S.L. 2004. Enemies everywhere: terrorism, moral panic, and U.S. civil society, in *Critical Criminology*, 12, 327–50.

Smelser, N.J. 2004a. Psychological trauma and cultural trauma, in *Cultural Trauma and Collective Identity*, edited by J.C. Alexander, R. Eyerman, B. Giesen, N. Smelser, and P. Sztompka. Berkeley: University of California Press, 31–59

Smelser, N.J. 2004b. Epilogue: September 11, 2001, as Cultural Trauma, in *Cultural Trauma and Collective Identity*, edited by J.C. Alexander, R. Eyerman, B. Giesen, N. Smelser, and P. Sztompka. Berkeley: University of California Press, 264–82.

Thompson, K. 1997. Regulation, de-regulation and re-regulation, in *Media and Cultural Regulation*, edited by K. Thompson. London: Sage Publications, 9–52.

Thompson, K. 1998. *Moral Panics*. Key Ideas. Milton Park: Routledge.

Thompson, K. 2011. Foreword, in *Moral Panics and the Politics of Anxiety*, edited by S.P. Hier. London: Routledge, vii–xi.

Tiryakian, E.A. 2009. Durkheim, Solidarity and September 11, *For Durkheim: Essays in Historical and Cultural* Sociology, by E.A. Tiryakian. Farnham: Ashgate, 131–48.

2002. *Uniform Crime Reports: Hate Crime Statistics 2002. Federal Bureau of Investigation* [Online]. Available at: http://www.fbi.gov/about-us/cjis/ucr/hate-crime/2002 [accessed: October 23, 2011].

Uricchio, W. 2001. Television Conventions. *re:constructions: reflections on humanity and media after tragedy* [Online, September 16] Available at: http://web.mit.edu/cms/reconstructions/interpretations/tvconventions.html [accessed: October 23, 2011].

Victor, J.S. 2006. Why the terrorism scare is a moral panic, *The Humanist*, July 1 [Online]. Available at: http://www.thefreelibrary.com/_/print/PrintArticle.aspx?id=148674633 [accessed: January 19, 2011].

Weigel, M. 2001. *Terrorism and the Sublime, or, Why We Keep Watching* [Online, September 17]. Available at: http://www.margaretweigel.com/comment/portSublime.pdf [accessed: October 23, 2011].

Williams, R.M. 1951. *American Society: A Sociological Interpretation*. New York: Alfred A. Knopf.

# Moral Panics over the Environment? "Climate Crisis" and the Moral Panics Model

Amanda Rohloff

This chapter utilizes the example of climate change to explore some of the core assumptions about moral panics and in doing so will begin to answer the question as to whether or not there can be moral panics about the environment. Several authors have argued that reactions to "risk society" issues such as climate change cannot be termed *moral* panics, as they are real, risk-based, and have little or no moral basis. Through an analysis of various sources of empirical data, this chapter illustrates that climate change is constructed within a strong moral basis. In regard to *panic*, this chapter contextualizes recent campaigns about climate change within long-term processes of changes in understandings about the environment and society.

Drawing on the work of German sociologist Norbert Elias and others, I use a revised notion of disproportionality to counter the claim that moral panic research on climate change must constitute a form of climate change "denial" (the charge of denial certainly indicates much about commonly held doubts concerning the concept of moral panic) (for useful introductions to Elias's work, see Mennell 1998, Fletcher 1997, van Krieken 1998, Kilminster 2007, and Hughes 2008.).

## Climate Change and Moral Panics

Sheldon Ungar (1992, 1995, 1998, 2001, 2011) has written several papers exploring climate change from a moral panic framework, attracting some criticism along the way (Goode and Ben-Yehuda 2009). In 2011, I published an article arguing that the phenomenon of climate change can be used to extend the concept of moral panic (Rohloff 2011a). Reactions to this idea are still emerging, though a reviewer of an earlier version of the manuscript termed it a piece of climate change denial. For some, it appears, the mere association of moral panics with climate change equates with denial. More recently, Stanley Cohen (2011) has suggested that reactions to climate change could be conceived of as "good" moral panics, but acknowledged that these types of important issues are less likely to gain the attention that other issues, such as that of immigration, receive.

Despite more than 20 years of moral panics over climate change (Ungar 2011), the topic has been largely avoided by moral panic researchers. This perhaps tells us something about the concept of moral panic, as David Garland (2008: 24–5) notes with reference to sociologists' reluctance to characterize reactions to 9/11 as a moral panic:

> The primary reason for this reluctance to invoke the idea of 'moral panic' was, I think, an ethical one. These sociologists were unwilling to challenge the moral sentiments that drove the social reaction. They were unwilling to play the debunking skeptics in the face of such intense grief and fear and so many murdered victims. It seems likely … that they saw the attribution of 'moral panic' as analytically appropriate but ethically taboo.

Could something similar conceivably be occurring in regard to climate change? Garland's very use of the term "debunking skeptic" proves problematic when applied to climate change, where "skeptic" is rebranded "denier." Do we need to think of ourselves as something other than a debunking skeptic? Perhaps the example of climate change can provide a means to rethink both the concept of moral panic and approaches to moral panic research.

## Norbert Elias

One way to rethink moral panic is by utilizing the work of sociologist Norbert Elias to take a long-term approach to the development of climate change as a perceived social problem (see Rohloff 2008, 2011a, 2011b, Rohloff and Wright 2010). In *The Civilizing Process* (2000), Elias shows that changes in standards of behavior and in habitus are interconnected with changes in wider (social and natural) processes, including processes of state formation. He argues that as societies become increasingly interdependent, individuals become more reliant on each other. This brings about changes in the ways people behave toward others:

> The more differentiated [social functions] become, the larger grows the number of functions and thus of people on whom the individual constantly depends. … As more and more people must attune their conduct to that of others, the web of actions must be organized more and more strictly and accurately, if each individual action is to fulfill its social function. Individuals are compelled to regulate their conduct in an increasingly differentiated, more even and stable manner. (Elias 2000: 367)

Elias describes individual regulation of behaviors in processes of civilization as "the social constraint towards self-constraint," whereby behavior comes to be increasingly regulated by the self, rather than external forces (a shift from social control to self-control). These changes go hand in hand with increasing mutual identification, and a decrease in cruelty and violence towards others. Along with changes in behaviors, Elias (2007) also writes about the gradual shift away from magico-mythical knowledge towards reality-congruent knowledge. Crucially, he regards these processes of civilization as neither inevitable nor unilinear:

> The armour of civilized conduct would crumble very rapidly if, through a change in society, the degree of insecurity that existed earlier were to break in upon us again, and if danger became as incalculable as it once was. Corresponding fears would soon burst the limits set to them today (Elias 2000: 532).

These processes of *decivilization* occur when civilizing processes go into reverse (Mennell 1990). During moral panics, perceived or actual crises may contribute to the reversals, with corresponding changes in behaviors and growing divisions among people.

These long-term changes in standards of behavior, and the interplay between social constraint and self-constraint, can be likened to the field of moral regulation—a recent addition to moral panic research (see, for example, the recent work of Chas Critcher and sociologist Sean P. Hier). But unlike studies of moral regulation, Elias's work provides us with both conceptual tools and an approach to research to help us overcome political problems associated with moral panics. First is the notion that social processes are dialectical, that is, that civilizing processes are not unilinear. Elias argues that the process of civilization is "in a continuous conflict with countervailing, decivilizing processes. There is no basis for assuming that it must remain dominant" (2008: 4). Sociologist Robert van Krieken, in discussing the concept of civilizing offensive (derived from Elias), argues "for a more *dialectical* understanding of social relations and historical development, one which grasps the often contradictory character of social life" (1998: 132). He is referring here to the idea that civilizing processes can contribute to decivilizing processes in the form of "civilized barbarism" (van Krieken 1998: 107, see also Elias 1996), a sort of fusion of civilizing and decivilizing trends. Exploring processes in such a complex way provides a means to avoid a simplified categorizing of a given moral panic as "bad."

Second, the concepts of involvement-detachment and secondary involvement provide guidelines for conducting research that can counter charges of mere debunking skepticism. Elias (2007: 72–3) argues that researchers should seek to achieve a balance between involvement and detachment—the interest in research may be sparked by one's involvement, and indeed the research may be aided by one's involvement, but that this should be accompanied by a continuous stepping back from the research so as to see it at a distance, in an attempt to avoid as much as possible the intrusion of "heteronomous evaluations" (such as those associated with wanting to liberate a disadvantaged group). For moral panics, through a process of "secondary involvement" (Elias 2007: 40, 48, 52), the researcher may utilize what they have found to contribute to a more "reality-congruent knowledge" (Elias 2007: 17) about the topic, and in the case of moral panics perhaps communicate whether reactions were appropriate (or not) and the ways that things might be improved. To avoid the charge of being merely a debunking skeptic, such judgment should be formed after the research and not before (though often one often has an inkling about the eventual results of research, hypotheses must continually be reflected upon critically).

# Where Are the "Moral," the "Panic," and the "Folk Devil?"

## Moral?

The very idea of moral panic research on climate change raises several possible problems, including the following:

1. The focus on the *science* of climate change may lead some to argue that it cannot be regarded as a *moral* panic as it is a *risk*-based issue.
2. The disproportionality and "debunking" commonly associated with moral panic may lead some to judge moral panic research on climate change as an example of climate change denial.
3. The apparent absence of an easily identifiable and marginalized folk devil may prove problematic, in some people's minds, for classifying reactions to climate change as "moral panics."

For some moral panic researchers, the moral is somehow seen as a separate sphere; for example, Kenneth Thompson argues that "Sometimes panics about food (for example, the BSE scare about infected beef) or health have been confused with panics that relate directly to morals" (Thompson 1998: vii). Such a stance suggests that "panics about food" cannot contain a moral element; it is a question of moral panics *versus* risk panics (Ungar 2001). In his introduction to the third edition of *Folk Devils and Moral Panics: The Creation of the Mods and Rockers*, Cohen (2002: xxxvi) argues that technical risks can be transformed into moral panics when the risk "becomes perceived as *primarily* moral rather than technical (the moral irresponsibility for taking this risk)." While the issue of climate change has been informed by science, and carries with it elements of technical risk, I wish to argue that it has become increasingly moralized over time.

An example of this increasing moralization is the award-winning climate change documentary *An Inconvenient Truth* (2006). I was one of many who saw it in 2006, when it was released in theaters. A friend dragged me along to the theater — at the time I had no desire to see it. I was immediately struck by how moralized the risk of climate change was throughout the documentary: I remember leaving the theater contemplating whether or not this could indeed be a prime case to explore from a moral panic perspective. Examples of the moralization throughout the documentary include the following statements by Al Gore (quoted in Guggenheim, *An Inconvenient Truth*, 2006):

"The moral imperative to make big changes is inescapable."

"Ultimately, this is really not a political issue so much as a moral issue. If we allow [the projected CO2 concentrations after 50 years of unrestricted fossil fuel burning] to happen, it is deeply unethical."

"This is what is at stake, our ability to live on planet earth, to have a future as a civilization. I believe this is a moral issue. It is your time to seize this issue. It is our time to rise again to secure our future."

Returning to Cohen, the "moral irresponsibility of taking this risk" becomes further apparent when Gore compares the development of the science of global warming and a lack of action, with initial responses to the scientific literature linking tobacco smoking with lung cancer—in the case of tobacco, Gore argues that the slow response resulted in the deaths of many, implying that a slow or inadequate response to climate change could have devastating consequences. He also draws comparisons between the storm brewing in Nazi Germany and the storm brewing in the form of Hurricane Katrina.

While *An Inconvenient Truth* received a great deal of attention at the time, it is only one of many, exemplifying a wider discourse surrounding climate change, also represented in such texts as other eco-documentaries, popular books about climate change, guides on "how to live green," "save the planet" and "stop global warming," eco-makeover lifestyle reality TV shows, and manners podcasts dedicated to "green living." For example, a *Scientific American* audio podcast episode, "Anesthesiologists Can Help Cut Climate Change," suggests that climate change should be on the mind of anesthesiologists, "because the gasses used to knock you out contribute to global warming." The presenter, Cynthia Graber (2010, emphasis in original) describes a study of three gasses commonly used by anesthesiologists, noting that two of the gases leave a significantly smaller carbon footprint than the third: "If a choice can be safely made, anesthesiologists should go with the one that's kindest to the climate."

Similarly, on an episode of the audio podcast series *Make-It-Green-Girl's Quick and Dirty Tips for an Earth Friendly Life* titled "Dry Clean Dilemma," the presenter, Anna Elzeftawy, discusses the problem of "eco-guilt" associated with dry cleaning, urging listeners to choose dry cleaners that use "environmentally friendly" solvents. This "eco-guilt" is manifested clearly in the *Guardian* blog, *Ask Leo and Lucy: Your Green Questions Answered* (Hickman and Siegle), where readers submit questions such as "Can I use perfume and be green?" "Do dimmer switches really save energy when lighting a room?" "What is the most eco-friendly alcoholic drink?" "What's the best form of carbon offsetting?" "How green is your pension?" and so on. While some of these questions are about "living green" and being "kind to the environment" in general, many relate back to climate change and carbon footprints.

An additional source of information on "green" questions is the recent proliferation of "green guides." These texts typically contain prescriptions and proscriptions about how to modify one's behaviors to combat climate change. The following examples are taken from several of these green guides: *I Count: Together We Can Stop Climate Chaos: Your Step-By-Step Guide to Climate Bliss* (2006) has a strong focus on the individual management of behavior to decrease individual carbon footprints. Some sections include a list of "good" things to do on one page, with a list of "bad" things that are done on the opposite page, directly comparing the impact these are calculated to have on carbon emissions.

*I Count: Together We Can Stop Climate Chaos: Your Step-By-Step Guide to Climate Bliss* (2006: 52) lists several steps one can go through to try to "stop climate chaos." Step ten is called "Reject the Ridiculous":

> On occasion we are all ridiculous. But this step will help. It works like this. Next time you are about to buy something, simply ask yourself if your purchase of that crazy packaged up beef burger is worth planetary chaos, mass starvation and general unpleasantness. Almost magically you will know the answer. So, repeat after me. I do not need my oranges individually wrapped; I believe their existing skin to be adequate. I do not need to heat the outside of my house with a gas-fired patio heater; I am capable of going inside.

And in another section of the same guide:

> Some habits kind of feel like they're good, but they aren't. Flying, for instance. There's no way around this. Aircraft just pipe greenhouse gases into our upper atmosphere, where they immediately do most damage. Let's get this in perspective: fly to Athens and to make up for your climate impact you will have to go without heating, cooking, lighting and all forms of motorised transport for 2 years and 3 months. Which you don't really fancy, do you? So you have to promise. I hereby solemnly swear that: I won't fly when I can take the train or boat. I will take more holidays in my lovely, comfy UK. I will use video conference technology. I will take at least one less flight a year. (*I Count* 2006: 58)

In these guides, there is also an emphasis on a perceived trend towards increasing overconsumption. In *How to Live a Low-Carbon Life: The Individual's Guide to Stopping Climate Change*, Chris Goodall writes, "As responsible members of prosperous societies, we have a duty to curb our own consumption rather than to rely on ineffectual governments and profit-seeking companies" (Goodall 2007: 4). Here, the perception is that not only are individuals failing to regulate their consumption (presumably the reason we need these guides) but states and corporations are also failing to regulate carbon emissions. There is a perceived crisis, and something must be done before it is too late.

The following quotation is a blurb for *The Virgin Green Guide: The Easy Way to Save the Planet and Save £££s* (2007):

> Global warming and environmental issues are front-page news, but a few simple changes to your lifestyle can lead to huge benefits to the health of our planet.
>
> The Virgin Green Guide is a practical, no-nonsense and timely guide to help you do your bit for the environment – and save some cash at the same time. Find out how much you could be wasting – from gas and electricity to food and water – and what you can do to stop it.

And here is a blurb from *The Climate Diet: How You Can Cut Your Carbon, Cut Costs, and Save the Planet* (2008):

> The atmosphere is getting fat on our carbon and other greenhouse gas emissions and it needs our help. We live in a world of excess, consuming too much of everything – food, clothes, cars, toys, shoes, bricks, and mortar. Our bingeing is often so extreme that it threatens our own health and wellbeing. And we are not the only ones who are getting sick. The Earth, which provides the food, air, water, and land that sustains us, is also under severe pressure. We either take steps to put our personal and planetary systems back into balance or we suffer the consequences. So, what does any unhealthy overweight person do when the doctor tells him or her that they are eating themselves into an early grave? Go on a diet!

This diet metaphor, contrasting excess in eating or drinking with excess consumption in general (that is, a "high carbon" lifestyle), draws parallels with other wider discourses and practices for moderating ones behavior. This is perhaps in an attempt to establish a moderation of "carbon consumption" as a status aspiration (see, for example Aarts, Goudsblom, Schmidt, and Spier 1995)

Similarly, another genre, that of the eco-makeover lifestyle reality TV show, consistently comments on climate change. In these shows that have been made in many countries around the world, including *No Waste Like Home* (United Kingdom, 2005), *Carbon Cops* (Australia, 2006), and *Wa$ted* (New Zealand, 2007), "experts" go into people's homes, workplaces, and so on and carry out carbon audits. In some of these eco-makeover shows, participants are described as "eco-criminals," and their actions "eco-crimes." There occur "naming and shaming" processes in some of these shows, in which incidents of "eco-deviance" are exposed and attempts are made to transform them into "eco-friendly" practices (see Lewis 2008). Throughout, various suggestions appear to the audiences (anyone who might be watching the shows) about what they can do (or should do) to cut down their own carbon emissions.

## Moral Panic?

Erich Goode and Nachman Ben-Yehuda (2009: 82, emphasis in original) argue that "the very word 'panic' *implies* disproportion" as a refutation of Ungar's contention that disproportionality is not an essential feature of moral panic. However, assessing disproportionality as a feature of moral panic depends on our definitions both of disproportionality and of moral panic. Goode and Ben-Yehuda mention several indicators of disproportion, one of which is "changes over time." They argue, "If the attention paid to a given condition at one point in time is vastly greater than that paid to it during a previous or later time, without any corresponding increase in objective seriousness, then, once again, the criterion of disproportion may be said to have been met" (Goode and Ben-Yehuda 2009: 46).

In relation to climate change, it is not only the natural crisis of global warming, but also the social crisis of our relationship with the environment, including patterns of consumption, that determine whether certain responses constitute moral panics. As I have argued elsewhere (Rohloff 2008, 2011a, 2011b), moral panic can be reconceptualized as a heightened campaign or sense of concern about a particular issue or set of issues, when a perceived crisis in the "civilizing" of the self and the other exists, the regulation of one's own or another's behavior is seen to be failing or out of control, or it is believed that to avoid a crisis a drastic change in the regulation of the self and the other is needed. Seen in this way, moral panics over climate change clearly both emerge from, and relate to, long-term ecological, social, and psychological processes. The campaigns surrounding climate change— books, guides, documentaries, reality TV shows, and other media mentioned earlier—that seek to both educate people and bring about changes in behavior can be conceptualized as a civilizing offensive; campaigns to "civilize" the self or the other. In this way, moral panics in general can perhaps be seen as civilizing offensives. However, depending on the historical development of given social processes, different civilizing offensives may accompany moral panics, ranging from civilizing all of us (as in the case of climate change), to civilizing some (making "them" more like "us"), to more exclusionary campaigns that seek to make society more "civilized" by excluding those deemed too "uncivilized."

Panic also has a flipside: denial (see Cohen 2001, 2002, 2011). As witnessed in the aftermath of "Climategate," as well as the development of so-called climate change skeptics or climate change deniers, along with existing research interviewing people about their thoughts about climate change, the growing awareness of the "exaggeration and distortion" in the media, combined with multiple media sources (McRobbie and Thornton 1995), suggests that generating both concern and changes in behavior can prove difficult in some cases. In this regard, moral panic research can be tremendously informative in assessing the adequacy, appropriateness, and success of past and current campaigns and interventions, that is, in assessing whether they will have more intended than unintended outcomes.

Possible interrelations between gradual change and moral panics can be explored by utilizing the concept of ecological civilizing processes (Quilley 2004, 2009, Schmidt 1993). Ecological civilizing processes include the gradual development of ecological sensibilities—this could include such things as changes in manners regarding littering and recycling, the treatment of other animals, developments in the ecological sciences (and other sciences), and changes in the way people see themselves in relation to the biosphere. If we then contrast ecological civilizing processes with reactions to and campaigns surrounding climate change, we can see a noticeable difference where the latter is concerned with a crisis. (It is artificial to separate them like this—ecological civilizing processes and moral panics—for they are not discreet processes but are intertwined: ecological civilizing processes feeding into, and being transformed by, moral panics about climate change.)

Like other moral panics, the "climate crisis" is more than a crisis about the changing climate. It is also a crisis about overconsumption, industrialization, capitalism, and how we see ourselves in relation to each other, other animals, and the biosphere as a whole. This climate crisis entails a sense of urgency, to act now before it's too late (if it isn't already too late). Discourses about climate change include the "new catastrophism" (Urry 2011), predicting catastrophic consequences of high-carbon lives, expressing the perception that civilizing processes are either not developing at a fast enough rate (to counter other processes) or have gone into reverse.

Perhaps civilizing processes themselves have contributed to decivilizing consequences in the form of, according to sociologist John Urry (2010: 201), "excess capitalism" and overconsumption. We can witness trends towards increasing moderation and self-control (changes in long-term patterns of eating and smoking) (Mennell 1996, Hughes 2003), but can also see the growing emergence of multiple sites of excess consumption, and the increasing "freedom to become 'addicted,' to be emotionally and/or physically dependent upon excessive consumption of certain products and services of global capitalism, legal, illegal or semi-legal" (Urry 2010: 204).

These decivilizing consequences may be contributing to the detriment of the environment and social life as a whole (see Ampudia de Haro 2008), including the development of anthropogenic climate change. To counter this, climate change campaigns could potentially be utilized as good moral panics or civilizing offensives, to bring about a civilizing spurt or an acceleration in ecological civilizing processes. However, the notion of good moral panics is not so straightforward— these campaigns also have the potential to have decivilizing consequences, for example if "good" and "bad" behaviors developed into "good" and "bad" people. We can already witness this in the notions of eco-criminals and eco-deviants mentioned earlier, two labels that feature prominently in eco-makeover lifestyle reality TV shows.

## Folk Devil?

In the most recent edition of their *Moral Panics: The Social Construction of Deviance*, Goode and Ben-Yehuda (2009: 42) argue,

> Threatening, dangerous or risky conditions ... [such as] nuclear energy, swine flu, *E. coli*, global warming, the shrinking ozone layer ... and so on ... may cause anxiety, concern, or fear but in the absence of folk devils or evildoers do not touch off *moral* panics.

Goode and Ben-Yehuda acknowledge that others have argued that we should look at moral panics in relation to such scientific issues, but they disagree with such assessments. As I have tried to show, despite Goode and Ben-Yehuda's doubts, folk devils can indeed be formed in relation to climate change, these folk devils differ significantly from those seen in other, "classic" moral panics and the social implications of this difference are great.

In contrast with some classic examples of moral panics—those over youth, the working class, and other marginalized groups, for example—climate change provides us with new types of folk devils: (1) climate skeptics/deniers, (2) big corporations (including, but not limited to, those of the energy industry), (3) governments, (4) the affluent, SUV driving, gas-guzzling consumer with a large carbon footprint, and (5) the extremely rich who consume to "excess" in sites of "excess consumption" (see Urry 2010: 204). As the power ratios between these new types of folk devils and the control culture are less unbalanced than those between more marginalized groups and the control culture, we witness a different type of governance. On one hand, we see an increase in the development of nongovernmental interventions such as the campaigning of environmental organizations, celebrities, scientists, and the increasing occurrence of activism and participation in protests and demonstrations. On the other hand, as well as these notional (or difficult-to-regulate) folk devils, individuals are also called upon to regulate and reassess their own behaviors, to examine the contributions they themselves make to climate change. Trends towards analyzing current practices of consumption—and the guides (books, reality TV, documentaries) that have been produced to provide people the means to change their behaviors, "save the planet" and "stop global warming"—are similar to both the etiquette books and the environmental literature of the past, but they also differ from them to the extent that they are interconnected with a perceived crisis.

While the trend towards self-governance is directed at everyone, marginalizing concepts of eco-deviance and eco-crime also emerge. As with smoking and drinking, one's own deviant behavior may affect the well-being of many others (Hier 2008, 2011). In the case of climate change, one person's choices may have an impact on the whole world, most explicitly in regard to carbon footprints. Therefore, deviant behaviors associated with climate change may become established, the gap between the eco-friendly and the eco-deviant may widen, and new folk devils may emerge.

## Concluding Remarks

In this chapter, I have argued that moral panic researchers must be reflective about the examples they choose to focus on and, more importantly, the ones they choose to ignore. Through a sociology of the sociology of moral panics, greater insights into the strengths and limitations of moral panic research and about the most effective ways to extend and develop the concept can be gained. I have focused on the climate crisis to introduce the possibility of utilizing moral panic in researching social problems about the environment, employing concepts derived from Norbert Elias's work to do so. Exploring both civilizing and decivilizing processes involved in reactions to climate change, we can examine moral panics as highly complex developments encompassing contradictory trends. Combining this effort with a pre-existing approach to research—situating climate change within the long-term development of ecological sensibilities, industrialization, technization, and so on— we can gain insight into the appropriateness of particular responses to climate change and other perceived crises. Through combining novel empirical examples with conceptual innovation, the notion of moral panic can be refined so that it lasts another 40 years.

## References

Ampudia de Haro, F. 2008. *Discussing Decivilisation: Some Theoretical Remarks*. Paper to the First ISA Forum of Sociology: Sociological Research and Public Debate, Barcelona, Spain, September 5–8.

Anesthesiologists can help cut climate change. 2010. *Scientific American: 60-Second Science*, December 6. Podcast.

Aarts, W., Goudsblom, J., Schmidt, K., and Spier, F. 1995. *Toward a Morality of Moderation: Report for the Dutch National Research Programme on Global Air Pollution and Climate Change*. Amsterdam: Amsterdam School for Social Science Research.

*Carbon Cops* (dir. Sean Cousins and Sophie Meyrick, 2006).

Cohen, S. 2001. *States of Denial: Knowing About Atrocities and Suffering*. Cambridge: Polity Press.

Cohen, S. 2002 (1972, 1980). *Folk Devils and Moral Panics: The Creation of the Mods and Rockers*. 3rd Edition. London: Routledge.

Cohen, S. 2011. Whose side were we on? The undeclared politics of moral panic theory. *Crime, Media, Culture*, 7(3), 237–43.

Elias, N. 1996 (1989). *The Germans*. Cambridge: Polity Press.

Elias, N. 2000 (1939). *The Civilizing Process: Sociogenetic and Psychogenetic Investigations*. 2nd Edition. Oxford: Blackwell.

Elias, N. 2007 (1983). *Involvement and Detachment*. Dublin: University College Dublin Press.

Elias, N. 2008 Civilisation, in *Essays II: On Civilising Processes, State Formation and National Identity*. Dublin: University College Dublin Press, 3–7.

Fletcher, J. 1997. *Violence and Civilization: An Introduction to the Work of Norbert Elias*. Cambridge: Polity Press.

Garland, D. 2008. On the concept of moral panic. *Crime, Media, Culture*, 4(1), 9–30.

Goodall, C. 2007. *How to Live a Low-Carbon Life: The Individual's Guide to Stopping Climate Change*. London: Earthscan.

Goode, E., and Ben-Yehuda, N. 2009 (1994). *Moral Panics: The Social Construction of Deviance*. 2nd Edition. Chichester: Wiley-Blackwell.

Harrington, J. 2008. *The Climate Diet: How You Can Cut Carbon, Cut Costs, and Save the Planet*. London: Earthscan.

Hickman, L. and Siegle, L. Ask Leo and Lucy: your green questions answered. The *Guardian* [Online]. Available at: www.guardian.co.uk/environment/series/ask-leo-lucy [accessed: November 23, 2011].

Hier, S. P. 2008. Thinking beyond moral panic: risk, responsibility, and the politics of moralization. *Theoretical Criminology*, 12(2), 173–90.

Hier, S.P. 2011. Tightening the focus: moral panic, moral regulation and liberal government. *British Journal of Sociology*, 62(3), 523–41.

Hughes, J. 2003. *Learning to Smoke: Tobacco Use in the West*. Chicago: University of Chicago Press.

Hughes, J. 2008 (1998). Norbert Elias, in *Key Sociological Thinkers*. 2nd Edition, R. Stones (ed.). Houndmills: Palgrave Macmillan, 168–83.

2006. *I Count: Together We can Stop Climate Chaos: Your Step-by-Step Guide to Climate Bliss*. London: Penguin Books.

*An Inconvenient Truth: A Global Warning* (dir. Davis Guggenheim, 2006).

Kilminster, R. 2007. *Norbert Elias: Post-Philosophical Sociology*. London: Routledge.

van Krieken, R. 1998. *Norbert Elias*. London: Routledge.

van Krieken, R. 1999. The barbarism of civilization: cultural genocide and the "stolen generations." *British Journal of Sociology*, 50(2), 297–315.

Lewis, T. 2008. Transforming citizens? green politics and ethical consumption on lifestyle television. *Continuum*, 22(2), 227–40.

*No Waste Like Home* (dir. Simon Ludgate, 2005).

Dry clean dilemma. 2008. *Make-It-Green-Girl's Quick and Dirty Tips for an Earth Friendly Life*, September 18, episode 20. Podcast.

McRobbie, A. and Thornton, S.L. (1995). Rethinking 'moral panic' for multi-mediated social worlds. *British Journal of Sociology*, 46(4), 559–74.

Mennell, S. 1990. Decivilising processes: theoretical significance and some lines of research. *International Sociology*, 5(2), 205–23.

Mennell, S. 1996 (1985). *All Manners of Food: Eating and Taste in England and France from the Middle Ages to the Present*. 2nd Edition. Urbana: University of Illinois Press.

Mennell, S. 1998 (1989). *Norbert Elias: An Introduction*. 2nd Edition. Dublin: University College Dublin Press.

Quilley, S. 2004. Social development as social expansion: food systems, prosthetic ecology and the arrow of history. *Amsterdams Sociologisch Tijdschrift*, 31(3), 321–47.

Quilley, S. 2009. The land ethic as an ecological civilizing process: Aldo Leopold, Norbert Elias, and environmental philosophy. *Environmental Ethics*, 31(2), 115–34.

Rohloff, A. 2008. Moral panics as decivilising processes: towards an Eliasian approach. *New Zealand Sociology*, 23(1), 66–76.

Rohloff, A. 2011a. Extending the concept of moral panic: Elias, climate change and civilization. *Sociology*, 45(4), 634–49.

Rohloff, A. 2011b. Shifting the focus? moral panics as civilizing and decivilizing processes, in *Moral Panic and the Politics of Anxiety*. London: Routledge, 71–85.

Rohloff, A. and Wright, S. 2010. Moral panic and social theory: beyond the heuristic. *Current Sociology*, 58(3), 403–19.

Schmidt, C. 1993. On economization and ecologization as civilizing processes. *Environmental Values*, 2(1), 33–46.

Thompson, K. 1998. *Moral Panics*. Key Ideas. Milton Park: Routledge.

Ungar, S. 1992. The rise and (relative) decline of global warming as a social problem. *Sociological Quarterly*, 33(4), 483–501.

Ungar, S. 1995. Social scares and global warming: Beyond the Rio Convention. *Society and Natural Resources*, 8(4), 443–56.

Ungar, S. 1998. Bringing the issue back in: comparing the marketability of the ozone hole and global warming. *Social Problems*, 45(4), 510–27.

Ungar, S. 2001. Moral panic versus the risk society: The implications of the changing sites of social anxiety. *British Journal of Sociology*, 52(2), 271–91.

Ungar, S. 2011. The artful creation of global moral panic: climatic folk devils, environmental evangelicals, and the coming catastrophe, in *Moral Panic and the Politics of Anxiety*, edited by S.P. Hier. London: Routledge, 190–207.

Urry, J. 2010. Consuming the planet to excess. *Theory, Culture and Society*, 27(2–3), 191–212.

Urry, J. 2011. *Climate Change and Society*. Cambridge: Polity Press.

2007. *The Virgin Green Guide: The Easy Way to Save the Planet and Save £££s*. London: Virgin Books.

2007. *Wa$ted!* (dir. Lisa Pringle et al., 2007).

# Practicing Moral Panic Research:
# A Hybrid Model with Guidelines
# for Its Application*

## Brian V. Klocke and Glenn W. Muschert

The social unrest of the 1960s in the United States, Britain, and elsewhere led to increasing social control efforts by states to criminalize youth subcultures, especially minority youth. Sociologist Howard S. Becker (1963) identified the efforts of "moral entrepreneurs" to label particular individuals and groups as deviants and criminals and to utilize media exposure to pressure the police to exercise their moral authority to crack down on deviants. In response, critical sociologists deconstructed these dynamics of power, arguing that extreme measures of social control, rather than simply responding to deviance, also created it, "by labeling more actions and people" as a threat to the dominant moral order (Cohen 2002: xxiv).

Stanley Cohen's (2002) seminal work, *Folk Devils and Moral Panics: The Creation of Mods and Rockers*, first published in 1972, emphasized the crucial role of media interacting with control agents (such as police), politicians, action groups (moral entrepreneurs), and the public to construct the youth groups identified as the mods and the rockers as an exaggerated threat to society that greatly disturbed moral hegemony. Cohen alleged that the over-reaction from the police and others was actually counterproductive as folk devils often relished their new outsider status as social rebels. A few years later, the moral panic of mods and rockers faded into obscurity. However, Cohen indicated that the standardization of symbols representing their "devilish" behaviors provided the framework for the emergence of future moral panics.

Thus, the origins of the term moral panic are grounded in the social construction of deviance and an analysis of the social control of real or perceived threats to the moral social order. In the innovative book, *Policing the Crisis: Mugging, the State, and Law and Order*, Stuart Hall et al. (1978) drew upon Cohen's concept of moral panic

---

\* Portions of this chapter were adapted from Klocke, B.V. and Muschert, G.W. 2010. "A Hybrid Model of Moral Panics: Synthesizing the Theory and Practice of Moral Panic Research." *Sociology Compass*, 4(5), 295–309.

to articulate the role of ideology in the media's contribution to the signification of deviant groups through the mobilization of "common sense" (Gramsci 1971) in order to secure hegemony. Moral panics, they theorized, develop particularly during times of crisis, serving to draw the public attention away from social and economic troubles and toward the particular subject of the moral panic to gain support for increasing forms of social control.

Erich Goode and Nachman Ben-Yehuda's (1994b) book, *Moral Panics: The Social Construction of Deviance*, extended the concept of moral panic into an attributional model. Whereas Cohen focused on a five-part process to moral panics (as outlined in table 23.1), Goode and Ben-Yehuda centered their model on operationalizing the elemental characteristics of a moral panic (as outlined in table 23.2).

**Table 23.1    Elements of Cohen's Model of Moral Panics**

| C1. | Behavior by folk devils is defined as a threat to societal values and interests. |
|---|---|
| C2. | The threat is depicted in a recognizable dramatic form by the media. |
| C3. | A rapid build-up of public concern arises. |
| C4. | Authorities, politicians and moral entrepreneurs call for a strong solution to the problem. |
| C5. | The panic recedes or results in social and institutional changes. |

*Source*: Klocke, B.V. and Muschert, G.W. 2010. "A Hybrid Model of Moral Panics: Synthesizing the Theory and Practice of Moral Panic Research." *Sociology Compass*, 4(5), 295–309. Reprinted with permission of Wiley Publishing.

**Table 23.2    Elements of Goode and Ben-Yehuda's Model of Moral Panics**

| G1. | Concern: There is heightened level of *concern* over the behavior and social consequences of a certain group. |
|---|---|
| G2. | Consensus: There is a general *consensus* that the threat is real, serious and caused by the wrongdoing of group members and their behavior. |
| G3. | Hostility: An increased level of *hostility* develops towards the deviants whose behavior is seen as threatening to society. |
| G4. | Disproportionality: The public concern is in excess of what is appropriate if concern were directly proportional to objective harm. |
| G5. | Volatility: Panics are by their nature fleeting, often subsiding as quickly as they erupt. |

*Note*: G1 through G5 are really descriptive elements of all stages of the operation of a moral panic. However, G4 and G5 are best assessed empirically after the dissolution of a moral panic.

*Source*: Klocke, B.V. and Muschert, G.W. 2010. "A Hybrid Model of Moral Panics: Synthesizing the Theory and Practice of Moral Panic Research." *Sociology Compass*, 4(5), 295–309. Reprinted with permission of Wiley Publishing.

These tables outline the primary aspects of the moral panic concept in two important strains of thought, roughly in the British tradition (Cohen) and the American tradition (Goode and Ben-Yehuda). In the following sections, we outline some conceptual criticisms of the current development of moral panic concepts, which serve as a lead-in to our presentation of a holistic model that combines the strengths of these two dominant strains in moral panic theory. Ultimately, our combined hybrid model leads us to provide the reader with some concrete suggestions about applying the concept in empirical research.

## Conceptual Clarifications

The widespread application of the concept of moral panic in both academia and the media (Altheide 2009) in recent decades has obscured its conceptual coherence and left scholars questioning where the conceptual boundaries of a moral panic begin and end. Some critics argue that its overlap with so many "adjacent concepts" (for example, the risk society, moral regulation, public anxieties, media rituals, or social problems) has "stretched so far beyond the original limits" that the term "has lost most of its conceptual ground" (Cornwell and Linders 2002: 313–14) and "analytical precision" (Cottle 2006: 417).

Not all constructions of a social problem can qualify as a moral panic, nor does the term apply to every situation of public anxiety in a risk-focused society. Jewkes (2004: 78, emphasis in original) indicates, "The term has become a shorthand description for *any* widespread concern." The distinction of moral panics from similar typologies of public concern needs to be considered and moral panics should be seen as one aspect of a broader range of moral regulation, public anxieties, and ideological discourses of social control, but not totally subsumed by any one of these concepts.

For conceptual clarity, we believe, it is important to situate moral panics within the sociology of deviance and social control. We follow Jock Young's (2009: 13) explanation that moral panics involve "a process of mass stigmatization" and "a widely circulated narrative on the genesis, proclivity and nemesis of a particular deviant group that tends to amplify in intensity over time" and eventually recedes. Not all social problem constructions are moral panics, for not all panics are about moralization and social control of a group labeled as deviant.

Additionally, we argue that for an example of public anxiety to be considered a moral panic, it must resonate with a broad audience. Successful moral panics, while widespread, can vary in scale. They need not grip "everyone or even a majority of the members of a given society at a given time" (Goode and Ben-Yehuda 1994a: 157). However, they need to establish interactive resonance with the media, social control agencies, moral entrepreneurs, politicians, action groups, and the public to a level of intensity that would stimulate collaborative, non-routine responses to the real or perceived threat. While Goode and Ben-Yehuda rightly indicate that moral panics can be driven primarily by elites, the grassroots, or interest groups, we emphasize that all these groups are present in each successful moral panic.

Moral panics may be sparked by a particular event at a local level, but in order to become a full-blown moral panic, we argue that its scope of concern must expand beyond the local level and a singular event to comprehend institutional and public concern of sustained intensity, over claimed immoral behavior seen as a threat to good citizens, or even to society as a whole. Since moral panics rely on a particular social group identified as deviant, we see moral panics as distinguishable from conditions and episodes involving just one individual, or from a more abstract, unpersonified threat, such as political scandals (for example, President Clinton's affair with Monica Lewinsky), consumer panics (health scares, product recalls, Y2K), industrial accidents (oil spills), economic crises (global recession), and natural disasters.

## Why a Hybrid Model Is Needed

In the almost four decades since the development of Cohen's model of moral panics, major changes have occurred in the media, the main institution through which the moral panics are communicated. Since Cohen and Goode and Ben-Yehuda developed their respective moral panics models, the fragmentation of media spawned by new communication technologies has opened up spaces for counter-media narratives, yet at the same time the increasing concentration of media ownership by corporations trying to increase their profits, and the development of a competitive 24-hour news cycle has made news sensationalism more prominent. Thus, the complexity and intensity of the interaction of news media production and audience reception dynamics have increased.

Reflecting this understanding, recent scholars have criticized Cohen's and Goode and Ben-Yehuda's models as alternately assuming predetermined media dynamics and effects and under-conceptualizing the central role of media not only in the broadcasting of a moral panic, but in the shaping of its discourse as well. The classic models of moral panics would be strengthened by an expanded account of the social conditions that give rise to, sustain and result in the success or failure of moral panics as well as an examination of the outcomes of a moral panic. A strong model needs not only to identify *what* happens during a moral panic but also *how* it happens. It also needs to allow for the possibility of counter-narratives not only from folk devils but also from other voices in the fragmented mediascape, while considering the impacts of a moral panic beyond its volatile media lifespan.

Additionally, moral panics do not just act to control folk devils, but also, as many social scientists have pointed out (see, for example, Ajzenstadt 2009, Critcher 2008, Hier 2008), serve to affirm and normalize dominant society and govern its boundaries. In the cauldron of competing claims makers from moral entrepreneurs to folk devils, people are not only controlled or reactive, but are also drawn to identify with differing ideological frames. They are "guided by the groups they belong to, the roles they occupy in the social structure, and the interests and understandings they develop in interactions with others" (Cornwell and Linders 2002: 309). This does not mean, however, that social interaction operates on a level playing field. So, it is surprising that many critiques of moral panics seem to avoid a critical analysis of dynamics of social status, social and cultural capital, and political and economic power infused into the processes of moral panics and disproportionately distributed across social groups. A thorough analysis of a moral panic must include the sort of critical formulation of material, symbolic, and discursive power that was a hallmark of Cohen's classic study.

# Hybrid Model of Moral Panics

In order to develop a more elaborate and useful model for analyzing contemporary moral panics, we combine Cohen's process-based model and Goode and Ben-Yehuda's element-based model into an expanded, hybrid model (see table 23.3) that examines social conditions and interactive social processes before, during, and after a moral panic, with a focus on the media as the nexus for public discourse surrounding moral panic as well as a key institution in affecting how that discourse unfolds.

**Table 23.3 Hybrid Model of Moral Panics**

1. Cultivation: the emergence of conditions, actors and discourse that make the growth of a moral panic more likely, such as:
   - Conflict among competing moral universes or rapid social change
   - Economic or political crisis
   - Media attention to related social problems
2. Operation: processes that function during a moral panic
   a. Episode (C1, C2, G1) – coverage of the shocking event or series of events that identify "the problem"
      i. Distortion – descriptions of the event and the deviants are exaggerated
      ii. Prediction – there is a prediction of future deviance
      iii. Symbolization – dramatic images and symbols are attached to the problem behavior.
   b. Magnification (C3, G2, G3) – the period of intense attention and prolonged media coverage of the causes and consequences of the threat, represented by a shift from media inventorying the episode to value-laden sense-making activities.
      i. Moralization – identification of the folk devils and why they are a threat to the social order, and typification of their behavior as representative of their inherent evil nature.
      ii. Officiation – increasing involvement of police, experts, other officials, moral entrepreneurs, and community leaders through media interviews, press releases, or public statements.

        iii.   Amplification – Coverage of the panic becomes themed and a re-occurring feature. Media focus on heightened public concern evidenced by opinion polls, letters to editors, protests, web pages, or blogs.
    c.   Regulation (C4, G4) – calling for strong measures of social control to deter, manage or eradicate the threat.
        i.   Surveillance – calls for law enforcement, other officials and the public to be vigilant and to report suspicious behavior
        ii.   Mobilization – gathering of people and resources for civic, legislative, and law enforcement action.
        iii.   Institutionalization – implementation of new structures of governance or enforcement, creation of social movement organizations, passage of new laws or tougher penalties.
3.   Dissolution: as a moral panic recedes there are several possibilities of the causes and results of the decline. (C5, G5)
    • Normalization – a new hegemony is established
    • Transformation – the panic results in social, ideological or institutional change
    • Dissipation – the panic burns out (panic is challenged or debunked, offending behavior drops off, or another pressing social problem takes its place)

*Note*: Parts a, b, and c in the operation stage are not meant to be discrete or linear steps.

*Source*: Klocke, B.V. and Muschert, G.W. 2010. "A Hybrid Model of Moral Panics: Synthesizing the Theory and Practice of Moral Panic Research." *Sociology Compass*, 4(5), 295–309. Reprinted with permission of Wiley Publishing.

Our suggestions for applying the hybrid model to moral panic research (see table 23.4), which we discuss in the next section, attempts to account for the indeterminacy and volatility of contemporary moral panics and the capacity of folk devils to resist, while acknowledging the disproportionality of social and institutionalized power. Our model also recognizes the ability of ideological and discursive patterns and structures to cultivate future moral panics and to have lasting cultural and institutional outcomes.

## Cultivation Stage

For a moral panic to take place, a conflict between two or more competing moral universes must be articulated by moral entrepreneurs who have been busy in creating a public perception of the particular problem, setting the stage for its possible development into a moral panic. These moral entrepreneurs may come from elite segments of society, the media, interest groups, or grassroots organizations but, regardless, are most likely to attract media coverage and garner institutional support when they have relative social privilege, status and capital. More broadly, moral crusades frequently occur during times of rapid social change and "growing social pluralism," that "create(s) increasing potential for value conflicts and lifestyle clashes between diverse cultural groups, which turn to moral enterprise to defend or assert their values against those of other groups" (Thompson 1998: 11). Economic (for example, recession) and political crises (war or threat of war), or other challenges to social hegemony (social movements, youth, or subcultures) can also provide conditions ripe for a moral panic. Additionally, past moral panics can cultivate future ones. The moral panic over one "crime wave," such as the one over LSD, can provide a familiar narrative or discursive genre for a later hybridized moral panic such as the crack panic.

Current deviant behavior is often depicted through the interplay of moral crusaders, folk devils, and media in ways that draw on previously existing images and symbols. A moral panic is more likely to emerge when folk devils are of marginalized social status (for example, race, class, or gender) or disavow their own social status and values of their dominant culture (John Walker Lindh and the American Taliban, hippie culture). News media have a particularly significant role in alerting the public to risks and dangers. Many scholars (see, for example, Best 1999, Stabile 2006) conclude that for journalistic and economic reasons, the media have an interest in reporting crimes especially when they appear to be a new category of crime or threats to the dominant culture.

Moral panics are more likely to happen when large-scale structural and value-oriented changes occur in a society. Youth are the ones that often most quickly reflect these changes (Young 2009) and become the scapegoat of moral crusades. Social problems are less likely to develop into moral panics when the deviance is invisible, the media do not have access to the deviants, and it seems that agents of control are effectively handling the social problem caused by a limited number of deviants.

## Operation Stage

*Episode Substage* Often, when a moral panic commences a precipitating event with a strong element of inherent drama occurs. News coverage immediately inventories the event and identifies a social problem and suspected or known troublemakers. Descriptions of the event and of the deviants are dramatized and usually exaggerated or distorted. Predictions of future problem behaviors on the part of the deviants are made and dramatic images and symbols are attached to the problem behavior.

*Magnification Substage* The panic over the moral threat becomes magnified through the focused discourse surrounding the threat. The folk devils are identified and their behavior is explained to be a threat to the existing social order. News media shift from detailing the "facts" of the episode to sense-making journalism, while public officials and moral entrepreneurs mobilize their resources to speak out about the problem. Officials and "experts" become increasingly involved, giving press conferences, and the media use official sources as the "primary definers" (Hall et al. 1978: 58) of the moral panic. Government officials, social institutions, and action groups use "rhetorical heat" (Goode 2008: 542), often revealing atrocity tales to emphasize the threat and typify the behavior of folk devils as representative of their inherent evil nature. Folk devils may speak out, usually eliciting more concern or possibly mitigating the moral panic. The media may construct themed taglines or headline frames in their expanded coverage and focus on heightened public concern evidenced by opinion polls, letters to editors, protests, web pages, blogs, and so on.

*Regulation Substage*   In conjunction with the magnification of the moral panic come calls for strong measures of social control to deter, manage, or eradicate the threat, including by taking pre-emptive action. Law enforcement widens its net of surveillance and encourages the public to be vigilant and report any suspicious behavior to officials. Agents of social control and action groups mobilize financial and human resources to take corrective legislative, civic, and law-enforcement measures against the new threat. Mobilization of regulatory forces may become institutionalized, creating new formal organizations such as neighborhood crime-watch groups or law enforcement task groups, passing new laws or tougher penalties, and taking other regulatory actions.

However, such extreme actions are likely to spark counter-movements to resist these new measures of social control. A moral panic and attempts at social control are most likely to resonate with individuals, groups, and organizations that are already a part of, or affiliate with, the social identities (for example, race, class, gender, religion, or nationality), social status, or ideology of the groups that appear to be threatened. If folk devils or their sympathizers have enough cultural and social capital to be successful in making counter-claims and offering explanations, they will impede or dissolve a moral panic. As interactive and volatile processes, the resonance of a moral panic with particular social groups may shift as more information is revealed and either deflate or inflate the moral panic, like the regulator on a steam engine.

## Dissolution Stage

As a moral panic recedes there are several possibilities of the causes and results of the decline. One possibility is the normalization of the threat, and attempts at regulation become an accepted part of daily life. Another possibility is that moral panic results in longer-lasting social or institutional transformation, either in support of the moral regulation of folk devils or against it, accepting them as part of a changing democratic culture. Factors that contribute to the receding of a moral panic are also factors that hinder it from developing into a moral panic from the start. Media may drop their coverage of the social issue or become critical of past coverage of the issue. A moral panic may dissipate into obscurity when its legitimacy is challenged by experts, investigative journalists, or a successful counter-social movement, debunking it as more myth than fact. The targeted deviant group may be successful in countering their antagonists' claims or a bigger or more pressing social problem, even perhaps another moral panic, may start dominating media coverage and public discourse. Moral panics can also fade away if the offending behavior drops off or disappears (see Jenkins 2009).

Moral panics also have the capacity to leave legacies in discursive and ideological forms. The descriptions, frames, and causal statements made in media accounts concerning previous moral panics can contribute and influence the way that the media portray similar social problems in the future. In severe cases, a place name, date, or other, usually innocuous label can become endowed with extraordinary meaning. Pearl Harbor, Columbine, and 9-11 are now triggers for much deeper emotional meanings than their place names or dates alone would suggest.

## Recipe for Moral Panic Research

For a scholar employing our Hybrid Model of Moral Panics, sitting down to begin a study of a particular iteration of moral panic (or its components), it may be difficult to know how to start and what to include. We propose a rough guide for moral panic research, which if followed may lead the investigator along the road toward producing palatable moral panic research.

**Table 23.4   Suggestions for Researching Moral Panics**

1. Cultivation Stage
   - Describe existing value conflicts.
   - Describe pre-existing problem frames.
   - Identify and describe pre-existing folk devils from earlier panics.
   - Identify and describe key interest groups and moral entrepreneurs.
   - Measure perceptions of relevant social problems or threats and identify social-historical conditions cultivating them.
   - Examine mass media reporting of the problem or threat prior to the panic.
2. Operation Stage
   a. Episode Substage
      - Describe the precipitating event(s), identifying key responders and their actions (for example, agents of social control).
      - Identify key commentators (agents of social control, experts, or community leaders) and analyze their characterizations of the event(s).
      - Interpret and analyze dramatic images and symbols attached to the deviants.
      - Identify predictions about the future recurrence of the problem or threat.
   b. Magnification Substage
      - Describe efforts to characterize the broader meaning of the precipitating event in value-laden terms and interpret the needs and interests of various stakeholders.
      - Identify efforts to connect the current problem or threat with other past problems or threats or to create a new folk devil.
      - Analyze official statements and media discourse about the extent of the problem or threat as well as its causes and solutions. Identify any discursive patterns typifying the

behavior of the folk devils. Analyze any statements from the folk devils and reactions to them.

- Analyze media coverage of the social problem and compare it to past coverage. Identify recurring themes or frames and elements of the coverage.

c. Regulation Substage
- Identify the social group(s) targeted for surveillance and the methods and means of social regulation attempted.
- Identify sources of mobilization and justifications for civic, legislative and enforcement action, as well as any groups mobilized and campaigns created to counter the moral panic.
- Analyze the processes and outcomes of key social control responses undertaken to mitigate the problem or threat.

3. Dissolution Stage
- Analyze the factors and conditions leading to the decline of the moral panic.
- Identify institutional legacies of the panic (new organizations, policies, or laws).
- Identify symbolic legacies (new or continuing problem frames and symbols or images) that may cultivate future moral panics or dissuade them.

*Source*: Klocke, B.V. and Muschert, G.W. 2010. "A Hybrid Model of Moral Panics: Synthesizing the Theory and Practice of Moral Panic Research." *Sociology Compass*, 4(5), 295–309. Reprinted with permission of Wiley Publishing.

Like any other recipe, ours specifies both the ingredients to be included and suggests the way in which these ingredients should be combined in the research process. Recognizing the inductive and hermeneutic nature of much moral panic research, these general guidelines are to be taken as such and are expected to be adapted to the particular disciplinary contexts and training of the researcher. We also offer a disclaimer that, like all recipes, this one at times may not turn out as intended. As always, the palatability of the result depends on a variety of factors, including the ingredients (of varying consistencies and purities), the preparation (at varying levels of sophistication), the presentation (in varying venues), and the tastes of the consumers (whose academic concerns may vary depending upon the discipline[s] in which they operate).

## Ingredients of Moral Panic Research: A Series of Guiding Questions

Asking quality questions is a fundamental aspect of scholarly endeavor and in moral panic research this may especially be the case. Given a lack of consensus on a specific methodology, the investigator may incorporate other approaches exhibited by foundational and contemporary studies. We offer guiding conceptual and analytical charges that, if accomplished, provide the raw materials (that is, the ingredients) for moral panic scholarship.

*Cultivation Stage*    If we are to study moral panics as sociological phenomena, we must make the assumption that they arise from pre-existing conditions conducive to their development. The cultivation stage is the period prior and leading up to a moral panic. When examining this stage, the investigator concentrates on the antecedents and underlying conditions, identifying existing value conflicts among competing moral universes and the pre-existing problem frames related to aspects of those conflicts. Potential participants or agents provocateurs of moral panic phenomena should be identified. These are frequently interest groups or moral entrepreneurs working to demonize selected aspects of social behavior. It is crucial to identify those groups that already bear stigmas from earlier moral campaigns and are potentially identifiable as responsible for threats to moral order. Concerning the cultivation stage, it is also important to examine claims and perceptions about related social problems, including public discourses (which can take place in media or in other discursive venues).

*Operation Stage: Episode Substage*    Although the antecedents of moral panic phenomena may be temporally longstanding, the early stages of a moral panic itself (that is, the substages of the operation stage) typically occur when a precipitating event (or an apparent series of episodes) triggers a social control response. A moral panic scholar should identify and describe the precipitating event (what happened and in what moral contexts it happened) as well as the key participants, both those who transgress norms and those who respond, whether formally or informally, to transgression. A crucial facet of social control responses can be found in the discursive attributes of moral panics, as key commentators (media personnel, agents of control, or symbolic leaders) analyze and define the precipitating event. Future prognostication of the meaning, persistence, and possible escalation of the threat posed by the precipitating event is of particular concern. Such predictions often stimulate increased fear and calls for increased control responses. Within these discursive aspects, the investigator might also identify dramatic images and symbolic meanings attached to those deviants presumed responsible for the precipitating event.

*Operation Stage: Magnification Substage*    As concern about the presumed threat posed by those responsible for the deviant behavior grows, a moral panic enters the magnification stage. Typically, the current threat becomes linked to past social problems and at least one group is identified as the folk devils whose behaviors threaten the existing moral order. Investigators can concentrate on discursive efforts to describe the broader meanings of the precipitating event (and the threat it poses) by identifying value-laden descriptions and interpretations. Frequently, current discourses are related to past social problems or threats and thereby connected to the behaviors of past folk devils, who may be the same or a different group perceived to be responsible for the current putative threat. Discursive features surrounding the specific and ancillary deviant traits of the identified folk devils, including statements made by those in authority positions, must be investigated. Additionally, the rhetorical efforts of folk devils to resist labeling must be analyzed. In this regard, the researcher should examine public discourses (often, media discourses) about the targeted groups or behaviors and also compare them with past coverage of similar problems or threats, which often reveals recurring themes.

***Operation Stage: Regulation Substage*** A noted aspect of moral panic phenomena is the mobilization of a strong social control response, often disproportionately severe compared with a rational assessment of the threat posed by the folk devils or their presumed deviant behaviors. The techniques employed to control targeted social groups should be identified. Since social control responses are usually sanctioned by legitimate authorities, it is also necessary to identify sources of material and symbolic support for control responses, support that often takes the form of civic, legislative, or law enforcement rhetoric and action. Of particular concern are integrated campaigns involving a variety of public and private resources to undertake the establishment of new standards for behavior or control practices. The moral panic scholar may assess the outcomes and consequences of such social control efforts, considering whether they were effective in achieving their stated purpose of reducing perceived harmful behaviors and whether they effectively mitigated the problem or threat. Also of concern are negative, unintended consequences of moral panics regulation, which in some cases may be ineffective or even exacerbate the situation.

***Dissipation Stage*** Finally, there is much to examine as moral panic subsides and perhaps leaves legacies. In particular, much attention has been placed on the eruption and growth of moral panics, while comparatively less scholarship has examined their decline. Specifying the factors that correspond to the waning of moral panic can be of great value. The issue-attention cycle (Downs 1972) or similar concepts indicating the tendency for issues to wax and wane in public concern presumably play a part in the decline of moral panic.

However, it is also crucial to examine those facets within moral panics that contribute to their dissipation. In some cases, folk devils may be able to mobilize sufficient material or symbolic resources to defend themselves against the moral panic or moral campaigners, or control agents may lose resources or legitimacy. In documenting the dissipation of a moral panic, the researcher should note how the resolution (whatever form it takes) has decreased overt conflict among groups representing competing moral positions or worldviews. Therefore, scholars should examine the legacies left by moral panics, including new institutional relations such as organizations, new policies, or new or revised laws, recognizing that these may alternately support the interests of the moral campaigners, the folk devils, or, to an extent, both.

A moral panic's symbolic legacies should be documented because they, though more abstract than material or institutional relations, are nonetheless necessary to understanding the episode's resolution. They also serve as potential symbolic and ideological fodder for future moral campaigns and moral panics.

## Concluding Remarks: The Future of Moral Panic Research

We hope that the conceptual clarifications we have discussed in relation to our hybrid model, while not resolving all questions, will nevertheless encourage empirical research in moral panics that combines British and American perspectives. Importantly, the moral panics model should not be applied only after research is completed, but must inform the research design from the outset. Our guidelines for applying the hybrid model provide a practical point of departure for a more systematic approach to research design guided by continual conceptual advancements in the field. We ground our model in the origins of the concept of moral panic within the sociology of deviance and social control, while allowing for interdisciplinary critical approaches to researching moral panics. We believe that the concept of moral panic continues to be a significant and useful tool for all social scientists in understanding dynamic processes in the social construction of deviance and social control, especially in recurring episodes of the moral regulation of youth subcultures and socially constructed threats to established cultural and moral ideologies around the world.

## References

Ajzenstadt, M. 2009. Moral panic and neo-liberalism: the case of single mothers on welfare in Israel. *British Journal of Criminology*, 49(1), 68–87.

Altheide, D. 2009. Moral panic: from sociological concept to public discourse. *Crime, Media, Culture*, 5(1), 79–99.

Becker, H.S. 1963. *Outsiders: Studies in the Sociology of Deviance*. New York: Free Press of Glencoe.

Best, J. 1999. *Random Violence: How We Talk about New Crimes and New Victims*. Berkeley: University of California Press.

Cohen, S. 2002 (1972). *Folk Devils and Moral Panics: The Creation of Mods and Rockers*. 3rd Edition. New York: Routledge.

Cornwell, B. and Linders, A. 2002. The myth of moral panic: an alternative account of LSD prohibition. *Deviant Behavior*, 23(4), 307–30.

Cottle, S. 2006. Mediatized rituals: beyond manufacturing consent. *Media, Culture and Society* 28(3), 411–32.

Critcher, C. 2008. Moral panics analysis: past, present and future. *Sociology Compass*, 2(4), 1127–44.

Cromer, G. 2004. "Children from good homes": moral panics about middle-class delinquency. *British Journal of Criminology*, 44(3), 391–400.

Downes, D., Rock, P., Chinkin, C., and Gearty, C. (eds). 2007. *Crime, Social Control and Human Rights: From Moral Panics to States of Denial*. Cullompton: Willan.

Downs, A. 1972. Up and down with ecology: the "issue-attention cycle." *The Public Interest*, 28, 38–50.

Goode, E. 2008. Moral panics and disproportionality: the case of LSD use in the sixties. *Deviant Behavior*, 29(6), 533–43.

Goode, E. and Ben-Yehuda, N. 1994a. Moral panics: culture, politics, and social construction. *Annual Review of Sociology*, 20, 149–71.

Goode, E. and Ben-Yehuda, N. 1994b. *Moral Panics: The Social Construction of Deviance*. Oxford: Blackwell.

Gramsci, A. 1971. *Prison Notebooks*. New York: International Publishers.

Hall, S., Critcher, C., Jefferson, T., Clarke, J., and Roberts, B. 1978. *Policing the Crisis: Mugging, the State, and Law and Order*. Critical Social Studies. Houndmills: Palgrave Macmillan.

Hier, S. 2008. Thinking beyond moral panic: risk, responsibility, and the politics of moralization. *Theoretical Criminology*, 12(2), 173–90.

Jenkins, P. 2009. Failure to launch: why do some social issues fail to detonate moral panics? *British Journal of Criminology*, 49(1), 35–47.

Jenks, C. 2011. The context of an emergent and enduring concept. *Crime, Media, Culture*, 7(3) 229–36,

Jewkes, Y. 2004. *Media and Crime*. Thousand Oaks: Sage Publications.

Klocke, B.V. and Muschert, G.W. 2010. A hybrid model of moral panics: synthesizing the theory and practice of moral panic research. *Sociology Compass*, 4(5), 295–309.

Stabile, C. 2006. *White Victims, Black Villains: Gender, Race, and Crime News in US Culture*. New York: Routledge.

Thompson, K. 1998. *Moral Panics*. Key Ideas. Milton Park: Routledge.

Young, J. 2009. Moral panic: its origins in resistance, ressentiment and the translation of fantasy into reality. *British Journal of Criminology*, 49(1), 4–16.

# Appendix I
# Alternative Thematizations
# for Classroom Use and Course
# Reading Lists

## History

Natália De' Carli and Mariano Pérez Humanes, "Hidden in Plain Sight: Moral Panics and the *Favelas* of Rio de Janeiro."

Bryan E. Denham, "Intermedia Agenda Setting and the Construction of Moral Panics: On the Media and Policy Influence of Steven Soderbergh's *Traffic*."

Mary deYoung, "Considering the Agency of Folk Devils."

Alan Hunt, "Assemblages of Moral Politics: Yesterday and Today."

Charles Krinsky, "From Nickel Madness to the House of Dreams: Moral Panic and the Emergence of American Cinema."

Chrysanthi S. Leon and John J. Brent, "Public Punitiveness, Mediation, and Expertise in US Sexual Psychopath Policies."

Jaime McCauley, "The Demise of the Same Sex Marriage Panic in Massachusetts."

Máire Messenger Davies, "Moral Panics and the Young: The James Bulger Murder, 1993."

Patricia Molloy, "Sexual Predators, Internet Addiction, and Other Media Myths: Moral Panic and the Disappearance of Brandon Crisp."

Magdalena Rek-Woźniak and Wojciech Woźniak, "Children Pushed Aside: Moral Panic over the Family and the State in Contemporary Poland."

Pamela D. Schultz, "Revelation and Cardinals' Sins: Moral Panic over 'Pedophile Priests' in the United States."

Samantha A. Smith and Simon A. Cole, "MyMoralPanic: Adolescents, Social Networking, and Child Sex Crime Panic."

Kenneth Thompson, "Cultural Trauma and Moral Panic: 9/11 and the Mosque at Ground Zero Affair."

Tuukka Toivonen, "Moral Panics versus Youth Problem Debates: Three Conceptual Insights from the Study of Japanese Youth."

Sheldon Ungar, "Is This One It? Viral Moral Panics."

Grazyna Zajdow, "I Vote and I Tote: Moral Panics, Resistance, and the Failure of Quiet Regulation."

## Children and Youth

Bryan E. Denham, "Intermedia Agenda Setting and the Construction of Moral Panics: On the Media and Policy Influence of Steven Soderbergh's *Traffic*."
Mary deYoung, "Considering the Agency of Folk Devils."
Charles Krinsky, "From Nickel Madness to the House of Dreams: Moral Panic and the Emergence of American Cinema."
Máire Messenger Davies, "Moral Panics and the Young: The James Bulger Murder, 1993."
Patricia Molloy, "Sexual Predators, Internet Addiction, and Other Media Myths: Moral Panic and the Disappearance of Brandon Crisp."
Magdalena Rek-Woźniak and Wojciech Woźniak, "Children Pushed Aside: Moral Panic over the Family and the State in Contemporary Poland."
Pamela D. Schultz, "Revelation and Cardinals' Sins: Moral Panic over 'Pedophile Priests' in the United States."
Samantha A. Smith and Simon A. Cole, "MyMoralPanic: Adolescents, Social Networking, and Child Sex Crime Panic."
Tuukka Toivonen, "Moral Panics versus Youth Problem Debates: Three Conceptual Insights from the Study of Japanese Youth."
Grazyna Zajdow, "I Vote and I Tote: Moral Panics, Resistance, and the Failure of Quiet Regulation."

## Governance

Natália De' Carli and Mariano Pérez Humanes, "Hidden in Plain Sight: Moral Panics and the *Favelas* of Rio de Janeiro."
Bryan E. Denham, "Intermedia Agenda Setting and the Construction of Moral Panics: On the Media and Policy Influence of Steven Soderbergh's *Traffic*."
Mary deYoung, "Considering the Agency of Folk Devils"
Alan Hunt, "Assemblages of Moral Politics: Yesterday and Today."
Charles Krinsky, "From Nickel Madness to the House of Dreams: Moral Panic and the Emergence of American Cinema."
Chrysanthi S. Leon and John J. Brent, "Public Punitiveness, Mediation, and Expertise in US Sexual Psychopath Policies."
Jaime McCauley, "The Demise of the Same Sex Marriage Panic in Massachusetts."
Patricia Molloy, "Sexual Predators, Internet Addiction, and Other Media Myths: Moral Panic and the Disappearance of Brandon Crisp."

Magdalena Rek-Woźniak and Wojciech Woźniak, "Children Pushed Aside: Moral Panic over the Family and the State in Contemporary Poland."

Amanda Rohloff, "Moral Panics over the Environment? 'Climate Crisis' and the Moral Panics Model"

Pamela D. Schultz, "Revelation and Cardinals' Sins: Moral Panic over 'Pedophile Priests' in the United States."

Willem Schinkel, "Governing Through Moral Panic: The Governmental Uses of Fear."

Tuukka Toivonen, "Moral Panics versus Youth Problem Debates: Three Conceptual Insights from the Study of Japanese Youth."

Sheldon Ungar, "Is This One It? Viral Moral Panics"

Grazyna Zajdow, "I Vote and I Tote: Moral Panics, Resistance, and the Failure of Quiet Regulation."

# Media Studies

Natália De' Carli and Mariano Pérez Humanes, "Hidden in Plain Sight: Moral Panics and the *Favelas* of Rio de Janeiro."

Bryan E. Denham, "Intermedia Agenda Setting and the Construction of Moral Panics: On the Media and Policy Influence of Steven Soderbergh's *Traffic*."

Mary deYoung, "Considering the Agency of Folk Devils."

Erich Goode and Nachman Ben-Yehuda, "The Genealogy and Trajectory of the Moral Panic Concept."

Charles Krinsky, "From Nickel Madness to the House of Dreams: Moral Panic and the Emergence of American Cinema."

Máire Messenger Davies, "Moral Panics and the Young: The James Bulger Murder, 1993."

Toby Miller, "Tracking Moral Panic as a Concept."

Patricia Molloy, "Sexual Predators, Internet Addiction, and Other Media Myths: Moral Panic and the Disappearance of Brandon Crisp."

Magdalena Rek-Woźniak and Wojciech Woźniak, "Children Pushed Aside: Moral Panic over the Family and the State in Contemporary Poland."

Samantha A. Smith and Simon A. Cole, "MyMoralPanic: Adolescents, Social Networking, and Child Sex Crime Panic."

Kenneth Thompson, "Cultural Trauma and Moral Panic: 9/11 and the Mosque at Ground Zero Affair."

Tuukka Toivonen, "Moral Panics versus Youth Problem Debates: Three Conceptual Insights from the Study of Japanese Youth."

Grazyna Zajdow, "I Vote and I Tote: Moral Panics, Resistance, and the Failure of Quiet Regulation."

# Moral Panics Models

## The Grassroots Model

Brian V. Klocke and Glenn W. Muschert, "Practicing Moral Panic Research: A Hybrid Model with Guidelines for its Application."

Máire Messenger Davies, "Moral Panics and the Young: The James Bulger Murder, 1993."

Amanda Rohloff, "Moral Panics over the Environment? 'Climate Crisis' and the Moral Panics Model."

Willem Schinkel, "Governing Through Moral Panic: The Governmental Uses of Fear."

Pamela D. Schultz, "Revelation and Cardinals' Sins: Moral Panic over 'Pedophile Priests' in the United States."

Samantha A. Smith and Simon A. Cole, "MyMoralPanic: Adolescents, Social Networking, and Child Sex Crime Panic."

Kenneth Thompson, "Cultural Trauma and Moral Panic: 9/11 and the Mosque at Ground Zero Affair."

## The Elite-Engineered Model

Joel Best, "The Problems with Moral Panics: The Concept's Limitations."

Chas Critcher and Julia Pearce, "A Missing Dimension: The Social Psychology of Moral Panics."

Bryan E. Denham, "Intermedia Agenda Setting and the Construction of Moral Panics: On the Media and Policy Influence of Steven Soderbergh's *Traffic*."

Brian V. Klocke and Glenn W. Muschert, "Practicing Moral Panic Research: A Hybrid Model with Guidelines for its Application."

Magdalena Rek-Woźniak and Wojciech Woźniak, "Children Pushed Aside: Moral Panic over the Family and the State in Contemporary Poland."

Willem Schinkel, "Governing Through Moral Panic: The Governmental Uses of Fear."

Kenneth Thompson, "Cultural Trauma and Moral Panic: 9/11 and the Mosque at Ground Zero Affair."

Grazyna Zajdow, "I Vote and I Tote: Moral Panics, Resistance, and the Failure of Quiet Regulation."

## The Interest-Group Model

Mary deYoung, "Considering the Agency of Folk Devils."

Brian V. Klocke and Glenn W. Muschert, "Practicing Moral Panic Research: A Hybrid Model with Guidelines for its Application."

Charles Krinsky, "From Nickel Madness to the House of Dreams: Moral Panic and the Emergence of American Cinema."

Amanda Rohloff, "Moral Panics over the Environment? 'Climate Crisis' and the Moral Panics Model."

Willem Schinkel, "Governing Through Moral Panic: The Governmental Uses of Fear."

## Race, Gender, and Sexuality

Chas Critcher and Julia Pearce, "A Missing Dimension: The Social Psychology of Moral Panics."

Natália De' Carli and Mariano Pérez Humanes, "Hidden in Plain Sight: Moral Panics and the *Favelas* of Rio de Janeiro."

Mary deYoung, "Considering the Agency of Folk Devils."

Chrysanthi S. Leon and John J. Brent, "Public Punitiveness, Mediation, and Expertise in US Sexual Psychopath Policies."

Jaime McCauley, "The Demise of the Same Sex Marriage Panic in Massachusetts."

Máire Messenger Davies, "Moral Panics and the Young: The James Bulger Murder, 1993."

Patricia Molloy, "Sexual Predators, Internet Addiction, and Other Media Myths: Moral Panic and the Disappearance of Brandon Crisp."

Magdalena Rek-Woźniak and Wojciech Woźniak, "Children Pushed Aside: Moral Panic over the Family and the State in Contemporary Poland."

Pamela D. Schultz, "Revelation and Cardinals' Sins: Moral Panic over 'Pedophile Priests' in the United States."

Samantha A. Smith and Simon A. Cole, "MyMoralPanic: Adolescents, Social Networking, and Child Sex Crime Panic."

Kenneth Thompson, "Cultural Trauma and Moral Panic: 9/11 and the Mosque at Ground Zero Affair."

Tuukka Toivonen, "Moral Panics versus Youth Problem Debates: Three Conceptual Insights from the Study of Japanese Youth."

## Research Concepts and Methods

Joel Best, "The Problems with Moral Panic: The Concept's Limitations."

Chas Critcher and Julia Pearce, "A Missing Dimension: The Social Psychology of Moral Panics."

Mary deYoung, "Considering the Agency of Folk Devils."

Erich Goode and Nachman Ben-Yehuda, "The Genealogy and Trajectory of the Moral Panic Concept."

Alan Hunt, "Assemblages of Moral Politics: Yesterday and Today."

Brian V. Klocke and Glenn W. Muschert, "Practicing Moral Panic Research: A Hybrid Model with Guidelines for its Application."

Jaime McCauley, "The Demise of the Same Sex Marriage Panic in Massachusetts."

Toby Miller, "Tracking Moral Panic as a Concept."

Amanda Rohloff, "Moral Panics over the Environment? 'Climate Crisis' and the Moral Panics Model."

Tuukka Toivonen, "Moral Panics versus Youth Problem Debates: Three Conceptual Insights from the Study of Japanese Youth."

# Appendix II
# Moral Panic: A Bibliography

Adam, B.D.2003. The Defense of Marriage Act and American exceptionalism: the "gay marriage" panic in the United States. *Journal of the History of Sexuality*, 12(2), 259–76.

Adler, J.S. 1996. The making of a moral panic in 19th-century America: the Boston garrotting hysteria of 1865. *Deviant Behavior*, 17(3), 259–78.

Adler, P.A., Adler, P., and O'Brien, P.K. (eds). 2012. *Drugs and the American Dream: An Anthology*. Chichester: Wiley-Blackwell.

Agamben, G. 2005 (2003). *State of Exception*, translated by K. Attell. Chicago: University of Chicago Press. Originally published as *Stato di eccezione. Homo sacer, Volume 2, Part 1*. Torino: Bollati Borighieri.

Alexander, J., Eyerman, R., Giesen, B., Smelser, N., and Sztompka, P. 2004. *Cultural Trauma and Collective Identity*. Berkeley: University of California Press.

Al-Natour, R.J. 2010. Folk devils and the proposed Islamic school in Camden. *Continuum*, 24(4), 573–85.

Altheide, D.L. 2002. *Creating Fear: News and the Construction of Crisis*. Hawthorne: Aldine de Gruyter.

Altheide, D.L. 2006. *Terrorism and the Politics of Fear*. Lanham: AltaMira Press.

Altheide, D.L. 2009. Moral panic: from sociological concept to public discourse. *Crime, Media, Culture*, 5(1), 79–99.

Altheide, D.L. and Snow, R.P. 1991. *Media Worlds in the Postjournalism Era*. Communication and Social Order. Hawthorne: Aldine de Gruyter.

Altman, D. 1986. *AIDS and the New Puritanism*. London: Pluto Press.

Altman, D. 2001. *Global Sex*. Chicago: University of Chicago Press.

Andrew, D.T. 2010. 'How Frail are *Lovers vows*, and *Dicers oaths*': gaming, governing and moral panics in Britain, 1781–1782, in *Moral Panics, the Media and the Law in Early Modern England*, edited by D. Lemmings and C. Walker. New York: Palgrave Macmillan, 176–94.

Ansell, N. 2008. Substituting for families? Schools and social reproduction in AIDS-affected Lesotho. *Antipode*, 40(5), 802–24.

Anthony, T. 2009. Manifestations of moral panics in the sentencing of Palm Islander Lex Wotton. *Current Issues in Criminal Justice*, 20(3), 466–75.

Armstrong, E.G. 2007. Moral panic over meth. *Contemporary Justice Review*, 10(4), 427–42.

Armstrong, E.M. and Abel, E.L. 2000. Fetal Alcohol Syndrome: the origins of a moral panic. *Alcohol and Alcoholism*, 35(3), 276–82.

Arnold, M. 1869. *Culture and Anarchy: An Essay in Political and Social Criticism.* London: Smith, Elder and Company. Originally published as a series of essays in *The Cornhill Magazine*, 1867–8.

Avdela, E. 2008. 'Corrupting and uncontrollable activities': moral panic about youth in post-civil-war Greece. *Journal of Contemporary History*, 43(1), 25–44.

Baerveldt, C., Bunkers, H., De Winter, M., and Kooistra, J. 1998. Assessing a moral panic relating to crime and drugs policy in the Netherlands: towards a testable theory. *Crime, Law and Social Change*, 29(1), 31–47.

Baker, P. 2001. Moral panic and alternative identity construction in Usenet. *Journal of Computer Mediated Communication*, 7(1), 427–46.

Barker, M. 1984. *A Haunt of Fears: The Strange History of the British Horror Comics Campaign.* London: Pluto Press.

Barker, M. (ed.). 1984. *The Video Nasties: Freedom and Censorship in the Media.* London: Pluto Press.

Barker, M. 1992. Stuart Hall: *Policing the Crisis*, in *Reading into Cultural Studies*, edited by M. Barker and A. Beezer. London: Routledge, 81–99.

Barker, M., Arthurs, J., and Harindranath, R. 2001. *The Crash Controversy: Censorship Campaigns and Film Reception.* London: Wallflower Press.

Barker, M. and Petley, J. (eds) 2001 (1997). *Ill Effects: The Media/Violence Debate.* Communication and Society. 2nd Edition. London: Routledge.

Barkun, M. 2011. *Chasing Phantoms: Reality, Imagination, and Homeland Security since 9/11.* Chapel Hill: University of North Carolina Press.

Barlow, M.H. 1998. Race and the problem of crime in "Time" and "Newsweek" cover stories, 1946 to 1995. *Social Justice*, 25(2), 149–83.

Barrett, R. T. J. 1997. Making our own meanings: a critical review of media effects research in relation to the causation of aggression and social skills difficulties in children and anorexia nervosa in young women. *Journal of Psychiatric and Mental Health Nursing*, 4(3), 179–83.

Barron, C. and Lacombe, D. 2005. Moral panic and the nasty girl. *Canadian Review of Sociology/Revue canadienne de sociologie*, 42(1), 51–69.

Bartie, A. 2010. Moral panics and Glasgow gangs: exploring 'the new wave of Glasgow hooliganism', 1965-1970. *Contemporary British History*, 24(3), 385–408.

Bauer, M.W. and Gaskell, G. 1999. Towards a paradigm for research on social representations. *Journal for the Theory of Social Behaviour*, 29(2), 163–86.

Bauman, Z. 2000. Scene and obscene: another hotly contested opposition. *Third Text*, 14(51), 5–15.

Bauman, Z. 2000. *Liquid Modernity.* Cambridge: Polity Press.

Bauman, Z. 2006. *Liquid Fear.* Cambridge: Polity Press.

Bauman, Z. 2007. *Liquid Times: Living in an Age of Uncertainty.* Cambridge: Polity Press.

Bayman, A. 2010. Cross-dressing and pamphleteering in early seventeenth-century London, in *Moral Panics, the Media and the Law in Early Modern England*, edited by D. Lemmings and C. Walker. New York: Palgrave Macmillan, 63–77.

Bearfield, D. 2008. The demonization of patronage: folk devils, moral panics and the *BostonGlobe*'s coverage of the terrorist attacks of 9/11. *International Journal of Public Administration*, 31(5), 515–34.

Beck, U. 1992 (1989). *Risk Society: Towards a New Modernity*, translated by M. Ritter, introduction by S. Lash and B. Wynne. London: Sage Publications. Originally published as *Risikogesellschaft: auf dem Weg in eine andere Moderne*. Frankfurt am Main: Suhrkamp.

Becker, H.S. 1963. *Outsiders: Studies in the Sociology of Deviance*. New York: Free Press of Glencoe.

Becker, H.S. (ed.). 1964. *The Other Side: Perspectives on Deviance*. New York: Free Press of Glencoe.

Beckett, K. 1994. Setting the public agenda: "street crime" and drug use in American politics. *Social Problems*, 41(3), 425–47.

Beckett, K. 1997. *Making Crime Pay: Law and Order in Contemporary American Politics*. Studies in Crime and Public Policy. New York: Oxford University Press.

Behlmer, G.K. 2003. Grave doubts: Victorian medicine, moral panic, and the signs of death. *Journal of British Studies*, 42(2), 206–35.

Béland, D. 2011. The unhealthy risk society: health scares and the politics of moral panic, in Ben-Yehuda, N. 1980. The European witch craze of the 14th and 17th centuries: a sociological perspective. *American Journal of Sociology*, 86(1), 1–31.

Ben-Yehuda, N. 1983. The European witch craze: still a sociologist's perspective. *American Journal of Sociology*, 88(6), 1275–9.

Ben-Yehuda. N. 1985. *Deviance and Moral Boundaries: Witchcraft, the Occult, Science Fiction, Deviant Sciences and Scientists*. Chicago: University of Chicago Press.

Ben-Yehuda, N. 1986. The sociology of moral panics: toward a new synthesis. *Sociological Quarterly*, 27(4), 495–513.

Bessant, J. 1991. Described, measured and labelled: eugenics, youth policy and moral panic in Victoria in the 1950s. *Journal of Australian Studies*, 15(31), 8–28.

Best, J. 1989 (ed.). *Images of Issues: Typifying Contemporary Social Problems*. Social Problems and Social Issues. Hawthorne: Aldine de Gruyter.

Best, J. 1990. *Threatened Children: Rhetoric and Concern about Child-Victims*. Chicago: University of Chicago Press.

Best, J. 1999. *Random Violence: How We Talk about New Crimes and New Victims*. Berkeley: University of California Press.

Best, J. 2001. *How Claims Spread: Cross National Diffusion of Social Problems*. New York: Walter de Gruyter.

Best, J. 2004. *Deviance: Career of a Concept*. Belmont: Wadsworth.

Best, J. 2011. Locating moral panics within the sociology of social problems, in *Moral Panic and the Politics of Anxiety*, edited by S.P. Hier. Milton Park: Routledge, 37–52.

Best, J. and Horiuchi, G. 1985. The razor blade in the apple: the social construction of urban legends. *Social Problems*, 32(5), 488–99.

Biltereyst, D. 2004. Media audiences and the game of controversy: on reality TV, moral panic and controversial media stories. *Journal of Media Practice*, 5(1), 7–24.

Binhammer, K. 1996. The sex panic of the 1790s. *Journal of the History of Sexuality*, 6(3), 409–34.

Boethius, U. 1994. Youth, the media and moral panics, in *Youth Culture in Late Modernity*, edited by J. Fornas and G. Bolin. London: Sage Publications, 39–57.

Bonn, S.A. 2010. How an elite-engineered moral panic led to the U.S. war on Iraq. *Critical Criminology*, 19(3), 227–49.

Bonn, S.A. 2010. *Mass Deception: Moral Panic and the U.S. War on Iraq.* Critical Issues in Crime and Society, foreword by M. Welch. Piscataway: Rutgers University Press.

Bonnet, F. 2004. The aftermath of France's last moral panic and its sociology. *International Journal of Social Research*, 28(4), 948–51.

Bose, N. 2010. The Central Board of Film Certification correspondence files (1992–2002): a discursive rhetoric of moral panic, "public" protest, and political pressure. *Cinema Journal*, 49(3), 67–87.

Bourdieu, P. 1984. *Distinction: A Social Critique of the Judgment of Taste.* Cambridge: Harvard University Press.

Bourdieu, P. 1993. *The Field of Cultural Production: Essays on Art and Literature*, edited by R. Johnson. New York: Columbia University Press.

Bourdieu, P. and Wacquant, L. 1992. *An Invitation to Reflexive Sociology.* Chicago: University of Chicago Press.

Bourke, J. 2006. *Fear: A Cultural History.* London: Virago.

Bovenkerk, F. and van San, M. 2011. Loverboys in the Amsterdam red light district: a realist approach to the study of a moral panic. *Crime, Media, Culture*, 7(2), 185–99.

Boyden, J. 2007. Children, war and world disorder in the 21st century: a review of the theories and the literature on children's contributions to armed violence. *Conflict, Security and Development*, 7(2), 255–79.

Brackenridge, C.H. 2001. *Spoilsports: Understanding and Preventing Sexual Exploitation in Sport.* Ethics and Sport. New York: Routledge.

Bratich, J.Z. 2008. *Conspiracy Panics: Political Rationality and Popular Culture.* Albany: State University of New York Press.

Bray. A. 2008. The question of intolerance: "corporate paedophilia" and child sexual abuse moral panics. *Australian Feminist Studies*, 23(57), 323–41.

Brayton, S. 2006. An American werewolf in Kabul: John Walker Lindh, the construction of race, and the return to whiteness. *International Journal of Media and Cultural Politics*, 2(2), 167–82.

Brittle, S. and Snider, L. 2011. "Moral panics" deflected: the failed legislative response to Canada's safety crimes and markets fraud legislation. *Crime, Law and Social Change*, 56(4), 1–15.

Bromley, D.G., Shupe, A.D., and Ventigmilia, J.C. 1979. Atrocity tales: the Unification Church and the social construction of evil. *Journal of Communication*, 29(3), 42–53.

Brookbanks, W. 2002. Moral panics and the lure of anticipatory containment. *Psychiatry, Psychology and Law*, 9(2), 127–35.

Brown, E. 2008. Race, space, and crime: the city, moral panics, and "risky" youth, in *Moral Panics over Contemporary Children and Youth*, edited by C. Krinsky. Aldershot: Ashgate, 203–24.

Brown, M. 2008. "Aftermath: living with the crisis": from *PTC* to Governing Through Crime. *Crime, Media, Culture*, 4(1), 131–6.

Buchanan, D., Shaw, S. Ford, A., and Singer, M. 2003. Empirical science meets moral panic: an analysis of the politics of needle exchange. *Journal of Public Health Policy*, 24(3/4), 427–44.

Buckingham, D. 1996. *Moving Images: Understanding Children's Emotional Responses to Television*. Manchester: Manchester University Press.

Buckingham, D. 1999. Superhighway or road to nowhere? Children's relationships with digital technology. *English in Education*, 33(1), 3–12.

Buckingham, D. 2000. *After the Death of Childhood: Growing Up in the Age of Electronic Media*. Cambridge: Polity Press.

Burgess, J. and Green, J. 2009. *YouTube: Online Video and Participatory Culture*. Digital Media and Society. Cambridge: Polity Press.

Burgett, B. 2009. Sex, panic, nation. *American Literary History*, 21(1), 67–86.

Burke, L. 2010. One punch can start moral panic: an analysis of news items about fatal assaults in Queensland between 23 September 2006 and 28 February 2009. *Queensland University of Technology Law and Justice Journal*, 10(1), 87–105.

Burns, R. and Crawford, C. 1999. School shootings, the media, and public fear: ingredients for a moral panic. *Crime, Law and Social Change*, 32(2), 147–68.

Campos, P., Saguy, A., Ernsberger, P., Oliver, E., and Gaesser, G. 2006. The epidemiology of overweight and obesity: public health crisis or moral panic? *International Journal of Epidemiology* 35(1), 55–60.

Canaday, M. 2011. *The Straight State: Sexuality and Citizenship in Twentieth-Century America*. Politics and Society in Twentieth-Century America. Princeton: Princeton University Press.

Carby, H.V. 1992. Policing the black woman's body in an urban context. *Critical Inquiry*, 18(4), 738–56.

Carr, P. 2005. *Clean Streets: Controlling Crime, Maintaining Order, and Building Community Activism*. New Perspectives in Crime, Deviance, and Law. New York: New York University Press.

Carrabine, E. 2008. *Crime, Culture and the Media*. Crime and Society. Cambridge: Polity Press.

Chadwick, D.L. 1994. A response to "The Impact of 'Moral Panic' on Professional Behavior in Cases of Child Sexual Abuse." *Journal of Child Sexual Abuse*, 3(1), 127–32.

Chambliss, W.J. 1994. Policing the ghetto underclass: the politics of law and law enforcement. *Social Problems*, 41(2), 177–94.

Chambliss, W.J. 1995. Crime control and ethnic minorities: legitimizing racial oppression by creating moral panics, in *Ethnicity, Race, and Crime: Perspectives across Time and Place*, edited by D.F. Hawkins. New Directions in Crime and Justice Studies. Albany: State University of New York Press.

Chambliss, W.J. and Sbarbaro, E. 1993. Moral panics and racial oppression. *Socio-Legal Bulletin*, 8, 4–13.

Chan, W. 2005. Crime, deportation and the regulation of immigrants in Canada. *Crime, Law and Contemporary British History*

Chapman, J. 2008. "Sordidness, corruption and violence almost unrelieved": critics, censors and the post-war British crime film. *Social Change*, 22(2), 153–80.

Chauncey, G. 1993. The postwar sex crime panic, in *True Stories from the American Past*, edited by W. Graebner. New York: McGraw-Hill, 160–78.

Chibnall, S. 1977. *Law and Order News: An Analysis of Crime Reporting in the British Press*. London: Tavistock.

Chiricos, T. 1996. Moral panics ideology: drugs, violence and punishment in America, in *Justice with Prejudice: Race and Criminal Justice in America*, edited by M.J. Lynch and E.B. Patterson. New York: Harrow and Heston, 19–48.

Chiricos, T., Padgett, K., and Gertz, M. 2000. Fear, TV news, and the reality of crime. *Criminology*, 38(3), 755–85.

Chunn, D.E. and Gavigan, S.A.M. 2004. Welfare law, welfare fraud, and the moral regulation of the "never deserving" poor. *Social and Legal Studies*, 13(2), 219–43.

Clarke, J. 2008. Still *Policing the Crisis? Crime, Media, Culture*, 4(1), 123–9.

Clarke, L. and Chess, C. 2008. Elites and panic: more to fear than fear itself. *Social Forces*, 87(2), 993–1014.

Cohen, A.K. 1955. *Delinquent Boys: The Subculture of a Gang*. Glencoe: Free Press of Glencoe.

Cohen, A.K. 1965. The sociology of the deviant act: anomie theory and beyond. *American Sociological Review*, 30(1), 5–14.

Cohen, A.K. 1966. *Deviance and Control*. Englewood Cliffs: Prentice Hall.

Cohen, C.J. 2009. Black sexuality, indigenous moral panics, and respectability: from Bill Cosby to the down low, in *Moral Panics, Sex Panics: Fear and the Fight over Sexual Rights*, edited by G. Herdt. New York: New York University Press, 104–30.

Cohen, C.J. 2010. *Democracy Remixed: Black Youth and the Future of American Politics*. Transgressing Boundaries: Studies in Black Politics and Black Communities. New York: Oxford University Press.

Cohen, P. 1997. *Rethinking the Youth Question*. London: Macmillan.

Cohen, S. (ed.). 1971. *Images of Deviance*. Harmondsworth: Penguin.

Cohen, S. 1991. *Visions of Social Control: Crime, Punishment and Classification*. Cambridge: Polity Press.

Cohen, S. 1999. Moral panics and folk concepts. *Paedagogica Historica*, 35(3), 585–91.

Cohen, S. 2002 (1972, 1980). *Folk Devils and Moral Panics: The Creation of the Mods and Rockers*. 3rd Edition. Milton Park: Routledge.

Cohen, S. 2011. Whose side were we on? The undeclared politics of moral panic theory. *Crime, Media, Culture*, 7(3), 237–43.

Cohen, S. and Young, J. (eds). 1973. *The Manufacture of News: Deviance, Social Problems, and the Mass Media*. London: Constable.

Cohen, S. and Young, J. 2004. Comments on Simon Cottee's 'Folk Devils and Moral Panics: "Left Idealism" Reconsidered', in *Theoretical Criminology*, 6(4). *Theoretical Criminology*, 8(1), 93–7.

Cole, S. 2000. From the sexual psychopath statute to Megan's Law: psychiatric knowledge in the diagnosis, treatment, and adjudication of sex criminals in New Jersey, 1949–1999. *Journal of the History of Medicine and Allied Sciences*, 55(3), 292–314.

Collins, V.E. 2012. Dangerous seas: moral panic and the Somali pirate. *Australian and New Zealand Journal of Criminology*, 45(1), 106–32.

Connell, J. 2003. Regulation of space in the contemporary postcolonial Pacific city: Port Moresby and Suva. *Asia Pacific Viewpoint*, 44(3), 243–57.

Cook, D.T. 2001. Exchange value as pedagogy in children's leisure: moral panics in children's culture at century's end. *Leisure Sciences*, 23(2), 81–98.

Cornwell, B. and Linders, A. 2002. The myth of "moral panic": an alternative account of LSD prohibition. *Deviant Behavior*, 23, 307–30.

Corrigan, P. 1981. On moral regulation: some preliminary remarks. *Sociological Review*, 29(2), 313–37.

Corrigan, P. and Sayer, D. 1985. *The Great Arch: English State Formation as a Cultural Revolution*. Oxford: Blackwell.

Corrigan, R. 2006. Making meaning of Megan's Law. *Law and Social Inquiry*, 31(2), 267–312.

Cottee, S. 2002. *Folk Devils and Moral Panics*: "left idealism" reconsidered. *Theoretical Criminology*, 6(4), 387–410.

Cressey, D.R. and Ward, D.A. (eds). 1969. *Delinquency, Crime, and Social Process*. New York: Harper and Row.

Critcher, C. 2002. Media, government and moral panic: the politics of paedophilia in Britain 2000–1. *Journalism Studies*, 3(4), 521–35.

Critcher, C. 2003. *Moral Panics and the Media*. Issues in Cultural and Media Studies. Maidenhead: Open University Press.

Critcher, C. 2008. Making waves: historical aspects of public debates about children and mass media, *International Handbook of Children, Media and Culture*, edited by K. Drotner and S. Livingstone. London: Sage, 91–104.

Critcher, C. 2008. Moral panic analysis: past, present and future. *Sociology Compass*, 2(4), 1127–44.

Critcher, C. 2009. Widening the focus: moral panics as moral regulation. *British Journal of Criminology*, 49(1), 17–35.

Critcher, C. (ed.). 2010 (2006). *Critical Readings: Moral Panics and the Media*. 2nd Edition. Issues in Cultural and Media Studies. Maidenhead: Open University Press.

Critcher, C. 2010 (2006). Introduction: more questions than answers, in *Critical Readings: Moral Panics and the Media*. 2nd Edition, edited by C. Critcher. Maidenhead: Open University Press, 1–24.

Critcher, C. 2010. Media, government and moral panic: the politics of paedophilia in Britain 2000–1. *Journalism Studies*, 3(4), 521–35.

Critcher, C. 2011. Drunken antics: the gin craze, binge drinking and the political economy of moral regulation, in *Moral Panic and the Politics of Anxiety*, edited by S.P Hier. Milton Park: Routledge, 171–89.

Critcher, C. 2011. For a political economy of moral panics. *Crime, Media, Culture*, 7(3), 259–75.

Cuordileone, K.A. 2004. *Manhood and American Political Culture in the Cold War*. New York: Routledge.

Currier, A. 2010. Political homophobia in postcolonial Namibia. *Gender and Society*, 24(1), 110–29.

Curtis, B. 1997. Metaphorical capital and the field of disinterest. *Canadian Journal of Sociology*, 22(3), 303–18.

Cyr, J.L. 2003. The folk devil reacts: gangs and moral panic. *Criminal Justice Review*. 28(1), 26–46.

Darnton, R. 1984. *The Great Cat Massacre and other Episodes in French Cultural History*. New York: Basic Books.

Dauvergne, C. 2008. *Making People Illegal: What Globalization Means for Migration and Law*. Law in Context. Cambridge: Cambridge University Press.

David, M., Rohloff, A., Petley, J., and Hughes, J. 2011. The idea of moral panic—ten dimensions of dispute. *Crime, Media, Culture*, 7(3), 215–28.

Davis, J. 1980. The London garrotting panic of 1862: a moral panic and the creation of a criminal class in mid-Victorian England, in *Crime and the Law: The Social History of Crime in Western Europe since 1500*, edited by VA.C. Gatrell, B. Lenman, and G. Parker. London: Europa, 190–213.

Davis, J.C. 1986. *Fear, Myth and History: The Ranters and the Historians*. Cambridge: Cambridge University Press.

Davis, M.T. 2010. The British Jacobins: folk devils in the age of counter-revolution? In *Moral Panics, the Media and the Law in Early Modern England*, edited by D. Lemmings and C. Walker. New York: Palgrave Macmillan, 221–44.

Davis, N.J. and Stasz, C. 1990. *Social Control of Deviance: A Critical Perspective*. New York: McGraw-Hill.

Dean, M. 1994. "A social structure of many souls": moral regulation, government and self-government. *Canadian Journal of Sociology*, 19(2), 145–68.

Dean, M. 1999. *Governmentality: Power and Rule in Modern Society*. Los Angeles: Sage.

Dean, R.D. 2003. *Imperial Brotherhood: Culture, Politics, and the Cold War*. Amherst: University of Massachusetts Press.

de Coninck-Smith, N. 1999. "Danger is looming here": moral panic and urban children's and youth culture in Denmark 1890–1914. *Paedagogica Historica*, 35(3), 643–64.

Dei, G.J.S. 2010. Politicizing the contemporary learner: implications for African schooling and education. *Teaching Africa*, 9, 104–13.

D'Emilio, J. 1989. The homosexual menace, in *Passion and Power: Sexuality in History*, edited by Peiss, K., Simmons, C., and Padgug, R.A. Philadelphia: Temple University Press, 226–40.

D'Emilio, J. 1998 (1983). *Sexual Politics, Sexual Communities: The Making of a Homosexual Minority in the United States, 1940–1970*. 2nd Edition. Chicago: University of Chicago Press.

Denham, B. 2008. Folk devils, news icons and the construction of moral panics. *Journalism Studies*, 9(6), 945–61.

Denham, B.E. 2004. *Sports Illustrated*, the mainstream press, and the enactment of drug policy in major league baseball: a study in agenda building theory. *Journalism*, 5(1), 51–68.

Denham, B.E. 2010. Amplifications of deviance surrounding illicit drug use: conceptualizing a role for film. *Communication, Culture and Critique*, 3(4), 485–502.

Denham, B.E. 2010. Toward conceptual consistency in studies of agenda-building processes: a scholarly review. *Review of Communication*, 10(4), 306–23.

De Venanzi, A. 2008. Social representations and the labeling of non-compliant youths: the case of Victorian and Edwardian hooligans. *Deviant Behavior*, 29(3), 193–224.

deYoung, M. 1997. The devil goes to day care: McMartin and the making of a moral panic. *Journal of American Culture*, 20(1), 19–25.

deYoung, M. 1998. Another look at moral panics: the case of satanic day care centres. *Deviant Behaviour*, 19(3), 257–74.

deYoung, M. 2004. *The Day Care Ritual Abuse Moral Panic*. Jefferson: McFarland.

deYoung, M. 2007. Two decades after McMartin: a follow-up of 22 convicted day care employees. *Journal of Sociology and Social Welfare*, 34(4), 9–33.

deYoung, M. 2008. Speak of the devil, in *Moral Panics over Contemporary Children and Youth*, edited by C. Krinsky. Aldershot: Ashgate, 127–42.

deYoung, M. 2008. "The devil's walking parody": a follow-up of 12 convicted women day care providers. *Contemporary Issues in Criminology and the Social Sciences*, 2(1), 33–59.

deYoung, M. 2011. Folk devils reconsidered, in *Moral Panic and the Politics of Anxiety*, edited by S.P. Hier. Milton Park: Routledge, 118–33.

Dewey, S. and Kelly, P. (eds). 2011. *Policing Pleasure: Sex Work, Policy, and the State in Global Perspective*. New York: New York University Press.

Dickson, D.T. 1968. Bureaucracy and morality: an organizational perspective on a moral crusade. *Social Problems*, 16, 143–56.

Di Mauro, D. and Joffe, C. 2009. The religious right and the reshaping of sexual policy: reproductive rights and sexuality education during the Bush years, in *Moral Panics, Sex Panics: Fear and the Fight over Sexual Rights*, edited by G. Herdt. New York: New York University Press, 47–103.

Ditton, J., Chadee, D., Farrall, S., Gilchrist, E., and Bannister, J. 2004. From imitation to intimidation: a note on the curious and changing relationship between the media, crime and fear of crime. *British Journal of Criminology*, 44(4), 595–610.

Doezema, J. 2000. Loose women or lost women? The re-emergence of the myth of white slavery in contemporary discourses of trafficking in women. *Gender Issues*, 18(1), 23–50.

Dolby, N. 2006. Popular culture and public space in Africa: the possibilities of cultural citizenship. *African Studies Review*, 49(3), 31–47.

Doran, N. 2008. Decoding "encoding": moral panics, media practices and Marxist presuppositions. *Theoretical Criminology*, 12(2), 191–221.

Dorman, B. 2005. Pana wave: the new Aum Shinrikyô or another moral panic? *Nova Religio*, 8(3), 83–103.

Downes, D., Rock, P., Chinkin, C., and Gearty, C. (eds). 2007. *Crime, Social Control and Human Rights: From Moral Panics to States of Denial, Essays in Honour of Stanley Cohen*. Cullompton: Willan.

Downes, D. and van Swaaningen, R. 2007. The road to dystopia? changes in the penal climate of the Netherlands, in *Crime and Justice in the Netherlands*, edited by M. Tonry and C. Bijleveld. Crime and Justice: A Review of Research, Vol. 35. Chicago: University of Chicago Press, 31–71.

Dowsett, G.W. 2009. The "gay plague" revisited: AIDS and its enduring moral panic, in *Moral Panics, Sex Panics: Fear and the Fight over Sexual Rights*, edited by G. Herdt. New York: New York University Press, 130–56.

Doyle, V. 2008. How to make "kiddie porn" in Canada: law enforcement, the media and moral panic in the age of AIDS, in *Moral Panics over Contemporary Children and Youth*, edited by C. Krinsky. Aldershot: Ashgate, 77–94.

Drotner, K. 1992. Modernity and media panics, in *Media Cultures: Reappraising Transnational Media*, edited by M. Skovmand and K.C. Schrøder. London: Routledge, 32–62.

Drotner, K. 1999. Dangerous media? Panic discourses and the dilemmas of modernity. *Paedagogica Historica*, 35(3), 593–619.

Drotner, K. and Livingstone, S. (eds). 2008. *International Handbook of Children, Media and Culture*. Los Angeles: Sage Publications.

Durington, M. 2007. The ethnographic semiotics of a suburban moral panic. *Critical Arts*, 21(2), 261–75.

Dworkin, S.L. and Wachs, F.L. 2009. *Body Panic: Gender, Health, and the Selling of Fitness*. New York: New York University Press.

Edwards, S. and Lohman, J. 1994. The impact of "moral panic" on professional behavior in cases of child sexual abuse: an international perspective. *Journal of Child Sexual Abuse*, 3(1), 103–26.

Eide, M. and Knight, G. 1999. Public/Private service: service journalism and the problems of everyday life. *European Journal of Communication*, 14(4), 525–47.

Eldridge, J., Kitzinger, J., and Williams, K. 1997. *The Mass Media and Power in Modern Britain*. Oxford Modern Britain. Oxford: Oxford University Press.

Elias, H.M. 1994. The impact of "moral panic" on professional behavior in cases of child sexual abuse: review, commentary and legal perspective. *Journal of Child Sexual Abuse*, 3(1), 137–40.

Elias, N. 2000 (1939). *The Civilizing Process: Sociogenetic and Psychogenetic Investigations*. 2nd Edition. Oxford: Blackwell.

Englund, H. 2006. *Prisoners of Freedom: Human Rights and the African Poor*. California Series in Public Anthropology. Berkeley: University of California Press.

Ericson, R. and Doyle, A. (eds). 2003. *Risk and Morality*. Green College Thematic Lecture Series. Toronto: University of Toronto Press.

Erikson, K.T. 1962. Notes on the sociology of deviance. *Social Problems*, 9(3), 307–14.

Erikson, K.T. 1966. *Wayward Puritans: A Study in the Sociology of Deviance*. New York: John Wiley.

Erjavec, K. 2003. Media construction of identity through moral panics: discourses of immigration in Slovenia. *Journal of Ethnic and Migration Studies*, 29(1), 83–101.

Ess, C. 2009. *Digital Media Ethics*. Digital Media and Society. Cambridge: Polity Press.

Etherington, N. 1988. Natal's black rape scare of the 1870s. *Journal of Southern African Studies*, 15(1), 36–53.

Farmer, S. 2010. Criminality of black youth in inner-city schools: "moral panic", moral imagination, and moral formation. *Race, Ethnicity and Education*, 13(3), 367–81.

Farrall, S., Bannister, J., Ditton, J., and Gilchrist, E. 2000. Social psychology and the fear of crime. *British Journal of Criminology*, 40(3), 399–413.

Farrall, S. and Lee, M. 2008. Critical voices in an age of anxiety: a reintroduction to the fear of crime, in *Fear of Crime: Critical Voices in an Age of Anxiety*. Milton Park: Routledge-Cavendish, 1–11.

Feeley, M.M. and Simon, J. 2007. *Folk Devils and Moral Panics*: an appreciation from North America, in *Crime, Social Control and Human Rights: From Moral Panics to States of Denial, Essays in Honour of Stanley Cohen*, edited by D. Downes, P. Rock, C. Chinkin, and C. Gearty. Cullompton: Willan, 39–52.

Fejes, F. 2008. *Gay Rights and Moral Panic: The Origins of America's Debate on Homosexuality*. New York: Palgrave Macmillan.

Ferguson, C.J. 2008. The school shooting/violent video game link: causal relationship or moral panic? *Journal of Investigative Psychology and Offender Profiling*, 5(1–2), 25–37.

Ferrell, J. 1999. Cultural criminology. *Annual Review of Sociology*, 25, 395–418.

Ferrell, J., Hayward, K., and Young, J. 2008. *Cultural Criminology: An Invitation*. London: Sage Publications.

Filler, D.M. 2003. Terrorism, panic, and pedophilia. *Virginia Journal of Social Policy and the Law*, 10(3), 345–82.

Finney, N. and Robinson, V. 2008. Local press, dispersal and community in the construction of asylum debates. *Social Cultural Geography*, 9(4), 397–413.

Fishman, M. 1978. Crime waves as ideology. *Social Problems*, 25(5), 531–43.

Fitzgerald, M.H. 2005. Punctuated equilibrium: moral panics and the ethics review process. *Journal of Academic Ethics*, 2(4), 315–38.

Flores-Yeffal, N.Y., Vidales, G., and Plemons, A. 2011. The Latino cyber-moral panic process in the United States. *Information, Communication and Society*, 14(4), 568–89.

Fordham, G. 2001. Moral panic and the construction of national order: HIV/AIDS risk groups and moral boundaries in the creation of modern Thailand. *Critique of Anthropology*, 21(3), 259–316.

Foucault, M. 1977 (1975). *Discipline and Punish: The Birth of the Prison*, translated by A. Sheridan, London: Allen Lane. Originally published as *Surveiller et punir: naissance de la prison*. Paris: Editions Gallimard.

Foucault, M. 1978 (1976). *The History of Sexuality, Vol. 1: An Introduction*, translated by R. Hurley. New York: Pantheon Books. Originally published as *Histoire de la sexualité 1: la volonté de savoir*. Paris: Editions Gallimard.

Foucault, M. 1985 (1984). *The History of Sexuality, Vol. 2: The Use of Pleasure*, translated by R. Hurley. New York: Pantheon Books. Originally published as *Histoire de la sexualité 2: l'usage des plaisirs*. Paris: Editions Gallimard.

Foucault, M. 1986 (1984). *The History of Sexuality, Vol. 3: The Care of the Self*, translated by R. Hurley. New York: Pantheon Books. Originally published as *Histoire de la sexualité 3: le souci de soi*. Paris: Editions Gallimard.

Foucault, M. 2003 (1997). *"Society Must Be Defended": Lectures at the Collège de France, 1975–1976*, translated by D. Macey. New York: Picador. Originally published as *Il faut défendre la société. Cours au Collège de France, 1976*. Paris: Seuil/Gallimard.

Francis, B. 2006. Heroes or zeroes? The discursive positioning of "underachieving boys" in English neo-liberal education policy. *Journal of Education Policy*, 21(2), 187–200.

Freedman, E.B. 1987. Uncontrolled desires: the response to the sexual psychopath, 1920–1960. *The Journal of American History*, 74(1): 83–106.

Furedi, F. 2006 (1997, 2002, 2005). *The Culture of Fear Revisited: Risk-Taking and the Morality of Low Expectation*. 4th Edition. London: Continuum.

Furedi, F. 2005. *Politics of Fear: Beyond Left and Right*. London: Continuum.

Furedi, F. 2011. The objectification of fear and the grammar of morality, in *Moral Panic and the Politics of Anxiety*, edited by S.P. Hier. Milton Park: Routledge, 90–103.

Gabilondo, J. 2006. Financial moral panic! Sarbanes-Oxley, financier folk devils, and off-balance sheet arrangements. *Seton Hall Law Review*, 36, 781–850.

Gadd, D. and Jefferson, T. 2008. Anxiety, defensiveness and the fear of crime, in *Fear of Crime: Critical Voices in an Age of Anxiety*, edited by M. Lee and S. Farrall. Milton Park: Routledge-Cavendish, 125–42.

Gardner, S. 1984. A feminist critique of *The Grass Is Singing* as a "moral panic" novel. *Social Dynamics*, 10(1), 52–6.

Gardner, S. 1985. Is racism "sexism extended?" Feminist criticism, "moral panics" and The Grass Is Singing. *Hecate*, 11(1), 75–97.

Garland, D. 1985. *Punishment and Welfare: A History of Penal Strategies*. Aldershot: Gower.

Garland, D. 1996. The limits of the sovereign state: strategies of crime control in contemporary society. *British Journal of Criminology*, 36(4), 445–71.

Garland, D. 2000. *Mass Imprisonment: Social Causes and Consequences*. London: Sage Publications.

Garland, D. 2002. *The Culture of Control: Crime and Social Order in Contemporary Society*. Chicago: University of Chicago Press.

Garland, D. 2003. The rise of risk, in *Risk and Morality*, edited by R.V. Ericson and A. Doyle. Toronto: University of Toronto Press, 48–86.

Garland, D. 2008. On the concept of moral panic. *Crime, Media, Culture*, 4(1), 9–30.

Gaskill, M. 2010. Fear made flesh: the English witch-panic of 1645–7, in *Moral Panics, the Media and the Law in Early Modern England*, edited by D. Lemmings and C. Walker. New York: Palgrave Macmillan, 78–96.

Gerassi, J. 1966. *The Boys of Boise: Furor, Vice, and Folly in an American City*. New York: Macmillan.

Gilbert, J. 1986. *A Cycle of Outrage: America's Reaction to the Juvenile Delinquent in the 1950s*. New York: Oxford University Press.

Gilman, S.L. 2008. *Fat: A Cultural History of Obesity*. Cambridge: Polity Press.

Gilroy, P. 1982. The myth of black criminality. *Socialist Register*, 19, 47–56.

Gilroy, P. 1987. *There Ain't No Black in the Union Jack: The Cultural Politcs of Race and Nation*. London: Hutchison.

Giroux, H.A. 2003. Racial injustice and disposable youth in the age of zero tolerance. *Qualitative Studies in Education*, 16(4), 553–65.

Girvin, B. 2008. Contraception, moral panic and social change in Ireland, 1969–79. *Irish Political Studies*, 23(4), 555–76.

Glassner, B. 1999. The construction of fear. *Qualitative Sociology*, 22(4), 310–19.

Glassner, B. 2009 (1999). *The Culture of Fear: Why Americans Are Afraid of the Wrong Things: Crime, Drugs, Minorities, Teen Moms, Killer Kids, Mutant Microbes, Plane Crashes, Road Rage, and So Much More*. 2nd Edition. New York: Basic Books. First published as *The Culture of Fear: Why Americans Are Afraid of the Wrong Things*.

Goffman, E. 1961. *Asylums: Essays on the Social Situation of Mental Patients and Other Inmates*. New York: Anchor Books.

Goffman, E. 1963. *Stigma: Notes on the Management of Spoiled Identity*. Englewood Cliffs: Prentice-Hall.

Golding, P. and Middleton, S. 1982. *Images of Welfare: Press and Public Attitudes to Poverty*. London: Martin Robinson.

Goldson, B. 1997. Children, crime, policy and practice: neither welfare nor justice. *Children and Society*, 11(2), 77–88.

Good, P. and Burstein, J. 2010. A modern day witch hunt: the troubling role of psychologists in sexual predator laws. *American Journal of Forensic Psychology*, 28(4), 23–49.

Goode, E. 1978. *Deviant Behavior: An Interactionist Perspective*. Englewood Cliffs: Prentice-Hall.

Goode, E. 1990. The American drug panic of the 1980s: social construction or objective threat? *International Journal of the Addictions*, 25(9), 1083–98.

Goode, E. 2000. Review Essay: No need to panic? A bumper crop of books on moral panics. *Sociological Forum*, 15(3), 543–52.

Goode, E. 2008. Moral panics and disproportionality: the case of LSD use in the sixties. *Deviant Behavior*, 29(6), 533–43.

Goode, E. and Ben-Yehuda, N. 1994. Moral panics: culture, politics, and social construction. *Annual Review of Sociology*, 20(1), 149–71.

Goode, E. and Ben-Yehuda, N. 2009 (1994). *Moral Panics: The Social Construction of Deviance*. 2nd Edition. Chichester: Wiley-Blackwell.

Goode, E. and Ben-Yehuda, N. 2011. Grounding and defending the sociology of moral panic, in *Moral Panic and the Politics of Anxiety*, edited by S.P. Hier. Milton Park: Routledge, 20–36.

Goodman, R. 2012. The 'discovery' and 'rediscovery' of child abuse (*jidō gyakutai*) in Japan, in *A Sociology of Japanese Youth: From Returnees to NEETs*, edited by R. Goodman, Y. Imoto, and T. Toivonen. Abingdon: Routledge, 98–121.

Goodman, R. 2012. From pitiful to privileged? The fifty-year story of the changing perception and status of Japan's returnee children (*kikokushijo*), in *A Sociology of Japanese Youth: From Returnees to NEETs*, edited by R. Goodman, Y. Imoto, and T. Toivonen. Abingdon: Routledge, 30–53.

Goodman, R. 2012. Shifting Landscapes: the social context of social problems in an ageing nation, in *A Sociology of Japanese Youth: From Returnees to NEETs*, edited by R. Goodman, Y. Imoto, and T. Toivonen. Abingdon: Routledge, 159–73.

Goodman, R., Imoto, Y., and Toivonen, T. (eds). 2012. *A Sociology of Japanese Youth: From Returnees to NEETs*. Nissan Institute/Routledge Japanese Studies. London: Routledge.

Gordon, L. 1988. The politics of child sexual abuse: notes from American history. *Feminist Review*, 28, 56–64

Gould, C. 2010. Moral panic, human trafficking and the 2010 Soccer World Cup. *Agenda*, 24(85), 31–44.

Gramsci, A. 1971. *Selections from the Prison Notebooks*, edited by Q. Hoare and G. Nowell Smith. New York: International Publishers.

Green, L. 2002. *Technoculture: From Alphabet to Cybersex*. Crows Nest: Allen and Unwin.

Greer, C., Ferrell, J., and Jewkes, Y. 2008. Introduction: investigating the crisis of the present. *Crime, Media, Culture*, 4(1), 5–8.

Griffiths, R. 2010. The gothic folk devils strike back! Theorizing folk devil reaction in the post-Columbine era. *Journal of Youth Studies*, 13(3), 403–22.

Grisso, T. 2007. Progress and perils in the juvenile justice and mental health movement. *Journal of the American Academy of Psychiatry and the Law*. 35(2), 158–67.

Guy, L. 2009. "Moral panic" or pejorative labelling? Rethinking the Mazengarb inquiry into underage sex in the Hutt Valley in 1954. *Journal of Religious History*, 33(4), 435–51.

Haas, J.L. 1994. "Moral panic": an attorney's perspective. *Journal of Child Sexual Abuse*, 3(1), 141–4.

Hall, L.A. 1991. Forbidden by God, despised by men: masturbation, medical warnings, moralpanic, and manhood in Great Britain, 1850–1950. *Journal of the History of Sexuality*, 2(3), 365–87.

Hall, S., Critcher, C., Jefferson, T., Clarke, J., and Roberts, B. 1978. *Policing the Crisis:Mugging, the State, and Law and Order*. Critical Social Studies. Houndmills: Palgrave Macmillan.

Hallsworth, S. 2008. Street crime: interpretation and legacy in *Policing the Crisis*. *Crime, Media, Culture*, 4(1), 137–43.

Hammond, J.L. 2011. Immigration control as a (false) security measure. *Critical Sociology*, 37(6), 739–61.

Harris, T. 2010. 'A sainct in shewe, a Devill in deede': moral panics and anti-Puritanism in seventeenth-century England, in *Moral Panics, the Media and the Law in Early Modern England*, edited by D. Lemmings and C. Walker. New York: Palgrave Macmillan, 97–116.

Hawdon, J.E. 2001. The role of presidential rhetoric in the creation of a moral panic: Reagan, Bush, and the war on drugs. *Deviant Behavior*, 22(5), 419–45.

Hay, C. 1995. Mobilization through interpellation: James Bulger, juvenile crime and the construction of a moral panic. *Social and Legal Studies*, 4(2), 197–223.

Heilborn, M.L., Brando, E.R., and Cabral, C.D. 2007. Teenage pregnancy and moral panic in Brazil. *Culture, Health and Sexuality*, 9(4), 403–14.

Herdt, G. 2009. Gay marriage: the panic and the right, in *Moral Panics, Sex Panics: Fear and the Fight over Sexual Rights*, edited by G. Herdt. New York: New York University Press, 157–204.

Herdt, G.. 2009. Introduction: moral panics, sexual rights, and cultural anger, in *Moral Panics, Sex Panics: Fear and the Fight over Sexual Rights*, edited by G. Herdt New York: New York University Press, 1–46.

Herdt, G. (ed.) 2009. *Moral Panics, Sex Panics: Fear and the Fight over Sexual Rights*. Intersections: Transdisciplinary Perspectives on Genders and Sexualities. New York: New York University Press.

Herndon, A.M. 2005. Collateral damage from friendly fire? Race, nation, class and the "War against Obesity." *Social Semiotics*, 15(2), 127–41.

Hickman, M. 1982. Crime in the streets—a moral panic: understanding "get tough" policies in the criminal justice system. *Southern Journal of Criminal Justice*, 8, 7–22.

Hier, S.P. 2002. Conceptualizing moral panic through a moral economy of harm. *Critical Sociology*, 28(3), 311–34.

Hier, S.P. 2002. Raves, risks and the ecstasy panic: a case study in the subversive nature of moral regulation. *Canadian Journal of Sociology*, 27(1), 33–57.

Hier, S.P. 2003. Risk and panic in late modernity: implications of the converging sites of social anxiety. *British Journal of Sociology*, 54(1), 3–20.

Hier, S.P. 2008. Thinking beyond moral panic: risk, responsibility, and the politics of moralization. *Theoretical Criminology*, 12(2), 173–90.

Hier, S.P. 2011. Tightening the focus: moral panic, moral regulation and liberal government. *British Journal of Sociology*, 62(3), 523–41.

Hier, S.P., Lett, D., Walby, K., and Smith, A. 2011. Beyond folk devil resistance: linking moral panic and moral regulation. *Criminology and Criminal Justice*, 11(3), 259–76.

Hilgartner, S. and Bosk, C.L. 1988. The rise and fall of social problems: a public arenas model. *American Journal of Sociology*, 94(1), 53–78.

Hill, A. 2002. Acid house and Thatcherism: noise, the mob, and the English countryside. *British Journal of Sociology*, 53(1), 89–105.

Hill, J.H. 2008. *The Everyday Language of White Racism*. Blackwell Studies in Discourse and Culture. Chichester. Wiley-Blackwell.

Hill, M. 2003. The making of a moral panic: religion and state in Singapore, in *Challenging Religion: Essays in Honour of Eileen Barker*, edited by J.A. Beckford and J.T. Richardson. London: Routledge, 104–15.

Hofstadter, R. 1964. The paranoid style in American politics, in *The Paranoid Style in American Politics and other Essays*. New York: Alfred A. Knopf, 3–40.

Holland, J., Ramazanoglu, C., and Scott, S. 1990. AIDS: from panic stations to power relations: sociological perspectives and problems. *Sociology*, 24(3), 499–518.

Holloway, S. and Valentine, G. 2001. *Cyberkids: Youth Identities and Communities in an On-Line World*. London: Routledge.

Hollway, W. and Jefferson, T. 1997. The risk society in an age of anxiety: situating fear of crime. *British Journal of Sociology*, 48(2), 283–98.

Hollywood, B. 1997. Dancing in the dark: ecstasy, the dance culture and moral panic in post cease-fire Northern Ireland. *Critical Criminology*, 8(1), 62–77.

Horiguchi, S. 2012. *Hikikomori*: how private isolation caught the public eye, in *A Sociology of Japanese Youth: From Returnees to NEETs*, edited by R. Goodman, Y. Imoto, and T. Toivonen. Abingdon: Routledge, 122--38.

Horsfield, P. 1997. Moral panic or moral action? The appropriation of moral panics in the exercise of social control. *Media International Australia*, 85, 32–9.

Humphries, D. 1999. *Crack Mothers: Pregnancy, Drugs, and the Media*. Columbus: Ohio State University Press.

Humphrey, M. 2007. Culturalising the abject: Islam, law and moral panic in the West. Australian *Journal of Social Issues*, 42(1), 9–25.

Hunt, A. 1997. 'Moral panic' and moral language in the media. *British Journal of Sociology*, 48(4), 629–48.

Hunt, A. 1997. Moral regulation and making up the new person: putting Gramsci to work. *Theoretical Criminology*, 1(3), 275–301.

Hunt, A. 1998. The great masturbation panic and the discourses of moral regulation in nineteenth- and early twentieth-century Britain. *Journal of the History of Sexuality*, 8(4), 575–615.

Hunt, A. 1999. *Governing Morals: A Social History of Moral Regulation*. Cambridge: Cambridge University Press.

Hunt, A. 2003. Risk and moralization in everyday life, in *Risk and Morality*, edited by R. Ericson and A. Doyle. Toronto: University of Toronto Press, 165–92.

Hunt, A. 2011. Fractious rivals? Moral panics and moral regulations, in *Moral Panic and the Politics of Anxiety*, edited by S. P. Hier. Milton Park: Routledge, 53–70.

Husbands, C.T. 1994. Crises of national identity as the 'new moral panics': Political agenda-setting about definitions of nationhood. *Journal of Ethnic and Migration Studies*, 20(2), 191–206.

Ibarra, P.R. and Kitsuse, J.I. 1993. Vernacular constituents of moral discourse: an interactionist proposal for the study of social problems, in *Constructionist Controversies: Issues in Social Problems Theory*, edited by G. Miller and J.A. Holstein. Hawthorne: Aldine de Gruyter.

Ingebretsen, E. 2001. *At Stake: Monsters and the Rhetoric of Fear in Public Culture*. Chicago: University of Chicago Press.

Innes, M. 2004. Signal crimes and signal disorders: notes on deviance as communicative action. *British Journal of Sociology*, 55(3): 335–55.

Introvigne, M. 2000. Moral panics and anti-cult terrorism in Western Europe. *Terrorism and Political Violence*, 12(1), 47–59.

Irvine, J.M. 2006. Emotional scripts of sex panics. *Sexual Research and Social Policy*, 3(3), 82–94.

Irvine, J.M. 2009. Transient feelings: sex panics and the politics of emotions, in *Moral Panics, Sex Panics: Fear and the Fight over Sexual Rights*, edited by G. Herdt. New York: New York University Press, 234–76.

Jackson, J. 2008. Bridging the social and the psychological in the fear of crime, in *Fear of Crime: Critical Voices in an Age of Anxiety*, edited by M. Lee and S. Farrall. Milton Park: Routledge-Cavendish, 143–67.

Jackson, S. and Scott, S. 1999. Risk anxiety and the social construction of childhood, in *Risk and Socio-Cultural Theory*, edited by D. Lupton. Cambridge: Cambridge University Press, 86–107.

Jasper, J.M. 1999. *The Art of Moral Protest: Culture, Biography, and Creativity in Social Movements*. Chicago: Chicago University Press.

Jefferson, T. 2008. *Policing the Crisis* revisited: the state, masculinity, fear of crime and racism. *Crime, Media, Culture*, 4(1), 113–21.

Jefferson, T. and Hollway, W. 2000. The role of anxiety in fear of crime, in *Crime, Risk and Insecurity*, edited by T. Hope and R. Sparks. London: Routledge, 31–49.

Jenkins, P. 1992. *Intimate Enemies: Moral Panics in Contemporary Great Britain*. Social Problems and Social Issues. Piscataway: Aldine Transaction.

Jenkins, P. 1994. 'The Ice Age': the social construction of a drug panic. *Justice Q*, 11(1), 7–31.

Jenkins, P. 1996. *Pedophiles and Priests: Anatomy of a Contemporary Crisis*. Oxford: Oxford University Press.

Jenkins, P. 1998. *Moral Panic: Changing Concepts of the Child Molester in Modern America*. New Haven: Yale University Press.

Jenkins, P. 1999. *The Cold War at Home: The Red Scare in Pennsylvania, 1945–1960*. Chapel Hill: University of North Carolina Press.

Jenkins, P. 1999. *Synthetic Panics: The Symbolic Politics of Designer Drugs*. New York: New York University Press.

Jenkins, P. 2001. *Beyond Tolerance: Child Pornography on the Internet*. New York: New York University Press.

Jenkins, P. 2009. Failure to launch: why do some social issues fail to detonate moral panics? *British Journal of Criminology*, 49(1), 35–47.

Jenkins, P. and Maier-Katkin, D. 1992. Satanism: myth and reality in a contemporary moral panic. *Crime, Law and Social Change*, 17(1), 19–48.

Jenks, C. 2011. The context of an emergent and enduring concept. *Crime, Media, Culture*, 7(3), 229–36.

Jewkes, Y. 1999. *Moral Panics in a Risk Society: A Critical Evaluation*. Studies in Crime, Order and Policing. Leicester: Scarman Centre for the Study of Public Order.

Jewkes, Y. 2010 (2004). *Media and Crime*. Key Approaches to Criminology. 2nd Edition. London: Sage Publications.

Jewkes, Y. 2010. Much ado about nothing? Representations and realities of online soliciting of children. *Journal of Sexual Aggression*, 16(1), 5–18.

Jewkes, Y. and Andrews, C. 2005. Policing the filth: the problems of investigating online child pornography in England and Wales. *Policing and Society*, 15(1), 42–62.

Johnson, B. and Cloonan, M. 2008. *Dark Side of the Tune: Popular Music and Violence*. Ashgate Popular and Folk Music. Aldershot: Ashgate.

Johnson, D.K. 2004. *The Lavender Scare: The Cold War Persecution of Gays and Lesbians in the Federal Government*. Chicago: University of Chicago Press.

Jones, K. 2008. Professional politicians as the subjects of moral panic. *Australian Journal of Political Science*, 43(2), 243–58.

Jones, P. 1997. Moral panic: the legacy of Stan Cohen and Stuart Hall. *Media International Australia*, 85, 6–16.

Kaarsholm, P. 2005. Moral panic and cultural mobilization: responses to transition, crime and HIV/AIDS in KwaZulu-Natal. *Development and Change*, 36(1), 133–56.

Katz, K. 2011. The enemy within: the outlaw motorcycle gang moral panic. *American Journal of Criminal Justice*, 36(3), 231–49.

Kehler, M. and Martino, W. 2007. Questioning masculinities: interrogating boys' capacities for self-problematization in schools. *Canadian Journal of Education*, 30(1), 90–112.

Kelly, L. 1988. What's in a name? Defining child sexual abuse. *Feminist Review*, 28, 65–73.

Kelly, P. 1999. Wild and tame zones: regulating the transitions of youth at risk. *Journal of Youth Studies*. 2(2), 193–211.

Kelly, P. 2000. The dangerousness of youth-at-risk: the possibilities of surveillance and intervention in uncertain times. *Journal of Adolescence*, 23(4), 463–76.

Kelly, P. 2001. The post-welfare state and the government of youth at-risk. *Social Justice*, 28(4), 96–113.

Kelly, P. 2001. Youth at risk: process of individualization and responsibilization in the risk society. *Discourse*, 22(1), 21–33.

Kendrick, J. 2009. *Film Violence: History, Ideology, Genre*. Short Cuts. London: Wallflower Press.

Kepplinger, H.M. and Habermeier, J.H. 1995. The impact of key events upon the presentation of reality. *European Journal of Communication*, 10(3), 371–90.

Killingbeck, D. 2001. The role of television news in the construction of school violence as a "moral panic." *Journal of Criminal Justice and Popular Culture*, 8(3), 381–95.

King, P. 2003. Moral panics and street crime 1750–2000: a comparative perspective, in *Comparative Histories of Crime*, edited by B.S. Godfrey, C. Emley, and G. Dunstall. Cullompton: Willan, 53–71.

Kinsella, S. 2012. Narratives and statistics: how compensated dating (*enjo kōsai*) was sold, in *A Sociology of Japanese Youth: From Returnees to NEETs*, edited by R. Goodman, Y. Imoto, and T. Toivonen. London: Routledge, 54–80.

Kitsuse, J.I. and Spector, M. 1973. Toward a sociology of social problems: social conditions, value-judgements, and social problems. *Social Problems*, 20(4), 407–19.

Kittrie, N.N. 1971. *The Right to Be Different*. Baltimore: Johns Hopkins University Press.

Kitzinger, J. 1999. The ultimate neighbour from hell? The media representation of paedophilia, in *Social Policy, the Media and Misrepresentation*, edited by B. Franklin. London: Routledge.

Kline, S. 2011. *Globesity, Food Marketing and Family Lifestyles*. Consumption and Public Life. New York: Palgrave Macmillan.

Klocke, B.V. and Muschert, G.W. 2010. A hybrid model of moral panics: synthesizing the theory and practice of moral panic research. *Sociology Compass*, 4(5), 295–309.

Knight, G. and Roper, J. 2011. When harm is done: panic, scandal and blame, in *Moral Panic and the Politics of Anxiety*, edited by S.P. Hier. Milton Park: Routledge, 208–23.

Knoll IV, J.L. 2008. The recurrence of an illusion: the concept of "evil" in forensic psychiatry. *Journal of the American Academy of Psychiatry the Law*, 36(1), 105–16.

Kramer, R. 2010. Moral panics and urban growth machines: official reactions to graffiti in New York City, 1990–2005. *Qualitative Sociology*, 33(3), 297–311.

Krinsky, C. 2008. Introduction, in *Moral Panics over Contemporary Children and Youth*, edited by C. Krinsky. Aldershot: Ashgate, 1–8.

Krinsky, C. 2008. The moral panic that never was: news media, law enforcement, and the Michael Jackson trial, in *Moral Panics over Contemporary Children and Youth*, edited by C. Krinsky. Aldershot: Ashgate, 111–22.

Krinsky, C. (ed.). 2008. *Moral Panics over Contemporary Children and Youth*. Aldershot: Ashgate.

Lamers-Winkelman, F. 1994. Moral Panic in the Netherlands? A Commentary. *Journal of Child Sexual Abuse*, 3(1), 1994, 145–150.

Lancaster, R.N. 2011. *Sex Panic and the Punitive State*. Berkeley: University of California Press.

Lawson, T. and Comber, C. 2000. Censorship, the Internet and schools: a new moral panic? *Curriculum Journal*, 11(2), 273–85.

Lea, J. and Young, J. 1993 (1984). *What Is to Be Done about Law and Order?* 2nd Edition. London: Pluto Press.

Le Bon, G. 1979 (1895). The crowd, in *Gustave Le Bon: The Man and His Works*, edited by A. Widener. Indianapolis: Liberty Press, 55–101.

Lee, M. 2007. *Inventing Fear of Crime: Criminology and the Politics of Anxiety*. Cullompton: Willan.

Lee, M. and Farrall, S. (eds). 2008. *Fear of Crime: Critical Voices in an Age of Anxiety*. Milton Park: Routledge-Cavendish.

Lemert, E. 1951. *Social Pathology: A Systematic Approach to the Theory of Sociopathic Behavior*. New York: McGraw-Hill.

Lemert, E. 1967. *Human Deviance, Social Problems, and Social Control*. Englewood Cliffs: Prentice Hall.

Lemmings, D. 2010. Conclusion: moral panics, law and the transformation of the public sphere in early modern England, in *Moral Panics, the Media and the Law in Early Modern England*, edited by D. Lemmings and C. Walker. New York: Palgrave Macmillan, 245–66.

Lemmings, D. 2010. The dark side of enlightenment: *The London Journal*, moral panics, and the law in the eighteenth century, in *Moral Panics, the Media and the Law in Early Modern England*, edited by D. Lemmings and C. Walker. New York: Palgrave Macmillan, 139–56.

Lemmings, D. 2010. Introduction: law and order, moral panics, and early modern England, in *Moral Panics, the Media and the Law in Early Modern England*, edited by D. Lemmings and C. Walker. New York: Palgrave Macmillan, 1–21.

Lemmings, D. and Walker, C. (eds). 2010. *Moral Panics, the Media and the Law in Early Modern England*. New York: Palgrave Macmillan.

Lent, J. 1999. *Pulp Demons: International Dimensions of the Postwar Anti-Comics Campaign*. Madison: Fairleigh Dickinson University Press.

Leon, C.S. 2011. *Sex Fiends, Perverts, and Pedophiles: Understanding Sex Crime Policy in America*. New York: New York University Press.

Lester, E. 1992. The AIDS story and moral panic: how the Euro-African press constructs AIDS. *Howard Journal of Communications*, 3(3–4), 230–41.

Lett, D., Hier, S.P., Walby, K., and Smith, A. 2011. Panic, regulaton, and the moralization of British law and order politics, in *Moral Panic and the Politics of Anxiety*, edited by S.P. Hier. Milton Park: Routledge, 155–70.

Levi, M. 2009. Suite revenge? The shaping of folk devils and moral panics about white-collar crimes. *British Journal of Criminology*, 49(1), 48–67.

Levi, M. and Wall, D.S. 2004. Technologies, security, and privacy in the post-9/11 European information society. *Journal of Law and Society*, 31(2), 194–220.

Levi, S.C. 2010. *The Great Red Scare in World War One Alaska: Elite Panic, Government Hysteria, Suppression of Civil Liberties,Union-Breaking, and Germanophobia, 1915– 1920*. Palo Alto: Academica Press.

Liew, K.K. and Fu, K.2006. Conjuring the tropical spectres: heavy metal, cultural politics in Singapore and Malaysia. *Inter-Asia Cultural Studies*, 7(1), 99–112.

Linnemann, T. 2010. Mad men, meth moms, moral panic: gendering meth crimes in the Midwest. *Critical Criminology*, 18(2), 95–110.

Little, M.H. 1994. "Manhunts and bingo blabs": the moral regulation of Ontario single mothers. *Canadian Journal of Sociology*, 19(2), 233–47.

Livingstone, S. 2009. *Children and the Internet*. Cambridge: Polity Press.

Lombardo, R.M. 2004. The Black Hand: a study in moral panic. *Global Crime*, 6(3), 267–84.

Loo, D. 2008. The "moral panic" that wasn't: the sixties crime issue in the US, in *Fear of Crime: Critical Voices in an Age of Anxiety*, edited by M. Lee and S.Farrall. Milton Park: Routledge-Cavendish, 12–31.

Lumby C, 1997. Panic attacks: old fears in a new media era. *Media International Australia*, 85, 40–6.

Lumby, C. and Funnell, N. 2011. Between heat and light: the opportunity in moral panics. *Crime, Media, Culture*, 7(3), 277–91.

Lundström, R. 2011. Between the exceptional and the ordinary: a model for the comparative analysis of moral panics and moral regulation. *Crime, Media, Culture*, 7(3), 313–32.

Luzia, K. 2008. Day care as battleground: using moral panic to locate the front lines. *Australian Geographer*, 39(3), 315–26.

Lynd, R.S. and Lynd, H.M. 1929. *Middletown: A Study in Contemporary American Culture*. New York: Harcourt, Brace, and Company.

Lynd, R.S. and Lynd, H.M. 1937. *Middletown in Transition: A Study in Cultural Conflicts*. New York: Harcourt, Brace, and Company.

Lyon, D. 2003 *Surveillance After September 11th*. Cambridge: Polity.

Macek, S. 2006. *Urban Nightmares: The Media, the Right, and the Moral Panic over the City*. Minneapolis: University of Minnesota Press.

MacGowen, R. 2010. Forgers and forgery: severity and social identity in seventeenth-century England, in *Moral Panics, the Media and the Law in Early Modern England*, edited by D. Lemmings and C. Walker. New York: Palgrave Macmillan, 157–75.

MacKay, C. 2003 (1841). *Extraordinary Popular Delusions and the Madness of Crowds.* Petersfield: Harriman House. Originally published as *Memoirs of Extraordinary Popular Delusions.*

MacLeod, M. and Saraga, E. 1988. Challenging the orthodoxy: towards a feminist theory and practice. *Feminist Review,* 28, 16–55.

Maguire, M. and Singer, J.K. 2011. A false sense of security: moral panic driven sex offender legislation. *Critical Criminology,* 19(4), 301–12.

Maneri, M. 2001. Moral panic as a device in the transformation of insecurity. *Rassegna Italiana di Sociologia,* 42(1), 5–40.

Marone, J.A. 2003. *Hellfire Nation: The Politics of Sin in American History.* New Haven: Yale University Press.

Martino, W. and Kehler, M. 2006. Male teachers and the 'boy problem': an issue of recuperative masculinity politics. *McGill Journal of Education,* 41(2), 113–31.

Marshall, K. 1985. *Moral Panics and Victorian Values: Women and the Family in Thatcher's Britain.* London: Junius.

Matsamura, J. 2007. Unfaithful wives and dissolute labourers: moral panic and the mobilisation of women into the Japanese workforce, 1931–45. *Gender and History,* 19(1), 78–100.

Matsuda, M. 2005. Discourses of *keitai* in Japan, in *Personal, Portable, Pedestrian: Mobile Phones in Japanese Life,* edited by M. Ito, M. Matsuda, and D. Okabe. Cambridge: The MIT Press, 19–40.

Mawby, R.C. and Gisby, W. 2009. Crime, media and moral panic in an expanding European Union. *Howard Journal of Criminal Justice,* 48(1), 37–51.

McCorkle, R.C. and Miethe, T.D. 1998. The political and organizational response to gangs: an examination of a "moral panic" in Nevada. *Justice Quarterly,* 15(1), 41–64.

McCorkle, R.C. and Miethe, T.D. 2001. *Panic: The Social Construction of the Street Gang Problem.* Criminal Justice and Police Training. Upper Saddle River: Prentice Hall.

McCreery, C. 2010. A moral panic in eighteenth-century London? The 'monster' and the press,in *Moral Panics, the Media and the Law in Early Modern England,* edited by D. Lemmings and C. Walker. New York: Palgrave Macmillan, 195–220.

McEnery, T. 2006. The moral panic about bad language in England, 1691–1745. *Journal of Historical Pragmatics,* 7(1), 89–113.

McIntosh, M. 1988. Introduction to an issue: family secrets as public drama. *Feminist Review,* 28, 6–15.

McKernan, L., 2010. XXIII IAMHIST conference, Aberystwyth, Wales, July 8–11, 2009: social fears and moral panics – a personal view. *Historical Journal of Film, Radio and Television,* 30(1), 111–15.

McLaren, P. 1993/1994. Moral panic, schooling, and gay identity: critical pedagogy and the politics of resistance. *High School Journal,* 77(1/2), 157–68.

McLaughlin, E. 2008. Hitting the panic button: policing/'mugging'/media/crisis. *Crime, Media, Culture,* 4(1), 145–54.

McLean, A.L. and Cook, D.A. (eds). 2001. *Headline Hollywood: A Century of Film Scandal*. Communications, Media, and Culture. New Brunswick: Rutgers University Press.

McNally, M. 2011. *Identity Theft in Today's World*. Global Crime and Justice. Westport: Praeger Publishers.

McRobbie, A. 1994. Folk devils fight back. *New Left Review*, 203, 107–16.

McRobbie, A. 1994. *Postmodernism and Popular Culture*. London: Routledge.

McRobbie, A. and Thornton, S.L. 1995. Rethinking 'moral panic' for multi-mediated social worlds. *British Journal of Sociology*, 46(4), 559–74.

Meades, J. 2011. The duality of the devil: realism, relationalism and representation, in *Moral Panic and the Politics of Anxiety*, edited by S.P. Hier. Milton Park: Routledge, 134–52.

Mercer, D. 1999. The higher moral panic: academic scientism and its quarrels with science and technology studies. *Prometheus*, 17(1), 77–85.

Messenger Davies, M. 2001. *'Dear BBC': Children, Television Storytelling and the Public Sphere*. Cambridge: Cambridge University Press.

Messenger Davies, M. 2010. *Children, Media and Culture*. Issues in Cultural and Media Studies. Maidenhead: Open University Press.

Meylakhs, P. 2004. The discourse of the press and the press of discourse, in *Journal of Sociology and Social Anthropology*, 4(28), 135–51.

Miller, A.L. 2012. *Taibatsu*: from educational solution to social problem to marginalized non-issue, in *A Sociology of Japanese Youth: From Returnees to NEETs*, edited by R. Goodman, Y. Imoto, and T. Toivonen. London: Routledge, 81–97.

Miller, D. and Kitzinger, J. 1980. AIDS, the policy process and moral panics, in *The Circuit of Mass Communication: Media Strategies, Representation and Audience Reception in the AIDS Crisis*, edited by D. Miller, J. Kitzinger, K. Williams, and P. Beharrell. London: Sage Publications, 200–18.

Miller, G. and Holstein, J.A. (eds). 2006. *Constructionist Controversies: Issues in Social Problems Theory*. Social Problems and Social Issues. Piscataway: Aldine Transaction.

Miller, L. 2004. Those naughty teenage girls: Japanese kogals, slang, and media assessments. *Journal of Linguistic Anthropology*, 14(2), 225–47.

Miller, N. 2002. *Sex-Crime Panic: A Journey to the Paranoid Heart of the 1950s*. Los Angeles: Alyson Books.

Miller, P.G. 2007. Media reports of heroin overdose spates: public health messages, moral panics or risk advertisements? *Critical Public Health*, 17(2), 113–21.

Miller, T. 2006. A risk society of moral panic: the US in the twenty-first century. *Cultural Politics: An International Journal*, 2(3), 299–318.

Miller, T. 2008. Panic between the lips: attention deficit hyperactivity disorder and Ritalin®, in *Moral Panics over Contemporary Children and Youth*, edited by C. Krinsky. Aldershot: Ashgate, 143– 66.

Miller, T. and Leger, M.C. 2003. A very childish moral panic: Ritalin. *Journal of Medical Humanities*, 24(1), 9–33.

Millie, A. 2008. Anti-social behaviour, behavioural expectations and an urban aesthetic. *British Journal of Criminology*, 48(3), 379–94.

Monaghan, L.F., Hollands, R., and Pritchard, G. 2010. Obesity epidemic entrepreneurs: types, practices and interests. *Body and Society*, 16 (2), 37–71.

Montana, R. 2009. Prosecutors and the definition of the crime problem in Italy: balancing the impact of moral panics. *Criminal Law Forum*, 20(4), 471–94.

Morgan, G. 2012. *Global Islamophobia*. Global Connections. Farnham: Ashgate.

Morgan, G. and Dagistanli, S. 2010. Global fears, local anxiety: policing, counterterrorism and moral panic over 'bikie gang wars' in New South Wales. *Australian and New Zealand Journal of Criminology*, 43(3), 580–99.

Morris III, C.E. 2002. Pink herring and the fourth persona: J. Edgar Hoover's sex crime panic. *Quarterly Journal of Speech*, 88(2), 228–44.

Morrison, B. 2011 (1997). *As If*. 2nd Edition. London: Granta Books.

Murray, T. and McClure, M. 1995. *Moral Panic: Exposing the Religious Right's Agenda on Sexuality*. Listen Up! London: Cassell.

Nadel, A. 1995. *Containment Culture: American Narratives, Postmodernism, and the Atomic Age*. New Americanists. Durham: Duke University Press.

Nathan, D. and Snedeker, M. 1995. *Satan's Silence: Ritual Abuse and the Making of a Modern American Witch Hunt*. New York: Basic Books.

Nava, M. 1988. Cleveland and the press: outrage and anxiety in the reporting of child sexual abuse. *Feminist Review*, 28, 103–121.

Neuilly, M-A. and Zgoba, K. 2006. Assessing the possibility of a pedophilia panic and contagion effect between France and the United States. *Victims and Offenders*, 1(3), 225–54.

Niehaus, I. 2010. Maternal incest as moral panic: envisioning futures without fathers in the South African lowveld. *Journal of Southern African Studies*, 36(4), 833–49.

Nietzsche, F. 1996 (1887), *On the Genealogy of Morals*, translated by D. Smith. Oxford World's Classics. New York: Oxford University Press. Originally published as *Zur Genealogie der Moral: Eine Streitschrift*. Leipzig: C.G. Naumann.

Nilsson, A. 2011. Cause for concern or moral panic? The prospects of the Swedish mods in retrospect. *Journal of Youth Studies*, 14(7), 777–93.

Noi, C. 2009. *Jungle Book: Thailand's Politics, Moral Panic, and Plunder, 1996–2008*. Chiang Mai: Silkworm Books. Authored pseudonymously by P. Phongpaichit and C. Baker.

Nussbaum, M.C. 2004. *Hiding from Humanity: Disgust, Shame, and the Law*. Princeton: Princeton University Press.

Nussbaum, M.C. 2010. *From Disgust to Humanity: Sexual Orientation and Constitutional Law*. Inalienable Rights. New York: Oxford University Press.

Nyberg, A.K. 1998. *Seal of Approval: The History of the Comics Code*. Studies in Popular Culture. Jackson: University of Mississippi Press.

O'Malley, P. 1992. Risk, power, and crime prevention. *Economy and Society*, 21(3), 252–75.

O'Malley, P. 1996. Post-Keynesian policing. *Economy and Society*, 1996, 25(2), 137–55.

O'Malley, P. 1999. Volatile and contradictory punishment. *Theoretical Criminology*, 3(2), 175–96.

Ortiz, A.T. and Briggs, L. 2003. The culture of poverty, crack babies, and welfare cheats: the making of the healthy white baby crisis. *Social Text*, 21(3), 39–57.

Osgerby, B. 2004. *Youth Media*. Milton Park: Routledge.

Ost, S. 2002. Children at risk: legal and social perceptions of the potential threat that possession of child pornography poses to society. *Journal of Law and Society*, 29(3), 436–60.

Ost, S. 2009. *Child Pornography and Sexual Grooming: Legal and Societal Responses*. Cambridge Studies in Law and Society. Cambridge: Cambridge University Press.

Parton, N. 1979. The natural history of child abuse: a study in social problem definition. *British Journal of Social Work*, 9(4), 431–51.

Parton, N. 1981. Child abuse, social anxiety and welfare. *British Journal of Social Work*, 11(1), 391–414.

Parton, N. 1985. *The Politics of Child Abuse*. London: Macmillan.

Paterson, B. and Stark, C. 2001. Social policy and mental illness in England in the 1990s: violence, moral panic and critical discourse. *Journal of Psychiatric and Mental Health Nursing*, 8(3), 257–67.

Patry, W. 2009. *Moral Panics and the Copyright Wars*. New York: Oxford University Press.

Patton, C. 2005. Outlaw territory: criminality, neighborhoods, and the Edward Savitz case. *Sexuality Research and Social Policy*, 2(2), 63–75.

Payne, R. 2008. Virtual panic: children online and the transmission of harm, in *Moral Panics over Contemporary Children and Youth*, edited by C. Krinsky. Aldershot: Ashgate, 31–46.

Pearce, J.M. and Charman, E. 2011. A social psychological approach to understanding moral panic. *Crime, Media, Culture*, 7(3), 293–311.

Pearson, G. 1983. *Hooligan: A History of Respectable Fears*. Basingstoke: Macmillan.

Pearson, G. 2006. Hybrid law and human rights? Banning and behaviour orders in the appeal courts. *Liverpool Law Review*, 27(2), 125–45.

Pijpers, R. 2006. Help! The Poles are coming? Narrating a contemporary moral panic. *Geografiska Annaler: Series B, Human Geography*, 88(1), 91–103.

Pike, E.C. J. 2011. The active aging agenda, old folk devils and a new moral panic. *Sociology of Sport Journal*, 28(2), 209–25.

Piper, H. and Stronach, I. 2008. *Don't Touch! The Educational Story of a Panic*. Milton Park: Routledge.

Platt, A. 1996. The politics of law and order. *Social Justice*, 21(3), 3–13.

Pontikes, E., Negro, G., and Rao, H. 2010. Stained red: a study of stigma by association to blacklisted artists during the "Red Scare" in Hollywood, 1945 to 1960. *American Sociological Review*, 75(3), 456–78.

Poole, W. Scott. 2009. *Satan in America: The Devil We Know*. Lanham: Rowman and Littlefield.

Poole, W. Scott. 2011. *Monsters in America: Our Historical Obsession with the Hideous and the Haunting*. Waco: Baylor University Press.

Posel, D. 2005. The scandal of manhood: "baby rape" and the politicization of sexual violence in post-apartheid South Africa. *Culture, Health and Sexuality,* 7(3), 239–52.

Potter, G.W. and Kappeler, V.E. (eds). 2006 (1998). *Constructing Crime: Perspectives on Making News and Social Problems.* 2nd Edition. Lexington Heights: Waveland Press.

Potter, R.H. and Potter, L.A. 2001. The Internet, cyberporn, and the sexual exploitation of children: media moral panics and urban myths for middle-class parents? *Sexuality and Culture,* 5(3), 31–48.

Poveda, T. 1972. The fear of crime in a small town. *Crime and Delinquency,* 18, 147–53.

Poynting, S., Noble, G., and Tabar, P. 2001. Middle Eastern appearances: "ethnic gangs", moral panic and media framing. *Australian and New Zealand Journal of Criminology,* 34(1), 67–90.

Quigley, M. and Blashki, K. 2003. Beyond the boundaries of the sacred garden: children and the Internet. *Information Technology in Childhood Education Annual,* 2003(1), 309–16.

Ranulf, S. 1938. *Moral Indignation and Middle-Class Psychology: A Sociological Study.* Copenhagen: Levin and Munksgaard.

Rasmussen, M. 2010. Revisiting moral panics in sex education. *Media International Australia,* 135, 118–30.

Reader, I.J. 2001. Consensus shattered: Japanese paradigm shifts and moral panic in the post-Aum era. *Nova Religio,* 4(2), 225–34.

Reddy, V. 2002. Perverts and sodomites: homophobia as hate speech in Africa. *Southern African Linguistics and Applied Language Studies,* 20(3), 163–75.

Reinarman, C. and Levine, H.G. 1989. The crack attack: politics and media in America's latest drug scare, in *Images of Issues: Typifying Contemporary Social Problems,* edited by J. Best. Hawthorne: Aldine de Gruyter, 115–37.

Richardson, J.T., Best, J., and Bromley, D.G. (eds). 1991. *The Satanism Scare.* Social Institutions and Social Change. Hawthorne: Aldine de Gruyter.

Richardson, J.T. and Introvigne, M. 2007. New religious movements, countermovements, moral panics, and the media. *Teaching New Religious Movements,* 1(6), 91–113.

Richardson, J.T., Reichert, J., and Lykes, V. 2009. Satanism in America: an update. *Social Compass,* 56(4), 552–63.

Robinson, D. 2010. New immigrants and migrants in social housing in Britain: discursive themes and lived realities. *Policy and Politics,* 38(1), 57–77.

Robinson, K. 2008. In the name of "childhood innocence": a discursive exploration of the moral panic associated with childhood and sexuality. *Cultural Studies Review,* 14(2), 113–29.

Robson, E. 2005. Portraying West Africa's children: moral panics, imagined geographies andglobalisation, in *West African Worlds: Paths through Socio-Economic Change, Livelihoods and Development,* edited by R. Cline-Cole and E. Robson. Harlow: Pearson Education, 65–85.

Rocheron, Y. and Linné, O. 1989. Aids, moral panic and opinion polls. *European Journal of Communication,* 4(4), 409–34.

Rodger, J. 1995. Family policy or moral regulation? *Critical Social Policy*, 15(43), 5–25.

Rodwell, G. 2011. One newspaper's role in the demise of the Tasmanian Essential Learnings Curriculum: adding new understandings to Cohen's moral panic theory in analyzing curriculum change. *Journal of Educational Change*, 12(4), 441–56.

Rohloff, A. 2011. Extending the concept of moral panic: Elias, climate change and civilization. *Sociology*, 45(4), 634–49.

Rohloff, A. 2011. Shifting the focus? Moral panics as civilizing and decivilizing processes, in *Moral Panic and the Politics of Anxiety*, edited by S.P. Hier. Milton Park: Routledge, 71–85.

Rohloff, A. and Wright, S. 2010. Moral panic and social theory: beyond the heuristic. *Current Sociology*, 58(3), 403–19.

Roman, L.G. 1996. Spectacle in the dark: youth as transgression, display, and repression. *Educational Theory*, 46(1), 1–22.

Rosie, M. and Gorringe, H. 2009. "The anarchists' world cup": respectable protest and media panics. *Social Movement Studies*, 8(1), 35–53.

Rothe, D.L. and Muzzatti, S. 2004. Enemies everywhere: terrorism, moral panics and US civil society. *Critical Criminology*, 12(3), 327–50.

Rous, T. and Hunt. A. 2004. Governing peanuts: the regulation of the social bodies of children and the risks of food allergies, *Social Science and Medicine*, 58(4), 825–36.

Rowbotham, J. and Stevenson, K. (eds). 2003. *Behaving Badly: Social Panics and Moral Outrage-Victorian and Modern Parallels*. Aldershot: Ashgate.

Rowbotham, J. and Stevenson, K. (eds). 2005. *Criminal Conversations: Victorian Crimes, Social Panic, and Moral Outrage*. Columbus: Ohio State University Press.

Rowe, D. 2010. The concept of the moral panic: an historico-sociological positioning, in *Moral Panics, the Media and the Law in Early Modern England*, edited by D. Lemmings and C. Walker. New York: Palgrave Macmillan, 22–40.

Rubin, G.S. 1994 (1984). Thinking sex: notes for a radical theory of the politics of sexuality, in *The Lesbian and Gay Studies Reader*, edited by H. Abelove, M.A. Barale, and D.M. Halperin. New York: Routledge. First published in slightly different form in *Pleasure and Danger: Exploring Female Sexuality*, edited by C.S. Vance. Boston: Routledge and Kegan Paul, 267–319.

Ruonavaara, H. 1997. Moral regulation: a reformulation. *Sociological Theory*, 15(3), 277–93.

Samara, T.R. 2005. Youth, crime and urban renewal in the Western Cape. *Journal of Southern African Studies*, 31(1), 209–27.

Samara, T.R. 2008. Marginalized youth and urban revitalization: a moral panic over street children in Cape Town, in *Moral Panics over Contemporary Children and Youth*, edited by C. Krinsky. Aldershot: Ashgate, 187–202.

Sandywell, B. 2006. Monsters in cyberspace: cyberphobia and cultural panic in the information age. *Information, Communication and Society*, 9(1), 39–61.

Schack. T. 2011. Twenty-first-century drug warriors: the press, privateers and the for-profit waging of the war on drugs. *Media, War and Conflict*, 4(2), 142–61.

Schaefer, N.A. 2002. The BBC and an American "faith healer": the making of a folk devil? *Journal of Contemporary Religion*, 17(1), 39–59.

Schinkel, W. 2010. *Aspects of Violence: A Critical Theory*. Houndmills: Palgrave Macmillan.

Schissel, B. 1997. *Blaming Children: Youth Crime, Moral Panics and the Politics of Hate*. Halifax: Fernwood.

Schissel, B. 1997. Youth crime, moral panics, and the news: the conspiracy against the marginalized in Canada. *Social Justice*, 24(2), 165–84.

Schissel, B. 2009. Justice undone: public panic and the condemnation of children and youth, in *Moral Panics over Contemporary Children and Youth*, edited by C. Krinsky. Farnham: Ashgate, 15–29.

Schultz, P.D. 2005. *Not Monsters: Analyzing the Stories of Child Molesters*. Lanham: Rowman and Littlefield Publishers.

Schultz, P.D. 2008. Naming, blaming, and framing: moral panic over child molesters and its implications for public policy, in *Moral Panics over Contemporary Children and Youth*, edited by C. Krinsky. Aldershot: Ashgate, 95–110.

Scott, S., Jackson, S., and Backett-Milburn, K. 1998. Swings and roundabouts: risk anxieties and the everyday worlds of children. *Sociology*, 32(4), 689–705.

Seekings, J. 1996. 'The lost generation': South Africa's 'youth problem' in the early-1990s. *Transformation*, 29, 103–25.

Sela-Shayovitz, R. 2011. Neo-Nazis and moral panic: the emergence of neo-Nazi youth gangs in Israel. *Crime, Media, Culture*, 7(1), 67–82.

Semati, M. 2007. *Media, Culture and Society in Iran: Living with Globalization and the Islamic State*. Iranian Studies. Milton Park: Routledge.

Settles, T. and Lindsay, B.R. 2011. Crime in post-Katrina Houston: the effects of moral panic on emergency planning. *Disasters*, 35(1), 200–219.

Shepard, B. 2007. Sex panic and the welfare state. *Journal of Sociology and Social Welfare*, 34(1), 155–71.

Showalter, E. 1998. *Hystories*. New York: Columbia University Press.

Sikes, P. 2008. At the eye of the storm: an academic('s) experience of moral panic. *Qualitative Inquiry*, 14(2), 235–53.

Sikes, P. and Piper, H. 2009. *Researching Sex and Lies in the Classroom: Allegations of Sexual Misconduct in Schools*. Milton Park: Routledge.

Simon, J. 2007. *Governing Through Crime: How the War on Crime Transformed American Democracy and Created a Culture of Fear*. Studies in Crime and Public Policy. New York: Oxford University Press.

Sindall, R. 1987. The London garotting panics of 1856 and 1862. *Social History*, 12(3), 351–59.

Sjoberg, R.L. 2000. The catechism effect: child testimonies during a 17th-century witch panic as related to educational achievement. *Memory*, 8(2), 65–9.

Skelton, T. and Valentine, G. (eds). 1998. *Cool Places: Geographies of Youth Cultures*. London: Routledge.

Smith, E. 2003. Failing boys and moral panics: perspectives on the underachievement debate. *British Journal of Educational Studies*, 51(3), 282–95.

Smith, E. 2003. Understanding underachievement: an investigation into the differential attainment of secondary school pupils. *British Journal of Sociology of Education*, 24(5), 575–86.

Smith, J. 2007. 'Ye've got to 'ave balls to play this game sir!' Boys, peers and fears: the negative influence of school-based 'cultural accomplices' in constructing hegemonic masculinities. *Gender and Education*, 19(2), 179–98.

Smith, S.J. 2005. *Children, Cinema and Censorship: From Dracula to Dead End*. Cinema and Society. London: I. B. Tauris.

Soothill, K. and Francis, B. 2002. Moral panics and the aftermath: a study of incest. *Journal of Social Welfare and Family Law*, 24(1), 1–17.

Soothill, K., Peelo, M., Pearson, J., and Francis, B. 2004. The reporting trajectories of top homicide cases in the media: a case study of *The Times*. *Howard Journal of Criminal Justice*, 43(1), 1–14.

Spooner, L. 1875. Vices are not crimes: a vindication of moral liberty, in *Prohibition a Failure or, The True Solution of the Temperance Question*, edited by D. Lewis. Boston: James R. Osgood. Authored anonymously.

Springhall, J. 1998. Censoring Hollywood: youth, moral panic and crime/gangster movies of the 1930s. *Journal of Popular Culture*. 32(3), 135–54.

Springhall, J. 1998. *Youth, Popular Culture and Moral Panics: Penny Gaffs to Gangsta Rap, 1830–1996*. Houndmills: Macmillan.

Springhall, J. 1999. Violent media, guns and moral panics: the Columbine High School massacre, 20 April 1999. *Paedagogica Historica*, 35(3), 621–41.

Springhall, J. 2008. "The monsters next door, what made them do it?" Moral panics over the causes of high school multiple shootings (notably Columbine), in *Moral Panics over Contemporary Children and Youth*, edited by C. Krinsky. Aldershot: Ashgate, 47–70.

Stabile, C.A. 2001. Conspiracy or consensus? Reconsidering the moral panic. *Journal of Communication Inquiry*, 25(3) 258–78.

Stabile, C.A. 2006. *White Victims, Black Villains: Gender, Race, and Crime News in US Culture*. New York: Routledge.

St Cyr, J. 2003. The folk devil reacts: gangs and moral panics. *Criminal Justice Review*, 28(1), 26–46.

Sullivan, M.L. 2001. Maybe we shouldn't study "gangs": does reification obscure youth violence? *Journal of Contemporary Criminal Justice*, 21(2), 170–90.

Sutherland, E. 1950. The diffusion of sexual psychopath laws. *American Journal of Sociology*, 56(2), 142–8.

Sutherland, E. 1950. The sexual psychopath laws. *Journal of Criminal Law and Criminology*, 40(5), 534–44.

Sutter, G. 2000. 'Nothing new under the sun': old fears and new media. *International Journal of Law and Information Technology*, 8(3), 338–78.

Swadener, B.B. and Lubeck, S. 1995. The social construction of children and families "at risk": an introduction, in *Children and Families "at Promise": Deconstructing the Discourse of Risk*, edited by B.B. Swadener, and S. Lubeck. New York: State University of New York Press, 1–16.

Szablewicz, M. 2010. The ill effects of "opium for the spirit": a critical cultural analysis of China's Internet addiction moral panic. *Chinese Journal of Communication*, 3(4), 453–70.

Tait, G. 1995. Shaping the "at-risk youth": risk, governmentality and the Finn Report. *Discourse*, 16(1), 123–34.

Tan, K.P. 2007. Youth: every generation's moral panic, in *Renaissance Singapore? Economy, Culture, and Politics*, edited by K.P. Tan. Singapore: National University of Singapore Press, 219–30.

Tan, M.L. 2000. AIDS, medicine, and moral panic, in *Framing the Sexual Subject: The Politics of Gender, Sexuality, and Power*, edited by R. Parker, R.M. Barbosa, and P. Aggleton. Berkeley: University of California Press, 143–64.

Terrio, S. J. 2008. New savages in the city: moral panics, delinquent hoodlums, and the French juvenile court, in *Moral Panics over Contemporary Children and Youth*, edited by C. Krinsky. Aldershot: Ashgate, 225–47.

Tettey, W.J. 2008. Globalization, cybersexuality among Ghanaian youth, and moral panic, in *Neoliberalism and Globalization in Africa: Contestations on the Embattled Continent*, edited by J. Mensah. Houndmills: Palgrave Macmillan, 157–76.

Thompson, K. (ed.) 1997. *Media and Cultural Regulation*. London: Sage Publications.

Thompson, K. 1997. Regulation, de-regulation and re-regulation, in *Media and Cultural Regulation*, edited by K. Thompson. London: Sage Publications, 9–52.

Thompson, K. 1998. *Moral Panics*. Key Ideas. Milton Park: Routledge.

Thompson, K. and Sharma, A. 1998. Secularization, moral regulation and the mass media. *British Journal of Sociology*, 49(3), 434–55.

Thornton S. 1994. Moral panic, the media, and British rave culture, in *MicrophoneFiends: Youth Music and Youth Culture*, edited by A. Ross and T. Rose. New York: Routledge, 176–92.

Thornton, S. 1996. *Club Cultures: Music, Media, and Subcultural Capital*. Hanover: Wesleyan University Press.

Tiffen, R. 2004. Tip of the iceberg or moral panic? Police corruption issues in contemporary New South Wales. *American Behavioral Scientist*, 47(9), 1171–93.

Titus, J. 2004. Boy trouble: rhetorical framing of boys' underachievement. *Discourse*, 25(2), 145–69.

Toivonen, T. 2011. "Don't let your child become a NEET!" The strategic foundations of a Japanese youth scare. *Japan Forum*, 23(3), 407–29.

Toivonen, T. 2012. NEETs: the strategy within the category, in *A Sociology of Japanese Youth: From Returnees to NEETs*, edited by R. Goodman, Y. Imoto, and T. Toivonen. London: Routledge, 139–58.

Toivonen, T. and Imoto, Y. 2012. Making sense of youth problems, in *A Sociology of Japanese Youth: From Returnees to NEETs*, edited by R. Goodman, Y. Imoto, and T. Toivonen. London: Routledge, 1–29.

Tomsen, S. 1997. Youth violence and the limits of moral panic. *Youth Studies Australia*, (16)1, 25–30.

Tonry, M. 2001. Unthought thoughts: the influence of changing sensibilities on penal policies. *Punishment and Society*, 3(1), 167–81.

Tonry, M. 2006. *Thinking about Crime: Sense and Sensibility in American Penal Culture*. Studies in Crime and Public Policy. New York: Oxford University Press.

Toor, S. 2007. Moral regulation in a postcolonial nation-state. *Interventions: International Journal of Postcolonial Studies*, 9(2), 255–75.

Trevor-Roper, H. 1967. *The European Witch Craze of the 16th and 17th Centuries.* Harmondsworth: Penguin.

Uggen, C. and Inderbitzin, M. 2010. Public criminologies. *Criminology and Public Policy*, 9(4), 725–49.

Ungar, S. 1990. Moral panics, the military-industrial complex, and the arms race. *Sociological Quarterly*, 31(2), 165–85.

Ungar, S. 1992. The rise and (relative) decline of global warming as a social problem. *Sociological Quarterly*, 33(4), 483–501.

Ungar, S. 1995. Social scares and global warming: beyond the Rio Convention. *Society and Natural Resources*, 8(4), 443–56.

Ungar, S. 1998. Bringing the issue back in: comparing the marketability of the ozone hole and global warming. *Social Problems*, 45(4), 510–27.

Ungar, S. 2001. Moral panic versus the risk society: the implications of the changing sites of social anxiety. *British Journal of Sociology*, 52(2), 271–91.

Ungar, S. 2008. "Don't know much about history": a critical examination of moral panics over student ignorance, in *Moral Panics over Contemporary Children and Youth*, edited by C. Krinsky. Aldershot: Ashgate, 167–82.

Ungar, S. 2008. Global bird flu communication: hot crisis and media assurance. *Science Communication*, 29(4), 472–97.

Ungar, S. 2011. The artful creation of global moral panic: climatic folk devils, environmental evangelicals, and the coming catastrophe, in *Moral Panic and the Politics of Anxiety*, edited by S.P. Hier. Milton Park: Routledge, 190–207.

Valentine, G. 1996. Angels and devils: moral landscapes of childhood. *Environment and Planning D: Society and Space*, 14(5), 581–99.

Valentine, G., Holloway, S., Knell, C., and Jayne, M. 2008. Drinking places: young people and cultures of alcohol consumption in rural environments. *Journal of Rural Studies*, 24(1), 28–40.

Valier, C. 2002. Punishment, border crossings and the powers of horror. *Theoretical Criminology*, 6(3), 319–37.

Valverde, M. 1994. Moral capital. *Canadian Journal of Law and Society*, 9(1), 213–32.

van Dijk, R.A. 2001. "Voodoo" on the doorstep: young Nigerian prostitutes and magic policing in the Netherlands. *Africa*, 71(4), 558–86.

van Krieken, R. 1991 The poverty of social control: explaining power in the historical sociology of the welfare state. *Sociological Review*, 38(1), 1–25.

Van Loon, J. 2002. *Risk and Technological Culture: Towards a Sociology of Virulence.* London: Routledge.

Vasta, E. 2007. From ethnic minorities to ethnic majority policy: multiculturalism and the shift to assimilationism in the Netherlands. *Ethnic and Racial Studies*, 30(5), 713–40.

Veno, A. and Van Den Eynde, J. 2007. Moral panic neutralization project: a media-based intervention. *Journal of Community and Applied Social Psychology*, 17(6): 490–506.

Victor, J.S. 1989. A rumor-panic about a dangerous satanic cult in Western New York. *New York Folklore*, 15(1–2), 23–49.

Victor, J.S. 1989. A rumor-panic about satanic cults. *Western Folklore*, 49(1), 51–81.

Victor, J.S. 1993. *Satanic Panic: The Creation of a Contemporary Legend*. Chicago: Open Court Press.

Victor, J.S. 1998. Moral panics and the social construction of deviant behavior: a theory and application to the case of ritual child abuse. *Sociological Perspectives*, 41(3), 541–65.

Villanueva-Russell, R. 2009. Chiropractors as folk devils: published and unpublished news coverage of a moral panic. *Deviant Behavior*, 30(2), 175–200.

Vincent, L. 2009. Moral panic and the politics of populism. *Representation*, 45(2), 213–21.

von der Lippe, G. and MacLean, M. 2008. Brawling in Berne: mediated transnational moral panics in the 1954 football World Cup. *International Review for the Sociology of Sport*, 43(1), 71–90.

Wacquant, L. 2009. *Punishing the Poor: The Neoliberal Government of Social Insecurity*. A John Hope Franklin Book. Durham: Duke University Press.

Waddington, P.A.J. 1986. Mugging as a moral panic: a question of proportion. *British Journal of Sociology*, 37(2), 245–59.

Waiton, S. 2008. *The Politics of Antisocial Behavior: Amoral Panics*. Routledge Advances in Criminology. New York: Routledge.

Walby, K. and Spenser, D. 2011. How emotions matter to moral panics, in *Moral Panic and the Politics of Anxiety*, edited by S.P. Hier. Milton Park: Routledge, 104–17.

Waldron, D. 2005. Role-playing games and the Christian right: community formation in response to a moral panic. *Journal of Religion and Popular Culture*, 9.

Walker, B.A. 2010. Essay: deciphering risk: sex offender statutes and moral panic in a risk society. *University of Baltimore Law Review*, 40.2, 183–213.

Walker, C. 2010. 'Remember Justice Godfrey': The Popish Plot and the construction of panic in seventeenth-century media, in *Moral Panics, the Media and the Law in Early Modern England*, edited by D. Lemmings and C. Walker. New York: Palgrave Macmillan, 117–38.

Walkowitz, J. 1992. *City of Dreadful Delight: Narratives of Sexual Danger in Late-Victorian London*. Women in Culture and Society. Chicago: University of Chicago Press.

Walsham, A. 2010. 'This newe army of Satan': the Jesuit mission and the formation of public opinion in Elizabethan England, in *Moral Panics, the Media and the Law in Early Modern England*, edited by D. Lemmings and C. Walker. New York: Palgrave Macmillan, 41–62.

Watney, S. 1987. *Policing Desire: Pornography, AIDS, and the Media*. London: Methuen.

Watney, S. 1988. AIDS, 'moral panic' theory and homophobia, in *Social Aspects of AIDS*, edited by P. Aggelton and H. Homans. London: Falmer Press, 52–64.

Weeks, J. 1981. *Sex, Politics and Society: The Regulation of Sexuality since 1800*. Themes in British Social History. London: Longman.

Weeks, J. 1985. *Sexuality and Its Discontents: Meanings, Myths and Modern Sexualities*. London: Routledge and Kegan Paul.

Weeks, J. 1989. AIDS: the intellectual agenda, in *AIDS: Social Representations, Social Practices*, edited by P. Aggleton, G. Hart, and P. Davies. London: Falmer Press, 1–13.

Weiss, K.J. and Watson, C. 2008. NGRI and Megan's Law: no exit? *Journal of the American Academy of Psychiatry and the Law*, 36(1), 117–22.

Weidner, R.R. 2009. Methamphetamine in three small Midwestern cities: evidence of a moral panic. *Journal of Psychoactive Drugs*, 41(3), 227–39.

Weitzer, R. 2007. The social construction of sex trafficking: ideology and institutionalization of a moral crusade. *Politics and Society*, 35(3), 447–75.

Weitzer, R. 2009. Legalizing prostitution: morality politics in Western Australia. *British Journal of Criminology*, 49(1), 88–105.

Welch, M. 2000. *Flag Burning: Moral Panic and the Criminalization of Protest.* Piscataway: Transaction Publishers.

Welch, M. 2002. *Detained: Immigration Laws and the Expanding I.N.S. Jail Complex.* Philadelphia: Temple University Press.

Welch, M. 2003. Ironies of social control and the criminalization of immigrants. *Crime, Law and Social Change*, 39(4), 319–37.

Welch, M. 2004. Trampling human rights in the War on Terror: implications to the sociology of denial. *Critical Criminology*, (12)1, 1–20.

Welch, M. 2006. *Scapegoats of September 11th: Hate Crimes and State Crimes in the War on Terror.* Critical Issues in Crime and Society. Piscataway: Rutgers University Press.

Welch, M. 2007. Moral panic, denial, and human rights: scanning the specturm form overreaction to underreaction, in *Crime, Social Control and Human Rights: From Moral Panics to States of Denial, Essays in Honour of Stanley Cohen*, edited by D. Downes, P. Rock, C. Chinkin, and C. Gearty. Cullompton: Willan, 92–106.

Welch, M., Fenwick, M., and Roberts, M. 1997. Primary definitions of crime and moral panic: a content analysis of experts' quotes in feature newspaper articles on crime. *Journal of Research in Crime and Delinquency*, 34(4), 474–94.

Welch, M., Price, E.A., and Yankey, N. 2002. Moral panic over youth violence: wilding and the manufacture of menace in the media. *Youth and Society*, 34(1), 3–30.

Welch, M. and Schuster, L. 2005. Detention of asylum-seekers in the US, UK, France, Germany, and Italy. *Criminology and Criminal Justice*, 5(4), 331–55.

Whitfield, S.J. 1996 (1991). *The Culture of the Cold War*. The American Moment. 2nd Edition. Baltimore: Johns Hopkins University Press.

Wieringa, S.E. 2009. Postcolonial amnesia: sexual moral panics, memory, and imperial power, in *Moral Panics, Sex Panics: Fear and the Fight over Sexual Rights*, edited by G. Herdt. New York: New York University Press, 205–33.

Wilkins, L.T. 1964. *Social Deviance: Social Policy, Action and Research*. London: Tavistock.

Williams, E.L. 2011. Moral panic: sex tourism, sex trafficking, and the limits of transnational mobility in Bahia, in *Policing Pleasure: Sex Work, Policy, and the State in Global Perspective*, edited by S. Dewey and P. Kelly. New York: New York University Press, 189–200.

Williams, J.A. 2001. Ecstasies of the young: sexuality, the youth movement, and moral panic in Germany on the eve of the First World War. *Central European History*, 34(2), 163–90.

Williams, P. and Dickinson, L. 1993. Fear of crime: read all about it? *British Journal of Criminology*, 33(1), 33–56.

Wood, B. 1999. Panic, what panic? The moral deficit of new right politics in Aotrearoa New Zealand. *New Zealand Sociology*, 14(1), 85–110.

Woodiwiss, M. and Hobbs, D. 2009. Organized evil and the Atlantic Alliance. *British Journal of Criminology*, 49(1), 106–28.

Wright, S. and Richardson, J. (eds). 2011. *Saints under Siege: The Texas State Raid on the Fundamentalist Latter Day Saints*. New and Alternative Religions. New York: New York University Press.

Yeomans, H. 2011. What did the British temperance movement accomplish? Attitudes to alcohol, the law and moral regulations. *Sociology*, 45(1): 38–53.

Yılmaz, F. 20011. The politics of the Danish cartoon affair: hegemonic intervention by the extreme right. *Communication Studies*, 62(1), 5–22.

Young, J. 1970. The zoo keepers of deviancy. *Catalyst*, 5, 38–46.

Young, J. 1971. *The Drugtakers: The Social Meaning of Drug Use*. London: MacGibbon and Kee.

Young, J. 1971. The role of the police as amplifiers of deviancy, negotiators of reality and translators of fantasy: some consequences of our present system of drug control as seen in Notting Hill, in *Images of Deviance*, edited by S. Cohen. Harmondsworth: Penguin Books, 27–61.

Young, J. 1988. Radical criminology in Britain: the emergence of a competing paradigm. *British Journal of Criminology*, 28(2), 159–83.

Young, J. 2007. Slipping away: moral panics each side of 'The Golden Age', in *Crime, Social Control and Human Rights: From Moral Panics to States of Denial, Essays in Honour of Stanley Cohen*, edited by D. Downes, P. Rock, C. Chinkin, and C. Gearty. Cullompton: Willan, 53–65.

Young, J. 2007. *The Vertigo of Late Modernity*. London: Sage Publications.

Young, J. 2009. Moral panic: its origins in resistance, ressentiment and the translation of fantasy into reality. *British Journal of Criminology*, 49(1), 4–16.

Young, J. 2011. Moral panics and the transgressive other. *Crime, Media, Culture*, 7(3), 245–58.

Zajdow, G. 2008. Moral panics: the old and the new. *Deviant Behavior*, 29(7), 640–64.

Zatz, M. 1987. Chicago youth gangs and crime: the creation of a moral panic. *Contemporary Crises*, 11(2), 129–58.

Zgoba, K. M. 2004. Spin doctors and moral crusaders: the moral panic behind child safety legislation. *Criminal Justice Studies*, 17(4), 385–404.

Žižek, S. 2002. *Welcome to the Desert of the Real: Five Essays on September 11 and Related Dates*. New York: Verso.

# Index